Haywire

ANDREW HINDMOOR

Haywire

A Political History of Britain since 2000

ALLEN LANE
an imprint of
PENGUIN BOOKS

ALLEN LANE

UK | USA | Canada | Ireland | Australia
India | New Zealand | South Africa

Allen Lane is part of the Penguin Random House group of companies
whose addresses can be found at global.penguinrandomhouse.com

First published 2024
001

Copyright © Andrew Hindmoor, 2024

The moral right of the author has been asserted

Set in 10.2/13.87pt Sabon LT Std
Typeset by Jouve (UK), Milton Keynes
Printed and bound in Great Britain by Clays Ltd, Elcograf S.p.A.

The authorized representative in the EEA is Penguin Random House Ireland,
Morrison Chambers, 32 Nassau Street, Dublin D02 YH68

A CIP catalogue record for this book is available from the British Library

ISBN: 978–0–241–65171–1

For Asha Hindmoor

Contents

CONTENTS

CONTENTS

List of Figures

List of Tables

I

Britain on the Edge

GETTING HERE

Vladimir Lenin, an occasional resident of North London who went on to other things, has been credited (perhaps apocryphally) with once saying that there are decades where nothing happens but weeks when decades happen. The first twenty-five years of this twenty-first century have had plenty of those kinds of weeks. Indeed, our recent history has at times resembled nothing so much as an episode of *Casualty*, the long-running BBC hospital drama in which every hedge trimmer slips, every gas pipe leaks, every piece of scaffolding collapses and everyone ends up in intensive care.

At the start of the new millennium everything looked reasonably rosy. A stable government with a large majority led by a young and still popular(ish) prime minister; an economic boom; a peace settlement in Northern Ireland; and devolution in Wales and Scotland. After which events took a dramatic turn for the worse. The Iraq War, the 2008 financial crisis, recession, austerity, the Brexit impasse, Covid-19 and the slow-motion unfolding of a new Cold War are the headline, haywire, moments. Beneath these Grade 1-listed crises are, however, a long supporting cast of terrorist attacks, MPs' expenses, phone hacking, Windrush, #MeToo, Liz Truss, galloping inflation and rising interest rates, alongside the slow burn of a broken social care system, a failing housing market and eye-watering levels of public, private and corporate debt. Behind all this, finally, can be seen the approaching calamity of climate change.

A quarter of the way through a new century Britain looks a lot like a person who has, whilst trying to cross the road, got hit by an on-rushing car, only to get up, dazed, and stumbled backwards, to then be hit by a lorry. It is not simply that one crisis has quickly followed another. Rather, the impact of one crisis has compounded the next. The financial crisis and the Labour government's response to it provided the context for austerity. The financial crisis, the MPs' expenses scandal and austerity paved the way for the Brexit vote. Brexit then changed the terms of the debate about Scottish independence and Irish reunification. And Covid-19 exposed and exacerbated almost everything which had come before.

This book tells a history, primarily a political history but one which leaves plenty of elbow room for economics and social history, of the deluge of events that have rained down on the United Kingdom of Great Britain and Northern Ireland since the year 2000, and the ways in which they and the responses to them have changed the country. It is divided into seven parts: *Millennium* (2000–2005), *Boom* (2004–08), *War* (2001–07), *Crash* (2008–10), *Union* (2010–14), *Splintering* (2014–19) and *Quartered* (2019–24).

Millennium, which opens late on the evening of 31 December 1999, with the Dome's ill-fated debut performance, deals with Tony Blair and New Labour's plate-spinning efforts to build and defend against all comers a 'Third Way' centre-ground framed as an alternative to hard-nosed, callous, chauvinistic, neoliberal Thatcherism to its right and old school, spendthrift, trade-union appeasing, business-hating socialism to its left. It documents New Labour's strengths and weaknesses; the waxing and waning of its electoral fortunes; and the way in which David Cameron, the self-styled 'heir to Blair', came to decide partial imitation might prove to be the sincerest form of flattery.* *Boom* describes some of the causes and effects and virtues and vices of the economic boom which Blair inherited in 1997. Beyond the fact of the boom itself, the common theme of these chapters, which start in Morecambe Bay, Lancashire, in February 2004 and finish with the Champions League Final in Moscow in May 2008, is globalization. New Labour

---

* Cameron reportedly described himself as the 'heir to Blair' at a dinner with newspaper executives the evening before his 2005 Conservative Party conference speech, the starting point of Chapter 6. Cameron's press advisors initially denied the story; then ignored it; and then broadly accepted it. Cameron himself, during the 2010 General Election campaign, eventually said he regretted using the phrase. Andrew Pierce, 'Horror as Cameron brandishes the B word', *The Times* (5 October 2005); Andrew Pierce, 'At last they admit my "Heir to Blair" scoop', *Daily Telegraph* (2 June 2007); and Tim Shipman, 'I should never have called myself "the Heir to Blair"', *Daily Mail* (5 May 2010).

bet the bank on a conviction that globalization was not only unavoidable but could be reconciled with its version of social justice. These chapters look at the stresses and strains this relationship posed.

The third part, *War*, starts with the September 11 terrorist attacks and chronicles the Afghan and Iraq wars and the 7/7 terrorist attack in London, before turning to the end of the IRA's armed struggle and the TB-GBs, the weaponized clashes between Tony Blair and Gordon Brown. *Crash* is centred upon the causes and consequences of the 2008 financial crisis and the 2009 MPs' expenses scandal. In terms of both its chronology and significance, *Crash* sits at the centre of the book. It is the moment at which New Labour's centrism was discredited, the boom went bust, and everything started to go wrong at an accelerating rate. All roads in the second half start here. The first of these, *Union*, covers the Coalition years between 2010 and 2015 and Cameron's on–off efforts to create a new kind of political centre ground and a new kind of austerity economics. The second, *Splintering*, turns to the before, during and after of the Brexit referendum and the way in which it exposed political fault lines around age, education, political geography and values. The final part, *Quartered*, opens in December 2019, the month in which the Brexit stalemate was broken by a decisive general election, and the same month in which, five thousand miles away, patients were arriving at hospitals in Wuhan with breathing difficulties.

MODERN MISERABILISM

The tone I have adopted so far has been consistently downbeat and might therefore sound strikingly familiar. There is a long tradition in British politics, a tradition I will return to and discuss in a later chapter (pp. 309–10), of arguing that the country is in decline and that everything is getting worse. Over the last decade or more, that sense of degradation, whether or not always justified, has grown stronger and now offers a shared point of reference between those on the left, right and centre; between libertarians and social authoritarians; environmentalists and climate sceptics; and Leavers and Remainers. Democracy, by its nature, necessarily produces losers and winners. Yet Britain, it would seem, has become a country in which everyone thinks they are, and have for a long time been, on the losing side and everything is getting worse. In 2008, just before the financial crisis began, polling showed only around 12 per cent of Britons thought youngsters would have a *worse* quality of life than their parents. That figure has since risen to over 40 per cent.[1]

In his anguished memoirs, a case study in modern miserabilism, the former deputy prime minister and leader of the Liberal Democrats, Nick Clegg, recounts the story of a focus group the Liberal Democrats convened in 2013 with voters who had switched from voting for the Lib Dems to supporting the UK Independence Party (UKIP). All of the participants were disappointed with the Coalition that Clegg and Cameron had conjured into existence but, digging deeper, all of them, it turns out, were equally upset with every other aspect of modern British life, ranging from aggressive drivers to loud music in supermarkets:

> Towards the end of the session one of the somewhat exasperated Lib Dem researchers asked the group: 'Can anyone perhaps tell me of one thing they actually like in modern Britain?' A long silence ensued. And then a man raised his hand and said: 'Yes, I know. The past.'[2]

This kind of glass-half-empty despondency is easy to mock and can easily be pushed too far. Blunders, Snafus and crises are not twenty-first-century innovations. Just about every episode listed so far as exemplars of the kind of things that have gone badly wrong over the course of the last few decades have had prequels. For Iraq, think Suez. For the fractures opened by Brexit, think the 1984–5 miners' strike. For the financial crisis, think of the seventeenth-century tulip mania or the 1825 banking crisis in which it got so bad that the Banque de France had to bail out the Bank of England. For the cost-of-living crisis in the early 2020s refer back to the collapse of the Bretton Woods system and the OPEC oil embargo in the early 1970s and, eventually, the 'Crisis, what crisis?' breakpoint of 1979.[3]

No matter how many things have gone wrong, and no matter how badly they have gone wrong, a sunny-side optimist might reasonably maintain that Britain remains, everything considered, a relatively prosperous, liberal, democratic and peaceful country. The last quarter of a century has not, by any measure, been another belle époque. But neither has it been a non-stop disaster story. As of early 2023, Britain still had the world's sixth-largest economy measured in terms of gross domestic product (GDP) and, depending on which set of criteria and which set of data you use, something like the twentieth-highest quality of life.[4] Britain routinely gets a top three podium position when it comes to 'soft power' rankings.[5] The Northern Ireland peace settlement has just about held. The rates of most kinds of crime and of pensioner poverty have fallen dramatically. The 2012 London Olympics was regarded as a huge success. The post-referendum Brexit impasse stressed and strained the political system – no less than a figure than the last governor of Hong Kong and chancellor of Oxford University, Chris Patten, suggested it risked turning Britain into a failed state.[6] Yet that impasse was eventually broken by an election rather than a Washington-style insurrection. Britain led the world when it came to setting ambitious targets to cut carbon emissions and British scientists played key roles in developing Covid-19 vaccines.

There is, it might be suggested, a further problem with miserabilism. It relies too heavily upon the superpower of hindsight. Governing is an incredibly difficult activity, one which requires the constant bashing of square pegs into round holes. The problem with too many of the most scathing arguments about what has gone wrong and what could have been done differently is that they tacitly assume that information was perfect, when it is always imperfect and uncertain, and that trade-offs could have been overcome or wished away, when they are in fact inescapable. In the following chapters I try and highlight the tough choices politicians faced and the reasons why crucial bits of information, which now appear obvious, might sometimes have been genuinely difficult to see. I try, in other words, not to set the bar too high when it comes to reaching after-the-fact judgements. But the whole point of looking back is, at some level, to exercise hindsight: to acknowledge the difficulties inherent in making policy decisions whilst also making a reasoned case about why particular decisions were mistaken.

The premise of this book is that a measure of anguish about the twists and turns of the last quarter of a century is warranted. The crises Britain has experienced since the year 2000 have been large in number and lastingly destructive in terms of their effects on Britain's international reputation, people's faith in politicians, the integrity of the United Kingdom itself and, most directly, on the lives of millions of people living in it. Britain is not, by any measure, a failing or failed state. Neither, however, has it simply been the victim of a particularly prolonged run of bad luck that will, sooner or later, come to an end. Far from it. Rather, the way in which the British state is organized and decisions within it are taken, has, I will go on to argue, exacerbated and at times caused crises that other countries have either avoided altogether or successfully mitigated. For this reason, the what? when? and whys? of the crises Britain has experienced deserve to be put at the front and centre of our recent history. This does not mean wallowing in misery or focusing exclusively on the worst moments. That would make for a tough read. Indeed, there are several chapters where I return to and look more closely at some of the good news stories listed above. But, equally, trying to understand what has gone badly, and why, is important, not least because it can tell us something about the likely challenges of what comes next.

I WOULDN'T START FROM HERE

There is an old joke that used to be told by (amongst others) the late Irish comedian Dave Allen about a tourist in the countryside who is lost and approaches a local for directions. 'I wouldn't start from here if I were you' is the reply. That feels like a reasonable-enough assessment of Britain's current situation after the events of the last decade or so. Britain is sagging under the weight of three linked problems: low political trust; contested political boundaries; and economic stagnation. In the chapters that follow I'll explore the development of these problems over time. In what follows next I'll simply provide a brief overview of where we are now.

There has never been a golden age of politics in Britain in which people were grateful for and overjoyed with the politicians they had and entirely trusting of them. In 1944, at a time when the normal rhythms of party politics had been suspended because of the war, a poll asked people whether politicians were out for themselves or their party, or were there to do the best for their country; 35 per cent said themselves, 22 per cent said their party, and 36 per cent said their country.[7] In the mid-1990s, at a point when the Conservatives were being undone by a non-stop cabaret of scandal and sleaze, a large and now often-forgotten part of New Labour's appeal was bound up with its promise of a fresh start and the recovery of lost trust. We know how that movie ended. New Labour's decline and fall was played out to the backdrop of the Hutton inquiry into the death of Dr David Kelly (pp. 160–63) and the 'cash for coronets' (p. 254) and MPs' expenses scandal. Party political parity and a sense of 'Déjà vu all over again' were then restored, a decade later, by the suspension of Owen Paterson from the House of Commons for breaching its rules on paid advocacy (and by Boris Johnson's abortive efforts to protect him); Barnard Castle; Abba parties in 10 Downing Street; sexual misbehaviour ranging from the questionable to the obviously inappropriate, through to the criminal; and the resignation, in the space of a few months in 2023, of the chairman of the Conservative Party, Nadhim Zahawi, for failing to disclose that he was being investigated by HM Revenue and Customs, and the deputy prime minister, Dominic Raab, for his 'unreasonably and persistently aggressive' behaviour towards civil servants.[8]

In the 2022 edition of its longstanding 'Veracity Index', the polling company Ipsos found that just 12 per cent of the public said they trusted politicians to tell the truth.[9] The year before, the British Social Attitudes Survey found only 23 per cent trusted politicians to put the national interest ahead of their party interest.[10] There have, it is worth adding, been times when low trust in politicians in Britain has co-existed with reasonable levels of faith in the British system of representative democracy. That may be changing. In 2019, when 'Partygate' was a coinage still waiting to happen, the Hansard Society found that 63 per cent of people agreed that the British system of government was rigged to advantage the rich and powerful, and that whilst only 15 per cent thought 'the people in power are good but the system prevents them from making the right decisions', a further 38 per cent thought 'neither the system nor the people making the decisions are good enough'.[11]

To a remarkable extent, political and economic power in Britain, devolution notwithstanding, remains concentrated within a couple of square miles of central London running from Buckingham Palace to Downing Street and Whitehall and Threadneedle Street and the City of London. Despite all the rhetorical praise heaped upon the concept of parliamentary sovereignty during the Brexit debate, the executive can still routinely bypass or browbeat Parliament. In most parts of Britain, local government enjoys the same level of autonomy as inmates in the kind of American high-security prisons Louis Theroux makes documentaries about. Centralized decision-making can, sometimes, make it easier for governments to respond to and manage a crisis. That was, as we will see, probably the case with the 2000 fuel crisis and the 2008 financial crisis. By privileging the appearance of decisive action over deliberation, compromise and adaptation, however, Britain's centralized system, combined, as it is, with the tightening grip of political parties – or, more precisely, the currently winning factions within political parties – also makes it much more likely a political drama will result in a crisis in the first place.

Britain's system of centralized 'partyocracy', as I will call it, breeds short-term, sometimes compulsive, decision-making; group think; and a woeful combination of intransigence and sudden lurches in policy when the political music temporarily stops and one set of characters within a political party are ousted and replaced by their sworn enemies. Centralized partyocracy gives little or no opportunity, let alone incentive, to opposition parties to participate in policy-making debates and so to support decisions taken about wickedly difficult and longstanding policy challenges like social care, housing or climate change. This is one reason why, from the vantage point of an incumbent government, it makes sense to place such issues on the highest political shelf at the back of the garage in the hope that nobody notices them. The great claim that used to be made on behalf of the British political system was that it generated strong and stable government. Even that now feels a tad too buoyant. The 2010, 2015 and 2017 general elections did not give any single party a large-enough majority to pass the legislation it wanted. As for the stable part of the strong-and-stable equation, Tony Blair, David Cameron, Theresa May and Boris Johnson won general elections before being disposed of by their own party in circumstances very much not of their own choosing. Intra-party factional fighting, marked by ceaseless plotting and negative briefings to favoured political correspondents, and ministerial appointments and reshuffles driven by assessments of political loyalty rather than actual talent, consume huge amounts of energy and political capital.

Later chapters keep returning to and highlighting the trust-sapping and crisis-inducing consequences of centralized partyocracy. For now, savour this one vignette. One of my colleagues at the University of Sheffield, Kate Dommett, convened a series of focus groups to explore people's attitudes towards political parties whilst researching her book *The Reimagined Party*. At the start of these sessions, she asked participants to write down three words they associated with political parties. In the order of the frequency of their appearance, the most common were 'divided',

'London-centric', 'not listening', 'short-termist', 'self-interested', 'argumentative', 'ideologically driven', 'insular', 'out of touch' and 'aloof'. That constitutes a notably damning (if not entirely surprising) assessment. But what was really striking were the responses when she asked the same question of a group of *party activists*. Their chosen words were 'unrepresentative', 'corrupt', 'divided', 'tribal', 'self-serving', 'self-interested', 'undemocratic', 'unfair/unjust' and 'unresponsive'.[12] Even those who have gone to the trouble and expense of joining a political party really don't like political parties.

It took a long time to bolt the United Kingdom together. Anglo-Norman lords arrived in Ireland in the twelfth century. English soldiers marched into Wales in the late thirteenth century. Cromwell invaded Ireland in 1649.[13] A political union with Scotland was negotiated in 1707 and the United Kingdom conjured into existence against a backdrop of Scottish near-bankruptcy, threats and bribery made more palatable by the promise of continued religious, legal and educational autonomy.[14] A few decades later, the Jacobite uprising, led by the 'Young Pretender' to the throne, Charles Edward Stuart, was crushed in the Battle of Culloden. The Irish Parliament was abolished on 31 December 1800 and the United Kingdom of Great Britain and Ireland established the following day. Having fought a three-year war, the Irish Free State was constituted in December 1922, leaving behind the United Kingdom of Great Britain and Northern Ireland. In the early 2000s, the Union looked to be in reasonably good shape. Devolution seemed to have taken the sting out of the Scottish independence campaign. The 1998 Good Friday Agreement had broken the political impasse in Northern Ireland and was eventually followed, in July 2005, by the IRA formally ordering an end to its armed struggle. Yet, within a few years, nothing seemed as certain. The 2014 Scottish referendum, far from settling the issue of Scottish independence, sealed the Scottish National Party's ascendancy. After the high-water mark of the unexpectedly positive political relationship between two previously sworn political enemies, Ian Paisley and Martin McGuinness, the 'Chuckle Brothers' as they were rechristened, the Northern Irish peace process stalled before being broadsided by Brexit.[15]

None of this means that the break-up of the United Kingdom is now inevitable. Far from it. Support for Scottish independence has rarely exceeded 50 per cent for sustained periods of time. Ever since the 2021

Scottish Parliament election, where Nicola Sturgeon's party won more than twice as many seats as any other party, the Scottish National Party appears to have been running backwards at an accelerating rate. Support for Irish unification within Northern Ireland waxes and wanes but opinion polls show it may only be the preference of a slim majority of self-identified nationalist voters, let alone of all voters in Northern Ireland.[16] As of March 2023, support for Welsh independence was hovering at around 20 per cent.[17] It is nevertheless difficult to imagine a situation in which, over the next decade or so, the future of the Union does not still arouse intense political passions and simply disappears as a frontline political issue. What's more, the boundaries of the British state continue to be contested when it comes to the management of Britain's post-Brexit trade relationship with the European Union and, separately, the arrival, across the English Channel, of small boatloads of migrants. Whilst the sun has long since set on the British Empire, arguments about its legacy, about statues of slave traders and imperialists and the contents of the British Museum, have, if anything, become more acute.

New Labour inherited an economy in which growth was high, inflation was low, and unemployment was falling. This economic boom, the subject of the second part of the book, made possible a simultaneous rise in take-home income and public expenditure (although that rise in household income was far less than it would have been if New Labour had come close to fixing the cluster-bomb disaster of the British housing market – the subject of the opening chapter in Part Four). It did not last. The financial crisis triggered a recession; which led to an age of state-shredding austerity; which, somehow, got combined with around £370 billion in state-expanding quantitative easing (QE) by 2016 (pp. 248–50); which was followed by a Covid-induced economic lockdown; which was followed by another £400 billion of QE; and, eventually, and following the Russian invasion of Ukraine, a surge in inflation and interest rates.[18]

The World Bank records that in 2021 Britain ranked 132nd out of 161 countries in terms of its levels of gross capital investment formation.[19] The Paris-based think tank and economic consultancy the Organization for Economic Co-operation and Development (OECD) estimates that GDP growth per hour worked, a standard measure of productivity, rose by just under 2 per cent in Britain between 2015 and 2021, putting Britain in 36th place on a list of 41 member countries.[20]

Public sector national debt rose from £334bn in March 2000 to £1,145bn in March 2010 (following the financial crisis), and to £2,216bn by March 2022.[21] Higher public debt has not been enough to paper over income cracks. In the seven years between 2000/1 and 2007/8 median household income *after* housing costs increased by 16 per cent. Over the next fourteen years it rose by just 9 per cent.[22] These figures on household income include the effect of government transfers such as tax credits. If you look at average pay, then the picture starts to look *really* bleak. Between January 2000 and December 2007 average real, seasonally adjusted total pay (adjusted for inflation and at 2015 prices), grew by just under 21 per cent from £425 to £513 a week. The financial crash took some of the sheen off that figure. By the end of 2010 average pay had fallen by 4 per cent to £492. Since then, and through to the end of 2022, average pay has risen by a grand total of 0.6 per cent to £495 – in other words, to below the level it had been in 2007.[23] *Stagnation Nation*, a report published by the Resolution Foundation in 2022, offers a rather grim but telling observation about Britain's economic position.

> We might think of ourselves as a country on a par with France and Germany, but we need to recognise that, except for those at the top, this is simply no longer true when it comes to living standards. Low-income households in the UK are now 22 per cent poorer than their counterparts in France, and 21 per cent poorer than low-income households in Germany. It's important to comprehend just how material these gaps are: the living standards of the lowest-income households in the UK are £3,800 lower than their French equivalents.[24]

TOO EARLY TO TELL

For a lot of people, the year 2000, our formal starting point, is going to feel as distant as light escaping from a faraway galaxy. Around 17 million people, getting on for a third of the country's population, were not born in 2000. For those who were already alive and kicking 2000 will by now, probably, be at best half-forgotten. It was, after all, a long time ago. In May 2000 *Gladiator* was released at cinemas, cementing the status of Russell Crowe as one of the world's biggest movie stars. In August, Robbie Williams released *Sing When You're Winning*.

In October, the old Wembley Stadium hosted its final football match, a
1–0 loss to Germany. Kevin Keegan promptly resigned as England manager. In November, George W. Bush and the hanging chads beat Al Gore
to become the US president. Barack Obama, a freshman Illinois State
senator, was not a household name beyond his own household. Donald
J. Trump was already a name but seemed doomed to political obscurity
having tried and failed to get himself nominated as the presidential candidate for the consistently obscure American Reform Party. David
Cameron, Theresa May, Boris Johnson and Nick Clegg had not yet been
elected to Parliament. Keir Starmer, eight years away from being
appointed director of public prosecutions, was best known for his pro
bono legal advice to the defendants in the so-called 'McLibel' trial being
pursued by McDonald's against two environmental activists, Helen
Steel and David Morris.[25] Meanwhile, video cassettes for watching films
and CDs for listening to music were being challenged for the first time
by the cutting-edge technology of DVDs.

Yet, at the same time, and by the standards of university modern
history courses, which open in the seventeenth or eighteenth centuries,
the year 2000 is not really history at all. All written histories are provisional. As archives open and diaries are published, our understanding
of what happened and of what people thought they were doing and
why changes. As events unfold and political values shift, the way we
look at and interpret the past alters. During President Nixon's visit to
China in February 1972 the Chinese premier, Zhou Enlai, hosted a diplomatic lunch during which he was asked by one diplomat what he
thought about the French Revolution. He is famously recorded as
having replied that 'it was too early to tell'. This line has stuck because
it seems to say something quite important. History is complicated.
Take your time. Don't rush to judgement. Wait and see. Which, if true,
does not bode well for a history as contemporary as this, where the full
implications of events such as the Iraq War and the 2008 financial
crisis, let alone Covid-19 or the Russian invasion of Ukraine, are still
being played-out.

There is, however, a surprise ending to this story. During a seminar
in Washington DC in 2011, Chas Freeman Jr, a senior US diplomat
who had acted as Nixon's interpreter during his visit to China, said
he had been present when Zhou had said 'too early to tell'. He added
that Zhou had almost certainly been talking not about the French

Revolution *circa* 1789 but, instead, about the much more recent May 1968 student-led protest movements.[26] It is not hard to see how this might have happened. Zhou was a lifelong Communist who had first read Marx whilst studying in Japan in the immediate aftermath of the October 1917 Bolshevik Revolution before moving to Marseilles in December 1920 and co-founding the European branch of the Chinese Communist Party.[27] To him, the events of 1968 probably *did* look like a revolution in the making. So, it would hardly be a surprise if they were the first thing which came to his mind. In which case why would he want to say so little about them? It seems unlikely that Zhou did not have any views about left-wing, anti-capitalist, student-led protests in France, Germany, Italy and Mexico. Everyone else did. Yet Zhou had good reason to keep his thoughts to himself. The lunch at which he said 'too early to tell' was being held during the early stages of the rapprochement between the United States and China. It was neither the time nor place for Zhou to say what he really thought about the 1968 protests in front of a bunch of Western diplomats who were one of the targets of those revolutionaries. The lesson I draw from this is to proceed, rather like Zhou, with caution. Twenty-five years is not very long. But 'too early to tell' is also too strong. Our sense of history is important because it shapes how we think about who we are.[28] Getting a provisional sense of that history down on paper sooner rather than later feels like a risk worth taking.

That the year 2000 seems so long ago and that so much has happened since suggests one simple reason for writing this history. When it comes to events like the 2000 fuel crisis, the collapse of the Northern Rock bank in September 2007 and the Rose Garden press conference in May 2010 to launch the Coalition, all the subject of later chapters, we have all had time to forget a lot of what happened. It is true that many of the most significant events of the last few decades – the Iraq War, the financial crisis, Brexit and Covid – are already the subjects of detailed individual histories and reflections. A second reason for writing this book, therefore, is to show how and why these different slices of Britain's recent history link together and how, as I have already suggested is the case, we can now see how one crisis seeded the ground for and compounded the next. Lots of the events I focus on in the chapters that follow include descriptions of events in Westminster, Whitehall or the White House. But I also want to show how national and international politics intersects with, falls upon, or is occasionally driven by what happens at a local level. That constitutes a third reason for writing this book and is why the opening sections of subsequent chapters are set, amongst other locations, in Ellesmere Port, George Square in Glasgow, the Bilash Bengali restaurant in Wolverhampton, Morecambe, Aberystwyth and downtown Basra. Finally, and having shown how centralized partyocracy exacerbates or sometimes causes crises, I also want to use the concluding chapter to address Lenin's 'What is to Be Done?' question by suggesting some distinctly un-Leninist fixes to Britain's political system.[29]

HOUSEKEEPING

The rest of the book is composed of thirty-five chapters, divided into seven parts followed by a conclusion. Each chapter contains a varying mixture of historical description and commentary and analysis intended to say not only what happened at particular moments but, as far as possible, why it happened and its significance. Overall, the chapters follow a broadly chronological sequence (albeit imperfectly), starting on 31 December 1999 and ending in the summer of 2023. The first three parts, *Millennium*, *Boom* and *War*, do however jump back and forth. The final chapter of *Millennium* starts with David Cameron's election as Conservative Party leader in 2005 and runs through until the 2010 General Election. The first three chapters of *Boom* then go back to 2004. The first chapter of *War* goes back even further, to September 2001. Then, in the sixth part of the book, *Splintering*, Brexit, the subject of two standalone chapters, leaks into the prior discussion of Jeremy Corbyn's rise and fall. I don't do this to prove a postmodern point about the fluidity of time, but to establish some common themes running between the different chapters. A timeline of key events, together with a glossary of abbreviations, are included at the end of the book.

The subject of this book is the United Kingdom of Great Britain and Northern Ireland. I occasionally, and for specific reasons, sometimes refer to UKGBNI. More often, I talk about Britain or Great Britain and the British whilst recognizing the complicated history of those terms and the political tensions they give rise to. In the seventeenth century 'settlers' (to use a polite term) in the Jacobean plantations of Ulster often described themselves as being British or as being from British stock.[30] Yet, as the historian Linda Colley documents, when the United Kingdom of Great Britain was established by the Act of Union in 1707, there was no clear sense of a shared and unifying British national identity in either country.[31] That only started to emerge during the wars the new United Kingdom fought during the rest of the eighteenth century, wars that required a centralized army and a centralized system of taxation to pay for it. Skip forward another century or so and a Greater Britain, and a growing sense of shared Britishness, came, to many people, to be associated with a global, imperial identity. Great Britain was not just the United Kingdom by another name. It was a string of places, scattered across the globe, many of whose people felt themselves to be wholly British.

As the British Empire decayed, it was replaced by what was routinely and sometimes officially described as the British Commonwealth. It was only in the 1960s, by way of a Cabinet discussion paper written by the then secretary of state for Commonwealth relations, Duncan Sandys, that the idea of a Greater Britain and Greater Britishness extending well beyond the borders of UKGBNI was formally put to bed and the British Commonwealth became simply the Commonwealth. What was the day-to-day name that ought to be given to the island left behind? As Sandys pointed out, the United Kingdom (let alone the United Kingdom of Great Britain and Northern Ireland) was 'totally lacking in popular appeal and inspires no emotions of affection or loyalty'.[32] So, as Stuart Ward demonstrates in his book *Untied Kingdom*, Britain and the British became the default factory setting. I have followed the same logic here in deciding to talk about Britain and Britishness rather than UKGBNI or United Kingdom-ers. Needless to say, later chapters nevertheless track the post-devolution interplay between British and Scottish, English, Welsh, Northern Irish and Irish political and cultural identities and their relationship to the British state.

Finally, a word of explanation about the title, or, rather, its etymology. British farmers have traditionally used twine to bale hay. American farmers tended to use wire, hay wire. That wire was kept bound in tight coils, which, if not enough care was taken, would whip around dangerously when released, before then becoming impossibly tangled. So, at some point in the early 1900s, Americans started to talk about machines or work situations 'going haywire' – becoming erratic, chaotic, malfunctioning and out of control. Humble hay wire was, however, important enough to American life to give rise to a second everyday expression, albeit one that is now largely lost in the mists of time. On American farms and, it would seem, lumber camps hay wire was used, rather like duct tape today, not only to bale hay but as an all-purpose tool for making temporary, makeshift repairs to whatever needed fixing. As a result, and for a while, particularly in New England, people would talk about a 'hay wire outfit': a slightly contemptuous term for any team of workers with poor equipment, slipshod standards and a reputation for patching things up rather than trying to fix them properly. It is with both these meanings in mind that I joyfully landed on *Haywire* as offering a single word description of modern Britain.

PART ONE

Millennium

In January 2000 Anthony Charles Lynton Blair was forty-six years old. He had been a Member of Parliament for seventeen years; leader of the Labour Party for six; and prime minister since May 1997. Most importantly, he looked untouchable. New Labour, it was true, was widely seen to have over-promised and under-delivered during its first term. Blair's reputation as, in his own words, a 'pretty straight kind of a guy', had also taken a significant hit when he had been less than straightforward about a £1 million donation to the Labour Party from the Formula One chief executive Bernie Ecclestone.[1] These bumps and scrapes did not however seem, at this point at least, to have done any real lasting damage. Blair, in his early days as Labour leader, had been dismissed as a political novice and a lightweight. 'Bambi' had however grown into the role of prime minister and was making a difference.[2] He had led the negotiation of the Good Friday Agreement (pp. 188–9). He had successfully introduced a windfall tax on privatized utility companies and a minimum wage, and had worked with his chancellor, Gordon Brown, to make the Bank of England operationally independent. The immediate future looked bright. The Conservatives were divided; the economy was booming; and in a political world in which the party thought to be occupying the centre ground usually won, New Labour was still seen as being slap bang in the political middle.

Looking back at New Labour in the early 2000s is rather like watching the first hour or so of James Cameron's 1997 movie *Titanic*. Everything is ticking along and everyone is happy, but you know the iceberg is dead ahead. The first of these icebergs, Iraq, plays the leading role in Part Three, *War*. The second, the 2008 financial crisis, takes centre stage in Part Four, *Crash*. The chapters here are perhaps, by comparison, a little humdrum. When it came to domestic policy, that is what New Labour sometimes was. Indeed, after the bangs and crashes of Thatcherism and the Conservative Party's breakdown under John

Major, humdrum may have been what many voters wanted. As Alan Partridge observed of the *Titanic*: 'people forget that on the *Titanic*'s maiden voyage there were over a thousand miles of uneventful, very pleasurable cruising before it hit the iceberg.'*

After the doom and gloom of the introductory chapter, I start here, by way of a little light relief, with the Millennium Dome and a Dome-themed review of the political identity of New Labour. I've just said that one of the things New Labour had going for it in the early 2000s was the sense that it sat at the centre ground of British politics. Chapter 4 looks at what this means and why it mattered and, more importantly, why, for a moment in September 2000, during the fuel crisis, it looked like it might not matter quite as much as everyone had thought. Chapter 5 charts the progress of devolution, as an exemplar of New Labour's Third Way, centrist, split-the-difference politics and, later, the rise of the Scottish National Party. The final chapter of Part One describes the emergence of another, eventually fatal threat to New Labour's electoral ascendancy, a modernizing Conservative Party.

* This line comes from the opening episode of *Knowing Me, Knowing You* when Keith Hunt, the former host of the *Loony Breakfast Show* on Radio Leeds, and now the host of *This is Your Life*, irritates Alan first by grandstanding his catchphrase 'Am I right?' (Audience – 'You're not wrong') and by then mocking Alan's catastrophic phone interview with Roger Moore, 'Does the word Titanic mean anything to you?'

2

A Dome with No Point

GOING OUT, OUT

On the early evening of 31 December 1999 Queen Elizabeth was taken by boat to the Millennium Dome in Greenwich. There, she was met by Tony and Cherie Blair. The assembled guests were then entertained with performances from, amongst others, Jools Holland, Mick Hucknall and two acrobats who performed a lovers' duet. With time ticking away, the Millennium Star, a 203-carat De Beers diamond, was placed at the centre of the stage and targeted by laser beams, which filled the arena with light. As the clock struck midnight, the Queen was visibly over-joyed and joined hands with the duke of Edinburgh and Tony Blair to sing *Auld Lang Syne*. At the end of the night, Blair, who had promised a celebration 'so bold, so beautiful, so inspiring that it embodies . . . the spirit of the future', expressed himself filled with joy.[1] New Labour had shown not only that it could flawlessly organize a major event but that it was the political embodiment of Britain's renaissance. Everyone went home happy, and the newspaper reports the next day were glowing.

Except, of course, that did not happen. Instead, almost everything that could have gone wrong went wrong. The Millennium Wheel at Southbank, aka the London Eye, failed a safety inspection and did not operate. The 10.8-second-long 'River of Fire' along the Thames was so underwhelming most people failed to notice it happening. There were long queues to collect tickets. These were then followed by even longer queues to get on Tube trains and through security checks. The Metro-politan Police, it transpired, had provided just one X-ray machine for the evening. When guests finally made it inside, the Dome was freezing cold. The food and drink were poor. The acrobats were 'cheap and vulgar' and wore sheer body stockings, which made them appear naked.[2] The Queen, several commentators observed, did not appear particularly pleased to be there. Neither, as it turns out, was Blair.

> The rest of the evening passed in a blur. We finally got home around 2 a.m. 'I thought the evening was rather fun,' Cherie said as we clambered into bed. 'Darling,' I replied, 'there is only one thing I am going to thank God for tonight, and it is that they only come around every thousand years.[3]

The problem was that it was not over.

For the next year the Dome remained open as a visitor attraction and a public relations disaster. The Y2K Bug, which lots of people thought might destroy every computer in the world, cause planes to drop out of the sky and hospital ventilators to turn themselves off, turned out to be a non-event.[4] But the Dome was a lasting headache. At £50 for a family (about £100 in 2023 prices), the tickets were seen as expensive. There were queues everywhere. The various zones within the Dome lacked any 'wow factor' and the temperature inside remained somewhere between refreshing and Arctic. It got worse. The Dome had to attract 12 million visitors to cover its construction costs. It did not come close. So, the Millennium Dome Project, which was running things, kept running out of money and had to be bailed out. The Dome's chief executive resigned. Then, in May, its chairman followed. In June, a large hole appeared in the Dome's roof. Then the Dome ran out of money – again. In November an armed gang attempted to steal the De Beers diamonds. At least someone wanted to visit, the joke went.

As the cultural historian Stephanie Barczewski observes, Britain is and has for some time been a country whose national heroes and cherished heroic moments – the Light Brigade, Scott of the Antarctic, Dunkirk – are all associated with failure.[5] Even though it got to appear in the 1999 Bond movie *The World Is Not Enough*, there was nothing particularly heroic about the Dome's failure. After twelve months and a total outlay of around £628 million, much of it in the form of government grants, the Dome closed.[6] The *Guardian* interviewed several staff.[7] Jan Anderson was a business strategy manager. 'There have been so many days when we've just sat here and cried. I've lost count.' Sholto Douglas-Home was the marketing director. 'It was like launching a new restaurant and giving everyone food poisoning on the first night.' Matt Costain was a trapeze artist who performed every day in the main arena. 'I've stopped telling taxi drivers what I do. I tell them I'm a tax inspector.'

NEW LABOUR: LEFT, RIGHT AND DULL

The Dome was a bit of a mess and cost a bit of money. But it was not *that* big a deal.[8] The Queen did not catch pneumonia on the opening night. None of the trapeze artists fell to their death. Most people who visited the Dome went away reasonably happy with what they had seen.[9] Years later, politicians sometimes invoked the spectre of the Dome as a horrible warning of policy failure. But it is probably fair to say that Iraq and financial deregulation just about edged it in terms of lessons to be learned. Besides, over the longer haul, it did not end up working out too badly. The Dome was eventually bought by a private company, rebranded as the O2 Arena, and hosted pop concerts, the ATP Tennis finals and auditions for the *X Factor*. None of this, however, was enough to stop the Dome from becoming its very own self-sustaining political metaphor.

For Blair, New Labour was a new and different political force in British politics. It offered a 'Third Way' for a country tired of old ideological debates.* New Labour was about combining a commitment to the free market, globalization and private ownership with social justice. New Labour was at the 'radical centre'[10] and daring to be different: 'I want us to be a young country again with a common purpose, ideals we cherish and live up to, not resting on past glories, fighting old battles and sitting back, hand on mouth, concealing a yawn of cynicism.'[11]

---

* Tony Blair, *The Third Way: New Politics for the New Century* (London, 1998). Blair's Third Way was the British leg of a broader political alliance that included Bill Clinton's New Democrats, the German Chancellor Gerhard Schröder, the Dutch prime minister Wim Kok and a succession of centre-left coalitions in Italy. The late Colonel Gaddafi used to enjoy discussing his own version of the Third Way with Blair but, somehow, never received an invitation to one of the international conferences where Blair, Clinton and others met to discuss their ideas. Anne Mellbye, 'A brief history of the Third Way', *Guardian* (10 February 2003). On the Libyan connection see Jeremy Wilson, 'Tony Blair says he used to listen to Colonel Gaddafi's theories about politics', Business Insider (11 December 2015). Blair's meetings with Gaddafi came as a result of his eventually successful efforts, starting in 2004, to persuade the Libyan leader to abandon his efforts to buy weapons of mass destruction in exchange for closer economic and trade links.

New Labour wanted to challenge the miserabilism of the left and the social callousness of the right and show that Britain could change. It wanted the country to be less ideological and policy to be evidence-based. It wanted a fresh start.

New Labour's Conservative opponents argued, on the one hand, that the Third Way was gibberish. In 1995 Boris Johnson, at that point assistant editor and chief political columnist at the *Daily Telegraph*, described it as 'spin-driven vanilla flavoured candy floss nothingness'.[12] On the other, they also argued that New Labour was not really new and that Blair and New Labour could not be trusted. Blair looked and sounded different. But in reality he was just another in a long line of Labour leaders who would increase taxes, redistribute money and tell people how to lead their lives. The only difference was that New Labour was hyper-incompetent and overly obsessed with its own image. Enter the Dome as Exhibit Number 1. Its costs had escalated. Its contents had disappointed, and it had become a financial black hole into which public money was being flung. Here, for example, is the then Conservative Party leader, William Hague, standing outside the Dome on the day of the launch of Labour's 2001 election manifesto, delivering a speech called, not at all chillingly, 'Remember the Dome':

> The Dome was to be the first paragraph of today's manifesto, instead it stands as the last word on why Britain cannot afford another four years of Labour . . . it is a monument to their contempt for the priorities of ordinary people . . . they have spent the last years consumed by their own self-image rather than getting to grips with the problems this country faces.[13]

From the other side of the political ledger, the left-wing, socialist, objection to Blair and New Labour was that Blair was really a Conservative and that New Labour had sold-out to free-market, state-shrinking, Thatcherite neoliberalism. Blair was a privately educated, upper-middle-class lawyer who had convinced himself he could turn Britain into a classless society by the simple expedient of endlessly saying that Britain was a classless society. New Labour was promising to end the cycle of 'boom and bust' but had little interest in reducing inequality or challenging big business. The Labour Party was meant to represent ordinary workers. New Labour had no real interest in doing so. As Peter Mandelson, one of its ideological high priests, had said, New Labour was 'intensely relaxed about people getting filthy rich'.[14]

The Dome was a small but typical part of this story. It had started life as a Conservative folly: the brainchild of Michael Heseltine. Labour, whilst in opposition, had ridiculed it as a waste of money. Yet, typically, New Labour, once elected, had decided to press on regardless. The Dome offered a glimpse of New Labour's one-sided efforts to forge partnerships with business: the money-making temple at which New Labour wanted to worship and be accepted. Large corporations had been collared to sponsor zones within the Dome. BAE Systems and Marconi, both major defence contractors, sponsored the Mind Zone; Tesco the Learning Zone; the City of London the Money Zone; Ford the Journey Zone; and British Airways and the British Airports Authority the Home Planet.[15] This was bad enough but, in return for their hard cash, the companies were then given a say in what was to be exhibited. Unsurprisingly, the Home Planet Zone did not go hard on climate change, and the Money Zone did not ask tough questions about high bank profits, financialization and short-term investment horizons.

Blair and New Labour had plenty of critics. The most important thing to say about them is that their criticisms did not add up in the early 2000s (the other important thing to say is that they started to make a lot more sense a few years later). The key problem with the Conservative's argument that New Labour was no different from Old Labour was that New Labour, during its first three years in office, had kept its promise to stick to the previous Conservative government's spending plans. Public expenditure, measured as a share of GDP, had, as a result, *fallen* since the 1997 General Election.[16] As for the left-wing objections, Blair probably didn't care. After only a few years in office New Labour could point to some solid and sometimes distinctly left-looking policy achievements: not only the windfall tax and the minimum wage, but devolution, working families tax credits, Sure Start centres and the Macpherson inquiry into the murder of Stephen Lawrence. This was never going to be enough for New Labour to make it onto the shortlist for the most revolutionary socialist government of the year award. But that did not matter one bit to Blair, who had long ago reached the settled view that revolutionary socialism was not going to win Labour many marginal constituencies in the South of England.

There is, however, a third political parable that might be extracted from the Dome. New Labour was all about being radical. 'We're at our best when at our boldest,' Blair told the 2002 Labour Party confer-ence.[17] This was a very Tony Blair thing to say. Yet, looking back, New Labour was perhaps a little like Coldplay. A lot of people were listening to it and sometimes humming the tunes they had heard, even if a lot of those same people were convinced it was all a bit dull. The Dome had no real point. It was there to celebrate the millennium but did not really say anything about the future. It looked like it ought to be educational, but it fell well short of the Natural History Museum or the Science Museum. It was meant to be *FUN (!!)* but it was not a fun park like Alton Towers or Blackpool Pleasure Beach. The various business-sponsored zones into which the Dome was divided were not awful. They were, however, full of interactive displays that did not work and which, when they did work, were not all that interesting.

Stephen Bayley, who was the Dome's creative director before resign-ing in 1998, reflected on how 'I wanted the best brains, artists and architects in the world to work on this. They said: "no, you can't have them". Instead, they got a lot of people who usually do trade fairs in Harrogate.'[18] Ouch. Lord Richard Rogers, who had made his name as one of the architects of the Pompidou Centre before turning his hand to the Dome, argued that the designers had spent too much time trying to be popular rather than focusing on quality: 'There was no really vision-ary person with a clear belief in charge of it . . . We needed a ringleader with a vision, cultural or sports-related didn't matter, but we didn't have that. You can't just say, "I want to make the most popular place."'[19]

Here, then, was perhaps the real structural flaw in New Labour's Third Way. It was not awful. It was not socialist. It was not neoliberal Thatcherism. But it was at times just a little bit underwhelming. Blair took a booming economy and a huge parliamentary majority and God-given buckets of political charisma and did . . . a lot of good things, but perhaps not nearly as much as he could have.

Whilst he was leader of the opposition, Blair had attacked the short-termism of British business and called for the creation of a 'stakeholder' economy (pp. 486–7).[20] When the Conservatives argued this showed how Blair really wanted, deep down, to nationalize everything, stake-holding was immediately abandoned. Blair toyed with the idea of some sort of pact with the Liberal Democrats to realign British politics and create a lasting anti-Conservative majority but decided against it when it became apparent that New Labour would not need any electoral help

(p. 269). He talked about fundamentally transforming the British state but got cold feet when it came to the House of Lords. He contemplated joining the European single currency but changed his mind (p. 206). He ducked reform of the social care system (p. 35) and housing (p. 217). After the September 2000 fuel crisis, he became warier of radical options for reducing carbon emissions (p. 49). He failed to ask tough questions – indeed, any questions – about the financial system (p. 100). New Labour had a lot of good and lasting achievements, including those listed a few paragraphs above, which later chapters will say more about (starting, next, with the NHS). When it came to domestic politics, New Labour was, however, consistently risk-averse. There are worse epitaphs for a government than this. But if New Labour was right to suggest in its 1997 General Election campaign song by D:Ream (featuring a young Professor Brian Cox) that 'things can only get better', it is also the case that they could have been better still.

THE CAPITAL OF EVERYTHING

One other lesson that might be drawn from the Dome's life and not very pleasant times was that, in a highly centralized country, London is, in terms of its relative size and gravitational pull, England's Death Star. In 2000 London's population of 10.5 million was greater than that of Manchester, Birmingham, Leeds, Newcastle, Glasgow, Liverpool, Sheffield, Nottingham, Bristol and Edinburgh combined.[21] The civil service, the law, finance and the arts were all based in London. As were most broadcasters. If you lived anywhere other than London, the news where you were came after the news where they were.[22] There was nothing particularly new in any of this. London had gone through a rough patch in the 1970s when its population had fallen and the West End had been the world capital of shabbiness. Yet, one way or another, London had been England's largest population centre long before William the Conqueror set up shop in the Palace of Westminster and built the Tower of London a few miles to the east.

London was the largest city. It was also overcrowded, polluted, expensive, massively unequal and far from being a happy place. When the Office for National Statistics started to measure well-being and life satisfaction in the early 2010s, it found that eight of the twelve areas with the lowest levels of well-being, as measured in terms of levels of life satisfaction, happiness and anxiety, were in London. Step forward Lambeth, Hackney, Islington, Camden, Lewisham, Greenwich, Haringey and Southwark.[23] The happiest places were the Orkney Islands, Na h-Eileanan an Iar (the Western Isles), Fermanagh and Omagh, the Shetland Islands, the Causeway Coast and Ribble Valley. None of which, you will have noticed, are anywhere near London.

Which probably misses the point. People may not have liked London, but they wanted to live there, and they wanted to live there because London was the centre of everything in a way the Orkney Islands were not. Between 2000 and 2012 London's population increased by a further 15 per cent.[24] When brains drained, they drained to London, which offered the best jobs and the best prospects of making a lot of money.[25] It had the hipster heavens of Shoreditch, Hackney and Brixton.[26] It had the most ethnically diverse population.[27] The best restaurants.[28] The best galleries; the tallest buildings; and the most popular tourist attractions.

In theory, the Dome could have been built anywhere. The ready and waiting National Exhibition Centre in Birmingham was the early front-runner, and Derby also made it onto the shortlist.[29] The eventual decision to build the Dome in London was not exactly a shock result, however. In the 1880s an international conference held in Washington DC voted to accept Greenwich, the site of the Royal Observatory founded by Charles II in 1675, as the Prime Meridian. London was the centre of the world then and it remained, by some distance, the centre of the country in 2000. As a part of the millennium celebrations Manchester got the Lowry Centre, Cornwall got the Eden Project, Leicester got the National Space Centre, and Scotland and Wales got refurbished sports stadia. On 31 December 1999 it was, however, London which grabbed all the attention. *Plus ça change*, as the French probably didn't say when, in 2005, it was announced that London had beaten Paris in the race to hold the 2012 Olympics.

A CULTURE OF SPIN: NEW LABOUR AND THE PRESS

New Labour had a love-hate relationship with the press which would have done justice to any of the long list of rom coms released in the early 2000s hot on the heels of *Bridget Jones's Diary*. In 1995 Blair flew to Hayman Island, Queensland, to address a News Corporation conference and Rupert Murdoch. This paid off when the *Sun* later endorsed New Labour (albeit at a point when Labour was already way ahead in the polls). It nevertheless remained a founding item of faith within New Labour that the *Daily Mail*, *Daily Telegraph* and *Daily Express* would take every opportunity they could to blame New Labour for anything and that Murdoch would follow their lead if he thought doing so made commercial sense. Having seen Old Labour lose the 1992 election, when Neil Kinnock had been repeatedly attacked in the tabloid press, New Labour felt it had no alternative but to spin policy announcements, drip-feed exclusives and attack its opponents – including those within the parliamentary Labour Party who did not subscribe to the philosophy of the Third Way.

New Labour's advancement of party-political fighting to a new twenty-four hours a day, seven days a week, level sometimes worked. The government's Strategic Communications Unit, led by Alastair Campbell, centralized media management, shaped the flow and tone of the media and pulled the government out of more than a few holes along the way. Spin-doctoring nevertheless came at a cost. By the turn of the millennium, the idea that New Labour would say or do anything in order to get elected and could not be trusted to tell the truth had become a commonplace. As a result, any new policy initiatives were routinely dismissed as being 'all spin and no substance'.

There are plenty of academics who have spent their working lives looking at this issue and, overall, the idea that the tabloid press directly influences how people vote does not get too much support. Most people either read a paper which fits with their existing views or largely discount what they read. In particular, the British Election Study found no evidence Labour had lost in 1992 because of anything the *Sun* or the other tabloids had said.[30] Yet there is a broad academic consensus that the press does, nevertheless, exercise a great deal of agenda-setting power. Day to day, before, during and after an election campaign, editors choose what issues to cover; how to frame them; and whether to put the resulting stories on the front page or buried on the sixth. Some days, something happens which is so important every paper ends up reporting on the same story in broadly the same way. On other days, editors have a great deal of discretion about which headlines to lead with and which stories to commission. Moreover, these choices can influence the stories covered by TV news channels.[31] Newspapers don't directly influence how people vote. But they influence what people think are the most important issues. And what people think are the most important issues influences, in turn, how they vote. So, as much as New Labour's efforts to manage the press ended up looking self-defeating, it is hard to see what alternatives there were available to it.

Which brings us back to the Dome. Long before it opened, the press decided the Dome was going to be a disaster and that this should be a headline story. It was therefore particularly unfortunate that, on New Year's Eve, newspaper editors were amongst the hundreds left waiting hours to collect their tickets and clear security checks. The former editor of *The Times*, Peter Stothard, reports how when Blair was told about what was happening, as it was happening, he collared Lord Charlie Falconer, the minister in charge. 'Please tell me you didn't have the media coming here by Tube from Stratford just like ordinary members of the public.' Falconer replied, 'Well, we thought it would be more democratic that way.' Blair responded, 'Democratic? What fool thought that? They're the media, for Christ's sake. They write about the people, they don't want to be treated like them.'[32] For the next year, the Dome did not come close to a favourable headline.

THE ROYAL FAMILY'S IMPROVING FORTUNES

One final footnote to the Dome's tribulations relates to the standing of the Royal Family. In 1992 the Queen's self-styled *annus horribilis* featured 'compromising' tabloid photographs of the Duchess of York and her financial advisor; the tell-all publication of *Diana: Her True Story*; the formal announcement of Charles and Diana's separation; and a fire at Windsor Castle. Then, in 1997, public mourning over Diana's death gave way to anger at the Royal Family for its apparent failure to publicly mourn her in a sufficiently performative manner. For a moment, the Royal Family's position looked a little shaky. The Queen herself seemed to acknowledge this when, during a speech to mark her fiftieth wedding anniversary in 1997, she said that the monarchy 'exists only with the support and consent of the people'.[33]

By December 1999, when the Queen led the celebrations at the Dome, the monarchy once again looked secure. Blair's talk of making Britain a 'young country' probably did not go down well in Buckingham Palace. Cherie Blair also ruffled feathers by deciding not to curtsy when she met the Queen at Balmoral in 1997.[34] Tony Blair was, however, no more likely to initiate a debate about the future of the monarchy than he was to nationalize Asda. Republicans still argued that an unelected head of state who was supreme governor of the Church of England made no sense in a democratic and secular age (pp. 301–2) and that change was possible. There were few takers. Hereditary succession was not an easy principle to defend but monarchism had, by this point, increasingly morphed into Queenism: the conviction that Queen Elizabeth worked hard and cared deeply, and that nothing else really mattered. Questions about Charles's suitability to be king if the Queen ever abdicated remained but were largely dispelled by the Queen's own announcement, in 2002 during the Golden Jubilee, that she had no intention of resigning and handing Prince Charles the Crown. This left republicans few places to go, and even the live broadcast, that June, of the execrable Party at the Palace, featuring Ricky Martin, S Club 7, Atomic Kitten and Brian May playing 'God Save the Queen' from the roof of Buckingham Palace, did not provoke much in the way of civil unrest.

Over the next decade, whilst New Labour crumbled, 'The Firm' continued its recovery. The Queen's initially awkward relationship with Tony Blair stabilized. A culling of public payments to minor royals in 2005 generated a positive set of headlines about modernization and prudence. There were still a few problems to overcome. The government found itself wading through a set of court cases relating to the publication of Charles's 'black spider' letters to ministers (so-called because of the prince's handwriting) on assorted political issues of the day. In 2010, Sarah Ferguson, the duchess of York, was caught telling a *News of the World* reporter, posing as a businessman, that she could 'open any door you want' if paid sufficiently.[35] A year later, her former husband, then known (in his happier days), as 'air miles Andy', resigned from his position as a trade envoy amidst questions about his relationship with the sex offender Jeffrey Epstein.[36]

Yet, during a period in which so many other institutions of British national life were being laid low by one crisis or another, the Royal Family was on a good run. The Queen was seen as trustworthy in a way few, if any, politicians were.[37] Looking back years later, in 2018, *The Economist* highlighted this change in fortune.

> The Queen represents stability in an unstable world, as well as unity in a polarised one. She has spent 66 of her 92 years on the throne and has survived 12 prime ministers and innumerable political crises. The royal household has done a good job of moving Prince Andrew and his ilk into the background and replacing them with a new generation. Prince William and Kate Middleton look exactly like the dignified mannequins that Bagehot's constitution demands. The marriage of Prince Harry and Meghan Markle is likely to be another brilliant chapter in this story of renewal. There are blemishes; Ms Markle's family look almost as strange as the Windsors. But the happy couple nevertheless offer the dignified branch a chance to reinvent itself for a more multicultural and touchy-feely age.[38]

As it turns out, *The Economist*'s timing was not great. This article was published in May 2018. Eighteen months later, Prince Andrew decided it would be a good idea to offer an interview to the BBC *Newsnight*'s Emily Maitlis. Not long after, Harry and Meghan declared a 'thanks but no thanks' Mexit. This is, however, a story for a much later chapter.

In 1669, the same year as the Battle of Cádiz during the Anglo-Spanish War, Edward Chamberlayne, a Fellow of the Royal Society, published *Angliae Notitia: Or, The Present State of England*. It radiated a Panglossian sense of sunny optimism: 'O happy and blessed Britannie, above all other Countries in the World, Nature have enriched thee with all the blessings of Heaven and Earth. Nothing in thee that is hurtful to Mankind, nothing wanting in thee that is desirable.'[39]

The mood was not quite as cheery in 2000. But, after the ideological bearbaiting of the 1980s and the sleaze and recession of John Major's administration in the early 1990s, there was, broadly, and the Dome notwithstanding, a general sense, if not of contentment, then at least of 'I've seen worse' faint praise for New Labour.

3

The NHS: An Expensive Breakfast

'A FIRST CLASS FARE'

After he turned down a contract offer from Nottingham Forest to play professional football, David Frost graduated from Cambridge in 1961 with a third-class degree in English before becoming a trainee at Associated-Rediffusion, the London ITV franchise. Not long after, the writer and producer Ned Sherrin asked Frost to host the satirical *That Was the Week That Was*. After then presenting the eponymous *Frost Report* and launching the careers of Ronnie Barker, Ronnie Corbett and John Cleese, Frost secured his global reputation by interviewing the former president Richard Nixon in 1977. The film telling the story of those interviews, *Frost/Nixon*, was released in 2008 with Michael Sheen playing the role of Frost. After returning to Britain as one of the presenters of ITV's *TV-am* in the early 1980s, Frost moved to the BBC and hosted *Breakfast with Frost* on Sunday mornings between 1993 and 2005. On Sunday, 16 January 2000, with the Dome already operating as a fully functioning negative publicity machine, Frost's guest at BBC Television Centre in West London was Tony Blair. He answered questions about the European Union; a possible future referendum on proportional representation and co-operation with the Liberal Democrats; Cherie Blair's recently announced pregnancy; police stop-and-search powers; Ken Livingstone's bid to be London mayor; and, first and foremost, on the NHS.

During the 1997 General Election campaign New Labour had promised to save the NHS from Conservative underfunding and privatization. It made a promising enough start. In the early 1990s the Conservatives had established an 'internal market' for healthcare by giving new NHS Trusts budgets to purchase health services from local providers. New Labour abolished this quasi-market and, in its place, promised to reduce waiting lists. By 2000, however, the government was struggling to meet the expectations it had raised. The core issue was money. New Labour had promised to stick to the Conservatives' spending plans and those plans were frugal. The health secretary, Frank Dobson, argued in a private memorandum to Blair that, 'if you want a first-class service, you have to pay a first class fare – and we're not doing it'.[1] Extra money looked like it might make good political sense. Data collected by the British Social Attitudes survey showed that getting on for 60 per cent of people said they favoured paying more taxes in order to increase public spending.[2] Blair was sympathetic but unconvinced. There was, he thought, a big difference between what people said and what they really thought. Tax levels were already right at the edge of what the public would tolerate. In October 1999 Dobson, feeling increasingly disillusioned, resigned from Parliament to run against Ken Livingstone for London mayor. He lost.

In the winter of 1999, the NHS started to run off the rails. A flu epidemic led to the cancellation of emergency operations and to refrigerated lorries being used as emergency morgue facilities. Newspapers picked up the story of seventy-three-year-old Mavis Skeet, whose surgery had been cancelled four times and whose cancer had, as a result, become inoperable.[3] Suddenly, the looming NHS crisis had a human face. To add fuel to the fire, Lord Winston, the fertility expert and media personality, gave an interview to the *New Statesman* in which he described inadequacies in the treatment his own mother had received and said that the NHS was 'slowly deteriorating'.[4] For a political party which went out of its way to create the impression it cared about every single news headline, this was a disaster. Healthcare was, in New Labour's view, a political banker: *its* issue and *its* stick with which to beat the Conservatives whenever it wanted.

THE AVERAGE OF THE EUROPEAN UNION

Frost opened his interview with the prime minister by quoting a letter from Mavis Skeet's daughter, Jane, to Blair:

How can you justify the loss of a life because of the lack of a suitable bed? I know you are a decent man so please tell me how you can allow all this to happen and I beg you not to let anyone go through the same agonies we must suffer in these coming weeks.[5]

Blair, who looked visibly uncomfortable, did his thing of appearing sympathetic and reasonable. He spoke about short-term pressures and Conservative cuts. He pleaded for a 'sense of balance' and suggested newspapers were going out of their way to create an unfair impression 'nobody was getting care within the Health Service'. None of this was hugely convincing. Then, suddenly, Blair started to talk about how economic growth would, over the next few years, allow the government to commit 'substantial extra resources for the Health Service': 'At the end of the [next] five years we will be in a position where our Health Service spending comes up to the average of the European Union, it's too low at the moment so we'll bring it up to there.'

Blair's entirely unexpected and surprisingly specific promises about spending increases were repeated by Downing Street press advisors, led that evening's news bulletins and were widely welcomed in even the Conservative-supporting press. Michael Gove, a political columnist at *The Times* and still five years away from being elected to Parliament, was reduced to complaining that Frost had gone 'so soft' on Blair his programme should have been sponsored by Lenor.[6]

Gordon Brown had been planning to say something about NHS expenditure in his March 2000 budget. For this reason, he reacted to Blair's announcement with all the enthusiasm of someone being told their train from Birmingham to Plymouth was going to be turned into a replacement bus service.[7] The result was a few days of political infighting and policy paralysis. On the following Tuesday, Blair's promise to raise NHS expenditure to the European average was redescribed by officials and spin doctors as an 'aspiration'.[8] Then it became apparent nobody in 10 Downing Street knew what the European spending average was and so could not say what it would take to raise Britain to that level.[9] Suddenly, Blair's promises began to look like an exercise in spin, with policy being made on the hoof in order to calm a political squall. By Prime Minister's Questions on Wednesday, the Conservative leader, William Hague, was taunting Blair about 'Frost on Sunday, panic on Monday, U-turn on Tuesday and waffle on Wednesday'.[10] All of which made for an uncomfortable few days for Labour. Looking back, the Frost interview was, nevertheless, a turning point. For the very first time Blair had publicly recognized New Labour was going to need to pin its colours to the mast of higher public expenditure and from this, as we will see, a lot of other things followed.

THE SPENDING STARTS

Sure enough, in the Budget two months later, Gordon Brown commissioned a long-term review into the NHS's funding needs. This was a very New Labour thing to do. Knowing the public did not trust politicians or New Labour's spin cycle, employing an expert to deliver a non-partisan assessment was a politically clever way of not appearing too political. The problem came in knowing which expert to press-gang. The Treasury initially spoke to the former director general of the Confederation of British Industry, Adair Turner. It soon became clear though that Turner wanted to assess whether a taxpayer-funded healthcare system was the most efficient option. Turner, it seemed, thought the answer to this question was yes, but he nevertheless wanted to be seen to be asking the question. The Treasury did not want him to do so. So, instead, Derek Wanless, who had recently stepped down as group chief executive at NatWest, was approached. Wanless was perfect. His record as a senior banker would give any recommendations he made about increasing NHS spending more credibility. What's more, he was happy to take the existence of the NHS in its then form as a given.[11] Two years later, and to nobody's great surprise, the Wanless review concluded that the government 'must expect to devote a significantly larger share of its national income to healthcare over the next twenty years'.[12] In accepting the report's recommendations, Brown said he was prepared to raise National Insurance contributions to pay for it.

Between 2000/1 and 2008/9 real public-sector expenditure on health, adjusted for inflation and at 2021/2 price levels, increased by over 60 per cent, from £85 billion to £138 billion (or from 4.9 per cent of GDP to 6.9 per cent).[13] Given that public health expenditure had only risen in real terms by 50 per cent between 1980 and 2000, this constituted, by any measure, a significant shift in policy direction and it made a real difference. Joseph Stalin was reported to have once said of the Red

Army that quantity has a quality all of its own. The same was true of the NHS in the 2000s. The number of people per General Practice doctor fell from 1 in 1,627 in 2000 to 1 in 1,336 in 2010.[14] Sixty-eight new hospitals were built. In 1997 the average age of NHS buildings was older than the NHS itself. By 2005 that was true of only a quarter of NHS buildings.[15] The average waiting time for in-patient NHS appointments, which had fallen only marginally from fourteen weeks in 1997 to thirteen weeks in 2000, plunged to just four weeks in 2009.[16] Avoidable mortality fell from 293 per 100,000 people to 227 per 100,000 over the same period.[17] Infant mortality fell from 5.6 per 1,000 births in 2000 to 4.2 in 2010.[18] One-year cancer survival rates rose from 64 per cent in 2000 to 70 per cent in 2010.[19]

This did not mean New Labour got everything right. Something like £10 billion was lost on a failed IT project to modernize patient records.[20] New contracts with GPs were generous in the extreme and resulted in a £300 million overspend.[21] Huge, scandalous, failings in healthcare at the Alder Hey Children's Hospital, Staffordshire Hospital and Furness General Hospital went undetected. Public spending may have been increasing in Britain, but it was still lagging a long way behind France and Germany.[22] Preventative health and mental healthcare services were still significantly underfunded, and the government struggled to come close to meeting the targets it had set to reduce health inequalities. New Labour also ducked taking tough decisions when it came to social care. It established a Royal Commission on the subject in 1998, which recommended the introduction of free personal care. New Labour welcomed the report but then did nothing about it until its 2010 General Election manifesto, by which time it was too late.[23] In July 2010 the incoming Coalition government asked Andrew Dilnot, the former director of the Institute for Fiscal Studies and warden of Nuffield College, to chair a review into the funding of social care. Dilnot recommended significant funding changes, including a cap on the maximum amount any individual would have to spend on social care. The Coalition welcomed the report but delayed implementing its recommendations. In the 2017 General Election Theresa May revised and replayed Dilnot. Labour denounced her 'dementia tax' and May abandoned her position in real time. By the time the Covid-19 pandemic began, social care was not a disaster waiting to happen: it was already a disaster.

Blair and Brown (and Wanless) nevertheless made the right call on the

NHS. As money poured in and outcomes slowly improved, public sat-isfaction with the NHS rose from around 45 per cent in the early 2000s to 50 per cent by 2005 and 70 per cent by 2010.[24] The 2000s were the period during which the NHS became its own national icon. The former Conservative chancellor Nigel Lawson famously once said that the NHS was the closest thing 'the English have to a religion' (he presum-ably meant British).[25] Under New Labour this religion went evangelical. The NHS became a living symbol of trust, duty and commitment. The NHS logo, designed in the early 1990s with its Pantone 300 (NHS Blue) colour and Frutiger font, became an increasingly visible brand, featuring heavily in the 2012 London Olympics' opening ceremony (p. 312). Ever since, the NHS has come out on top in polls asking people what makes them proud to be British.* In narrowly party-political terms New Labour could now headline any election campaign by argu-ing it had saved the NHS and that the Conservatives would destroy it overnight. You could reasonably argue the NHS was just one policy and just one part of New Labour's domestic political statecraft. You might as well argue Iraq was just one strand of New Labour's foreign policy. Twenty years on, if you wanted to argue that, all things con-sidered, New Labour was a force for good, increased NHS spending is almost certainly going to be top of your list of its achievements.

NHS REFORM AND SOCIAL DEMOCRACY

Let's go back to the Frost interview. After Blair had said his piece about future spending increases, he went on to argue that 'it's not just a ques-tion of resources' and 'we also need reform and change in the structure'.[26]

---

* A 2020 poll for the *Daily Mail* asking people what made them proud to be British put the NHS on 71%, followed by fish and chips on 58%, a full English breakfast on 52%, the Queen on 48% and the British countryside on 44%, with sarcasm, the perennial underachiever of British national culture, and James Bond limping along behind on 30% and 28% respectively. Jennifer Newton, 'Britons reveal the top 50 things that make them proud to be British', *Daily Mail* (2 April 2020). A 2022 poll by Ipsos MORI put the NHS on 55%, ahead of 'our history' (33%), 'the Royal Family' (28%), 'the British Army' (24%), 'our culture and arts' (21%), 'British sports teams' (15%), 'the BBC' (12%), 'our position in the world' (11%), 'having a free press' (10%) and 'British business' (6%). Ipsos, 'What makes us proud to be British?' (15 August 2022) (https://www.ipsos.com/en-uk/what-makes-us-proud-be-british).

At the time, this got largely overlooked. It should not have been. Nothing could have been more Third Way than extra spending *and* tough reforms. For Blair, 'modernisation requires money. But money without modernisation is money not well spent ... [and so] is not an optional extra. It is a "must do".'[27]

The case for reform was, in many respects, a respectable one. New Labour could spend more money but, with a rising and ageing population, demand was, as the Wanless review recognized, always in danger of outstripping supply.[28] Although it was not, strangely, something Wanless mentioned, the NHS was also particularly vulnerable to the 'Baumol Effect'. In the 1960s the American economist William Baumol observed productivity tends to rise more in some parts of the economy than others. This is because in some industries, for example car manufacturing, there are far more opportunities to replace people with machinery. This matters because when productivity rises, companies can afford to pay higher wages. This is a good thing. Nevertheless, it also creates a problem. Industries where productivity gains are lower because there are fewer opportunities to replace people – healthcare, social care and teaching being obvious examples – will also come under pressure to pay higher wages in order to attract staff. As a result, their overall costs will rise.[29]

In the United States, where healthcare is largely privately provided, rising costs mean a constant pressure to increase healthcare insurance premiums. In Britain, where healthcare is largely publicly provided, rising costs mean a constant pressure to raise taxes. An ageing population then kicks in on top. Governments can compensate for the Baumol Effect by choosing to provide fewer health services for free, or they can provide a lower quality service with longer waiting times. Alternatively, they can try to prevent public-sector wages from rising as quickly as those in the private sector and risk industrial action. New Labour did not want to do any of these. Instead, it opted for higher taxes but also, with one eye on the future, NHS reform.

The problem Blair initially faced, according to Peter Mandelson (who, between 1999 and 2001 was secretary of state for Northern Ireland) was that, whilst he knew he wanted to reform and modernize the NHS, 'neither he, nor the rest of us, were quite sure how to achieve this'.[30] The NHS was, after the US Defense Department, the Chinese People's Liberation Army, Walmart and McDonald's, the world's largest employer.[31] Reforming it was never going to be easy. That said, it was an organization which, in England at least, could be managed from White-hall and, as time passed, and in theory, from 10 Downing Street.[32] Initially, and in a fit of public-sector managerialism, New Labour went all out for top-down targets as a means of making a difference and improving best practice. When it came to some issues – most notably waiting times – targets made a positive difference.[33] They were, how-ever, also vulnerable to gaming. A hospital with a target to discharge patients within a certain number of days would sometimes discharge them just before the cut-off point, regardless of whether they were fully recovered, only for them to have to be readmitted shortly after, a prob-lem, needless to say, compounded by the underfunding of the social-care system.

Targets and the cult of 'delivery' were *very* New Labour, and target-setting became one of the political and cultural motifs of the age. Everything and everyone could be measured, inspected, ranked and exhorted to perform better if provided with the right kind of inspir-ational management, clear enough objectives and a self-motivating commitment to excellence. In the 1960s, during the Cultural Revolu-tion, young Chinese people, including the Communist Party's future general secretary, Xi Jinping, were sent to the countryside to live and work in rural areas as a part of the less-fun-than-it-sounds Down to the Countryside programme. In the 2000s a Managerial Revolution in the UK doomed countless public-sector middle managers to endless strategy-forming away-days in anodyne hotels or conference centres.

New Labour never entirely lost its ardour for inspection and rank-ings, establishing the Commission for Health Improvement, the Healthcare Commission and the Care Quality Commission as new regulatory bodies. Blair's thinking nevertheless evolved and became increasingly fixed on large-scale, structural, reform. The first move came with the establishment of a new breed of 'foundation hospitals', to be given more local autonomy and the freedom to borrow money to fund capital investments. This proved controversial with Gordon Brown, in the name of socialist virtue and Treasury prudence, winning a battle to limit the amount any hospital could borrow.[34] Blair then raised the stakes further, promoting, from about 2005 onwards, the development of a quasi-market in healthcare, which shared many of the features of the Conservative internal market New Labour had abolished in the late

1990s. But this time round New Labour also made it clear that Primary Care Trusts could, if they wanted, negotiate contracts with private healthcare providers.

What does the twin-track of higher budgets and NHS reform tell us about New Labour's political identity? How new and how different was New Labour? As we have seen, the Conservative argument was that it was no different from its Labour predecessors. The socialist argument was that Blair was utterly different to any previous Labour leader. This brings us to a key figure in Labour's intellectual history: Anthony Crosland. Crosland was first elected as a Member of Parliament in 1950; was a candidate for Labour's leadership in 1963 and 1976; and sat in the Cabinet as, variously, president of the Board of Trade, secretary of state for local government, secretary of state for the environment and eventually, and prior to his sudden death in February 1977, foreign secretary.

Crosland's lasting achievement was *The Future of Socialism*, published in 1956 as a consciously revisionist tract for Labour's right-wing.[35] Capitalism, Crosland argued, had changed and the Labour Party needed to change with it. Markets and competition were generating economic growth and increases in income. The case for public ownership, which had underpinned the socialist case for nationalization and economic planning in the 1930s and 1940s, was, as a result, no longer as relevant. Instead, he argued, a social democratic Labour Party should focus on using tax revenues to improve public services and promote equality. Crosland's argument was hugely influential and Crosland-ite social democracy became the dominant (but not uncontested) governing philosophy of the Labour Party under Harold Wilson and James Callaghan.[36]

Blair argued that New Labour was still a social democratic party; that he was intent on improving the NHS; and that the evidence of his good faith was his willingness to increase public spending on it. To many of his supporters, he was, in this sense, just another in a long line of centrist, social democratic, Labour leaders happy to leave the free market to do its thing and to spend the resulting proceeds. It was in this vein that Blair described the 'Third Way' as a 'modernised' form of social democracy.[37] To his most passionate left-wing critics, Blair was something very different and much less palatable: a free-market, state-shrinking, neoliberal Thatcherite. At that time, however, there was a second, softer but more persuasive version of that left-wing critique. Blair believed markets and competition were not only the best thing for the private sector, as Crosland had argued, but *also* the best thing for the public sector because they were the key to higher productivity. Hence the NHS reforms. For the right of the Labour Party this was something new, and for some of New Labour's supporters and architects, including Gordon Brown, it was a step too far and a retreat from Labour's proud, social democratic history. The injection of market forces into the public sector was wrong in principle, would not work in practice and amounted to a form of privatization.

I'll return to this argument about the demands of social democracy in a later chapter about the personal and ideological battles between Blair and Brown. For now, there is one more point worth making. Looking back from the 2020s, it is easy to talk about 'Blair' or 'New Labour' as if he or it were one fixed thing. They were not. Blairism, if there was such a thing, went through several different stages.[38] The Blair who talked about 'stakeholding' in 1996 was not the Blair who extolled the virtues of free markets and globalization in later years. The Blair who acquiesced in Robin Cook's proclamation of an 'ethical dimension' to British foreign policy was not the Blair who pressured his attorney general, Lord Goldsmith, to abandon a Serious Fraud Office investigation into corrupt payments to a number of Saudi princes by the defence firm BAE Systems.[39] Similarly, the Blair who entered office in 1997 determined to abide by the Conservative government's spending plans was not the same one who appeared on *Breakfast with Frost* in 2000, or the one who later extolled the virtues of foundation hospitals or quasi-markets.

PRESIDENT BLAIR?

Blair's handling of the NHS also tells us something about the location of political power in Britain's hyper-centralized political system. In the 1980s Margaret Thatcher was often described as being a de facto British president, who could be relied upon to ride roughshod over her Cabinet.[40] Her replacement, John Major, who lacked such an overwhelming parliamentary majority and inherited an ideologically divided Cabinet, was more circumspect. Long before he had arrived in 10

Downing Street, Blair's chief of staff, Jonathan Powell, had warned civil servants Blair's arrival would signal a return to a 'Napoleonic system'.[41]

He was not kidding. Blair and Brown decided, between themselves, to give the Bank of England operational independence. 'They'll agree with it. You don't need to put this to Cabinet,' Blair told the Cabinet secretary.[42] Not long after, Blair announced he wanted to press ahead with the Dome and invited the rest of the Cabinet to agree with his assessment.[43] Blair sidelined the secretary of state for Northern Ireland, Mo Mowlam, during the Good Friday peace talks.[44] He made health policy on the hoof when being interviewed by David Frost. He 'gripped' (a favourite Blair word) the fuel protests in 2000 and, later, the political management of the Afghan War and the run-up to the Iraq War. The Cabinet still met every week to discuss events, but it was not always clear what difference those meetings made. Key decisions were instead squared, in advance, with ministers in bilateral meetings: 'sofa government' as it became known.* By 2000, the political observer and historian Peter Hennessy was ready to conclude that the Cabinet system of collective government, which, in his view, even Margaret Thatcher had abided by for the most part, had 'gone', to be replaced by a new 'command model'.[45]

Was Blair operating, as many people argued, more as a president than a prime minister?[46] He created a new Strategic Communications Unit in Number 10, through which all government press releases and policy statements had to be cleared, and gave its director, Alastair Campbell, the authority to issue direct orders to civil servants. He established a set of new policy units within 10 Downing Street with a political reach extending into government departments. These included 'The

---

* John Prescott says Blair treated the Cabinet like it was the Shadow Cabinet, 'making his decisions with his chums on the sofa'. He is honest enough to admit he only complained when he realized he was no longer being invited to sit on the sofa with him: Prescott, *Prezza: My Story*, p. 255. Prescott instead was forced to rely upon Billy the Big Mouth Bass to know who Blair was meeting with. Billy was a life-size model of a fish which Prescott had given Blair as a present. When a button was pressed, Billy would sing Bobby McFerrin's 'Don't Worry, Be Happy'. Blair placed the present on top of the television set in his office in Number 10. After hearing Billy sing, visitors could be relied upon to ask Blair where he had got the fish from and to then tell Prescott what has happened. 'I bought it as a bit of a laugh. But it is the only bloody way I can keep up with who he is seeing. They all come out and say "I saw your bloody fish, John"'. Michael White, 'Prescott goes fishing for undercover information', *Guardian* (18 September 2000).

Prime Minister's Delivery Unit' led by Michael Barber (who returned to Downing Street to review government delivery in 2021).[47] Blair even got as far as planning to purchase a prime ministerial jet – 'Blair Force One' as it was immediately dubbed.[48]

Blair also *personalized* the business of being prime minister in a way that, at times, felt rather American presidential-ish.[49] As the person who had rescued the Labour Party from the political wilderness and won the 1997 election, Blair believed that he, uniquely, knew what the public mood was on any issue; hence his absolute conviction, in the late 1990s, that the public would not tolerate tax rises to pay for the NHS.[50] More than that, he cast himself, his background and personality, as embodying national characteristics and values in a way typical of aspiring or incumbent US presidents. Blair, as he kept reminding people, was a father of young children and had a wife who worked. He was someone who was prepared to do his share around the house. He was a football fan and supporter of Newcastle United. He was an affable guy and not remotely pompous: 'Call me Tony.'[51] Above all, in his early days, Blair managed to convey the image he was not really a politician at all but had, somehow, ended up as a Labour MP by accident. His Conservative rival, William Hague, had, aged sixteen, addressed the 1977 Conservative Party conference. Blair, for his part, avoided politics at university and was, like most voters, he seemed to suggest, intensely un-ideological. All of this was, of course, carefully crafted. Blair was not an ordinary bloke. He had been to Oxford, had become a pupil barrister and had first stood for Parliament in a by-election in Beaconsfield when he was twenty-nine. Blair did not drive a car, cook a meal, or do his own laundry after he became prime minister.[52] Blair was, however, extraordinarily good when he needed to be at the political art of stylized ordinariness.

For this reason, the idea of President Blair has some merit; in other respects, the presidential analogy was entirely misleading. Blair may have dominated the Cabinet, but he had to contend with a chancellor who had his own power base in the Treasury and, increasingly, his own policy agenda and ambitions. Blair, as we will see later, at one point toyed with the idea of breaking up the Treasury in order to secure the supremacy of 10 Downing Street (p. 202). He backed away having decided that the costs involved in antagonizing Brown and perhaps provoking his resignation were too great.

No American or French president would have had to (just about) tolerate Gordon Brown in the way Blair did. On the other hand, and unlike his American counterpart, Blair did not have to worry about negotiating with a legislature controlled by another party (or, for that matter, with strong English regional governments with political minds of their own). With an overall majority of 179 seats after the 1997 election, and 167 seats after 2001, Blair did not, day to day, have to spend too much of his time negotiating with recalcitrant MPs from his own party in a way Bill Clinton, Barack Obama and Joe Biden, whatever the trappings of presidential power, all had to do in order to get new policies approved (Donald Trump, for the most part, did not even try). Blair lost the support of many of his MPs when he reinterpreted social democracy and pushed for the injection of market forces into the NHS. Yet, in the end, Blair, although he was often risk-averse, nevertheless used his parliamentary majority to get done the things he most wanted to do – and did so with a political ease that most American presidents could only have dreamed about.

4

Fuel on a Fire

THE SPARK AT STANLOW

The Stanlow Refinery at Ellesmere Port sits between the River Mersey and the M56, around 15 miles to the south and east of Liverpool city centre. It is a huge site, the size of three hundred football pitches, and one of half a dozen major oil refineries in Britain.[1] Late on the evening of 7 September 2000 a group of around one hundred protestors, most of them farmers, arrived at the refinery and blocked its entrance, preventing lorries from entering or leaving the next day. This was the ignition point for a sudden and spectacular protest about the price of fuel that, for a short while, looked like it would do real damage to New Labour.

It all started back in June 1992 when John Major had attended the Earth Summit in Rio de Janeiro and signed the Climate Change Convention. Rio was the first moment climate change had really grabbed the headlines in Britain. Major appeared on evening news broadcasts from Rio in shirt sleeves talking about the future dangers the world faced if carbon emissions were not reduced. A little over a year later his chancellor, Norman Lamont, introduced a fuel escalator, which increased, dramatically, the level of tax on fuel, whilst committing to further above-inflation increases in the future. This was presented as an affordable and necessary environmental measure. New Labour, when it assumed office, left the policy in place. As petrol prices continued to rise in the late 1990s, partly because of the fuel escalator and partly because of an increase in the global price of oil (following an earlier period of decline), opposition to the escalator steadily grew. The Conservatives, now in opposition, framed it as one of a large number of new 'stealth taxes'. Road hauliers and farmers argued the cost of fuel was destroying their businesses and costing jobs.

In his November 1999 pre-Budget report, Gordon Brown announced that he was planning to suspend the fuel escalator and was roundly condemned for doing so by environmental groups. Petrol prices, pushed upwards by global demand, nevertheless continued to rise. Some Labour MPs blamed the fuel companies for price gouging. Hauliers and farmers, with the wind in their sails after Brown's apparent U-turn, blamed the government for not cutting fuel duty, and kept hammering home the point that Britain still had Europe's highest fuel prices.[2] Some hauliers organized go-slow convoys on motorways. Then, in late August, fuel protests began in France and Spain, where prices had also been rising.[3] At first, these were of interest to the British press mostly because they had left some tourists stranded at blockaded ferry ports ('typical French, protest about anything', and so on). Then, on the evening of Monday 4 September, Brynle Williams, a fifty-one-year-old farmer from the village of Cilcain, North Wales, helped organize a protest meeting at Ruthin cattle market. After a lot of angry speeches, not much happened. A few days later, a second meeting was held at St Asaph livestock market at which someone suggested blocking the entrance to the Stanlow refinery 25 miles to the east and, as Williams himself put it, something just 'went click'.[4]

A SENSE OF CRISIS

The Stanlow protest worked. Tanker drivers, whether out of a fear for their own safety or out of sympathy with the protestors, or both, refused to cross the picket line. Reporters who arrived to cover the story issued warnings that, within a day or two, if the protests continued, garages would run out of fuel. Spurred on by these stories more protestors arrived at Stanlow's gates. As did the police. Everyone expected they would remove the protestors. They did not. The protestors remained and the fuel tankers were left parked. Everything then spiralled. Copycat protestors appeared outside other refineries. Long queues appeared at garages as drivers reacted to news bulletins by deciding they had better buy as much fuel as possible as soon as possible. Supermarket managers warned they would soon run out of food if the lorries they depended upon to make deliveries ground to a halt.

Sometimes, politicians leap to call something a crisis because, by doing so, they can justify taking an otherwise difficult course of action. When the Stanlow refinery was blockaded the first reaction of New Labour's media managers was very different. They argued everything would resolve itself soon enough and that, essentially, there was nothing to see. Tony Blair was on a self-styled 'listening' tour of the north of England, which looked like a warm-up act for the General Election widely expected to be called shortly after. On the evening of 11 September, he was in Hull where he was guest of honour at a dinner at Mr Chu's Chinese restaurant to mark the thirtieth anniversary of the first election of his deputy prime minister, John Prescott, as the local MP. It did not go to plan. The police advised Blair it was not safe to go to the dinner because of the presence of an irate group of fuel and fox hunting protestors. He ended up eating a bag of fish and chips in the back of his car.[5] The next morning, he abandoned his tour and returned to London to chair a meeting of the Civil Contingencies Committee, COBRA, a kind of cut-price White House Situation Room.[6] Taking an upbeat line, Blair reassured journalists everything was under control and that deliveries to petrol stations would resume within twenty-four hours.

This looked, by any measure, a rash promise to make. The first problem the government faced was that the protests looked to be attracting quite a lot of support. The Richard Scarry Rule (named after the children's author) holds that politicians ought never to mess with workers whose jobs are depicted in children's books.[7] Farmers therefore constituted a big problem. The Conservative leader William Hague, seizing the moment, described the protestors as 'fine upstanding citizens' and suggested they had been left with no alternative but to protest because the government had refused to listen.[8] The next big problem was that police chief constables, who could have ordered their local forces to clear the picket lines, made it clear they did not want to intervene in what looked like a political dispute. Labour MPs – and some ministers – were not best pleased, given that the police had expressed no such qualms during the miners' strike in the 1980s. At first, it looked like there might be a way out. The police hinted they might get involved if refinery managers told them the protestors were trespassing. The oil company executives were, however, reluctant to be seen to be demanding police action for fear of alienating public opinion.

For a couple of days, it all looked a bit bleak. Blair's chief of staff, Jonathan Powell, described pulling 'every lever available' only to find 'none of them seemed to be connected to anything'.[9] Ministers discussed mobilizing the Army.[10] Alastair Campbell, in his diaries, records Blair as saying: 'if we don't get things moving pretty quickly, I'll have to let someone else take it on.'[11] But just when it looked like there would be no easy way out, it began to turn around. The key to it turned out not to be the police or the oil executives but leaning into the sense of crisis and turning this against the protestors. Blair started to get some traction with an argument that the protestors were a threat to democracy and the rule of law. 'We cannot and will not alter government policy on petrol through blockades and pickets ... that's not the way to make policy in Britain and as far as I'm concerned it never will be.'[12] Friendly trade-union leaders were then lined up to repeat the same messages about lawful protest and, behind the scenes, to talk to local union organizers about the damage being done by the protests.[13] Next, the health secretary, Alan Milburn, was deployed with all the subtle force of a brick to argue that the protests were crippling the NHS and putting lives at risk because staff could not get to work and ambulances could not be refuelled. To underline just how serious this all was, the NHS was put on Red Alert and non-emergency operations cancelled.[14] Meanwhile, and if that were not enough, Gordon Brown was sent on a tour of news studios to assure voters the government was listening, whilst hinting at fuel price tax cuts in the next budget.[15]

This was all quite clever, and it was all highly co-ordinated. Public opinion began to shift, and the protest leaders found themselves under acute pressure to answer some difficult questions to which they had no clear answers and no media team to help. Shortly after 5 p.m. on Thursday 14 September, a week after the protest had started, Brynle Williams called the whole thing off. 'We are backing down in the interest of the general public ... we have won a moral and just victory.'[16] He added the protests would resume in sixty days if the government did nothing to address their demands. The remaining blockades were dismantled and deliveries to petrol stations, more than 90 per cent of which had been forced to close, resumed shortly after.

The world went back to normal. Ministers emerged, blinking, from the news studios in which they had been trapped, looking like people walking out of a cinema in the afternoon only to discover it is still light outside. The NHS reinstated the operations it had cancelled or had threatened to cancel. Supplies at supermarkets held up. Within a few weeks the news caravan had moved on to cover flooding, the closure of the MG Rover Longbridge plant in Birmingham and the Hatfield rail crash on 17 October, which killed four people and eventually pushed the private company that owned and ran the rail track and signalling systems, Railtrack, into administration, to be replaced by the publicly owned Network Rail. A few days before Williams's self-imposed deadline, Gordon Brown announced a freeze in fuel duty until 2002 and a set of other support measures for drivers and hauliers. Some of the September protestors were mollified. Others said Brown's concessions were a token gesture and threatened more direct action. A slow-moving convoy of lorries in early November, designed to disrupt traffic on the A1, did not amount to much. A public spat between Williams and David Handley, one of the other co-organizers of the September protests, then complicated matters further. The second wave of protests fizzled out (as they did again in 2005 and 2007).[17] As for Brynle Williams, he eventually joined the Conservative Party and was elected to the Welsh Assembly, where he served as shadow minister for rural affairs. In 2010 he was misdiagnosed as suffering from ulcerative colitis when, in fact, he had cancer of the colon. He died in April 2011.

For a few months in the autumn of 2000, newspaper commentators remained convinced Labour's election prospects had been irreparably damaged.[18] In October a handful of polls put the Conservatives ahead of Labour, the first time this had happened since 1993. By November, Labour had, however, started to recover the ground it had lost. Between February and March 2001 a mass outbreak of foot-and-mouth disease led to the closure to the general public of large parts of the British countryside; the slaughter of around 6 million cows and sheep; and huge economic losses to the tourist industry, which lost an argument with the National Farmers Union about whether vaccinations offered a better option for dealing with the disease. It also led to the postponement of the General Election, widely expected to take place in early May. When that election eventually took place, on Thursday 7 June, New Labour comfortably won a second term. If there was a highlight to this otherwise dour campaign in which turnout fell by 12 percentage points and very few seats changed hands, it came when John Prescott thumped a local agricultural labourer, Craig Evans, who had thrown an egg at him during a campaign trip to Rhyl. Evans, it transpired, was a pro-hunting activist who had participated in the Stanlow blockade.[19] Prescott, it turned out, had boxed when he was younger. The events in Rhyl constituted, as he later put it, one way of connecting with the electorate.*

The fuel crisis had a lasting legacy in terms of environmental policy. New Labour continued to talk about the importance of climate change (Chapter 10) but became a lot more cautious about the nuts and bolts of environmental policy. A new road-building programme was launched. Later, in 2007, a national road-pricing scheme was abandoned at the last minute for fear of the likely reaction amongst motorists, nearly 2 million of whom had signed a parliamentary petition to express their anger.[20] The fuel tax escalator was, meanwhile, quietly parked in a corner. The fuel crisis probably also helped to convince Blair, if he needed any convincing, that the best way of dealing with a crisis was for him to lead from the front by taking personal control of decision-making. In the grand scheme of things, the fuel crisis did not end up looking all that important at the time. It nevertheless tells us something about emerging fault lines in British politics and New Labour's vulnerabilities.

THE POLITICS OF DRIVING

In July 1895 Evelyn Ellis drove an imported French Panhard et Levassor car from Micheldever in Hampshire to his home in Berkshire. In the 1890s the first cars were built in Britain by Fred Simms, a London engineer who, through a connection with the German industrialist Gottlieb Daimler, had acquired the rights to build Daimler engines. His cars were not cheap and for the next century car ownership remained

* John Prescott, *Prezza: My Story, Pulling no Punches* (London: Headline Review, 2008), p. 246. Prescott, when he was much younger and working as a ship's steward, had been a good-enough boxer to have won a boxing contest on a cruise liner. He had been awarded his winner's medal by former prime minister Anthony Eden, who was holidaying on the same boat. Andy McSmith, 'Prescott the Labour heavyweight v Craig Evans, the gentle giant of Rhyl', *Daily Telegraph* (18 May 2001). For a moment it looked like Prescott, who had earlier got into a fight whilst at the BRIT awards, might have to resign. In the end, he attracted a fair bit of public support, along with letters of endorsement from Sean Connery and Alex Ferguson (Prescott, *Prezza: My Story*), p. 250.

strongly linked to income. The richer a family was, the more likely it was to drive a car. By 2000 that relationship had not only broken down but was on the way to reversing itself.[21] Younger people, and people living in cities, had become much less likely to own a car, regardless of their income.[22] Meanwhile, people living in small towns and rural areas had become much more likely to own a car, with rates of ownership increasing at the fastest rate in families with below-average household incomes.[23]

This did not mean money was unimportant when it came to driving. Quite the opposite. Because more people on lower incomes were relying upon their car, car ownership increasingly went from being a symbol of affluence to a key cause of financial stress, with insurance premiums and petrol prices becoming for many people make-or-break expenditure items. Add in high-profile arguments about climate change and it is not hard to see why car ownership and the price of fuel was a big enough political issue to trigger significant protests in 2000.

The issues at stake were, however, cultural and political as well as economic. The term 'white van man' had been around in Britain since the 1990s. In the 2000s it acquired a real political edge when the *Sun* started to run a white-van-man column offering common-sense political opinions on issues of the day. Then, in October 2002, the BBC motoring series *Top Gear*, which had been running since the late 1970s, was relaunched with Jeremy Clarkson and Richard Hammond (and, later, James May). For the next decade, *Top Gear* was one of the BBC's biggest commercial successes, broadcast in more than two hundred countries.[24] In its heyday the programme was consistently slick, sometimes funny, always blokey and often deliberately controversial. One recurring part of this controversy centred upon repeated accusations of homophobia and racism about the way in which Clarkson, egged-on by Hammond, parodied, variously, Mexicans, Asians, Argentinians and Americans.[25] This was not all. *Top Gear* was not only about fast cars and the joys of driving. It was also about mocking anyone who did not like fast cars and driving and used public transport or cycled or droned on about climate change (and who, for all these reasons, were precisely the kind of people most likely to support the fuel escalator). A lot of this, when it was not simply offensive, was silly and some of it came close to self-parody. The programme's producers were, however, clever enough to know that driving had the potential to become a bit of a culture-war issue ahead of its time. Indeed, looking back, Clarkson even got his moment of being 'cancelled' when, in 2015, the BBC decided not to renew his contract following a physical altercation with one of the programme's producers. All three presenters promptly decamped to Amazon Prime.[26] (Clarkson then went from strength to strength, combining a new TV hit, *Clarkson's Farm*, with a newspaper column in which he described how he hated Meghan Markle more than the child murderer Rose West (p. 458).) By the time of the 2019 General Election, the Conservatives were recording a 17-percentage point lead amongst car owners and Labour an equivalent lead amongst those without a car.[27]

THE POLITICS OF US AND THEM

In the introduction to this part of the book I said that one of New Labour's political assets in the early 2000s was the sense it occupied the political centre ground. Blair's thinking on this was straightforward. Most political activists tend to have stridently left-wing or right-wing views. Most voters, on the other hand, are instinctive moderates. Labour had lost the 1983, 1987 and 1992 elections because it was regarded as being too far to the left. To win it had to move to the right. As Alastair Campbell records Blair as saying in his diaries: 'We have to stay bang in the centre ground. I am where the country is. Hague is more right-wing than the country and GB [Gordon Brown] is more left wing than the country.'[28]

Blair was right that, in 1997, most voters self-identified as being at the political centre and most of them voted Labour.[29] That had not changed by the early 2000s. Figure 1, which uses data taken from the 2001 British Election Study (BES), shows how a representative sample of voters responded when asked to place themselves and the Labour Party along an 11-point scale, running from 0 (left-wing) to 10 (right-wing). The black (self-placement) line is where people placed themselves and the grey (Labour placement) line shows where they thought New Labour was. The results are a Labour strategist's dream come true. The two lines are basically the same shape. Most voters saw themselves as being at the centre ground, and most voters also thought this was where New Labour was.

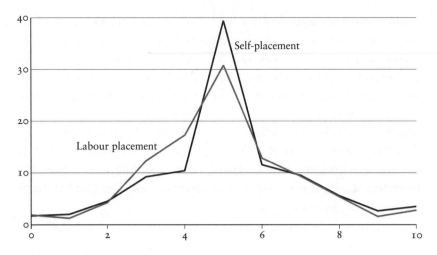

Figure 1. Left–Right Position in the 2001 General Election

The horizontal axis shows spatial positions running from far left (0) to far right (10). The vertical axis shows the % of respondents selecting particular positions.

British Election Study, 2001: Cross-Section Survey, questions Bq38a and Bq38f (via http://nesstar.ukdataservice.ac.uk/webview/).

The centre ground is, all other things being equal, generally a good place to be in politics. But being there is not the end of the story.[30] For a start, and as Jeremy Corbyn forcefully argued once he became Labour leader in 2015, the position of the centre ground changes and can be changed by political argument (p. 352). What's more, a lot of voters don't really have a clear sense of what left or right is, or whether a particular party is to the left or right of another. Something like 20 per cent of the respondents to this BES survey did not or could not answer this question about spatial position.[31] Alternatively, voters may prioritize competence over political position, or vote for the political leader who, to them, seems most trustworthy or who they can identify with and they think best understands the problems they face.

All of which brings us back to the fuel crisis. There can be no doubt that, in September 2000, many of the fuel protestors, Brynle Williams included, saw themselves as being to the right of New Labour. The fuel crisis was not, however, necessarily about left and right. The political nerve the protestors were touching on – and that *Top Gear* also hit when the presenters berated bus lanes, bicycles and speed cameras – took a different form. It was about the pretensions of a self-serving political, metropolitan, out-of-touch elite who did not understand ordinary people and what they liked and the difficulties they had doing something as simple but important as filling up their car at a garage. In other words, the reason why the 2000 fuel protests were so important is that they offered the first glimpse, in the period covered by this book, of a populist politics that viewed the existing political system as rotten and the country as being divided not into left, right and centre, but into a relatively small, corrupt, untrustworthy elite and a vast swathe of ordinary people whose values and interests were being ignored.[32]

New Labour may have colonized the centre ground, but it was vulnerable, hugely vulnerable, to this populist attack. For a start, the protestors were right to argue New Labour was, increasingly, a political party of the largest, increasingly non-driving, metropolitan cities. In the 1997 election New Labour had, in winning a landslide, swept the board in Britain's largest cities.[33] Yet, even at this moment of maximum success, New Labour's appeal was not geographically broad. It won only one seat in rural Lincolnshire, a minority of the seats in North Yorkshire and none in Dorset. What's more, and to its populist critics, New Labour was not simply a party of the large cities but, specifically, a party driven by the interests of London – the elite power centre to which its representatives and apparatchiks, no matter where they had come from, had defected to. Blair was the MP for Sedgefield, County Durham, but to almost everyone he looked and sounded like someone who had lived in North London for most of his adult life, as indeed he had.

To its critics, New Labour was also increasingly and obviously middle class: full of the kind of people who, as the protestors often argued, could easily afford higher fuel prices. In September 2000 the Cabinet included three people – John Prescott, John Reid and David Blunkett – who had either grown up in real poverty or had, for a long time, worked in manual jobs before going to university. On the other side of the ledger, it also included six people who had attended fee-paying independent schools; six people who had studied at Oxbridge; five former university lecturers; a solicitor; three barristers; and the daughter of a former prime minister.[34] One of those barristers, the prime minister, later confessed in his memoirs he should have seen the fuel crisis coming because 'the children's nanny, Jackie, had been complaining about [fuel costs] for weeks before the crisis broke'.[35] Yes, really. As for the broader Parliamentary Labour Party, the number of MPs from working-class occupational backgrounds had fallen from around one in three in the 1960s to around one in ten.[36]

To all of this can be added one more problem for the largest political parties in general and, given that it was in government, for Labour in particular. Surveys show that most voters prefer and are more likely to vote for a candidate standing to be an MP who has a strong prior local connection, all else being equal.[37] It is not hard to see why this might be so. Local representatives are, voters might think, more likely to have had similar experiences and to understand local needs. In other words, they are less likely to be part of an out-of-touch and untrustworthy elite who only care about their own career. Yet only around a half of all MPs in 2001 (although, to be fair, 58 per cent of Labour MPs) had a direct connection to their local constituency by way of having been born, educated or worked there before, or having served as a part of its local government.[38]

SAVED BY THE ECONOMY

All of which begs a question. If New Labour was vulnerable to the kind of populist challenge offered by the fuel protestors, why, with the partial exception of the campaign against English regional devolution (pp. 64–5), did that challenge then fade away before reappearing with a vengeance in the 2010s? Why was there no blockbuster sequel to the fuel protests?

It probably helped that immigration – another issue which could arouse a populist 'us and them' set of political reactions – only really started to top the charts of the issues voters most cared about from around 2004 onwards, and that when this happened the Conservatives promised to reduce net migration dramatically, and were believed to be capable of doing so (it became a very different story in the 2010s when the Conservatives failed to make good on this commitment). It probably also helped that, when it came to another of those issues where politics was not just about left and right – Europe – New Labour decided against holding a referendum on joining the European

Single Currency (p. 207). More than anything else, though, it was probably the economy, the boom, which capped the political appeal of populism in the 2000s. Between 1992 and 2008 Britain recorded sixty-two successive quarters of economic growth. Inflation was low. Unemployment was falling and average household income was rising. This was, by any standards, an impressive economic record and one which gave New Labour a platform from which it could argue that its centrist, Third Way, social democratic strategy was working for everyone.

The populist counter-argument at the time was that the boom had only really benefited a small, middle-class, university-educated, city-dwelling elite and that ordinary people were struggling like they had not had to struggle before because of 'stealth taxes' and because of higher immigration driving down wages (p. 92). Yet, in some respects, the proceeds of the boom were, in fact, evenly distributed. The Institute for Fiscal Studies collects data on household income and how it varies over time across different income groups, ranging from the poorest 5 per cent to the richest 5 per cent of households.[39] In 2000/1 it shows the average monthly income *before* housing costs of the richest 5 to 10 per cent of households (£944) was 4.15 times greater than that of the poorest 5 to 10 per cent of households (£227). That ratio remained constant over the course of the boom years. By 2006/7 the average income of the richest 5 to 10 per cent (by then £1,059) was still 4.15 times greater than that of the poorest 5 to 10 per cent (£255). Yet, over this same period, and with the notable exception of the very poorest 5 per cent of households, average income *increased* by the same percentage amount across all households. Indeed, if anything, it grew by slightly more in the poorest 50 per cent of households than it did in the richest 50 per cent.[40]

In later chapters I'll return to this headline conclusion and add some important caveats, showing how economic growth varied across the country; how wealth inequality continued to rise during the 2000s; and how increased housing costs depressed income growth. For now, the interim conclusion is, nevertheless, an important one. New Labour did not reduce overall levels of income inequality in Britain. But the proceeds of the boom did *not* simply accrue to the richest households. The economic good times in the 2000s were just about good enough and lasted just about long enough to blunt the edge of the populist challenge represented by the fuel protests, keeping New Labour afloat. But the 2008 financial crisis wiped out a part of the gains from the boom, and the 2009 expenses scandal then supercharged the conviction that politicians – all politicians, but especially New Labour ones – were on the make and could not be trusted. Having spluttered in the 2000s, populism made a strong comeback in the 2010s.

5
Devolution

A SETTLED WILL

In Chapter 1 I referenced Linda Colley's argument that, at the time of the Act of Union in 1707, there was, initially, no strong, shared sense of British identity in England or Scotland (p. 15).[1] Daniel Defoe, the author of *Robinson Crusoe*, put it more robustly, observing how 'a firmer union of policy with less union of affection has hardly been known in the world'.[2] In the nineteenth century British identity became tied to the fortunes of the pan-national British Empire. Another historian, David Edgerton, persuasively argues that the Second World War and the start of the gradual loss of Empire strengthened the sense of British national identity in the late 1940s and 1950s; he goes so far as to argue, in a beautiful rhetorical flourish, that Great Britain might be 'usefully seen as one of the new nations which arose from the dissolution of the Empire'.[3] On this reading, the Labour government that was elected in 1945 with strong support in Scotland and Wales was as much a (British) nationalist force as it was a socialist one, with industry, health and welfare and economic planning all being literally nationalized. The 1950s and 1960s offered, for this reason, tough times for Scottish and Welsh nationalists. Plaid Cymru, which had been formed in 1925, and the Scottish National Party (SNP), formed a decade later after the merger of two other Scottish nationalist parties, still contested elections. They did not, however, get very far. In the 1955 General Election, Plaid Cymru contested 11 seats and won an average of just over 4,000 votes in each of them. The SNP, its coffers empty, contested just 2 seats and secured a grand total of just over 12,000 votes.

The political weather began changing in the 1970s when economic recession and deindustrialization undercut the traditional, tried and tested argument that the Union was a source of economic strength from which Scotland and Wales more than benefited. In the October 1974 General Election, the SNP won 30 per cent of the vote in Scotland (more than the Conservatives) and eleven seats. In Wales, Plaid won three seats but came second in five others. For a short while, it looked like 'the break-up of Britain', to use the title of an influential book by the Scottish political economist Tom Nairn, might be on the cards.[4] But it did not work out that way. The Labour government, looking to find ways of weakening support for the SNP and Plaid, became late converts to the cause of devolution.[5] Eventually, and after a lot of planning and parliamentary to-ing and fro-ing, legislation was approved and referenda held in March 1979 on whether to create a Scottish Parliament and Welsh Assembly. Scotland voted narrowly against.[6] Wales voted decisively against. Shortly after, Labour lost a vote of no confidence (in which the SNP voted against the government) and, in the general election that followed, the SNP's vote collapsed and the Conservatives were elected. Devolution was wrapped in plastic and put in a storage freezer.

Devolution made it back onto the political agenda in the aftermath of the 1987 General Election, when the Conservatives won a large majority in Westminster despite haemorrhaging support in Scotland and Wales. In Britain, with its London-based centralized partyocracy, this resulted in some difficult questions being asked about political legitimacy. Why, in a country with a strong sense of its own national identity such as Scotland, should the Conservatives be able to exercise untrammelled political power with only minimal political support? The eventual answer, proposed by way of a Scottish Constitutional Convention with representatives from Scottish Labour, the Liberal Democrats, the Greens, trade unions, churches and local government, was that they should not. The Scottish people had a 'sovereign right ... to determine the form of government best suited to their need'.[7]

The Conservatives secured a fourth term of office in 1992 despite winning only eleven of seventy-two parliamentary seats in Scotland. The Labour Party's new leader, John Smith, declared a Scottish Parliament to be the 'settled will of the Scottish people'.[8] Smith died suddenly in May 1994 and was replaced by Tony Blair. Blair recognized and broadly accepted the democratic case for devolution: Scotland and

Wales ought to be given the chance to govern themselves. Indeed, in many ways devolution looked very on-brand as a part of Blair's Third Way philosophy: a split-the-difference alternative to the extreme and unpalatable options of either independence or direct rule from Westminster. Blair was nevertheless cautious. The Labour Party, in the 1970s and, once again, under John Smith, had championed the cause of devolution not only for reasons of political legitimacy but for party-political advantage. The SNP and Plaid did well out of arguing that Scotland and Wales were being trampled on by the English Conservatives. The SNP had won 21 per cent of the vote in Scotland in the 1992 General Election and looked like it might be in a position to take more votes away from Labour in the future. The calculation was therefore that devolution would, in the words of George Robertson, Labour's shadow Scottish secretary of state prior to the 1997 General Election, kill nationalism 'stone dead'.[9] Blair was, however, worried. Devolution might, he thought, prove a 'dangerous game to play', one that could provide the SNP with a base camp from which they could mount a campaign for full independence.[10] So, contrary to the spirit of the 'settled will' line, Blair insisted on referenda being held in Scotland and Wales to endorse Labour's plans. On 11 September 1997, on a turnout of 60 per cent, devolution was approved by three-quarters of those Scots who voted.[11] A week later, 50.3 per cent of the 50.2 per cent of people who voted in the Welsh referendum voted to establish a Welsh National Assembly. Even then, Blair went out of his way to remind anyone who would listen that, even after devolution, sovereignty would still reside in Westminster.

This was true. In theory, Westminster, having voted to create a Scottish Parliament and Welsh Assembly, could simply decide to abolish them. Seizing on this, the SNP leader, Alex Salmond, suggested the devolved Parliament was a 'deceit which would return Edinburgh less power than an English parish council'.[12] This was pushing it a bit far. As part of the devolution settlement, Westminster retained reserved powers in relation to the constitution, foreign affairs, defence, financial and economic matters, trade and industry, social security, abortion, genetics, surrogacy and medicines. But that still left the Scottish Parliament with control over a wide range of domestic policy, including health, education, economic development, local government, law, policing and prisons, transport, the environment, agriculture and housing, together with an annual budget of around £20 billion, rising to about £30 billion by 2004/5.[13]

BACK AFTER A BREAK

The first elections to the new Welsh Assembly and Scottish Parliament were held on 6 May 1999. In Scotland (which is the primary focus of this chapter because it is in Scotland that the argument for independence led to a referendum in 2014), Labour won the most seats but fell short of an overall majority and formed a coalition with the Liberal Democrats. In Wales, where turnout was just 46 per cent, the same thing happened. The Scottish Parliament met for the first time a week later. The new Parliament's glorious new building, in Holyrood, at the base of Arthur's Seat, was still several years away from being completed. So, making do, the Parliament met in the General Assembly Hall of the Church of Scotland at the other end of the Royal Mile, underneath the shadow of Edinburgh Castle. A few months later, on 1 July, in the presence of the Queen, the opening address at the Scottish Parliament's official launch party was delivered by Scotland's new first minister, Donald Dewar. He did not knowingly understate the significance of this moment.

> Today, we look forward to the time when this moment will be seen as a turning point: the day when democracy was renewed in Scotland, when we revitalised our place in this our United Kingdom. This is about more than our politics and our laws. This is about who we are, how we carry ourselves.[14]

This was not simply political hyperbole. Under the terms of the Act of Union, Scotland had retained its own, distinctive, legal, educational, local government, university and religious systems. Through a long-standing system of administrative devolution, Scotland had also had a secretary of state for Scotland and a separate Scottish Office.[15] The Scottish Parliament had, however, been on a break since 1707.

When he was leader of the opposition, Tony Blair spoke a lot about transforming the British political system to help restore trust in politicians.[16] In office, New Labour was more cautious. The government passed freedom of information legislation but added to it a long list of exemptions. Blair came to believe that even that bare minimum had been a huge mistake. 'You idiot. You naive, foolish, irresponsible nincompoop. There is really no description of stupidity, no matter how vivid, that is adequate. I quake at the imbecility of it.'[17] New Labour abolished the automatic right of hereditary peers to sit and vote in the House of Lords, but ducked wholesale reform of the second chamber. It created the position of London Mayor and waxed lyrical about empowering local government, even creating elected regional authorities. Yet, when push came to shove, New Labour refused to give local authorities the powers to raise more local taxes to fund local expenditure. The government, it is true, gave the Bank of England operational independence and, in 2009, created a Supreme Court. On the other hand, Blair created a 'Napoleonic' system with key decisions across a range of issues being taken, more than ever before, in and by 10 Downing Street (p. 41). All in all, therefore, devolution was important because it was the first and only clear-cut way in which New Labour, during its time in office, really did anything to significantly alter the otherwise hyper-centralized balance of power in British politics.

DEVOLUTION IN PRACTICE

Once the Scottish Parliament was established, the Labour and Liberal Democrat coalition carved out a distinctive political space a little to the left of New Labour, which, over time, came to look a lot like Gordon Brown's old-school social democratic version of New Labour (p. 40). This coalition was comfortable enough with capitalism and the free market; preached the virtues of higher public expenditure; spoke a lot about the importance of equality; and, crucially, distanced itself from the idea the public sector would benefit from an injection of market forces and competition. It was not socialist. Far from it. But neither was it quite Blairite.

This meant the Scottish NHS blocked the introduction of foundation hospitals and opposed the use of privately owned hospitals to deliver public services. It meant a commitment to fund social care on a universal rather than means-tested basis.[18] It meant the abolition of top-up university fees in favour of a graduate endowment (a one-off payment of £2,000 made a year after graduation; in other words, you might say, a fee). It meant a generous pay settlement with the largest teaching unions in Scotland. It meant a national free bus-fare scheme for pensioners, along with free eye tests and free prescriptions and a freeze on Council Tax rises. When it came to the environment and transport, it meant a lot of talk about congestion charging and Scottish climate-change targets. Finally, when it came to law and order, it translated into a scepticism towards the use of Anti-Social Behavioural Orders (ASBOs) and prioritizing new legislation relating to sexual violence, the management of offenders and sectarian marches.[19] Some of these policies worked. Others attracted sustained criticism. Cumulatively, what they showed was that the Scottish Parliament and executive offered a lot more than a talking shop. By 2004, at a moment when trust in Blair and New Labour was evaporating, a report found that, whereas only 22 per cent of Scottish voters trusted the British government to 'just about always' or 'most of the time' look after Scotland's interests, 52 per cent trusted the Scottish executive to do so.[20]

In Wales, it was a similar story. The Welsh Assembly did not initially have as many powers or responsibilities as the Scottish Parliament. The Labour leader and first minister, Rhodri Morgan, nevertheless worked hard to put some 'clear red water' between Wales and England.[21] He eulogized the universal provision of public services and kicked back against school league tables, early years testing and foundation hospitals. With constant reminders that devolution was a 'process and not an event', Morgan also worked long, hard and successfully to persuade London to give more law-making and policy-setting powers to the Welsh Assembly, or, as it was eventually to become, the Senedd (Parliament).[22]

In the 1990s there had been a lot of talk in the Scottish Constitutional Convention about not only creating a Scottish Parliament but creating one that would look and sound very different to Westminster; with much more power-sharing, deliberation and public consultation and a far more prominent role for cross-party parliamentary committees. What was wrong with the British system, it was argued, was not simply the fact that it was hyper-centralized but that it was dominated by institutionally antagonistic and increasingly unrepresentative political parties. What Scotland needed was not only its own Parliament but a more pluralistic kind of politics. Some of this came to pass. Elections to the Scottish Parliament were via the semi-proportional Additional

Member system, which made it harder for a single party to win enough seats to govern alone. Hence the need for Labour to form a coalition with the Liberal Democrats in 1999, despite winning just under 39 per cent of the vote (more than Labour secured nationally in the 2005 General Election in return for an overall majority of sixty-six seats). The debating chamber in the new Scottish Parliament building, when it eventually opened, was designed in a horseshoe shape, eschewing the face-to-face, confrontational layout of the House of Commons. Finally, the political parties in Scotland went out of their way to secure a more representative gender balance. Fully 40 per cent of the Members of the Scottish Parliament (MSPs) elected in 2003 were women (more than double the proportion at that time in the House of Commons).[23]

Yet, for the most part, hopes the Scottish Parliament would offer an alternative to the partyocracy of Westminster and Whitehall were dashed.[24] Labour and the Liberal Democrats governed in a coalition but agreed on shared policy positions behind closed doors and then whipped their backbenchers into supporting what they had agreed. Parliamentary committees tasked with holding the Scottish executive to account were, for the most part, kept firmly at arm's length. Instead of a more deliberative, power-sharing political culture MSPs, like their counterparts at Westminster, spent a lot of their time calling their opponents names and scoring party political points. Devolution constituted an important challenge to and limitation upon the centralization of British political power. It is nevertheless striking how, given the opportunity to go its own way, Scotland ended up creating its own similar-looking version of the party-dominated political system it had worked so hard to escape from.

If you had stopped the clock at the time of the second set of elections to the Scottish Parliament, in May 2003, the big story would, however, have been the way in which, as George Robertson had predicted would be the case, devolution had flattened nationalism. After an achingly dull election campaign, Labour lost six seats in 2003 but remained, by some distance, the largest party in the Scottish Parliament. Its leader, Jack McConnell, promptly renewed his coalition vows with the Liberal Democrats. The SNP, which was just emerging from a period of bitter infighting, secured 24 per cent of the vote and lost eight seats. Meanwhile, in Wales, where just 38 per cent of people voted at all, Labour gained two seats in the 2003 election; it fell just short of an overall majority and eventually decided to form a minority administration. Plaid Cymru won 21 per cent of the vote and lost not only five seats but, temporarily, its leader, Ieuan Wyn Jones, who resigned shortly after the results had been announced.[25]

In the early 2000s there was a fear not only that devolution would fuel independence but that it would vitalize English nationalism. For a long time, that argument also looked like it was plain wrong. There was, it was true, a lot of talk about the growing strength of English national identity. The *Sun* ran a long campaign to promote St George's Day.[26] English flags and 'In-ger-land' chants became standard fare at England football matches. And by 2007 opinion polls suggested that, when forced to choose between describing themselves as English or British, more than 40 per cent of people in England said they were English. This looked significant, but it probably wasn't; the number opting for English when forced to choose had not really changed since devolution. Moreover, when people were given a longer list of options, and were not forced to choose unless they wanted to, only 19 per cent of people said they were English and not British.[27] There was a sense in England that Scotland got more than its fair share of resources. In particular, there was some resentment at the continuing use of the so-called Barnett Formula, which, since the late 1970s, had been used to determine the size of the block grant given to Scotland and was calculated in such a way the Scottish executive could count on being able to spend something like an extra £1,500 per person.[28] Finally, when the English were asked, point blank, whether it was fair Scotland had its own Parliament when there were no separate political arrangements for England, there was a patchy agreement that it was not.[29]

There was, however, very little sense in the first decade of the 2000s that the English really cared to any great extent, one way or another, about Scottish or Welsh devolution, let alone that they were desperate to copy it (or, for that matter, reverse it). Indeed, when New Labour proposed establishing elected English Regional Assemblies intended to complement Scottish and Welsh devolution, the result was a bit of a mess. In November 2004 Labour held the first of what it anticipated would be a series of local referenda to rubber-stamp its plans. This one was held in the Northeast where it was thought support for a new elected body would be strongest. It did not work out like that. The 'Northeast Says No' campaign, led by one Dominic Cummings, argued a new assembly would simply mean more politicians and more party-political hot air, when what was needed was more doctors and nurses and better roads.

Eventually, getting on for a million people, a creditable 48 per cent of registered voters, went to the polls to express their views. Only 22 per cent voted in favour of an elected assembly. Cummings had tapped into a common set of populist attitudes towards politics which could not have been more different to those of the constitutional reformers wanting to decentralize and pluralize political power. In effect, the belief that politics is dull and when it is not dull it is duplicitous. Elections are a good thing because they put the people in charge. Once an election has taken place politicians just need to then get on and do what they have said they will do.[30] In Scotland and Wales, in the late 1990s, voters did not trust the British government and so voted for political reform in the shape of devolution. A few years later, in England, low (if not lower) trust in politicians went hand in hand with opposition to political reform because political reform would mean more politicians. In other words, whilst there was some sense of a strengthening English national identity in the 2000s, there was very little sense of a growing English nationalism intent upon redrawing the boundaries of the state to secure English political power for the English nation.

THE SCOTTISH NATIONAL PARTY RESPLENDENT

Despite coming out on top in the 2003 Scottish elections, Scottish Labour aged badly. Jack McConnell struggled to persuade voters that Scottish public services were improving, and that Scottish Labour had nothing to do with an increasingly unpopular New Labour government south of the border. Scotland continued to do well economically. Between 2000 and 2007 GDP per head grew at a faster rate in Scotland than in Wales, Northern Ireland, London, or any of the other eight regions of England (p. 93).[31] This was not enough to reverse Labour's slow slide in the opinion polls, which began in 2004 and did not stop for several years. The Scottish Conservatives were not able to exploit Labour's troubles. In the May 2005 General Election, the Conservatives came fourth in Scotland with just 16 per cent of the vote. A few months later, their leader, David McLetchie, was forced to resign having spent £11,500 of taxpayers' money on taxi fares.[32] So, with Labour down and the Scottish Conservatives apparently out, it was, instead, the SNP, with a new leadership team of Alex Salmond and Nicola Sturgeon, which staged a political comeback.

Salmond had been elected to the Westminster seat of Banff and Buchan in 1987 and became the SNP leader for the first time in 1990. Having once been seen as a radical within the party, Salmond used his time as leader to reposition the SNP as a pro-European, moderate, left-of-centre, social democratic party whose nationalism took a civic rather than ethnic form. To be Scottish, on this account, had nothing to do with having parents or grandparents who were Scottish. The Scots were the people living in Scotland, regardless of where they had been born. In 1997 he courted controversy within his party by campaigning in support of devolution on the grounds it offered – as Blair worried might be the case – a potential staging point to independence. All was going well. Then, in 2000, Salmond, who had assumed the role of leader of the opposition in the Scottish Parliament, on top of his role as a Westminster MP, found himself over-extended and quit as SNP leader. With more time on his hands, Salmond became a regular guest on the BBC's *Have I Got News for You* and a racing tipster for the *Scotsman* and Channel 4's *The Morning Line*.[33]

By the time Salmond stood again for the SNP leadership in 2004, following the party's shellacking in the 2003 Scottish Parliament elections, he was an instantly recognizable figure. To many Scottish voters he seemed authentic and ordinary whilst also being experienced and capable of standing up for Scottish interests.[34] Just like Tony Blair in the late 1990s, Salmond was a politician who could attract support to his party from people who, otherwise, would never have supported it – including, in the Scottish context, Catholic voters living in the West of Scotland who had traditionally eschewed the SNP. He was not, by any stretch, short of detractors. Many saw him as arrogant and conceited. There were stories, lots of stories, about his temper and alleged bullying.[35] There were, at this point, no stories circulating about sexual harassment. It was, however, already clear that Salmond struggled to attract the same level of support with women voters that he did with men.[36] This was one reason why, above and beyond her own obvious political talents, having Nicola Sturgeon as his deputy was politically advantageous.

For a while, with the Salmond/Sturgeon leadership team firing on all cylinders, it looked like the SNP might easily win the 2007 Scottish Parliament elections. But Labour began to pull itself out of the electoral hole into which it had fallen with an argument that the SNP could not be trusted to govern effectively and would pursue independence at any economic cost. The SNP's lead narrowed and on the night of 3 May the two parties found themselves tied on forty-six seats. It all came down to the Western Isles constituency, the results of which were delayed when a helicopter sent to collect the ballot boxes was grounded by bad weather. Eventually, the SNP won it with a majority of just under seven hundred. Everyone expected Salmond to then negotiate a coalition with the Liberal Democrats. The talks between the two parties ran aground though, and Salmond eventually decided to form a minority administration.[37]

A NEW THIRD WAY

The SNP's election, coinciding as it did with Welsh Labour's decision to join a coalition with Plaid Cymru after the 2007 Welsh Senedd elections, was seen at the time as a huge deal.[38] Far from devolution having killed nationalism stone dead, nationalism now seemed to be winning. Lacking a working majority in the Scottish Parliament, however, Salmond and Sturgeon had to back away from some of the more controversial items in their manifesto, including a proposed referendum on independence. Instead, they settled for a 'national conversation' on independence, which eventually, and in a turn of events nobody could have seen coming, reached the conclusion that independence would be a good idea.[39]

With independence off the table for the foreseeable future, the SNP got on with the business of governing and, as a part of this, of cutting deals with the other parties. The graduate endowment on tuition fees was abolished. Road bridge tolls, including the always controversial Skye Bridge toll, were abolished. New investments were made in the social and mental healthcare systems and in alternative energy. Prison sentences of under six months were effectively replaced with community service. This was not revolutionary stuff and did not look like the gateway to the kind of Socialist Republic Alex Salmond had once dreamed of in his youth. They were, however, popular policies and the SNP made them appear more than the sum of their parts by garlanding them with an argument they were standing up for Scotland. By late 2010, after the Conservative–Liberal Democrat coalition had replaced Labour at Westminster and the SNP was able to portray itself as the one last thing protecting Scotland from Über-austerity, its lead, ahead of the 2011 Scottish Parliament elections, already looked unassailable. Labour voters who had, for the first time in their lives, switched to another party in 2007, now found little reason to go back. Scotland was, in this respect, the first brick to crumble in Labour's Red Wall.[40]

What also helped the SNP in all this was that Scotland was now well past the point where it had started to look and sound a lot like a nation-state. In 2003, when the Scottish Parliament was still finding its feet, only 21 per cent of respondents to a Scottish Social Attitudes survey had said that the Scottish executive had the most influence in how Scotland was run, compared to 79 per cent who cited the British government.[41] By 2010, after three years of SNP minority government, this gap had narrowed greatly, with 45 per cent now saying the Scottish executive and 55 per cent the British government. Moreover, most Scots now saw themselves as either Scottish and not British, or more Scottish than British.[42] Recall here, one more time, Linda Colley's argument that a strong British identity emerged after the creation of the British state. In the 2000s history repeated itself but this time in the reverse direction. Political devolution strengthened the sense of Scottish identity and made the Scottish Parliament, rather than London, the locus of Scottish politics. There was however little sign that support for Scottish independence was rising along with support for the SNP. Indeed, depending on the precise nature of the question asked, support for independence was flatlining at or around 30–35 per cent in 2010.[43] Many voters, it seemed, had reached the view they could have the best of all worlds: a competent Scottish government which was willing, when the time was right, to stick it to the British government and the English but without all the possible risks of independence. This was not the kind of Third Way Blair would have wanted when, with more than a few reservations, he had given the green light to devolution in the mid-1990s. Nevertheless, it was, in its own way, a split-the-difference centrism.

6

Centrism: The Sort of Sequel

AM I SWEATING TOO MUCH?

Nobody really won the May 2005 General Election. Turnout was just 61 per cent. New Labour lost forty-eight seats but did enough to secure an overall majority of sixty-six. Polls showed just 10 per cent of voters regarded Blair as being more honest than most politicians, whilst only 6 per cent trusted New Labour to keep its promises.[1] The sense that Blair's days were numbered was palpable. For their part, the Conservatives won thirty-three new seats and the largest number of votes in England but only managed to improve their overall share of the vote by three-quarters of one percentage point. After eight years in opposition, this was a miserable return. Shortly after the results had been declared, the Conservative leader, Michael Howard, announced he would step down. There was no shortage of candidates to replace him. Kenneth Clarke, an MP since 1970 and a senior Cabinet minister in the late 1980s and 1990s, was the tried-and-tested, been there and done it, pro-European, leftish candidate. David Davis was cast as the Eurosceptic libertarian and keeper of the Thatcherite flame. Liam Fox, Alan Duncan, Malcolm Rifkind and David Cameron also announced they would be standing.

The key moment in the campaign came at the Conservative Party conference at Blackpool in October. Each of the candidates was given the opportunity to address the delegates. Cameron, the thirty-eight-year-old shadow secretary for education and skills, spoke on the morning of Tuesday 4 October. Cameron was a very traditional-looking Conservative. His father was a stockbroker and distantly related to royalty. He was educated at Eton and Oxford where, along with Boris Johnson, he had been a member of the Bullingdon Club.

After graduating with a first-class degree in Politics, Philosophy and Economics, he had worked for the Conservative Research Department and had helped John Major prepare for Prime Minister's Questions. In 1994, he had left front-line politics to become director of corporate affairs at Carlton Communications, a media company, before contesting and winning the Oxfordshire constituency of Witney in the 2001 General Election. One of the first recorded national newspaper references to Cameron came when *The Times* reported how, whilst he was out canvassing, an elderly constituent told him she could not stop to talk because she had lost her dog. Cameron asked whether he could help her look for the animal. 'No, she just died,' he was told.[2] Less than eighteen months later, the *Sunday Times* was describing Cameron as someone 'displaying the potential' to be a future prime minister.[3]

In early 2005 Cameron was asked to play a lead role in drafting the party's manifesto. After the Conservatives had lost, he was appointed shadow education secretary. Shortly after, he decided to stand for the leadership. His campaign was a slow burn. By the middle of the summer, he had only secured the support of around a dozen or so MPs.[4] His formal campaign launch on 29 September, accompanied with pop music, fruit smoothies and chocolate brownies, was well received but Cameron remained a rank outsider. One of his few supporters, Oliver Letwin, who later went on to become chancellor of the Duchy of Lancaster, records how he had to introduce Cameron at his launch because 'there wasn't anyone else of equivalent seniority in the party to do so', and how he remembered thinking at the time 'this is clearly a hopeless cause'.[5] That was about to change at Blackpool. Talking without notes or the support of an autocue, Cameron started with some spiky but ritualistic attacks on Labour:[6]

> We meet in the shadow of a third consecutive election defeat. Defeated by a government that has complicated the tax system, dumbed down the education system, demoralised the health system and bankrupted the pension system. It made promises that no one believes, passed powers to a European Union that nobody trusts and set up Regional Assemblies that nobody wants, and nobody ever voted for.

That done, Cameron went on to outline the case for the Conservative Party's modernization:

There are some people who say all we've got to do is wait for the economy to hit the rocks, for Gordon Brown to be more left-wing than Blair. All we need is 'one more heave'. I think that's a pathetic way for a great party to behave. One more heave means one more defeat.

We have to change and modernise our culture, attitudes and identity. When I say change, I'm not talking about some slick rebranding exercise. What I'm talking about is fundamental change . . . a modern compassionate Conservatism is right for our times, right for our party and right for our country.

Young, confident and projecting an air of approachability and normality, Cameron, at the end of his speech, received a standing ovation from the audience, during which his wife, Samantha, walked onto the stage, allowing David to pat her pregnant stomach. The scene was complete when he leaned across and, newspapers reported, whispered 'I love you' in her ear. She later suggested that what he had in fact said was: 'Am I sweating too much?'[7]

The following day, the press reports were gushing. In the *Daily Mail* Peter Oborne described Cameron as a 'front-rank British politician, who will bestride Westminster for the next quarter of a century'.[8] In the *Daily Telegraph* Matthew D'Ancona said Cameron looked to be a 'change maker' and had pulled off 'the hardest task that faces any party moderniser before his own members, which is to challenge them without causing offence'.[9] It only got better when Kenneth Clarke addressed the conference and did nothing to hide his pro-European sympathies, and when David Davis then gave a speech that was described as 'boring', 'flat' and 'lacklustre'.[10] Alan Duncan withdrew from the race and switched his support to Cameron. Other Conservative MPs followed and, suddenly, as snap opinion polls of Conservative Party members confirmed, David Cameron was the frontrunner.[11] There were a few more moments of political turbulence ahead, some of them relating to Cameron's semi-admission that he had used drugs when he was younger.[12] In the final ballot of party members, after the other candidates had been eliminated, Cameron nevertheless beat Davis by a margin of two to one.[13]

BACK TO THE CENTRE

From the moment he launched his leadership campaign, Cameron was routinely compared with, and likened to, Tony Blair. This was no accident. On the evening before his Blackpool conference speech, Cameron described himself as the 'heir to Blair' (p. 2). Blair, for his part, later observed 'he's being me . . . it's an impersonation of me'.[14] The parallels were obvious.

Both men appeared immensely comfortable in their own skins and in front of television cameras. Both could project a feeling that they could quite happily have done without the hassle of a life in politics. Both represented non-metropolitan constituencies but had lived in the capital for most of their adult lives. Both were obviously vulnerable to a populist attack that they were privileged know-nothings. Both had acceded to party leadership as one half of a political double act: Blair with Gordon Brown and Cameron with George Osborne. Both presented themselves as being – and, more importantly, were seen by many voters as being – inherently practical and pragmatic politicians who were entirely un-ideological and reasonable.[15] Both were elected to lead parties that had lost successive general elections and had come to be regarded, by some commentators, as unelectable. Both were derided by their opponents as inexperienced and superficial and willing to say or do anything they could to get elected. Rupert Murdoch, after meeting Cameron for the first time in 2006, said, 'he's charming, he's very bright, and he behaves as if he doesn't believe in anything other than trying to construct what he believes will be the right public image.'[16] Finally, both were effective parliamentary performers with a knack of being able to present their incumbent rival as hopelessly dated and out of touch. 'I want to talk about the future, he was the future once' as Cameron said of Blair on his debut as leader of the opposition at Prime Minister's Questions.[17]

Above all, Cameron, like Blair, was convinced that, in order to win, the Conservatives had to be seen to be occupying the centre ground of British politics. The only alternative, Cameron believed, would be 'irrelevance, defeat and failure'.[18] Labour, Blair believed, had gone backwards whilst it was in opposition in the 1980s by re-fighting old arguments about ideology, rather than looking to see how the electorate had changed and how it could credibly position itself as a moderate, competent and centrist alternative. Cameron, it seemed, thought much the same. The Conservatives had been seduced by the ferocity of the opposition to Blair from newspapers like the *Daily Mail* and had moved steadily to the right. As a result, whilst dazzling their own core supporters, they had made themselves look deeply unattractive to those at the centre. In Chapter 4 we saw how, during the 2001 General Election, most voters saw themselves (and the Labour Party) as being at the political centre. That had not changed by 2005. Asked once again by the British Election Study survey to place themselves along an 11-point scale running from 0 to 10, 62 per cent of voters placed themselves at positions 4, 5 or 6 (the broad centre ground). Asked where New Labour was, 60 per cent said it was at one of those same points. Only 34 per cent of voters thought the Conservatives were at the centre.[19]

Cameron was not, by any means, the first Conservative leader to think his party had to be seen to be at the centre ground. In the nineteenth century, Benjamin Disraeli had patented the idea of the 'one nation' party. In the twentieth, Stanley Baldwin and, later, Harold Macmillan, the latter an early exponent of a self-styled 'middle way' politics, had pursued the same strategy.[20] The former prime minister John Major, the one-time arch-Thatcherite Michael Portillo and, on occasion, the departing leader Michael Howard had all argued that the Conservatives needed to be seen as occupying the centre ground.[21] In his opening address at the start of the 2005 Blackpool conference, the Conservative Party chairman, Francis Maude, had made the same point – as had, the following day, one of Cameron's rivals, Malcolm Rifkind.[22] Even David Davis, Cameron's supposedly hardcore right-wing rival, had argued the Conservatives needed to be a one nation party that could appeal to women and ethnic minorities.[23]

Cameron, in presenting the case at Blackpool for modernization and electoral moderation, was not, therefore, swimming against the tide. Far from it. But it was Cameron, and Cameron alone, who managed to find a way of presenting the case for change and modernization in a way that avoided sounding defeatist and came across as credible and authentic. In the place of Blair's musings on the 'Third Way', Cameron ran with the idea of a 'Compassionate Conservatism', which he described in terms of trust, responsibility, inclusiveness and the need to rebuild society.[24] The Conservatives, he argued, had been entirely mistaken to make it look like they did not care about poverty and inequality. They did care. The problem was that Labour, in exclusively relying on the state and top–down redistribution, had failed to change anything. The Conservatives had to show there was another way of addressing social problems, by trusting churches, families, local communities and charities to change society at a local level.

SPIN AND SUBSTANCE

New Labour reacted to Cameron's election by arguing that nothing had really changed. Cameron was all spin and no substance. The Conservatives, if they were ever elected, would lurch back to the right, privatize the NHS and slaughter the first-born child of every family in the North of England. This attack line had worked when William Hague, Iain Duncan Smith and Michael Howard had been Conservative leaders. The problem Labour now faced was that Cameron, once he had been elected, was willing to back his talk of moving the Conservatives to the centre ground with some changes in policy. True, there was no single Clause IV moment of the kind Blair had engineered after he became leader, facing down his party to demand it formally renounce its commitment to 'common ownership of the means of production, distribution and exchange'.[25] Cameron was however willing to talk about different issues and to talk about them in different ways in a concerted effort to change the Conservatives' image. In April 2006 he flew to the Arctic Circle to show how much he cared about climate change. Only a few months before, he had delivered his so-called 'hug a hoodie' speech about understanding the social causes of crime.[26] Cameron joined a live web chat on mums.net; ordered his ministerial team to switch to green energy tariffs; co-opted Bob Geldof on to one of his policy reviews; ordered Fairtrade coffee for Conservative Central Office; and was photographed buying a copy of the *Big Issue* and cycling to work (it was later reported his driver had followed him carrying his shoes and briefcase).[27]

There were also some substantive changes in policy. During the 2006 Conservative Party conference Cameron signalled his tacit support for gay marriage and tough carbon-reduction targets, and warned that tax cuts would not be a priority for a government he led.[28] The following year, he seemed to suggest he would veto the creation of any more grammar schools whilst also ditching Conservative proposals to extend consumer choice and private provision through NHS and pupil 'passports'. Meanwhile, and to the dismay of many Conservative local associations, he pressed ahead with plans to introduce an 'A list' of approved candidates for winnable seats, at least 50 per cent of whom were to be women and 10 per cent from ethnic minority backgrounds.[29] Finally, and taking a leaf straight out of New Labour's 1990s Greatest Hits list, the shadow chancellor, George Osborne, sought to defuse Labour's accusations the Conservatives would slash public spending by promising, in September 2007, to stick to Labour's own spending plans if they were elected.[30]

Cameron's efforts to show that the Conservatives were changing were helped when he was attacked by his party's right-wing. Edward Leigh, an old-school Conservative, was quoted as saying he wanted to meet with Cameron 'to tell you to your face that you are the anti-Christ'.[31] A few months later Norman Tebbit wondered out loud whether Cameron was the Conservatives' 'Chairman Mao or Pol Pot, intent on purging even the memory and name of Thatcherism before building a New Modern Compassionate Green Globally Aware Party'.[32] Nigel Farage, who had been elected the leader of the United Kingdom Independence Party (UKIP) in September 2006, argued that Cameron was intent on betraying Conservative voters and embracing European federalism. This was just what Cameron wanted. UKIP was flatlining in the polls at around 1–2 per cent support, which meant describing it (as Cameron did) as a party full of 'fruit cakes, loonies and closet racists' looked like offering a centre-ground political reward at minimum political cost.[33]

By early 2008 the signs were that all this was working. Opinion polling showed that around 40 per cent of voters agreed that 'the Conservatives under David Cameron are more moderate than they used to be under Michael Howard and Iain Duncan Smith' (21 per cent disagreed and 38 per cent were not sure).[34] This, plus the perception that Gordon Brown – who had replaced Blair as prime minister in June 2007 – was not only significantly to the left of the centre ground but visibly struggling in his new role, was enough for the Conservatives to close the political gap on Labour for the first time since the 2000 fuel crisis.

ETON AND A LAND OF OPPORTUNITY.

When Cameron first emerged as a serious leadership candidate, much was made of his Eton College background. No Conservative leader since Alec Douglas-Home, selected in 1963, had been to Eton. When Douglas Hurd stood for the leadership in 1990, he had been roundly pilloried for attending the school. 'I thought I was running for the leadership of the Conservative Party, not some demented Marxist sect,' he protested in one interview, before being beaten by John Major who had left school at sixteen.[35]

Cameron was also forced to defend himself for having gone to Eton – especially when David Davis, his leadership rival in 2005, peppered his campaign speeches with references to his upbringing in a working-class council home. Cameron nevertheless played it well. In interviews, he didn't deny he was privileged. That would not have worked. Rather, he argued that he was, in other respects, perfectly normal: someone who paid a mortgage, changed nappies, watched *Desperate Housewives* and listened to Snow Patrol and The Smiths (a strange combination but one which presumably provided a knowing nod to different groups of people).[36] This was exactly the kind of 'call me Tony' political signalling Blair had excelled at. Cameron used it to make a broader political point:

> In the sort of politics I believe in it shouldn't matter what you've had in the past, it's what you are going to contribute in the future, and I think that should be true of everybody, from all parts of society, all colours and ages and races, and I hope that goes for Old Etonians too.[37]

British politics should not, Cameron argued, be about class envy and spite. Anyone who attacked him was simply betraying their own prejudices. However, the Eton connection never really went away. In 2007 there was a rush of stories about Cameron having nearly been expelled from the college for smoking cannabis.[38] In the run-up to the 2010 General Election Gordon Brown made a big point of arguing that the Conservatives' tax plans had been drafted on the 'playing fields of Eton'.[39] Later, the story became the rivalry between Cameron and his fellow Etonian Boris Johnson, who had been there at the same time as Cameron.

Overall, however, Cameron received a whole lot more flak for his membership of the all-male, consistently obnoxious Bullingdon Club at Oxford than he did for attending Eton.[40] Blair, in pushing New Labour towards the holy grail of the centre ground, had already declared the class war to be over.[41] This made it much harder for him to attack Cameron for his background. Besides, Blair had attended Fettes College, a private school in Edinburgh sometimes described as 'the Eton of the north' or 'the Scottish Eton' (as well as being the school Ian Fleming had described James Bond as attending and J. K. Rowling's inspiration for Hogwarts). Gordon Brown was readier than Blair to pick away at some old class-war wounds. Yet Brown, the son of a minister of the Church of Scotland, had been raised in comfort in Kirkcaldy in Fife. He was not alone. The days when most Labour MPs came from steadfastly working-class backgrounds had long gone. The Parliamentary Labour Party was middle class (p. 54). In the British class system Cameron was several notches above middle class. To a lot of voters, however, the difference between 'posh' and 'really very posh' might not have seemed all that meaningful.

Besides, Cameron might have added, Eton, like the Conservative Party, was in the throes of modernizing itself. Once mocked as a kind of mixed-ability comprehensive for the landed classes, Eton had, in the 1990s, started to emphasize academic excellence. By 2002 applicants, regardless of whether their parents had attended, had to pass a competitive exam to secure a place. Moreover, and to counter accusations that it remained a bastion of privileged wealth, Eton increased the number of scholarships it offered to pupils from poorer backgrounds and co-sponsored a sixth-form college, the London Academy of Excellence, in Newham, East London.[42] In 2020 Eton even committed itself to decolonizing its curriculum.[43] Yet the suspicion remained, as it did with David Cameron, that less had changed at Eton than met the eye. Most pupils still paid the full college fees of around £45,000 a year. Eton held a £300 million investment and property portfolio despite receiving a £40 million annual public subsidy from claiming charitable status.[44] Meanwhile, the school's 1,300 pupils continued to benefit from a pupil–staff ratio of 10:1 and the presence of 24 science laboratories, 3 language laboratories, a natural history museum, several theatres, 20-plus rugby and football pitches, tennis courts, an Olympic-standard rowing lake, a golf course and indoor and outdoor swimming pools.[45]

Even amongst the 'bursary boys' it was not at all clear that a new age of social mobility had dawned. 'We tried to identify the bursary boys who are with my son', remarked a pupil's mother, 'but his year group includes two oligarchs' sons and a family with four children all at different English boarding schools. Our suspicions fell on the parents of an Indian boy but then we bumped into them while skiing in Val d'Isère.'[46]

A CONSERVATIVE CENTRE

Coming back to David Cameron's time as leader of Her Majesty's Most Loyal Opposition, it all, so far, looks reasonably clear-cut. Blair, the king of split-the-difference political centrism, was on the way out. Cameron, it seemed, was the next centrist cab off the rank. Only it was a bit more complicated than that.

Blair's Third Way centrism was about splitting the difference between Old Labour socialism on the one hand and Thatcherism on the other. Cameron, for his part, was splitting the difference between Blairism and Thatcherism and this left him plenty of room for an unwavering commitment to the traditional Conservative values of parliamentary sovereignty, the monarchy and constitutional conservatism, and low taxes, stable finances and business-friendly regulation. On these issues, Cameron, for all his talk of modernization, ticked all the standard Conservative boxes. He always had. In his autobiography, Cameron talks about the sense of personal freedom Eton gave him and the debt he owed to the teachers who had piqued his interest in current affairs and economics. He then goes on to reveal something of his early political views:

> To me at least, right from the start it was the radical monetarists and free marketeers who seemed to have the new and exciting ideas. There was a radical Institute of Economic Affairs pamphlet we were encouraged to read, 'What Price Unemployment?', which rejected all the old ideas about pumping more government spending into the economy and trying to control wages and prices. I think we were told to read it so that we could critique what was seen at the time as dangerous nonsense. I thought it made pretty good sense.[47]

This reads like it might be a clever self-parody. But it wasn't written that way.

This does not mean Cameron was a fake. He wasn't. He wanted to modernize the Conservatives. But modernization was, for Cameron, a means to an end. In October 2002 Theresa May, the party's chairman, had described the Conservatives as having a reputation for being 'the nasty party'.[48] It still had that reputation in 2005. Cameron was convinced that Conservative MPs spent too much of their time talking about Europe, immigration and welfare fraud – issues which excited core voters on the right but left others cold.[49] The Conservatives, Cameron maintained, had to earn the 'right to be heard' about the things they really cared about by talking less about fringe issues.[50] Only when the Conservatives had detoxified themselves and shown they felt comfortable talking about increasingly mainstream issues, such as the environment and gender equality, could they then run with a traditional Conservative message around lower taxes and spending and deregulation, and – up to a point and within reason – crime, immigration and Europe, without being seen to be to the right of Attila the Hun.

Cameron's strategic analysis of what the Conservatives needed to do and, crucially, the order they needed to do it in, gave his leadership a particular dynamic. In his first few years as leader, Cameron was a whirl of modernizing initiatives and shock announcements. This irritated the right-wing of his party but slowly lifted the Conservatives in opinion polls. From around 2008 onwards, Cameron then changed direction. He backed away from his earlier thoughts about vetoing new grammar schools and shelved talk of the 'A list' and of new environment taxes. Instead, he started to talk more about welfare reform, reducing immigration, tackling crime, the failings of state multiculturalism and the need for a referendum before transferring any more powers to the European Union. In doing so Cameron was trying to play to the Conservatives' traditional areas of electoral strength: the ones Michael Howard had based his campaign around in 2005. There was however a difference. Cameron was emphasizing the same issues as Howard had but was doing so at a point when he thought he had done enough to change the Conservatives' underlying image.

Then, in the autumn of 2008, the financial crisis played into Cameron's hands. Gordon Brown nationalized some of Britain's largest banks and increased public spending. Cameron and George Osborne agreed that an emergency response to the crisis was needed, but argued New Labour had created the mess in the first place. It had failed to regulate the banks and had, during the boom years, spent too much money and accumulated too much debt. In November 2008, Cameron therefore abandoned his earlier commitment to stick to Labour's spending plans. The NHS and overseas aid would be protected. Otherwise, budgets would have to be cut. 'They have splashed the cash like there's no tomorrow – but the trouble is, there is a tomorrow, and it's got to be paid for.'[51] Having earned the right to be heard, the Conservatives, he felt, could now afford to push traditional Conservative arguments about the need for stable finances and low taxes.

In 2010 Cameron increased the Conservatives' overall share of the vote from 32.4 per cent to 36.1 per cent and gained (adjusted to the 2005 constituency boundaries) ninety-six seats. He then formed a coalition with the Liberal Democrats and pursued a self-styled policy of austerity via an Emergency Budget which cut public spending and increased taxes. That policy is the subject of a later chapter. One point to note here is that Cameron was constantly accused during this period of having misled voters and abandoned the centre ground. But that was not quite right. When it came to modernizing the Labour Party in the 1990s, Blair's position was Taliban-esque. He wanted to change as much as possible in the party he led, as quickly as possible. This was not true of Cameron. He wanted to modernize the Conservatives and thought party activists and the right-wing of his Parliamentary Party needed to take a long look at themselves and stop talking in public. However, he did not aim to remake the Conservatives in the same way Blair had remade Labour. Cameron really did just want to modernize the Conservatives, rather than recreate them afresh.

PART TWO

Boom

Between 2000 and 2007, the world economy, helped along by low interest rates and inflation, easy credit, lower energy prices and, above all, China's rapid economic globalization, grew by an average of 3.6 per cent a year.[1] The British economy did not quite match this, averaging 2.7 per cent a year. Yet, within Europe, Britain was a star performer, pulling ahead of France (2.1 per cent average growth), Germany (a sluggish 1.5 per cent) and the Eurozone economies overall (2.2 per cent). Sustained growth and, crucially, rising levels of private sector investment and rising productivity resulted in falling unemployment and rising living standards. Median household disposable income, before housing costs and adjusted for inflation, increased by 14 per cent between 2000 and 2008.[2] The number of people living in poverty in Britain (defined by the Institute for Fiscal Studies in this case as 60 per cent of the 1996/7 national median income after housing costs), fell from nearly 21 per cent of the population in 1999/2000 to 13.4 per cent in 2007/8.[3]

There was never a point when everyone in Britain just sat back and concluded the economy was doing well and would continue to do well and that was the end of it. Far from it. Lots of people argued that the British economy was being damaged by excessive debt, over-regulation, income inequality, inadequate skills-training, regional imbalances, spiralling house prices and the absence of a clear industrial strategy. The idea that economic growth and higher living standards were unalloyed goods also came under fire. One argument here – the subject of a heavyweight commission established by the French government and chaired by the 2001 Nobel Prize-winning American economist Joseph Stiglitz – was that GDP, the key metric of economic growth, ignores the negative effects of environmental pollution, longer and more stressful working hours, higher inequality and so on.[4] A broader argument, popularized in Britain by the psychologist, author and broadcaster Oliver James, was that economic growth exacerbates 'affluenza', a disease caused by placing too high a value on acquiring money, which results in a profound unhappiness marked by low self-esteem and poor mental health.[5]

The following chapters seem sometimes to exhibit a similar level of caution about the downsides of growth. The first, on immigration, opens with the story of the entirely avoidable deaths of at least twenty people in Morecambe Bay. The second, on banking, identifies some of the *pre*-crisis social and economic detriments of London's financial boom. The third, on Apple and the Internet, dwells on the working conditions in the factories making iPhones. The fourth, on climate change, takes as its backdrop the immense, existential threat posed by rising global temperatures. Yet I also highlight the opportunities economic growth created. The economic boom was not perfect, but it was preferable to the crash that followed.

7
Immigration

MORECAMBE BAY

Morecambe Bay is the large estuary to the north of Blackpool, stretching from Heysham in Lancashire to Barrow-in-Furness in Cumbria. The bay's broad, funnel-like shape and shallow depth affects its tidal ebb, creating currents that can move faster than a person can run.[1] This makes travelling across or working in the bay very dangerous: one reason why, in 1548, official guides were appointed by the Crown to escort travellers across the bay and why the post of the King's Guide to the Sands still exists.[2]

Fishing for flukes, a kind of flatfish, or gathering cockles has been a mainstay of Morecambe Bay's local economy for centuries. In the late 1990s, groups of Chinese workers, operating in organized gangs of twenty or more, began to appear on the bay to do this work. There were tensions between these groups and locals over who could work in which areas and at what times. Then, in August 2003, seven Chinese workers were rescued from the rising tide and treated for hypothermia.[3] Another thirty were rescued in January 2004. A few weeks later, on 5 February, the disaster many had expected finally happened at Warton Sands, just a few miles north of the town of Morecambe. Locals stopped work at 7 p.m. to avoid the incoming tide. A group of Chinese workers remained. At 9.30 p.m. twenty-eight-year-old Guo Bing Long called 999 to say he and others in his group were trapped. A rescue operation was launched.[4] By the next afternoon nineteen bodies had been recovered.[5]

Years later, Li Hua, the sole survivor from the group which had been trapped by the incoming currents, described what had happened. 'The water covered the wheel and the vehicle couldn't move. Everyone was panicking, they got out of the vehicle and tried to swim . . . But the water was flooding so quickly some were dragged right away under the water.'[6] The police recovered a Mercedes van that had transported the workers to the bay. Its owner was traced to a house in Liverpool, where up to sixty people were sleeping on concrete floors without heating. Many had paid upwards of £15,000 to be smuggled out of China and illegally into Britain. Half of this sum had to be paid in advance. The rest was taken from their wages once deductions for food and accommodation had been made. The workers were trapped. If they fled, their Chinese relatives would have been forced to pay their debts. Following the conclusion of the police investigation, the gangmaster, Lin Liang Ren, was tried and sentenced to fourteen years in prison for manslaughter and perverting the course of justice. Two Englishmen who directed the Liverpool Bay Fishing Company, David Eden and his son, also David, argued that whilst they bought the cockles from the Chinese they were not involved in their exploitation. They were acquitted.[7]

The Morecambe Bay tragedy, which came only a few years after fifty-eight people had died in the back of a lorry in Dover, served as a discomforting reminder of the dangers illegal immigrants encounter and of the dark side of globalization.[8] Anger about what had happened in Morecambe Bay led, not long after, to legislation requiring gangmasters to register with a new regulatory body and, in doing so, to comply with labour and health and safety standards. Whether or not those new rules had made any real difference was still being debated a decade later.[9] The Morecambe Bay disaster also fed into a more general argument about the scale and consequences not just of illegal but also of legal immigration to Britain. That link was established early on with the *Daily Mail* and *Express*, amongst others, reporting on what had happened in Morecambe Bay in the context of an increase in the overall number of people arriving to live and work in Britain.[10] A few weeks after the Morecambe Bay disaster, the Conservative Party leader, Michael Howard, visited Morecambe to talk with senior police officers, before travelling to Burnley, the scene of riots in 2001 (p. 179), where he delivered a speech about asylum and immigration.[11] For the next few years, these two issues were never far from the forefront of political debate.

A POSITIVE-SUM GAME

When New Labour first arrived in office, the pressing policy issue it inherited related not to immigration but to asylum. Propelled by wars in the Balkans, Somalia, Iraq and Afghanistan, the number of people seeking asylum in Britain had jumped to around 70,000 a year, and applications were taking years to process. Labour, to the chagrin of many of its supporters, adopted a tough approach. Asylum-seekers were dispersed around the country and issued with vouchers that could only be used in certain shops. The right of appeal against rejected asylum claims was curtailed. Eventually the backlog was reduced, and the numbers claiming asylum started to fall when immigration control was tightened on the Eurostar and the Sangatte refugee camp on the French coast was closed in 2002 to new arrivals.[12]

What happened next was, in this context, unexpected. New Labour moved, quite suddenly, towards encouraging higher levels of immigration. Existing permit schemes were relaxed, and new visas introduced for skilled and unskilled workers. In 2004, the same year as the Morecambe Bay tragedy, when the Czech Republic, Estonia, Hungary, Latvia, Lithuania, Poland, Slovakia and Slovenia joined the European Union, Britain, along with Sweden and Ireland, waived its right to impose transitional border controls on workers from these new EU member states. In New Labour's 'Napoleonic' system of government, there was no detailed discussion about immigration strategy in the Cabinet.[13] The decision to waive transitional border controls was instead taken by Blair prior to a European Council meeting in Copenhagen, in December 2002, in which he was keen to rebuild some diplomatic bridges in the run-up to the Iraq War. Nor was any consideration given to the possibility of working with local councils to increase spending in the areas with the highest numbers of new migrants, let alone to create a policy regime where immigrants would be encouraged to move to areas where there were the most job vacancies or housing.

It is money which best explains the change in policy. Business organizations were telling the government that their members could not fill the job vacancies they had and that, if the boom was going to be sustained, immigration would need to be increased. In an interview in March 2021 Alastair Campbell described how

[o]ne of the messages that business was giving us the whole time was that there were labour shortages, skill shortages, and we were going to need more immigrants to come in and do the job. Particularly those jobs that British people did not want to do, or that they were not necessarily skilled in doing.[14]

New Labour, eager to be seen as pro-business, accepted this logic. Britain, the Home Office minister Barbara Roche argued, was in a global 'competition for the brightest and best talents'.[15] Higher immigration would be a positive-sum game. It would benefit those coming to Britain. It would benefit employers. It would also benefit consumers because higher immigration would keep prices down. Meanwhile, with businesses growing, tax revenues would be higher, allowing more to be spent on health and education and all the other areas New Labour wanted to spend money on. Ministers were aware of the counter-argument that higher immigration might drive down wages and cost jobs. The Treasury's advice, backed by professional economists, was that this would not happen. There were more than enough jobs to go round.

What really mattered here was globalization. New Labour supported higher immigration for the same reason, deep down, that it supported free trade, financial integration, foreign direct investment, political engagement with China and, when it came to climate change and the perceived threat posed by weapons of mass destruction (WMD), co-ordinated international action. Globalization was a twenty-first-century fact. It was both inevitable and desirable. Blair changed his mind about a lot of things. He never changed his mind about that: 'The driving force of economic change today is globalisation . . . travel, communications, and culture are becoming more international' (1994);[16] 'We accept the global economy as a reality and reject the isolationism and "go-it-alone" policies of the extremes of right or left' (1997);[17] 'The issue is not how to stop globalisation . . . because the alternative to globalisation is isolation' (2001);[18] 'I hear people say we have to stop and debate globalisation. You might as well debate whether autumn should follow summer' (2005);[19] 'Globalisation is a force of nature, not a policy: it is a fact' (2019).[20]

Figure 2 shows estimated levels of immigration and net migration (immigration minus emigration, a number which can be either positive or negative) in Britain from 1991 until 2010. In the early 1990s net migration was less than +100,000 people a year. Levels of both emigration and immigration then rose and by 2000 net migration was +220,000. Net migration then rose to a peak of +349,000 in 2004 and immigration to a peak of 513,000 in 2006. In 2010 an estimated 498,000 people immigrated to Britain and net migration stood at +294,0000. In total, between 2000 and 2010 just over 5 million immigrants arrived in Britain. Total net migration over the same period amounted to just under 3 million additional people. The decision, in 2004, to waive transitional border controls had a particular impact here. The initial estimate was that somewhere between 5,000 and 13,000 additional workers would arrive in Britain each year. However, that assessment assumed more EU countries would also waive transitional controls.[21] This did not happen and, as a result, the estimate proved wildly inaccurate. Between 2004 and 2008 something like 750,000 East European workers arrived in Britain, nearly three-quarters of them from Poland.[22]

The impact increased immigration had on different parts of the country was uneven.[23] By 2010, 34 per cent of London's population had been born outside the United Kingdom. Yet London was, in this respect

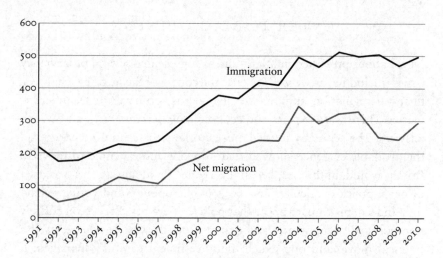

Figure 2: Estimates of Immigration and Net Migration to the UK, 1991–2010 (exclusive of British citizens) (in thousands)

Madeleine Sumption and Peter Walsh, 'Net migration to the UK', The Migration Observatory (20 Dec. 2022), Figure 2, p. 6.

(as in so many others), an outlier. In the Southeast, the East of England and the East and West Midlands the figure was around 10 per cent. In Scotland, Northern Ireland, the Northeast and Wales it was below 7 per cent. Overall, immigration was highest in the largest cities. By 2010 there were ten London boroughs where more than 40 per cent of residents had been born overseas. In Manchester as a whole 25% had been born outside Britain; in Birmingham 20%; in Edinburgh 13%; in Bristol 12%; and in Glasgow and Sheffield 11%. In more rural areas, like West Devon, Erewash, Copeland, Ayrshire and South Lakeland, that proportion remained below 2%. Higher levels of immigration changed Britain socially. It made the country younger than it would otherwise have been. It created new national stereotypes like the 'Polish plumber'. It changed the social fabric of some small towns, such as Boston, Lincolnshire, which was a hub for seasonal agricultural workers. It changed the kind of food sold in shops and restaurants and the kind of people working in care homes. Immigration also changed, for both better and worse, the lives of hundreds of thousands of people who came to work in Britain during this time and whose fictionalized stories were told in novels like Rose Tremain's *The Road Home*, published in 2007.

ENTER PUBLIC OPINION

New Labour presented immigration, as it presented several other policy issues (including, as we will see over the course of the next few chapters, financial regulation and climate change) as, primarily, a technocratic matter. There were experts and economic models and right and wrong answers. The economy needed more workers to sustain the boom and the available evidence showed that allowing more people to move to Britain would, in the end, benefit everyone. Yet alongside this was a set of party-political calculations about public opinion and voting behaviour. Indeed, making it appear that policies were being taken on entirely non-political, technocratic and expert grounds was, of course, itself a political move, and one which the government carefully managed. It chose the experts it listened to, whether Derek Wanless (p. 34) or Sir Nicholas Stern (Chapter 10). It chose how to interpret their evidence and whether and how to act upon it. In the case of the Bank of England, which was granted operational independence in 1997, the government set its inflationary objectives. The problem for New Labour when it came to immigration was not that it adopted a technocratic tone, but that it embraced a high-risk political strategy.

In 1995, when inward net migration stood at something like +76,000, two-thirds of people thought immigration was too high and should be reduced, by either a little or a lot. By 2003, when net migration had increased to +185,000, that had climbed to three-quarters. By 2008 that number had peaked at around 80 per cent.[24] Younger people, university graduates and people living in the largest cities, where immigration was highest, were much more likely to think immigration was benefiting Britain economically and culturally.[25] Yet, overall, public opinion was largely hostile. By 2009 38 per cent of people thought it 'strongly likely' – and a further 40 per cent 'likely' – that more immigration would result in higher crime, whilst 35 per cent thought it 'very likely' and the same number 'likely' that higher immigration would result in people born in Great Britain losing their jobs.[26]

That is the first part of the story when it comes to public opinion. The second part is that people came to feel increasingly strongly about this issue. In December 1997 only 4 per cent of people mentioned immigration and race relations when asked by the polling company Ipsos what the most important issue facing the country was. By January 2000 that figure had risen only slightly to 7 per cent. By December 2004 it had climbed to 25 per cent and by December 2006 to 38 per cent (higher than any other issue).[27] Increasingly, those who cared about immigration *really* cared about immigration and believed it posed a profound threat to the entire country. Here, writing in the *Daily Mail* in 2006, is the broadcaster and journalist Richard Littlejohn:

> There's a deep well of anger and frustration at Labour's venality, incompetence and cultural vandalism. And it just keeps on coming ... more evidence has emerged of this government's fanatical determination to change irrevocably the face of England ... Blair's government has been firing cultural Katyusha missiles into Middle England since May 1997 ... mass immigration – legal and illegal – has transformed parts of England into foreign countries.[28]

To its critics, high immigration was not just about immigration. It was about something bigger. It was, just as the fuel crisis had been before, about the failure of politicians in general, and New Labour ones in particular, to take seriously the experiences and views of the people they were meant to represent. Experts might be saying the economy needed higher immigration and that there were no downsides to this. Simple common sense showed this was not the case. High immigration was pushing down wages and placing unsustainable pressures upon local hospitals and schools. The only reason New Labour's politicians and experts were saying otherwise is because they lived in a world of leafy suburbs and secure jobs and regular pay rises and did not really care.

DEBATING THE PUBLIC

Why did the Labour government not change its immigration policy when public opinion was so hostile? New Labour, after all, had a history when it came to compromising with public opinion and seeking the centre ground. Indeed, for a time, in the late 1990s and early 2000s, the accusation routinely levelled against it was that it had no underlying principles or values and would say or do anything to get elected and then re-elected. Why, if this was the case, was immigration different?

The simplest answer is that New Labour was convinced a more liberal immigration policy was the right policy for the country and the economy and that, in the end, it was the health of the economy which *really* mattered to voters. If the government could, via higher immigration, deliver sustained economic growth which would allow it to keep spending more on public services, voters would ultimately reward it. If, on the other hand, the government cut immigration, then growth would fall, inflation would rise and household incomes would stagnate. If this happened, voters, regardless of whether or not they approved of the U-turn on immigration policy, would punish the government and remove it from office. That was the high-risk political strategy.

Ministers and their advisors and supporters also suspected that hostility to immigration was being whipped up by tabloid papers and reflected, at least in part, simple racism, which ought not be pandered to. The Conservatives, Labour politicians argued, were defined by, and could not escape from, Britain's often racist past and, as a result, could only conceive of immigration as a threat. At a moment when novels like Zadie Smith's *White Teeth* (2000) and Andrea Levy's *Small*

Island (2004) and films like *Bend It Like Beckham* (2002) were celebrating British multiculturalism, New Labour wanted to present Britain as open-minded and Britishness as a fluid identity.

New Labour had a point. A lot of newspapers *were* writing numerous stories about just how awful immigration was. What's more, a lot of these stories were, without doubt, often silly and frequently downright malicious. As for the accusation of racism, the bottom line is that there *was* a fair bit of racism to go round and that this did impact people's views on immigration. In 2004 Ipsos found nearly or more than 20 per cent of people in Wales, Scotland and most English regions (but only 5 per cent of people in London and 12 per cent of people in the Southeast) *disagreed* with the statement 'it is a good thing that Britain is a multiracial society'.[29] A report using British Social Attitudes data found that in the same year around 30 per cent of people were prepared to describe themselves as being either very prejudiced or slightly prejudiced against people of other races.[30]

There is, however, a big difference between arguing that the tabloid press and racism were a part of the problem when it came to immigration and arguing that they *were* the problem. True, the level and intensity of opposition to immigration amongst voters *was* rising in line with the number of tabloid stories being published on the subject. But correlation does not equal causation. The number of tabloid stories about immigration was also rising in line with increases in overall net migration.[31] As for the link to racism, it is striking that, for the most part, anxiety about immigration was being publicly expressed not in terms of race or cultural homogeneity but wages, jobs and pressure on public services. In 2002 the British Social Attitudes survey found that 48 per cent of people who described themselves as being somewhat or very racially prejudiced thought immigration was having a negative cultural impact on Britain, and that 59 per cent thought it was having a negative economic impact. By 2011 these numbers had risen to, respectively, 68 per cent and 71 per cent. That is hardly surprising. Yet the survey also found that in 2002 26 per cent of those who described themselves as having no racial prejudice thought immigration was having a negative cultural impact, and that 36 per cent thought it was having a negative economic impact. By 2011 those numbers had risen to 42 per cent and 35 per cent.[32]

As for the economy, whilst high net migration was probably not the difference between boom and bust, it probably helped make the boom a little bit boomier. For employers, it covered up gaping cracks in Britain's skills training, cracks which New Labour spent a great deal of time talking about but never properly addressed. For consumers, high levels of net migration meant the economy could continue to grow without price inflation taking off and interest rates having to rise. For skilled workers, higher net migration probably pushed up wages by increasing demand for their services. For unskilled workers, particularly those employed in hotels, restaurants, building sites, bars, cleaning firms and care homes, high net migration probably depressed wage levels. This does not mean unskilled workers were necessarily worse off because of high immigration levels. Losses in terms of wages must be balanced against gains from lower prices. But immigration did have a significant distributional impact.[33] It also eroded levels of public trust not only in New Labour but, it would seem, in Britain's political system. Taking account of a range of other possible explanatory factors, people's changing levels of concern with immigration do not simply correlate with, but seem to be predictive of, declining levels of public trust.[34]

BACK TO MORECAMBE

In discussing the long-term impact of the fuel crisis, I argued earlier that the populist assault on New Labour was, in the end, tempered by the economic boom and rising household incomes. That conclusion might be called upon again here to argue that, in the end, New Labour's high-risk political strategy paid off. High levels of net migration *were* good for the economy, which is one reason why the boom was sustained. What's more, a good economy was, in the end, good for New Labour's electoral polling. That is why New Labour won the 2005 General Election (albeit with a reduced majority) even though the Conservatives had prioritized the immigration issue in their campaign.

There is, however, a catch here to do with the geography of growth. We know, overall, that the boom benefited low-income households as well as high-income ones (p. 55). But different parts of the country did not grow at anything like a similar rate. Here, I want to look at data not on household income, as I did in Chapter 4, but instead on changes in

GDP per head across different parts of the country.[35] One reason for doing so is that household income figures include welfare transfers and payments, applied at a national level. Growth figures can, however, give us a clearer sense of the economic vitality of different areas.

If we start at the broadest level, using data on Scotland, Wales, Northern Ireland and the eight English regions, then, broadly speaking, economic growth levels were not all that different.[36] Across UKGBNI, GDP per head, adjusted for inflation, grew by 35 per cent during the boom years between 2000 and 2007. It grew by more than this in Scotland (43%), the Northeast (41%), London (41%), the Northwest (38%), Yorkshire and Humberside (38%) and Northern Ireland (36%). It grew by less than this in Wales (34%), the Southwest (34%), the East of England (32%), the East Midlands (31%), the Southeast (29%) and the West Midlands (28%).

Clearer differences start to emerge, however, at a more fine-grained level of analysis. The broad pattern here is that growth was highest in London and Britain's other largest cities. Hotspots included Camden (64%), Tower Hamlets (61%), Edinburgh (60%), Belfast and Liverpool (51%), Glasgow (50%), Sheffield and Southampton (49%), Newcastle (46%) and Manchester (44%). In fact, the only major city which did not grow at the same rate as the average for the country was Birmingham (34%). At the other end of this scale, many (but not all) of the areas with the lowest rates of growth were smaller towns or rural areas: notable cold spots including Herefordshire (16%), Dorset (18%), West Sussex (20%) and Hertfordshire (24%).

The economic boom was not simply confined to the largest cities (or the South of England). It was, however, concentrated in the largest cities, so creating a sense of *relative* geographic deprivation. Towns like Morecambe are an important part of this story. Morecambe is only 5 miles and a 20-minute drive away from Lancaster. It is, however, nearly 60 miles away from Manchester. Historically, this had not proved a hindrance. With its view of the Lakeland hills and a direct train connection to Yorkshire, a thriving tourist industry had developed in Morecambe at the start of the twentieth century that, along with fishing on Morecambe Bay, provided plenty of jobs. In the 1950s, in an effort to compete with Blackpool, 25 miles to the south, Morecambe began hosting the 'Miss Great Britain' beauty contest. In the 1970s, as package holidays became more widely available, the numbers visiting Morecambe began to fall and did not recover. Seafront buildings closed; the West End Pier was damaged in a storm in 1977 and demolished the following year. In 1991 the Central Pier, once improbably dubbed the 'Taj Mahal of the North', was damaged in a fire and then removed.[37] In 1994 Lancaster Council agreed a deal with Noel Edmonds, then at the very peak of his Saturday night light entertainment fame, to open a new tourist attraction, Crinkley Bottom, in the town. It closed a few months later. The subsequent legal battle cost the council a couple of million pounds.[38] By the early 2000s, Morecambe, with its population of around 34,000 people, was in deep trouble. In 2003 it made it to number three in the *Crap Towns* list of the worst fifty places to live in the UK:

> Poor old Morecambe. The seaside town they should never have opened. Where a silent and grey day comes as a blessed relief from the gales of black depression that generally batter its desolate promenades ... I can't possibly think why anyone would ever go to Morecambe, unless of course they are unlucky enough to live there, or are attracted to misery and squalor in the same way hearty moor-walking Victorians used to be attracted to graveyards and consumption.[39]

This was not simply poetic excess.* A 2009 benchmarking study of seaside towns for the Department for Communities and Local Government found that Morecambe, along with Bridlington, Clacton, Great Yarmouth, Ilfracombe, Lowestoft, Penzance and Skegness, was one of the more deprived areas anywhere in England in terms of housing, health and disability, education and skills, and income.[40]

So New Labour's argument that high levels of net migration were good for the economy – and thereby good for its own electoral popularity – was flawed. Economic growth in the 2000s was uneven and some areas, to use a term popularized once New Labour had left office, were 'left behind'. The obvious irony though is that economic growth was, for the most part, highest in the areas with higher immigration and lower in the places with lower immigration. That is one reason

---

* In 2009, the beautiful art-deco Midland Hotel, with views right over the bay, was renovated and reopened. In 2013, one of the co-authors of *Crap Towns*, Sam Jordison, returned to Morecambe, his hometown, and, possibly with a sense of a debt to repay (and possibly fearing retribution from family members), described it as having 'turned a corner'. Sam Jordison, 'Morecambe's revival: how the original crap town turned itself around', *Guardian* (10 October 2013).

why, over time, Labour lost ground in places like the parliamentary seat of Morecambe and Lunesdale, where 95 per cent of the population was British-born at the time of the 2011 Census.[41] Labour had won this constituency for the first time in a long time in the 1997 General Election but then lost it again in the 2010 General Election to the Conservatives, and then kept on losing it over the next decade.

8

All the Money in the World

AN OPENING EVENT

On the morning of 5 April 2004 the chancellor, Gordon Brown, was driven from Number 11 Downing Street to 25 Bank Street, Canary Wharf, to open the new European headquarters of the American investment bank Lehman Brothers. No. 25 Bank Street was a 32-storey building with its own broadcast studio, a 400-seat auditorium, a gym and fitness centre and four open-plan floors for financial trading. When construction work had begun, the intended tenant was the giant American energy firm Enron. Enron had, however, declared bankruptcy in 2001. Lehman Brothers, which had been spun off from American Express in the 1990s to become, along with Goldman Sachs, Morgan Stanley, Merrill Lynch and Bear Stearns, one of the big five American investment banks, was the Plan B.

Brown had been asked to open Lehman's new offices by the chairman of Lehman's European Advisory Board, Lord Christopher Tugendhat, the former Conservative MP for the Cities of London and Westminster. Tugendhat already knew Brown personally.[1] But in terms of making sure the invitation was gratefully received, it must have helped that Lehman Brothers had sponsored a seminar series on, ironically enough, 'Civilised Capitalism', organized by the Smith Institute, a small think tank named after the Labour Party's former leader John Smith, to which Brown had himself contributed.[2] Brown would not have needed much encouragement to attend, however. Banking in general, and Lehman Brothers especially, was a huge success story almost any politician would, at that time, have worked hard to associate themselves with.

Brown opened his speech with some specific words of praise for Lehman's:

> I would like to pay tribute to the contribution you and your company make to the prosperity of Britain. During its one hundred and fifty-year history, Lehman Brothers has always been an innovator, financing new ideas and inventions before many others even began to realise their potential. And it is part of the greatness not just of Lehman Brothers but of the City of London, that as the world economy has opened up, you have succeeded not by sheltering your share of a small protected national market but always by striving for a greater and greater share of the growing global market.[3]

He then got down to the more serious business of lauding New Labour's pro-business, pro-globalization, pro-finance record. He told his audience that the government had just fought and won a battle with the European Commission over the Investment Services Directive and its proposed tax harmonization measures. He promised to continue fighting for a 'Europe that recognises that it is no longer a trade bloc isolated from the rest of the world, but a Europe that must be outward looking'. He hinted at future tax breaks for the City and promised that 'in all the decisions we make, the Government will continue to do all in our power to ensure that London remains a pre-eminent financial centre'.[4] That done, and with some easy headlines secured, he was driven back to Downing Street.

THE CITY OF LONDON

The City of London fell upon tough times in the aftermath of the Second World War when austerity, domestic credit regulations, foreign currency exchange controls and the inexorable rise of the US economy and Wall Street flattened profits. The good times started to roll again in the late 1960s when British banks led the way in processing US dollar transactions held by investors based outside the United States (and away from the eyes of American regulators). The 'Eurodollar markets', as they became known, were good for business and, within a few years, the opportunity to recycle petrodollars from the Middle East further boosted the City of London's profits.[5] In the early 1970s, the Bank of England lifted restrictions on credit creation, allowing banks to lend more money (and to profit from doing so). One immediate consequence was the 'Secondary Banking Crisis' of 1973–5 in which the Bank of England had to intervene to save upwards of thirty smaller banks which had lent heavily and lost a lot of money when property prices fell.[6] Nevertheless, in the longer term, deregulated credit provided the stimulant for a new era of financialization.

By the early 2000s the City of London and the banks which populated it were experiencing a boom like no other. Commercial, or high street, banks have traditionally made most of their money from lending money for mortgages or to businesses. Investment banks, or merchant banks as they were called in Britain, had, on the other hand, made most of their money by offering financial advice to their wealthiest customers, raising capital for businesses and arranging mergers and acquisitions. Starting in the early 1970s, American investment banks had however discovered new ways of making money by trading either their clients' money or their own money in foreign currency exchange markets, derivatives markets (where you can take a position on the likely future price of an asset), or, as time passed, more specialist markets in creating, buying or selling securitized assets (where assets such as mortgages are bundled together and sold to other investors and/or traded) or credit default swaps (where you can insure yourself against losses on an asset and, if you want, trade that position).

The financial boom of the early 2000s really began in Britain when ordinary commercial banks like Barclays and the Royal Bank of Scotland (RBS), which, in the year 2000, successfully launched a takeover bid for NatWest, began mimicking the American investment banks by supplementing their traditional source of income from lending with the high-octane profits of financial trading. Banks, to be clear, were still lending money for mortgages. Indeed, as house prices rose, they were lending more money than ever before to homeowners, businesses and property developers. Yet, for several of the largest British and American banks financial trading became, in the words of one senior bank executive, 'the basic business of banking'.[7] By 2007 RBS, for example, held derivative assets with an estimated market value of £337,410 million, around 18 per cent of the total value of its assets.[8]

The City of London had always operated on a global scale, offering insurance for trade and investing money overseas. In the 2000s the City hyper-globalized, with banks trading currencies, shares and financial assets of all imaginable shapes, sizes and locations. By 2006 London held a 49 per cent share of the global market in foreign exchange derivatives and a 34 per cent share in interest rate derivatives.[9] The largest British banks also expanded overseas. RBS bought the retail arm of Pittsburgh-based Mellon Financial for £1.5bn in 2001; Charter One Financial for £6bn in 2004; and the giant Dutch bank ABN Amro for £16bn in 2007. As a result of these and other purchases, RBS had become, by 2007, the largest bank in the world when measured in terms of its total assets. Barclays, for its part, had become the world's fourth largest.[10]

The globalization of the City's financial industry also meant that London increasingly became the place where shady money – up to £100 billion a year according to the National Crime Agency – could be laundered for a profit.[11] This did not happen by accident. As Oliver Bullough notes in his book *Butler to the World*, successive British governments had engaged in a 'decades-long effort to encourage' financial skuldug-gery.[12] This involved an investor-visa scheme that offered people with a few million pounds to spare the opportunity to buy British residency with very few questions asked; libel laws that made it really easy to intimidate anyone asking awkward questions about where someone's money had come from through the threat of a financially ruinous court case; and a host of legal firms willing to do everything they could to help anyone do almost anything they wanted if the fees were high enough.[13] Meanwhile, behind the City of London but closely connected to it, were a gaggle of British Overseas Territories, including the British Virgin Islands, the Cayman Islands and Bermuda, where light-touch regulation pretty much gave way to clear-cut non-regulation.

A LIGHT TOUCH

Banking and finance were a global growth industry in the 2000s. London was, however, ahead of the rest of the pack. Indeed, such was the City's success that, in 2007, New York's mayor, Michael Bloomberg, sponsored a report on 'Sustaining New York's and the US' Global Financial Services Leadership', one of the conclusions of which was that

'New York has become less attractive relative to London'.[14] London was in a convenient time zone which straddled the American and Asian markets. It was seen as glamorous and cosmopolitan in a way other European financial centres (Frankfurt, Geneva) were not. It was also the home of an array of IT, legal and accountancy firms and private schools which could make life easier for the banks and their senior employees.

London also benefited from its conscious cultivation of a reputation for light-touch regulation. Light touch was not a New Labour invention. Far from it. In the nineteenth and twentieth centuries the Bank of England had operated on the assumption that the chaps working in the City could be trusted to do the right thing and to always keep their word and that the best thing the Bank could do was to keep out of their way. Formalizing but nevertheless sustaining this system, Margaret Thatcher had, in the 1980s, as a part of the City's 'Big Bang' deregulation, given the green light to a new system of self-regulation organized through the Securities and Investment Board.[15] It did not work. The spectacular collapse of the Bank of Credit and Commerce International in 1991 and then of Barings Bank in 1995 brought self-regulation into fatal disrepute. New Labour decided on a new approach and, in 1997, gave the Bank of England its independence whilst stripping it of its responsibility for day-to-day financial regulation, giving it to a new body, the Financial Services Authority (FSA). This was all very controversial at the time. Indeed, the then governor of the Bank, Eddie George, came within a whisker of resigning over the issue.[16]

Yet whilst the names on the door had changed the overall ethos of easy-going financial regulation had not. The FSA conducted plenty of audits and reviews but worked on the assumption that the banks themselves had the best information and the strongest incentives to manage their own risks and for these reasons ought not to be second-guessed. In this way, the 'efficient markets hypothesis', the idea that financial markets would price financial assets correctly, became the 'working ideology' of regulators.[17] Just to make things even clearer, the FSA was given a legislative responsibility to avoid 'damaging the UK's competitiveness' when exercising its powers.[18] Everything possible had to be done to make London as attractive a location as possible to overseas investors and banks. As such, the typical starting point of any discussion about banking and bank regulation was the question, asked in 2006 by Ed Balls, the Treasury's economic secretary and Brown's key lieutenant:

'what more can I do . . . to support and enhance the critical role that the banking industry plays in our economy?'[19]

Britain was not alone in adopting a light-touch regulatory approach. It did nevertheless go further and faster down that road than just about any other country. In the United States, for example, whilst regulations relating to derivatives trading were steadily eliminated, the Securities and Exchange Commission was still seen by the largest banks as a thorn in their side. This is one reason why the American banks, Lehman Brothers included, were so keen to open new offices in London. According to the writer Peter Gowan, London, during the boom years, became to New York what Guantanamo Bay was to Washington: a bolthole where you could do things out of sight that you would not be allowed to do at home.[20]

Given what happened in 2008 when the financial markets imploded it might be tempting to think the FSA and the government knew they were taking a chance in promoting a light-touch approach but thought the risk was worth it. The reality was different. Nobody really saw the risks of what was being done. The banks, it was assumed, had every reason to avoid taking excessive risks, and the banks themselves were convinced they knew what they were doing. Risk managers had been employed in their thousands to monitor traders and lenders. Complex algorithms had been designed to measure the precise risks banks were being exposed to. Capital buffers had been put in place to cover any potential losses (pp. 232–3). Crucially, the banks also believed they could minimize the risks on their own balance sheets by selling their own securitized assets to other banks and financial institutions in the event of any future financial problems.

In 2002 the American billionaire and investor Warren Buffett described derivatives as 'financial weapons of mass destruction'.[21] In 2006 JP Morgan's chief executive, Jamie Dimon, who had grown concerned about balance-sheet risk, ordered his traders to reverse some of their positions.[22] A year later, the American hedge-fund manager Michael Burry, immortalized in the film *The Big Short*, found a way of using credit default swaps to bet that the subprime housing market would collapse.[23] Closer to home, the Liberal Democrat MP Vince Cable consistently asked a lot of awkward questions about credit, debt and lending. Elsewhere, a few senior economists, including William White, at the Bank for International Settlements, and Raghuram Rajan, the chief economist at the IMF, pointed to deteriorating credit standards and growing trading exposures. They were, for the most part, ignored or rebuked.[24] Most of the people involved in the financial system – the FSA, the banks themselves, the credit-rating agencies, politicians and financial journalists – believed the system was safe.[25] As Alistair Darling notes in his account of his tenure as chancellor, 'many people have claimed to have predicted what was going to happen. Most of them failed to mention it at the time.'[26]

'THAT'S WHERE THE MONEY IS'

We know why the banks liked London and New Labour, but why, for its part, did New Labour want the banks? In 1952 the American bank robber Willie Sutton was supposedly asked by a reporter why he robbed banks. 'Because that's where the money is,' he replied.* In a similar vein, New Labour wanted the banks because the banks made money and paid the bills and, in doing so, made Third Way, split-the-difference, election-winning, centre ground social democracy possible. By 2006 the financial sector was employing over a million people, generating around £70 billion in tax revenue (14 per cent of the UK tax total).[27] That paid for a whole lot of public sector expenditure and a whole lot of new public sector jobs. This was not just about the NHS (p. 34). Between 2000/1 and 2008/9 'real' (that is, inflation-adjusted) public expenditure (at 2021/2 prices) on education rose from £72bn to £105bn; on social protection (welfare) from £202bn to £259bn; on public order and safety (policing and justice) from £32bn to £43bn; on housing from £8.6bn to £19.5bn; on defence from £40bn to £47bn; and on transport from £14bn to £27bn. Overall 'total managed expenditure' rose from £613bn to £873bn.[28]

Higher public expenditure offered New Labour a strong line of defence against the argument that it was, in essence, no different from Thatcherism (p. 22). It offered a party-political opportunity to bait the Conservative opposition with pictures of and numbers about new hospitals and schools and nurses and teachers. The City's success also bought status and prestige. It was, for ministers, a living, breathing

* Sutton's Law, named in his honour, is a medical maxim that when making a diagnosis it is always best to start with the simplest explanation.

proof that Britain was back; that globalization paid off; that a Labour government could work with and do well by business; and that the Third Way was the best way. That is why, ultimately, Gordon Brown was so keen to open Lehman's new headquarters in 2004 and why, in his final annual Mansion House speech as chancellor in June 2007, shortly before moving next door to 10 Downing Street, he pulled out all the rhetorical stops:

> I congratulate you Lord Mayor and the City of London on these remark-
> able achievements, an era that history will record as the beginning of a
> new golden age for the City of London ... And I believe it will be said of
> this age, the first decades of the twenty first century, that out of the great-
> est restructuring of the global economy, perhaps even greater than the
> industrial revolution, a new world order was created.[29]

No hostages to fortune there.

Political economists sometimes talk about the 'structural power' of business and the extent to which businesses, particularly in a globalized world, will play governments off against each other, demanding tax breaks and favourable regulation in return for a promise to invest and create jobs.[30] We can sometimes see that with the banks. HSBC threat-ened, during the 2000s, to leave London and relocate to Hong Kong. The British Bankers' Association, for its part, spent a lot of time warn-ing that overseas banks in Britain would leave unless regulation was further reduced.[31] Yet, in the end, British government ministers did not need to be threatened to give the banks what they wanted. They wanted to give the banks what they wanted, because they seemed to be doing so well and because they seemed to be such a great advert for Britain and for New Labour.

THE DARK SIDE OF THE MOON

The British economy crashed headlong into a brick wall after the global financial system fell apart in September 2008 (Chapter 19, pp. 240–41). Yet, even when the good times were rolling and the money was flowing into the Treasury, a case can be made that the City's dizzying success came with some notable economic downsides.

As we have seen at the end of Chapter 4, the growth in household income during the 2000s benefited poorer and richer households. But, whilst providing plenty in the way of tax revenue, the financial boom nevertheless exacerbated inequalities at the very top of the income scale. The Office for National Statistics calculated that in 2001 the richest 1 per cent of people earned 7.8 per cent of all income. By 2008 this had risen to 9.8 per cent.[32] A sizable slice of that money was being earned by bankers. At the top end of the scale the average take-home pay of chief executives in the banking sector had risen to over £4 million a year by 2007.[33] Further down the financial food chain, 'golden hello' payments to poach staff from rival companies and generous bonus payments linked to a bank's overall, short-term, performance meant financial traders were routinely making more than £1 million a year. One study estimates that annual bank bonuses accounted for two-thirds of the increase in the share of earnings going to the richest 1 per cent of workers in Britain in the 2000s.[34] So whilst the evidence suggests that, overall, New Labour stabilized the growth in income inequality, in London and, to a lesser extent, regional financial centres such as Edinburgh and Leeds, it would not necessarily have felt that way. At the very top, the income distribution was becoming more unequal. John Lanchester's 2012 state-of-the-nation novel *Capital*, set in a fictional street in Clapham, Pepys Road, during the boom and its immediate aftermath, captures this perfectly. It features an elderly widow, Petunia, an investment banker and his shopaholic partner, Roger Hunt and Arabella, two Pakistani immigrants who run the local corner store, Ahmed and Rohinka Kamal, a talented footballer about to make his debut in the Premier League, Freddy Kamo, and a Polish builder, Bogdan, who fixes things in their homes. Lanchester conveys the sense of a city whose inhabitants occupy different worlds even when they are living in the same physical space.[35]

Putting to one side for now the issue of income, banking and finance were also driving significant increases in wealth inequality. To use the simple two-part equation employed by Thomas Piketty in his best-selling tome, also called *Capital*, wealth inequality increases when the rate of return on wealth – that is, the amount of money you can make from having money – exceeds the rate of growth in the economy $(r > g)$.[36] When a heavily regulated City of London was struggling in the aftermath of the Second World War, the rate of return on wealth was low. Interest rates were capped; marginal rates of taxation were high;

and foreign exchange controls were strict. Financial deregulation and globalization changed this. The explosion in financial trading in the 2000s transformed it again. In the 2000s the British economy was growing by an average of 2.7 per cent a year. This was impressive, but shares in the stocks of many leading companies were offering annual returns of around 9 per cent a year and investments in securitized mortgage assets more than that. In other words, no matter how high g was, r, thanks to the efforts of the City of London, was now much higher. The result was increasing wealth inequality. Piketty estimates that in 1910 the wealthiest 10 per cent of people in Britain held around 90 per cent of the total wealth of the country. By 1970 that share had fallen to just over 60 per cent. By 2010 it had increased to 70 per cent and the share of the wealthiest 1 per cent had risen to nearly 30 per cent.[37]

One of the most interesting reflections on the economic effects of the role of the banking sector within the British economy was published in 2015 by Adair Turner, the former director general of the Confederation of British Industry and chairman of the FSA between 2008 and 2013.[38] Turner argues that, during the 2000s, mortgage lending became an easy source of profits for the banks because default rates on mortgages were so low. As a result, banks fell over themselves to make more and larger loans. This had the effect of pushing average house prices higher than they would otherwise have been. This, in turn, had the effect of pushing up average levels of household debt. By 2009, just as the economy was sliding into recession, gross household debt was an average of nearly 170 per cent of household income.[39] Finally, the easy money to be made from household lending (and, it might be added, financial trading) also had the effect, Turner argues, of crowding out business lending:

> Lending to finance non-real estate business investment requires difficult and expensive assessment of project prospects and future cash flows: and if the project fails, the assets financed often have little resale value. But real estate, whether commercial or residential, usually has value for many alternative users. Taking security against real estate therefore seems to simplify risk assessment. Banks seeking rapid market share growth nearly always focus on real estate; safely expanding other types of lending requires the gradual and difficult build-up of customer relations and knowledge.[40]

Economists and politicians sometimes talk about 'the Resource Curse', the idea that the sudden discovery of natural resources – oil being the most obvious example – can harm a country. Natural resources generate windfall profits and tax revenue that can be used to fund long-term development. More often, however, the discovery of natural resources has the effect of destabilizing a country's politics by encouraging corruption and fuelling inflation.[41] In a similar way, Britain, it might be argued, has endured a 'Finance Curse'.[42] Whilst the banks were booming, billions of pounds of extra tax money funded billions of pounds of public expenditure. For a while, it looked like this benefited everyone. Yet, in fact, banking had the effect of turning London into a money-laundering capital whilst distorting and undermining its economy and driving greater inequality. That is, by any measure, a despairing reading of events. The one thing Britain seemed to have a comparative economic advantage in turned out to be something which was doing it a great deal of harm. It is also an argument whose merits you would have struggled to persuade many people of whilst the banks were recording huge profits and the economy was growing. In June 2004 Lehman Brothers was the poster child of finance and being lauded by the chancellor of the Exchequer. But the future has a habit of arriving even when you don't want it to. A little over four years later, Lehman's was, as we will see in a later chapter, ground zero for the financial crisis.

9
Opening the Apple

'IT'S MORE LIKE GOING TO SEE A POP GROUP'

In the early nineteenth century the Prince Regent, later to become King George IV, sponsored the architect John Nash and the property developer James Burton to redesign and rebuild a stretch of land owned by the Crown between Marylebone Park (now Regent's Park) and Carlton House into one of Britain's first purpose-built shopping streets. Regent Street was an immediate commercial success. In fact, it generated so much revenue that, a few decades later, most of the original buildings designed by Nash were demolished and replaced with five-storey buildings made from Portland Stone. Many of these still remain. In the late 1990s, the Crown Estate, which still owned the land, sought new investors and tenants to kick-start another phase of redevelopment.[1]

No. 235 Regent Street, just to the south of Oxford Circus Tube station, was one of the buildings which attracted the most commercial interest. It had been built in 1898 and had once been occupied by Salviati, a globalized glassmaking and mosaic firm from the island of Murano in Venice. In the early 2000s, and as a part of the building's refurbishment, Salviati's motif, a mosaic incorporating two lions and four coats of arms, representing the cities of London and Westminster and the Venetian islands of Murano and Burano, had been restored. After several years of negotiations Apple eventually bought the lease on the building and opened its first-ever store outside the United States there on 20 November 2004. The new shop was 24,000 square feet large and had been designed by the architects Foster and Partners (he, Foster, of the Pompidou and the Dome) with grey Italian stone floors, a 23-foot-tall grand hall and a glass staircase. On the ground floor, display tables surrounded a forum for invited experts to deliver presentations. Upstairs, a mezzanine hosted Apple's Genius Bar for tech support and a boardroom for meetings. Customers queued for over a day to be one of the first to enter the store. Matt Duffy, a thirty-four-year-old from Clydebank, was one of those interviewed by journalists:

> I'm just about as loyal as you can get. I spend a lot of the day using the Mac for the web, e-mail and gaming mainly . . . following Apple is a full-time job in itself. I was at the San Francisco store opening too . . . It's more like going to see a pop group. They are really cool, and they know what they are doing.[2]

Within a few years, Apple, Regent Street, was deemed by analysts to be the most profitable shop in Britain.[3]

It was impossible to go a long time in the early 2000s without bumping into references to the new knowledge economy. In March 2000 Tony Blair gave an opening address to the Knowledge 2000 Conference at which he assured the assembled delegates (who probably did not need much persuading) that 'the knowledge economy is the future . . . it is here, and it is now'.[4] As speeches go, this was about as clichéd as you can get. Yet it was not wrong. Computing and the Internet were changing the economy, and Apple was one of the companies doing it. In 1994 Timothy Leary, the former psychology professor at Harvard who had become one of the strongest proponents of the recreational use of LSD, had published *Chaos & Cyber Culture*, a futuristic account of the possible impact of computing on people. In it he pronounced the Apple Macintosh to be an equivalent to 'the opposable thumb . . . the Model T Ford and the printing press'. Owning it, he argued, 'defines you as a member of a new breed – post-industrial, post-biological, post-human'.[5] That was, by pretty much anyone else's standards, wildly overblown. It does nevertheless go some way towards explaining why, for so many people, the opening of a new shop in central London was so important and why Apple and the Internet were an important part of the economic boom.

THE HOMEBREW COMPUTER CLUB

Steve Jobs was born in San Francisco in 1955 and attended Homestead High School in southern Los Altos. In 1973 he dropped out of Reed College in Portland, Oregon, and later travelled around India studying Zen Buddhism. After he returned home and resumed his old job at Atari, as a technician fixing circuit boards, Jobs started to work more closely with Steve Wozniak, another former Homestead student with an interest in computing. In 1975, after attending a meeting of the Homebrew Computer Club, Wozniak began building a crude computer with a typewriter-like keyboard that could be connected to a TV screen. Jobs christened it Apple because he thought the name sounded 'fun, spirited and not intimidating'.[6] Jobs and Wozniak founded Apple Computer on 1 April 1976 and went on to sell around five hundred of the original Apple computers (they now sell at auction for upwards of half a million pounds).[7]

Jobs and Wozniak used the money they had made from their first joint venture to develop the Apple Macintosh. Ridley Scott, who had directed *Alien* and *Blade Runner*, was hired to make the accompanying television advert, which was first played during a third-quarter timeout in the 1984 Super Bowl. Scott decided to play with some of the themes in George Orwell's *1984* with the premiss that, this time, it was Apple users rather than Winston Smith who were challenging convention and authority.[8] The advert was filmed at Shepperton Studios, a few miles south of Heathrow. Scott recruited local skinheads to play the conformist non-Apple users. When he could not find enough skinheads, he paid people to shave their heads.[9] The Macintosh was a huge commercial success, with 70,000 units being sold within four months. However, Wozniak decided to leave Apple in 1985, and, shortly after, Jobs, who had fallen out with Apple's chief executive, John Sculley, also departed. Over the next decade, Apple established its reputation as a leading technology company, but its financial position deteriorated. In the second quarter of 1996 Apple lost over $700 million.[10] When Michael Dell, the founder of Dell Computers, was asked what he would do with Apple if he was running it, he answered he would 'shut it down and give the money back to shareholders'.[11]

Jobs eventually returned to the fold in February 1997 when Apple bought NeXT, the company Jobs had founded after he had quit. Within a few months Jobs had convinced Apple's directors to appoint him as the company's new chief executive. To cut costs, he immediately closed several new product lines and fired, often abruptly, a lot of people. Guy Kawasaki, one of the people responsible for marketing the Macintosh, once remarked: 'Steve proves that it's OK to be an asshole.'[12] But there was no immediate turnaround. In 2000 Apple was still recording losses. What eventually made the difference was the launch of a range of new, beautifully designed, high-margin products: the iMac in 1998; the iPod in 2001; the Macbook Pro in 2006; the iPhone in 2007; and the iPad in 2010. Jobs became the public face of Apple during these years, standing alone on a stage to launch a new product in front of an invited audience. All computers do, he once explained, is fetch and shuffle numbers, but do it fast enough and 'the results appear to be magic'.[13] It worked. In 2010, the year before Jobs was killed by the neuroendocrine cancer with which he had first been diagnosed in 2003, Apple sold 13 million Macs and 40 million iPhones to record, overall, $65 billion in total sales and a profit of $14 billion.[14] Apple was, by this point, the third largest company by market capitalization in the world. By 2020 it was briefly valued at $3 trillion.

Jobs was, undoubtedly, one of the single most important reasons why Apple was, and still is, so successful. Yet there was also a broader story at play. In 1983 Jobs remarked to a journalist, Steven Levy, that 'computers and society are out on a first date in this decade, and for some crazy reason, we're in the right place at the right time to make that romance blossom'.[15] This was right. Apple's commercial success needs to be understood in the context of the development and, in the 2000s, mass roll-out of broadband Internet access; the development of global supply chains that allowed companies like Apple to reduce their costs and rationalize their tax base; and, finally, of the economic boom of which Apple, like other major technology firms, was both a cause and beneficiary.

THE INTERNET

You can take your pick of the possible dates when the Internet was invented: 1969, when the first computers were connected through the Advanced Research Projects Agency Network; or 1972, when Ray

Tomlinson, an American computer programmer, developed the first system allowing emails to be sent between users on different hosts; or possibly 1973, when University College London and the Norwegian Royal Radar Establishment connected to the American Advanced Research Projects network. Or maybe it was 1983, when the domain name system with its familiar .com, .org, .edu, .gov suffixes were introduced. Or 1990, when Tim Berners-Lee, a scientist at CERN, the European Organisation for Nuclear Research, developed HyperText Markup Language – HTML – as a standard way of displaying documents on web browsers.

It was, however, in the late 1990s and early 2000s that the Internet became an increasingly indispensable and, for some people, defining part of their lives. In 1998 the launch of Google gave users a way to navigate across and find different websites. But it was connectivity that made the real difference. In 2000 Britain's first broadband service was launched as an alternative to and replacement for dial-up connections. Then, in 2003, 3G wireless technology was rolled out, allowing mobile Internet access via phones and laptops. Shortly after, Internet providers began offering Wi-Fi to homes and businesses. By 2010 70 per cent of households had access to the Internet from home. Around the same number had a home computer and by 2015 95 per cent were using a smartphone.[16] For firms like Apple, the availability of fast mobile broadband access was essential. The iPhone, Macbook and iPad all became far more attractive with broadband and Wi-Fi. Better Internet access made possible the development of the 'Web 2.0', populated by websites using user-generated content, such as Facebook (established in 2004), YouTube (2005), WhatsApp (2009) and Instagram (2010). These sites gave more people more reason to spend more time online whilst mobile Internet also made Apple's iTunes (2001) service and App Store (2008) more appealing and, of course, more profitable.

As for the Internet itself, whilst other technologies – the printing press, electric lighting, the motor car – have had a similar impact in terms of the way economics and society are organized, it is difficult to think of any other technology which has had such an *immediate* impact on almost every aspect of life.* If, as a result of falling into the plot of a

* The first printing press was imported to England by William Caxton in the 1470s. It was not until the nineteenth century that printing was fully mechanized and popularized. In

Channel 5 sci-fi drama, a younger you time-travelled from the mid-1990s to today, a lot of things would feel familiar: the same political parties; the same arguments about tax and spending; the same football teams (give or take) at the top of the Premier League; and the same newspaper stories each summer about A levels and grade inflation. One obvious exception would be the Internet, which, in the chapters to follow, is an ever-present supporting actor. It was the Internet that made it possible for someone in Whitehall to plagiarize several paragraphs from a 2002 academic article in the *Middle East Review of International Affairs* by Ibrahim al-Marashi, a PhD student in Oxford, for inclusion in the 2003 'dodgy dossier' on weapons of mass destruction (pp. 160–61). It facilitated the collection of data about and the modelling of future climate change undertaken by the Intergovernmental Panel on Climate Change (IPCC). It allowed for the instantaneous global communication of information about falling subprime asset prices at the start of the financial crisis. It provided a handy medium to abuse strangers in Britain's culture wars (p. 461). It allowed scientists to map and then share with the rest of the world the genomic sequence of Covid-19 within a few weeks of the start of the pandemic, and it allowed the *Daily Star* to livestream an iceberg lettuce in a death race with Liz Truss (p. 485).

APPLE AND GLOBALIZATION

Apple's headquarters, at 1 Apple Park Way, Cupertino, 30 miles southeast of San Francisco International Airport, is less than 10 miles away from where Steve Jobs lived as a child. Yet whatever its hometown origins, Apple is also, obviously, now one of the world's most globalized companies. By 2020 Apple had opened stores in twenty-five countries and achieved 100 per cent recognition in US and European and 90 per cent recognition in Asian markets.[17]

This begs the question, why Apple? Or rather, how and why did

---

1879 Mosley Street in Newcastle was provided with electric street lighting. It was not until after the First World War that electric lighting became the norm. The first car was driven in Britain in 1895 (p. 49) Yet, by the early 1950s, fewer than 15 per cent of households owned a car. Penicillin is probably the one innovation which had both a more significant and quicker impact than even the Internet. Penicillin was discovered in 1928 and first used to treat a patient in 1930, although it was not mass-manufactured until the early 1940s.

American firms – Apple, Microsoft, Dell, IBM and HP – come to dominate the British market? This now feels like a slightly silly question to ask. British computing firms? Really? But code-breaking at Bletchley Park during the Second World War had put Britain in a strong position when it came to the post-war development of computing.[18] The world's first commercially available computer, the Ferranti Mark I, based on a prototype built at the University of Manchester, was developed by a British firm and launched in February 1951.[19] By the end of that decade, British Tabulating Machines, Elliott Brothers, English Electric, Ferranti and Leo Computers were all important players in the growing domestic market. Indeed, it was not until the 1960s, when IBM first emerged as a global leader, that the British computing industry began to really struggle. By 1968, when the existing British firms were merged to form ICL, it was probably already too late.

In the late 1970s and early 1980s, the British computing industry had a bounce when Sinclair (via the seminal and largely dysfunctional ZX80 and ZX81), Amstrad and ACORN (via a contract for the BBC Micro) found a ready market to sell cheap personal computers.[20] This proved short-lived. In 1984 Michael Dell founded the Dell Computer Corporation and the following year Bill Gates launched the first retail version of Microsoft Windows. Apple survived and thrived. The British industry did not. In 1990 Fujitsu acquired an 80 per cent stake in ICL and bought it outright in 1998. The brand name ICL was dropped in 2002 and, when it came to the production of British-made computers, that was just about that.

A British-based semiconductor industry did, however, survive, with cutting-edge firms such as Imagination Technologies (founded in 1985), ARM (1990), PicoChip (2000) and Cambridge Semiconductor and Icera (both founded in 2002) securing global sales – including, in the case of Imagination Technologies, for a graphics processor chip to be used in the iPhone. Yet, over time, nearly all these firms were sold to overseas buyers: Icera and, eventually, ARM to the American firm Nvidia; Cambridge Semiconductor to another American firm, Power Integrations; PicoChip to the Californian Mindspeed Technologies (and then to Intel); and Imagination Technologies to a private equity firm, Canyon Bridge Capital Partners, based in Beijing. In total, and between 2010 and 2020 alone, British semiconductor firms valued at around £35 billion were sold to overseas companies.[21] This was not a one-off story. In the 2000s foreign takeovers of British-owned firms became the new normal, with O2, Boots, the British Airports Authority, Powergen, Thames Water, P&O and Corus all being bought. Then, in early 2010, the American firm Kraft launched a takeover bid for Cadbury, the British confectionary firm founded in 1824 in Birmingham by the Quaker John Cadbury. Kraft promised to keep Cadbury's Somerdale factory, near Bristol, open. A few weeks after the deal went through, it announced Somerdale would close.[22]

New Labour argued that none of this really mattered. Foreign investment was creating new British jobs and British firms were buyers as well as sellers in this global market. Others were not so sure. The economist and journalist Will Hutton, whose arguments about the failings of British capitalism and the need for a 'stakeholder' economy had, if only for a brief moment, struck a chord with Blair in the mid-1990s, kept talking about the economic costs of overseas ownership.[23] He was treated in government policy-making circles as you might a distant relative who had let themselves go but occasionally had to be invited to family gatherings.

Apple also offers a good example of the rise of global value chains. Trade does not just consist of trade in finished products. It also consists in the movement and assembly of different parts of what will eventually become one finished product. Indeed, this intermediate form of trade now accounts for something like 80 per cent of total global trade.[24] Whilst Apple directly employs around 163,000 people worldwide, a far larger number, close to 700,000, are engaged in designing, selling, manufacturing and assembling its products.[25] Apple's resulting supply chain includes 4 companies based in the UK; 2 in France; 8 in Germany; 14 in Singapore; 22 in South Korea; 28 in Taiwan; 42 in Japan; and 156 in China.[26] Most Apple products are now mostly assembled and manufactured in China (with the notable exception of Apple's central processing unit chips, which are manufactured in the Taiwan Semiconductor Manufacturing Company). According to Horace Dediu, a former Nokia executive who now runs a market intelligence group, the value of Apple's machinery in China is now greater than that of all Apple's buildings and retail stores put together.[27]

The globalization of trade and supply chains has had a significant impact on British manufacturing employment. Put simply, the overwhelming force of competition from low-wage economies such as China makes it harder to sustain low-productivity, high-employment production. That is one (but only one) reason why the share of manufacturing jobs in Britain fell from about 12 per cent of total employment in 2000 to 8 per cent by 2010.* In terms of the underlying trade economics, perhaps the key point to note is that the globalization of production has not been accompanied by an equivalent globalization of profits. The cost of the raw materials used to make an iPhone amount to something like 20 per cent of its retail price. The wages of Chinese workers are equivalent to around 2 per cent. Apple's profit, on the other hand, amounts to around 58 per cent.[28] The lesson to be drawn is that, as Hutton has argued, ownership matters. Britain and China occupy very different positions in high-tech value chains. Yet when it comes to the transfer of profits to a company like Apple, both are net exporters.

The human implications of globalized supply chains were highlighted in 2010 with reports of a rash of suicides in the factory making iPhones run by the giant Taiwanese company Foxconn, in Longhua, Shenzhen. The Longhua factory, which employed nearly half a million people, was reported to have had eighteen suicide attempts and fourteen confirmed deaths. Managers, in response, installed large nets on the outside of buildings to prevent suicide attempts and hired counsellors. Helpfully, employees were also required to sign pledges stating they would not attempt to kill themselves.[29] Foxconn and Apple promised to review conditions whilst arguing that their factories were carefully regulated and provided workers access to restaurants and cinemas.

In 2012, and then once again in 2016, workers at the Longhua factory gathered on a rooftop at the factory and threatened to jump unless they were provided with improved conditions.[30] Yet, as is often the way with such stories, media attention waned. Instead, it was Apple's globalized taxation arrangements which began to attract attention. Apple

---

* Technological advances allowing more to be produced using fewer people had, overall, more of an impact on levels of manufacturing employment than globalization. The important point to note here is that the total output of the British manufacturing sector continued to rise in the 2000s even as its overall contribution to employment fell. That said, Britain struggled to maintain its global market share in manufacturing industries where competition was driven primarily by considerations of quality and reliability rather than cost. This is one reason why, in 2010, 18 per cent of German workers were still engaged in manufacturing. For a general discussion of the relationship between employment, globalization and technology see Martin Sandbu, *The Economics of Belonging* (Princeton, NJ, 2020), pp. 73–82.

opened its international headquarters in Cork in the early 1980s. A decade later it became one of the first companies to make use of the so-called 'Double Irish' corporate tax tool devised by the Irish state. The Double Irish allowed companies to channel profits from international sales through Ireland and on to low-tax havens and so minimize their overall tax payments.[31] For a long time, this remained largely hidden from view. It became headline news when, in 2016, the European Commission ruled that Ireland had, over an extended period, granted Apple illegal tax benefits and ordered the company to pay €13 billion in unpaid Irish taxes from between 2004 and 2014. Two years later, the campaign group Tax Justice Network reported that Apple may have paid as little as 1 per cent tax in the European Union between 2015 and 2017.[32] In 2019 *The Times* reported that Apple's tax bill from £1.2 billion of sales in British shops may have been as little as £3.8 million.[33]

THE MILKMAN OF HUMAN KINDNESS

The economic boom of the 2000s was characterized, above all else, by high and stable levels of economic growth. The orthodox economics textbook account of why growth is good relates to the capacity to satisfy preferences subject to a budget constraint. The simplified but not particularly misleading version of this argument is that growth is good because it allows more people to buy more of what they want and to go to more of the places they want to go to.

In the early 2000s it was possible to buy a relatively cheap laptop for around £400 (not hugely different to the price in the early 2020s).[34] Apple operated in a different market, its computers being promoted based on their design, durability and functionality. For Steve Jobs everything was about taste: about 'trying to expose yourself to the best things humans have done and then trying to bring those things into what you are doing'.[35] As a result, when the Apple Macintosh went on sale in 1984, it was priced at $2,500 (at a point when the exchange rate was around $1.40 to £1). Over the next decade, most Apple computers, whether the Powerbook G4 Series launched in the late 1990s or the Macbook Pro launched in 2006, were sold for around £1,800 in Britain.[36] For committed users, Apple computers represented great value. Yet buying one still required a great deal of money. So, on this reading, the economic boom was a good thing because it gave more people the opportunity to be the kind of free-thinking, creative, Mac users Apple wanted them to be and profited from.

As I said in the introduction to this part of the book, the 2000s were also a decade in which the idea that growth was an unalloyed good came under intense challenge (pp. 81–2). We have already seen how New Labour argued that immigration was good for the economy. This was challenged by people who, for a variety of reasons, did not think higher immigration was a price worth paying for growth (as well as plenty of others who questioned the idea that immigration *would* lead to higher growth). In the next chapter we will see how economic growth in the 2000s coincided with the development of further evidence about the long-term consequences of increased carbon emissions. The working conditions in the factories assembling iPhones also speaks to the basic intuition that growth can be costly. What applies to Apple also applies, even more clearly, to the Internet. Drug dealing, human trafficking, arms dealing, and money laundering existed long before the Internet was developed. The Internet has, however, made it possible to undertake these welfare-destroying activities on a far grander scale – which also makes them far harder to stop.

But the Internet has also made it much easier for more people to co-operate with each other, in a decentralized way removed from a market environment driven by price and profit, to use their abilities and energies in ways that are not effectively captured in GDP figures but which are, nevertheless, hugely beneficial. One such example is open-source software. In the early 2020s, the average salary for a computer programmer in Britain was around £31,000. Apple paid something closer to an average of £58,000.[37] Yet tens of thousands of computer programmers routinely offer their time, free of charge, to the development of open-source software like the Apache web server, Android, LibreOffice, the VCL media player, the Firefox browser and WordPress that anyone can use, study, improve and distribute for free. A 2021 report by OpenUK estimated the value of open-source software to British businesses to be over £45 billion.[38]

Wikipedia offers a second example of an Internet-driven collaboration. Wikipedia was founded in 2001 and now contains over 60 million separate articles. According to one estimate, American consumers put a value of around $150 a year on being able to use Wikipedia, which, if correct, would make it worth somewhere around $40 billion.[39] Yet Wikipedia is run not as a profit-making company but as a non-profit charity which depends on charitable grants and donations and the free labour of over 130,000 editors, who compile its pages using guidance intended to ensure entries are on noteworthy topics and described using independent sources from a neutral standpoint.[40] The founders of Wikipedia, Jimmy Wales and Larry Sanger, initially conceived of Wikipedia as a way of uncovering and promoting a definitive version of the truth of a subject. Over time, and whilst accuracy remains important, the honest presentation of balanced viewpoints has come to be emphasized more. Studies, including a 2005 paper in *Nature* that received a lot of publicity at the time, have ranked Wikipedia as being as accurate as the *Encyclopaedia Britannica*, which it has largely replaced and which cost, in its final print edition in 2010, around £800 to buy.[41]

10

A Changing Climate

'A CHORUS OF GRATITUDE'

In the mid-2000s Britain was one of a number of countries seeking to attract international support for a new climate change treaty to replace the Kyoto Treaty, negotiated in the aftermath of the 1992 Rio 'Earth Summit' (p. 44). One of the delicate problems Britain faced in doing so was the steadfast reluctance of President George W. Bush and a Republican-controlled Congress to sign an international treaty requiring the US to cut carbon emissions. To try and move things forward Gordon Brown commissioned the economist Sir Nicholas Stern, the second permanent secretary at the Treasury and former chief economist at the World Bank, to write a report on the economics of climate change. By focusing on the baseline economics of how best to address climate change, rather than the climate change science itself, Brown hoped to persuade American policymakers that reducing emissions made sense. This was, for New Labour, a tried-and-tested way forward. Technocratic expertise was going to be called in like a precision airstrike to clear a political obstacle. Stern was going to do for climate change what, in a very different context, Derek Wanless had done for the NHS.

At the time, the invitation to draft a report on climate change was seen as something of a sideways move for Stern who, it was widely reported, had previously angered Brown by publishing a critical review of Britain's tax system during his time at the World Bank.[1] Whatever the truth of those reports (and fair to say, annoying Gordon Brown was not a difficult thing to do), it soon became clear Stern was delighted to be given the opportunity to make a lasting contribution in relation to an issue he cared passionately about. The son of a German Jew who had fled to Britain in 1938, Stern said that whilst the crisis faced by his father's generation was one of 'fighting fascists', 'ours is fighting climate change'.[2] On 26 October 2006 Stern presented a summary of his key findings to the prime minister and the Cabinet. A few days later, with the prime minister, the chancellor and the secretary of state for the environment, food and rural affairs, David Miliband, in attendance, Stern spoke at the formal launch of his 700-page review.[3]

The Stern Review evaluated and endorsed the existing scientific evidence on the causes and likely future scale of global climate change. It also presented a hard-nosed economic case that the costs of co-ordinated international action to reduce emissions – estimated by Stern to amount to something like 1 per cent of global GDP – would be a lot less than the costs of doing nothing. Reducing carbon emissions was not, Stern argued, an alternative to economic growth. It was a prerequisite for it:

> The evidence shows that ignoring climate change will eventually damage economic growth ... tackling climate change is the pro-growth strategy for the longer term, and it can be done in a way that does not cap the aspirations for growth of rich or poor countries. The earlier effective action is taken, the less costly it will be.[4]

This was a powerful message. Moreover, in arguing that market-based solutions like emissions trading offered an economically efficient way of minimizing the costs of climate change action, Stern could not simply be dismissed as the kind of woolly-headed leftie environmentalist *Top Gear*'s Jeremy Clarkson delighted in mocking. The Stern Report had its critics. The American Enterprise Institute argued his proposed measures would flatten developing economies.[5] The *Sun*, on the day of the launch, carried a picture of Tony Blair under the headline 'I'M SAVING THE WORLD ... YOU LOT ARE PAYING'.[6] Some economists also argued that Stern had got his cost–benefit analysis wrong by attaching too low a discount rate to the welfare of future generations and, as a result, was asking current generations to pay too high a price to protect future ones.[7] These dissenting voices were nevertheless the exception. At a time when the economy was booming and capitalism seemed to have all the answers, the Stern Review, with its argument that, left to its own devices, capitalism was unsustainable, was widely applauded. *The Economist* observed that Stern had been 'greeted with such a chorus of gratitude that one might have thought the distinguished economist had single-handedly rescued the planet from certain destruction'.[8]

AN EXPERT CONSENSUS

Margaret Thatcher, a trained chemist, first spoke about the dangers of climate change and global warming in a lecture at the Royal Society in 1988.[9] Two years later, in one of her final speeches as prime minister, Thatcher told the World Climate Conference in Geneva that 'the danger of global warming is as yet unseen, but real enough for us to make changes and sacrifices, so that we do not live at the expense of future generations'.[10] Her successor, John Major, was an active participant in the Rio Summit, in the aftermath of which his government introduced several new environmental policies, including the fuel duty escalator.

By the mid-1990s, when the Kyoto Protocol was being negotiated, a broad policy consensus was emerging within governments and international organizations about the significance, causes and best possible responses to climate change. One important part of that consensus was the idea that climate change constituted a giant market failure. Most of the time competitive markets do a reasonable job of ensuring that those who benefit from producing something, whether it be an item of clothing or a house, also bear the costs of its production. The problem with climate change, the economic argument went, was that producers had no incentive to take account of the long-term costs of carbon emissions in the prices of the products they sold. Governments needed to intervene to correct that failure. The best and most efficient way of doing so was via an overall target to reduce emissions, backed by either new taxes on emissions and/or emissions trading schemes to ensure that emissions occurred at an optimal economic level.

Slowly, this expert consensus about the need to address climate change and the best way of doing so found its way into the manifestos of the leading British political parties. In the 1997 General Election campaign the Conservatives promised to 'provide leadership in Europe and internationally on environmental issues' and to cut greenhouse gas emissions by 10 per cent of 1990 levels by 2010.[11] The Liberal Democrats went further, promising to cut emissions by 30 per cent.[12] New Labour, no surprise, split the difference with a centrist commitment to cut emissions by 20 per cent.[13] Given just how entrenched culture war battles around climate change and climate change protests became in the early 2020s, this expert-led, cross-party consensus on climate change now looks quite remarkable. Climate change scepticism was a thing. The former chancellor Nigel Lawson inveighed against climate change policies in the House of Lords and at meetings of the Institute of Economic Affairs, and eventually published, in 2008, *An Appeal to Reason: A Cool Look at Global Warming*.[14] Yet for the most part, climate change was not seen as a party-political killing zone because the broad acceptance of the market failure argument meant that being *for* government-led climate change action did not mean being *against* any and all kinds of capitalism.

After winning the 1997 General Election, New Labour pressed ahead with assorted policy measures to address climate change. In 2001 the Climate Change Levy linked the amount of tax energy producers paid to the targets they had set to improve energy efficiency. This was then buttressed with a legal obligation upon electricity providers to source an increasing proportion of their supplies from renewable energy sources. In March 2002, and in advance of a planned European Union scheme, Britain then launched one of the world's first emissions trading schemes.[15] By the middle part of the decade, Britain remained on course to meet its Kyoto obligations with emissions 12 per cent below their 1990 levels.[16]

As headline figures go, this was not unimpressive. In many respects there was, however, slightly less to it than met the eye. For a start, the 12 per cent figure related to emissions generated within the British Isles; it excluded carbon emissions associated with the consumption of goods in Britain produced in other countries. There was nothing underhand about this. The targets in the Kyoto Treaty related to territorial emissions. But carbon emissions are emissions no matter where they come from, and between 2000 and 2005 Britain's overall carbon footprint, imports included, rose slightly.[17] Putting this to one side, ministers, when pushed, also had to admit that, insofar as Britain's territorial-produced emissions had fallen, this was largely as a result of a market-led shift away from the use of coal towards gas, which had very little to do with arguments about, or policy in relation to, climate change.[18] Moreover, with the 'dash to gas' largely complete, it was becoming increasingly clear that progress was stalling and that the government was going to fall far short of meeting its own 20 per cent target.[19]

With the economy booming, Britain would have been well placed to have invested heavily in wind power or battery technology at this time, to try and develop a comparative economic advantage whilst creating a pathway to lower emissions. New Labour's Crosland-ite social democratic centrism (p. 39) did not extend as far as a seriously interventionist industrial strategy to significantly reshape British capitalism, however, and this opportunity was lost. In terms of the party politics involved, it did not help that the Conservatives, whilst still committed to reducing overall emissions, were now arguing that New Labour was using the environment as a smokescreen for endless new stealth taxes. To add to the list of difficulties, international negotiations were becoming mired in arguments about the level at which to set an overall emissions reduction target; the way this would then be matched to individual national targets; and whether and to what extent large developing economies, particularly China and India, should be expected to contribute to that process. Add to this the hearty climate scepticism of President Bush and there was, all in all, a loss of momentum, a sense of words and promises speaking louder than actions. This was the political context in which Sir Nicholas was invited to prepare his report.

TIED TO THE MAST

In the end, the Stern Review did not have the impact Brown had hoped it would have on the American negotiating position. For the Americans, the key issue was not about whether there were attractive market-based solutions to reducing carbon emissions. They cared far more about whether China and India would be required to cut their emissions and the potential damage that would be done to American industry if they were not. Instead, Stern had far more of an impact on British public opinion and policy-making.

To an extent few had expected, the publication of the Stern Report became, for several weeks, a headline media story. This, together with the release a few months before of Al Gore's film *An Inconvenient Truth*, meant that, for a brief while, climate change came to be regarded by the public as one of the most important issues facing the country.[20] In shifting public opinion, Stern also changed the policy-making dynamics. New Labour's approach to climate change had been largely technocratic and top-down. Expertise would save the day. Yet Stern gave pressure groups an opportunity to mobilize public opinion and lobby for policy change. The 'Big Ask' used Stern as a rallying-point to demand an annual 3 per cent cut in carbon emissions. By November 2006 412 of the 600-plus MPs in the House of Commons had pledged their support for this target. Many business leaders, via the Prince of Wales's Corporate Leaders Group on Climate Change, also publicly backed Stern's analysis and called for more government action.

A second political factor was at play here. Nine months before Sir Nicholas had published his report, David Cameron was elected Conservative Party leader and set about trying to show voters how much he and the Conservatives cared about issues like climate change in order to 'earn the right to be heard' (p. 79). In April 2006 Cameron visited the Scott Turner glacier in the Arctic Circle to highlight the impact of climate change. The resulting pictures of Cameron hugging a husky made newspaper front pages.[21] Then, when the government announced, in December 2006, that it was going to double the Air Passenger Levy, rather than playing the usual stealth tax card, Cameron argued that it needed to set a more ambitious target. In the end, and as the 2010 General Election approached, Cameron's interest in environmental issues faded as he focused on the more traditionally Conservative-friendly issues of the economy, taxation, immigration and crime. Yet his initial enthusiasm had already made a difference. As one of environment secretary David Miliband's advisors later observed, 'it's only with Cameron's election [as party leader] that the domestic agenda really took off and, frankly, you could say to Number 10 and the Treasury "look, you're in a political race" and that's why you would win certain battles'.[22] It is probably worth pausing for a second to contemplate the significance of this point. In a 'centralized partyocracy' in which the shadow of the future does not extend much further than the next general election, a key consideration when it came to addressing the long-term consequences of climate change was the short-term party-political tactics of an opposing party.

On the day the Stern Report was published in October 2006, Miliband announced he would be seeking parliamentary approval for a law requiring the British government to reduce emissions generated within Britain by 60 per cent, relative to 1990 levels, by 2050. In June 2008, with the preparatory work having been completed, the Climate Change Bill was tabled in the House of Commons. This was no small feat. To get to this point Miliband had had to see off the Treasury, which had argued any British target ought to be made conditional upon other countries also cutting their emissions.[23] That, however, proved to be Miliband's largest obstacle. To many people's surprise the bill received cross-party support, with only five Conservative MPs voting against.[24]

New Labour had cut its teeth in 1997 by giving the Bank of England its independence in the hope of taking day-to-day politics out of interest rate management, handing over responsibility for making potentially unpopular decisions to unelected experts.[25] A decade later, the Climate Change Bill did something similar. The bill did not just create a target to reduce emissions. It imposed a legal requirement upon future governments to set five-year carbon budgets consistent with that target and created a new technocratic body, the Committee on Climate Change, charged with issuing annual reports on the government's progress which had to be debated in Parliament. Homer's Odysseus, when approaching the island inhabited by the Sirens, orders his crew to put beeswax in their ears and to bind him to the mast of his own boat. This way, he reasons, he can listen to the Sirens' beautiful voices without being lured onto the rocks and shipwrecked. The Climate Change Bill was intended to serve the same function. Once it was the law of the land it would force future governments to do the right thing, whatever short-term party-political temptations they faced.

In December 2009 the UN Climate Change Conference convened in Copenhagen to agree on a successor to the Kyoto Treaty. It turned into something of a soap opera. In sub-zero temperatures delegates were herded into a giant exhibition centre where they spent hour after hour disagreeing about what needed to be done and who needed to do it. The Danish organizers were accused of being out of their depth. At various points lots of countries accused other countries of acting in bad faith. To add to the confusion, there were various fake press releases and even a spoof press conference. At one point President Obama, who had unexpectedly arrived on Air Force One, gate-crashed a meeting being attended by the Chinese premier, Wen Jiabao, to demand the Chinese demonstrate more leadership.

Then, just when it looked like the conference would end in acrimony, thirty countries, including the United States, China and India, reached a self-styled 'meaningful agreement' between themselves that actions needed to be taken to keep any global temperature increase below

2 degrees Celsius. They did not say very much about how they planned to meet this target, or whether and how it was going to be made legally binding for those countries which had not yet enacted an equivalent of Britain's legislation. This was nevertheless progress.[26] It was the first time a 2-degrees target had been agreed. Moreover, it was a target America *and* China had agreed to. Within a year, more than two-thirds of all countries had signed up to the Copenhagen Accord and nearly a dozen, representing over 80 per cent of global emissions, had publicly committed themselves to meeting the Copenhagen target.[27]

AN UNDERCURRENT OF SCEPTICISM

Between the publication of the Stern Report in 2006 and the conclusion of the Copenhagen summit in December 2009 a great deal had changed in relation to both the domestic and the international politics of climate change. Yet there was still an obvious problem. Nearly two decades on from the Rio Earth Summit, British public opinion on climate change was lagging a long way behind. For a start, and except for a brief moment following the publication of the Stern Review, climate change was not seen by most of the public as a particularly important issue. In the early 2000s, Ipsos found that only 3 or 4 per cent of people mentioned the environment when asked what the most important issues facing the country were. By 2007 this had risen to just over 10 per cent. By 2009, with the global financial crisis in full flow, it had fallen to around 6 per cent.[28]

There was more to this than a lack of interest. The British Social Attitudes survey found that the proportion of people who considered climate change to be very or extremely dangerous actually fell, from 51 per cent in 1993 to 50 per cent in 2000 and then to 43 per cent in 2010.[29] Meanwhile, over the same period, the numbers who thought 'we worry too much about the future of the environment and not enough about prices and jobs today' rose from 35 per cent to 43 per cent.[30] There was a link here to political affiliation. Whereas 49 per cent of people who said they identified with the Labour Party in 2010 believed the rise in global temperatures caused by climate change was 'very dangerous' or 'extremely dangerous', the equivalent figure for Conservative identifiers was 38 per cent. Dig a bit deeper into these

numbers and it was age, education and income differences that mattered more, however: 48 per cent of people aged eighteen to fifty-four
believed climate change was very or extremely dangerous. Amongst
those aged sixty-five or over that fell to 28 per cent. For those with a
degree the figure was 63 per cent, whilst for those with no qualifications
the figure was 28 per cent. For those whose incomes were in the highest
quartile the figure was 52 per cent and for those in the lowest quartile it
was 37 per cent.[31] These differences in attitudes looked similar to those
for immigration and, looking ahead, for those around Brexit, and they
posed a significant political challenge for Labour by making it much
harder to forge a 'catch-all', centrist political position.[32] In adopting a
strong pro-immigration and strong climate change agenda, Labour
risked alienating a large part of its traditional support base – older
voters and people on lower incomes without a degree.

A lot of people tied themselves to an argument that climate scepticism was driven by a mixture of ignorance and apathy. People don't
really understand the science and are not prepared to make any
changes to their own lifestyles. These people then get manipulated by
'us and them' populists who insinuate that scientists are part of a
middle-class, metropolitan elite who don't understand and don't care
about ordinary people.[33] Yet there is another and more interesting part
to this story. In the late 1960s and 1970s academic sociologists
developed an influential critique of natural science that, in certain
respects, had ploughed a similar furrow in seeking, in the words of one
of its proponents, Sheila Jasanoff, to take scientific and technical
knowledge down a few pegs.[34] Science, far from being the process of
discovering immutable facts and truths embedded within an external
reality, is a social construction. What gets studied and what gets
funded to be studied are social and political processes. Who gets to be
counted as an expert and why is a political move. Science itself is
steeped in hierarchies and power-plays. Facts are the results, not the
causes, of the resolution of scientific disputes. Science and knowledge
are never as certain and uncontroversial as they are made to appear
when being communicated to non-scientists. Scientific claims are
always provisional and are often shown, later, to be incorrect. There
are different kinds of valid expertise, including lay expertise. In short,
science – let alone social science – is not infallibly God-like but irre-
deemably social and human.

Very few people would have directly encountered this academic critique in the 2000s. But, in a context in which political trust was low and still falling and in which New Labour was reliant upon an expert, technocratic consensus to justify its approach when it came to monetary policy, NHS spending, immigration and climate change, critics who wanted to question what ministers were saying drew upon a very similar set of ideas that often put scientists and experts on the side of an untrustworthy elite establishment. So when New Labour pressed for a self-styled evidence-based approach to the use of genetically modified crops, critics, including environmental groups and backed by newspapers which ran and ran with stories about Frankenstein food, argued the science could not be trusted.[35] When ministers and health experts argued there was no evidence of a link between the MMR vaccine and autism, significant numbers of people, supported once again by a significant number of newspapers, demurred.[36] Something similar happened with arguments about climate change. New Labour relied upon scientific expertise as a trump card to make its case for policy change. But in many people's eyes, this approach was suspect. Experts disagree with each other and their disagreements are, in part, recognizably political. They have vested interests in particular outcomes. Scientific knowledge is flawed. It is derived from and is overly dependent upon abstract models which are used to generate predictably incorrect predictions. Those claiming the mantle of expertise often lack common sense, practical experience and a real understanding of the lives or values of ordinary people.

This undercurrent of populist scepticism, elements of which came to the surface during the 2000 fuel crisis, found a focal point in 2009 when hacked email correspondence between members of the Climatic Research Unit at the University of East Anglia was leaked. Selective quotes seemed to show scientists complaining that 'there should be even more warming: but the data are surely wrong'; boasting of a 'trick' to 'hide the decline' in reported temperature changes; worrying about how negative news stories would compromise funding bids; and of balancing the 'needs of the science and the IPCC'. 'Climategate' (as it inevitably became known) attracted the interest of Republican Congressmen in America, and prompted the lead Saudi Arabian negotiator at the Copenhagen conference, Mohammad Al-Sabban, to declare 'it appears from the details of the scandal that there is no relationship whatsoever between human activities and climate change'.[37]

Another academic, Harry Collins, who, along with Sheila Jasanoff, had been one of the key figures in developing the sociological critique of science, later argued, persuasively, that all Climategate had done was to show how scientists had always worked and had always spoken to each other and had revealed absolutely nothing which brought into question the basic validity of the peer-reviewed science of climate change. Instead, and in a partial recanting of his earlier views, Collins argued that what the incident showed was just how little most people understood about science, and how precious and difficult to acquire true expertise is.[38] The problem was 'technological populism'.[39] Yet to many people, operating with a view that scientists are, if they are doing their jobs properly, heroic figures doing no more than battling to discover the truth, Climategate seemed to show something different. That these scientists could not necessarily be trusted because they were chasing funding, bending results and working, undercover, as political activists. That was not the case. There is no evidence the climate scientists at the UEA acted improperly, let alone that they faked their evidence. Yet as Mark Brown, a professor in the Department of Government at the California State University, argues, what is true is that their emails reveal a group of scientists who were acting with an underlying desire to reinforce the rationalist, linear model of science in which knowledge is always certain; a model that Collins and others had previously cast doubt upon.[40]

New Labour, as we have already seen, relied heavily upon a political strategy of employing experts to deliver advice which it could then present as being non-partisan. This sometimes worked. The Wanless Review into the long-term funding of the NHS probably helped New Labour make the case for higher health spending. The Stern Review helped pave the ground for the 2008 Climate Change Act. Yet there were risks involved. Because New Labour was not trusted, the expertise it invoked also risked being viewed as tainted. Michael Gove's comment, during the Brexit referendum, that 'the people of this country have had enough of experts', a comment we will return to later (pp. 373–4), had, in this respect, a backstory.

BOOM

SOLDIERING ON

Despite significant public scepticism about the causes and importance of climate change, the 2008 Climate Change Act had a lasting impact. After making his name by hugging a few huskies, David Cameron's relative lack of interest in environmental issues prior to the 2010 General Election sustained itself once he became prime minister. He did not deliver a major speech on this issue after 2010. In 2012 he appointed Owen Paterson, a noted climate change sceptic, to lead the Department of Environment, Food and Rural Affairs.[41] In 2013, he reportedly told aides to 'cut the green crap'.[42] In 2015 he scrapped a proposed regulation that would have required all newly built homes in Britain to be carbon-neutral and, not long after, amended planning regulations in ways which made it close to impossible to get permission to build onshore windfarms.[43]

Yet the Coalition, and the Conservative governments which followed it, did not repeal – and did not come close to trying to repeal – the Climate Change Act. The cross-party, expert-led, technocratic consensus that was stitched together in the 2000s and given political impetus by Nicholas Stern and David Miliband just about held. In 2013 the Coalition introduced a new carbon tax for the power-generation industry which had the effect of rendering the burning of coal uncompetitive. In June 2019, following a recommendation from the Committee on Climate Change, Parliament agreed to a new and more ambitious 'net zero' target, of cutting emissions by 100 per cent relative to their 1990 levels by 2050.[44] Meanwhile, the proportion of energy generated through renewable sources rose from 7 per cent in 2010 to 43 per cent by 2020.[45] Largely as a result, Britain met the targets contained in its first (2008–12) and second (2013–17) carbon budgets, and by 2018 could report that overall carbon emissions were 44 per cent below their 1990 levels despite the economy being 60 per cent larger.[46] This did not mean the government had done everything it could to cut emissions. Yet compared with, for example, the United States, Japan and Australia, where carbon emissions had risen relative to 1990 levels, Britain's record was, in many respects, an impressive one.[47] The question was whether it could last, and in 2023 the Climate Change Committee concluded that it had not (p. 482).

Outside the technocratic black box the 2008 Climate Change Act had established, climate change also risked becoming, in the early 2020s, part of Britain's broader culture wars (Chapter 34). On the one hand, groups like Extinction Rebellion and Just Stop Oil staged high-profile protests such as throwing soup at Vincent van Gogh's 'Sunflowers' at the National Gallery and orange powder paint over one of the tables at the Snooker World Championships in Sheffield.[48] On the other, the former UKIP leader Nigel Farage returned to the political fray in order to launch a campaign to hold a referendum on the net zero target.[49]

As for broader public opinion, the percentage of people regarding pollution and the environment as one of the most important issues facing the country grew steadily from a low of 5 per cent in 2013 to around 10 per cent in 2018, before reaching 20 per cent in 2021 and then dipping slightly to around 15 per cent in 2022.[50] As for underlying views on climate change, the 2018 edition of the British Social Attitudes survey found that 93 per cent of respondents believed the climate was definitely or probably changing and that only 9 per cent believed this was happening because of mainly or entirely natural reasons un-related to human activity. These numbers are suggestive of, if not a sea-change, then at least a shift in public attitudes relative to those from 2010. Yet, at the same time, only 6 per cent of people said they were 'extremely' worried about climate change and only a further 19 per cent 'very' worried (the very middling 'somewhat' worried being the pre-ferred response of 45 per cent).[51] If you compared this with the warning in the summary of the 2023 IPCC report, that 'Human-caused climate change is already affecting many weather and climate extremes in every region across the globe' and that 'this has led to widespread adverse impacts and related losses and damages to nature and people', you could not help but notice the difference.[52]

I I

A Global Game

A SHOOT-OUT

At 10.45 p.m. local time on the evening of 21 May 2008, the final of the UEFA Champions League kicked off in front of a crowd of 67,000 people inside the Luzhniki Stadium in Moscow. For the first ever time the final was being contested between two English teams: Manchester United, who had just won their tenth Premier League title, and Chelsea, who had finished second. In many ways, the 2008 final was a powerful testimony to the quality of English football and of the English Premier League. Yet, whilst both clubs certainly had deep roots in English football – Manchester United could trace its history back to the creation of Newton Heath Lancashire and Yorkshire Railway Football Club in 1878, and Chelsea to a foundational meeting at the Rising Sun pub (now the Butcher's Hook) opposite the main entrance to the club's ground at Stamford Bridge in 1905 – the 2008 Champions League final was, above all else, a powerful symbol of globalization.

Manchester United was owned by the American billionaire Malcolm Glazer. Chelsea was owned by the Russian billionaire Roman Abramovich, who had bought the club in 2003 (and remained its owner until he was sanctioned by the British government following the Russian invasion of Ukraine in 2022). Manchester's season had started the previous July with a brand-enhancing tour of the Far East, which included games against Urawa Red Diamonds, FC Seoul, Shenzhen FC and Guangzhou FC. Chelsea had started with three games in California against the Mexican team Club América, the South Korean team Suwon Bluewings and Los Angeles Galaxy, then captained by one David Beckham, the former Manchester United and England footballer whose marriage to 'Posh Spice' Victoria Adams had redefined the boundaries of what could be done to commercialize marriage, fame and masculinity. The starting line-ups of the Moscow final featured ten English players alongside three Frenchmen, two Portuguese, a Dutchman, a Serbian, an Argentinian, a Czech, a Ghanian, a German and an Ivorian. United were managed by the Glaswegian Alex Ferguson and Chelsea by the Israeli Avram Grant, who had replaced the Portuguese José Mourinho earlier that season.

The game itself, with an estimated 25,000 British fans in the stadium, was tense but, for long periods, a little dull. Cristiano Ronaldo scored in the 26th minute for United before the Romford-born Frank Lampard equalized in the final minute of the first half. Not much then happened. During the penalty shoot-out to decide the result, Ronaldo missed United's third kick, giving the Chelsea and England captain, John Terry, the chance to win the title. He slipped and hit the post. Edwin van der Sar then saved Nicolas Anelka's penalty and Manchester United won 6–5. A few weeks later Chelsea sacked Grant. A little while after that, Ronaldo, agitating for a move to Real Madrid, described his position in Manchester as being like that of a slave.[1]

A GLOBAL GAME

The term globalization was coined by an American academic, Theodore Levitt, in 1983.[2] He defined globalization in terms of changes in social behaviour and technologies allowing companies to sell the same products around the world. Today, globalization is used far more generally to describe the process by which countries, companies and people are becoming more connected as a result of improvements in transport and communications, enabling people, goods capital and information to move across the world. We tend to think of globalization (a common theme of the chapters in this Part), as a defining hallmark of the late twentieth and twenty-first centuries. Yet a race to globalize the English state in search of treasure, security and status began in the Elizabethan Age, with the East India Company being formed in 1600. The first British Empire came and went in the eighteenth century.[3] It was succeeded by a second Empire, which sustained not only a complex system of international trade but, for some of its inhabitants, including those in England, a pan-national sense of imperial identity.[4] Writing in 1919, in the immediate aftermath of the globalization-destroying First World War, John Maynard Keynes looked back on this period, in the late nineteenth and early twentieth centuries, as being, for those with enough money, one of accelerated globalization.

> The inhabitant of London could order by telephone, sipping his morning tea in bed, the various products of the whole earth, in such quantity as he might see fit, and reasonably expect their early delivery upon his doorstep; he could at the same moment and by the same means adventure his wealth in the natural resources and new enterprises of any quarter of the world, and share, without exertion or even trouble, in their prospective fruits and advantages ... [or] He could secure forthwith, if he wished it, cheap and comfortable means of transit to any country or climate without passport or other formality.[5]

It was during this same period that British fans, players and coaches were playing a globalizing role in the development of football, the game whose origins, in England, are seen as predating the reign of King Henry IV (1399–1413), before culminating in the formation of the world's oldest still-existing football club, Sheffield FC, in 1857. The inaugural French football league was won in 1894 by Standard Athletic, a British social club in Paris (which went on to represent France at cricket in the 1900 Olympics). In Spain, in 1898, Athletic Bilbao was one of several clubs founded by expatriate British workers.[6] In Italy, Juventus was founded in 1897 and initially wore pink shirts. A few years later, one of their players, an Englishman called John Savage, persuaded some friends living in Nottingham to send him some black-and-white striped Notts County shirts. The club continues to play in these colours. Arthur Johnson, who was born in Dublin but identified himself as an Englishman, was Real Madrid's first coach between 1910 and 1920. Jack Reynolds, who was born in Pilkington, Lancashire, managed Amsterdam's Ajax for a total of twenty-seven years between 1915 and 1947 and is credited with the development of its pioneering style of 'total football'.[7]

Despite the strength of these connections, the English game eventually turned inwards. England refused to join the Fédération Internationale de Football Association (FIFA) when it was established in 1904, and in 1931 the English Football Association introduced a new rule requiring players to have been resident in the country for at least two years before they could play for an English club. In the years following the Second

World War, non-British professional players were few and far between within the English game, one of the most famous exceptions being Bernhard 'Bert' Trautmann, who had won an Iron Cross on the Eastern Front before he was captured and sent to a prisoner-of-war camp in Cheshire. He signed for Manchester City as a goalkeeper in 1949, playing in – and completing – the 1956 FA Cup, which the club won despite him being knocked out and cracking a vertebra in a collision fifteen minutes before the end of the game.

When the European Cup, the forerunner of the Champions League, was established in 1955, British clubs struggled to make much of an impact; Real Madrid, Benfica, AC Milan and Inter Milan won the first eleven finals. Eventually, the tide began to turn. Celtic beat Inter Milan 2–1 in the 1967 final in Lisbon and in 1968 Manchester United, captained by the late Bobby Charlton, matched this success, beating Benfica 4–1 at Wembley Stadium. The British teams that contested these two finals were, however, distinctly un-globalized. All eleven of the 'Lisbon Lions' who started the 1967 final for Celtic were born within 30 miles of Celtic Park in Glasgow.[8] Manchester United's starting line-up a year later featured seven Englishmen, two Irishmen, a Scot and the shimmering Northern Irishman George Best. Over the following years Bayern Munich and Ajax dominated the European Cup. Then, in the 1970s and early 1980s, three English teams – Liverpool, Nottingham Forest and Aston Villa – won the European Cup seven times over the course of eight years, before English teams were banned for five years from all European football competitions following the Heysel Stadium disaster in 1985. They did so with teams composed almost entirely of British players. In the 1984 final at the Stadio Olimpico in Rome, Liverpool beat Roma with a starting line-up of ten British or Irish outfield players alongside the Zimbabwean goalkeeper Bruce Grobbelaar.

THE GLOBAL POWER OF MONEY

Economically, Britain began to re-globalize in the 1960s with the development, in the City of London, of the Eurodollar markets (p. 97). When Margaret Thatcher abolished exchange controls in 1979 economic globalization accelerated. British football remained largely and blissfully unaffected. In the 1980s the Argentinian players Osvaldo 'Ossie'

Ardiles and Riccado 'Ricky' Villa and the Dutchmen Arnold Mühren and Frans Thijssen played for and became stars at, respectively, Tottenham Hotspur and Ipswich Town. They were, however, the exceptions to a very British, un-globalized, rule. At the start of the inaugural Premier League season in August 1992 there were just thirty-seven overseas players registered to play for one of the Premier League's twenty-two teams.[9]

English football was globalized from around the mid-1990s onwards by money. That money came from Sky TV's regular payments to broadcast Premier League matches. When the chairmen (they were all men) of the English Football Association First Division teams voted to create a breakaway Premier League in 1992, Sky agreed to pay £304 million a year to broadcast its games. At the time, this was an unimaginably large sum. It turned out to constitute great value for money. When Sky renewed its contract in 1997 it paid £670 million a year. In 2001 this rose to £1.1 billion a year, when the Premier League was earning another billion pounds each year from selling broadcast rights to more than a hundred other countries across the world.[10] By 2008 seven of the twenty richest clubs in the world, a list which of course included Manchester United and Chelsea, were English.[11] An estimated 4.8 billion people across more than two hundred countries watched the Premier League. Indeed, in February 2008 the Premier League's administrators had even proposed adding an additional round of games each season – to be hosted in international cities which would pay for the privilege.

Money globalized football because it gave clubs the opportunity to buy more and better players and managers from abroad. On 26 December 1999 Chelsea became the first ever team in Premier League history to name a starting eleven composed entirely of non-British players. Nearly a decade on, when Chelsea played Manchester United in Moscow, four of Chelsea's players (and six of Manchester United's) were English. That was unusually high. In the 2007/8 season, 63 per cent of the Premier League's players had been born overseas: the highest proportion of any of the major European leagues.[12]

As English football globalized itself on the pitch and, as a result, became more successful, an increasing number of clubs were also bought by overseas investors, out to make a profit or acquire free publicity. In Chapter 9 I observed how New Labour's pro-globalization, free market position led it to turn a relaxed blind eye to overseas takeovers of British firms. Football was no different. In the early 2000s, voices could be heard arguing that the influx of foreign players was coming at the expense of the development of English talent. At other times overseas players were accused of destroying the moral fabric of the English national game by either diving or feigning injury or eating pasta. Yet, for the most part, the globalization of English football teams proved relatively uncontroversial.

Foreign ownership of clubs remained, it is true, an occasional flashpoint. The Glazer family's takeover of Manchester United sparked intense protests, which led some fans to launch the breakaway club FC United of Manchester. In 2007, the takeover of Liverpool by two other American billionaires, George Gillett and Tom Hicks, proved equally divisive. Yet fans' objection did not seem to be to foreign ownership per se but, rather, to certain foreign owners. The Glazers and Hicks and Gillett were pilloried not for being American, but for the way they had financed their purchases by loading debts onto their new clubs' balance sheets.[13] Mike Ashley, the English owner of Newcastle United between 2007 and 2021, was just as unpopular with his club's fan base because of his lack of spending and ambition. On the other hand, and almost without exception, local fans welcomed the takeover, in August 2008, of Manchester City by the Abu Dhabi Group, led by Sheikh Mansour, the deputy prime minister of the United Arab Emirates and a member of Abu Dhabi's royal family.

The Premier League's rise and rise in the 1990s and 2000s was a political godsend for New Labour. It offered, along with the City of London, cast-iron evidence that globalization paid off and that Britain was back. Critics like Will Hutton might have fretted about British-owned industries being sold to the highest bidder, but football showed that globalization was a force for good.[14] Yet if the Moscow Champions League final, which came a year after Blair had left Downing Street, can be seen as symbolizing a high-point of globalization, there were soon signs the world might be changing.

In April 2008, at a summit meeting in Bucharest, NATO invited Albania and Croatia to open accession talks and, in its final communiqué, 'welcomed Ukraine and Georgia's Euro-Atlantic aspirations for membership and agreed that these countries will become members of NATO'.[15] In August, Russian troops invaded the disputed territory of

South Ossetia on the border with Georgia. If the Champions League final had been an advert for globalization, the war between Russia and Georgia over South Ossetia represented, in a very specific and niche way, a repudiation of it. In 1999 the three-time Pulitzer Prize-winning American journalist Thomas Friedman, riffing on Immanuel Kant's 1795 *Toward Perpetual Peace* theory, advanced the 'golden arches theory of conflict prevention'.[16] Globalization, Friedman argued, meant, first and foremost, economic growth. Economic growth resulted in the emergence of a prosperous and politically influential middle class with a vested interest in consumerism. At the cusp of the twenty-first century, the acme of consumerism was McDonald's. Hence, Friedman advanced, no two countries with McDonald's franchises in their country had ever gone to war with each other. Written down, this sounds silly. But it also turned out to be true. At least, it was true until August 2008 when Russia, whose first McDonald's had opened in Pushkinskaya Square in Moscow in 1990, attacked Georgia, whose first franchise had opened on Rustaveli Avenue in Tbilisi in 1999.

Then, in September 2008, Lehman Brothers filed for bankruptcy in a New York courthouse. The financial crisis was, in many ways, testimony to the power of globalization. Financial data from Wall Street was communicated across the rest of the world in seconds, leading to the collapse of banks everywhere and all at once. But, after governments across the world had sought, after a difficult start, to co-ordinate their responses, the financial crisis became a moment when the boundaries of the nation-states became more important and globalization became an economic problem rather an answer. As the central banker and economist Charles Goodhart observed, banks are 'international in life and national in death'.[17] When they imploded in 2008, it was national governments that had to decide whether and how to bail them out and how to pay for doing so.

A BRITISH FIELD

This chapter has not only focused upon the English Premier League but has come perilously close to presenting football as an English game. Yet the Foot-Ball Club of Edinburgh (founded in 1824) and the Dublin University Football Club (founded in 1854) would both dispute Sheffield

FC's claim to being the world's oldest football club. Moreover, it was a Scotsman, William McGregor, the president of Aston Villa, who had first suggested that England's leading clubs form their own league.[18]

By the 2000s, however, football was thriving in England in ways and to an extent that was not true of the other home nations. In Wales, rugby, not football, remained the national game, with the Welsh team winning the Six Nations Grand Slam in 2005 and 2008. The national football team failed to qualify for any major tournament in the 2000s (although it did reach the semi-finals of the 2016 European Championships). At club level, the semi-professional League of Wales was established in 1992 but immediately became embroiled in an intense legal and political tussle with the 'irate eight': established non-league clubs based in Wales who wanted to remain in the English system.[19] Further up the football pyramid, the larger, professional Welsh clubs – Cardiff, Swansea and Wrexham – also continued to play in the English Football League. In August 2000 a Lebanese businessman, Sam Hammam, purchased Cardiff City and pledged to rename the club the Cardiff Celts and make the team the fulcrum of a new 'Welsh identity and pride'.[20] Hammam was probably right to see the potential for a stronger Welsh identity for Welsh football, but it was the deep local enmity between Cardiff and Swansea which, in the end, continued to generate the most intense passions amongst fans.[21]

In Northern Ireland, football had historically offered another outlet for sectarian conflict, pitching Protestant Linfield and Glentoran against predominantly Catholic Cliftonville.[22] The 1998 Good Friday Agreement, the subject of Chapter 15, eased some of those tensions whilst also making it easier for supporters and some players to follow the example set by Derry FC, which had switched from the Northern Irish to the Irish Football League in 1985. In the new political environment, local teams pledged to oppose sectarianism, with Linfield signing Catholic players and severing its connections to militant Loyalist groups.[23] Yet some of those old divisions remained. In 2000 Neil Lennon, a Northern Irishman and Catholic, signed for Celtic, the Glasgow team founded in 1888 to raise money for a Catholic charity, the Poor Children's Dinner Table. Lennon was repeatedly booed when he subsequently played for Northern Ireland in front of the predominantly Protestant home crowd at Windsor Park, Belfast. He had received death threats from members of the Loyalist Volunteer Force, it was reported, before

he announced his retirement from international games.[24] When the historically Protestant club Glasgow Rangers edged out Celtic on the final
day of the 2008/9 season to win the Scottish Premier League, Loyalists
in Coleraine took to the streets to celebrate. Kevin McDaid, a Catholic
community worker and his wife, Evelyn, a Protestant, were attacked
and Kevin was killed by a mob outside their house.[25]

Scotland was an economic success story in the 2000s, experiencing
the highest rate of growth of any part of UKGBNI (p. 93). The same
could not however be said of Scottish football. In 1998 Scotland qualified for the World Cup in France, losing narrowly to Brazil and drawing
with Norway before being hammered by Morocco during the final
game of their group. Scotland did not then qualify for another major
tournament for over twenty years At a club level, the Glasgow duopoly
of Rangers and Celtic, which had been temporarily broken by Sir Alex
Ferguson's Aberdeen in the mid-1980s, reasserted itself until Rangers
were relegated to the Third Division in 2012 following a financial meltdown, which also had the effect of derailing talk of the two clubs joining
the English Premier League.[26] Sky continued to sign deals to show live
Scottish Premier League games, although the amounts they were willing
to pay were a small fraction of those paid for the English Premier
League.[27] Less money meant fewer expensive foreign players, increasingly run-down stadiums and the constant threat of losing players and
managers south of the border.

In England, footballing success was also concentrated within a relatively small number of clubs. It was a part of the appeal of the English
Premier League that 'on any given day', as the television cliché had it,
'anyone could beat anyone', whilst promotions and relegations gave
any team at any level the opportunity to prosper. In 2021 it was this
sense of the significance of the principle of an equality of opportunity
that drove fans, including fans of the largest clubs, to successfully
oppose a breakaway European league in which some teams, by virtue of
their size and historic success, would have been guaranteed places in
perpetuity.[28] That notion of an equality of opportunity was not entirely
without foundation. Of the twenty teams in the 2000/1 iteration of the
English Premier League, only twelve were still there by the start of the
2007/8 season. Yet this turnover masked a great deal of continuity at
the very top where larger stadiums, a larger slice of television revenue
and participation in European competitions ensured that, between

them, Manchester United, Chelsea, Arsenal and Liverpool finished in four of the top five positions over six consecutive seasons between 2003/4 and 2009/10. Meanwhile, outside the Premier League in the financially lost zones of League 1 and League 2, clubs struggled to survive. Hull City, Bury, Halifax Town, Bradford City, Notts County, Barnsley, Port Vale, Darlington, Rotherham United, Wrexham, Chester City and Stockport County all went into administration in the 2000s.

What was true of English football was true of British society. In his efforts to distance New Labour from its socialist past, Tony Blair preached the virtues not of equality of outcome, but of equality of opportunity. So, for example, in a speech he delivered in Hackney in 2002 to mark the publication of the government's fourth annual report on poverty, he described how 'our goal is a Britain in which nobody is left behind; in which people can go as far as they have the talent to go; in which we achieve true equality – equal status and equality of opportunity rather than equality of outcome'.[29] Yet, whilst New Labour went some way towards stabilizing levels of income inequality in the 2000s, there is little evidence it achieved a greater measure of social mobility. Indeed, a report from the Independent Commission on Social Mobility in 2009 concluded that 'Britain is a society of persistent inequality' and that the 'life chances of people in Britain today remain heavily dependent upon the circumstances of their birth'.[30] The following year, a report published by the OECD echoed this analysis. It looked at the extent to which a son's earnings correlated with his father's. It found that in Denmark, a father's income could explain 15% of the variance in a son's income. In Australia, it could explain 16%; in Norway 17%; in Canada 19%; in Sweden 28%; in Germany and Spain 32%; in France 41%; in the United States 48%; in Italy 49%; and in the United Kingdom 50%.[31]

INCLUSION, EXCLUSION

I have suggested that the English Premier League was so successful in the late 1990s and 2000s because it could use the money it received to internationalize its players, managers and global appeal. There is, however, another important part of the story here. Football, as it had developed in England and the other home nations in the nineteenth and twentieth centuries, was packaged and to a significant extent made into something largely white and male. That exclusiveness had been consistently challenged. However, in the 2000s those challenges not only became more common but, for the first time, were being embraced – if sometimes inconsistently – by the Football Association and the English Premier League.

There is some debate about it, but the first black professional football player in England was probably Arthur Wharton, who was born in what is now Accra, in Ghana, before moving to England in 1882 and playing for Rotherham and Sheffield United.[32] By the late 1970s, however, when Viv Anderson became the first black player to be awarded a full England international cap, racial abuse was a pervasive part of terrace football culture.[33] Vince Hilaire, who played for Crystal Palace between 1977 and 1984, once described how racist abuse was so common that if the police had ever done anything about it 'up to the mid-1980s, there'd probably be no one left watching football'.[34] The 1991 Football Offences Act made racist or indecent chanting at a football match a criminal offence. The Let's Kick Racism Out of Football campaign was established in 1993 and eventually attracted support from the Football Association. The number of black players increased steadily in the 2000s. Eight of the starting twenty-two players at the Moscow Champions League final were black. By 2010 between 20 and 25 per cent of all professional footballers in England came from a black or minority ethnic background.[35] Two years later, the Culture, Media and Sport parliamentary select committee could credibly claim 'racism in football has become significantly less common in the United Kingdom' and that 'the atmosphere experienced by those attending football matches has changed hugely since the 1970s and 80s when racial and other forms of abuse were common'.[36]

Yet racism in football, as in the broader society within which it existed, did not simply disappear in the 2000s. Whilst 20 per cent of all professional players might have been black, there were still remarkably few professional players from an Asian background. Moreover, the presence of a significant number of black players made the dearth of black football executives or managers more striking. In 2005 all 103 members of the Football Association Council were white. In June 2008, the former England captain Paul Ince became the first black English manager of a Premier League club. He was sacked in December.

On 15 October 2011 the Liverpool striker Luis Suárez racially abused the Manchester United defender Patrice Evra and was banned for eight games and fined £40,000. Just two weeks later, the Chelsea and England captain John Terry, who had played in the 2008 Moscow final, was accused of racially abusing an opposing player, Anton Ferdinand. Terry was eventually acquitted by a court but found guilty by the FA of using abusive and/or insulting words which included a reference to colour and/or race.[37] He was stripped of the England captaincy – a decision which led England's Italian manager, Fabio Capello, to resign. The player who was the victim of Terry's invective, Anton Ferdinand, was repeatedly attacked on social media whilst eggs and bricks were thrown at his mother's house.[38]

In the late nineteenth century, thousands of fans regularly attended women's football games. In 1920 a Boxing Day match between Dick, Kerr Ladies and St Helen's Ladies drew a crowd of over 50,000 to Goodison Park in Liverpool.[39] In 1921, at a moment when it was already pushing back against the globalization of the game, the Football Association banned clubs affiliated to it from hosting women's games. That ban was overturned in 1971 but for a long while after women, whether as fans, players, managers or football administrators, were rendered invisible.[40] In 1995 Sepp Blatter, the president of FIFA, declared that 'the future is feminine' (although, somewhat patronizingly, he went on to add that female payers contributed a 'distinctive style of play, characterized by a certain elegance which has prevailed over a more robust impersonation of the man's game'). In 2002 the film *Bend It Like Beckham*, the story of a young English girl of South Asian descent, Jessindra 'Jess' Bhamra, drew greater attention to women's football at a time when the largest clubs were seeking to broaden their support base. By the middle of that decade Premier League surveys suggested up to 20 per cent of fans were women.[41] In 2009, a year prior to the establishment of the Women's Super League, several of whose teams were entirely professional, over a million people watched the England women's football team play Germany in the final of the European Championships.

Yet as David Goldblatt observes, there were still plenty of people who remained entirely happy to talk about the essential maleness – 'it's a man's game' – of football.[42] With plenty of fans ready to rail against the commercialization of football, a backlash against female participants accompanied a steady stream of sexist football coverage.

This ranged from Soccer AM's 'Soccerettes' feature to ITV's *Footballers' Wives* and the wall-to-wall coverage of Victoria Beckham, Coleen Rooney and other WAGS (wives and girlfriends) of the England men's team during the 2006 World Cup finals in Germany. In 2006 the Luton manager Mike Newell was warned, but not sacked, after a verbal outburst at Amy Rayner, the Football League's first female assistant referee: 'She shouldn't be here. I know that sounds sexist. But I am sexist.'[43] In January 2011 Sky's television commentator Andy Gray and presenter Richard Keys were, at a moment when they thought their microphones had been switched off, recorded saying someone needed to explain the offside rule to Sian Massey-Ellis and asking, 'why is there a female linesman?'[44] In fact, it was not until 2022, when the England Lionesses won the European Football Championship final – and followed this up by making the final of the 2023 World Cup – that women's football fully stepped out of the shadow into which it had been cast.

The economic boom and accelerated globalization came, for a while, to seem entirely normal in the 2000s. Football, the banks, computer firms like Apple and the climate all seemed to be operating on an ever-larger scale. That world did not come to an end in the 2010s, and nor did it come to an end, a decade later, with Covid. But after the financial crash and the Russian invasion of Georgia, globalization never looked quite as obvious and inevitable again. I will tell the story of the financial crash in some detail in the fourth part of the book. Before then, I turn back to 2001 and a moment of global terror.

PART THREE

War

Part Three is where the dam bursts. The opening chapter starts with al-Qaeda's attacks on mainland America on 11 September 2001 and George W. Bush's declaration of a 'War on Terror'. Chapter 13 describes the unravelling of the British military occupation of Basra in southern Iraq and Helmand Province in Afghanistan and the death of Dr David Kelly in July 2003. Addressing the Labour Party Conference in October 2001 Tony Blair argued that the terrorist attacks on New York and the threat of further terrorism were a 'moment to seize', one which provided an opportunity to 're-order this world around us'.[1] Looking back, that is exactly what then happened, albeit not in the way he intended. The invasions of Afghanistan and Iraq changed the international system, transformed Blair and Blair's premiership and, to an extent that had not been true of the Korean, Suez, Falklands or First Gulf War, divided and defined the government.* In his final resignation speech, delivered at the Trimdon Labour Club in May 2007, Blair acknowledged that the Iraq War had been 'bitterly controversial' but argued it had been the right thing to do, and added 'we can't fail it'.[2] The problem, at this point, was not simply that most people disagreed with Blair about whether the invasion of Iraq had been the right thing to do. Rather, the

---

* The Suez crisis is often seen as a turning-point in Britain's post-war decline but that was not nearly so obvious at the time. It led to the resignation of Anthony Eden as prime minister, but events moved on and Suez was barely mentioned during the 1959 General Election campaign, which the Conservatives won. Andrew Jones, 'How significant was the Suez Crisis?', History Extra (24 July 2020). That the Conservatives and Margaret Thatcher only won the 1983 election because of the 'Falklands Factor' is still regarded (at least by critics of Margaret Thatcher) as an item of faith. It is probably untrue. The 1983 election was a decisive moment in the development of Thatcherism, but, whether due to good decisions, good luck or careful electoral-economic engineering, the Conservatives were on-track to win the election long before Argentinian scrap-metal merchants landed on South Georgia on 19 March 1982. David Sanders, 'Government popularity and the Falklands War: a reassessment', *British Journal of Political Science*, 17, 3 (1987): 281–313.

problem was that most people had, by this time, decided that Britain had *already* failed.

Chapter 14 begins with the terrorist attacks on central London on 7 July 2005 and the police investigation that followed. Chapter 15 is about the end of a war rather than its start. It starts with the IRA's announcement, in July 2005, that it was ceasing its armed struggle and ends with the swearing-in of Ian Paisley and Martin McGuinness as first minister and deputy first minister of Northern Ireland. The final chapter of this part covers Blair's deteriorating relationship with his long-time chancellor Gordon Brown and eventual downfall. The key question it addresses is whether the 'TB-GBs', the on-going conflict between Blair and Brown, was all about personality, ambition and weapons-grade sulking, or whether it *also* revolved around a substantive political disagreement about what New Labour was and what it should be.

12

Giving War a Chance

11 SEPTEMBER 2001

At 8.46 a.m. Eastern Standard Time on 11 September 2001, five hijackers flew American Airlines Flight 11 into the nineteenth floor of the North Tower of the World Trade Center in New York. Seventeen minutes later, a second plane was flown into the South Tower. Half an hour after, terrorists crashed a plane into the Pentagon. Finally, following a ferocious struggle, terrorists then crashed Flight 93, from Newark to San Francisco, into a field in Pennsylvania. When the first plane hit the World Trade Center Tony Blair was in a suite at the Grand Hotel in Brighton making last-minute preparations for a speech he was due to deliver to the Trades Union Congress (TUC). Blair's advisors told him what had happened, but everyone assumed it was just a horrible accident and he returned to work. When the second plane hit the South Tower and it became instantly clear America was being attacked, Blair left the hotel to deliver a short address to conference delegates, in which he described 'mass terrorism' as the 'new evil in our world'.[1]

When Blair made it back to Downing Street there was a surfeit of confusion. There were intelligence reports of other imminent attacks.[2] Communications with Washington were patchy. The Cabinet's Civil Contingencies Unit were on an away-day in Yorkshire. Nobody was quite sure who had the authority, if it were needed, to give the order to shoot down an airliner over British airspace. Over the next few days, as it became clear that the Islamist group al-Qaeda, based in Afghanistan, had planned and executed the attacks, the question of what America would do next and what Britain ought to say and do to influence it became more pressing. On 20 September, during a fleeting visit to America, Blair told a press conference the terrorist attacks on America had been an attack on the 'whole of the democratic and civilised and free world'. Britain, he added, would support America's fight against international terrorism 'for as long as it takes'.[3] Quite often, when politicians say things like this, they both mean and don't mean it. Blair *really* meant it. That evening, he watched as President Bush delivered a joint address to Congress in which he thanked Blair for his support, delivered an ultimatum to the Taliban government in Afghanistan to 'hand over the terrorists' or 'share in their fate', and warned that 'our war on terror begins with al-Qaeda, but . . . will not end until every terrorist group of global reach has been found, stopped and defeated'.[4]

IRAQ, VIA AFGHANISTAN

On 7 October the al-Qaeda leader, Osama bin Laden, broadcast a message celebrating the attacks on America and calling on Muslims to attack their enemies. That same day the United States, with the backing of British forces, and in the absence of any clear United Nations (UN) authorization, launched 'Operation Enduring Freedom' to topple the Taliban and eliminate al-Qaeda in Afghanistan.[5] After the initial onslaught, it looked, for a while, as if the military campaign might grind to a halt. American planes ran out of targets to bomb and the Northern Alliance, the military group that had been fighting the Taliban since 1996, seemed to be stalling. Then, just when it seemed that nothing was going to happen other than the winter, the Taliban fell apart. On 13 November Northern Alliance troops, joined for the day by the BBC's John Simpson, entered Kabul and the Taliban fled.[6] In December, Hamid Karzai was sworn in as interim chairman of the Afghan administration, and in January 2002 a NATO-led international security force, including 2,000 British troops, was deployed to maintain security, oversee economic development projects and prevent the return of the Taliban. Meanwhile, the business of hunting senior al-Qaeda figures was left to the Americans and some British special forces units. Bin Laden escaped.

American attention then turned back to Iraq.* In his State of the

---

* On the afternoon of 11 September, at a point when President Bush had yet to return to Washington, the defence secretary, Donald Rumsfeld, told the vice-chairman of the Joint Chiefs of Staff that America should consider a wide range of options, and that his personal

Union Address in January 2002 Bush named Iraq, along with North Korea and Iran, as members of an 'axis of evil' whose ongoing plans to develop and deploy weapons of mass destruction (WMD) posed a 'grave and growing danger'.[7] In April, at another post-summit press conference with Tony Blair, this one in Crawford, Texas, where the president had a home, Bush confirmed that 'the policy of my government is the removal of Saddam'. Blair, for his part, was a bit more nuanced. He agreed that 'the region, the world, and not least the ordinary Iraqi people would be better off without the regime of Saddam Hussein'. But, he added, 'how we approach this, this is a matter for discussion . . . a matter for considering all the options'.[8] On 10 October the US House of Representatives voted by 296 to 133 to authorize the use of force against Iraq. Blair, left with little alternative but to respond, did not rule out British involvement in any future war but made it clear he wanted the Americans to seek UN approval. Bush eventually agreed. British diplomats, led by Britain's permanent representative at the UN, Jeremy Greenstock, then went into overdrive, drafting and redrafting resolutions intended to attract maximum support and to appease the concerns of France, Russia and China, three of the five permanent members of the UN Security Council, who were, at best, sceptical about the case being made for war and wary of American military expansionism. Somehow it worked. On 8 November the Security Council unanimously voted to adopt Resolution 1441. This described Iraq as being in breach of previous UN resolutions and gave it 'a final opportunity' to allow UN weapons inspectors to enter the country and check whether there was any evidence of an ongoing programme to develop or store WMD.[9]

For a brief moment events seemed to be going Blair's way. Britain had led the debate at the UN. The Parliamentary Labour Party was anxious but partially reassured by Resolution 1441, while the Conservatives were adopting a bipartisan approach. There was, however, a problem. The countries who had voted for 1441 had very different ideas about how the resolution should be interpreted and what ought to happen next. America maintained Iraq's possession of WMD was beyond

instinct was to attack Saddam Hussein and Iraq as well as Bin Laden and Afghanistan. On 15 September the British Embassy in Washington reported that key figures in the American administration were convinced Iraq would have known about, and perhaps might even have facilitated, the 11 September attacks and were actively discussing options for an invasion.

dispute and that, if Iraq failed to admit this and disarm, 1441 would automatically create a legal mandate for invasion. France and Russia were equally clear that 1441 included no references to war and that it was up to the weapons inspectors to decide whether Iraq was violating 1441 and, if it were, for the UN to decide what to do next.

On 13 November 2002 Saddam Hussein said Iraq would comply with 1441 and allow weapons inspectors into the country. But shortly before they arrived, he submitted a multi-volume document to the UN denying that Iraq possessed any WMD or still had plans to develop them. Bush, who had been told by the director of the Central Intelligence Agency, George Tenet, that it was a 'slam dunk case' that Iraq had WMD, described Saddam's declaration as 'patently false'.[10] The weapons inspectors were then deployed; after a few weeks they had found nothing. Two decades later one of them was interviewed by the BBC's Gordon Corera for the Radio 4 documentary series *Shock and War*. Asked about their search for mobile biological laboratories – a key focus of American and British intelligence reports – he was dismissive. 'It was just basically glorified ice cream trucks and a flatbed. There were some cobwebs.'[11] The UN asked for more time to continue the inspections. Russia and France backed them. The US argued that Iraq was self-evidently deceiving the inspectors and that there was no plausible alternative to war.

On 3 February 2003 Blair told the House of Commons that Iraq was not co-operating with the UN inspectors and so had breached 1441. Rather than follow the Americans in arguing this made war inevitable, Blair argued that the UN now needed to pass a second resolution approving military intervention. In doing so, the prime minister had one eye on domestic politics. Opinion polls showed around a third of people were against military action, regardless of what happened, but that similar numbers thought war could already be justified based on the first UN resolution. A large middle ground, however, thought that the legitimacy of the war and of British involvement in it would depend on whether clear-cut evidence of Iraqi WMD emerged and on a second UN resolution.[12]

Blair did not get what he wanted. France and Russia, who were already annoyed by the way in which America had interpreted 1441, refused to play ball. On 16 March Britain, blaming everything on the French, announced it was abandoning its search for a second resolution.

Blair's split-the-difference centrist option was now no longer available. The alternatives were either going to war without a second resolution, or sitting out the American invasion that everyone now knew was coming. On 17 March the attorney general, Lord Goldsmith, published a short legal note saying that the invasion would be legal under international law without a second resolution. Shortly after, the leader of the House of Commons and former foreign secretary, Robin Cook, resigned telling the House of Commons 'Iraq probably has no weapons of mass destruction in the commonly understood sense of the term'.[13] That evening, in a televised address, President Bush gave Saddam Hussein a 48-hour deadline to leave Iraq. The following day, Parliament voted to authorize the use of British force.[14] Early on the morning of 20 March 2003 the invasion began.

WHAT WERE THEY THINKING?

So much for the basic timeline of events. The key question is why things happened the way they did. What did Blair and other key figures like Jack Straw (the foreign secretary), Geoff Hoon (the defence secretary), Jonathan Powell (Blair's chief of staff) and David Manning (Blair's foreign policy advisor) think they were doing? What did they believe?

Not long after he became prime minister, Blair had started to express concerns about Iraq's WMD. During private discussions in November 1997, he told the Liberal Democrat leader Paddy Ashdown that he had seen some 'pretty scary' intelligence briefings on Iraq and that Saddam should not be allowed to 'get away with it'.[15] In December 1998 Blair approved British military involvement in a four-day bombing campaign to pressure Iraq to co-operate fully with UN weapons inspectors. When Bush became president in January 2001 Blair told MPs he had raised the issue of Iraq's WMD with him during their first meeting.[16] Blair never seemed to give any credence to American speculation about Iraq's direct or indirect involvement in the 11 September attacks. Those attacks did however seem to confirm his own worst fears about WMD.*

---

* It is worth emphasizing that these fears, although subsequently proven to be entirely wrong, were grounded in a reality. Although WMD were not deployed during the First Gulf War in 1991, in the aftermath of Iraq's military defeat and flight from Kuwait it became

In the aftermath of the Crawford summit in April 2002, in which he had agreed with George Bush that the world would be better off without Saddam, Blair warned that allowing WMD 'to be developed by a state like Iraq without let or hindrance would be to grossly ignore the lessons of September 11'.[17] In September 2002 he told the TUC, on the anniversary of his visit the year before, that 'I do not want it on my conscience that we knew of the threat, saw it coming and did nothing'.[18]

There is of course an alternative account available here. Blair knew all along that there were no WMD. The war was really all about imperialism, oil and British subservience to America. This was the view of the Stop the War Coalition and of many of the hundreds of thousands who marched against the war in London and other British cities on 15 February 2003. It was also the view of the distinctly un-Trotskyite Conservative MP Kenneth Clarke, who thought WMD was a 'pretext' and that what Blair really wanted was regime change.[19] The idea that Blair was lying and knew he was lying is the most rhetorically powerful claim, but it is also the hardest to pin down. What we can say is that Blair had been repeatedly advised by the intelligence services, including, on the eve of the invasion, by the chair of the Joint Intelligence Committee, John Scarlett, that Iraq *did* possess chemical and biological WMD and the means to deliver them.[20] Blair might have wanted to be told this, and may have been responsible for creating an environment in which he would be likely to be told it, but that does not necessarily mean he was lying. Why knowingly lie when that lie was so quickly going to get found out once the invasion had happened?

The argument that the war was really about oil is a trickier one. It would be naive to argue that, historically, American involvement in the Middle East has had nothing to do with the region's oil reserves. It would be equally implausible to think that British politicians and officials were unaware of Iraq's oil reserves and the potential opportunities they offered to British firms to develop and profit from them.[21] It is however quite a leap from this to concluding that oil was the real reason Britain went to war, and that everything else was camouflage. After all, Britain (and, for that matter, the United States) were, at this time, easily getting access to the oil they needed through the simple expedient of

---

clear that it had a WMD programme that was much more advanced than Western intelligence agencies had appreciated.

paying for it on the market. In 2001 crude oil prices, adjusted for inflation and at 2023 prices, were around $55 a barrel, well below their level in the late 1970s and 1980s when they had reached a peak of $150 a barrel.[22]

However, there is one part of the argument that the war was not really about WMD which feels unimpeachable. At some point between September 2001 and March 2003, perhaps in the immediate aftermath of the Crawford meeting in April 2002, Blair seems to have decided that he would not allow Britain to adopt a different position to America's. Looking back, Blair himself confirms he knew 'in the final analysis I would be with the US'.[23] Shortly before the invasion began, when it looked possible the government might lose the forthcoming vote in the House of Commons, President Bush gave Blair the option of not committing British troops to the invasion force but, instead, entering Iraq as part of the clear-up operations. Blair was not interested. It was unambiguously in Britain's national interest to remain in lockstep with America and, in doing so, to show it was prepared to back its words with deeds and 'boots on the ground'. 'I was sure that our alliance depended on us doing this together.'[24] Britain had to be seen to be a big-enough world power to put troops on the ground in order to demonstrate that it was a dependable junior partner.

Blair also believed that he, personally, was in a uniquely strong position to be a bridge between Europe and America. He thought he could persuade the German Chancellor Gerhard Schröder and French President Jacques Chirac to tone down their anti-American rhetoric and eventually, if only grudgingly, back the Americans at the UN. He believed he could temper America's go-it-alone zeal and persuade President Bush to work with other countries when it came to Iraq, and to resume and prioritize Palestinian peace talks – these being, in Blair's view, the essential prerequisite to a lasting peace in the Middle East. Blair knew enough to know that Britain was no longer a major military power. But he thought Britain could play a valuable role in helping make Europe and America, as he saw it, better versions of themselves.

There was one more combustible element to Blair's reasoning. By the early 2000s he had come to the view that, in an increasingly globalized and interdependent world, the old idea that state sovereignty was sacrosanct was outdated, immoral and counterproductive. In a speech in Chicago in April 1999, delivered during the Kosovan War, Blair argued that democracies should not turn a blind eye to atrocities being committed elsewhere. The West, he argued, had been wrong to stand and watch from the sidelines during the Rwandan genocide in 1994 and the Srebrenica massacre in 1995. Increasingly, democracies would find that the best way of protecting their own citizens would be to protect those in other countries.

> We live in a world where isolationism has ceased to have a reason to exist. By necessity we have to cooperate with each other across nations. Many of our domestic problems are caused on the other side of the world ... we cannot turn our backs on conflicts and the violation of human rights within other countries if we want to still be secure.[25]

At the time, this looked like very new and radical stuff: a new theory of international relations for a new, globalized age. But, just as keeping close to America was a longstanding principle of British foreign policy, Blair's 'liberal interventionism' had a long, and not always very glorious, history going back to William Gladstone's campaign to persuade the British public of the case for intervening to protect Bulgaria's Christians in the 1870s.[26] Blair was, in this respect, a very modern kind of back-to-the-future British leader.

'THAT'S ALL HISTORY, MIKE'

There were no WMD in Iraq. As the report on the Chilcot Inquiry into the Iraq War later observed, the intelligence community simply failed to consider the possibility Iraq had no WMD.[27] A lot of the apparent evidence pointing to an ongoing WMD programme was not only wrong but fabricated. Claims that Saddam was trying to purchase uranium from Africa were based on a forgery.[28] A source who convinced British Intelligence that Iraq was continuing to mass-produce anthrax took his inspiration from the 1996 Sean Connery film The Rock.[29] The Americans, for their part, had fallen hook, line and sinker for an Iraqi defector codenamed 'Curveball', who the German intelligence services had already decided was completely unreliable. Large parts of the 2003 British 'dodgy' dossier on Iraq: Its Infrastructure of Concealment, Deception and Intimidation, a report name-checked by US Secretary of State Colin Powell, in his presentation to the UN in February 2003, were plagiarized from a PhD thesis (p. 112).

Blair had asked people to trust him when he said Iraq had WMD. He authorized the release of some very general intelligence information but implied that, behind this, there was sensitive but compelling information he could not reveal. In fact, and as the Butler Review into WMD intelligence chaired by the former Cabinet secretary Robin Butler concluded, the available intelligence information was 'sporadic and patchy', whilst the version of it being presented to the public went to the 'outer limits' of what was reasonable.[30] Blair, it appeared, had already decided Iraq had WMD and so seemed to ignore all the caveats in the intelligence he was given, and failed to ask any difficult questions about what it all amounted to. As a result, and, in the reported words of the director general of MI6, Richard Dearlove, to his American counterparts during the run up to the invasion, 'the facts were being fixed around the policy'.[31] Blair was not lying about WMD. He thought Iraq had them and was continuing to develop them. But that was because he and his key allies allowed worst-case intelligence assumptions to become just assumptions.

Blair was also wrong about the difficulties of occupying and simultaneously trying to rebuild an already broken country. He was warned about the likelihood of internal conflict in Iraq and the possibility of civil war. He was warned about the likely difficulties of sustaining a military occupation. He was warned about the potential for Iranian interference. He was warned about the absence of any detailed US planning for post-invasion Iraq.[32] These warnings were, however, ignored. Blair was always eager to be briefed on the latest military intelligence on WMD but was largely uninterested in the details of post-war planning.[33] When a Foreign Office expert, Michael Williams, briefed him on the history of ethnic and religious schisms in Iraq he replied: 'That's all history, Mike. This is about the future.'[34]

Finally, Blair wildly overestimated his influence on America. As Colin Powell's deputy at the State Department, Richard Armitage, observed, the problem with Blair's strategy of always remaining supportive of the US in public was that it was too easy to hear the 'yes but forget the but'.[35] Blair had his moments. He was someone who was listened to in Washington in a way that was not true of other European leaders. He played a key role in persuading George Bush to back the idea of trying to rebuild Afghanistan. He persuaded the president to press for renewed Palestinian peace talks and to take his case for the invasion to the UN.

These were runs on the board for British diplomacy. They did not, in the end, amount to that much though. When it came to Afghanistan, America basically said that, if other countries wanted to do nation-building, it would not stand in their way. When it came to the Middle East, Bush sometimes endorsed Blair's view that new peace talks were needed. But he never really made them a priority. Going to the UN was, as far as Bush was concerned, a 'favour' he was happy to offer Blair.[36] It was not a costly thing to do. The Americans never said they would be bound by any decision the UN made. The failure to secure a second resolution was a major diplomatic setback for Britain. For the Americans it was largely neither here nor there.

THE GHOST OF FUTURE IRAQ

The question we are left with is, how did Blair get it so wrong and come to believe so many things which now seem so unbelievable? Blair was a political optimist, who believed events would work out as he wanted them to if he tried hard enough. He believed he could persuade the French to go along with the Americans; the Americans to push the Israelis to agree a new peace settlement with Yasser Arafat, the president of the Palestinian National Authority; the Labour Party to accept the moral–humanitarian case for going to war; and the Afghan and Iraqi people that Britain was coming armed with good intentions and that an invasion was not really an occupation. On his better days he may even have thought he could persuade Gordon Brown to wear a 'I love Tony' badge. Given what then happened, this now looks not just arrogant but stupid. It does however need to be remembered that Blair was, at this point, on a roll. He had rebuilt the Labour Party and made it electable. He had, against the odds, brokered a relatively stable peace in Northern Ireland. He had faced down criticism about civilian casualties and the lack of a clear UN mandate and had seen through and made a reasonable success of military intervention in Serbia and Kosovo. To cap it all, he had then shown that the Taliban could be removed from power and a new and more democratic government put in their place. Blair may, all things considered, have often been a consistently risk-averse politician (pp. 23–5). But foreign policy in the period between the 2001 General Election and the unravelling of the Iraq occupation from around April 2003 onwards were notable exceptions to this general rule.

Blair and his key advisors had also fallen into the habit of thinking that anyone who criticized them was out to get them. This is, up to a point, how politics operates, and it is certainly how New Labour operated. Blair knew a lot of the Labour Party thought he was too right-wing and could not wait for him to fail. This applied to Robin Cook, who had never been viewed as a true New Labour believer. It also applied to Clare Short, the international development secretary, who had described Blair's approach to Iraq as 'reckless' in a radio interview on 9 March 2002 and resigned a few months later.[37] What feels notable here, however, is that Blair created an atmosphere in which even his closest supporters felt they would be best advised to say very little. By 2002 Peter Mandelson, Blair's one-time political soulmate and advisor, references to whom are dotted throughout this book, was out of office but still in regular contact with Blair and angling for a return to the Cabinet. He broached some concerns about Iraq, but Blair dismissed them and Mandelson was left feeling that 'those who had reservations of the sort I had raised were lumped together in his mind with anyone who he felt wasn't 100 per cent on board'.[38]

Finally, Blair's overconfidence and reluctance to listen to criticism car-crashed into a hyper-centralized, winner-takes-all political system. It is true that Iraq was discussed at a significant number of Cabinet meetings between February 2002 and March 2003.[39] It is also true that Blair kept Parliament updated on developments, published the attorney general's legal advice and repeatedly made himself available to hostile questioning from the media. Yet, looked at more closely, critical debate about Iraq had been hollowed out. Blair for the most part avoided discussing his strategy in the Cabinet Committee on Overseas Policy and Defence because he found it 'too formal' and 'insufficiently focused'.[40] Instead, he made sofa-based decisions via a series of bilateral and often unrecorded meetings with politicians and key officials (p. 41).[41] The Cabinet talked about Iraq but it was never offered the opportunity for a no-holds-barred discussion on whether invading the country made sense and what other options might be available. Blair tended simply to update Cabinet on what was happening before moving on.[42] As for the attorney general's advice, Blair told Cabinet there was no time to discuss the short written document they had been given, and ministers were not told Lord Goldsmith had previously written a private thirteen-page memorandum to Blair in which he had said a 'reasonable case' could be made that an invasion would be legal but that there were also risks of a successful legal challenge.[43] Blair's defence secretary, Geoff Hoon, has claimed he was told to burn his copy of that initial advice.[44]

In the end, and as the Chilcot Report concluded, Britain went to war at a point when diplomatic options had not been exhausted.[45] The country went to war because Tony Blair decided going to war was the right thing to do and because Britain's centralized partyocracy gave him the opportunity to do what he wanted. If Tony Blair had gone to sleep on 17 March 2003, the night before the parliamentary vote on war, and had been visited by the ghost of the future of Iraq and told there were no WMD and that the occupation would go disastrously wrong, and had decided, on this basis, to reverse his position, he would, no doubt, have faced some awkward questions from his Cabinet, the intelligence services and his advisors about what had happened. The Conservatives would have accused him of lacking backbone and of jeopardizing Britain's national interest. The Americans would have been disappointed. The chiefs of the Armed Forces would have been dismayed. It is, however, hard to imagine a situation in which Parliament would have decided to press ahead regardless.

13
Iraq and Afghanistan: Downhill all the Way

A DAY IN THE SUN

Iraq had a huge army with plenty of experience of war. Its soldiers were fighting in defence of their own territory. Plenty of people expected a long and bloody war culminating in street fighting in Iraq's major cities. It did not happen. On 3 April 2003, less than two weeks after the invasion had begun, troops from the US Army's 3rd Infantry Division captured Baghdad airport. The next day, American troops drove through central Baghdad. On the afternoon of 9 April, a group of Iraqi civilians attacked and, with assistance from American troops, eventually toppled the 40-foot-high statue of Saddam Hussein in Firdos Square. On 1 May President Bush landed on the aircraft carrier USS *Abraham Lincoln*, moored 30 miles off the coast of San Diego, California, and gave a short speech whilst standing in front of a banner declaring, triumphantly, 'MISSION ACCOMPLISHED'.[1]

On Thursday 29 May Tony Blair became the first Western leader to visit Iraq. He landed at Basra, the largest city in the south of Iraq and one which British troops now occupied. He was met by Paul Bremer, who had been appointed by George Bush to lead the Office for Reconstruction and Humanitarian Assistance. After talks with Bremer and local leaders, Blair visited Khadija al-Kubra primary school where he was presented with flowers by a group of children. He was then taken to Basra Palace, one of Saddam's former homes, which was being used as a makeshift headquarters by the British 7th Armoured Division. Blair, wearing a dazzlingly white and crisp shirt, addressed a group of soldiers. He promised that British troops would stay to help rebuild Iraq and that he would continue to work for a broader Middle East peace process.[2] Having stayed for an hour to talk to the soldiers, Blair was then flown to meet the crew of a minesweeper, HMS *Ramsey*, moored at Umm Qasr, 25 miles to the south.

Blair was riding high. The Chilcot Report was later to conclude that Britain's military contribution to the invasion had been 'largely discretionary'.[3] That was not how it was spun at the time. British troops had fought hard and played a vital role. Television reports had shown crowds of Iraqis celebrating Saddam's downfall. Robin Cook's resignation as foreign secretary had been largely forgotten. Opinion polls now showed that nearly 60 per cent of British people thought that it had been right to take military action.[4] There had been no humanitarian disaster and during his flying visit Blair had expressed absolute confidence that evidence of Iraq's WMD programme would soon be uncovered.[5] Basra was at the very southern tip of Iraq. Nevertheless, after Blair had left it was downhill all the way.

SEXING IT UP

On the very day Tony Blair was in Basra, Andrew Gilligan, the BBC's defence and diplomatic correspondent, appeared on the Radio 4 *Today* programme. Within government circles, Gilligan was already viewed unsympathetically, to put it mildly, thanks to some of his earlier stories about faulty and inadequate equipment being provided to British troops. That was just a warm-up to the main act. In September 2002 the government had published a dossier on Iraq's WMD based, it was said, on the work of the intelligence services. The dossier, and Blair's foreword to it, played heavily upon a claim that Iraq's 'military planning allows for some of the WMD to be ready within 45 minutes of an order to use them'.[6] Gilligan said he had been told 'by a British official who was involved in the preparation of the dossier' that the dossier was:

> transformed in the week before it was published to make it sexier. The classic example was the claim that weapons of mass destruction were ready for use within 45 minutes. That information was not in the original draft. It was included in the dossier against our wishes, because it wasn't reliable. Most of the things in the dossier were double-sourced, but that was single sourced, and we believe that the source was wrong.[7]

In a piece for the *Mail on Sunday*, a few days later, Gilligan went further. When he had asked one source how the 45-minute claim had come about, 'the answer was a single word: Campbell.'[8] At this point, the Campbell in question, Alastair, Blair's director of communications, exploded and demanded the BBC apologized for this attack upon his integrity.

The idea that the government had tried to sex-up its various dossiers promoting the war did not seem entirely far-fetched. What's more, Gilligan's timing was spot-on. Blair's promise, whilst in Basra, that WMD would soon be found had been prompted by a report, a few days before, that Donald Rumsfeld, the American defence secretary, had said that they might have been destroyed before the war had begun.[9] On the other hand, it was, as Campbell observed, far from ideal that Gilligan's story appeared to be based on a single source too, and that Gilligan himself had wavered between saying the government knew the 45-minute claim to be false in his unscripted *Today* report and saying, in later interviews, that it was 'questionable'.

In Iraq, the immediate and increasingly pressing challenge was to find any evidence of any WMD. In London, the key question was about the identity of Gilligan's source – and whether or not they had been in a position to know if the dossier had been 'sexed-up'. On 30 June, Dr David Kelly, a Ministry of Defence employee, a government advisor on biological warfare and a former weapons inspector in Iraq, wrote to his line manager to say he had held an unauthorized meeting with Gilligan in which he had discussed Iraq's weapons programme in broad terms.[10] Kelly could have been Gilligan's source. He was not only exceptionally well informed about WMD but had commented upon early drafts of the 2002 dossier. That said, it did not seem likely Kelly could have known whether Alastair Campbell had directly intervened to correct the 45-minute claim. That would have happened during the final stages of the dossier's preparation. Kelly, for his part, directly denied making any allegations about the circumstances in which the dossier had been prepared, and said he was certain he could not have been Gilligan's source.

Kelly was repeatedly interviewed by Ministry of Defence officials who, in the end, accepted his version of events. On 4 July he was told that disciplinary action would not be taken against him, but that this decision might be reviewed if new facts came to light casting doubt on his account.[11] Events then spiralled. Downing Street welcomed the news that Kelly had admitted talking to Gilligan because they thought it showed Gilligan had over-egged his story. Fatally, a decision was then taken during a series of largely un-minuted meetings, some of which Blair attended, that, if a journalist asked directly whether Kelly had been Gilligan's source, it would be confirmed he was.[12] By an amazing coincidence, a journalist asked, shortly after, whether Kelly was the source and was told yes.[13] As a result, Dr Kelly suddenly found himself at the centre of an intense media storm and was summoned to appear before the Foreign Affairs Select Committee where he was asked some leading and difficult questions, including several about whether he had spoken to other journalists. Kelly said he had not. This was not true. He had in fact also spoken to two other BBC reporters.[14]

On the afternoon of 17 July Kelly went for a walk. When he did not return home, his family called the police. The next morning his body was found in the nearby countryside. Kelly had cut his left wrist and hastened his death by taking co-proxamol tablets. He had not left a suicide note. Many people, including the Liberal Democrat MP Norman Baker, seizing upon a comment Kelly had made to a friend that he would 'probably be found dead in the woods' if Iraq was invaded, maintained he might well have been murdered.[15] Kelly was, however, also under intense pressure. In particular, he had reason to fear that disciplinary action would be taken against him once it became apparent that he had spoken to other journalists. Robert Lewis, a novelist who wrote a biography of Dr Kelly, suggests Kelly may have briefed Gilligan and other journalists to ensure it was the government and not the intelligence services who were blamed when no WMD were found in Iraq, but then despaired when he received little support in return.[16]

Blair was flying to Japan from the United States for a trade mission when he was told about Dr Kelly's death. At a press conference in Tokyo, he was asked by a *Mail on Sunday* journalist, Jonathan Oliver, whether he had 'blood on his hands' and whether he was going to resign.[17] It did not seem an unreasonable question to ask given the reports which were already circulating about Blair's own involvement in the leaking of Dr Kelly's name. Blair looked – and almost certainly was – distraught. But he did have an immediate way out, which was to announce that a public inquiry into Kelly's death would be chaired by the former lord chief justice of Northern Ireland, Brian Hutton. Blair gave evidence to that inquiry in August 2003 and accepted 'overall responsibility' for the leaking of Kelly's name. He also said that, after an initial round of meetings, he had handed the matter over to the Ministry of Defence and played no further part.[18] None of this looked great. By October only 6 per cent of voters said they trusted the government more than the BBC to be telling the truth.[19] Yet when Lord Hutton's report was eventually published, on 28 January 2004, the government and prime minister were exonerated. Hutton concluded Kelly had not told Gilligan the 45-minute claim was false; that there was no underhand or reprehensible government conspiracy to name Kelly as Gilligan's source; that the dossier containing the 45-minute claim had been published in good faith and with the approval of the intelligence services; that it had been appropriate for Campbell and others to make suggestions about the wording of the dossier; and that the BBC was at fault for allowing Gilligan to broadcast his claims without first checking what he was going to say.

Blair survived. Campbell, who had left his government role in August 2003, was absolved. Gilligan resigned and the BBC's chairman, Gavyn Davies, and director general, Greg Dyke, followed him out of the door. If the government won the battle on this issue, it nevertheless lost the war. Long before Hutton published his report it had become clear that the pre-war claims about WMD had been entirely erroneous. Hutton's report, which, at its most critical, spoke of how 'the desire of the Prime Minister to have a dossier which, whilst consistent with the available evidence, was as strong as possible' may have 'subconsciously influenced' senior intelligence officials to 'make the wording of the dossier somewhat stronger than it might otherwise have been', was widely derided and largely dismissed.[20] Blair had invited people to trust him when it came to WMD. He had argued the intelligence material he had access to was unambiguous. But, in fact, it was wrinkled with doubts and caveats that had been airbrushed out to make the case for war stronger than it would otherwise have been. A centralized and conviction-driven decision to go to war had, entirely unsurprisingly, been supported by a Downing Street operation to present that decision in the best possible light.[21]

THE ROAD TO A NEW ACCOMMODATION

Within a few weeks of the formal end of the Iraq War, the American occupation was already failing. In April and May there was looting and a wave of sectarian murders in Baghdad. On 19 August a suicide truck-bomb attack on the UN headquarters in the city killed twenty people, including the UN's special representative in Iraq, Sérgio Vieira de Mello. Shortly afterwards, the UN pulled all its personnel out of Iraq. On 29 August an attack on the Shia Imam Ali Mosque marked the start of something approaching a civil war within Baghdad and some of Iraq's other ethnically or religiously mixed cities. Within a few months, insurgent attacks on American military convoys in the so-called 'Sunni triangle' to the north and west of Baghdad accelerated. In April 2004 American troops fought a pitched battle in the city of Fallujah in which they deployed white phosphorus, a chemical weapon.[22] In that same month, evidence of the systemic abuse of Iraqi prisoners by US troops in Abu Ghraib prison emerged. In August, the Americans were drawn into another major urban battle in Najaf.

The view in Downing Street and in the British base at Basra was that things were going wrong in Iraq because the Americans were making some horrible mistakes. American troops had stood by to let looting happen in Baghdad at the end of the fighting. Paul Bremer had dissolved the Iraqi Army and disbanded the governing Ba'ath Party and barred any of its members from roles in the new government. American administrators, trapped within the relatively safe 'Green Zone' in Baghdad, had no idea what was happening in the country they were meant to be governing.[23] And the American military had failed to consider how its aggressive tactics might alienate Iraqi civilians.

There was a lot of truth in all this. However, Britain was in no position to point the finger. It made plenty of its own mistakes and had made them right from the start. British troops had not had to fight their way into Basra. They had been welcomed. Yet in the days after their arrival there had been extensive looting and British troops had lost a lot of goodwill when the commander of the 7th Armoured Division, Brigadier Graham Binns, lacking clear orders, decided not to intervene.[24] Too many troops were then withdrawn too quickly from Basra City and the surrounding areas. Many of those who remained were suffering from severe diarrhoea and vomiting. A lot of the British equipment did not work. Problems mounted when, in May 2003, shortly before Blair's visit, British troops had abused and beaten locals who had been caught trying to steal food.[25] It was around this time that regular attacks on British troops began. The Shia population in and around Basra thought of themselves as having done as much as they could to resist Saddam's rule and resented – profoundly – being marginalized and treated as potentially hostile by a British occupying force. A former soldier offers this account of his time in Basra:

> The highest temperature I remember was 56 Celsius, but mainly it was in the high 40s. It took a long time to get used to it, and we all spent a lot of time drinking water – and then peeing it out. I used to dream of finding a cold bottle of water on the wagon but because of the heat and the engines they were always warm . . . [W]hen we first went there, it felt like we were doing something worthwhile – the people would run up to us and cheer – but after a couple of weeks that changed. We had stuff thrown at us by Iraqis in the street.[26]

Blair knew this. Indeed, on his return from Iraq, he had told ministers there were problems in Basra and that Britain needed to return to a 'war footing' to 'avoid losing the peace'.[27] Amazingly, nothing then happened, and the planned withdrawal of troops continued. Blair did not follow-up his instructions. The situation then deteriorated. In June 2003 six military police were killed in the small town of Majar al-Kabir about 60 miles to the north of Basra. In April 2004, Jaysh al-Madhi – the Mahdi Army – led by the thirty-year-old Muqtada al-Sadr and backed, it was thought, by Iran, launched a popular uprising in and around Basra against the British and the local government co-operating with them. British troops came under regular attack whenever they left their base. Any hopes of undertaking development work or holding confidence-building meetings with residents were shelved. By August 2003 there was, at most, about ten hours of electricity a day in Basra.[28] Eventually, the Mahdi uprising was just about contained but the British position never really recovered. Local military commanders came to the view that venturing out of their bases to patrol the streets simply provoked more attacks, resulting in more casualties, and so opted to remain locked-down until they could leave.

In September 2005 Iraqi police arrested two British special forces soldiers dressed in civilian clothes who had been carrying out surveillance. British soldiers then attacked the police station where they had been detained. The two soldiers, it transpired, had been handed over to local militants. More fighting followed during which several civilians were killed. The two British soldiers were eventually rescued but Basra's provincial government suspended all co-operation with British forces. In May 2006 Blair was told about 'rumblings from within the US system about the UK's failure to grip the security situation' and its apparent determination to exit as soon as practicable.[29] There was some truth to this. The number of British troops deployed in southern Iraq had fallen from 46,000 during the initial invasion to just 8,000 by early 2006. Meanwhile, the Mahdi Army was back with a vengeance and in day-to-day control of Basra. By October that year, Graham Binns, the new overall British commander of the forces in Iraq, had concluded that 'time for the UK was running out'.[30]

The end came not with a bang but a whimper. British commanders on the ground, whose headquarters in Basra Palace were now being attacked almost every day, negotiated a deal with the Mahdi Army. In return for the release of detainees, British troops would be allowed to leave their base and withdraw to the airport outside the city. One problem with the terms of this deal was that as soon as the last detainee had been released the attacks on British forces resumed, albeit on their airport base which was much easier to defend. The more serious problem was that the existence of this deal, the 'accommodation' as it became known, had not been revealed to either the American or Iraqi governments, who, when they found out what had happened, were apoplectic. Britain did not formally hand over military control to the Americans until April 2009, but it had left the stage long before then. In March 2008, when the Iraqi prime minister, Nouri al-Maliki, launched the 'Charge of the Knights' Operation to regain control of Basra and tackle the militia groups, American troops provided the firepower. British troops were effectively left as spectators.[31]

HELMAND PROVINCE: PLAN B

For a while, when Britain was fighting but losing the occupation in Iraq, Afghanistan was regarded as being militarily winnable and politically palatable. Al-Qaeda had been defeated and the Taliban vanquished.

America had committed itself to a new 'Marshall Plan' for Afghanistan to rebuild the country, and women's rights were being promoted and local democracy supported. The streets of Kabul were relatively tranquil. There were still reasons to be wary, however. The American and British view was that anyone who was not their enemy, the Taliban, was their friend and deserved support. But the Afghan government they were supporting, led by Hamid Karzai, was staggeringly corrupt and almost entirely dependent, outside Kabul, on the support of exceptionally violent warlords, who were terrorizing their local populations. Nevertheless, in the mid-2000s Afghanistan did not look like the kind of lost cause Iraq already appeared to have become. Which was the cue for a moment of hubris.

In 2005 plans emerged for a new NATO-led international security force to deploy across Afghanistan to rebuild the country and repel the Taliban forces who were starting to infiltrate back into the country from Pakistan. In January 2006, at around the time the Americans were starting to complain about British disengagement in Iraq, the Cabinet agreed to deploy more than three thousand troops to Helmand Province in the south of Afghanistan. The idea was that the soldiers would expel the Taliban, support local government and promote development. The British envoy to Kabul, Sir Sherard Cowper-Coles, later told MPs he had been told by the head of the Army, General Sir Richard Dannatt, that the Army was also keen to redeploy in order to avoid further cuts to its numbers.[32]

The result was another military and political failure. British troops were initially deployed in a series of small towns and villages along the banks of the Helmand river. The idea was to secure these areas and then spread outwards.[33] Instead, the troops, once deployed, were left isolated, attacked and frequently outgunned by Taliban forces. In order simply to survive they had to summon air strikes, which resulted in large numbers of civilian casualties. To the local inhabitants they were meant to be protecting, the troops were unequivocally seen as an uninvited occupying force. Mike Martin, a former officer deployed to Helmand, describes the British approach as 'so far removed from the Helmendi understanding that [they] considered them to be trying to destroy the province through an alliance with the Taliban'.[34] British troops were woefully underequipped. There were not enough helicopters to move troops around Helmand. Troop carriers, lacking sufficient armour, were highly vulnerable to improvised explosive devices (IED). One by one, British troops were forced to withdraw from the towns and villages they had been deployed to. What followed was a kind of stalemate.[35] British troops could defeat the Taliban in an open firefight, but could not prevent them from intruding into towns and villages and could not provide the security which would have sustained meaningful local economic development work.

In February 2009 President Obama reluctantly authorized a temporary troop surge in Afghanistan to regain control.[36] The US Marine Corps were deployed to Helmand and led a series of military engagements to push the Taliban out of their strongholds. 'They [the British] were here for four years. What did they do?' asked one marine.[37] A BBC *Panorama* programme broadcast in 2022 reported that it was during this period that British special forces teams routinely murdered Afghan prisoners and civilians.[38] If, as a result of the American 'surge' the military position in Helmand was improving, the overall strategic position nevertheless remained largely hopeless. The Afghan central government and Helmand's provincial government were feared and despised by most of the local population.[39] The Taliban had been pushed out of the largest towns in Helmand but still held the countryside, and could count on the support, tacit or otherwise, of the government in Pakistan. At the start of the 'surge', Obama had said that troop levels would increase but that this would be a temporary arrangement and that the longer-term goal was to pull all American troops out of the country. The Taliban knew they could wait things out. 'You have the watches, we have the time,' as one Taliban commander had said years previously.[40] Above all, there was no serious political strategy, no attempt to see if a deal could be struck with parts of the Taliban to share power. At various points, American military commanders acknowledged the need to hold talks but any serious efforts to start negotiations were immediately vetoed by President Karzai.[41] As a result, once he became prime minister David Cameron came quite quickly to the conclusion that the war in Afghanistan was unwinnable. Claiming that the recruitment and training of Afghan army and police forces was running ahead of schedule, Cameron announced the start of a withdrawal in July 2011. The last British combat troops pulled out of Helmand in October 2014.

After a chaotic and visibly corrupt election, Ashraf Ghani replaced

Karzai as Afghan president in September 2014. In 2018, following an upsurge in violence, he finally proposed unconditional peace talks with the Taliban. A ceasefire was agreed, but the Taliban refused to negotiate directly with the Afghan government. Instead, direct talks in Qatar between the Americans and the Taliban began in October. Eventually, in February 2020, the Americans and the Taliban signed a peace agreement. The Taliban pledged to prevent al-Qaeda from operating in areas under its control and to open talks with the Afghan government. The Americans, in return, agreed to continue reducing their number of soldiers and to withdraw entirely by September 2021 if the Taliban kept to its side of the bargain.

In April 2021, and without any prior consultation with the British, the new US president, Joe Biden, who had opposed Obama's troop surge when it had first been proposed, confirmed that all American troops would indeed be withdrawn, according to the agreed schedule. The Americans assumed that the Afghan Army would be more than capable of repelling the Taliban once they had departed. In fact, more than two-thirds of the troops in that purportedly 300,000-strong Army did not actually exist. They had been invented so local commanders could claim their wages. When the Taliban attacked in July 2021, when American troops had started to evacuate, there was a rout. Lashkar Gah, the capital of Helmand Province, was captured by the Taliban on 13 August. Kabul fell a few days later. Over the next week, over 100,000 people were evacuated from Kabul airport, the last part of Afghanistan to remain under American military control. Major General Chris Donahue, commander of the 82nd Airborne Division, was the last American soldier to leave, boarding a C-17 transport plane under cover of darkness on Monday 30 August.[42] Prime Minister Boris Johnson praised British military efforts to evacuate staff and vulnerable Afghan nationals who had worked for the British. This air of triumph was tempered by reports that the foreign secretary, Dominic Raab, had delayed returning from a beach holiday in Greece to oversee the evacuation effort; that the prime minister had intervened to help a charity evacuate stray cats and dogs; and that large numbers of Afghanis who had worked with the British had been left behind.[43]

THE COST OF WAR

A total of 457 British military personnel died in Afghanistan and another 179 in Iraq. As early as 2006 an article in *The Lancet* estimated that 654,000 Iraqis had died during and in the years immediately following that country's invasion.[44] In Afghanistan, it was estimated 66,000 Afghan soldiers and police, 47,000 Afghan civilians and 50,000 Taliban fighters had died, alongside 444 aid workers, 72 journalists, 2,448 American servicemen, 3,846 American contractors and 1,144 other NATO troops.[45] In addition, by 2019 more than 45,000 American soldiers who had served in Iraq had committed suicide.[46]

By just about any measure, Britain's military engagements in Iraq and Afghanistan were disastrous.* Yet Iraq and Afghanistan were relatively peripheral issues in terms of day-to-day politics from 2004 onwards. The Conservatives condemned the government's failure to equip troops properly but did not demand an earlier and faster withdrawal. There were relatively few debates in Parliament about what was happening in either Iraq or Afghanistan. In the 2005 General Election, Reg Keys, a founder member of the campaign group Military Families against the War whose son, Tom, was one of the military policemen killed in Majar al-Kabir, stood against Tony Blair in his Sedgefield constituency and won over 4,000 votes. From around 2007 onwards, large numbers of mourners gathered in and around the town of Wootton Bassett to mark the repatriation of the bodies of soldiers being taken from RAF Lyneham to the John Radcliffe Hospital in Oxford. The tone at these gatherings was however one of respect and sadness, rather than of anger. There were very few anti-war, bring-back-the-troops marches. In the late 2000s internecine 'poppy wars' erupted over the failure of some footballers, minor celebrities, or occasional politicians to wear a Remembrance Day poppy deemed to be of an acceptable size at an early enough moment.[47] For the most part, the fighting in Iraq and Afghanistan remained, for most people, very distant.

It is nevertheless clear that Iraq and Afghanistan deeply wounded

---

* The chief of the defence staff between 2010 and 2013, Sir David Richards, says in his memoirs that 'with the benefit of hindsight, I now side with those who view [Iraq] as a grand strategic error'. David Richards, *Taking Command* (London, 2014), p. 171.

Blair and New Labour. Blair's personal reputation for honesty, which had already taken a battering by 2003, never recovered after Iraq. Between 2004 and 2006 the numbers of people who said they considered him to be more honest than most politicians struggled to make it to double figures.[48] It is quite possible that a poll of Blair's colleagues in the Parliamentary Labour Party, taken any time after June 2003, would have yielded similar results. The idea that New Labour was a politically progressive party became increasingly hard to sustain. The idea that New Labour was capable and competent and was good in a crisis was fatally compromised. Newspapers that felt they had been manipulated over WMD became more hostile. Labour MPs who had voted against the war felt vindicated and became more trenchant in their criticisms. Blair's refusal to apologize for anything he had said or done when it came to Iraq became a story in its own right.[49] Any political credit Blair thought he might have gained in Washington from supporting the invasion was lost when Britain failed to hold either Basra or Helmand and then pushed for an early exit. The Iraq War did not reduce the global threat from WMD. Iraq did not have any. Iran and North Korea, however, were given good reason to get them whilst they could in order to deter an invasion. The occupation of Iraq and Afghanistan made terrorist attacks on Britain more, rather than less, likely (p. 176). Moreover, the botched US withdrawal from Afghanistan in 2021 probably helped persuade President Putin that the West was weak and would do very little to oppose a Russian invasion of Ukraine.

In an article published in the *New Statesman* in March 2023, Peter Ricketts, who served as chair of the Joint Intelligence Committee in 2000/1 before later becoming Britain's first national security advisor in 2010, concluded that the unravelling of the international order, engineered by Vladimir Putin since 2008 (pp. 137–8), had begun with Iraq. 'By disregarding the principles of the UN Charter in 2003, the US and the UK ceded their moral authority to promote the rule of law, and emboldened authoritarians to act illegally when it suited them.'[50] In almost every imaginable respect, Iraq and Afghanistan were political, diplomatic and military failures of the highest order.

14
The Home Front

7 JULY 2005

On Saturday, 2 July 2005, London's Hyde Park hosted, in bright sunshine, the Live 8 Concert to press for more action on debt relief and climate change at the forthcoming G8 summit at the Gleneagles Hotel in Auchterarder, Scotland. Four days later, the International Olympic Committee, meeting in Singapore, announced that London had beaten Paris, Madrid, New York and Moscow in the race to host the 2012 Summer Olympics.

At 4 a.m. on Thursday 7 July, Mohammad Sidique Khan, Shehzad Tanweer and Hasib Hussain left Leeds in a rented blue Nissan Micra to drive to London. They stopped at the Woodall Services on the M1, a few miles after Sheffield, to buy petrol and snacks. They then drove to Luton Station where they met with a fourth man, Germaine Lindsay, who had been waiting for them. They put on rucksacks and boarded a train to King's Cross Station. When it arrived, they were seen hugging in the station concourse area. Three of the men went to the Tube. Khan boarded a westbound Circle Line train towards Paddington. Tanweer boarded an eastbound train and Lindsay a Piccadilly Line train. They detonated the bombs they were carrying in their rucksacks just before 8.50. The fourth man, Hussain, bought a battery from the WHSmith shop in King's Cross before walking onto Euston Road where he caught a number 30 bus and sat on the upper deck. Having possibly mistaken a passing traffic warden for a policeman, he detonated his bomb at 9.47 a.m. near Tavistock Square.[1] In total, fifty-six people, including the four terrorists, were killed.

The backgrounds of those who were killed were predictably varied. Carrie Taylor was twenty-four. She had graduated with a degree in drama and theatre from Royal Holloway. She had worked at the English National Opera, and on 4 July had been offered a permanent job at the Royal Society of Arts. She commuted with her mother:

> We travel together every day. I know it sounds silly, but we have a little farewell ritual. Carrie gives me a kiss goodbye before we go our separate ways. Then I watch her as she heads off for the Tube. Every few steps she turns and waves before she disappears into the crowd. I always watch until she's out of sight. It's a funny little mum's habit – but I'm so very glad that the last picture I have of her is smiling and waving at me.[2]

Atique Sharifi was a twenty-four-year-old refugee. He had fled the war in Afghanistan in which his parents had died. He settled in Hounslow in 2002, where he attended the West Thames College to learn English and worked in a takeaway pizza restaurant to support his sister, Farishta, who was still in Afghanistan.[3] Lee Harris and Samantha Badham lived in London where they worked as an architect and a web content designer, respectively. They had arranged to meet friends that morning in Soho. Medics found Samantha and Lee lying next to each other on the tracks. Lee was taken to the Royal Free Hospital where he was in a coma for eight days. Samantha's body was recovered from the wreckage a day later. They were buried together in Ledbury on the edge of the Malvern Hills.[4] Giles Hart was born in Sudan to English parents in 1949. His parents moved to London when he was five. He worked for the Civil Service and, later, British Telecom. He was secretary and chairman of the Polish Solidarity Campaign and later founded the Polish Refugee Rights Group, which helped support people who had fled martial law in Communist Poland to settle in Britain. His daughter, Marlya, remembered him as someone who hated 'fundamentalism and totalitarianism'. After his death he was awarded the Knight's Cross of the Order of Merit of the Republic of Poland for his services to democracy.[5]

UNORGANIZED TERROR

After the bombs had been detonated, London froze. Mobile phone networks were suspended, along with public transport.[6] Offices closed and workers walked home. There were numerous false reports of other attacks. Tony Blair joined the other G8 leaders to condemn the attacks before returning to the capital. A fortnight later, just as things had returned to normal for most people, there were failed suicide attacks on three other Tube stations. In the wake of those attacks the Metropolitan Police shot dead a young Brazilian man, Jean Charles de Menezes, who they believed, entirely mistakenly, to be a terrorist. In December 2008 a jury at the inquest into his death rejected Scotland Yard's claim that he had been lawfully killed as part of an anti-terrorism operation and, having been precluded by the coroner from ruling that the killing had been unlawful, recorded an open verdict.[7]

The investigation into who had committed the King's Cross bombings proceeded, by comparison, relatively smoothly. At 11.40 p.m. on 7 July, a police officer whose job it was to collate evidence from the scenes of the attacks called investigators to say cash and membership cards in the name of Sidique Khan and a Mr S Tanweer had been found at Aldgate.[8] A few minutes later, Khan was identified as the account holder for a credit card found at the site of the Edgware Road bombing. On 12 July police searched several premises in West Yorkshire, including the homes of Khan, Tanweer and Hussain. The same morning, investigators received a report that four people had been seen putting on rucksacks at Luton Station car park. The police had already started to work on an assumption that there must have been a link back to King's Cross, as the three trains on which the bombs had exploded had been equidistant from the station. Later that day, police identified a CCTV image of four men carrying rucksacks at King's Cross on the morning of the attack. Tanweer was identified using a record of his driving-licence photograph. Working backwards, the same four men were identified on CCTV recordings at Luton Station.

Over the following weeks, a great deal was learned about the backgrounds of the bombers. Mohammad Sidique Khan, thirty, was assumed to be the de facto leader of the group. He was married and had a daughter. He worked as a primary school teacher and youth worker and had been interviewed in the *Times Educational Supplement* in 2002 about his job.[9] As a young man Khan had seemed to have cast off parts of his Muslim background, calling himself Sid and wearing a leather jacket and cowboy boots after a visit to America. In 1999 he had encountered and been influenced by the radical cleric Abdullah el-Faisal, who was later convicted of soliciting murder and fomenting racial hatred. In 2001 Khan was one of forty people suspected of being connected to terrorist activity caught on CCTV during an outward-bound expedition to the Lake District.

Shehzad Tanweer, twenty-two, had been raised in a relatively affluent family in the suburb of Beeston, Leeds, where Khan had also grown up. He had been close to completing a degree in sports science but had dropped out in 2003 and had worked at his family's restaurant. He completed the Hajj to Mecca, and then had travelled with Khan to Pakistan in November 2004 to complete a course in Islamic studies at a madrasa in Muridke, near Lahore. The third bomber, Hasib Hussain, eighteen, had left school without any qualifications and had previously run into trouble having been caught using soft drugs. He lived in Holbeck, a couple of miles away from Beeston, and was a member of local football and cricket teams. Germaine Lindsay, nineteen, was the outsider to this group. He had been raised in Huddersfield by his mother, before she moved to America leaving Lindsay to fend for himself. Whilst still at school, Lindsay had been disciplined for handing out leaflets in support of al-Qaeda. Later, he, like Khan, had been influenced by Abdullah el-Faisal. Lindsay, who worked as a carpet fitter and earned extra money by selling mobile phone covers, married Samantha Lewthwaite, a native of County Down, Northern Ireland. They lived in Aylesbury, Buckinghamshire, with their daughter and were expecting a second child. In 2012 the Kenyan authorities issued an arrest warrant for Lewthwaite, who was accused of conspiring to cause explosions.

Once Khan, Tanweer, Hussain and Lindsay had been identified, the police and security services searched for evidence of a network of supporters, a link back to al-Qaeda and a mastermind behind the attacks. In the end, not much was uncovered. It was possible Khan and Tanweer had met with people connected to al-Qaeda during their visit to Pakistan, but no clear links were ever established. The four men seemed to be self-starters who had planned the attacks on a budget of less than £10,000 and had learned what they needed to know about bomb-making from the Internet.[10]

Ministers denied, and went on denying, that the attacks had anything to do with Afghanistan or Iraq. This never seemed plausible. On 1 September 2005 the television station Al Jazeera played a message recorded by Khan shortly before the 7 July attacks. 'Until we feel security, you will be our targets. And until you stop the bombing, gassing, imprisonment and torture of my people we will not stop this fight.'[11] On the first anniversary of the attack Al Jazeera played a second video statement, this one from Shehzad Tanweer. 'What you have witnessed now is only the beginning of a string of attacks that will continue and become stronger.' The attacks, he warned, will continue 'until you pull your forces out of Afghanistan and Iraq'.[12] In May 2006 the official report into the King's Cross bombings concluded that the four bombers had been motivated by a 'fierce antagonism to perceived injustices by the West against Muslims and a desire for martyrdom'.[13] In 2010, during the evidence she gave to the Chilcot Inquiry into the Iraq War, the former director general of MI5, Eliza Manningham-Buller, the embodiment of a Civil Service culture of speaking truth to power, argued that the Iraq invasion had radicalized 'people who saw [it] as an attack upon Islam'. The invasion, she suggested, had 'undoubtedly' increased the terrorist threat in Britain.[14] She also confirmed that the Joint Intelligence Committee had warned, in February 2003, that invading Iraq would increase the level of threat posed by al-Qaeda.[15]

A STRONG STATE GETTING STRONGER

In the immediate aftermath of the London bombings, Blair held a press conference in which he argued that the 'rules of the game' in relation to fighting terrorism needed to change.[16] In the future, he warned, extremist Muslim clerics would be deported without appeal and mosques closed if those in them preached hatred. The use of terrorist control orders would be extended to British nationals advocating terrorism. A new Terrorism Bill was drafted that would have allowed the police to detain people suspected of terrorism offences for up to ninety days without charge. That legislation was defeated in November 2005 when forty-nine Labour MPs voted against the government: Blair's first parliamentary defeat as prime minister. Parliament later agreed to extend the detention period to twenty-eight days.[17]

The logic justifying these new anti-terrorism measures, one which had obvious parallels to the arguments used to justify the invasion of Iraq, was that, in a new age of mass terrorism, the police had to prevent attacks before they happened. In a lecture he delivered in 2007, Peter Clarke, the head of the Metropolitan Police Counter Terrorism Command, argued that 'we can no longer wait until the terrorist is at or near the point of attack before intervening'. To do so, he argued, would put the public at too great a risk.[18] Clarke maintained that what was needed – and what the police got – were new powers to combat and prevent future terrorist attacks. New legislation broadened, dramatically, the definition of terrorism to include the provision of material support and the planning of terrorist activity regardless of what stage those preparations were at and whether a specific intent to commit a terrorist act could be proven. The 'encouragement' and 'glorification' of terrorist acts was criminalized, as was the distribution of any publication which could prove useful to a person in the commission or preparation of acts of terror.[19] New surveillance powers were authorized, along with measures relating to terrorist financing, the detention of foreign suspects, restrictions on overseas travel for those suspected of plotting terrorist offences, and new stop-and-search powers. The number of armed police patrolling the largest British cities was increased. Counter-terrorism work was increasingly centralized within the Metropolitan Police Anti-Terrorist Branch and MI5.

The government argued the measures it had taken to prevent terrorist attacks were both necessary and proportionate. This view was, for the most part, endorsed in annual reports by the government-appointed independent reviewer of terrorism legislation.[20] There were however dissenters. In 2008 the Conservative MP David Davis, the shadow home secretary, resigned over proposals to extend the detention period from twenty-eight days (the status quo that had been agreed upon in 2005) to forty-two days. Yet, for the most part, polls seemed to show that the measures being taken to curb terrorism were popular with voters. In this respect, it is perhaps telling that two of the more controversial applications of anti-terrorism legislation during this period related to actions taken against two non-Muslim men: Walter Wolfgang, who was ejected from the Labour Party conference in September 2005 after heckling the foreign secretary, Jack Straw; and Paul Chambers, who sent a satirical tweet threatening to blow up Robin Hood Airport in South Yorkshire if his holiday flight was delayed. Eventually, Chambers with the support of, amongst others, Stephen Fry, won a High Court challenge against his earlier conviction. Sitting in front of the nominatively determined lord chief justice Lord Judge, Chamber's barrister argued his tweet could not really, seriously, be considered to have been menacing or threatening and, if it really were, that John Betjeman's line about asking friendly bombs to fall on Slough and Shakespeare's invocation to kill all the lawyers would also need reviewing.

In some of the earlier chapters I have discussed the extent to which Tony Blair and New Labour can best be understood as Thatcherite retreads. At the time, my focus was almost exclusively on economics. Yet Thatcherism was a broader political project connected to the extension of Britain's global role and the strengthening (rather than rolling-back) of the state and this was a political trajectory Blair seemed consistently happy to embrace.[21] Blair first made his name as shadow home secretary in the early 1990s by promising to be 'tough on crime and tough on the causes of crime'.[22] As prime minister he passed wave after wave of new legislation relating to crime, targeting in particular anti-social behaviour. When it came to defence and foreign policy, Blair believed, as he had made clear in his 1999 Chicago speech on the 'Doctrine of the International Community' (pp. 153–4), that there were times when the frontiers of the British state should be rolled forward and rolled over other states. When it came to the threat of terrorism, Blair never suggested arguments about civil liberties should simply be dismissed out of hand. He did, however, share Peter Clarke's view that the threat posed by radical Islamic terrorists, willing to sacrifice their own lives in the pursuit of killing as many other people as they could, justified the acquisition and use of new state powers.[23]

THE 2001 RIOTS

The events of 11 September 2001 are a hugely important part of the background to the 7 July attacks in London. Yet there is an earlier and often forgotten part of this story. In the summer of 2001, a few months before the 11 September attacks, there were riots in several towns in northern England. The first to be affected was Oldham. On the evening of Saturday 26 May, an argument between a group of Asian and white boys began outside the Good Taste chip shop in Glodwick. A number of white adults arrived; the violence escalated and the homes of several Asian families living in the area were attacked. Later that evening, drinkers in, ironically enough, a pub called Live and Let Live were attacked by a group of Asian men. A stand-off with the police followed, during which petrol bombs were thrown.[24] On the Monday, the offices of the *Oldham Evening Chronicle* newspaper were attacked. Reports of threats and fights rumbled on for several days and, weeks later, someone threw a petrol bomb at the home of Oldham's deputy mayor, Riaz Ahmad, whilst he and his family were asleep inside.

On 5 and 6 June there were disturbances in Harehills, Leeds, after the arrest of a local Asian man. Then, a few weeks later in Burnley, on Saturday 23 June, there were reports of fights between white and Asian gangs that the police connected to disputes over drug dealing. Early the next morning, an Asian taxi driver was attacked with a hammer by a group of white men. That evening, the Duke of York pub in Colne Road was attacked by a group of Asian men who believed those drinking inside were planning to attack them. There was a fight, with both sides at one point attacking the police. Sporadic fighting continued over the following days. In total, around four hundred people were involved in the fighting and one hundred people injured.[25] Finally, on 8 and 9 July, riots involving upwards of a thousand people took place in Bradford, during which the Manningham Labour Club was firebombed whilst people were inside. Nearly two hundred people were charged with rioting and Mohammed Ilyas, a forty-eight-year-old local businessman, was jailed for twelve years for the firebomb attack.[26]

In the aftermath of the riots, the home secretary David Blunkett commissioned the former chief executive of Nottingham City Council, Ted Cantle, to write a report on the causes of the riots and the measures which needed to be taken to prevent them from recurring. The Cantle Report argued that the riots needed to be seen in the context of long-term economic decline. Oldham, Burnley and Bradford had all been hit by the closure of textile factories in the 1970s and had never fully recovered.[27] A lack of opportunities meant many young people left 'as soon as they could'. Those who remained, Cantle argued, in one of the earlier uses of the term in this context, were 'left behind' and often found themselves caught in a downward spiral of low income, debt and poor housing.[28]

As we have seen, average household income increased during the boom years of the 2000s (p. 81). Yet household income levels continued to show significant racial disparities. By 2008, of families headed by a person reporting their ethnic status as being Black, 31 per cent had incomes that placed them amongst the lowest 20 per cent of all households nationally. The equivalent figure for families with an Asian head of household was 38 per cent.[29] That ethnic inequality ran headlong into and was compounded by the uneven economic geography of growth, which was highest in London, the Southeast, Scotland and the largest cities in the North of England but lower in smaller northern towns. In the year 2000, the government's Index of Multiple Deprivation, drawing on data related to income, work, health, housing, education, crime and the physical environment, ranked Oldham 338th out of 355 districts across England in terms of overall deprivation. Bradford ranked 339th and Burnley 335th.[30]

The 2001 riots were partly due to economic factors. Yet Cantle also argued that the riots, which had taken place along ethnic lines, were reflective of the prior separation of the communities within the towns. People were, he suggested, living parallel lives in separate ethnic communities. They lived in separate parts of towns, went to separate schools, worked in different places, worshipped in different places and had separate social lives. The Executive Summary of the Cantle Report includes this passage:

> A Muslim of Pakistani origin summed this up: 'When I leave this meeting with you I will go home and not see another white face until I come back here next week.' Similarly, a young man from a white council estate said: 'I never met anyone on this estate who wasn't like us from around here.' There is little wonder that the ignorance about each other's communities can easily grow into fear; especially where this is exploited by extremist groups determined to undermine community harmony and foster divisions.[31]

In its response to the Cantle Report, the government promised to invest more money in community cohesion programmes and in economic regeneration. Yet, over time, the ground slowly shifted. Cantle had described the communities affected by the riots largely in terms of their ethnicity and geographic origins, as Asian or Pakistani or Indian and so on. After the 11 September attacks the same sets of divisions came, increasingly, to be described in religious terms. Asians, Pakistanis and Indians became, increasingly, Muslims linked by their Islamic faith.[32] Looking back, the leader of the British National Party, Nick Griffin, whose members were active in Burnley and Oldham during the summer of 2001, had helped establish this frame. Griffin, who was invited to appear on the BBC *Today* Programme on 30 June 2001, used the language of a 'clash of civilizations', popularized by the American political scientist Samuel Huntingdon, to argue that Islam posed an existential threat to white working-class communities.[33]

The 2005 London attacks accelerated this process. Most obviously this was because, in their recorded messages, Khan and Tanweer used their religious faith and what they regarded as Western attacks on Islamic countries to justify their actions. It was also because, in the aftermath of the attacks, a series of newspaper reports, drawing on opinion-poll surveys, seemed to show that as many as 16 per cent of British Muslims felt some sympathy for the motives of the suicide bombers.[34] The obvious point here – that there is a world of difference between sympathizing with someone's motives and condoning their actions – got lost, as did the fact that non-Muslim people were, by and large, as likely to sympathize with those motives as Muslims.[35] Broader polling of attitudes showed British Muslims were often more socially conservative than British non-Muslims, but reported a strong sense of belonging to their local community and a stronger sense than the national average of feeling British.[36]

The frame of Islamic terrorism, together with a growing awareness within New Labour of the extent of public opposition to high levels of immigration (p. 89), led to a rhetorical rowing back on New Labour's commitment to and celebration of multiculturalism. At its simplest, multiculturalism might be understood as an empirical claim that there are people with lots of different cultures in Britain and that this is unlikely to change.[37] In the 2000s, multiculturalism was, however, turned into a normative for-or-against political value. New Labour argued that increased immigration was not only good for the economy but was good for British society. In 2001 Robin Cook, the foreign secretary, offered a robust defence of the benefits of multiculturalism and immigration using a culinary example:

> Chicken Tikka Masala is now a true British national dish, not only because it is the most popular, but because it is a perfect illustration of the way Britain absorbs and adapts external influences. Chicken Tikka is an Indian dish. The Masala sauce was added to satisfy the desire of British people to have their meat served in gravy.[38]

This speech was delivered a few months before the 11 September terrorist attacks in America. In October 2005, a few months after the

7 July attacks, his successor at the Foreign Office, Jack Straw, wrote a column in his local newspaper in which he said he was increasingly concerned about the number of women in his Blackburn constituency choosing to wear the niqab as a 'visible statement of separation and difference'.[39] In December 2006, Blair gave a speech in which he argued multiculturalism was still to be valued, but that the 7 July attacks had thrown the concept into 'sharp relief'; that a new and virulent form of Islam posed a problem in a minority of the Muslim community; and that, as a consequence, more emphasis needed to be placed on the promotion of common values.[40]

THE TROJAN HORSE

During his time as leader of the opposition, David Cameron was a strong critic of New Labour's statism. He favoured the concept of the 'Big Society' – empowering local communities, families and churches to work together to address social problems. Once in 10 Downing Street, the Big Society slowly faded from view whilst the frontiers of the state were rolled further forward. Troops were deployed to Libya in 2011, in an operation which deposed Colonel Gaddafi but led to civil war and economic collapse.[41] In terms of the domestic threat posed by terrorism, the Coalition government established a new National Security Council and passed legislation in 2015 allowing authorities to seize the passports of those they thought were travelling abroad to support a terrorist organization; issue temporary exclusion orders; and monitor more closely Internet traffic in pursuit of terrorist conspiracies. The Coalition also broadened the definition of extremist ideology used within the counter-radicalization 'Prevent' programme to include strong but non-violent statements of opposition to British foreign policy.[42] Finally, Cameron extended the attack on multiculturalism by picking up on points in Ted Cantle's report and arguing that New Labour had encouraged different cultures not only to 'live separate lives' but to tolerate 'segregated communities behaving in ways that run completely counter to our values'.[43]

The secretary of state for education, Michael Gove, also placed himself at the forefront of the multiculturalism debate during what became known as the 'Trojan Horse Affair'. In late 2013 extracts from a letter were sent to Birmingham City Council which purported to be from a report on the progress of a conspiracy to gain control of some Birmingham schools with a view to running them on Islamic principles. The council viewed the letter as a crude forgery. It nevertheless commissioned Ian Kershaw, the chief executive of the Northern Education Trust, to examine whether some of the allegations being made were true.[44] Gove then became involved. In 2006 he had published a book, *Celsius 7/7*, arguing that 'Islamism poses a challenge to Western values, indeed to universal human values of freedom, dignity and equality, just as potent as past totalitarianisms.'[45] Gove commissioned Peter Clarke, who had now retired as head of the Metropolitan Police Counter Terrorism Command, to also investigate the allegations. In his report, published in July 2014, Clarke concluded there was 'clear evidence that there are a number of people, associated with each other and in positions of influence in schools and governing bodies, who espouse, endorse or fail to challenge extremist views'.[46] Fourteen teachers and the chairman of the Park View Education Trust were banned from teaching or working in schools.

The Trojan Horse Affair remains exceptionally controversial. Supporters point to evidence, largely in the form of WhatsApp exchanges between several male teachers, the 'Park View Brotherhood', which either expressed or failed to challenge sexist views about female teachers and the merits of gender segregation in the classroom. They also point to Kershaw's findings that 'elements' of the plot alleged in the Trojan Horse letter were 'present in a large number of the schools considered'.[47] Critics, including the producers of a *New York Times* podcast series *The Trojan Horse Affair*, Brian Reed and Hamza Syed, argue that Clarke failed to understand the role of Education Trusts or the rules relating to the teaching of religion in all schools. They also argue it is inconceivable Gove would have responded in the same way to a letter purporting to detail a Christian plot to subvert schools, let alone commissioned a former anti-terrorist police officer to investigate them.[48] Yet one thing here is entirely clear. The Trojan Horse letter and the responses to it, including the Kershaw and Clarke reports, as well as the subsequent debates around their findings, understood the issues at stake not in the way the Cantle Report had primarily done so – in terms of ethnicity and geography – but in terms of religion and faith.

In the immediate aftermath of the 2001 terrorist attacks on New York, and after he had briefly addressed the TUC conference, Blair travelled back to London by train. He recalls thinking that 'what the terrorists would want was not merely to cause carnage by the original terrorist act, but to set in train a series of events, including setting part of the Muslim World against America'.[49] Two days later, during a Cabinet meeting, Blair argued that 'it was essential to reinvigorate the Middle East peace process to avert the possibility that battle lines were drawn up between the Muslim world and the West'.[50] This was an immensely prescient judgement. But stopping it from happening was never going to be easy. It did not help matters when, shortly afterwards, George Bush described his self-declared War on Terror as a 'crusade'.[51] The invasion and occupation of Afghanistan and Iraq; terrorist attacks on the West between 2001 and 2004; the 7 July bombings; later terrorist attacks undertaken in the name of Islam and attacks upon Muslims in Britain all contributed to the salience of a religious framing for the post-11 September world. Blair, to be fair, sought to assure anyone and everyone that he was in no way anti-Muslim and that his target was religious 'extremists of whatever faith'.[52] But he did also see the world in religious terms. In his memoirs he suggested that an 'uncomfortably' large number of Muslims 'buy into bits' of the terrorists' 'world view', and that those Muslims who 'unequivocally condemn terrorism' have struggled to develop 'an alternative narrative for Islam that makes sense of its history and provides a coherent vision for its future'.[53]

15
Northern Ireland: A Farewell to Arms

EXCLUSIVELY PEACEFUL MEANS

On 28 July 2005 the IRA issued a statement, by way of a DVD recording read by Séanna Breathnach, also known as Séanna Walsh. Breathnach was a member of the IRA who had served time in Her Majesty's Maze 'H Block' Prison on three separate occasions before eventually being released in 1998 as part of the Good Friday Agreement. Breathnach had been close friends with Bobby Sands, the first IRA prisoner to die during the 1981 Hunger Strikes in the Maze, and was married to Sinéad Moore, another former IRA prisoner. His credentials within the Republican movement were, in other words, beyond reproach. They needed to be. It was Breathnach's job to announce that the IRA was ending its armed struggle:

> The leadership of Óglaigh na hÉireann has formally ordered an end to the armed campaign ... All IRA units have been ordered to dump arms ... all volunteers have been instructed to assist the development of purely political and democratic programmes through exclusively peaceful means.[1]

Shortly after, Tony Blair and the Irish taoiseach, Bertie Ahern, issued a joint statement in which they described the IRA's decision as a 'momentous and historic development'.[2] Blair followed this up with a short individual statement. 'This may be the day when, finally, after all the false dawns and dashed hopes, peace replaces war, politics replaces terror on the island of Ireland.'[3]

It is easy to see the IRA's announcement as the natural and inevitable end point of a peace process that had resumed in earnest in the early 1990s. The formal end of the IRA's armed campaign was, on this reading, something that was always going to happen. Everyone knew there was a military stalemate. Everyone knew that, sooner or later, a compromise would have to be struck and that, in order to further advance its political cause via Sinn Féin, the IRA would have to build on its existing ceasefire by drawing a line under its armed struggle. This is only how it looks in hindsight. For the first five years of the new millennium, it looked, for much of the time, as if a breakdown in the ceasefire and a resumption of Northern Ireland's three decade-long civil war was just as likely an outcome, if not a more likely outcome, than the 2005 statement. There was nothing remotely inevitable about the IRA's disbanding. 'Peace came dropping slow.'[4]

THE ROAD TO GOOD FRIDAY

A purely modern history does not really cut it with Northern Ireland. In fact, even saying Northern Ireland does not really cut it. For a majority of Catholics and nationalists, Northern Ireland was never Northern Ireland but, rather, the North of Ireland: a secessionist regime composed of six of the traditional nine counties of Ulster, run by and for its Protestant majority. Inspired by the American Civil Rights movement, the Northern Ireland Civil Rights Association was formed in January 1967, which led to a march, in Derry, in October 1968 that was broken up by way of the breaking of protestors' bones by the Royal Ulster Constabulary. The following year the Irish Republican Army split and the Provisional IRA, 'the Provos', was formed. British troops were deployed to Northern Ireland in August 1969. The Provisional IRA first authorized attacks on British troops in 1971, and in 1972 the British Army killed thirteen unarmed people during a march in the Bogside area of Derry. By then both sides, Catholic and nationalist on the one and Protestant and unionist (or loyalist) on the other, felt themselves to be a beleaguered minority.[5] Catholics knew they were a minority in the North of Ireland and were convinced that the Protestant majority would continue to deny them rights or recognition. Protestants saw themselves as a religious minority on the island of Ireland and dependent upon a government in London which did not understand or care for them and would, if given the opportunity to do so, sell them out.

In December 1973 the Sunningdale Agreement looked, for a brief while, like it might offer a political way out via a devolved assembly in Northern Ireland, power-sharing and a Joint Council of Ministers with the Irish government. It fell apart in May 1974 after a general strike organized by the loyalist Ulster Workers' Council. For a while, leading unionist politicians toyed with the idea of pursuing an independent Northern Ireland outside the United Kingdom. In the end, this option was rejected and unionism grudgingly accepted the new status quo of direct rule from London. For the next decade politics was put on the back burner as the death toll mounted. A turning point of sorts came in 1981 when Bobby Sands, on hunger strike in the Maze, was elected as the MP for Fermanagh and South Tyrone. Sands' political success and the embarrassment it caused the British government convinced Gerry Adams, Sinn Féin's vice president and, simultaneously – many have claimed, although he has always denied it – a senior IRA commander, of the merits of a twin-track approach of mixing armed attacks with electoral politics.[6]

Margaret Thatcher's willingness to negotiate the 1985 Anglo-Irish Agreement, which gave the Republic of Ireland a formal role in the politics of Northern Ireland, helped persuade some figures on the nationalist side that the British government would not always block political progress.[7] It was within the context of this new political environment that, in January 1988, the leader of the nationalist Social Democratic and Labour Party (SDLP), John Hume, first met with Adams, now president of Sinn Féin, to talk about a peace process. In November 1990 Peter Brooke, the secretary of state for Northern Ireland, delivered a speech to the annual lunch of the Association of Canned Food Importers and Distributors in London (obviously) in which he acknowledged it was difficult to envisage a military defeat of the IRA, and that the British government had 'no selfish strategic or economic interest' in Northern Ireland and would accept unification if the people wished it.[8] Those few words were a big deal because, to the IRA, they signalled a willingness to recognize Northern Ireland's right to self-determination. In 1991, Martin McGuinness, a senior figure within Sinn Féin and a former IRA chief of staff, began 'back-channel' talks with the British security services.[9] Not long after these started, Gerry Adams wrote a long letter to John Major (who had replaced Margaret Thatcher as prime minister towards the end of 1990), setting out Sinn Féin's view of the peace process. That letter was initially delivered, mistakenly, to the 10 Downing Street which runs off the Shankill Road in Protestant Belfast. When that mistake was eventually corrected, Major concluded there was something of a 'flavour' to the letter which suggested Sinn Féin might be serious about restarting the peace process.[10]

In February 1993 the British government claimed it had received a message from McGuinness saying that 'the conflict is over, but we need your advice on how to bring it to an end'. McGuinness denounced this as black propaganda. It is, however, entirely possible McGuinness had said something positive about the peace process but that what he had said had been exaggerated, either by members of the British security services or one of the other intermediaries to their talks.[11] Either way, the Downing Street Declaration, issued by Major and the Irish taoiseach Albert Reynolds in December 1993, pushed the peace process further forward. It affirmed the right of the people of Ireland to self-determination and that Northern Ireland could become a part of a new unitary Irish state encompassing all of the island of Ireland if a majority of its people favoured such a change. This led, a few months later, to an IRA ceasefire. The momentum which had been gained then dissipated. Adams and McGuinness faced opposition to their strategy within the IRA Council.[12] At the same time John Major was coming under increasing pressure from Unionist MPs, whose support he increasingly depended upon in Parliament, and from his own Conservative backbenchers to concede no further ground to the IRA. Eventually, and with not much further progress having being made, the ceasefire broke down in February 1996 when the IRA detonated a bomb in the London Docklands, killing two people.

Multiparty talks, excluding Sinn Féin, began in June of that year but did not get very far. When Tony Blair was elected in May 1997, he promised to prioritize peace talks whilst presenting himself as someone who had 'no ideological or historical baggage' when it came to Northern Ireland.[13] In July 1997 the IRA declared a new ceasefire, and in August Sinn Féin was invited to join the peace talks. This led the Democratic Unionist Party (DUP), led by the Reverend Ian Paisley, to walk away. The talks, when they began, were, despite this, still not easy. Mo Mowlam, the secretary of state for Northern Ireland, describes how most of the time 'people just glared at each other . . . exchanged insults and tried to goad each other'.[14] In December a loyalist terrorist, Billy

Wright, was murdered by IRA prisoners in the Maze, which started a sequence of tit-for-tat sectarian murders. Nevertheless, in January 1998 a breakthrough came when the Irish and British governments reached an agreement on how power-sharing might work. Blair eventually flew to Belfast on the evening of 7 April and the Good Friday Agreement (or Belfast Agreement as it is also known) was concluded three days later.*

A START NOT AN END

The Good Friday Agreement ran to thirty-five pages and covered three main areas: the creation of a democratically elected Assembly in Northern Ireland; the creation of a North–South Ministerial Council; and the establishment of a British–Irish Council and British–Irish Governmental Conference.[15] Beyond all the institutional detail, the Agreement was, in essence, an elaborate and clever power-sharing compromise in which the nationalists and the unionists both gave up something they valued in return for something they wanted a little more.

The nationalist side, in the shape of the SDLP (still led by John Hume) and, eventually – and with a bucketful of reservations – Sinn Féin, accepted that any future unification of the island of Ireland would require majority support in Northern Ireland. In return, it secured the promise of a Northern Ireland Assembly and power-sharing executive (replacing direct rule from London), in which the first and deputy first ministers would represent the two different communities and have identical powers; the release of prisoners; demilitarization (including a massively reduced British Army presence); and greater cross-border political co-operation with the Republic. The unionist community and its largest political party, the Ulster Unionist Party (UUP), led by the barrister and former academic David Trimble, split over the Agreement. Trimble, who, as we will see, had his doubts about the Agreement,

* It is instructive to note the two sides struggled to even agree on a name for what they had done. Blair and the nationalist side spoke about the Good Friday Agreement. The unionist side referred to the Belfast Agreement. Two decades later, when negotiating its Brexit Deal with the European Commission, one of Theresa May's negotiating demands was that the final text refer to 'the Good Friday Agreement or Belfast Agreement' rather than simply the Good Friday Agreement. Gavin Barwell, *Chief of Staff: Notes from Downing Street* (London, 2021), p. 264.

nevertheless argued that it strengthened the Union. Others within his party, including a future leader of the DUP, Jeffrey Donaldson, who had been part of the negotiating team, came out strongly against it – as did Ian Paisley's DUP. Meanwhile, the Agreement recognized the 'birthright of all the people of Northern Ireland to identify themselves and be accepted as Irish or British, or both, as they may so choose'.[16] As for the border, it eventually turned into a replica of Schrödinger's famous cat. It was there and not there.[17] Because Britain and the Republic of Ireland were both members of the European Single Market, the border, whilst it still existed as an important political line, could, for the purpose of day-to-day travel and trade, be largely ignored once political violence had wound down and demilitarization had started.

The Good Friday Agreement was endorsed in referenda in the Republic (overwhelmingly) and Northern Ireland (comfortably, but with only the narrowest of majorities from unionist voters). John Hume and David Trimble were awarded the 1998 Nobel Peace Prize. Yet, from the start, there were problems. Northern Ireland remained a deeply divided society. In the first set of elections to the Northern Ireland Assembly in 1998, the avowedly non-sectarian and centrist Alliance Party secured just over 5 per cent of the vote. That same year, the Northern Ireland Life and Times Survey found that just 1 per cent of those who identified as Catholics supported either the UUP or the DUP, and that only 1 per cent of self-identified Protestants supported the SDLP or Sinn Féin.[18] The 2001 census showed that 67 per cent of Catholics and 73 per cent of Protestants lived in areas that were at least 90 per cent or more Catholic or Protestant.[19] That was not all. Sinn Féin had participated in the talks which had led to the Agreement but had then withheld its formal endorsement of it. The IRA, for its part, initially argued that the Agreement fell a long way short of offering a lasting settlement.[20] The DUP refused to have anything to do with it at all – and, given that its leader had once described Pope John Paul II as the Antichrist, nobody was expecting any change in that position any time soon.[21] To add to the problems, the UUP were split down the middle. Trimble, who had made his name by marching arm-in-arm with Paisley during an Orange Order march at Drumcree in July 1995, had put his name to the deal, but several of his most senior colleagues had already made it abundantly clear that he did not have their support. Blair, for his part, was sanguine, knowing that the Agreement was closer to being a starting point than an end point. 'Whereas the agreement could be described as art – at least in concept – the implementation was more akin to heavy manufacturing.'[22]

The fundamental problem everyone now faced, however, was that neither side really trusted the other and were dismayed when their opponents interpreted the contents of the Good Friday Agreement differently (as differently, in fact, as the Americans and the French were later to interpret UN Resolution 1441). The unionists were outraged when nationalists presented the Agreement as a stepping stone on the inevitable road to a united Ireland. The nationalists were incandescent when unionists said it showed unification was off the agenda. To add to this there were long and hard disagreements about the right of loyalists to march through nationalist areas; the future name, structure and composition of the Royal Ulster Constabulary (which, following the conclusion of the Independent Commission on Policing for Northern Ireland adroitly chaired by Chris Patten, the former governor of Hong Kong, eventually became the Police Service of Northern Ireland in 2001); and the powers and remit of the North–South Ministerial Council, established as part of the Agreement to give an Irish dimension to Northern Irish politics. It was, however, the argument about the link between Sinn Féin entering the power-sharing executive and IRA weapons decommissioning which nearly tipped Northern Ireland back into war.*

THE LONG AND WINDING ROAD OF DECOMMISSIONING

Decommissioning had always been a tough issue. 'The Provos' had split from the 'Official' IRA when the latter had failed to use its arms to protect nationalist communities in Ulster in 1969.[23] John Major had excluded Sinn Féin from the multiparty talks that had begun in 1996

---

* The Good Friday Agreement did not just require the IRA to decommission its arms. It made the same requirement of loyalist terrorist groups such as the Ulster Freedom Fighters, Ulster Volunteer Force and Loyalist Volunteer Force, some of whose leaders or associates also harboured political ambitions. This chapter nevertheless focuses on the IRA because its participation was central to the fortunes of the Good Friday Agreement in a way which was not as true of these other groups.

because the IRA had ended its ceasefire and had, prior to this, shown no inclination to decommission. With the Good Friday Agreement having been signed, the UUP and the DUP argued that it was completely unacceptable for the Northern Ireland Assembly to meet and the power-sharing Executive to start work unless and until the IRA had actually *started* physically to disarm its estimated stockpile of 1,000-plus rifles and 2 tonnes of plastic explosives. Quoting the text of the Good Friday Agreement, they argued that everyone participating in the peace process, Sinn Féin included, had committed themselves to the use of 'exclusively democratic and peaceful means of resolving differences on political issues' and to the 'total disarmament of all paramilitary organisations'.[24] Trimble also revealed that, when he had threatened to walk out of the peace talks, Tony Blair had personally promised him that decommissioning would start 'straight away', and to exclude Sinn Féin from the new Northern Ireland Assembly if this did not happen.[25]

The Irish government, the SDLP and, most vociferously, Sinn Féin held to a very different line. The Agreement, they argued, actually made no formal or immediate commitments in relation to decommissioning. Nor did it say decommissioning was a precondition for the establishment of a devolved assembly. All it said was that parties to the Agreement would work constructively and in good faith to achieve the decommissioning of all paramilitary arms within two years. Sinn Féin, for its part, went further: decommissioning was of little practical significance.[26] If the IRA ever wanted to fight it would find the weapons with which to do so. The unionists were fixated on the issue not because they wanted peace, but because they did not want to share power. Besides, Sinn Féin added, the party was not the same as, and did not control, the IRA and so should not be excluded from the democratic process. Finally, Sinn Féin also made the point that the decommissioning process was connected to the full implementation of the Good Friday Agreement, including British demilitarization in the province.

As disagreements go, this looked like a showstopper. Nevertheless, some progress was made. Sinn Féin earned itself some credit when, in August 1998, it unequivocally condemned the murder of twenty-nine people in Omagh in a bombing by the breakaway 'Real IRA'. In April 1999 George Mitchell, a former American senator and Senate majority leader, who had previously led talks about decommissioning whilst John Major had been prime minister, was parachuted back into

Northern Ireland and brokered a compromise agreement.[27] There would be no prior decommissioning but, instead, representatives from the paramilitary groups would meet with members of a newly established Independent International Commission on Decommissioning to start talks about decommissioning, and would do so on the same day that the newly established power-sharing Executive met for the first time.

This just about worked. Trimble got just enough votes from the UUP Council in late 1999 to join the Northern Ireland Executive and become First Minister and to do so without prior decommissioning. But that was never going to settle things for very long. The UUP continued to insist decommissioning had to start sooner rather than later and, in January 2000, with nothing having happened, Trimble threatened to walk away and, in so doing, to collapse the power-sharing Executive. In February 2000 Peter Mandelson, who had replaced Mo Mowlam as Northern Ireland secretary, suspended the Assembly before Trimble could end it first.[28] This provoked an unexpectedly positive reaction. In May, the IRA said, for the first time, that it was ready to start a process that would 'completely and verifiably' put its arms beyond use.[29] That was enough – just – to bring the UUP back into the power-sharing fold, and in June 2000 the former Finnish president Martti Ahtisaari and the anti-apartheid campaigner and African National Congress politician Cyril Ramaphosa confirmed that they had seen a large number of IRA weapons 'safely and adequately' stored in bunkers.[30] This was not, however, the same as actual decommissioning and the UUP remained largely unimpressed. Eventually, in July 2001, David Trimble resigned as Northern Ireland's first minister, citing the lack of progress over IRA decommissioning.[31]

In the words of Blair's chief of staff, Jonathan Powell, 11 September 2001 then 'changed everything'.[32] American politicians who had been vocal in their support for Sinn Féin before 11 September were now more wary of having any connection to any kind of terrorist or terrorist-connected group. The British now argued that a moment of decision had finally arrived for the IRA and that there was now no possible justification for them to still be holding on to their weapons. Sinn Féin might have been able to stall the British government, but it now came under pressure to act from a number of these previously supportive American politicians. On 15 September Gerry Adams got in touch with the British government to say that the IRA would decommission but needed more time. A few weeks later Adams issued an appeal to the IRA to commence decommissioning.[33] The next day, the Independent International Commission confirmed it had witnessed weapons being put 'beyond use'.[34]

In March 2002 there was a break-in at the Special Branch offices in the Castlereagh Police Station. It was reported that files containing the names of police informers had been stolen, and the police said they suspected the IRA of organizing the break-in.[35] Then, in April, the talk was once again of the unionists collapsing the power-sharing Executive.[36] In May, June and July there were riots across parts of Northern Ireland. In October a squad of armed police raided Sinn Féin's offices in the Stormont Assembly. The police said they were investigating a spy ring and had recovered material that could have been used to target politicians; Denis Donaldson, Sinn Féin's administrator within the Northern Ireland Assembly, was arrested.[37] Jeffrey Donaldson, one of David Trimble's fiercest critics within the UUP (and definitely no relation of Denis's), argued that the raids had 'totally discredited' Sinn Féin. The latest British secretary of state for Northern Ireland, John Reid, then suspended the Assembly once again. Martin McGuinness had already warned that Sinn Féin might well conclude that the Good Friday Agreement was now 'dead in the water'.[38]

A further problem was looming. From the early 1990s onwards, the British and Irish governments had regarded the SDLP and the UUP as being key to the peace process. Each party, they thought, would, deep down, be prepared to make compromises to achieve peace. The signing of the Good Friday Agreement had vindicated their faith. There was however a second part to their strategy. With a power-sharing agreement in place, the British and the Irish expected compromise to become a habit and voters' political attitudes to soften. As a result, it was assumed, the SDLP would, over time, take votes away from the more hard-line Sinn Féin whilst the UUP would marginalize the DUP.[39] In short, the hope was that, with the Agreement in place, centrifugal politics in Northern Ireland would become centripetal.

That did not happen. On the one hand, there were some signs of political attitudes having changed. The Northern Ireland Life and Times Survey found that in 2003 only 2 per cent of self-identified Catholics said they would find it impossible to accept a majority of people in Northern Ireland *never* voting for reunification. Conversely, the proportion of Protestants saying they would find it impossible to accept a majority of people in Northern Ireland voting *for* reunification fell from 23 per cent in 1998 to 14 per cent in 2004.[40] On the other hand, the idea that the Good Friday Agreement would transform the dynamics of party competition and strengthen the more moderate SDLP and UUP proved wide of the mark. In the 1998 elections to the Northern Ireland Assembly, the UUP won eight more seats than the DUP whilst the SDLP won six more seats than Sinn Féin. Yet, with the power-sharing Executive established, Sinn Féin and the DUP found that they could now attract support by lambasting their rivals for conceding too much ground. In the November 2003 Assembly elections, the DUP won three more seats than the UUP, and Sinn Féin won six more seats than the SDLP.

Political polarization posed an apparently acute problem. The DUP loathed the Agreement and were committed to its renegotiation.[41] Their position on decommissioning and the IRA was equally one of zero tolerance. In November 2004, in response to some comments from Gerry Adams that decommissioning needed to be done in a way that avoided humiliating the IRA, Ian Paisley responded by saying it 'needs to be humiliated'.[42] Sinn Féin's position was more nuanced. By now, it was publicly backing the Agreement and ruling out any renegotiation on terms set by the DUP. When it came to decommissioning, they argued that the IRA had already demonstrated its good faith and needed to be given more time. But Adams and McGuinness also kept warning the British and American governments that they had to move very carefully in order to prevent an open split within the IRA.

A MURDER AND A BREAKTHROUGH

By the end of 2004 the political prospects in Northern Ireland looked some way short of rosy. But Ahern and Blair kept at it – making phone calls, suggesting talks and looking for political openings. Blair also got it right in sticking with his argument that the IRA needed to fully commit to full disarmament and was undermining its own cause by refusing to do so. This stance was criticized by Sinn Féin and by some politicians within the SDLP. It nevertheless earned Blair some capital with the unionist parties: capital he used to persuade them that power-sharing would need to resume if and when the IRA did disarm.

It worked. Slowly, very slowly, Paisley and the DUP shifted their stance and in June 2005 Paisley told Blair, in one of a series of private meetings, that if the IRA fully disarmed 'everything would be possible'.[43] Paisley's willingness to compromise may have had something to do with his own sense of personal mortality following a serious illness in 2004. But there was also a political calculation at play. Paisley was increasingly concerned that, if he remained steadfast in his opposition to the resumption of power-sharing, the British and Irish governments would simply reach their own agreement: one which would result in the Irish government being given a more direct role in the governance of Northern Ireland. The Good Friday Agreement was bad; the alternative could be worse.[44] Besides, and more narrowly, Paisley knew that he and his party had now achieved a measure of political supremacy within the unionist community and that he could potentially look forward to being first minister.

The other difference-makers were Adams and McGuinness. They had developed the twin-track 'Armalite and ballot-box' strategy in the 1980s but had later come to accept that a military stalemate in Northern Ireland was inevitable. Having persuaded the largest part of the IRA and Sinn Féin to fully accept the Good Friday Agreement, Adams, when asked whether he could envisage a future without the IRA, had, on 26 October 2002, said yes.[45] A few days after, McGuinness had publicly confirmed that 'my war is over'.[46] Adams and McGuinness were very careful. They waited to be sure Blair and Ahern were not going to waver in their argument that the IRA had to disarm fully. They waited for the DUP to signal that power-sharing could resume. They waited until they were sure they had a strong-enough base of support within Sinn Féin and the IRA's army council. Perhaps most importantly, they also waited to be sure that their support within the United States was drying up and that George W. Bush and key congressional leaders were absolutely adamant that the IRA had to disband. When all of this had happened, they then threw their own personal support behind disarmament. So, in the end, whilst the strategy of building from the centre failed, insofar as the UUP and the SDLP had lost votes, it worked in that their apparently more hard-line replacements, the DUP and Sinn Féin, decided it just about made sense for them to reach a compromise in order to protect the principle of power-sharing.

There was one other and more immediate factor which tipped the scales. On 30 January 2005 Robert McCartney, a Catholic, a father and, it was reported, a Sinn Féin supporter, was stabbed to death outside a pub in Belfast following a brawl. McCartney's sisters, fiancée and friends maintained he had been killed by a senior member of the IRA and that the IRA had wiped the bar clean of any forensic evidence and made it bluntly clear to witnesses they should not speak to the police about what had happened. Sinn Féin came under pressure to denounce the attack. On 8 March the IRA issued a statement saying that four people had been involved in the murder and that they had made an offer to the McCartney family to shoot those involved.[47] This was a huge miscalculation. To many of their own supporters it made the IRA look like thugs. President Bush announced Sinn Féin was no longer a 'reliable partner for peace' and several congressmen, including Ted Kennedy, withdrew their public support from Adams and called upon the IRA to disband.[48]

All of which brings us back to the IRA's July 2005 announcement. In September of that year the Independent International Commission on Decommissioning announced not only that it had observed the destruction of a large quantity of arms, but that it believed this to have been all the arms in the IRA's possession. In October 2006 multiparty talks were held at St Andrews, on the east coast of Scotland, focused upon reforms to the police and justice system; the restoration of power-sharing; and the status of Gaelic as an official language. In November, a transitional Assembly was established. This was followed, in March 2007, by fresh elections to the Assembly. Sinn Féin and the DUP, who had said, in advance, that they would be willing to participate in a new power-sharing Executive, triumphed. The DUP won thirty-six seats and Sinn Féin twenty-eight (compared with eighteen seats for the UUP and sixteen for the SDLP).

In May 2007 Ian Paisley and Martin McGuinness were sworn in as, respectively, first and deputy first minister in a new power-sharing government. Members of the IRA were in the room whilst Westlife's *You Raise Me Up* – a slightly strange choice all things considered – was played as background music. Tony Blair, who was a few days away from confirming that he was going to step down as prime minister, spoke of the opportunity to 'make history anew, not as a struggle between warring factions but as a search for the future shared'.[49] Paisley, who recalled being arrested on the night the Good Friday Agreement had been concluded, declared that 'Northern Ireland has come to a time of peace, a time when hate will no longer rule'.[50]

Not all that many countries find themselves fighting a civil war. The United Kingdom did, and, between the start of 'The Troubles' in 1968 and the IRA's 2005 statement, that war led to the deaths of 3,720 people. The years since then have not been without violence. Between 2006 and 2015 the Conflict and Politics in Northern Ireland Archive attributes twenty-two deaths to the security situation in Northern Ireland.[51] In 2019 the murder of the journalist Lyra McKee, who was shot whilst reporting on a riot in the Creggan area of Derry, attracted worldwide condemnation. Yet, whilst Northern Ireland was not, to use a phrase which had become horribly familiar during the 1980s and 1990s, 'normalized' during the 2010s, it was transformed.

16

The TB-GBs

A BRIEF HISTORY OF A BAD RELATIONSHIP

Reporting on and speculation about the bad and constantly worsening relationship between Noel and Liam Gallagher, Jennifer Aniston and Brad Pitt, and Tony Blair and Gordon Brown seemed, at times, to consume all the oxygen the 2000s had to offer.

When John Smith unexpectedly died in May 1994 it seemed almost certain that either Blair or Brown would stand in the Labour leadership election to replace him. The worry for their supporters was that both would run, splitting their support, and both would thereby lose. Although they had entered Parliament together in 1983, and then shared an office, Brown, as the shadow chancellor, regarded himself as the senior partner in the relationship and expected Blair to step aside.[1] Blair, who was convinced he could appeal to voters in the South of England in a way Brown couldn't, moved first and announced he was standing. Brown agonized over what to do. His supporters were convinced he could win by presenting Blair as a posh, inexperienced, public schoolboy who did not really understand the Labour Party.[2]

It is the meeting between Blair and Brown in a London restaurant, Granita, which usually gets all the attention in terms of the way this stand-off played itself out. But the key meetings between Blair and Brown probably took place in Edinburgh. On the day before John Smith's funeral, the public service for which was held in Morningside, Blair met Brown at a house in Merchiston, another affluent suburb of Edinburgh, which belonged to one of Blair's school friends. They argued and only stopped arguing when Brown went to the toilet. In his telling of the story, Blair waited downstairs for fifteen minutes, feeling increasingly alarmed. Suddenly the phone in the house rang. He ignored it and it went to the answerphone. 'Tony, it's Gordon here ... I am upstairs in the toilet and I can't get out.' It transpired that during recent building work, the toilet door had been replaced minus an inside handle. Blair went upstairs. 'Withdraw from the contest, or I'm leaving you in there.'[3] Afterwards, the two spoke at Brown's house in North Queensferry, on the banks of the Firth of Forth. In Brown's account, Blair's mood when he arrived at the house 'was close to desperation'. He repeated a promise he had already made to give Brown unfettered control over economic and social policy as chancellor if he stood aside, and 'added another promise' to step down during his second term. Over the next few days Brown says he agreed to this deal because he was 'unwilling to see the party divided in a way that would endanger the prospects for reform'.[4]

With Blair elected as Labour's new leader, the Brown–Blair relationship looked, for a while, like it might just about go back to working. Brown had left Blair hanging out to dry when Blair unexpectedly threw his 'stakeholding' chips on the table in 1996. However, they had agreed on the contents of Labour's 1997 manifesto without any problems and had jointly presented to the rest of the Cabinet the fait accompli of Bank of England independence. Moreover, the early signs were that Blair would indeed allow Brown not only to run the Treasury but, as he had wanted, other economics-related departments.[5] Even then, it was obvious Brown was never going to win a most-helpful-employee-of-the-month award. Peter Mandelson describes how Brown used to sit in meetings of the Cabinet 'hardly ever looking at him [Blair], always scribbling on papers, always [bringing] a mound of paperwork into the Cabinet which he would look through, never [listening] to what anyone else was saying'.[6]

Europe became the first big policy issue over which the pair fell out. In its 1997 manifesto Labour had prioritized the completion of the Single Market, increasing the number of Member States, reform of the Common Agricultural Policy and retaining the national veto over 'key matters of national interest'.[7] All of which was very apple pie and ice cream. On the tougher question of whether Britain should join the European Single Currency, scheduled to be launched on 1 January 1999, Labour decided discretion was the better part of valour. Here the manifesto promised a referendum if a Labour government ever decided it should join, but that everything would depend on a 'hardheaded assessment of Britain's economic interests' at some future and unspecified point. Shortly after the 1997 election, the Treasury came up with five economic tests to assess whether joining or not joining was a good idea.* In the summer of 1997 a number of newspapers reported that the Treasury was edging towards a view that Britain had passed the tests, and that the Cabinet was edging towards a decision to join.

That was premature. Brown's press officer, Charlie Whelan, planted a story in *The Times* that the Treasury was in fact going to rule out joining until after the next election.[8] Blair was blindsided and had to phone the Treasury to find out who had said what and why. He was eventually patched through to Whelan, who was drinking in the Red Lion pub in Whitehall. None of this looked great. To the outside world it looked like policy was being made and unmade via leaks and spin and the financial markets reacted badly. After a lot of huffing and puffing, a compromise was eventually reached and announced to Parliament. The Treasury, it was confirmed, had reached the view that joining was not in Britain's immediate economic interest. The economic case would continue to be reviewed but, in the meantime, Britain would not be joining the single currency before the next general election, 'barring some fundamental and unforeseen change in economic circumstances'.[9]

This was a reasonable-enough decision, but, whilst it was not one Blair necessarily disagreed with, it was one he appeared to have been pushed into. The revenge of Blair's camp was served cold in January 1998 when Andrew Rawnsley, writing in the *Observer*, quoted a 'close ally' of Blair as saying the chancellor had 'psychological flaws'.[10] In July, Blair pushed things a little further by demoting several of Brown's key allies in a Cabinet reshuffle.[11] Once the 2001 election had been won, Brown began pressing Blair to say when he would resign. Blair declined to answer. He was riding high and felt under no pressure to say or do anything. He could probably even have got away with moving Brown from the Treasury at this point. Politics never stands still though, and the build-up to the Iraq War took a toll on Blair's health and political

---

* The five tests related to whether business cycles and economic structures had converged; whether there was sufficient flexibility to deal with economic problems if they emerged; whether monetary union would encourage long-term investment; what impact it would have on financial services; and whether, on balance, it would encourage economic growth.

standing.[12] By November 2002 Rawnsley was reporting that the 'TB-GBs index is now at an all-time low'.[13] In 2003 the failure to find WMD in Iraq and the death of Dr David Kelly put Blair further on to the political defensive. By the end of the year, at the conclusion of peace talks between the two men organized by John Prescott, Blair had (according to Prescott's later account) promised to leave before the next election if Brown supported him until then.[14]

In January 2004 the Hutton Report exonerated Blair from any direct blame in Dr Kelly's death (p. 163). Blair recovered some of his self-confidence and decided that he, and only he, was best placed to carry New Labour into and through a third term in government and that Brown had not offered him the support he had promised. On 30 September 2004, after months of speculation, Blair confirmed he would, if he won the forthcoming general election, continue to serve as prime minister, but would not lead the party into the following one. This was, on paper, a sort of resignation promise. It was, however, one that left open the mathematical possibility of Blair remaining as prime minister for another five or six years.[15]

To rub salt into Brown's wounds, Blair's allies started to develop a plan, called (incongruously) 'Operation Teddy Bear', to break up the Treasury and create a new Budget Management Office outside the chancellor's control.[16] There was a certain logic to this. In most countries economic responsibilities are divided between a finance ministry and an economics ministry. Moreover, there was a long-standing suspicion that, in its existing form, the Treasury prioritized budget frugality (the finance function) over measures to enhance growth and productivity (the economic ones) and that this was damaging the economy. The idea that the Treasury was a part of the problem rather than the solution to Britain's problems became Liz Truss's rallying cry during her brief time as prime minister in 2022: it led to her and her hapless chancellor, Kwasi Kwarteng, to foolishly sack the Treasury's highly regarded permanent secretary.[17] The sentiment she was expressing was, however, much the same one that had led Harold Wilson to create the Department of Economic Affairs as a counterweight to the Treasury in 1964 and which Blair now seemed to be toying with.[18]

To say Gordon Brown was unlikely to be persuaded by the merits of 'Operation Teddy Bear' would be an understatement. Indeed, when he got wind of what was happening, Brown declared political independence. He refused to give Blair any advance notice of Treasury announcements or spending decisions.[19] He banned Treasury officials from briefing the prime minister.[20] His supporters were encouraged to rubbish any minister who was still seen as being loyal to Blair and, to cap it all, Brown reportedly told Blair to his face he no longer believed anything he said.[21] But having come close to the point of no return, the two men just about managed to stop publicly arguing in front of the kids for a while. When Labour had a wobble in the polls before the 2005 General Election, Brown was brought back into the fold to assist with election planning – which, if nothing else, gifted the world a truly excruciating photoshoot during a campaign trip. On a sunny day in Kent, Blair was filmed walking towards the counter of an ice cream van and ordering a 99. After a few seconds he says, 'you better make that two.' He gives the second ice cream to Brown saying, 'it is not very often he gets something for free.' Brown sparkles by saying: 'You don't get much for nothing these days.' They then go their separate ways, Blair, inevitably, signing his name on a football. Shortly afterwards, Brown rejoins him minus the ice cream which, it would seem, he has either binned or gifted to an aide.[22] As inauthentic efforts to appear casual and authentic go, this was a classic, perfectly capturing a 'can't stand you, can't leave you' middle-aged political vibe.

THE CURRY HOUSE PLOT

After Labour had won the 2005 General Election – albeit with just over 35 per cent of the popular vote – Blair decided against sacking Brown or emasculating the Treasury. Whether this was because he felt he owed Brown something or feared provoking a leadership challenge, or was simply scared of confronting Brown (as John Prescott believed to be the case), is not clear.[23] But trouble was, soon enough, on its way. In August 2006, having just arrived back from a summer holiday in Cliff Richard's six-bedroom house in Barbados, Tony Blair gave an interview to *The Times* to set the political scene for the year ahead.[24] New Labour, Blair assured readers, had 'not [been] paralysed or run out of steam'. Far from it. He was brimming with energy; had a long policy to-do list; and could not wait to get started again. This was, by now, standard Blairite stuff. So, it was what Blair said about his own leadership that made the headlines. He was not, he said, planning to 'go on and on' as prime minister and would give his successor 'ample time' to settle in before the next general election. But he refused to say anything about when, exactly, he would resign. Instead, he gave the clear impression it would not be any time soon, and finished by saying people just needed to let him 'get on with the job'.[25]

The interview landed really badly within the Parliamentary Labour Party. At a moment when Labour was sagging in opinion polls and Blair had been widely criticized within the party for failing to press Israel to agree to a ceasefire following its invasion of Lebanon a few months earlier, it looked to many that Blair, who had been Labour leader for twelve years, was saying he *would* go on and on. A number of MPs, some of them previously on the loyal side of the New Labour ledger, went public with their concerns. Andrew Smith told the *Today* programme that 'the debilitating uncertainty over the leadership can't go on'.[26] Others, some describing themselves as 'implacable modernizers', sent Blair letters asking him to quit or set a precise timetable for leaving.[27] On 6 September, fresh from an evening meal with other local Labour MPs at The Bilash, an award-winning Bengali restaurant in Wolverhampton, Tom Watson, the parliamentary under-secretary of state for veterans, resigned, saying he shared 'the view of the overwhelming majority of the party and the country that the only way the party and the government can renew itself in office is urgently to renew its leadership'.[28] This looked like it might be the start of something bigger. Watson was close to Brown, and the Blairites were sure he would never have resigned without Brown's blessing.[29] Amidst reports that other ministers were drafting their resignation letters, Brown met with Blair and reportedly demanded that he announce a fixed and early departure date, running a joint premiership with him in the meantime. John McDonnell, a left-wing backbencher who was to become shadow chancellor a decade later, likened it all to an 'episode of *The Sopranos*'.[30]

On 7 September, during a visit to a North London school, Blair, recognizing he was in a weak position, publicly clarified his thinking. He did not set a resignation date but said that the Labour Party's conference later that month would be his last as leader.[31] This proved to be enough. There were no more resignations. On 10 May 2007 Blair announced he would resign as Labour leader and prime minister at the end of June. On 14 May nominations for the Labour leadership opened.

Most of the heavyweight candidates being touted as possible rivals to Brown – David Miliband, Charles Clarke, John Hutton, Alan Johnson and Alan Milburn (all of them notably male) – decided not to stand. John McDonnell and his fellow left-winger Michael Meacher did stand but could not attract enough nominations to force a vote. Blair, sounding like he had been kidnapped and forced by his tormentors to read from a prepared script, said Brown would make an 'excellent' prime minister.[32]

MORE THAN AN ADO ABOUT NOTHING

Many commentators and most of Blair's supporters in the Labour Party maintained that the TB-GBs had nothing to do with ideology or policy and everything to do with personality and with Brown's ambition. Brown, on this reading, just did not like Blair, finding him too glib and too obsessed with his own image. Blair, for his part, no doubt often found Brown overbearing, dogmatic, rude and quite possibly a bit of a bore. Add to this Brown's resentment at the way in which Blair had pushed him to one side a few days after John Smith's death and had repeatedly broken what he, Brown, considered to have been cast-iron assurances to resign, and it is not hard to see how their relationship had deteriorated so spectacularly. Andrew Adonis, a key minister in Blair's later years and nobody's fool, subscribes to the idea that, in the end, the TB-GBs were primarily about personality and ambition. To this end, Adonis observes that when he was a parliamentary secretary at the Department of Education, Brown routinely opposed everything he was doing. In May 2007, with Blair on the way out, Brown asked to meet Adonis and told him he was doing great work which he was keen for him to continue. Adonis describes leaving the meeting and 'walking around St James's Park in a daze admiring the pelicans and contemplating the peculiarity of politics'.[33]

Yet whilst there was, no doubt, a lot of personal politics at play in the TB-GBs, there were also elements of principled disagreement. Blair and Brown were foundational Labour Party modernizers in the 1990s but had come to hold very different views about what modernization would require going forward. Blair's view was, basically, that New Labour needed to *keep* modernizing. Brown had never really, properly, *got* New

Labour. To him, it had all been about winning elections.[34] As a result, if he ever became leader, Brown would pursue a 'kind of uneasy and ultimately muddled compromise, with, basically, Old Labour organisational politics, and bits of New Labour policy, together with trade-offs to the left'.[35] That was one side of the story. The other side, Brown's side, was that he had not changed and that he still believed in all the things he had always believed in when he first became shadow chancellor in 1994. It was Blair who had moved to the right and lost the plot. In *Apocalypse Now*, Francis Ford Coppola's Vietnam War reworking of Joseph Conrad's *Heart of Darkness*, Captain Benjamin L. Willard, played by Martin Sheen, is sent on a secret mission to assassinate Colonel Kurtz. Kurtz has resigned his command but remains very much in control of his men, refusing to return to base and terrorizing the local population. To Brown and his supporters, Blair, by the mid-2000s, had become a kind of Kurtz *redux*.

It is worth returning to the European leg of the story as well. In the late 1990s Brown seemed, at times, to be edging towards accepting the economic case for Britain joining the European Single Currency, whilst Blair seemed to be focused on the political problems a commitment to joining would pose. At some point prior to the 2001 General Election, the ground seemed to shift. With the British economy booming, Brown came to doubt the economic case for joining and feared that, if Britain joined at the wrong rate, it would do lasting damage to the British economy.[36] Blair, for his part, seems to have edged towards a view that Britain, if it was ever going to become a full and proper member of the European Union, just needed to get on with it. Blair told the 2001 Labour Party conference that Britain should adopt the Single Currency if the economic conditions were right.[37] Eighteen months later, shortly before the start of the Iraq War, he told the French ambassador that he wanted Britain to join before the next general election.[38]

For Blair to clear the way for Britain to join the Single Currency, the Treasury needed to look again at the evidence and decide that the economic indicators had changed and that joining was now in Britain's interest. That was a problem. Whatever else he controlled, Blair certainly did not control the Treasury. Sure enough, having gone back and looked at the issues again, the Treasury decided it had been right to rule against joining the first time and in April 2003 presented Blair with a draft assessment which said just that. Brown was happy. Blair was not.

At the end of the presentation accompanying the arrival of the report, there was a long silence, broken by Blair saying, 'I don't accept your conclusions.' He went on to demand revisions that would leave open the possibility of a referendum on the issue later in the year.[39] In the end, senior civil servants got involved and the draft was tweaked and toned down. The assessment that was eventually published nevertheless remained, on balance, sceptical of the case for joining the Single Currency.[40] For a brief while, it looked like this would lead to a political showdown. In the end, and when the issue was brought to Cabinet, Blair backed away.

This looks like a defeat for Blair, and it was. It can also be read as evidence of Blair's overriding sense of political caution. Blair knew enough to recognize that the Single Currency would be tough to sell to the British public, and that losing a referendum on the issue might fatally damage his leadership. He could have decided that it was a risk worth taking and promoted a technocratic, expert-driven case for joining; however, this would have been a difficult ask at a point when so many experts in the Treasury were opposed. Blair, in the end, called it a day. Given everything that went wrong in the Eurozone economies from 2010 onwards – problems the Treasury had partly anticipated in its assessment – the government probably dodged a bullet.[41]

One other obvious policy disagreement between Blair and Brown related to public-service reform. When it came to the NHS, Blair eventually reached a view that markets, competition and choice offered the right way forward (pp. 38–9). Brown, for his part, was not against the idea of NHS reform. He had been an enthusiastic supporter of setting targets – not least because it offered a way by which the Treasury could link the promise of future spending increases to better results and greater Treasury control. He was however suspicious of the case being made for foundation hospitals and outright hostile to Blair's talk of markets and competition. One of his arguments was that choice was largely meaningless in the public sector because it would require spare capacity in the hospitals with lower costs – which would be seen by the public as wasteful – and closures in areas where the hospitals were underperforming, which would be politically suicidal. Brown also argued that, when it came to the public sector in general, and the NHS in particular, 'there are values far beyond those of contracts, markets and exchanges'.[42] This was the classic old-school, non-Blairite social democratic position (pp. 39–40). Free markets, if regulated, can work. Some things are, however, too valuable to be left to the vagaries of the price mechanism. Blair, as far as Brown was concerned, was betraying the original New Labour cause.

This leads on to a final issue, equality. In Chapter 3 I gave Anthony Crosland's *The Future of Socialism* as the template for Labour's social democratic ideology. To recap, Crosland argued that Labour had over-invested in the socialist principle of public ownership and that, if the party stood for anything, it ought to stand for greater equality through higher public expenditure and redistribution. Brown remained absolutely convinced of the merits of this argument, going so far as to write a laudatory foreword to the fiftieth anniversary edition of *The Future of Socialism* in 2006.[43] As chancellor, Brown walked the walk, overseeing the implementation and championing the cause of the minimum wage, tax credits (up to £20 billion of tax credits a year by 2008/9), Sure Start centres, a 'windfall' tax on the privatized utility companies and increases in overseas aid, as well as higher public expenditure.[44]

New Labour often avoided taking difficult political decisions. But Brown's policies when he was chancellor were far from being either risk-averse or underwhelming. One study calculated that the net effect of central government tax and benefit reforms between 1997 and 2010 was such that the poorest 10 per cent of households gained, on average, an amount equal to just short of 13 per cent of their income, with the richest 10 per cent losing an amount equal to nearly 9 per cent of their net income.[45] This is one important reason why the proceeds of the economic boom were distributed across the income spectrum. It is also why the Gini Coefficient,* which had, in the case of income *before* housing costs were considered, risen significantly from 0.253 in 1979 to 0.333 in 1996/7, then stabilized, before rising fractionally to 0.352 in 2006/7.[46] Blair, for his part, was not against greater income equality per se. But when he spoke about equality, he tended to talk about equality of opportunity rather than equality of outcome. He was also convinced that New Labour would run into political quicksand if it raised and kept raising taxes. He was prepared to make exceptions to this rule, such as the increase in National Insurance Contributions to

---

* The Gini Coefficient, named after the Italian statistician and sociologist Corrado Gini, measures inequality on a scale running from 0 (completely equal) to 1 (perfectly unequal).

pay for more NHS spending. However, his general political position was that higher taxation was and always would be a death-trap for New Labour.

DID IT MATTER?

The TB-GBS are, undoubtedly, an important part of the history of New Labour. They are however also part of a wider political story. At a point when another relationship between another prime minister, Boris Johnson, and his chancellor, Sajid Javid, was disintegrating, the *Financial Times*'s chief political correspondent, Robert Shrimsley, argued that 'good government often depends on senior ministers – and the Chancellor in particular – being able to fight bad ideas'.[47] The Treasury tends to a view that all public spending is guilty and wasteful until proven innocent. The resulting creative tension, Shrimsley argued, ultimately makes for better policy. A prime minister who could do whatever they wanted, or a Treasury which could veto any and every policy idea, would end up making more mistakes. Geoff Mulgan, the director of the prime minister's Policy Unit between 1997 and 2004, has a similar view, arguing that competition between Blair and Brown was healthy because it 'provided a check on both of them from doing things that might be self-destructive'.[48] On this reading, the Treasury offers one of the few meaningful checks within a highly centralized winner-takes-all political system. Blair's greatest political misjudgement, the one which continues to define his legacy, is Iraq; and the problem with Iraq, it might be noted, was not that the Foreign Office was offering an alternative viewpoint and was too powerful, but that there was, in the end, only one voice which really counted – that of Tony Blair.

There is however a downside here. Principled arguments between 10 Downing Street and the Treasury may have their advantages, but in the British system, where there is little room for formal and open disagreements within the government, the arguments take place behind closed doors with only the drip-feed of hostile press briefings to keep the public half aware of what might be happening. This is not good for the health of a democracy and for the sense that policies, once agreed, are legitimate. Divisions at the top of the government are also exceptionally time consuming in an environment in which time is a scarce resource. John

Prescott talks about the 'hundreds of phone calls, meetings, pre-summits, summits and dinners on various Blair–Brown issues'.[49] Multiply this across dozens of ministers and you end up with a lot of people wasting a lot of time. It is also clear that, above and beyond the sheer time they consumed, the TB-GBs sometimes resulted in policy paralysis. Government departments across Whitehall found themselves caught in the crossfire and under pressure to choose a side. Gordon Brown would, meanwhile, in the view of Steve Robson, a former senior Treasury official, 'take an opposing view simply to bugger up Tony'.[50] Policy initiatives were sidelined not because they were necessarily intrinsically flawed, but because they were seen as originating in either Number 10 or Number 11.

All political parties are and always have been coalitions of people who disagree with each other about a lot of things but agree to stick together because they share certain values in common, as well as a shared loathing of the other political parties. Britain was still a partyocracy in the 2000s, but it was one in which the governing party fell apart, and Blair and Brown and their supporters got to re-enact a version of the English Civil War. The TB-GBs generated some great stories and amusing moments. Yet it offered a profoundly depressing advert for the state of British democracy. New Labour ended not with a bang, not even with a whimper. It ended as a trailer for *The Thick of It*.

PART FOUR

Crash

In the early hours of Monday, 15 September 2008, seven years, four days and a short ten-minute walk away from the Twin Towers, where on 11 September 2001 history had already turned, Lehman Brothers filed bankruptcy papers in a New York courthouse. Within a few days the global financial system had fallen apart. Not long after it became apparent that one political and economic age was ending and another, less pleasant one, was beginning. New Labour's boast of having ended the age of boom and bust was discredited. Labour's social democratic vision of standing back whilst the economy grew and then redistributing the proceeds was no longer viable. The question that remained was about what would come next. I start this story, however, not with Lehman Brothers but with the Northern Rock bank, whose collapse, a year earlier, was initially attributed to a mixture of bad management and bad luck. In fact, Northern Rock was operating a business model that contained baked-in vulnerabilities in its balance sheet. It turned out that it was not the only financial institution to do so. Hence the switch, in Chapter 19, from Newcastle, where Northern Rock was based, to New York.

For Gordon Brown, moments of haywire crisis seemed to appear nearly as often as new Gordon Ramsey television shows. The 2008 financial crisis was the big one and it was also the one which he was best equipped to deal with: working alongside the Bank of England to roll forward the frontiers of the state to protect the economy and – his critics would maintain – his own political future. Yet it was the MPs' expenses scandal, the subject of Chapter 20, which probably did him the most political damage. In May 2008 the *Daily Telegraph* began publishing stories about Cabinet ministers' (and, later, common-or-garden backbench MPs') expense claims (on more than a few occasions for their distinctly uncommon gardens). The expenses scandal was a huge political moment. It generated a real and genuine sense of anger and confirmed for a lot of people something they already thought they knew – that politicians are in it for themselves and can't be trusted.

Part Four is distinctive in that it only contains four chapters. One obvious consequence of the financial crisis was austerity and I examine the formation and fortunes of the Coalition government, which championed austerity and its economic consequences, in Part Five, *Union*. Before all that, however, I begin this Part by describing the nature and consequences of another policy hyper-failure of the 2000s: the British housing market. Margaret Thatcher bought herself much political capital in the 1980s with the 'right to buy' programme. The Northern Rock and other banks made a lot of money in the 2000s from home lending. And, as we will see, New Labour found a sure-fire way of wasting a lot of the proceeds of the economic boom through housing.

17
Broken Homes

LOCATION, LOCATION, LOCATION

The first episode of the first series of *Location, Location, Location* was broadcast on Channel 4 in May 2000. The format is very simple. The presenters, Kirstie Allsopp and Phil Spencer, sometimes tagged as the Mr and Mrs of Comfort TV, meet and work with a couple (in later series, two couples) who want to buy a home in a particular area.[1] *Location* was one of a number of housing/design/DIY programmes that became a fixture of daytime or early evening television schedules in the 2000s. Think *Changing Rooms* (1996–2004), *Property Ladder* (2001–9), *Homes Under the Hammer* (2003 onwards) and *Grand Designs* (1999 onwards). *Location* is unlikely to be cited alongside *The Sopranos* (1999), *The West Wing* (1999) or *The Wire* (2002) as examples of the start of what has sometimes been described as a second golden age for television.[2] But *Location* achieved solid ratings, no doubt made its production company a lot of money and offered occasionally interesting moments of human drama.

The narrative arc of each episode of *Location* begins with unrealistic expectations on the part of the couple about what they think they could buy. This is followed by dawning disappointment; brief despair and bickering; and then positive thinking, teamwork, creativity, compromise and, eventually, a last-gasp triumph. If Kirstie Allsopp and Phil Spencer are the stars, the best supporting-acting role in the 2000s was played by rising house prices. Prices were important because the programme would not really have worked if a couple had started out thinking they could buy a small flat in Acton only to be told by Kirstie they could in fact afford to buy a Georgian mansion in Chelsea. Instead, each couple had to start knowing what they wanted to buy and thinking they could, at a stretch, probably afford it – only to be told that they were not even close.

Luckily, house prices never let *Location* down. Inflation was low and stable in Britain for the 2000s at around 1–2 per cent a year. An independent Bank of England with a remit to raise interest rates if inflation ever exceeded its target (2.5 per cent) probably helped keep inflation low. China's membership of the World Trade Organization from December 2001 onwards, which resulted in a glut of cheap imports, also made a significant difference (pp. 465–6). Whatever the reason though, house prices were the notable exception to the rule. Between 2000 and 2007 they rose by an average of 11 per cent a year.[3] They rose faster in the South of England than they did in the Midlands or the North, and they rose faster in England than they did in Scotland, Wales or Northern Ireland.[4] But, with only a handful of exceptions, house prices rose faster than inflation and wages everywhere. In Edinburgh, where, in *Location*'s second episode, Jane and Hew were looking to buy, the average price of a detached house went from £140,000 in 2004 to £314,000 in 2007. In Bolton, where Susan and Neil wanted to buy in *Location*'s fourth episode, the average price of a semi-detached house went from £45,000 to £127,000 between 2000 and 2007. In Surrey (Fiona and James in the fifth episode) the price of a terraced house went from £119,000 to £256,000 over the same seven years. In Manchester (Colin and Anthony in the first episode of the second series) the price of a flat went from £40,000 to £124,000 and in Bristol (Nicky and Brian in the third episode of the second series) from £62,000 to £154,000.[5]

All of this came, eventually, to be seen as freakishly normal and a symbol of the economic boom and the rolling of the good times. Newspapers, most consistently the *Daily Express* and *Daily Mail*, celebrated rising prices one day before bemoaning the impossibility of getting on the property ladder the next. Everyone spent a lot of time talking about house prices and how they had a friend who had bought their flat in 1985 and was now a multi-millionaire who was thinking about buying a small Premier League football club. What tended to get lost in all of this was the fact that the housing boom was, largely, a very British thing. Canada was just about the only other G7 economy which had a housing boom. In Germany, not exactly an economic disaster story in the 2000s, house prices tracked retail inflation.[6] Indeed, one of the reasons why the Treasury decided, in 2003, that joining the Single Currency was not in Britain's economic interests (pp. 206–7) related to differences in the British and European housing markets and, in particular, the price of housing and its volatility. The resulting story about what went wrong in the housing market makes for grim reading. Housing became an income-destroying Ponzi scheme where large parts of the gains of the economic boom were dissipated.

A MATTER OF DEMAND AND SUPPLY

The basic reason why house prices went up by so much in the 2000s is that the demand for houses increased significantly whilst the supply of new housing largely stagnated.

Demand for housing rose for several reasons. The overall size of the British population increased by nearly 4 million people between 2000 and 2010.[7] Over this same period, the average number of people living in each home fell, with the number of single-person households rising by around 1½ million.[8] Demand to buy a house also went up because incomes were rising during the boom whilst interest rates remained relatively low. A five-year fixed-rate mortgage would have come attached with a 9 per cent-plus interest rate in the mid-1990s. By the mid-2000s they were available for 4 per cent, which made buying a lot more attractive. Moreover, lots of people were buying in the expectation prices would continue rising. David Miles of Imperial College London and Vladimir Pillonca of the International Monetary Fund estimate that up to a third of the increase in British house prices during the 2000s can be attributed to the expectation of capital gains.[9] Finally, we can add to this list of reasons the wall of money flowing into London, the South-east and a few other major cities from overseas buyers.[10] By the time Russia invaded Ukraine in 2022, Transparency International estimated that Russians suspected of having links to the Kremlin or to corruption owned £1.5 billion-worth of property in Britain.[11]

When it comes to the supply of new housing a little historical context is needed. In the late 1960s getting on for 400,000 new permanent dwellings were being completed each year in Britain.[12] By the late 1970s that had fallen to around 270,000. By the end of the 1980s it had fallen to around 220,000, and by the end of the 1990s it had fallen again, to just over 180,000. In the 2000s, for the first time in a long time, the numbers started to climb again. By 2007, just as the boom was getting close to popping, 215,000 new dwellings were being completed. That was, however, still well below the European average and, given the increase in demand, not nearly enough to stop average house prices from climbing.[13] To put this into a comparative perspective, in 2011 England had 434 dwellings per 1,000 people, compared to 510 in France and 495 in Germany.[14] Then, when the financial crisis began, the building market fell apart. By 2012 new completions had fallen to 133,000.

Which leads to the next obvious question: why were so few houses being built? This is where everything starts to get a little more contentious, but a series of reports published in the 2000s found the main problem was a planning system that was highly decentralized, expensive, complicated, time consuming and weighted against the approval of new developments.[15] The result, according to Anthony Breach of the Centre for Cities, is that Britain 'does not have a planning system, we have a rationing system'.[16] This was not about inefficient (or corrupt) bureaucrats. It was about local politics. In an otherwise highly centralized political system in which local government was sidelined, planning remained largely a local responsibility. To understand why local authorities were tardy when it came to building new homes we need to go back to the politics. No matter what powers local authorities hold in relation to planning, local government remains an appendage of the central state when it comes to taxation. By 2010 95 per cent of all taxes collected in Britain were collected at a national rather than local level (slightly up from 94 per cent in 2000). The average across the other six G7 countries (Canada, France, Germany, Italy, Japan and the USA) was just over 70 per cent.[17] Local authorities do not even come close to covering their own bills. Most of the money councils spend is allocated to them by central government.

This matters because it means local authorities do not really stand to gain a great deal from approving plans to build lots of new houses because most of the additional tax revenue from doing so will go to central government. Most of the complaints from existing residents about those new houses – the impact they have on local services, the views they block, the green land they take, the impact they have on the value of existing homes – will, however, end up being directed squarely at local councillors and local planning teams. All pain and very little gain does not make for a good system if what you want is more houses to be built. As such, the political logic for local councils and local councillors (who must, of course, stand for re-election) is to agree with the general principle that new homes are needed but oppose individual applications.

The other reason why the supply of new housing stagnated in the 1990s and 2000s is that local authorities basically stopped building new homes from the 1980s onwards, putting extra pressure on the private market. If we go back to the late 1960s, something like 40 per cent of all the new houses being built in Britain were being built by local authorities. A large part of that stock was sold in the 1980s and 1990s under the terms of the 'right to buy' scheme.[18] By 2019 a total of 2.6 million homes had been sold.[19] That was a huge jolt to the housing market. Just as importantly, however, local authorities stopped building new homes to replace those being sold. In 1999 just 320 new local authority homes were completed in Britain, and by 2007 this had fallen to 250.[20] Housing associations took up some of this slack. In 2000/1 there were 22,000 new housing association completions. By 2007/8 this had crept up to 28,000.[21] This was better than nothing but it was one or two hundred thousand new homes lower than it needed to be to have a chance of increasing overall supply in a way which might have come close to making a real difference to house prices.

New Labour knew about the structural flaws in the British housing market and spent a lot of time talking about the importance of building new homes. It devised new spatial strategies and set local targets within local development frameworks and did all sorts of other kinds of impressive-sounding planning.[22] It even set aside money to build new homes for key workers who were locked out of the London housing market. But New Labour ducked any radical changes. It could have decided to rip up the local planning system and replace it with a regional, or even national, one in which areas were zoned and housing developments fast-tracked within designated areas. It could have changed taxation rules in ways that would have given local authorities a proper incentive to build more new homes and enough money to compensate existing residents. Alternatively, and given how low interest rates were, the government could have borrowed money to allow new public housing to be built, or, failing that, allowed local authorities to do so.

The Labour government could also have significantly relaxed existing restrictions on housing development in the 13 per cent of the green belt land in England which girdles London and the other major cities (London's green belt is three times the size of the capital itself). This would have caused howls of political protest because opinion polls showed consistent support for existing green belt rules.[23] Politically tough as it would have been, ministers could, nevertheless, have pointed out that most green belt land consists not of woodlands, paths and fields – as many people imagine – but farming land, which, whilst obviously useful for growing things like food, has, at best, limited public access.[24] Similarly, when faced with arguments about how the country was already overrun with housing and full beyond bursting, ministers could have noted that less than 6 per cent of land in England is used for residential purposes and that golf courses occupy twice as much land as houses.[25] But after John Prescott had been derided for mis-speaking during a 1998 radio interview and saying 'the green belt is a Labour achievement and we mean to build on it', there was very little appetite within the government for a political battle over the green belt.[26] In the end, ministers looked at the political coalitions and the political imbalance between short-term costs and long-term benefits and decided to fiddle around the edges. In a centralized partyocracy, prioritizing the actual construction of additional tens of thousands of new houses did not make electoral sense, even if talking about doing so sometimes did.

WINNERS AND LOSERS

Housing consumes the largest part of the income of most households. For most people a house will be by far the single most expensive purchase they make in a lifetime. So, it is not surprising the housing boom created winners and losers. Let's start with the winners.

The largest housing development firms in what became, during this time, a highly concentrated market, did very well for themselves. Barratt Developments' pre-tax profits rose from £178 million in 2001 to well over £400 million by 2007. Persimmon's pre-tax profits topped £500 million. Going back to the earlier question about why so few houses were being built during this decade, the profits of some of these companies seem to have been boosted by 'land banking': the name given to the process by which building companies, in the expectation prices will continue to rise, sit on land which has planning permission rather than develop it. Land banking is potentially risky if prices fall but can boost long-term profits if they continue to rise. It certainly has the effect of reducing the number of housing completions. Estimates vary; however a detailed study by the Office of Fair Trading, published in 2008, concluded that 'overall, the evidence . . . suggests that homebuilders are not delaying building on permissioned land to an extent that would appreciably affect the rate of delivery of new homes'.[27]

With prices rising, owners of land with planning permission to build new houses also made windfall profits, measured in billions of pounds annually. In his detailed analysis of the rents extracted from land sales, the political economist Brett Christophers shows how one key group of beneficiaries were the privatized utility companies and their shareholders.[28] The Harworth Group (formerly UK Coal), Severn Trent Water, the Royal Mail and the National Grid all sold land that had previously been publicly owned for hundreds of millions of pounds during the 2000s. At the other end of the income scale, windfall profits of upwards of £70 billion also accrued to people who bought their council homes at a hefty government discount.[29]

Owner-occupiers as a group also generally did well from the boom. Because interest rates were relatively low in the 2000s, anyone who could afford to buy a home found that higher initial house prices could be offset against lower mortgage interest rates. Meanwhile, and in return, owners could sit back and watch whilst the value of their house rose each year. Some of this gain was of course illusory. Any first-time buyers who, on paper, had seen the value of their house double would, if they wanted to trade-up, still need to buy a larger house whose price would probably also have doubled. But anyone who had paid off either all or most of their mortgage before house prices had rocketed, made windfall gains from the housing boom. Two economists at Heriot-Watt University, Abdulkader Mostafa and Colin Jones, estimate that a first-time buyer in the mid-1970s would, by 2011, have had an average return of £12 for every £1 they initially invested in buying their house.[30]

Another way of looking at this is to say that one of the key groups of beneficiaries of the boom were the 'Baby Boomers' (born between 1946 and 1964) who had bought their houses when they were cheap, seen the value of their private pensions rise and, on top of this, benefited from a near doubling in the value of the State Pension in the 2000s, alongside the introduction of Pension Credit in 2003.[31] Overall, pensioner incomes grew by 28 per cent in real, inflation-adjusted terms between 2001 and 2009 (compared to 6 per cent growth for working-age households).

Indeed, by around 2010/11 the median income of a pensioner had over-taken that of the median working person.[32]

Finally, landlords were another group who did very well out of the housing boom. Because the supply of housing was so tight, private-sector rents rose by an average of over 40 per cent in England between 2000 and 2007.[33] The introduction of 'buy-to-let' mortgages, favour-able tax breaks and the steady elimination of assured tenancy contracts made renting out a property even more attractive. Some large compa-nies, including Grainger, the Grosvenor Group and Annington (which acquired a large part of the Ministry of Defence's housing stock in 1996), accumulated large portfolios of rental houses in the 2000s. Most rental properties were, however, owned by people who had bought one or two properties and were using the extra money they earned to either pay their own mortgage or supplement their pensions.[34]

The most obvious set of losers from the housing boom were people who were unable to get on the housing ladder in the 2000s, got on late and so missed out on most of the windfall gains, or could not afford to get on at all. Perhaps most obviously, anyone renting lost out. True, average rents did not rise as quickly as average house prices in the 2000s. Never-theless, they rose by enough to ensure that, by 2008, nearly a quarter of those who were renting were spending more than half of their income on rent.[35] Moreover, many of those tenants were paying sizable rents for poor-quality accommodation that had been subdivided to within an inch of its life. By 2008 44 per cent of all privately rented properties fell below the decent homes standard set by the government.[36]

No doubt there were lots of well-paid twenty- and thirty-somethings who were renting luxury flats with swimming pools, gyms and private balconies in the 2000s. For the most part, however, those who were renting were (and are) disproportionately the poor and the young who could not afford to buy. The simplest way of seeing this is to look at average household income by tenure. In 2008/9 average household income in England was £519 per week. For owner-occupiers with a mortgage the average was £804. For those renting privately it was £465 and for those renting from a local authority or from a housing associ-ation it was £235 and £240 respectively.[37] Unless they either fell into very well-paid jobs very quickly or could count on support from their parents or grandparents, 'Millennials' (born between the early 1980s and the mid-1990s), were particularly vulnerable.

This was one facet of what the former Conservative minister David Willetts labelled as *The Pinch* in a book published in 2010.[38] Demographics matter. Politicians are, for the most part, rational creatures. They go where the votes are – which means the policy agenda can become skewed towards the interests of the largest and loudest. The 'Boomers' constituted a large political constituency who, Willetts argues, politicians in all parties pandered to when it came to tax breaks, pensions and housing. The Boomers were the generation that was most likely to have made windfall gains from buying their houses cheaply, often on fixed-rate mortgages, in the late 1960s and 1970s. They were the group who could often afford to buy and rent a second property. The Millennials and their successors, 'Gen Z' (born since the mid-1990s), have been left holding the sharp end of this stick: paying university tuition fees; missing out on fixed-benefit pension schemes; and being forced to accept precarious, sometimes zero-hour contract jobs in the 'gig economy'. To add insult to injury, they have also become 'Generation Rent'.[39] In 1984, when the average Baby Boomer was in their late twenties/early thirties, two-thirds had already bought a home. For Generation X (born between 1965 and 1980) the equivalent figure was 59 per cent. For Millennials (1981–96) it was just 37 per cent.[40] As the Scottish comedian Hannah Fairweather puts it, 'By my age, my parents had a house and a family, and to be fair so do I, but it is the same house and the same family.'[41]

A REVERSE REDISTRIBUTION MACHINE

In Chapter 4 on the fuel crisis, I showed how the gains in household income during the boom years were evenly distributed across the income spectrum. The figures I used then related to *before* housing-cost income. Figure 3 shows just how different things look once the focus is upon income *after* housing costs. It does so by looking at the *proportion* of before housing-cost income different groups along the income scale spent on housing from 1961 through until 2006/7, for four different groups: the poorest 5 per cent of households in each year; the poorest 5–10 per cent of households; the median household; and the richest 5 per cent of households. Consider, as one example, the richest 5 per cent of households in 2006/7. The average weekly *before* housing-costs income of this group was £1,343. Its average income after housing costs was £1,225. The difference between these two is £118 and £118 as a percentage of the before housing-cost income of £1,343 is 8.8 per cent (which is, rounded-up, the number shown in the very bottom right-hand side of Figure 3). These numbers look complicated but the story here is simple. From the early 1960s through until the late 1970s the four groups in question spent a similar and stable proportion of their before housing-cost income on housing. Then, from the early 1980s, all hell breaks loose. The median household ends up, a quarter of a century later, spending a slightly lower proportion of its income on housing. The richest 5 per cent of households end up spending way less on housing, whilst the poorest households end up spending considerably more. By 2006/7, these differences were eye-watering. In that year, the median household spent 13 per cent of its before housing-cost income on housing; the poorest 5 per cent of households fully 39 per cent; the poorest 5–10 per cent of households 28 per cent; and the richest 5 per cent of households just 9 per cent.[42]

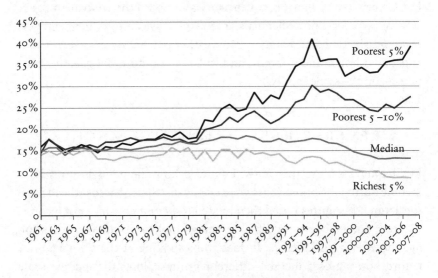

Figure 3. Housing Costs as a Percentage of *Before* Housing-Cost Income, 1961–2006/7

The data used in this table was taken from the Institute for Fiscal Studies, 'Living standards, poverty and inequality in the UK' (https://ifs.org.uk/living-standards-poverty-and-inequality-uk).[43]

We can now come to wealth. This is another part of the not-quite-as-good-as-it-might-have-seemed New Labour story. The Gini Coefficient measuring income inequality *before* housing costs flatlined in the 2000s, standing at 0.352 by 2006/7 (the scale running from 0, completely equal, to 10, perfectly unequal; p. 208). For household income *after* housing costs the figure was 0.393 by 2006/7 (growing to 0.404 by 2009/10).[44] However, that does not capture the full picture. Wealth inequality was increasing in the 2000s (pp. 104–5). Overall, the wealthiest 10 per cent of people held 64 per cent of the country's total wealth in 1990; 68 per cent in 2000; and over 70 per cent by 2010.[45] Housing was an important part of this story. The Gini Coefficient for wealth held in the form of property between 2006 and 2008 was 0.62.[46]

New Labour was a social democratic party that wanted to raise public expenditure and reduce inequality. In many ways, it delivered this. Public expenditure on health, education, social protection, the environment and public safety all dramatically increased in the 2000s. The minimum wage and tax credits went some way to stabilizing the growth in income inequality. However, what New Labour achieved with one hand, the housing boom took away with the other. Housing took money away from the poorest households and the young and gave it to the richest households and the old.

A HIGH PRICE TO PAY

The economic costs of rising house prices in the 2000s were masked by rising incomes and low interest rates. That is why the average proportion of income being consumed by mortgage repayments in households with a mortgage only increased slightly, from 19 per cent in 2000 to 21 per cent in 2007.[47] So it could be argued that people weren't worse off as a result of higher house prices than they would otherwise have been. But this would be pushing a glass-half-full argument beyond the point where the glass is going to shatter. What really counts is that things should have been a lot *better* and weren't, because large dollops of the growth in income resulting from the economic boom ended up being spent on deposits and mortgage payments on what was largely the same basic housing stock. That is key. People were not spending more money to get *better* houses. For the most part, they were spending more money to get the same thing.

In fact, it was worse. The new houses being built in the 2000s were not, overall, nicer houses. Quite the opposite. To try and keep the overall cost of a house somewhere approaching just about affordable when the costs of the basic land on which houses were being built was spiralling, developers kept their profit margins and economized on the costs of the houses they were building. One result, according to the Royal Institute of British Architects, was the proliferation of 'shameful shoebox homes'.[48] Houses got smaller, the materials used to build them got cheaper, and efforts to ensure all new homes met the highest insulation standards got pushed to the back of the queue.

Another result was higher debt. The amount of money people were paying each month on their mortgages might have remained broadly the same because interest rates were so low, but the total amount of the debt they were carrying was, because of house price inflation, much higher. In the first quarter of 2000 the value of total mortgage approvals for house purchases to individuals (excluding remortgages) stood at £14 billion. By the first quarter of 2008 it had more than doubled to £29 billion. Cumulatively, and over this entire period, total lending amounted to £1,104 billion.[49] To a significant extent, Britain's boom was built on, and fuelled by, debt in an economic system the political economist Colin Crouch described as a form of 'privatized Keynesianism' (I discuss Keynesianism in more detail in Chapter 22).[50]

The housing boom also cost taxpayers money. To try and make housing more affordable for low-income households, successive generations of governments – New Labour included – have thrown public money at, variously, mortgage interest tax relief, capital gains tax relief, stamp duty holidays and various grants and offers for first-time buyers. All of this made it seem like the government was doing something to make house-buying more affordable but, in reality, it achieved very little. Extra money created more demand. More demand meant higher prices. Higher prices meant more demand for more government action. Which started the cycle again. At the other end of the income scale, and to make renting more affordable, governments also spent huge amounts on housing benefit. During the longest economic boom in over a century, housing-benefit expenditure rose from just over £11 billion in 2000/1 to nearly £15 billion in 2006/7. When the recession came and the number of new houses being completed each year fell through the floor and rents rose further, housing-benefit expenditure increased to over £24 billion a year in 2013/14.[51] The result was a double whammy. The housing market failed, and the taxpayer paid for that failure. This was a very high price to pay for the light entertainment provided by *Location, Location, Location.*

18

The Run on the Rock

ENTER ROBERT PESTON, STAGE LEFT

On the evening of Thursday, 13 September 2007, the BBC's business editor, Robert Peston, reported that the Northern Rock building society was in trouble and had asked for emergency financial support from the Bank of England.[1] The next morning, queues of people wanting to close their accounts formed outside branches. There was an atmosphere of panic. In one incident, police were called to a branch in Cheltenham where two customers had barricaded the branch manager in her office after she had refused to allow them to withdraw a million pounds.[2] Those attempting to withdraw their money were not necessarily over-reacting (even if the Cheltenham couple probably were). Under the arrangements in place at the time, bank deposits were only fully insured up to a maximum limit of £2,000. If Northern Rock was in trouble, it made sense to act first and ask questions later.

The implosion of Northern Rock caught almost everyone completely unaware. There had not been a run on a bank on this scale in Britain since the late nineteenth century.[3] That said, the financial markets had been in turmoil for some time. The American housing market had been struggling for over a year. In June 2007 two large hedge funds run by the US investment bank Bear Stearns, which had invested heavily in subprime mortgages, had collapsed. On 9 August, the giant French bank BNP Paribas had told investors they could no longer withdraw their money from two of its funds. The same day, the European Central Bank had injected €95 billion into the banking market to add liquidity. Northern Rock itself had issued a profit warning that July, when its shares had lost a third of their value since the start of the year,[4] and Northern Rock managers had alerted their regulator, the Financial Services Authority

(FSA), and the Bank of England to the fact that it was struggling to raise money to fund its operations in mid-August. Efforts had immediately begun, behind the scenes, to find a buyer for the building society. Later that month, several other banks had approached the Bank of England asking for support.[5] The governor of the Bank of England, Mervyn King, was initially wary of being seen to be too supportive. If banks saw one of their own being bailed out they might, he thought, start taking more risks.[6]

The Court of the Bank of England* met on Friday 14 September to discuss their options. According to one of its members:

> We were told there would be a meeting of the Court. Instead of coming to the bank, where we would be photographed coming in the front door, we were all to meet outside the McDonald's in Liverpool Street where we would be picked up in a people carrier with darkened windows and driven in through the back of the bank. There were two problems with this. Firstly, Robert Peston had already broken the story about Northern Rock. Secondly, there were two McDonald's outside Liverpool Street. Half of us were outside one, and the rest of us were outside the other.[7]

Amidst fears the Northern Rock bank run could, if left unchecked, spread to other banks, fears of creating new 'moral hazard' risks via a bail-out were put to one side. Liquidity support, cash, was offered to Northern Rock – and to other banks that needed it – in return for collateral in the form of balance-sheet assets. When this looked like it might not be enough to calm things, the chancellor, Alistair Darling, announced on Monday 17 September that all the deposits in Northern Rock would be fully guaranteed by the government.

Darling's statement did the trick. The run on the Northern Rock ended and did not spread to other banks. A few weeks later the chairman of Northern Rock, Matt Ridley, announced his resignation. The bank's chief executive officer, Adam Applegarth, followed him in December, leaving with a £785,000 golden handshake, a £2.6 million pension and £10,000 to improve security at his £2.5 million Northumberland home.[8] Meanwhile, unsurprisingly, the government and the Bank of England were struggling to find anyone willing to buy Northern Rock. Eventually accepting the inevitable, the government announced,

* In effect the Bank's board of directors.

in February 2008, that it was rolling forward the frontiers of the state to take the bank into public ownership. Gordon Brown was not best pleased.[9] But by this stage Northern Rock was already an old and slightly dull story. The newspapers were leading on the norovirus stomach bug; the suspension from Parliament of a Conservative MP, Derek Conway, who had used his parliamentary allowance to employ his son to undertake research work without there being any evidence his son had actually done any work; and a coroner's inquest into the death of Diana Spencer, during which Mohamed Al-Fayed had accused the Royal Family, Tony Blair and the security services of a conspiracy to murder. The travails of the Northern Rock didn't really cut it. What nobody realized was that the collapse of the Northern Rock was simply one of the first scenes in a much larger play.

A 'NASTY BLEMISH'

In the eighteenth century small groups of local workers formed mutual societies to build and buy homes. At first, these societies were dissolved when all their members had been housed. But in the nineteenth century some of them became permanent building societies, open to new members. By the start of the twentieth century nearly two thousand local building societies had been established across Britain. For the next half century or more they continued to provide the largest share of mortgages across the country.

In 1965 the Northern Rock Building Society was formed from the merger of the Northern Counties Permanent Building Society and the Rock Building Society. In 1997, taking advantage of legislation passed in the mid-1980s, Northern Rock effectively privatized itself, buying out its members in return for cash payments. Demutualization, as this process was known, gave the bank's new executive managers greater freedom to borrow money and to grow further and faster. By 2006 Northern Rock had morphed into one of the largest mortgage providers in the country with assets of around £110 billion and annual pre-tax profits of over £600 million, and had become, for many people, a symbol of Britain's entrepreneurial transformation.[10]

At face value, Northern Rock was a very different kind of bank to Lehman Brothers and the other large overseas investment banks, the composition of whose balance sheets was briefly discussed in Part Two (pp. 98–9). In the first place, Northern Rock still looked like a regional rather than a global bank. Its headquarters were in Gosforth, Newcastle, and the bank made a great virtue of its sponsorship of Newcastle United and its local charitable work. Whilst the investment banks and large high-street banks like Barclays and the Royal Bank of Scotland (RBS) were lending money and buying assets on a global scale, Northern Rock was basically still a British bank lending to British people. Moreover, whilst Barclays and RBS were making huge profits during the boom from buying and trading derivatives and other complex financial instruments, Northern Rock was making most of its money from lending people money to buy their own homes.

In the aftermath of the bank's collapse, there were two explanations of what had happened. The first was that in a world in which expertise was everything, Northern Rock was run by a bunch of amateurs. The Northern Rock's chairman, Matt Ridley, a former senior journalist, science writer and a viscount whose father had been chairman before him, was, some suggested, out of his depth.[11] A second argument was that the executives had simply been too greedy. They had pushed too hard and tried to grow the bank too quickly. Executives had invested too heavily in online banking, where customers were notoriously fickle, rather than building more local branches. They had lent money to people with poor credit histories who were always likely to default on their loans, and they had placed managers under intense pressure to meet loan targets.[12]

These two arguments were, for regulators and politicians, comforting. What they implied was that Northern Rock was a bad apple and that there were no real problems with the banking system. In November 2007 an editorial in The Times argued that Northern Rock was no more than a 'nasty blemish on the reputation of Britain's financial system' and, as such, 'little more than an embarrassment'.[13] Not long after, in a speech to the Worshipful Company of International Bankers, Chancellor Alistair Darling highlighted the 'strength and depth of the talent that underpins our truly global financial services industry'; lauded the 'tremendous contribution' financial services make to the UK economy; and assured his audience that the government would not, in the aftermath of the Northern Rock debacle, now 'revert to more heavy-handed or mechanistic regulation'.[14]

The bad-apple argument was, however, off beam. Northern Rock may have *looked* different to the investment banks and largest commercial banks based in London. It may have had a British customer base and may have made most of its money from mortgages. But Northern Rock was, nevertheless, wired into the global financial system and shared with the other banks in it some fundamental flaws. It had borrowed too much money; had too small a capital buffer to protect it from losses; had become too blasé about the risks it was carrying on its balance sheet; had become too dependent upon growth; and was, whatever Alistair Darling was saying, wildly underregulated.

GOSFORTH IS A LONG WAY FROM CALIFORNIA

Banks lend people money. Traditionally, they get that money from taking customer deposits. People save their money in a bank and the bank uses that money to fund mortgages or other kinds of loan. The problem Northern Rock faced in the 1990s was that it wanted to make more loans than it had money in the coffers from its relatively small customer base. To get round this problem it did two things. First, it securitized its loans. Rather than keeping its mortgage loans on its own balance sheet, it sold them to investors across the world. These investors got the promise of a steady stream of repayments; the Northern Rock got large dollops of money which it could use to make more loans.[15] This was one of the crucial ways in which Gosforth and the Northern Rock were connected to the City of London and the global banking system. Northern Rock's securitized assets were sold to other financial institutions across the world. Second, to even out its cash flow between its regular sales of securitized mortgages and to fund further lending, Northern Rock also borrowed money from other banks and financial institutions on what was known as the wholesale funding market. And it had done so on a huge scale. In the late 1990s around 60 per cent of Northern Rock's funding came from deposits. By 2007 only 23 per cent did.[16]

For a long while, it looked like Northern Rock had, via securitization and wholesale borrowing, found a magic money tree. There was a steady stream of borrowers who wanted to take on new mortgages and a lot of investors who wanted to buy those mortgages when they had been securitized. The size of those mortgage loans was increasing because house prices were booming. However, Northern Rock had plenty of people ready to buy its securitized loans because its loan book looked incredibly safe. At a moment when the economy was booming, the proportion of Northern Rock's mortgage loans that were in arrears was low and stable. For the same reason, the bank had no problem borrowing money from other financial institutions across the world and, when it wanted, rolling over those loans. All of which turbo-charged its profits and growth.

In the autumn of 2006 the housing markets in Arizona, California, Florida and Nevada turned. Hundreds of thousands of homeowners, many of them subprime borrowers who had been sold so-called 'teaser loans' on which their interest payments were scheduled to rise dramatically, found themselves struggling to meet mortgage repayments on houses that were now worth less than the value of their loan. Thousands of people, literally, walked away.[17] As a result, the estate agents in an increasingly bloated market, where profits were dropping and fewer people were buying, ran into problems. Some of these estate agents were owned by the banks which had to carry the resulting losses. Other banks had lent money to the estate agents. Even more banks had bought and traded the securitized mortgages underpinning the loans. Whatever way you look at it, the bursting of the housing bubble was bad for the banks.

Gosforth is a long way from California and, unlike some of the other large British banks, Northern Rock had not issued and had not bought securitized subprime 'teaser' loans from other banks. But this did not matter. With the market turning and confidence collapsing, Northern Rock, from late 2006 onwards, found it increasingly hard to sell on its securitized mortgages. Securitization had been the flavour of the month. Now it wasn't. As a result, Northern Rock's previously stable cash flow started to wobble. The same thing happened in the wholesale funding markets. With everything going wrong in the American market, lenders across the world all suddenly became a lot more risk-averse. Northern Rock looked – on paper – as safe as houses, but nobody wanted to take a chance on lending the bank money when spare cash could instead be parked in US Treasury bonds or simply hoarded. So, at the same time as it was struggling to sell its securitized mortgages, Northern Rock was also struggling to borrow money and to roll over its existing loans at anything approaching its previous rate of interest. That was not, by any measure, a good combination.

Northern Rock was not uniquely exposed to the downturn in the securitization and wholesale funding markets. By 2006 around $4 trillion of assets were being securitized annually via the global financial markets and banks were both lending and borrowing money from each other on a huge scale.[18] Across the six largest British banks, customer deposits had fallen from being the equivalent of 57 per cent of bank sheet liabilities in 2000 to just 35 per cent by 2007. Some of the replacement loan money was borrowed on a long-term basis, which allowed banks to weather any short-term downturn. But by 2006, 50 per cent of bank borrowing was being done on a short-term, sometimes weekly, basis.[19]

This brings us to the next part of the story. Banking is and always has been an inherently risky business. To minimize this risk, banks hold capital – the money invested in banks by shareholders and the profits the banks retain which can be used to cover losses when they arise. There are different kinds of capital and different ways of counting capital, but the basic point is that the more capital a bank has relative to the size of its assets, the safer, all else being equal, it is. The problem Northern Rock faced, and – crucially – a problem its investors knew it faced, was that its capital buffers were extremely thin.

In its 2006 annual report, Northern Rock boasted of achieving 'capital efficiency [by] optimising the use of debt and equity capital'.[20] This sounded impressive. What it meant was that Northern Rock had done a good job of reducing the size of its capital buffers relative to its loan book. Northern Rock reported that it was holding £2,600 million in capital, which sounds like a huge sum. The problem was that Northern Rock had total assets of well over £100 billion. So, the bank could only afford to make losses equivalent to around 2 per cent or so of the value of the assets on its balance sheet before it became technically insolvent. True, Northern Rock could argue its loan book was very safe and that its rates of arrears were very low and that what had happened in the American housing market would not happen in Britain. This didn't really matter. In the early months of 2007 wholesale investors were in the same position Northern Rock's ordinary, high-street deposit holders found themselves in in September. Of course, Northern Rock might be fine, but why take the chance? After all, with such a low capital buffer, it would not take much to wipe the bank out, and if that happened it would be too late to do anything about it. Better to get out first.

Northern Rock was not the only bank to have reduced its capital buffers. Almost every other bank had done the same thing. In the nineteenth century, banks regularly held capital equivalent to the value of at least 30 per cent of their assets. As recently as the early 1970s, most banks were working with capital buffers of around 10 per cent of the value of their total assets.[21] Then, in the early 1990s, following the collapse of the wildly corrupt Bank of Credit and Commerce International, new international regulations, the so-called 'Basel rules', were introduced to ensure every bank had adequate minimum capital buffers. These rules did their job insofar as several banks were forced to raise more capital. But the Basel rules had an unanticipated side effect. Banks which were carrying *more* capital than the new Basel minimum interpreted these new rules as giving them permission to lower their capital buffers. As a result, the *average* size of capital buffers fell. To make matters worse, the run-up to the financial crisis coincided with the introduction of new 'Basel II' rules, which, following lobbying by the banks, allowed them to further reduce the size of the capital buffers they had to carry in relation to mortgage debt. As a result, by the mid-2000s nearly every major global bank had engineered its capital buffers right down towards the kind of levels seen at Northern Rock. Meanwhile, the huge 'shadow' banking system (consisting of lenders, brokers, hedge funds, venture-capital funds, money-market funds and other credit intermediaries outside the regulated banking system) was basically operating with something close to zero capital buffers.[22]

So, whilst Northern Rock may have looked like it was different from the globalized banks based in London, it wasn't. Not really. Far from being a bad apple, a one-off or an outlier, Northern Rock was, in many respects, entirely typical. There is a further point to make here. During the boom years the banking sector appeared highly decentralized and competitive. Not only were there lots of established high-street banks but there were lots of new challengers, like Northern Rock and RBS (which had successfully taken over NatWest in February 2000). Yet all the banks in this system behaved in remarkably similar ways. They had all reduced their capital buffers. They were all dependent upon wholesale funding. Many of them were increasingly dependent on securitization. Many of them (but not, to be fair, Northern Rock) had started to mimic the largest American investment banks by growing their financial trading operations. What looked like a highly decentralized system was, in fact, highly synchronized.

In January 2000 a particularly nasty flu epidemic had shown that the NHS lacked any spare capacity with which to withstand a surge in demand (p. 32). Nine months later, a lot of people, the prime minister included, suddenly discovered that a 'just-in-time' delivery system meant that the country could grind to a halt after only a few days of fuel blockades (p. 45). What the 2008 crisis showed was that the banks, which had made huge profits during the economic good times, had almost no capacity to withstand a downturn in their fortunes.

A POTEMKIN VILLAGE

Bankers are not stupid. Senior bankers are usually the very opposite of stupid. So, in the 2000s, plenty of people would have known banking crises had happened many times before. One possible reason why they acted as if the boom would go on forever is that they knew but did not care. They were making IBGYBG ('I'll be gone, you'll be gone') trades, where profits and bonuses could be booked immediately and everything else left to another day. There is, however, more to the story than this. Lots of executives truly believed that this time everything was going to be different and that risk had been sliced and diced and rendered safe. Banks thought they had developed algorithms which could tell them how many customers would default on what kinds of loans and at what rates. They thought that by creating securities and selling them to other investors, risk had been dispersed through the system. They thought they had effectively insured themselves against catastrophic losses by buying credit default swaps as a form of insurance. Finally, the banks were absolutely one hundred per cent sure that, if the worst did happen and default rates on loans climbed, they would be able to use the assets on their balance sheet as collateral to borrow whatever money they needed to cover their losses.[23]

All these assumptions turned out to be wildly mistaken. The IBGYBG trades came home to roost sooner rather than later. The algorithms proved to be good at predicting default rates in a booming market but useless at predicting what would happen in a downturn. Because banks had bought each other's securities and then traded them, risk had not been dispersed. Credit default swaps had been used not simply as a form of insurance but, far more often, as another trading instrument for making short-term profits. When the market turned, the firms that had been left holding the sticky end of the credit default stick, including the London-based financial products division of the American firm AIG (which found itself holding around $450 billion in credit default swaps), collapsed and had to be rescued.[24] To cap it all, just when the banks were sustaining losses and needed to either sell their assets, borrow more money or raise new capital, nobody proved willing to lend anything or to buy anything from anyone.

Bank executives, who had been under constant pressure to keep increasing their profits in order to sustain their share price during the boom years, ended up looking a lot less clever than they had appeared. But any bank executive could point to the fact that regulators knew most of what had been going on and had raised no objections. The collapse of Northern Rock showed that an elaborate-looking regulatory system was a Potemkin village. Northern Rock was one of the largest mortgage lenders in Britain. Yet FSA supervisors held no meetings with Northern Rock managers in 2005; one meeting in 2006; and, in 2007, at a time when we now know the bank was already starting to falter, seven meetings, two of them by phone. There were no written records of key meetings and a subsequent internal FSA audit found that those supervisors, when questioned, had only a limited understanding of what it was they were supposed to be doing.[25] After the horse had not only bolted but retired and bought a nice house in Surrey with the money it had made, Alistair Darling admitted that an ethos of light-touch regulation had degenerated into an 'anything goes philosophy', which led to a 'culture of lackadaisical supervision [and a] climate where too often regulators and boardrooms alike were happy to look the other way'.[26]

Light-touch regulation was, more than anything else, grounded on an assumption that the banks knew what they were doing and could, in a competitive market, be trusted to protect their own balance sheets. In its report into the failure of the RBS, several years later, the FSA admitted that, prior to the crisis, it had operated with 'an overt supervisory philosophy that it should, wherever possible, rely on a firm's senior management to ensure that risks were well-controlled'. Speaking after the crash had happened, Hector Sants, the FSA's former chief executive, spoke of a 'prevailing climate at the time and indeed, right until the crisis commenced, that the market does know best'.[27] The banks, for their part, had worked on the assumption that they had a green light to do anything the FSA had not told them they could not do.

The FSA was eventually left to carry the can when the crisis came and was dissolved in 2013. Yet, in its defence, it had been dealt a poor hand by a government that was itself determined to hear only good news and had passed legislation requiring the FSA to protect London's international position as a global financial centre (p. 100). As one of the FSA's other post-crisis, look-back-in-anger reports acidly observes, if one of its senior executives had suggested, in the mid-2000s, that existing regulations were inadequate, it would have run into extensive complaints that it was 'pursuing a heavy handed, gold-plating and unnecessary approach'.[28] On this at least the FSA and the Bank of England could find common cause. The Bank had never been remotely happy that New Labour had stripped it of its regulatory responsibilities in the late 1990s in return for its operational independence. Yet it may have managed to dodge a bullet. After all, any regulator who had sought to persuade politicians the banks were underregulated would, as Mervyn King observed, have confronted a 'massively difficult task'.[29]

RUNNING OVER THE CLIFF

Along with Tom and Jerry and Bugs Bunny, Wile E. Coyote and Road Runner were staples of children's TV cartoons in the 1970s and 1980s. Each episode revolved around the efforts of Coyote to catch the Road Runner, usually with the help of equipment mail-ordered from the Acme Corporation. Each plan backfired with the Road Runner escaping unharmed and Coyote being flattened. One running gag involved Coyote running off the edge of a cliff but not noticing he had done so. For a few moments he would defy gravity and carry on running, before looking down and noticing there was no ground beneath his feet. At this moment he froze in mid-air before plunging to the bottom of the canyon.

From around the summer of 2007 onwards, the global financial system had reached the stage where, like Coyote, it had run off the edge of the cliff but had yet to start falling. In January 2008 the US Federal

Reserve slashed interest rates to revive the economy. In February George Bush signed into law an economic stimulus package worth around $150 billion. In early March the Federal Reserve announced it was pumping $200 billion into the mortgage-backed securities markets to keep the funding system afloat. Not long after, Bear Stearns, America's fifth largest investment bank, failed and was bought by JP Morgan in a government-brokered deal. In April, RBS announced plans to raise an additional £12 billion in shareholder funding. In June, Barclays raised £4.5 billion via the Qatar Investment Authority. On 11 July the American IndyMac bank failed. On 21 July one of the largest British banks, HBOS, tried but failed to raise new capital. On 7 September the two giant, government-backed American mortgage lenders, Fannie Mae and Freddie Mac, had to be rescued and placed into 'conservatorship' – a government life-support system.

Which brings us back to Lehman Brothers, whose expensive new European headquarters Gordon Brown had opened in 2004. In June 2008 Lehman's announced a $3 billion second-quarter loss whilst hinting at more bad news to come. For a short while it seemed the Korean Development Bank might save the day and pump some capital in. On 9 September those talks fell apart, and on the 10th Lehman's new chief financial officer, Erin Callan, preannounced a third-quarter loss of $4 billion.[30] Lehman's chief executive officer, Dick Fuld, called Barclays' American-born boss Bob Diamond to ask whether he would be interested in buying the bank. Diamond flew to New York with a team of managers and auditors to inspect Lehman's books. Hank Paulson, the US Treasury secretary, and Timothy Geithner, the head of the New York Federal Reserve, summoned the chief executives of all the largest American banks to New York for emergency talks.[31]

For a few hours, a deal looked possible. Lehman's most toxic real estate assets would be spun-off into a separate company, which the other American banks would underwrite. Barclays would buy the rest of the bank. At the last possible moment, on Sunday, 14 September 2008, exactly a year and a day after Robert Peston's BBC report about the state of Northern Rock, the deal fell apart when the FSA and Alistair Darling made it clear they were, at best, sceptical about the Barclays deal and were not prepared to waive it through. Darling, not unreasonably, was concerned that if Lehman Brothers was in an even-worse shape than it had already admitted, British taxpayers would be left picking up the pieces. 'We don't want to import your cancer,' he told Paulson.[32]

With all other options exhausted, Lehman's was left to file for bankruptcy in a New York courthouse early on 15 September. (Shortly after, Barclays purchased Lehman's North American investment banking and capital markets business at the knock-down price of $1.75 billion.) For the next few days, people kept turning up for work at Lehman's London offices at 25 Bank Street. There was very little employees could do though, and not many people were keen to answer the phone. Eventually, Lehman Brothers Europe was put into administration with the loss of around four thousand jobs. Natalia Rogoff, who worked in international client sales, described the experience.

> The first emotion that hit very hard was disbelief . . . the bank collapsed, we are still in the building, there is no official news from the management, they are all behind closed doors, there's nothing from the US, everyone disappeared . . . the phones were ringing. The clients were ringing all day long, they were wanting to know – where is my money, what is going on?[33]

What had happened to Northern Rock had now happened, on a massively larger scale, to Lehman Brothers. This was, however, the end of the beginning rather than the beginning of the end.

19

Falling Down: The Financial Crisis

THE LEHMAN MOMENT

A financial crisis was already unfolding at the moment Lehman Brothers declared bankruptcy. The 'Lehman Moment', as it came to be called, was nevertheless significant because after the government-facilitated rescue of Bear Stearns, six months earlier, the American government had now let a major bank fail and declare bankruptcy. A point was going to be made. Lehman's shareholders had made a lot of money when the economic times were good and the bank had taken all sorts of risks. Now that everything had fallen apart they would have to bear the pain. No bank or financial institution should think it was 'too big to fail'. Moral hazard mattered and had to be addressed.

The US Treasury, led by Hank Paulson, a former chief executive of Goldman Sachs, knew that letting Lehman go under would send a strong signal. Paulson nevertheless underestimated just how strong that signal would be. From the second Lehman's declared bankruptcy, every investor, wholesale lender or financial institution knew that if one of the very largest banks had been allowed to fail, then anyone and everyone else might also fail. In a situation in which nobody was sure who owned precisely which assets; who, through credit default swap contracts, had insured whose assets; and who was already running out of cash, every bank decided the safest course of action was to minimize its exposures to any other institutions by hoarding cash and not lending money.

The sense of irrational exuberance which had driven the boom now turned to outright panic. Suddenly, banks found themselves unable to sell any of their assets at any price or to borrow money at any interest rate. The market froze, and once it had, banks who depended on borrowing money to fund their day-to-day operations found themselves, instantly, on the financial equivalent of death row. To make matters worse, credit-rating agencies who had previously thrown the highest-grade AAA ratings at almost any passing securitized asset, now downgraded banks' credit ratings, which triggered regulations requiring them to raise more capital at a moment when, of course, nobody was willing to invest capital in a bank.

The same day as Lehman's filed for bankruptcy, Bank of America announced it was going to buy, at a bargain-basement price, another major investment bank, Merrill Lynch. The next day, and with its determination to avoid spending any public money to bail out banks already shot, the Federal Reserve Bank of New York lent $85 billion to the giant American International Group, whose London-based trading office, AIG Financial Products, we encountered in the previous chapter. On 17 September Hank Paulson told US Treasury staff that America was facing an 'economic 9/11', and warned the world economy might conceivably collapse within another day or two.[1] On 25 September Washington Mutual (with assets of $327 billion) was pushed into foreclosure. In October, two other large banks – Wachovia (with assets of $812bn) and National City Bank ($150bn), were rescued via takeovers. Not long after, Citigroup (with eye-watering total assets of $2,187bn) and Bank of America (£1,052bn) were offered government help.

In a globalized financial system in which banks everywhere had lent money and bought and sold each other's assets, what had happened in America was never going to stay in America. In late 2019 and early 2020, Covid was spread via airports, cruise liners, ski resorts and football matches. The contagion of the financial crisis spread via computer terminals.[2] Following the collapse of Lehman Brothers, the Belgian banks Fortis and Dexia, the Swiss giant UBS, Anglo-Irish Bank, the Portuguese Banco Português de Negócios and the Icelandic banks Landsbanki, Glitnir and Kaupthing fell apart. London, one of the three largest global financial centres in the world, was also (as everyone instantly knew would be the case) in the line of fire. One senior official in the Cabinet Office, John Cunliffe, sent an email to colleagues warning 'if we don't do something now the whole system is going to go down'.[3] HBOS found itself on the brink of collapse and, with the government's blessing, was pushed into a shotgun-marriage with Lloyds TSB, which then had to be bailed out in turn because of the losses it incurred. The Bradford and Bingley building society was nationalized on 29 September. RBS came within a few hours of running out of cash and had to be rescued on 8 October.

The 2008 crisis did not involve bank runs of the sort that had felled Northern Rock in 2007. Banks did not fail because their ordinary customers with savings in the bank lost confidence and withdrew their money. That was because customer deposits were in fact no longer the key part of the system. What mattered in 2008, above all else, was the collapse of the wholesale lending markets that, in the boom years, had provided the funds to keep everything running (p. 232). The banks which fell apart were left with their shiny headquarters and balance sheets showing they had billions of pounds of assets in the form of loans owed to them. What they did not have was any cash. Everything which seemed solid had melted into air.[4]

This brings us to the question asked by Queen Elizabeth when she visited the London School of Economics to open a new building in November 2008. 'Why did nobody notice?'[5]A few economists and a handful of politicians had asked difficult questions about financial innovation, credit conditions and trading exposures long before the crisis began, but they were very much in a minority. As I have previously quoted the then chancellor Alistair Darling as saying: 'many people have claimed to have predicted what was going to happen. Most of them failed to mention it at the time.'[6] Many of the active participants in the financial system, those taking the actual risks, were dazzled by the rewards on offer and knew that playing it safe and avoiding excessive risks, far from paying off, would be likely to cost them their jobs. Andy Haldane, the executive director of financial stability at the Bank of England between 2009 and 2015 before becoming the Bank's chief economist, said this:

Times were good and it was very difficult for any firm individually to step back – to step out of the party . . . was too much business being written? Absolutely. They'd say, well we've got a friend who stopped two years ago and they're not in a job any more. So there was this locomotive that was steaming ahead, it was impossible to step off this profitability merry-go-round. People were conscious that that meant running a bit more risk than they'd like but they couldn't stop themselves because their loss would have been someone else's gain. So I think externally there was, at least towards the end, a pretty strong sense of the risks that were being piled up ... in a way that led, collectively, to everyone to pile over the cliff.[7]

Politicians and regulators were, meanwhile, in thrall to the idea that bank executives and the shareholders trusting them with their money knew best and should not be second-guessed lightly. Lord Adair Turner, a technocrat whose name has cropped up at several points in this book, was appointed chairman of the Financial Services Authority on 20 September 2008 and, subsequently, wrote a review into the causes of the financial crisis and the most appropriate regulatory response to it. At one point in that report, he describes the 'dominant philosophy of confidence in self-correcting markets'.[8] In a later lecture, delivered in 2011, he returned to this theme:

> It is striking in the pre-crisis years how dominant and how overconfident, at least in the arena of financial economics, was a simplified version of equilibrium theory which saw market competition as the cure to all problems, and mathematical sophistication decoupled from philosophical understanding as the key to effective risk management.[9]

There can be little doubt that, on top of this, New Labour and the Treasury became addicted to the tax revenues which the City offered. But that addiction needs to be understood in the context of New Labour's underlying and, as it proved, misplaced social democratic faith in markets to do their thing and generate growth.

'NOT FLASH – JUST GORDON'

Gordon Brown became prime minister in June 2007. For a short while he seemed to be doing reasonably well. He was credited with responding calmly to a terrorist attack on Glasgow Airport and to floods in Yorkshire in a way that allowed Labour's media spin doctors to cultivate his image of being 'not flash – just Gordon'.[10] Brown got a lot of credit for appointing non-politicians such as Digby Jones, the former director of the Confederation of British Industry (CBI), and Lord West, the former first sea lord and chief of the naval staff, to ministerial positions.

Brown's political fortunes changed from the autumn of 2007. He was derided for changing his mind about holding an early general election before the end of the year, and for denying opinion polls had in any way influenced his decision. He lost a lot of support within the Labour Party when he plagiarized Conservative proposals to cut inheritance tax. In April 2008 he was pushed into a U-turn over a budget decision to abolish the 10p starting rate of income tax. This was followed by heavy election defeats in the May 2008 local elections, and in October the government was defeated in its attempts to extend pre-trial detention for terrorist suspects. Two thousand and nine brought the MPs' expenses scandal; the PR disaster of the Gurkha Justice Campaign (in which former members of the Brigade of Gurkhas, with support from the television star Joanna Lumley, campaigned for all its veterans to be given a right of abode in Britain); the resignation of one of Labour's senior press officers, Damian McBride (whose emails discussing plans to invent rumours about the personal lives of opposition politicians and post them on a website were leaked); and accusations from a number of former chiefs of the defence staff that Brown was failing to protect and support the British Army and injured ex-servicemen.

Tony Blair's supporters and, eventually, Blair himself let it be known that Brown was living down to their expectations.[11] There were Cabinet resignations including, in June 2009, that of the work and pensions secretary, James Purnell, who called on Brown 'to stand aside to give Labour a fighting chance of winning the next election'.[12] There was endless speculation about leadership challenges, culminating in a slightly half-hearted and unsuccessful attempted putsch, the 'Great Goose Plot', led by two former Cabinet ministers, Margaret Hodge and Geoff Hoon, in January 2010 (so-called because the plan was hatched over a roast-goose dinner at Hodge's Suffolk weekend home).[13] There were constant reports Brown had fallen out with his chancellor, the governor of the Bank of England and just about anyone else whose surnames began with letters between A and Y. There were stories about Brown bullying staff in Number 10 and being spoken to about this by the Cabinet secretary.[14] The director of the National Bullying Helpline said people working for Brown had spoken to the organization.[15] Finally, there were endless stories about a lack of organization, an obsession with media headlines and Brown's inability to make decisions.

Yet when it came to the two most pressing policy issues of his tenure, climate change (Chapter 10) and the financial crisis, Brown, looking back, got more things right than he did wrong. He did not, as the Nobel

Prize-winning American economist Paul Krugman once suggested might have been the case, 'save the world financial system'.[16] In fact, during the financial crisis, Britain was sometimes consigned to its long-familiar role of welcoming American initiatives. Yet Brown, with a decade's experience of the international economy and the people who piloted it, nevertheless made a difference. With the free market suddenly looking less like the solution to a problem and more like the problem itself, Brown was ready – more ready than Tony Blair might have been – to embrace the idea of a strong, activist state and, in doing so, to pull New Labour further away from its social democratic salad days of letting the free-market economy tick along whilst spending the proceeds.

In the immediate aftermath of the collapse of Lehman's, Brown was also one of the first people, and certainly one of the first world leaders, to recognize that the financial crisis was systemic. Letting the market work out which banks had made bad decisions was not going to cut it. Shorn of any confidence, if left to its own devices the entire banking system was in danger of falling over and taking large parts of the rest of the world economic system with it.[17] Brown was also one of the first leaders to see that because the crisis was systemic, dealing with it would require co-ordinated international action. Brown's was a strong voice at the G20 summit meeting in Washington in November 2008 at a time when George Bush looked like the lamest of lame ducks and Barack Obama had not yet been sworn into office. Brown then went into battering-ram mode in preparing the agenda for the G20's April 2009 summit in London and lining up world leaders behind a $1 trillion-plus agreement to cut taxes, raise public spending, eschew new trade barriers and reform global bank regulation.[18]

At a time when the US Treasury was still wedded to the idea of buying the euphemistically named 'troubled assets' on bank balance sheets and storing them away far from sight (a part of the initial plan for dealing with Lehman's losses, p. 237), Brown and his advisors were quick to see that what the banks needed, above all else, was money in the form of new capital. In October 2008, British banks were told they had to raise new capital and that, if they could not do so through the stock market (which most of them could not), the government would require them to take its cash in return for a share of their ownership. This was a form of show-and-tell nationalization that led to £107 billion being pumped into RBS and Lloyds in return for, respectively, an

84 and 43 per cent share of each bank's ownership (total government support including cash and guarantees amounted to £256 billion for RBS and £276 billion for Lloyds). By any measure, this was a bail-out. Whatever it may have looked like at the time, it was not, however, a gift: the idea was that once the banks had recovered, the government would sell its shares and recover its money.[19]

Finally, Brown realized that protecting the real economy would require tax cuts and higher government spending to boost confidence and protect jobs. After a decade of free-market economics, Keynesian economics was back. John Maynard Keynes had been right to argue that the 1929 Wall Street Crash had morphed into a worldwide economic slump because governments had done nothing to prevent this slump from happening. A Labour government would prevent history from repeating itself. To stimulate the economy public spending would be increased and VAT would be cut. This would mean a significant increase in public borrowing in the short term, but doing so would save the economy in the longer term. Critics mocked Brown for rediscovering Keynesianism only in a crisis. This was, however, to miss the point. You don't need Keynesianism when times are good. Keynesianism *is* an economics of crisis.[20] It provides governments with a 'what to do' instruction sheet for moments when the free-market economy is crashing.

LENDER OF THE LAST RESORT

In late 2008 and early 2009 Labour rolled forward the frontiers of the state. Central banks, the Bank of England included, then rolled them further forward again. In the 1990s and 2000s central banks had spent their time nudging interest rates a few notches up or a few notches down to make sure inflation was under control. The financial crisis gave them a new and politically more high-profile role.

First, the banks cut interest rates and kept cutting them to encourage consumer borrowing: the flip side of government-led fiscal Keynesianism. In July 2007 the official Bank Rate set by the Bank of England was 5.75 per cent (exactly what it had been in January 2000). By March 2009 it had been cut to 0.5 per cent.[21] This was, however, only a slice of the story. During the height of the crisis in late 2008, when confidence was evaporating, the Federal Reserve opened 'swap deals' that allowed other central banks, the Bank of England included, access to US dollars (around 4,450 billion of them) at a time when, more than ever, the dollar was a symbol of security.[22] Even more impressively, it eventually became clear, a few years later, that the Federal Reserve had pumped dollars (in return for collateral) into foreign banks which had American subsidiaries, including an injection of $85 billion into RBS and $65 billion into Barclays. In this way, the Federal Reserve basically became the lender of last resort not only to American banks, but to most of the global financial system.

Central banks also took the post-crisis lead in reforming the financial system. The Financial Services Agency, the selected anti-hero scapegoat of 'light-touch' regulation, was abolished and overall responsibility for financial regulation returned to the Bank of England. Over the next few years, and against the backdrop of a constant chorus of complaints from the banking sector and their lobbyists, new and tougher rules relating to capital buffers, countercyclical capital buffers, cash reserves, the ring-fencing of commercial- and investment-bank assets, living wills and stress tests were introduced.[23] Bankers bemoaned a regulatory environment which, according to the chairman of RBS, Philip Hampton, had 'changed beyond recognition' and hemmed in their profit-making opportunities.[24] At the same time, these reforms, the imposition of which would have been simply unthinkable just a few years before, were also profoundly conservative.[25] They were intended to make the existing financial system work better and more safely. They were not intended to reshape the economy by making the banks smaller and the City of London a regional rather than a global financial centre. The banks were not being nationalized as a new socialist strategy. They were being sheltered within the public sector until they could be returned to the private sector.

Post-crisis, the balance sheets of the largest banks kept growing, and nobody found a way of stopping this from happening. What it meant was that the 'too big to fail' problem, which had led governments to calculate they had no alternative but to bail out the largest banks, remained stubbornly unfixed. Post-crisis, financial trading was hemmed-in and more carefully regulated by way of a 'ring-fence', introduced following a recommendation of the Independent Commission on Banking chaired by the economist Sir John Vickers.[26] But financial trading nevertheless remained an important part of the balance sheets of the largest banks.[27]

Which brings us back, yet again, to Lehman's European headquarters in London. After it had declared bankruptcy, another American bank, JP Morgan, eventually moved in to 25 Bank Street.[28] Its decision to do so was welcomed by London's recently elected mayor, Boris Johnson, who said it would 'help ensure the capital retains its position as a banking powerhouse . . . which attracts the brightest and best stars'.[29] Not long after, a trader based there, Bruno Iksil, the 'London Whale', completed a series of credit default swap trades that ended up costing his company, give or take, $6 billion.[30]

Once the immediate post-Lehman crisis had passed, the Bank of England's governor, Mervyn King, became an increasingly trenchant critic of the government's fiscal strategy and of the amount of money it continued to borrow. In June 2009 King delivered his annual Mansion House speech. He carefully avoided giving Chancellor Alistair Darling a copy of the speech in advance before proceeding to tell the government, in no uncertain terms, that it needed to develop a plan to reduce the deficit.[31] Given that the Conservatives were also arguing that Labour was borrowing far too much money, this was politically incendiary stuff. Darling, who, behind the scenes, was pressing Gordon Brown to set a clear timeline to reduce borrowing, was furious. In his memoirs he later accused King and the Bank of having come 'close to crossing a line between legitimate comment and entering the political fray'.[32] To add fuel to the fire, King met with George Osborne and David Cameron to discuss the Conservatives' economic plans. It later transpired that King had not been impressed (he had found them lacking experience and to have had 'a tendency to think about issues only in terms of politics, and how they might affect Tory electability').* But at the time, when the fact of their meeting became public, it looked like the Bank, or at least its governor, might be making a political statement about his lack of confidence in the Labour government by meeting with its political opponents.

---

* King offered an account of his meetings with Cameron and Osborne to the US ambassador to London. This account was forwarded to Washington where it eventually was revealed as a part of the WikiLeaks cables. David Leigh and Patrick Wintour, 'WikiLeaks cables: Mervyn King had doubts over Cameron and Osborne', *Guardian* (30 Nov. 2010).

QUANTITATIVE EASING

The 2009 Mansion House speech made King look, for better or worse, a small 'c' or even, possibly, a large 'C' conservative. Yet King was also the governor who gave the green light to the radical policy of Quantitative Easing (QE) which, in terms of pushing forward the frontiers of the state, was a kind of 'Advance to Mayfair' Monopoly moment. By 2009 interest rates had already been cut almost to zero. Yet economies across the world, Britain's included, were nevertheless still floundering. As the immediate emergency phase of the financial crisis wound down, the pressure upon central banks to do more to promote a recovery increased. Following an example set by Japan in the early 1990s, the Federal Reserve – followed by central banks in nearly twenty other countries, including Britain and, eventually, the European Central Bank in 2015 – found an answer to this question in QE.[33] Between March 2009 and 2013 the Bank of England went into the market and bought around £375 billion of assets held by corporations and pension funds, nearly all of them Treasury gilts, the bonds issued by the British government when it wants to borrow money.[34]

This was not an insignificant sum. In fact, £375 billion amounted to something like the equivalent of 14 per cent of GDP. But the Bank of England did not have to apply for an overdraft. It instead created the money electronically and placed the resulting debt (to itself) on its balance sheet.[35] The idea was that buying Treasury gilts on this scale would increase their market price and reduce their yield, and so make them less attractive to other investors. As a result, the theory went, borrowers would be encouraged to borrow more because of lower interest rates, and investors would spend more of their money on other kinds of assets, such as company shares, giving those companies more money to spend and invest.[36] Moreover (although this was rarely said out loud), QE would make it a lot easier for the government to continue to borrow money because it meant there would always be someone – the Bank of England – ready to buy its bonds if other people wanted to sell theirs.[37] Indeed by 2022, after another Covid-induced round of QE, the Bank of England owned around a third of all British government debt.[38]

The Bank of England's assessment, after the event, was that QE had worked – that it had boosted the economic recovery and minimized job losses.[39] Yet it remained controversial. One key argument here was that it was deeply unfair and regressive. QE had the effect of boosting share prices by as much as 25 per cent according to the Bank's own estimates.[40] So shareholders did very well at a moment when, otherwise, the times might have been tougher. Those shares were, up to a point, owned by huge numbers of people via pension funds. But looked at more closely and from an individual level, most of them were owned by already wealthy people. In other words, whilst QE might, in Keynesian fashion, have pump-primed the economy, it had offered a particular dollop of help to those who already had the most money. In 2012, the journalist Fraser Nelson, writing in the *Spectator*, a magazine not normally known for its left-leaning political economy, described QE as 'the ultimate subsidy for the rich'.[41] A few years later, during his 2015 Labour leadership campaign, Jeremy Corbyn picked up on this kind of analysis and proposed a 'People's Quantitative Easing', whereby the Bank of England would purchase bonds in a state-owned National Investment Bank to invest in skills training and to build more council houses.[42]

Meanwhile, for those still wedded to the discipline of the free market QE looked like the equivalent of burning the furniture to keep a house warm. It worked in the short term but was going to create a long-term mess. It was a political IBGYBG, no different to printing money. QE would encourage feckless governments to borrow and keep borrowing; which would drive up inflation; which, sooner or later, would mean higher interest rates and a debasing of the currency. It was habit-forming and character-destroying and basically every bit as bad as every other kind of socialism. At first, the free-market critique of QE was pushed (and pushed very hard) largely by the right-wing of the US Republican Party.[43] But from 2015 onwards, William Hague and Theresa May also started to express carefully worded Conservative public doubts about the long-term impact of what the Bank was doing.[44]

All this put the Bank of England in a potentially difficult spot. It was independent, and being independent was supposed to mean it was above the party-political fray. This was always a bit far-fetched. Central banks can't help but be political. The mandates they are given by governments, whether to keep inflation below a certain level, keep it within a certain range or to place an equal value on low inflation and high growth and high employment, are unavoidably political because they unavoidably create winners and losers. In the 2000s the politics of central banking were largely hidden because there was a cross-party consensus about prioritizing low inflation. The financial crisis and QE changed this and put the Bank of England on the political frontline, where it was to remain (p. 436).[45]

BACK TO BROWN

The global financial crisis was, by any measure, a huge, money-destroying calamity. By some measures, its immediate economic impact was worse than that of the 1929 Wall Street Crash.[46] Yet, in the end, a rerun of the Great Depression of the 1930s was avoided.[47] Lots of banks collapsed but the banking system as a whole recovered. There was no trade war.[48] Nor was there a global depression. Between September 2008 and September 2009 global GDP fell for the first time since 1946 but, the year after, it recovered.[49]

The world economy might have shaken off the impact of the financial crisis quicker than many had expected but Britain, with its outsized banking system, was not so fortunate. Between 1992 and early 2008, the country recorded sixty-two successive quarters of economic growth. In 2008/9 it then contracted for five successive quarters. During this recession the unemployment rate rose from 5.2 per cent in early 2008 to a peak of 8.4 per cent in late 2011, whilst median household income *after* housing costs fell by 3.3 per cent.[50] In terms of the raw numbers, this made what happened post-Lehman's worse than the mid-1970s' recession, the early 1980s' recession or the early 1990s' recession. Between 2000 and 2007 GDP grew by an average of 2.7 per cent a year. That was reasonably impressive. But if you add in the next two years' figures to take account of the growth-destroying impact of the financial crisis, that average falls to just 1.7 per cent.[51]

For a while, at the start of the financial crisis, Brown's polling ratings and those of the Labour Party rose. This proved to be a dead-cat bounce, however; by 2009 déjà vu had set in and New Labour was in all sorts of political trouble. For the most part, voters did not blame Brown for causing the financial crisis. The 2010 British Election Study found that only around 19 per cent of people held Brown responsible for the financial crisis, compared to about 93 per cent who blamed the banks.[52]

People did however blame the government for bailing out multibillion-pound banks and multi-millionaire bankers, and they were increasingly persuaded by the Conservatives' argument that higher borrowing was damaging the economy and that Brown was refusing to say how or when spending would be cut, mindful of the forthcoming general election.

In the end, that election, on 6 May 2010, was a lot closer than many had expected (pp. 267–8). Labour's share of the vote just about held up and the Conservatives failed to gain an overall majority. This did not, however, improve Gordon Brown's reputation. In 2010, a ranking of the effectiveness of post-war British prime ministers by academics writing about British politics or modern history, put Clement Attlee in top place (with an average rating of 8.1 out of 10) followed by Margaret Thatcher (6.9) and Tony Blair (6.4). Gordon Brown came third from last, with only Alec Douglas-Home (prime minister for a year before losing the 1964 election) and Anthony Eden (who lasted for a year and a half but lied about and lost the Suez War before being deposed by his own party) behind him.[53] Academics Brown could probably have ignored or laughed off. A 2013 survey of MPs really put the boot in though, confirming the positions of Attlee, Thatcher and Blair at the top but putting Brown flat bottom.[54] He must have been delighted when, in 2022, Liz Truss lowered the bar and gave him a chance to escape from under the pile.

20

An Expenses Business

HOT WATER

On Friday, 8 May 2009, the *Daily Telegraph* published the first of an avalanche of stories about MPs' expenses.[1] They began at the top. Gordon Brown had flipped the designated address of his second home in a way that allowed him to continue to claim expenses on it once he had moved into 10 Downing Street.[2] Jack Straw, the justice secretary, had claimed more than he was entitled to on his council tax and mortgage bills. The business secretary, Lord Mandelson of Foy in the County of Hertfordshire and of Hartlepool in the County of Durham, as he had become in 2008, had spent thousands of pounds improving his constituency home after announcing plans to step down as an MP, and had pocketed more money when the house was later sold. Alistair Darling, the chancellor, had flipped the address of his second home four times in four years and, by so doing, had been able to claim for improvements each time. Paul Murphy, the secretary of state for Wales, had claimed for the installation of a new plumbing system which made his hot water less hot. Margaret Beckett, the minister of state for housing and planning, had claimed over £600 on hanging baskets and pot plants. John Prescott, the former deputy prime minister, had claimed for two lavatory seats in two years and for mock Tudor beams to be attached to the front of his house.

After first focusing upon senior Labour figures, the *Telegraph* shifted its focus to several other MPs who had falsely claimed expenses on mortgage-interest payments. It then ran stories about the Conservatives. Several members of the Shadow Cabinet had flipped their second home addresses. Oliver Letwin, one of David Cameron's senior advisors, had claimed £2,000 to repair a leaking pipe beneath his tennis court. Other

Conservative MPs had claimed for swimming pool maintenance, moat cleaning and the salaries of domestic staff. David Willetts had claimed for someone to change a light bulb. To cap it all, Sir Peter Viggers had claimed £1,645 for a floating duck island. (The ducks, he later revealed, had never liked their new home, which had since been put into storage.)[3]

A handful of MPs, 'the Saints', as the *Telegraph* dubbed them, were lauded for the modesty of their claims.[4] Everyone else lived in fear they would be the next to be exposed. On 22 May, Nadine Dorries, the Conservative MP for Mid-Bedfordshire who, in 2013, was suspended from the Parliamentary Conservative Party for appearing on the TV show *I'm a Celebrity* whilst Parliament was sitting, said she and others expected an MP to commit suicide.[5] The following day, the archbishop of Canterbury, Rowan Williams, warned that 'the continuing systematic humiliation of politicians itself threatens to carry a heavy price in terms of our ability to salvage some confidence in our democracy'.[6] Nobody blinked. The expenses scandal seemed to confirm everyone's worst fears that MPs were out to feather their own nests and lived by a different set of rules to everyone else. In June 2009 an opinion poll found 95 per cent of respondents had heard of the expenses scandal, and it made 91 per cent of them 'very angry'. Nearly 60 per cent now agreed most MPs were corrupt.[7]

NOTHING NEW UNDER THE SUN

After they had unexpectedly won the 1992 General Election, the Conservatives fell apart after a decade in power. They did so for a number of reasons, but sleaze was one of the most important. At the 1993 Conservative Party conference, John Major had spoken about getting 'back to the basics' of common decency. From that moment on, a truckload of Conservative MPs seemed to throw themselves into an endless variety of financial and sexual scandals. New Labour would probably have won the 1997 election come what may, but its job was made considerably easier when it could start every press release with a reference to Tory Sleaze. New Labour, Blair promised, would offer a fresh start and higher standards. Any MP who so much as thought about underpaying a parking meter would find themselves ferried to Rockall, two hundred miles off the west coast of Scotland, and left there.

Since they had set the bar so high, New Labour found itself with further to fall. In 1997 Blair had to apologize when it transpired the government had exempted Formula 1 racing from a ban on tobacco advertising at sporting events not long after accepting a donation from its chief executive, Bernie Ecclestone. In 1998 Peter Mandelson resigned from government after failing to disclose a £373,000 loan advanced to him by the paymaster general, Geoffrey Robertson. Mandelson later resigned for a second time, in 2001, in relation to a passport application for a wealthy tycoon, S.P. Hinduja, who had injected some cash into the Millennium Dome. David Blunkett also resigned twice: once in relation to a work visa and then over a failure to consult an advisory committee about extra-parliamentary jobs. Meanwhile, 'Cheriegate', which involved the Blairs' purchase of a flat in Bristol with some sort of support from Carole Caplin, Cherie Blair's style advisor, and Peter Foster, her partner, an Australian con artist, fell a long way short of Watergate but was embarrassing.[8]

Next came the 'cash-for-honours' scandal. In 2006 the House of Lords Appointments Commission refused to approve the names of several people the Labour Party had nominated for peerages who, they suspected, had only been nominated because they had previously made donations to the Labour Party. A police investigation followed, during which Labour's senior fundraiser and Middle East envoy, Michael Levy, who was a close friend of Blair's, was arrested. Tony Blair himself was questioned by the police on three separate occasions although he was never cautioned. In the end, in July 2007, the Crown Prosecution Service decided against charging anyone, on the grounds that it would be exceptionally difficult to prove any formal agreements had been made to offer peerages in return for donations.[9] Which did not stop anyone and everyone from thinking that some kind of informal understanding had been reached. As Levy, who, even before this turn of events, had been known as 'Lord Cashpoint', later said in his memoirs, 'very few of the businessmen who gave large-scale donations to any of the parties did so without at least the vague hope that they might get some honour in return'.[10]

In February 2009 the *Sunday Times* recorded four Labour Party life peers offering to help make amendments to legislation in return for payments of more than £100,000.[11] By that time, the idea that Blair had lied about the Iraq War, along with a conviction that the government was ignoring people's views about immigration, that ministers had failed in their duties when it came to financial regulation, and that they had socialized the banks' losses when the banks collapsed, were pretty much baked-in. The 2009 expenses scandal was not, in other words, an unexpected bolt from the blue. It came at the end of a decade in which faith in New Labour had already frayed.

THE POWER OF A MEMORY STICK

An MP's basic salary in April 2009 was £64,000. This was less than the amount earned by an NHS general practitioner or the headteacher of a large school but getting on for three times the median salary. Moreover, this salary was supplemented by an exceptionally generous expenses scheme, which allowed MPs to claim for the costs of living in London for a part of the year whilst also maintaining a home in their constituency.

The rules relating to accommodation expenses were so light touch they would have startled the Financial Services Authority. MPs could buy a house and profit from selling it. They could furnish it and repair it and could do so without having to provide receipts for any expenses below £250. They could change the address of the house they were claiming against and submit a totally new set of expense claims to the Parliamentary Fees Office without any danger of being asked to justify what they had spent. Lots of people must have known the system was open to abuse. One reason why nobody sought to do anything about it, however, was that it was very difficult for public servants working in the Parliamentary Fees Office to raise concerns without risking damage to their careers.

Journalists had tried to write stories about the expenses scheme but had been hampered by the level of secrecy around it. The 2000 Freedom of Information Act – the one Blair later described himself as being an 'irresponsible nincompoop' for supporting (p. 61) – offered them a way forward. After a lot of legal advice had been offered and a lot of letters exchanged, the parliamentary authorities eventually agreed, in 2004, to release details of the *total* level of claims being made by MPs. That decision was followed by another legal battle about whether the details of individual claims being made by MPs could be released. In May 2008 the High Court ruled that they could.[12] The writing was now on the wall and the parliamentary authorities employed a team of casual workers to sift through the original expense claims and redact any information relating to individual addresses; the names and details of any people or companies mentioned; and any correspondence with the Fees Office. One of the workers employed to process the data, or, perhaps, one of the security guards paid to watch over them, copied the entire contents of the files onto a memory stick. This person approached John Wick, a former special forces officer who had founded a corporate intelligence company, to negotiate its release. After several months of stop-and-start negotiations with several papers, a deal was struck with the *Telegraph*.[13]

The publication of the expenses data was always going to be a matter of high political drama. Gordon Brown turned it into a crisis. His first reaction was one of anger. The *Telegraph* story about his expenses was misleading and part of a political witch hunt against him. His position was eventually vindicated, nine years later, when the Independent Press Standards Organization ruled against the *Telegraph* in a case brought by him.[14] But, at the time, Brown's palpable anger did not necessarily help the government's cause, given just how angry so many other people were about what they were reading. A few days later Brown argued that the problem lay not with the behaviour of MPs but in the complexity of the expenses system itself. MPs, the implication went, had not really understood what they could and could not claim for. As a line of defence this was, if nothing else, heroic. Brown then used a speech to the Royal College of Nursing to issue a half-baked apology 'on behalf of politicians of all parties for what has happened' without really saying what it was he thought had gone wrong or what he was apologizing for.[15]

On 19 May, the speaker of the House of Commons, Michael Martin, who had previously attacked the *Telegraph*'s coverage, announced his resignation. On 2 June, Jacqui Smith, who had been embarrassed by revelations she had claimed for the cost of an adult movie which had been watched by her husband, announced she would resign as home secretary and would not contest the next general election. The following day, the secretary of state for communities and local government, Hazel Blears, resigned. On 4 June Labour crashed to 23 per cent of the vote in local elections and to 15 per cent in the simultaneous European Parliament elections. On 5 June, Geoff Hoon, who had rented out his London home and claimed expenses on his constituency house, resigned as secretary of state for transport. On the same day, Tony McNulty, the minister of state for employment and welfare reform, who had admitted claiming expenses on a second home occupied by his parents, 8 miles away from his primary residence, also announced he would resign. Eventually, getting on for half of the MPs identified by the *Telegraph* or the *News of the World* as being among the worst offenders announced that they planned to retire rather than stand for election again.[16]

Expenses and Labour sleaze became the gift which kept on giving. In February 2010, just three months before the general election, the director of public prosecutions, Keir Starmer, announced that three Labour MPs and a Conservative peer would face criminal charges of false accounting. In the same month, a former senior civil servant, Sir Thomas Legg, who had been asked to investigate past expense claims, concluded that MPs had ignored their own rules to exploit a 'deeply flawed' expenses system and ordered three hundred MPs to repay money or to produce additional evidence supporting their claim.[17] In March, Channel 4's *Dispatches* programme broadcast the details of a sting operation it had run in which assorted MPs had offered to work for a fictitious lobbying firm in return for thousands of pounds of consultancy fees a day.[18] One of them, Stephen Byers, had described himself to an undercover reporter as being 'a bit like a sort of cab for hire'.[19]

In April 2009, at a point when Gordon Brown was chairing the G20 summit conference in London and promising to fix the global financial system, Labour was trailing the Conservatives by around 5 percentage points in opinion polls. By June 2009, in the immediate aftermath of the expenses scandal, that gap had more than doubled. Some of Labour's support leaked across to the United Kingdom Independence Party, which had been formed by an academic at the London School of Economics, Alan Sked, in 2003. UKIP had spent years arguing not only that Britain was being harmed by the European Union, but that a self-serving political elite in Brussels and Whitehall was lining its own pockets at everyone else's expense. In the 2009 European Parliament elections, held in early June, UKIP secured 16 per cent of the vote and won thirteen seats.[20] The expenses scandal also proved to be something of a blessing for the Conservatives. David Cameron was quick to offer a clear and unqualified apology on behalf of all MPs at a moment when Brown was floundering. Moreover, when the *Telegraph* turned its fire upon Conservative MPs, duck houses and all, he was quicker than Brown to sack senior colleagues who had transgressed. A poll published on 30 May 2009 found that 60 per cent of people thought Brown had been most damaged by the crisis, while only 5 per cent thought Cameron had been.[21]

AN ABSENCE OF TRUST

I have focused, so far, largely on the party politics of the expenses scandal. But there is a bigger story here about trust in politicians generally. In September 2009 the Royal College of Physicians published its annual 'Trust in Professions' survey.[22] The headline story was that, whilst 92 per cent of people trusted doctors to generally tell the truth and 88 per cent trusted teachers, the figure for politicians was just 13 per cent. Britain was not alone. By the end of the 2000s, overall levels of political trust were also eye-wateringly low in France, Germany, Australia, Japan and the United States.[23] Yet in Britain, the 13 per cent figure came as a real shock and created a sense that the expenses scandal had irreparably damaged not only Labour's political standing, but people's sense of the legitimacy of the overall political system.

There is, however, a caveat worth adding here. Whilst trust in politicians fell thanks to the expenses scandal, it had already started pretty much at sea level. In 1983, the first year the Trust in Professions survey was published, only 18 per cent of people said they trusted politicians to tell the truth. By 1993, with a glut of Conservative sleaze stories in the papers, that had fallen to 14 per cent. By 1999, following the election of a new government, levels of trust had recovered somewhat to 23 per cent but by 2007, with the cash-for-honours scandal still in the news, it had fallen again to 18 per cent.[24] In other words, whilst the expenses scandal made a difference, it did not make *that* much difference. Once the dust had settled and a new government had been elected in 2010, trust bounced back once again. By 2013 the proportion of people trusting politicians to tell the truth had risen to 18 per cent, the same as in 2007, and by 2015 had risen to the heady heights of 21 per cent.

It is also worth asking here whether and how a lack of trust matters. Academic studies show that low and falling levels of political trust are associated with a reduced willingness to support long-term policies that require some measure of personal sacrifice.[25] Yet low levels of trust did not prevent the Coalition government from persuading large parts of the electorate that austerity, painful as it might be, would be good for the country in the long run. Nor did it preclude high levels of initial compliance with Covid-19 lockdown rules in 2020 (at least up until the moment when Barnard Castle's suitability as the location for a mobile optician became a national talking-point).*

It is worth adding too, that, whilst many people were angry and disgusted at politicians, there is little evidence to suggest large numbers of them had, at this point at least, reached the point of questioning the basic merits of representative democracy, or of wanting to pluralize Britain's winner-takes-all political system by way of, for example, a new and more proportional voting system, an elected second chamber or further devolution to the English regions. Most voters operate with a 'stealth' conception of politics and democracy: one that we have already encountered in the context of Scottish devolution (p. 65).[26] The problem with British democracy is that politicians don't do what they promised they were going to do. They spend most of their time grandstanding, bickering or, it now seemed, fiddling their expenses. As a result, anger at individual politicians, and even a sense that all politicians were the same and were all in it for themselves, did not lead, in 2009–10, to a demand for any fundamental changes in the way politics was done. Individual politicians were at fault rather than the political system itself, and the answer to this problem was to get a new set of politicians.[27] The irony here is that the arrival of a Coalition government to replace Labour in May 2010, something which did constitute a potentially important departure in Britain's political system, happened not because of the expenses scandal or because of a demand for less winner-takes-all politics but because the Conservatives fell short of their own electoral expectations.

* Falling levels of trust in politicians in general, and in New Labour politicians in particular, might well form one part of the explanation of why turnout in general elections fell from 71% in 1997 to 59% in 2001, and only reached 61% in 2005. In a book on the enduring importance of class in British politics, Geoffrey Evans and James Tilley show that working-class voters who had voted for Labour in 1997 were disproportionately likely to have abstained from voting in 2001. Geoffrey Evans and James Tilley, *The New Politics of Class: The Political Exclusion of the British Working Class* (Oxford, 2017), p. 175.

This does not mean political trust is unimportant. A lack of trust in politicians, or at least in mainstream ones, was one of the drivers of the Brexit vote in 2016 and the success of Jeremy Corbyn and Boris Johnson in the 2017 and 2019 general elections, respectively. There are two parts to this story. First, a lack of trust in 'business as usual' politicians made people more willing to vote for apparently more authentic outsider politicians such as Corbyn and Johnson, who seemed to say what they really thought. Second, one consequence of low and falling levels of trust in the 2000s seems to have been falling levels of 'partisan identification'. Between 1989 and 2009 the share of the electorate reporting a strong level of attachment to a particular party fell from 51 per cent to 29 per cent, whilst the proportion reporting no partisan allegiance at all rose from 25 per cent to 47 per cent.[28] With lower levels of partisan attachment, more voters are more likely to change their minds more often about whether to vote and, if they do vote, who to support. Hence partisan de-alignment seems to be associated with higher levels of electoral volatility. In the mid-1960s, when levels of partisan identification were high, only around 10 per cent of voters who voted in two consecutive elections switched the party they voted for across those elections. As the number strongly identifying with a party fell, that proportion rose steadily to around 30 per cent in the 1997, 2001 and 2005 elections, before climbing to 40 per cent in 2015 (and then dipping to 33 per cent in 2017).[29] Lower levels of partisan alignment and higher levels of electoral volatility were one of the necessary preconditions for the haywire turmoil of the 2010s where voters swung, in large numbers, from one party to another and, in 2016, singularly failed to heed the advice of the leaders of all the largest political parties to vote Remain.

PRESSING THE POINT

If Gordon Brown, Michael Martin and Peter Viggers were the biggest losers from the expenses scandal, the *Daily Telegraph* was the most obvious winner. At the 2010 British Press Awards it won newspaper of the year, campaign of the year and journalist of the year.[30] The political scalps the *Telegraph* collected in 2009 marked the end of what had been a good decade for the printed press and the BBC. In the late 1990s the expectation had been that New Labour's 'spin machine' would steamroller journalism and lead to the publication of glorified party-political press releases: 'churnalism' as it was known at the time.[31] But, whilst New Labour delivered on its side of the bargain, spinning for all it was worth, parts of the press hit back. On radio and then in print Andrew Gilligan broke the 'sexed-up' story on Iraqi WMD. The *Observer*'s Andrew Rawnsley documented and dissected the TB-GBs. To the annoyance of its executives and everyone at the Financial Services Authority, Robert Peston broke the Northern Rock story.

Indeed, rather than being steamrollered, the media were, just as often, accused of playing to the gallery: of simply assuming, without good reason, that politicians were lying and, in doing so, of actively undermining public trust in politicians and democracy. In *What the Media Do to Our Politics*, published in 2004 at precisely the moment the Hutton Inquiry was still playing out, the commentator John Lloyd argued that

> the media have claimed the right to judge and condemn; more, they have decided – without being clear about the decision – that politics is a dirty game, played by devious people who tell an essentially false narrative about the world and thus deceive the people.[32]

Shortly before he resigned as prime minister, in June 2007, Tony Blair jumped straight in at the deep end of this argument.[33] He acknowledged that the relationship between the press and politicians had never been an easy one and that, in its early days, New Labour had made matters worse. But he also argued that the proliferation of news channels and, in particular, 24-hour rolling news channels, had massively intensified the pressure upon journalists to search for and, if necessary, manufacture scandal and controversy and to editorialize on the news stories being reported on. Just as intense competition and pressure from the capital markets pushed the banks to search for ever-higher profits in the 2000s, intense competition and the need to meet circulation targets, Blair argued, was driving the media to abandon balance and nuance in ways that were doing untold longer-term damage. The media did not, it is safe to say, offer Blair a round of collective applause and a promise to do better in the future. The *Independent* (which Blair had attacked at length in his speech) doubled down on its argument that Blair had knowingly misled the public when it came to Iraq and in doing so had destroyed faith in politicians.[34] Yet, once he had left office, Blair probably had the last laugh, as the media's fortunes seemed to track those of Gordon Brown.

The phone hacking scandal began in 2002, when the Information Commissioner's Office raided the offices of newspapers and a number of private investigators and found evidence that several hundred journalists had illegally purchased confidential personal information.[35] Then, in 2005, the *News of the World* published a couple of relatively innocuous stories about how Prince William had borrowed a portable editing suite and had made an appointment with a knee surgeon, the details of which, William concluded, could only have been unearthed as a result of his voicemails being accessed. This led to a Metropolitan Police investigation and the arrest and eventual sentencing, in January 2007, of the *News of the World* journalist Clive Goodman and a private investigator, Glenn Mulcaire, and, at the same time, the resignation of the *News of the World*'s editor Andy Coulson.

We now know that the practice of phone hacking was widespread. But the *News of the World* conducted an internal investigation and told the world that Goodman had been a bad apple.[36] Further investigations by the Press Complaints Commission and the Metropolitan Police, the latter a profoundly perfunctory exercise, reached the same conclusion. But, with details of the legal settlements the *News of the World* was reaching with other victims of phone hacking accumulating, the *Guardian* journalist Nick Davies, *Private Eye* and the *New York Times* kept pushing the story forward. In December 2010 the *Guardian* reported that some of the documents previously seized by the police implied that Glenn Mulcaire had been specifically instructed to hack phones by a previous editor of the *News of the World*, Ian Edmondson.[37] In January 2011 the Met. reopened its investigations into phone hacking. Shortly after, Andy Coulson, who had been hired by David Cameron after he had departed the *News of the World*, resigned from his position as the government's director of communications.

In July 2011, the *Guardian* reported that journalists working for the *News of the World* had, in the days after she had disappeared in March 2002, accessed the voicemail of the murdered schoolgirl Milly Dowler and that, in deleting messages, they had led her family to believe she might still be alive.[38] A story that had been slowly building now exploded. Over the course of the next month the FBI launched an investigation into whether the paper had hacked the phones of victims of the

11 September attacks; the *News of the World*'s ultimate owner, Rupert Murdoch, was summoned to appear before a parliamentary inquiry ('the most humble day of my life');[39] Rebekah Brooks, another former *News of the World* editor, resigned as the chief executive of News International; the *News of the World* was closed by Murdoch; and a judicial inquiry into the culture, practices and ethics of the British press, to be chaired by Lord Justice Leveson, was established.

Over the following years, thanks to parliamentary inquiries, the Leveson hearings and books like *Dial M for Murdoch* by the Labour MP Tom Watson and the journalist Martin Hickman, it was revealed that phone hacking had indeed been a widespread journalistic practice, across more than one newspaper, and that it had been sustained by widespread corruption within the police and other public bodies and by a ferociously competitive workplace environment that had driven journalists to find and publish stories.[40] A former senior reporter at the *News of the World*, Neville Thurlbeck, suggested that News International newspapers had been ordered to scour the private lives of members of the House of Commons Culture, Media and Sport Committee.[41] The former prime minister John Major told the Leveson Inquiry that, at a dinner he hosted prior to the 1997 General Election, Murdoch had asked him to change his government's policy on Europe and told him, if he did not, that his organization would withdraw its support.[42] We also learned that David and Samantha Cameron lived near to and socialized with Rebekah Brooks and her husband and with Murdoch's daughter, Elisabeth, as a part of the so-called 'Chipping Norton Set', and that David Cameron had met with Rupert Murdoch or senior executives from News International on at least twenty-six occasions during his first year as prime minister.[43] Indeed, in June 2011, just a fortnight before the story about Milly Dowler's phone being hacked broke, Cameron, along with Labour's new leader, Ed Miliband, and the shadow chancellor, Ed Balls, had attended News International's summer party.[44]

Nobody came out of this whole sorry affair looking anything other than sordid. Yet, in the 2010s, the bigger story for the press was the collapse in circulation figures.[45] In 2009 the *Sun* was selling around 3 million papers a day. By 2020 this had fallen to just over 1 million. Over the same period, *The Times*'s circulation fell from a little over 600,000 to 370,000; the *Guardian*'s from 358,000 to 132,000; and the *Mail*'s from over 2.1 million to 1.1 million. Between 2005 and 2020 more than 250 local newspapers closed.[46] This was not just about newspapers. By the end of the 2010s, around half of all adults and nearly 90 per cent of those aged between sixteen and twenty-four were using social media to get their news.[47] Of those using social media, the key sources of news information were Facebook (76%), Twitter (37%) and Instagram (31%).[48] When John Lloyd wrote about the dysfunctional relationship between the press and politicians in 2004, Twitter, which I will return to later (p. 461), was probably not what he had in mind as the solution to the problem.

PART FIVE

Union

The *Union* in the title of Part Five refers, variously, to the party-political union between the Conservatives and Liberal Democrats; the 'we're all in it together' framing of the economics of austerity; the institutional union of marriage; the shared 'imagined community' created by Danny Boyle for the Olympic Games' opening ceremony of 2012; the political union of the United Kingdom, which was at stake in the 2014 Scottish independence referendum; and, finally, the failure of that political union to treat the 'Windrush Generation' with a decent level of humanity.[1]

In some respects, the Coalition years between 2010 and 2015, the main focus of these chapters, austerity apart, now looks like a *relatively* uneventful interregnum between the crash and bang of the financial crisis and the constitutional nervous breakdown of the Brexit years. It is telling, in this respect, that a second common theme here, beyond the trope of union, is things which did not happen. Many political commentators expected the Coalition to fall apart. It didn't. Scotland did not vote for independence. The London Olympics were not the disaster it was widely assumed they would be. Legislation allowing for same sex marriage did not lead, as one Conservative local councillor, James Malliff, warned it would, to people being allowed to marry animals.[2] Finally, and despite the introduction of the 'hostile environment' policy that led directly to the Windrush scandal, the Conservatives failed to reduce net migration to 'the tens of thousands'.[3]

Yet many of the events discussed in this Part are, I hope, compelling insofar as they capture at least some of the ways in which high-end politics and public policy touched ordinary lives. This is perhaps most obviously true of austerity and of the 'hostile environment' policy that left hundreds of people who had lived in Britain for decades being required to pay for NHS medical treatment, refused employment, or detained and then deported. To take just one case, Judy Griffith came to Britain from Barbados as a child in 1963, but in 2014 was required by the Home Office to prove her citizenship. Because she was, in her own words, a 'hoarder' who had kept enough paperwork to satisfy the requirement imposed on her to supply four different pieces of identification for each year she had been living in the country, she was eventually able to do this. But she was nevertheless left traumatized by what had happened:

> Basically, I was told that I was an illegal immigrant, which was horror, shock, horror, shock, more horror, you know. Having lived and worked here all my life, I was like, well, something is obviously wrong. Initially I didn't really take it to heart because to me it seemed like an impossibility. I just could not get my head around it.[4]

Legislation allowing same sex marriage had a profound impact on many people's lives, whilst the Scottish independence campaign generated intense passions which contrasted with the worthy but slightly dull earlier years of devolution. Finally, and although it does not perhaps rank as a life-changing event, the London Olympics created lasting memories for the eight thousand torchbearers who carried the Olympic flame, the seventy thousand who were selected to work as volunteer 'games makers' and the millions who watched.[5]

21

The Coalition: No Bed of Roses

'BANTER AND BONHOMIE'

Nick Clegg's big breakout moment as the Liberal Democrat leader came on 15 April 2010 during the first leadership debate of that year's general election. Looking calm and collected and sounding passionate but reasonable, Clegg told his audience that Labour and the Conservatives were two peas in a pod. 'The more they attack each other the more they sound like one another.'[1] What followed, for a few brief days, was an 80 per cent approval rating and a Liberal Democrat polling surge. It did not last. Cameron and Brown turned their fire on Clegg, who struggled to answer the question always asked of Liberal leaders about what he would do in the event of a hung parliament. On 6 May, the day of the election, the Liberal Democrats secured 23 per cent of the vote, an improvement on their 2005 record, but lost five seats. The Conservatives secured 36 per cent of the vote, gained ninety-one new seats and comfortably saw off the expected threat from UKIP, which achieved just a 3.1 per cent vote share. The Conservatives nevertheless fell just short of securing an overall majority, which left Clegg and the Liberal Democrats holding a winning lottery ticket.

For a short while everyone waited to see what would happen. Gordon Brown, still in residence in Number 10, heroically seized the opportunity to do not very much. This gave Cameron, who had previously discussed the option of a coalition with George Osborne, the chance to make a 'big, open and comprehensive offer' to work with the Liberal Democrats.[2] In 2008 Cameron had described Clegg as his 'favourite joke'.[3] But in May 2010 the maths mattered more. Conservatives plus Liberal Democrats equalled a working overall majority. So, the two parties began talking and the talks went well. Then, at the eleventh hour,

Gordon Brown rose from his political slumber and confirmed that Labour was also interested in doing a deal. This looked like it might work. Labour was prepared to offer Clegg and his party a referendum on proportional voting when the Conservatives were only offering a committee of inquiry. Moreover, Labour looked and sounded a lot more pro-European than the Conservatives – and being pro-European was a Liberal Democrat priority. Gordon Brown even offered to resign as prime minister to make it all happen. But just when it looked like Labour might snatch victory from the jaws of defeat, the Conservatives returned to the negotiating table determined, in the words of William Hague, the Conservative's lead negotiator, to 'go the extra mile'.[4] In next to no time the Conservatives also agreed to a referendum on proportional voting, and sweetened the deal by confirming Clegg would become deputy prime minister.

On Wednesday 12 May, Cameron and Clegg held a joint press conference in the Rose Garden of 10 Downing Street to announce the formation of their new Coalition. The sun shone down and there was, in Cameron's words, lots of 'banter and bonhomie'.[5] Cameron revealed he and Clegg had initially spoken about a limited deal in which the Liberal Democrats would have supported the Conservatives on key votes in Parliament in return for policy concessions. They had, however, decided that a formal Coalition was what the country needed. With the public finances imploding and the financial markets wobbling, it was vital that the Conservatives and Lib Dems should be seen to be capable of putting their differences aside in order to work in the national interest to address Britain's economic emergency. The voters had spoken, and he and Clegg had listened and were offering a new kind of politics based on compromise and stability and all-round grown-upness.

GOING ORANGE

The Liberal Democrats were formed in 1988 from the wreckage of the political alliance between the Social Democratic Party and the Liberal Party, an alliance that had tried, but failed, to 'break the mould' of British politics in the 1980s.[6] In the 1992 General Election they and their new leader, the ex-special forces and ex-MI6 officer Paddy Ashdown, secured 18 per cent of the vote. This was reasonably impressive but counted for very little. Outside its traditional areas of strength – the Southwest of England, the Scottish Borders and the Scottish Highlands – the Liberal Democrats tended to come second to either the Conservatives (in the South of England) or Labour (in the North of England, Wales and Scotland). Basically, coming second in a first-past-the-post plurality system was right up there with winning a signed copy of a Piers Morgan DVD: 18 per cent of the vote translated into just twenty MPs.

Tony Blair, once he was elected Labour's leader in 1994, made matters worse. The Liberals' tried-and-tested political strategy was to present themselves as the sensible, moderate, centre-ground alternative to their hyper-ideological rivals. Yet this was a political position Blair was of course keen for New Labour to be seen to be occupying. As Ashdown said in his diary, 'Blair fills exactly the space I have been aiming at for the last seven years.'[7] For a while it looked like the Plan A-alternative for the Liberal Democrats might be for them to negotiate some sort of deal with New Labour, agreeing joint positions on key policies whilst promising not to contest constituencies which the other party was best-placed to win. Any such deal would have been wildly unpopular with the left of the Labour Party and Labour's deputy leader, John Prescott.[8] Yet it is not hard to see why Blair, in an effort to publicly demonstrate how Labour was changing and moving to the centre ground, might have been interested. However, in the end Plan A came to nothing. By 1995 New Labour was miles ahead in the opinion polls and clearly set to win the next election, regardless of whether or not it was nice to the Liberal Democrats. And having blown hot, Blair then went cold. He argued that the Liberal Democrats lacked the 'necessary fibre' to make tough decisions and that high-fibre New Labour would be better off without them.[9]

In 1999 Charles Kennedy, the MP for Ross, Skye and Inverness West, replaced Ashdown. His Plan B alternative was to present the Liberal Democrats as a more principled, less authoritarian left-of-centre alternative to New Labour.[10] The Liberals opposed the Iraq War; opposed new police powers; opposed market-driven public-sector reform; and argued that higher taxes on the richest were a necessary price for reducing inequality. This proved controversial. Plenty of Liberal Democrat MPs were happy to move to the left of New Labour. But a group of high-profile dissidents adopted a very different position. They maintained that the problem with New Labour was not that it was too right-wing but that it was too left-wing: too ready to raise taxes; too ready to invent new regulations; and too ready to go all 'nanny state' when it came to people's individual choices. In 2004 these nonconformists, including the MPs Vince Cable, David Laws and Ed Davey, and two up-and-coming Members of the European Parliament, Nick Clegg and Chris Huhne, contributed chapters to a book, *The Orange Book*, which made the Plan C Liberal Democratic case for more markets and more individual freedom.[11]

The 2005 General Election seemed to vindicate Kennedy's Plan B. The Liberal Democrats won 22 per cent of the vote and, thanks to a great deal of tactical voting, an impressive sixty-two seats, several of them in leftish, middle-class and student-heavy constituencies such as Manchester Withington, Sheffield Hallam and Birmingham Yardley. In an age of growing partisan de-alignment and higher electoral volatility (p. 260), the Liberal Democrats (and, it might be added, the Scottish National Party) had, it seemed, put themselves in a position to benefit from New Labour's various stresses and strains. Yet there was a downside. The Liberal Democrats had cuffed New Labour around the ears, but they had lost more seats to the Conservatives than they had gained from them, and the Orange Bookers were not happy. Kennedy's leadership came under increasing pressure. After he had publicly admitted to a drinking problem he resigned in January 2006 and was replaced by the former sprinter Menzies 'Ming' Campbell, who had competed in the 1964 Tokyo Olympics and once raced against O. J. Simpson.[12] Campbell, who kept faith with Kennedy's Plan B, was, however, pushed into resigning eighteen months later amidst a barrage of stories about his age and mental sharpness.

The Liberal Democrats' next leadership election, in 2007, was contested by two Plan C Orange Bookers: Chris Huhne and the newly elected Member of Parliament for Sheffield Hallam, Nick Clegg. Clegg won by a whisker, but then had to work out how to move his party from left to right at a point when most Liberal Democrat activists were happy with where they were. He did not manage to find an answer to this problem and, as a result, the Liberal Democrats' 2010 election manifesto was packed full of Plan B-promises to abolish university tuition fees, cancel the Trident nuclear missile submarine programme, introduce a 'mansion tax' on houses worth more than £2 million and cap NHS managers' pay. Yet some commentators had nevertheless realized just how far Clegg had drifted from his party. A profile published in the *Financial Times* in April 2010, just a few days before the first leadership debate and the burst of Cleggmania that followed it, noted David Cameron saw Clegg as a 'closet Tory' and that Chris Huhne had taken to describing Clegg as 'David Cameron's stunt double'.[13]

We can now go back to where we started. In May 2010 a lot of people assumed the Liberal Democrats would want to do a deal with Labour because the two parties seemed to be saying a lot of the same things. But Clegg did not necessarily want to be saying what he was saying. He was a lot closer to the modernizing David Cameron than he was to the left-of-centre born-again Keynesian Gordon Brown. So, Plan C won by the back door, and in the new Coalition four other Liberal Democrats joined Clegg in the Cabinet (as secretaries of state for business, innovation and skills, energy and climate change and Scotland and as the chief secretary to the Treasury).

PLAN C IN ACTION

The consensus was that the Coalition would not last.[14] Outside wartime emergencies, the British political system was basically designed around the assumption one party would win power. The Liberal Democrats and the Conservatives had spent too many years attacking each other and were too ideologically different. They would inevitably end up disagreeing about policy and airing their grievances in the media. One or other of them would eventually decide they ought to walk away. However, this view was quite myopic. It failed to take account of Clegg's *Orange Book* ideology and that, outside Westminster, coalitions had survived and even thrived within local government and the devolved Scottish, Welsh and Northern Irish executives.

The Coalition had its rocky moments. In October 2010 a review chaired by the former chief executive of British Petroleum, Lord Browne of Madingley, recommended the existing £3,920 cap on tuition fees be eliminated and that universities be allowed to set their own fees in a free market. Clegg and Cameron paused, took a deep breath and eventually agreed to keep the cap but to raise it to £9,000. The problem for Clegg came in squaring this with the Liberals' 2010 manifesto pledge to 'scrap unfair university tuition fees so everyone has the chance to get a degree, regardless of their parents' income'.[15] When the Higher Education Bill came to a vote in Parliament only twenty-seven of the fifty-seven Lib Dem MPs voted with the government of which they were a part. Shortly after, Vince Cable the business secretary, seen by many as a potential replacement for Clegg, was caught telling a visitor to his constituency office (in a sting operation mounted by the *Daily Telegraph*) that working in the Coalition was like 'fighting a war', one in which he reserved the option of taking the 'nuclear option' and resigning if it all got too bad.[16]

The Conservatives had promised the Liberal Democrats a referendum on the voting system. Rather than insist that the option on the table be the fully proportional Single Transferable Vote, Clegg ended up agreeing to a referendum on the Alternative Vote – a kind of half way, semi-proportional system that he himself had previously described as a 'miserable little compromise'.[17] In an era of partisan de-alignment and electoral volatility, there was a respectable case for switching to a more proportional voting system to make the membership of the House of Commons more representative. The Liberal Democrats had, after all, won 23 per cent of the vote in 2010 in return for just 9 per cent of the number of MPs. UKIP had secured over 900,000 votes and won the square root of nothing. Yet the argument for adopting a more proportional system was not a given. To Clegg's apparent surprise, the Conservatives, when the referendum campaign began, laid into the Alternative Vote on the grounds that it would result in more coalitions, a lack of electoral accountability and, with one knowing eye on the tuition fee increase, 'more broken promises'.[18] After a notably lacklustre campaign, the Alternative Vote gathered 6 million votes for and 13 million votes against on a turnout of just 42 per cent.[19]

Looking back, Cameron describes the AV referendum as a 'miserable little episode' after which 'things between our parties would never be quite the same'.[20] For Clegg, the referendum loss was the moment when 'the relationship between the two coalition partners changed for good' and became much more 'transactional'.[21] The Liberal Democrats would stick with the Coalition and, in doing so, honour the terms and conditions of the Partnership Agreement they had negotiated in May 2010. But otherwise, and when the opportunity arose, they would not hesitate to put the boot into the Conservatives. In December 2011 Clegg accused Cameron of caving in to his own Eurosceptic backbenchers after he had vetoed a new European Union Treaty (pp. 363–4). In July 2012, follow-ing a row over a botched proposal to reform the House of Lords, Clegg withdrew his support for a Boundary Commission review of parliamen-tary constituencies – a review which, it was expected, would have benefited the Conservatives.[22] Cameron says he and Clegg 'nearly came to blows' about how to respond to the results of the Leveson Inquiry into press regulation in March 2013.[23] In September of that year, during a speech to the Liberal Democrat conference, Clegg revealed he had blocked Conservative plans to cut inheritance tax, dilute the Human Rights Act and deregulate labour markets, and said that he would con-tinue to fight against 'Tory party dogma'.[24]

Yet the Coalition survived. There was lots of talk about someone challenging Clegg for the Lib Dem leadership, but nothing happened. Clegg himself apparently considered resigning in 2014 when the Lib Dems were at a particularly low ebb but eventually decided against doing so.[25] Indeed, even when it was at its lowest ebb, the Cameron–Clegg relationship remained a lot more amicable than the Blair–Brown one had been. At the first meeting of the new Coalition Cabinet in May 2010 Cameron said someone had told him that he and Clegg were the new Tony Blair and Gordon Brown of British politics. This, he added, was 'setting the bar rather low'.[26] This was a good line and it remained true. Their relationship deteriorated but they kept talking and neither tried to depose the other by way of a curry house coup.

The Coalition was held together in part by the Fixed Term Parlia-ment Act, which it had passed in 2011 and stipulated that a government must serve a full five-year term unless there was either a vote of no con-fidence in it or two-thirds of MPs voted for an early election. That legislation made it much harder for either the Conservatives or the Lib-eral Democrats to walk away and trigger a new general election. Day to day, the Coalition was also strengthened by the formal mechanisms put in place by the Civil Service to keep everyone involved on the same page, most notably via the weekly 'Quad' meetings between Cameron, Clegg, Osborne and the Liberal chief secretary to the Treasury, Danny Alexander. The irony here was that, in bypassing or pre-empting the Cabinet, these Quad meetings protected, in their own way, the central-ized ethos of winner-takes-all politics.

Above all, the Coalition was held together by austerity, the subject of the next chapter. Outside the Quad, various senior Liberal Democrats hinted that, given the option, they would have cut public spending more slowly and more carefully. But Clegg and Alexander never wavered in their conviction that government debt had to be reduced and that this would require significant cuts to public expenditure. Indeed, on some accounts, Alexander, with all the burning enthusiasm of a recent convert, wanted to move further and faster than George Osborne.[27] In his account of Tolstoy's view of history, Isaiah Berlin drew an influential distinction between two styles of intellectual thinking, citing, in doing so, a line from the Greek poet Archilochus: 'The fox knows many things, but the hedgehog knows one big thing.'[28] Clegg and Alexander were hedgehogs. They knew one big thing, that austerity was going to be painful but necessary and they did not waver in this belief. That is why the Coalition survived.

DISRAELI'S LAST LAUGH

So, the Coalition worked well enough as an exercise in government. But it eventually proved to be a Grade I political disaster for the Liberal Democrats. After the happy days of the Rose Garden in the spring, the turning point seemed to come with tuition fees in the autumn of 2010. Once he had been elected as party leader, Clegg had tried to persuade Liberal Democrat activists to soften their opposition to university tuition fees. He had failed and in 2010 publicly signed a pledge not to raise fees further, before then agreeing to raise them to £9,000 a year just a few months later.[29] George Osborne is reported to have thought Clegg had been 'nuts' to do this and, sure enough, Clegg was slaughtered by the press for breaking his promises.[30] Yet whilst many commentators, including the Liberal Democrat's next leader, Tim Farron, blamed the 'unfolding nightmare' of tuition fees for the party's loss of votes, the bottom line is that the party had already been haemorrhaging support before the tuition fees legislation came to the House of Commons. By July 2010 they were already down to 15 per cent support in opinion polls.[31] In the May 2011 local elections, held alongside the AV referendum, they remained on 15 per cent, losing, in the process, 750 of their 1,800 local councillors. In the 2014 European Parliament elections, where they lost ten of their eleven seats, they crashed to 6.6 per cent of the vote, coming fifth behind UKIP, Labour, the Conservatives and the Green Party. By this time, Clegg was reportedly the most disliked party leader in modern British political history.[32]

William Hague was of the view that the Liberal Democrats were doomed to disaster from the moment they entered the Coalition. When the Partnership Agreement between the two parties that he had helped to negotiate was eventually concluded, he reportedly told his wife, Ffion, 'I've just killed the Liberal Democrats'.[33] Clegg, for his part, recognized, from the very start, the danger that voters would end up punishing the Liberal Democrats for everything the Coalition did. Yet he also hoped that, over the longer term, the party might come to be respected for their willingness to compromise and make difficult decisions. Blair, recall, had thought the Liberal Democrats lacked the necessary fibre to make tough decisions. Joining the Coalition would show, once and for all, that the Liberals were a serious party willing to take difficult decisions. As Clegg said in September 2010:

> We have to hold our nerve. The prize is not now. We have to look ahead to 2015 when we can say, 'you may not have liked the coalition before and may have disagreed with what we had to do to restore the economy but now your children have got jobs to go to, you have a pupil premium, fairer taxes, a pension guarantee, a greener economy, a reformed form of politics, restored civil liberties . . .' I think that would be a record that people would say 'OK they took a risk for the benefit of the country and it paid off.'[34]

Various academic studies concluded that, relative to their parliamentary size, the Liberal Democrats had actually done pretty well out of the initial Coalition negotiations over how to turn two manifestos into one policy agenda.[35] Yet most voters had very little, if any, idea what policies the Liberals had or had not been responsible for. In 2010 they were seen as being, like Labour, a left-of-centre party.[36] So, voters tended to regard their willingness to jump into bed with the Conservatives as clear-cut evidence of their willingness to discard everything they believed in in order to achieve a slice of power. Clegg could argue politics was all about compromise and putting aside narrow party interests to work in the public interest and that he had struck a good deal for his party and its supporters, but his view was not widely shared. By 2015 only 7 per cent of voters trusted the Liberals to keep their promises.[37] As Clegg himself eventually recognized, after the Coalition had been dissolved: it had started to fall apart from the start. The Rose Garden press conference had seemed like a good idea at the time but it had come to symbolize the party's 'excessive willingness to compromise' and its loss of political identity.[38] That loss of identity might not have been quite as severe if the Liberal Democrats, rather than spreading themselves thinly across government with a few Cabinet positions and lots of junior ministers playing a 'watchdog' role in departments, had, instead, assumed control of one or two large areas of policy, perhaps education, and made a virtue of going their own political way.[39] But, as we have seen, and whatever voters may have thought in 2010, Nick Clegg and other senior figures in the party had, in fact, already moved well to the right by 2010.

If the Liberal Democrats had had a committed base of partisan supporters, they might have come closer to weathering the storm. But this is precisely what they did not have. In 2010 around 50 per cent of those who voted Liberal said they either had no sense of underlying identification with the party or had an underlying sense of identification with an entirely different party.[40] They had voted for the Liberal Democrats either because they were quite taken by Nick Clegg or because they passionately disliked the versions of the Conservatives and Labour which were on offer. There was very little chance these voters were going to give Clegg the benefit of the doubt.

When the Coalition was first formed, lots of commentators dug out their dictionaries of political quotations and, thumbing through, stumbled across Benjamin Disraeli's observation – delivered as the chancellor in a dying minority Conservative government in December 1852 – that 'England does not love coalitions'. This was, in fact, a bit selective. What Disraeli had actually said was that 'coalitions, although successful, have always found this, that their triumph has been brief. This too I know, that England does not love coalitions.'[41] In a sense, the Coalition was something of a triumph. Whilst lots of people expected it would fall apart, it lasted for five years. Yet, in the end, Disraeli had the last laugh. Plenty of people told polling companies they wanted to see political parties put the national interest above their own party interests and, in doing so, co-operate more with each other. Yet they also wanted parties, once they had promised to do something, to do it with no ifs or buts. This kind of 'stealth politics' view of what politics ought to be about proved impossibly difficult to reconcile with the realities of coalition politics and the give and take of bargaining over policies. It is of course the case that political parties are themselves coalitions often built on uneasy compromises. Before they joined the Coalition in 2010, Plan A, Plan B and Plan C Liberal Democrats all wanted different things despite being in the same party. Moreover, the post-election bargaining and compromise between the Conservatives and Liberal Democrats took place under a particularly harsh and public light – one that voters, as it turned out, did not particularly like.

In the mid-1990s, the Liberal Democrat's campaign director, Chris Rennard, wrote to Paddy Ashdown to warn him that if he negotiated some sort of Plan A-deal with New Labour, his party would be punished at the next general election, crashing to as little as 10 per cent of the vote. Rennard nevertheless argued that this might be a price worth paying if a deal with New Labour led to a switch to a proportional voting system and 'permanent influence'. However, without electoral reform, Rennard warned, any deal would be 'suicidal'.[42] That turned out to be about right.[43] In the 2015 General Election, and without the comfort blanket of a deal on proportional voting, the Liberal Democrats lost forty-nine of their fifty-seven MPs and 4.4 million votes. Danny Alexander, Vince Cable, Ed Davey and Charles Kennedy all lost their seats.

Nick Clegg narrowly held on to his Sheffield Hallam constituency in 2015 but lost it to Labour in 2017.[44] In 2019 he was made head of global affairs and communications at Facebook and moved to Atherton, on the south side of San Francisco Bay, only a few miles from where Steve Jobs had been raised. In explaining the move Clegg said he 'couldn't get my head round the idea that I was going to spend 20, 30 years possibly pontificating to absolutely no impact whatsoever'; 'sitting on a few company boards'; and 'popping-up on the *Today* programme as a ghost from the past'.[45] Facebook offered a new start. At first, a lot of people assumed the new job would be largely ceremonial and that Clegg had been appointed for his contacts. This, it turned out, was not right. When Donald Trump was suspended from Facebook for two years in January 2021 for praising the Washington Capitol Hill insurrection, Clegg appeared before the American media to explain the decision and to take the flak from those who thought Trump should have been banned for life or never removed in the first place. A few months later, when the data engineer and Facebook employee Frances Haugen leaked documents to the *Wall Street Journal* detailing concerns raised by employees to senior managers about the damage Facebook was doing to the state of American democracy and people's mental health, it was Clegg, rather than Facebook's founder, Mark Zuckerberg, who did the initial round of press interviews. Having, presumably, been seen to have done a good job in difficult circumstances, Clegg was promoted to a new role as president of global affairs at Facebook's new parent company, Meta.

The British press, when it first noticed that Clegg had moved to America, ran several snarky stories about his nice new house, large salary and sunny Californian winters.[46] Others pointed to the parallels between his role at Facebook, defending decisions ultimately taken by Zuckerberg, and his role as deputy prime minister defending decisions taken by David Cameron. This was, in some ways, unfair. According to Nathaniel Persily, a Stanford law professor, Clegg, far from simply following the established company line, had repeatedly pushed the case for tougher self-regulation within Facebook. Yet, Persily added, he had lost most of these key battles. This made the comparison with Clegg's former political life and times perhaps more understandable. 'He's fighting the good fight inside. But he's also fallen on his sword so many times that he's quite punctured at this point.'[47]

22

Calling an Austerity Emergency

COUNTRIES THAT CANNOT LIVE WITHIN THEIR MEANS

One important power governments have is the power to call something a crisis and to say what that crisis is about, who caused it and what needs to be done to resolve it. Governments might not always be believed, and their arguments might not always be accepted, but crisis-calling is a tried-and-tested political strategy. Sometimes, when times are particularly tough, governments don't simply call a crisis but label something as a national emergency and, in doing so, warn people of difficult times ahead and the need for everyone to make sacrifices. Tony Blair presented the threat posed by Iraq's weapons of mass destruction as an existential threat. Boris Johnson justified the Covid-19 national lockdown in equally stark terms. On 8 June 2010, during the Queen's Speech debate, the new Conservative chancellor of the Coalition government, George Osborne, presented austerity as the unavoidable solution to a national crisis:

> I have just returned from the G20 meeting in South Korea where I was representing the country with the worst budget deficit of any state round the table. Our national debt has doubled and is set to double again in the space of just five years. Those who believe that this is some abstract problem should pay heed to warning noises from the European continent. Countries that cannot live within their means face higher interest rates, greater economic shocks and larger debt interest bills.[1]

Britain was facing a national economic emergency and an impending debt catastrophe. Understatement was not possible. Doing nothing was not an option. It was time to put narrow party politics to one side and take decisions to protect Britain's long-term national interests. There was, as Margaret Thatcher had once said, no alternative.

With Conservative MPs wagging their fingers at their Labour opponents on the opposition benches and Liberal Democrat MPs nodding in support, Osborne later announced that government borrowing would be cut from £160 billion in 2010 to £37 billion by 2014/15 and that, to achieve this, spending would be cut and taxes raised. The NHS and the overseas aid budget would be exempt but other government departments would face 20 per cent-plus budget cuts. Public-sector wages would be frozen for anyone earning more than £21,000. A proposed rise in the pension age to sixty-six would arrive sooner rather than later. Welfare benefits would be increased in line with consumer price inflation rather than the retail price index. There would be a cap on the total amount which could be claimed through housing benefit. Tax credits would be cut. A bank levy would be introduced. VAT would increase and, whilst corporation tax would fall, capital gains tax would rise.

There was an element of self-flagellating political theatre in all of this. At the start of a new election cycle, Osborne, an acutely political chancellor, could afford to paint everything in the darkest of colours, knowing that all the blame could be heaped on the previous Labour government. For this reason, Osborne downplayed the extent to which spending cuts were going to be phased in over time. That said, there was no doubt the underlying numbers, theatre or not, were startling. Osborne had promised an emergency austerity budget and he delivered on that promise.

ARGUING ABOUT AUSTERITY

Austerity was, most obviously, a set of government policies centred upon spending cuts. But austerity was also an argument about what had happened to the British economy and what needed to be done to turn it around. After the 'right to be heard' phase of Cameron's early years as the Conservative leader (p. 79), these arguments were notably uncompromising.

Britain was in debt and debt was bad. Just as individuals need to live within their means, so, too, do countries. Labour had borrowed money in the short term to try and win an election and, in so doing, had pushed annual government borrowing up to eye-wateringly, completely unsustainable levels. Debt was bad for the economy. The government had borrowed so much that businesses, facing higher interest rates and taxes, were cutting back on investment. Austerity would be painful, but it would, in the medium term, boost growth. This was not simply a matter of ideological dogma. It was a hard-headed economic judgement endorsed by the OECD and the International Monetary Fund (IMF). Drawing upon the economic theory of the 'expansionary fiscal contraction', Osborne argued that a credible commitment to cutting spending and debt would increase business confidence, reduce interest rates and kick-start an economic recovery.[2] Debt was, however, not just an economic issue. It was also a moral one. Labour's profligate borrowing would have to be paid for by future generations and that was unconscionable. Austerity was the right thing to do to protect the future.

Austerity could not be postponed. There was only a narrow window in which the government could act. Labour wanted to keep on borrowing but if this happened then, sooner rather than later, investors would start to wonder whether the money they had lent would ever be repaid. When that happened, interest rates would shoot up, creating the possibility of a future and humiliating government default. This was not simply scaremongering. Greece was on everyone's mind. It had borrowed like there was no tomorrow and was, as a result, at just the moment George Osborne was delivering his budget, paying the price. Its lenders had lost confidence in it and the result – one playing out on the evening news broadcasts – had been riots, failing medical supplies and the rise of extreme nationalism. Britain needed to act now to avoid the risk of something similar.

Austerity could be done fairly. Labour had become addicted to spending and had wasted millions on bureaucracy and silly policy initiatives. The Coalition would have to make difficult decisions, but it would make those decisions fairly. The NHS would be protected. Pensioners would be protected. Banks and high earners would have to dig deep and those claiming welfare benefits would have to accept that they would be paid less than those who worked and that they had a responsibility to find work.

If the Conservative argument for austerity drew, consciously or not, upon arguments first developed in the 1930s and 1940s by the Austrian free-market economist (and future Nobel Prize-winner) Friedrich Hayek, austerity's opponents drew upon his great intellectual rival, John Maynard Keynes.[3] Keynes, it will be recalled, had argued amid the Great Depression that recessions destroyed confidence, spending and investment, and so risked becoming self-perpetuating. The invisible hand of the free market could not be relied upon. Instead, the very visible hand of government was needed to pull the economy out of recession via increased borrowing and spending.

Osborne argued that governments could not keep spending more than they earned, any more than individuals could. But this was contestable. In the 1930s Keynes had shown that if all households saved more and reduced their debt and did so at the same time, the result would be an economic slump as spending and employment fell.[4] By borrowing money, as the Labour government had done in the immediate aftermath of the financial crisis, the economy could be protected in ways that would allow growth to resume and borrowing to be repaid. This Keynesian argument was not just technical and economic. It was also moral. Protect the vulnerable now and invest for the future. The alternative to increased short-term borrowing was not, as George Osborne had argued, lower overall debt but lower long-term economic growth.[5]

The Coalition argued that Greece was a warning of what would happen if you borrowed too much. But this was comparing apples with coffee tables. Most of Greece's debt had been accumulated by its banks and private companies and not by its government.[6] Because it was part of the European Single Currency, the real problem Greece had was that it depended on Germany and the European Central Bank to finance its debt. Britain did not have the same problem. It was free to borrow money and the Bank of England, through quantitative easing, could keep interest rates low and keep funding government debt (pp. 248–50). Britain was borrowing a lot of money, but because interest rates were so low the total cost of that borrowing was manageable. That argument proved a difficult one to sell at the time, but it was eventually vindicated. In 2010 the government was paying around £39 billion in interest payments on its *total* debt, or, to put this another way, around a quarter of the amount it borrowed that year. By 2011/12 that sum had risen to £45bn. Over the next nine years it hovered at around £40bn. Expressed as a share of GDP, debt interest payments fell from

2.4 per cent in the early 2010s to 1.7 per cent in 2019/20.[7] Those are all high numbers. But in the context of an overall government budget of over £600 billion they were not unsustainable in the way that Greece's debt had been. Britain was borrowing a lot of money, but it was borrowing that money at a point when borrowing was relatively cheap.

Moreover, the argument that Labour had become addicted to spending could be overblown. By 2007, on the eve of the financial crisis, the government was borrowing about £40 billion a year, around 6 per cent of total public expenditure. That was not great, but neither was it obviously calamitous.* When the economy had started to stall, the government had borrowed more, but it had done so in order to minimize the impact and the length of the recession. Borrowing, in other words, was not the cause of the recession but one of its consequences.[8] When the economy had started to recover, tax revenues would have risen and welfare expenditure and borrowing fallen of their own accord. Austerity was attempting to fix a problem which would have gone a long way towards resolving itself.

Finally, the argument that austerity was being done fairly, that, in Cameron's words, 'we're all in it together', was a travesty. Faced with a choice between cutting spending or raising taxes, the Coalition had opted, overwhelmingly, for the former. By 2014/15 something like £8 billion was to be raised through tax rises, compared with £40 billion to be saved through spending cuts.[9] Spending cuts fell hardest on women and the poorest in society because they depended most on that money. The Fawcett Society pointed to a 'triple jeopardy' for women caused by cuts to public-sector jobs, cuts in wages and pensions, and cuts in public services – especially social care, which would leave family carers (most of them women) 'filling in the gaps'.[10] New Labour had made Britain a richer and fairer society. For all their talk of 'compassionate Conservatism', Cameron and Osborne were reverting to Thatcherite type and would load the costs of a recession caused by the very wealthiest bankers on to the most vulnerable.

---

* In 1994 and 1995 the Conservatives, under John Major, had run annual budget deficits of £45bn and £38bn.

'A CRASS MISTAKE'

Between 2010 and 2015 austerity had more than a few rough political moments. In 2011 there were large protest marches against spending cuts.[11] In that same year, Cameron announced a pause to a new set of market-driven NHS reforms.[12] In March 2012 Osborne's so-called 'omnishambles' budget – an expression previously coined by the writers of *The Thick of It* – resulted in a measure of confusion and an eventual U-turn on the imposition of VAT on hot snacks. Looking back and judging by the standards of Kwasi Kwarteng's mini budget in September 2022, Osborne's problems now look like small change. But, at the time, they offered a rare moment of political cut-through for Labour which poured scorn on a 'millionaire's budget' that had also seen a cut in the top rate of taxation from 50 to 45 per cent.[13] In April 2012, Nadine Dorries described Cameron and Osborne as 'two posh boys who don't know the price of milk' and show 'no remorse, no contrition and no passion to understand the lives of others'.[14] Then, in September, Andrew Mitchell, the chief whip, was accused of swearing at policemen guarding Downing Street and of calling one of them a 'pleb': a line which definitely failed the 'all in it together' vibe.* By February 2013 Labour had a 10-percentage point lead over the Conservatives in opinion polls.[15]

Yet, even when things got politically bad, they never got *that* bad. Osborne and Cameron stuck together and, in the end, and despite a fair bit of noise, the Conservative and Liberal Democrat coalition did the same. Moreover, whilst the Labour Party looked, for a while, as if it might win the next general election, austerity itself retained a broad measure of public support. On the one hand, polls showed that the proportion of people agreeing that spending cuts would be good for the

* Mitchell resigned the next month. In December 2012, a serving police officer, suspected of leaking a copy of the police log of the incident to the *Sun*, was arrested. Apparent discrepancies between the version of events in the police log and what witnesses to the incident said they had heard then emerged. One police officer was subsequently jailed and two others dismissed for gross misconduct. Mitchell sued the *Sun* for libel; in November 2014 he lost his case when the judge ruled he had, in all probability, used the word pleb. Loulla-Mae Eleftheriou-Smith, 'Plebgate: the timeline of events that left Andrew Mitchell's career in tatters', *Independent* (28 Nov. 2014).

economy fell from 53 per cent in June 2010 to just 29 per cent in September 2012 (before recovering to 45 per cent in the first few months of 2015). Meanwhile, the proportion agreeing that the Coalition's spending cuts were being done fairly stood at around 35 per cent in late 2010 before falling to just over 20 per cent in April 2012 (by early 2015 it had recovered to 27 per cent). That does not necessarily sound like an election-winning formula. The important number, however, was that 50–60 per cent of people consistently thought that the spending cuts, whether fair or not, were necessary, whilst more people consistently thought it was Labour rather than the Coalition who were to blame for them having to be made.[16]

To this extent, the key figure when it comes to understanding the politics of austerity was not George Osborne but the Labour MP Liam Byrne. If scientists had been able to build an archetypal New Labour MP using cloned DNA and the collected speeches of Anthony Crosland, Byrne was what you would have got. He was born in Warrington, raised in Harlow and graduated from the University of Manchester, where he studied Politics and Modern History, before gaining a Fulbright Scholarship and studying at Harvard for an MBA. He then worked for consultancy firms before founding his own IT company. In July 2004, aged thirty-four, he was selected as the Labour candidate for a by-election in Birmingham Hodge Hill. He won by a few hundred votes after a campaign organized by Gordon Brown's favourite Blair-basher, Tom Watson, that featured a leaflet warning voters that the 'Lib Dems are on the side of failed asylum seekers'.[17] In May 2006, Byrne was appointed minister of state for borders and immigration, where he argued the case for a points-based immigration system, ID cards and curbs on the arrival of Romanian and Bulgarian workers, as well as issuing a consultation paper on future immigration which referenced the need to create 'a much more hostile environment in this country' for illegal immigrants.[18] He was appointed minister for the Cabinet Office in October 2008, not long after suggesting that the August bank holiday be made the centrepiece of a national celebration of Britishness.

Finally, Byrne was appointed Labour's chief secretary to the Treasury in 2009 and, after Alistair Darling had just about persuaded Gordon Brown that the government needed to have a plan to cut the deficit in order to appease, amongst others, the governor of the Bank of England

(p. 247), Byrne led on negotiations to cut £32 billion from proposed future spending programmes. In May 2010 he comfortably held his seat in Birmingham Hodge Hill but Labour lost. As ministers often do when they leave office after losing an election, he left a note on his desk for his successor. This one was notably short.

Dear Chief Secretary,

I'm afraid there is no money.
Kind regards and good luck!

Liam

On 17 May 2010, the incoming chief secretary, the Liberal Democrat David Laws, mentioned the note at a press conference. Osborne's press secretary asked for a copy. Laws says he refused to hand it over.[19] If that is true, it made no difference. The *Sun* led with the story the next day. Needless to say, 'no money left' made it into Osborne's emergency budget statement.

Over the course of the next few years, the Labour Party changed. But it was not necessarily clear that it had changed in ways that discomforted the Conservatives or rendered references to Byrne's note redundant. After Gordon Brown had resigned, Ed Miliband, the former secretary of state for energy and climate change, had beaten his brother, David, as well as Ed Balls, Andy Burnham and Diane Abbott, to become Labour's new leader. In his first major policy speech, at the 2011 Labour Party conference, Miliband drew a clear line under New Labour's social democratic strategy *and* Gordon Brown's emergency-rescue Keynesianism (p. 245). Drawing on an academic literature on the 'Varieties of Capitalism' within political economy, Miliband argued that Britain had saddled itself with the wrong kind of capitalist model: short term, predatory, financialized and often exploitative. A future Labour government would need to confront vested interests, put an end to 'fast buck' capitalism and provide far more support for the 'producers' in the British economy.[20] Miliband did not reference 'stakeholding' but, in many respects, this was a back-to-the-future moment, rediscovering the road not taken by Blair. 'Red Ed', as he was dubbed by the Conservative-supporting press, followed this up with an argument that greater equality needed to be put at the very heart of the Labour project because inequality was bad for the economy, bad for democracy and bad for people's sense of self-worth.[21]

Yet having set an apparently clear ideological direction, Miliband nevertheless struggled. Even when Labour was ahead in the opinion polls, he never really created a strong sense he was going to win. He was easily caricatured, sometimes viciously, as a North London academic elitist.[22] He made a bit of a fool of himself by trying and failing to elegantly eat a bacon sandwich in a café.[23] Above all, he found himself torn between arguing that a future Labour government could be trusted to manage public spending and reduce the debt and arguing that the Conservatives' arguments about austerity were deeply unfair and economically illiterate. As a result, Byrne's note still retained a cult status within the Conservative Party.[24] David Cameron carried a copy of it with him wherever he went during the 2015 General Election campaign and brandished it to the cameras whenever he could. New Labour had pushed the country into debt. The Coalition had made the right decisions to cut the deficit. Ed Miliband could not be trusted with the public finances. This argument worked and the Conservatives emerged from the general election on 7 May 2015 with twenty-four additional seats and a narrow overall majority. Two days later, Byrne published a short article in the *Guardian* explaining why he had written the note and apologizing for having done so, describing it as a 'crass mistake' which made him burn with shame.[25] In August of that year, Jon Cruddas, who had served as Ed Miliband's policy co-ordinator, published the results of an independent inquiry he had chaired into the election campaign. Its key finding was that 'the Tories didn't win despite their commitment to cut spending and the deficit; they won because of it' and that Labour had lost not because it was seen to be offering a fairer, softer form of austerity but because it was perceived as being anti-austerity.[26]

ENTER THE OFFICE FOR BUDGET RESPONSIBILITY

Whilst austerity worked politically, it is not nearly as obvious that it worked economically. The basic argument for austerity was that cutting public spending would lead to higher economic growth and lower government borrowing. Let's start with the first part of this equation:

spending. Earlier, in Chapter 8, I showed how real, inflation-adjusted, public expenditure increased across most areas of government activity between 2000/1 and 2007/8. Between 2010/11 and 2015/16, *overall* 'real' (i.e., inflation-adjusted) public sector total managed expenditure (at 2021/2 prices) fell by a little under 1 per cent, from £916 billion to £908 billion. The impact of these cuts was not, however, even. Health expenditure increased by just over 6 per cent (from £148bn to £158bn) whilst public spending on education, defence and public order and safety (policing and the courts) was cut by 15, 14 and 17 per cent respectively.[27]

Perhaps the most interesting set of numbers here relates to social protection expenditure. From the start, the Coalition made a big play on cutting welfare expenditure and wrapping this in an argument that too much money was being spent helping people who were showing no inclination to help themselves. As Osborne put it at the 2012 Conservative Party conference, 'where is the fairness for the shift worker, leaving home in the dark hours of the early morning, who looks up at the closed blinds of their next door neighbour sleeping off a life on benefits?'[28] This proved wildly attractive to Conservative activists and the Conservative-supporting press but, whilst the Coalition was able to cut expenditure on Jobseekers Allowance, this constituted only a small fraction of overall welfare expenditure. The 'triple lock' on pensions, introduced in 2010, meant that public expenditure on the state pension rose from £69bn to over £90bn between 2010 and 2015, whilst overall public expenditure on social protection rose by nearly 7 per cent, from £284bn to £303bn, over the same period.[29] In the run-up to the 2010 General Election, Cameron had promised to reduce welfare expenditure and to promote the 'Big Society'. The opposite happened. Welfare expenditure increased whilst austerity hollowed out the voluntary bodies and the budgets of local authorities upon which the Big Society idea depended.

So, public spending did fall between 2010 and 2015 even if it did not, overall, fall by as much as the Conservatives and their political opponents sometimes suggested it had. It did fall by a large amount relative to Labour's long-term spending plans when they had been in office, but that was a very different thing. Moving on, another part of the austerity equation was inequality. Critics argued that austerity would massively increase levels of inequality. The evidence here is mixed. Using Institute for Fiscal Study data on household income, this time *after* housing costs, the income of the poorest 50 per cent of households grew by an average of 2 per cent between 2010/11 and 2015/16 whilst that of the richest 50 per cent grew by 4 per cent. Over the same period, the Gini Coefficient measure of income inequality *after* housing costs rose slightly, from 0.383 to 0.396.[30] More significantly, quantitative easing, by inflating the value of shares, housing and other assets, further inflated the wealth of the already wealthiest (p. 249). In a speech pointedly delivered in Port Talbot, one of the poorer areas in Wales in 2016, the Bank of England's chief economist, Andy Haldane, observed that increases in median wealth since 2007 had been concentrated in London and the Southeast; that those in the bottom two-fifths of the income distribution scale had seen virtually no gains in their wealth since 2010; that those in the bottom 20 per cent had seen their wealth fall over this period; and that those in the top quintile had seen their wealth increase by almost 20 per cent.[31] There was one more dimension to this debate. To its critics, austerity was not simply a matter of richer or poorer but of life or death. A paper published in the *British Medical Journal* in 2017 comparing mortality rates prior to and following the introduction of austerity, concluded that spending constraints, particularly in social care, might have been responsible for an excess of 45,000 deaths a year from 2012 to 2014.[32]

Part three of the equation was growth. Cut expenditure, the Coalition had argued, and growth would follow. This happened. After a sharp recession, the British economy had started to grow again in late 2009.[33] Between 2010 and 2015 GDP grew by an average of 2.0 per cent a year. That fell some way short of the 2.7 per cent average of the boom years but was not awful and compared well with the 1.7 per cent figure between 2000 and the *end* of the recession caused by the financial crisis. Average economic growth was higher in the United States (2.2%) and, by a narrow margin, across the G7 as a whole (1.8%), but Britain outperformed the average of the European Union (1.2%).[34] But in this case, one plus one did not necessarily equal two. Osborne predicted that spending cuts and growth would translate to a significant fall in the government's annual spending deficit by 2015/16. That did not happen. The deficit fell but by 2015 the government was still borrowing £97 billion a year in order to balance its books. As a result, *total* public sector debt, excluding the debts of the banks that had been effectively nationalized during the financial crisis, increased, from £1,145 billion to £1,557 billion.[35] If you wanted to be generous, you could argue that Britain's borrowing was off the scale in 2010 and that this was why reasonably solid economic growth was not enough to eliminate the deficit. But the bottom line here was that by 2015 the government was borrowing twice as much as it had in 2007.

At this point, austerity's outcome looks like a bit of a score draw. Growth was OK-ish. The deficit was down but not out. However, what starts to tip the argument the other way is the judgement of the Office for Budget Responsibility (OBR). This was the body established by George Osborne in 2010 to provide independent growth and budget forecasts and, in doing so, to make it harder for governments to massage budget numbers through over-optimistic Treasury forecasts. Over time, the OBR came to a view that austerity and spending cuts, far from boosting economic growth, had reduced GDP by something like 1.4 per cent. Moreover, when Cameron and Osborne publicly insisted otherwise, the OBR's chairman, Robert Chote, wrote to the prime minister to correct him.[36] The OBR was not alone in reaching this view. In 2016, the OECD, which had initially supported the idea of an 'expansionary fiscal contraction', changed its mind and concluded that, with interest rates having been so low, higher borrowing after 2010 would have strengthened demand and increased growth and could have done so on a sustainable basis.[37] None of this meant that, back in 2010, the deficit was a non-issue. But the idea that the deficit was a national emergency and all that really mattered, and that the only way of cutting the deficit was to drastically cut public expenditure, did not, in the end, look to have been the right one. The economy did not recover because of austerity. It recovered despite it.

We can now come to austerity's most significant legacy and one that has never really been resolved since – investment and productivity. Between 2010 and 2015, Gross Capital Formation (an overall measure of investment which takes account of both private- and public-sector investment) was 16.6 per cent of GDP in Britain. In Italy it was 18.2%; in the United States 20%; in Germany 20.2%; and in France 22.5%. Indeed, in the 174 countries for which the World Bank keeps records, Britain, over this period, came 150th.[38] The first point to note here is that, overall, profits in the private sector were reasonably buoyant during this period. The rate of return for private non-financial corporations was steady at a little over 10 per cent between 2010 and 2015.[39] Indeed profits, buoyed by quantitative easing which pushed down the cost of borrowing, were sufficiently high to sustain share dividends of £227 billion and a further £80 billion of share buyback schemes amongst the largest FTSE 100 publicly listed British companies between 2011 and 2015.[40] Just as the banks were focused on 'IBGYBG' market trades during the boom years, there can be a reasonable suspicion here that companies were also significantly focused on their short-term financial position. But, overall, whilst business investment fell off a cliff during the recession, it then broadly recovered. The Office for National Statistics presents data on business investment using a benchmark in which 1999 = 100. Using that measure, investment rose to a peak of 145 in Q2 of 2007 before falling to a low of 111 in Q3 of 2009. It then recovered to 130 by Q4 2011 and to 145 in Q4 of 2014.[41]

Instead, what stands out when it comes to overall levels of investment, is the other side of the ledger: public-sector investment. As we have seen, whilst overall public spending, adjusted for inflation, fell between 2010/11 and 2015/16, it did not fall by *that* much. This was not the case however with one particular category of public expenditure: public sector net investment. Between 2000/1 and 2007/8 public sector net investment grew, in real terms (and, once again, in 2021/2 prices), from a paltry £6 billion a year to £35 billion. That huge increase was never likely to be sustained during a downturn. Yet, showing a preference for the short term over the long term that would have done justice to the most rapacious of bankers, public investment was then cut, from £48 billion in 2010/11 to £36 billion in 2015/16 – numbers which are difficult to square with the Coalition's habit of justifying austerity in terms of the welfare of *future* generations.[42]

Investment matters because, ultimately, as the economist Paul Krugman puts it, 'a country's ability to improve its standard of living ... depends almost entirely on its ability to raise its output per worker'; that is, upon its rate of productivity growth.[43] In the 2000s Britain experienced, on some measures, the highest productivity growth of any of the G7 economies.[44] Productivity growth in just about every country took a hit during the financial crisis, but in Britain it never really recovered. Between 2010 and 2015 the OECD estimates that, across its member countries, productivity, measured in terms of GDP per hour worked, grew by 4.5 per cent. In Germany it grew by 5.3%; in France by 4.5%; in the United States by 4.5%; and in Japan by 6.2%. In Britain it grew by 1.8 per cent.[45] Largely as a result, typical household incomes were 16 per cent lower in Britain by 2018 than they were in Germany and 9 per cent lower than they were in France. In 2007, British household income had been higher.[46]

'CHOPPED UP IN BAGS IN MY FREEZER'

In the summer of 2014, the 'Ice Bucket' challenge became, for a few months, a viral craze. YouTube groaned under the weight of celebrities (including Donald Trump, accompanied by Miss USA and Miss Universe – of course) throwing ice-cold water over their heads before nominating someone else to do the same or pay a cash forfeit to the ALS Association to fund research into motor neuron disease (Trump nominated his sons and President Obama; the latter declined and paid the cash). Then, as happens with these things, saturation point was reached and everyone moved on.

The oddest thing about the austerity argument is not how politically potent it proved in the early 2010s but, rather like the Ice Bucket challenge of which it offered a fiscal equivalent, how quickly it then faded away. In their 2015 election manifesto, the Conservatives promised to go from 'stuck in the red, to back in the black' by cutting a further £30 billion of public expenditure and by running a budget surplus from 2018/19 onwards.[47] In his budget in July 2015, the first to be delivered by a Conservative chancellor in a Conservative-only government in eighteen years, Osborne, who had argued during the 2015 General Election campaign that Labour's talk of significantly raising the national minimum wage would destroy all known life on the planet, announced a Damascene conversion to a national living wage. He also said that because growth and tax revenues had been higher than forecast, he would be able to raise public spending in the short term. Yet, overall, austerity remained the name of the game. Public spending would continue to fall as a share of GDP in the medium term and the annual budget deficit would be eliminated by 2019/20.

The political mood then started to change. In March 2016, the work and pensions secretary, Iain Duncan Smith, resigned over proposed cuts to disability benefits. In doing so he voiced his concern that the government was increasingly being driven by calculations of political rather than national interest.[48] Not long after, polls showed that the proportion of people who thought spending cuts were good for the economy had fallen to just 33 per cent.[49] Following on from this, the British Social Attitudes survey found that, for the first time in a decade, the number of people who thought public spending and taxes should be increased exceeded the proportion thinking they should be left as they were.[50] The European Union referendum then happened. Cameron resigned and Osborne was sacked shortly after by Theresa May, who told him to 'go away and get to know the party better'.[51] Osborne's replacement as chancellor, Philip Hammond, wanted to keep Osborne's target of balancing the books but came under immediate pressure from May and her chief of staff, Nick Timothy, to start spending more (p. 361). The 2017 General Election proved a triumph for Jeremy Corbyn's anti-austerity arguments and in October 2018 May announced that the age of austerity had come to an end.[52]

To tie-up one last loose end, George Osborne did OK. In 2017 he was appointed editor of the *Evening Standard*. Having reportedly said that he would not rest until Theresa May was 'chopped up in bags in my freezer', Osborne now found himself in pole position to dish out some high-end political *Schadenfreude* as Theresa May's premiership unravelled.[53] After he resigned as an MP, Osborne's name was then linked with, variously, a possible run at London's mayoral election or an application to be either the managing director of the IMF or, later, the chairman of the BBC. None of them came to pass and in February 2021 Osborne became a full-time partner of the investment bank Robey Warshaw.[54] In June of that year he was appointed chairman of the British Museum.

23
Same Sex Marriage

THE TIES THAT BIND US

Twenty eleven began badly for David Cameron, the Conservatives and the Coalition. In January, Cameron's press secretary Andy Coulson, a former editor of the *News of the World*, was forced to resign because of his prior links to the phone hacking scandal (p. 262). He was eventually sentenced to eighteen months in prison. In the same month the rate of VAT was increased, and the Office for National Statistics announced the economy had contracted by 0.5 per cent. Opinion polls at the time put Labour at 42 per cent of the vote and the Conservatives at just over 30 per cent.[1] In March, up to 500,000 people marched through London to protest against austerity and spending cuts. Then, slowly, things started to stabilize. In February 2011 anti-government rallies by protestors angered by the arrest of a human rights lawyer, Fethi Tarbel, began in Benghazi, Libya. These escalated, and on 17 March a UN Resolution authorized member states to establish a no-fly zone over Libya and to use 'all necessary measures' to prevent attacks on civilians.[2] British armed forces were deployed and after several months of fighting, Colonel Gaddafi, who had been in power since 1979, was discovered hiding in a drainage pipe in Sirte and killed. The Libyan state and economy subsequently disintegrated,[3] but for a while Libya looked like a feel-good story about how, post-Iraq, Britain had done the right thing by protecting protestors against a brutal tyrant's murderous regime. To add to the list of good news, Cameron and the Conservatives comfortably won the referendum on the Alternative Vote on 5 May, cutting the Liberal Democrats down to size; and, in the same month, the Office for National Statistics confirmed that the British economy had started to grow again.

After summer holidays in Tuscany and Cornwall, Cameron went back to work in early September. In October, he delivered an hour-long address to the Conservative Party conference in Manchester.[4] The economy was, inevitably, the main order of business. Cameron celebrated and took credit for the resumption of growth but warned delegates it would take a long time to fix the economy because Labour had left it in such a mess. He derided the shadow chancellor Ed Balls for having denied, a few days earlier, that Labour had borrowed and spent too much money when it was in office. He ruled out joining the Single Currency; praised the NHS; called upon businesses to be more socially responsible; and looked ahead, with breath barely bated, to the London Olympics the following year.

All of this was standard and predictable stuff. The surprise came right at the end of his speech, when Cameron glided from his usual few lines about 'the Big Society', otherwise fading fast from view, and his hopes of encouraging civil citizenship and social volunteering, to marriage. He began by arguing that the institution of marriage was as relevant as ever. It is probably safe to say very few of those present in the audience would have wildly disagreed with him on that. Cameron then seemed to suggest, without actually saying anything specific, that more needed to be done to ensure the tax system provided people with incentives to get married. Next, he announced the government was going to launch a consultation about same sex marriage:

> And to anyone who has reservations, I say: Yes, it's about equality, but it's also about something else: commitment. Conservatives believe in the ties that bind us; that society is stronger when we make vows to each other and support each other. So I don't support gay marriage despite being a Conservative. I support gay marriage because I'm a Conservative.

The audience clapped and, with that done, Cameron concluded with a claim that the Conservatives had 'turned this country into a beacon of enterprise'. It was only afterwards, when Conservative Party media officers were dispatched to brief the press, that it became apparent that Cameron saw the same-sex marriage announcement as the pivotal part of his speech.

'ON THE WRONG SIDE'

New Labour had left office in 2010 with a strong, albeit incomplete, record when it came to homosexual equality. In 2000 legislation had lowered the age of consent for gay men to sixteen in England, Scotland and Wales.* In the same year, the ban on homosexuals serving in the Armed Forces was lifted. In 2001 the Criminal Injuries Compensation Board recognized the rights of same sex partners. In 2002 Parliament debated and approved a change allowing same sex couples to adopt children. In 2003, and after an earlier attempt had been derailed in the House of Lords, Section 28 of the 1998 Local Government Act, which prohibited councils from intentionally promoting homosexuality, was repealed. Then, in 2004, the government secured parliamentary support for legislation creating a new form of same sex legal union – the civil partnership – which was very similar, but not fully identical, to marriage.

On 5 December 2005 Chris Cramp and Matthew Roche became the first same sex couple to complete a civil partnership ceremony in Britain. They were given dispensation to do so ahead of the nationwide introduction of partnership ceremonies because Matthew was dying of bile-duct cancer and had only a few days left to live.[5] Where they led, plenty of others followed. By the end of 2011 over 53,000 civil partnerships had been registered in the UK. Civil partnerships were a very New Labour, centrist, split-the-difference kind of policy. On the one hand, Labour ministers could sense people's attitudes towards homosexuality were shifting. In the mid-1980s the number of people recorded by the British Social Attitudes survey as saying that same sex relationships were 'not at all wrong' was as low as 11 per cent. By 2000 this number had risen to over 30 per cent and was growing steadily.[6] Yet, at the same time, New Labour wanted to avoid the public fight it thought would result if it followed other countries (the Netherlands, Belgium, Spain, Canada and others) in legislating to allow same sex marriage. So it ended up creating a third way option which, in no time at all, became as wildly uncontroversial as an episode of *Countryfile*.

David Cameron, by his own admission, initially put himself on what

* The age of consent in Northern Ireland was not equalized to the age of sixteen until 2009.

he came to regard as 'the wrong side of the argument' about homosexual equality.[7] He abstained on the vote allowing gay couples to adopt and voted against the repeal of Section 28. But he voted for civil partnerships and, in 2006, in full-on modernizing mode, told the Conservative Party conference that the institution of marriage was worth defending 'whether you're a man and a woman, a woman and a woman or a man and another man'.[8] In 2009 Cameron became the first Conservative leader to address a Gay Pride event, apologizing for his party's past support for Section 28.[9]

In the run-up to the 2010 General Election, Cameron contemplated making a manifesto commitment to same sex marriage. He was dissuaded from doing so by Andy Coulson, who thought it would play badly with Conservative core voters.[10] That said, George Osborne told a meeting of gay Conservative activists during the campaign that he would be 'very happy' to consider same sex marriage if elected.[11] The Coalition Agreement negotiated between the Liberal Democrats and Conservatives following the election did not specifically reference same sex marriage. Yet, within a few months, it became clear that the Liberal Democrats, and specifically Lynne Featherstone, the parliamentary under-secretary for equalities, were going to push to making a formal commitment to same sex marriage. Meanwhile, the Scottish Executive had already announced it was going to launch a consultation on the issue. Cameron now felt he had to say something and decided to say something supportive.

Cameron's support for same sex marriage involved an element of political calculation. In the mid-2000s he had made his name as a socially liberal modernizer. As the 2010 General Election approached, he had reverted to a more traditional-looking Conservative agenda, and as prime minister he had doubled down on austerity and spending cuts. However, as his director of strategy, Andrew Cooper, argued, coming out in support of same sex marriage gave Cameron the opportunity to reboot his modernizing image.[12] This does not mean that Cameron's support was insincere. In the end, it seems clear, he backed same sex marriage because he believed it was the right thing to do. What was noteworthy was that, in having reached this decision, Cameron found himself being pushed into the very New Labour world of a language of rights and equality. These were concepts large parts of his own party were decidedly uncomfortable with, particularly when it came to the rights of asylum-seekers and the role of the European Court of Human Rights. Yet Cameron knew enough to know that the country was changing, and that Margaret Thatcher's brand of socially conservative, prurient individualism no longer fitted, even if the other parts of the Thatcherite consensus – the free market and the strong state protecting Britain from enemies within and without – still made sense.

A 'REAL DANGER POINT'

In March 2012 the Coalition launched a public consultation on proposals to allow same sex marriage in England and Wales and on allowing religious organizations to refuse to participate if they so wanted.[13] The results were announced on 17 December. Out of 228,000 responses, 53 per cent had been supportive of same sex marriage and 46 per cent had been opposed. The following day, the minister for equalities, the Conservative Maria Miller, confirmed that the government would move ahead with legislation to allow same sex marriage. Religious organizations that were opposed to the principle of doing so would not be required to conduct same-sex marriage ceremonies. Those religious groups which wanted to opt-in would, however, be allowed to do so.[14]

In 2004 Labour's Civil Partnership Act received overwhelming backing in the House of Commons, with only forty-nine MPs voting against it at the end of the key parliamentary debate. In late 2012 and early 2013 it looked, for a while, as if history might repeat itself, given that the leadership of the Conservatives, Labour, Lib Dems, SNP and Plaid Cymru were all officially in favour. Broadly speaking, opinion polls showed reasonable but not unambiguous levels of public support for same sex marriage. A House of Commons Library briefing paper published in January 2013 found that of sixteen recent opinion polls on the issue, ten had recorded majority support for the government's proposals and six had recorded more opposition than support.[15] Yet it was also clear that a majority of Conservative supporters – and a clear majority of Conservative Party activists – were steadfastly opposed.[16] Indeed by February 2013 newspapers were reporting that several local Conservative Party chairmen had resigned over the issue.[17]

Within the Conservative Parliamentary Party Cameron could count on the support of other modernizers, including Michael Gove and Boris

Johnson (at this point still London mayor), who established a campaign group to support the same-sex marriage legislation. They were, however, in a minority. Sixty Conservative MPs and members of the House of Lords signed a letter in the *Daily Telegraph* arguing that the government lacked a mandate for same sex marriage as neither the Conservatives nor the Liberal Democrats had referred to the issue in their 2010 manifestos.[18] Alan Duncan, one of a number of openly gay Conservative MPs, described Cameron's proposals as 'poison'.[19] The chairman of the Conservative backbench 1922 Committee, Graham Brady, argued that the issue posed a 'real danger point' for Cameron and that it was 'pretty much the universal advice of any colleague who spoke to him' that he ought to drop the proposals.[20]

The real problem for Cameron was that the opposition to him at this time was not only over same sex marriage. A lot of Conservative MPs felt that he had botched the 2010 General Election campaign and that the coalition with the Liberal Democrats was an abomination. Whilst there was very little opposition to the basic political principle of austerity, plenty of Conservative MPs were worried about the political impact of the cuts being made in their constituencies and the continuing fallout from the 'omnishambles' budget (p. 284). Above all, in a parliamentary party in which Euroscepticism had gone from being a minority taste to the new normal, Conservative MPs felt Cameron was far too soft and timid when it came to Europe. In June 2012 a hundred Conservative backbench MPs submitted a letter to Cameron demanding a referendum on Britain's membership of the European Union.[21] In October, fifty Conservative MPs went a step further: they voted against their party and with Labour on a vote relating to the approval of the European Union's budget.[22]

By early 2013 Cameron was under intense pressure, with talk of a leadership challenge growing. Pushed into a corner, he gave way. But he chose to do so over the issue of Europe. On 23 January he delivered a short speech at the Bloomberg news agency in which he promised to hold an in–out referendum on Britain's future membership of the European Union if the Conservatives were re-elected.[23] When it came to same sex marriage he held his nerve; he knew that, on this issue, the other parties would be unlikely to vote against him and his proposals in the way they would and had over Europe. That calculation proved correct. A House of Commons vote on 5 February 2013 split the

Conservative Party right down the middle, with 127 of its MPs voting in favour of same sex marriage; 136 voting against; and 40 either abstaining or voting both for and against.[24] Two Cabinet ministers – the environment secretary Owen Patterson and the Welsh secretary David Jones – voted against the Bill. Yet, overall, the legislation was comfortably approved, with 400 MPs voting in favour and 175 against.

On 29 March 2014 John Coffey and Bernardo Marti were the first same sex couple to marry. Their ceremony, at the Mayfair Library in Westminster, was timed to start at 11.30 p.m. so that the registrar, Tommy Hanover, could pronounce them married at the moment the clock struck midnight. Coffey, a television producer, spoke afterwards of how he remembered growing up in London and seeing white stickers placed on the walls of Tube stations offering a phone number to call for help if you were gay and alone. He described it as 'astonishing' that same sex marriage had been approved: 'five years ago I would never have believed it.'[25] On 31 December 2014 Susan and Gerrie Douglas-Scott became the first same sex couple to marry in Scotland.

After all the arguments they had caused, same sex marriages soon became largely uncontroversial.* In her 2016 Conservative Party leadership campaign Andrea Leadsom said she didn't like same sex marriage because of the 'clear hurt' it caused Christians.[26] But this argument did not get very far. Indeed, in many ways the biggest policy shift in later years came with a 2018 ruling by the Supreme Court in favour of a couple, Rebecca Steinfeld and Charles Keidan, who had argued that restricting civil partnerships to same sex couples was discriminatory and a breach of their human rights.[27] The result was a change in the law in England and Wales, and then Scotland, giving heterosexual couples the option of a civil partnership.

'WE DON'T DO GOD'

Outside the ranks of local Conservative Party associations, opposition to same sex marriage was led primarily by religious organizations and

---

* To which it is, once again, worth adding 'not in Northern Ireland'. Here, legislation relating to same sex marriage was effectively imposed by Westminster in 2019 at a moment when the Northern Ireland Executive was suspended.

pressure groups established by them. Some of these, diving right in at the deep end, argued that homosexuality was a sin and contrary to God's will. In its submission to the government's 2012 consultation, Christian Voice argued that Jesus Christ, as recorded in the Gospel of Matthew, clearly considered marriage to be a 'creation ordinance' between a male and a female, adding (for good measure) that whilst Jesus did not explicitly condemn homosexuality, neither did he condemn 'bestiality or incest in his earthly ministry'.[28] The Coptic Orthodox Church, the Evangelical Alliance, the Evangelical Presbyterian Church in England and Wales, the Free Presbyterian Church of Scotland, Keep Marriage Special, the Manchester Rabbinical Council, the Methodist Church in Britain, the Muslim Council of Scotland, the National Orthodox Association of Jewish Schools, and Sikhs in England also directly invoked scripture in their submissions against same sex marriage.[29]

In their public statements the Church of England, the Catholic Bishops Association, the Muslim Council of Britain and the Jewish Board of Deputies tended, instead, to frame their opposition in more secular terms. They argued that same sex marriage would weaken the institution of marriage; that it had little public support; that the government lacked a mandate for its proposals given the silence of both the Conservative and Liberal Democrat manifestos on the issue; and, finally, that assurances they would not be required to conduct same sex marriages would prove legally unsustainable. It is not hard to understand this approach. Religious organizations, with the notable exceptions of the Unitarians and Quakers, were passionate in their opposition to same sex marriage but recognized that, in an increasingly secular society, arguments invoking scripture were, as the then archbishop of Canterbury Rowan Williams observed, likely to be 'greeted as platitudinous or irrelevant'.[30]

Rowan Williams's view that Britain was an increasingly secular society was not without foundation. The 2011 Census asked a voluntary question about religion. It found that, in England and Wales, 33 million people, nearly 60 per cent of the population, described themselves as Christian; that in Scotland 57 per cent did so; and that in Northern Ireland nearly half of people saw themselves as being either Catholic or Protestant.[31] By comparison, 5% of the English and Welsh population identified as Muslim; 1.5% as Hindu, 0.8% as Sikh; 0.5% as Jewish; and 0.4% as Buddhist. At face value, this would seem to show that

Britain remained a largely Christian country. Yet those numbers were, in many ways, misleading. Asked what their religion is, plenty of people still say Christian because they think they are being asked to say something. But in this respect actions speak louder than words. Between 1980 and 2014 the number of people across Britain attending Church at least once a month declined from just over 5 million people to a little over 3 million.[32] There were exceptions to this general rule of decline. In London, attendance at religious services grew in the 2000s. This was largely as a result of the rapid growth of Pentecostalism, which emphasizes the work of the Holy Spirit and the direct experience of the presence of God, within African churches in the capital.[33] Yet, by one estimate, over 2,000 English parish churches had ten or fewer worshippers each week by 2010.[34] A global poll conducted by the Pew Research Center in 2014 found that Britain was one of the world's most irreligious countries, with only 30 per cent of those surveyed identifying themselves as being religious.

In many respects, Britain had, by the time of the 2011 Census, become a secular society in which faith was seen as a matter of individual choice and in which people could, without any obvious social penalties, live independently of any sense of religiosity.[35] Public debate about religion in the 2000s was led by 'new atheists' such as Richard Dawkins, Christopher Hitchens and the philosopher Daniel Dennett, who argued that religion, in all its forms, should not be tolerated but attacked and, in Dawkins' words, its 'vicious, dodgy, perniciously delusional, sanctimoniously hypocritical practitioners exposed'.[36] This remained too strong a position for many people. But it is telling that Danny Boyle, who had wanted to be a priest when he was younger, offered an account of Britain's past and present at the opening ceremony of the 2012 London Olympics which was almost entirely secular in tone and content.[37] For a post-Reformation state founded on its Protestantism and the Protestantism of its monarchy, this was noteworthy.

Party politics was also becoming increasingly secularized. Margaret Thatcher, who was raised as a Methodist before joining the Church of England, once described Britain as a nation 'whose ideals are founded on the Bible' and routinely offered theological justifications for capitalism and the free market.[38] Tony Blair, in his early years as Labour leader, lent heavily upon the theology of Christian Socialism as a prop for his political faith.[39] Nevertheless, as prime minister he largely adhered to Alastair Campbell's advice that British politicians 'don't do God' and that it would be a mistake to link his personal faith to policy decisions.[40] This is one reason why he waited until he had left office in 2007 to convert to Catholicism.[41] David Cameron also largely avoided talking about spiritual issues, describing his faith, when pressed, as one which 'comes and goes, rather like reception for *Magic FM* in the Chilterns'.[42] By the time of the 2015 election the fact that Ed Miliband and Nick Clegg openly described themselves as being atheists passed almost without remark. Instead, and in 2017, it was the personal Christian faith of the Liberal Democrat leader Tim Farron which became an election story in relation to his views on abortion.

It is easy to forget just how unusual Britain is in this respect. In the United States, a religious revival in the 1950s led by figures such as the evangelist Billy Graham eventually found a political outlet within the Republican Party, by way of a 'neoconservative' strand of its philosophy associated with figures like Irving Kristol. In the 1980s and 1990s, the Christian Right transformed American politics, with adherents such as the religious broadcaster Pat Robertson, who established the Christian Coalition and ran for the Republican presidential nomination in 1988, becoming mainstream and at times dominant political figures.[43] In 2022 more than 80 per cent of Americans said they believed in God, whilst 70 per cent reported attending a religious service at least once a month.[44] Moreover, 60 per cent of self-identified Republican supporters also said at this time that they would support a move to declare America to be a Christian country (compared with 17 per cent of Democrats and 38 per cent of all those polled).[45] This overt religiosity gives American politics a very different flavour to Britain's when it comes to, for example, 'culture war' battles over abortion or trans-rights, where those opposed to such policies can draw upon a wider base of support from church-attending and socially conservative Christians.[46]

A LASTING AFTERLIFE

Yet if Britain is an increasingly secular society, it is one in which religion still has a lasting afterlife. As the sociologist Grace Davie argues, whilst religious identification and Church attendance is falling, British society remains one in which, as she puts it, 'believing without belonging' is entirely normal.[47] Between a half and two-thirds of people continue to believe in some sort of God or supernatural force at least some of the time, whilst three-quarters agree there are things in life which cannot be explained through science or any other means.[48] Most people do not regularly attend religious services but most people do seem to want to engage with the Church at key moments in their lives, as witnessed by, for example, the growing visibility of chaplains within hospitals, as well as the more obvious examples of weddings and funerals.

A lot of this sense of religiosity, or at least of spirituality, is quite vague. It appeals to and connects with a sense of and need for beauty, whether expressed through Church architecture, organ music and choirs or ritual. That is one reason why cathedrals were also able to buck the overall trend of falling church attendance in the 2000s.[49] For other people it connects to a loose sense of spirituality and what Paul Heelas calls 'self-religions' centred upon knowing and being true to yourself. This is sometimes connected to a faith in an immanent rather than transcendent God or, at other times, in astrology, crystals or simply the spirit-affirming qualities of the countryside or of open-water swimming.[50]

Moreover, Christianity retains a political resonance whether or not individual political leaders are Christian. That is why the decision of the Occupy protest movement to pitch its tents in the gardens and square surrounding St Paul's Cathedral in the aftermath of the 2008 financial crisis and to denounce, in biblical terms, greed and inequality was so powerful.[51] Although the rise of the avowedly non-sectarian Alliance Party is a noteworthy development (p. 390), Northern Irish politics and the largest Northern Irish political parties still divide between Catholic and nationalist and Protestant and unionist. In Scotland, the unexpectedly strong challenge of Kate Forbes, an active member of the evangelical Calvinist Free Church of Scotland, with very socially conservative views on sex before marriage, same sex marriage and abortion, in the 2023 SNP leadership contest that followed Nicola Sturgeon's resignation, drew attention to a religious aspect of Scottish politics many left-of-centre English voters had not previously encountered.[52]

The Church of England, which has in the past been referred to as 'the Tory Party at prayer', retains a formal status within the British state as the Established Church.[53] In 2022 the archbishop of Canterbury, Justin Welby, criticized the government's plans to send asylum-seekers to Rwanda. The Conservative MP Ben Bradley attacked Welby, arguing that 'we separated the Church from the state a long time ago'.[54] He is, of course, mistaken. There are still twenty-six seats reserved for Church of England bishops in the House of Lords. Fourteen of them were present during the debate on the Same Sex Marriage Bill, nine voting in favour of an amendment to deny the Bill a Second Reading.[55] Later, in 2018, a number of bishops petitioned the government to offer an amnesty for the Windrush generation.[56] There are also around 4,500 Church of England schools (compared to around 200 Muslim ones);[57] moreover, the 1988 Education Reform Act continues to require the provision of a religious act of worship in all schools, which must be of a 'wholly or mainly' 'broadly Christian character'.[58] The interpretation of this requirement proved particularly contentious in relation to the so-called 'Trojan Horse' affair in 2014 (pp. 182–3). Finally, King Charles's coronation in May 2023, which involved swearing an oath of commitment to Protestantism and fidelity to the Church of England, of which he became supreme governor, was a reminder of just how entwined state and religion remain.[59]

Social attitudes and voting patterns also continue to bear a religious imprint. In 2013 opposition to same sex marriage was more than twice as high amongst self-identified Anglicans, Catholics and other Christians as it was amongst those with no religion.[60] Meanwhile, Table 1 overleaf, drawn from British Social Attitudes data, shows average Labour Party support in the 1980s, 1990s and 2000s for practising and non-practising Presbyterians and Catholics in Scotland (1a) and Anglicans (Church of England), Nonconformists (Methodists, Baptists, Quakers and Brethren) and Catholics in England (1b). The results are startling. Catholics in Scotland, whether practising or not, are far more likely to vote Labour than Presbyterians, with no real sign of that gap closing. In the 2014 independence referendum Scottish Catholics were also far more likely to vote for independence (54 per cent did so, compared to just over 39 per cent of members of the Church of Scotland and 51 per cent of those with no religious identity).[61] In England, non-practising Catholics are twice as likely as practising Anglicans to vote Labour with Nonconformists somewhere between these two extremes. What's more, these religious differences can't simply be accounted for in terms of underlying social class. Whilst it is true that Catholics are more likely than Anglicans to be working class, a religious difference remains even after this and other social factors are taken into account.[62]

Table 1. The Religious Basis to Voting

(a) Average *Labour Party* support from practising and non-practising Presbyterians and Catholics in Scotland for each decade, 1983–2010 (%)

Denomination		1980s	1990s	2000s
Presbyterian	Practising	29	30	37
	Non-Practising	52	50	57
Catholic	Practising	78	75	81
	Non-Practising	79	77	72

(b) Average *Labour Party* support from practising and non-practising Anglicans, Nonconformists and Catholics in England for each decade, 1983–2010 (%)

Denomination		1980s	1990s	2000s
Anglican	Practising	23	30	29
	Non-Practising	39	47	44
Nonconformist	Practising	24	42	43
	Non-Practising	53	50	47
Catholic	Practising	45	53	57
	Non-Practising	53	64	64

James Tilley, '"We don't do God"? Religion and party choice in Britain', *British Journal of Political Science*, 45, 4 (2015): 907–27

Finally, it is worth emphasizing the continued growth of other religions. In the 2011 Census, nearly 60 per cent of the English and Welsh population described themselves as Christian. By the time of the 2021 Census that had fallen to 46 per cent.[63] That is perhaps not entirely surprising. By 2022, post-pandemic, average weekly attendance at Anglican churches in England had fallen to just over 600,000 people, a little over 1 per cent of the population.[64] Over that same period, the number of people describing themselves as Muslim has increased from 2.7 to 3.9 million (or from 4.9 to 6.5 per cent of the population), and the number describing themselves as Hindu from 818,000 to 1 million (or from 1.5 to 1.7 per cent).

Moreover, research by Ridhi Kashyap and Valerie A. Lewis comparing the attitudes of self-identified young Christians and both younger and older Muslims suggests that, on average, younger and older Muslims regard their religion as being much more important to their identity than Christians and are much more likely to regularly attend religious services.[65] To tie this back to party politics, it is worth noting that 90 per cent of Muslims voted Labour in the 2017 General Election compared to just 25 per cent of Jewish people (the latter figure possibly skewed by the antisemitism row overshadowing Labour and Jeremy Corbyn at the time).[66]

Britain is, in most respects, becoming a more secular country. It is certainly becoming a less Christian one. It is also becoming a steadily more liberal one. I have focused in this chapter on attitudes towards gay marriage, but they are part and parcel of a larger shift in attitudes that has resulted from both generational cohort effects (each new generation has tended to be more liberal than its predecessor) and period effects (each generation has become more liberal as it has grown older). The political tensions which remain here, as made manifest in 'culture wars', are the subject of a later chapter. But it is worth running through some of the other basic numbers as revealed through successive editions of the British Social Attitudes survey. In 1983 only 42 per cent thought that premarital sex was not at all wrong. By 2000 that number had climbed to 62 per cent and by 2018 to 74 per cent.[67] The number disapproving of a couple having a child whilst cohabiting fell from 21 per cent in 2006/7 to 11 per cent in 20018/19.[68] As recently as 2012 over 80 per cent agreed that schools ought to teach children to obey authority. That number had fallen to 62 per cent by 2020.[69] The number believing that for some crimes the death penalty is the most appropriate sentence had fallen from over 70 per cent in 1980s to below 50 per cent by 2014.[70] In the 1980s between 40 and 50 per cent agreed that it was a man's job to earn money and a woman's role to look after the home and family. By the early 2010s that number had fallen to just over 10 per cent.[71] Lastly, and to return to the subject of this chapter, the number thinking that same sex relationships were not at all wrong, which had stood at 34 per cent in 2000, had climbed to 66 per cent by 2018.[72] As for same sex marriage, polling in June 2023 found that support was running at over 75 per cent.[73]

24
Isles of Wonder

DANNY BOYLE

Daniel Francis Boyle, the son of two working-class Irish Catholic parents, was born in 1956 in Radcliffe, Greater Manchester. Having considered the priesthood as an option when he was younger, Boyle eventually applied to study English and Drama at Bangor University. After graduating, he worked at the Joint Stock Theatre Company in London and at the Royal Court.[1] In 1987 he switched to television where he co-wrote and directed episodes of *Inspector Morse*. In 1994 Boyle released his debut film, *Shallow Grave*, a black comedy set in Edinburgh about a bunch of friends who discover the body of their mysterious new flatmate, played by Keith Allen, and a suitcase of money, shortly before a lot of other bad things start to happen. *Shallow Grave* was a success, but Boyle's real breakthrough came two years later with the release of *Trainspotting*, a film based on Irvine Welsh's novel of the same name. *Trainspotting* was a 'zeitgeist-stranglingly definitive' hit which launched the careers of Ewan McGregor, Kelly Macdonald, Robert Carlyle and Johnny Lee Miller.[2]

Over the following years Boyle went on to direct *A Life Less Ordinary* (1997), *The Beach* (2000), *28 Days Later* (2002), *Millions* (2004) and *Sunshine* (2007). These films were, in different ways and to different extents, successful but were all eventually overshadowed by *Slumdog Millionaire* (2008), the story of an eighteen-year-old boy, Jamal Malik, played by Dev Patel, who wins the Indian version of *Who Wants to Be a Millionaire? Slumdog* won eight Academy awards in 2009, including that for Best Picture. One of *Slumdog*'s many admirers, it transpired, was the former Olympic athlete and former Conservative MP Sebastian Coe, who had chaired London's successful bid to hold the 2012

Olympics. Not long after the film's release, Coe had written to Boyle to say how sad he was that his mother, Tina, who was of Indian descent, would not see the film and how he hoped his own children would learn about India by watching it.[3] In June 2010, a month after the new Coalition government had been formed, it was announced that Boyle would be artistic director for the games' opening ceremony.

TWENTY TWELVE

The announcement that London had beaten Moscow, New York, Madrid and Paris in its bid to host the Olympics was made shortly after midday on Wednesday, 6 July 2005, at a moment when Tony Blair had just travelled to Scotland to host the G8 summit at the Gleneagles Hotel, Auchterarder. The initial budget for constructing the new purpose-built stadium, at the site of an abandoned former industrial site in Stratford, a few miles to the north of Canary Wharf and the Millennium Dome, was put at £2.5 billion. That always appeared somewhat optimistic, to say the least. Sure enough, by 2007 the expected stadium costs had already nearly quadrupled to £9.3 billion.[4] Yet hosting the Olympics still seemed like a reasonably good idea. The British economy was booming, and the Olympics would bring the world to London's doorstep. Winning the bid showed that Britain had changed: that, in Blair's words, it was 'no longer the stuffy old Britain that used to be sent up in the comedy sketches of the 1970s but a nation proud, willing and able to go out and compete on its merits'.[5]

Timing is everything and the timing of the London Olympics was not great. The financial crisis, the MPs' expenses scandal, recession, austerity and, in August 2011, a series of riots which began in Tottenham, North London, but spread to Birmingham, Bristol, Coventry, Liverpool, Wolverhampton, Manchester, Leicester and Derby, flattened the Olympic mood and left a lot of people wondering whether spending billions of pounds on building new sporting venues was quite as good an idea as it had once seemed. In the opening chapter of this book, I noted that there is a long tradition in British politics of arguing that the country is in decline and everything is getting worse. It is now worth saying a little bit more about that disposition in the context of the London Olympics.[6]

In the 1880s, as American and German firms first started to cut into

British industrial profits, a Royal Commission on Trade and Industry pointed to the challenges the British economy was facing and predicted a long-term relative economic decline. In the aftermath of the disastrous Second Boer War at the turn of the century, this analysis became linked to a more general set of arguments about the health and well-being of the average British worker.[7] Declinism found a second wind in the 1920s and early 1930s during the Depression, before re-emerging in the early 1960s where it provided the animating spirit for Michael Shanks' *The Stagnant Society* and Arthur Koestler's *Suicide of a Nation?*[8] The conviction being expressed in these books, that Britain was falling behind, played a background role in Harold Wilson's 1964 election campaign (the country had to harness the 'white heat' of 'scientific revolution') and in popularizing the case for Britain joining the European Economic Community. In the 1970s, as the post-war consensus was failing and Keynesian economics was falling apart, declinism reappeared with arguments on the left that Britain needed more planning and more public ownership and, on the right, that it needed a strong dose of free-market medicine.[9]

Margaret Thatcher grounded her appeal on a promise to reverse Britain's economic, political and cultural decline. As the party's 1979 election manifesto put it, 'our country's relative decline is not inevitable. We in the Conservative Party think we can reverse it.'[10] Over the following decade Thatcher, in the eyes of her supporters, achieved exactly what she had promised. Critics argued that recapturing the Falkland Islands and pump-priming an economic boom via tax cuts for high-earners constituted a faded form of faux national glory. But, by the end of the 1980s, the language of decline and descriptions of Britain as the 'sick man of Europe' (a term first applied by Tsar Nicholas I to the Ottoman Empire) had, for the first time in a long while, become less common. Tony Blair, for his part, tended not to talk about Britain's decline but did promise to remake Britain as a 'young country', 'one not resting on past glories, fighting old battles and sitting back, hand on mouth, concealing a yawn of cynicism, but ready for the day's challenge, ambitious, idealistic, united'.[11] In 2010 the Conservatives returned once again to the declinist trope: promising to fix 'broken Britain' and arguing that 'there is no law that says we must accept decline'.[12] History doesn't always rhyme. Sometimes it plagiarizes.

By 2012 the country's bleak mood had not lifted. Data published by the Office for National Statistics showed that overall levels of life satisfaction and of day-to-day happiness had fallen significantly in 2010/11 and had not yet recovered.[13] The Olympics became a part of the backdrop to this sense of national anguish. On *Mock the Week* comedian Dara Ó Briain asked panellists: 'What was the bad news about the Olympics this week?' Frankie Boyle (no relation to Danny) replied: 'Is it that it's going to be held in Britain, so it's going to be completely rubbish?'[14] This felt about right. There were stories about rising security costs, expected terrorist attacks and the installation of surface-to-air missiles on the rooftops of tower blocks adjoining the Olympic Stadium.[15] There were reports that hotel bookings in London were down and that tourists were staying away for fear the city would be too crowded and expensive.[16] There were stories about the so-called 'Zil Lanes' which were going to be reserved for the exclusive use of Olympic athletes, officials, sponsors and journalists and the likely traffic chaos they would cause.[17] Then, with only a few days to go before the Olympics began, G4S, the firm engaged to provide on-site security at the games, announced that it had been unable to recruit enough workers and would be unable to meet the terms of its contract.[18] The Army had to be deployed in its place.

All of this took place against the backdrop of the screening of the second series of the BBC's mockumentary *Twenty Twelve*, which satirized the bureaucratic absurdities, management talk and all-round incompetence of a lightly fictionalized set of politicians and Olympic organizers, including that of 'Siobhan Sharpe', the hapless head of brand for the public relations firm 'Perfect Curve'. In the show's final episode, broadcast on 24 July 2012 just a few days before the actual opening ceremony, everything falls apart when it becomes apparent that the fireworks at the opening ceremony will trigger the surface-to-air missiles. That same day, in the real world, Mitt Romney, the US Republican presidential candidate, was forced to explain comments he had made during a visit to London about 'disconcerting' signs for the games.[19] Two days later, the organizers of the women's football tournament, which had started early, caused a diplomatic storm by mistakenly flying the South Korean flag to welcome the arrival of the North Korean team onto the pitch.[20]

AN IMAGINED COMMUNITY

The opening Olympic Ceremony, which provided an unexpectedly joyous moment of respite from the challenges of austerity economics, began at exactly 9 p.m. on Friday 27 July. It was called *Isles of Wonder* – the title offering a knowing nod to *The Tempest*, where Caliban refers to an 'isle full of noises, sounds and sweet airs, that give delight, and hurt not'. The task Danny Boyle had been given was to present an attractive, non-declinist image of Britain, not only to the rest of the world but to itself. In a politically divided country, which was used to arguing about its own history, this was no easy task. Boyle was known to be on the political left. Yet he was clear that he wanted to present Britain as a decent country with shared values and common points of reference:

> I felt very strongly when we were creating the opening ceremony – in a philosophical, theoretical and also practical way – that we are a decent country. One of our attributes is our self-criticism, which can sometimes stop us from really appreciating our basic decency. All sorts of people hijack the notion of being patriotic for all sorts of reasons, but that shouldn't stop us from acknowledging that whether you were born here or emigrated here, there are certain values that we all want to try and share. They're pretty sound values as well.[21]

During the ceremony itself this played out by way of a long tribute to the NHS and, in particular, to Great Ormond Street Children's Hospital, a few miles to the west of the Olympic Stadium. A troop of 600 NHS nurses, together with 1,200 volunteers and 300 children on hospital beds, some of which doubled as trampolines, jumped and twirled and danced. This morphed into a linked segment on British children's stories that began with J. K. Rowling reading from J. M. Barrie's *Peter Pan*. In 1929 Barrie had donated the copyright of *Peter Pan* to Great Ormond Street and in 1988 the House of Lords had voted for a special clause in the Copyright Designs and Patent Act which gave the hospital the right to royalties from the book in perpetuity. Boyle, who later suggested Conservative ministers had tried to pressure him to drop, or at least water down this sequence, used the NHS (and nursing in particular) as symbols of a shared British decency.[22]

Boyle's search for a shared common ground also meant a recurring link back to a self-deprecating British sense of humour, with the Queen apparently joining James Bond in parachuting into the Olympic Stadium and Rowan Atkinson, as Mr Bean, playing Vangelis's *Chariots of Fire* theme tune whilst running along a beach. Less obviously, it also meant a short clip of the moment in October 1987 when the BBC weather forecaster Michael Fish referenced 'a woman who had called the BBC to say that she had heard that there was a hurricane on the way' as a prelude to reassuring viewers that, in fact, the weather was going to be fine (it was not).

Boyle ducked away from the tougher moments in British history. The segment narrating the history of the Industrial Revolution, which concluded with Isambard Kingdom Brunel (played by Kenneth Branagh), lifting the Olympic Rings, did not dwell upon child labour, class conflict or land enclosures. The Armed Forces were largely absent. Whilst a pride in multiculturalism ran through the entire event, there were no noticeable references to the Empire, let alone to Britain's role in the slave trade. At the start of the evening youth choirs sang the informal anthems of the four home nations: 'Jerusalem', 'Flower of Scotland', 'Cwm Rhondda' and 'The Londonderry Air'. However, nothing was said about the ways in which the United Kingdom had been pulled together or about the history of 'The Troubles' in Northern Ireland (in his memoirs Cameron later said he had vetoed a planned element in the ceremony which featured Gerry Adams and Martin McGuinness).[23]

Above all, the search for common ground meant a focus on music, television programmes and films which constituted a shared cultural heritage, an 'invisible fingerprint' in Boyle's words, which 'everybody in Britain carries with them whether they know it or not'.[24] Boyle's tastes sometimes dated him, but nevertheless he got nearly everything right. *Isles of Wonder* opened with a video tracing the course of the River Thames from its source in the Cotswolds to the Olympic Stadium, played to a soundtrack that included the Sex Pistols singing 'God Save the Queen', the *EastEnders*' theme tune and 'London Calling' by the Clash. In the part of the show which most people now most clearly remember, two characters, June and Frankie (played by Jasmine Breinburg and Henrique Costa), go for a night out on the town with their friends, during which they meet and fall for each other to a background of music by The Jam, The Eurythmics, Soul II Soul, Amy Winehouse, The Bee Gees, Tinie Tempah, The Sugababes, Eric Clapton, The Who, The

Rolling Stones, The Kinks, New Order, the Prodigy, Blur, Dizzee Rascal, Queen, David Bowie, Led Zeppelin, The Beatles, Frankie Goes to Holly-wood and Underworld, interspersed with clips from *Kes*, *Doctor Who*, *Four Weddings and a Funeral*, *Trainspotting* (the pub toilet scene), *Brookside* (the kiss between Beth Jordache and Margaret Clemence in 1994) and *Emergency Ward 10* (one of the first interracial kisses shown on British television between Louise Mahler and Giles Farmer).

All of this was washed down with David Beckham arriving on a speedboat shepherding the Olympic Torch; Doreen Lawrence carrying the Olympic flag; Tim Berners-Lee working on a NeXT computer (p. 110) inventing the World Wide Web and tweeting 'this is for everyone'; a tribute to the victims of the 7 July 2005 terrorist attacks; and Mary Poppins, Pink Floyd and The Arctic Monkeys. At 10 p.m. the athletes of each country entered the stadium to more music, including 'West End Girls' by the Pet Shop Boys, 'Beautiful Day' by U2, 'Stayin' Alive' by The Bee Gees and, for the British team, 'Heroes' by David Bowie. Then, when everything looked like it was done, Paul McCartney appeared and closed the evening, shortly before one o'clock in the morning, with 'Hey Jude'.

Isles of Wonder largely ducked politics. But it worked and was seen as a huge success because it offered an attractive alternative to the idea that Britain was in decline. The Empire had gone. Britain and America had ended up being the bad guys in Iraq. The banks had crashed. MPs had fiddled their expenses. London had rioted. But Britain had been and still was a world leader when it came to popular culture. That was its non-threatening gift to the world. The obvious contrast here was with the trials and tribulations of the Millennium Dome. The Dome failed not only because it was draughty and expensive. It failed because it was presented as an exercise, in Blair's 'young country', of looking forward to the future and in Britain the future is not necessarily seen as a good thing. *Isles of Wonder*, on the other hand, worked not only because Danny Boyle and the team around him were exceptionally talented and had been given a large budget to play with, but because, in a country convinced that it had fallen into a hole, the theme of the evening was about days gone by. Recall here the line from the 2013 Liberal Demo-crat focus group I quoted in the opening chapter (p. 4). 'Can anyone perhaps tell me of one thing they actually like in modern Britain?' 'Yes ... the past.'[25] Danny Boyle doubled-down on that sentiment and extracted some great entertainment from it, along with a measure of reassurance for a country that seemed to have lost a large amount of confidence in itself.

SUPER SATURDAY

An estimated 900 million people watched the opening ceremony.[26] the British audience peaked at around 27 million, making it, to this day, one of the most-watched British television broadcasts of all time, behind the 1966 World Cup final, the Apollo 13 splashdown, the funeral of Princess Diana and, more recently, Boris Johnson's announcement of the first national lockdown in March 2020.[27] The instant reaction was ecstatic, transforming, in just a few hours, the mood around the Olympics.

The days after the night before came with a few early hiccups. There were a lot of empty seats at some events. British athletes who had been expected to do well fell short. After four days Britain had won only one silver and one bronze medal. 'The curse of Cameron' even became a thing as the prime minister developed a habit of arriving shortly before British athletes lost.[28] Yet the curse, if that is what it was, eventually lifted. There were no major security scares; the weather held; the public transport system worked; and British athletes came good, winning twenty-nine gold and eighteen silver and bronze medals. This put Britain in third place in the overall medal table, behind the United States and China but narrowly ahead of Russia, and a long way ahead of South Korea, France and Germany. Given that it had only managed a single gold medal in the 1996 Atlanta Games (Matthew Pinsent and Steve Redgrave in the men's rowing coxless pair) this was an impressive result, one vindicating the powers of lottery funding when combined with generational talent. The highlight of it all, 'Super Saturday', came on 4 August. In one day, Britain won six gold medals, starting with the men's coxless fours in rowing, followed by the women's lightweight sculls and the women's team pursuit in the cycling. This was before, in the space of less than an hour and in front of a capacity crowd, Jess Ennis won the heptathlon, Greg Rutherford won the long jump and, finally, Mo Farah sprinted clear in the 10,000 metres.

A few days prior to 'Super Saturday', the chairman of the British

Olympic Association, Colin Moynihan, observed that a disproportionate number of the athletes representing Britain at the Olympics had attended private schools.[29] That was entirely correct. In total around 20 per cent of all the British Olympic competitors (rising to a third in rowing, sailing and equestrian events) were privately educated. Ennis, Rutherford and Farah offered a different version of Britain as an imagined country. Jess Ennis was born in Highfield, Sheffield, in 1986, to Vinnie, a painter who had moved to Britain from Jamaica, and Alison Howell, a social worker. She started running, aged ten, at the Don Valley Stadium in Sheffield. Whilst still studying psychology at the University of Sheffield, she won a bronze medal at the 2006 Commonwealth Games in Melbourne. She then won the 2009 World Championships in Berlin before coming third in that year's BBC's Sports Personality of the Year award. Greg Rutherford was the great-grandson of Jock Rutherford, who, as a professional footballer, had won three First Division titles playing for Newcastle United in the early 1900s before moving to Woolwich Arsenal. Greg had been raised in Bletchley, Milton Keynes, in a family in which his parents, a builder and a nurse, were devout Jehovah's Witnesses. Rutherford later described an unhappy childhood in which he had dropped out of school and sometimes slept rough before discovering athletics and becoming the youngest ever winner of the long jump at the Amateur Athletics Association Championships in 2005.[30] Finally, Mo Farah was born in Gabiley, Somaliland. He moved to Britain aged nine. He attended Isleworth and Syon School in West London a few miles to the east of Heathrow and then Feltham Community College. After Farah showed early promise in cross-country races, the philanthropist Eddie Kulukundis then paid the legal fees needed to complete Farah's naturalization as a British citizen.

The Olympics concluded on 12 August with a concert in Hyde Park featuring Blur, New Order and The Specials and a closing ceremony in the Olympic Stadium with a live performance from The Who and a handover ceremony for the Olympic flag from the mayor of London, Boris Johnson, to the mayor of Rio de Janeiro. A few weeks later, the Paralympics began with over 4,000 athletes and an opening ceremony featuring, this time, 'Spasticus Autisticus', a riotously self-mocking song by the late Ian Dury, who had contracted polio at the age of seven. Ticket sales were strong, and Channel 4 offered sustained coverage, including the moment when Houssein Omar Hassan, Djibouti's first

Paralympic athlete, completed his 1,500-metre race at a crawling pace after injuring his ankle, urged on by a crowd performing a 'Mexican Wave' to keep him going.

After it was all over, the country came back to earth with a bang. In early October the Ministry of Defence announced that five Royal Marines had been charged with murder following the death of an insurgent in Afghanistan in 2011. A few weeks later, and a year after his death, the Metropolitan Police announced it was launching a formal criminal investigation into sexual abuse allegations made against the TV star and charity fundraiser Jimmy Savile. In early November, the former Labour MP Margaret Moran was found guilty of fifteen counts of false accounting in relation to £53,000 of her expenses claims. In January 2013 the Office for National Statistics reported that the British economy had shrunk by 0.3 per cent in the final three months of 2012.[31] Austerity was still the economic order of the day. Yet the lustre of the Olympics did not fade. An opinion poll in December 2012, which reminded respondents of the Olympics' £9 billion price tag, still found nearly 80 per cent thought it had been a positive and cheering experience.[32]

The official government report into the Olympics' legacy, soaked in a spirit of corporate self-promotion, threw some numbers into a pot and concluded the Olympics had been worth somewhere between £28 and £41 billion for the British economy.[33] That looked like something straight out of *Twenty Twelve* but the Olympics did accelerate the already ongoing regeneration of Stratford, Hackney, Tower Hamlets and Newham. London also avoided the usual Olympic fate of leaving behind empty and decaying stadiums. After protracted negotiations (which ended in a court battle), West Ham United bought a lease on the Olympic Stadium and sold their old ground, Upton Park, in Newham, for housing.

Not everything went so well. Only around 11,000 of the promised 40,000 new homes on and around the Olympic site were built.[34] A 2013 House of Lords report found that, at a time when local councils were closing sports centres, the Olympics had not led to more people participating in sports.[35] As time passed, it also became increasingly clear that the London Olympics had probably been the dirtiest in history.[36] During the games, 5,000 drug tests had been administered of which only a handful had been returned as positive. This proved to be entirely misleading. As samples were later analysed using more advanced techniques, one hundred and forty-nine athletes who had competed in London were found guilty of doping violations, with nearly fifty medals taken away from the people who had originally won them. In the women's 1,500-metres race, four of the initial top nine were later banned, including both the gold and silver medallists. Russia, whose state-sponsored doping programme was eventually exposed in 2015, was the largest offender with forty-eight violations; overall, however, athletes from thirty countries were sanctioned. To add to London's misery, a Parliamentary Committee was told, in 2017, that some of Britain's Paralympic athletes had misrepresented their disability in order to gain a sporting advantage.[37] Finally, a series of reports published from 2017 onwards revealed, within cycling and gymnastics, patterns of systemic bullying, driven by the search for competitive advantage.[38]

HEY DUDE

What happened next to some of the people most closely involved with the Olympics? In November 2014 Jess Ennis-Hill, as she had become, asked for her name to be removed from the stand named after her at Sheffield United's ground, Bramall Lane, after the club re-signed a player, Ched Evans, who had, at that point, been convicted of rape.* She, in turn, was abused on social media and, at one point, told that she should be raped.[39] She gave birth to a son, Reggie, in July 2014, and then returned to competition and won her third World Championship a year later in Beijing, before winning silver at the 2016 Rio Olympics. After announcing her retirement, she was made a Dame Commander of the Order of the British Empire in 2017. Greg Rutherford won more gold medals at the 2014 Commonwealth Games in Glasgow and the 2015 World Athletic Championships before finally retiring in 2018. In between these two events he was eliminated during the ninth round of voting on *Strictly Come Dancing* in 2016. In 2019 he won *Celebrity*

---

* Evans continued to protest his innocence and when new evidence emerged was granted a retrial. In October 2016 he was found not guilty and his conviction was quashed. In 2019 Evans accepted an £800,000 settlement from the legal firm which had represented him at his first trial.

MasterChef before, in April 2021, announcing that he had joined the British Bobsleigh team and was aiming to compete in the World Cup and Winter Olympics.[40]

Mo Farah was made a Commander of the British Empire in 2013 and won two gold medals at both the 2013 and 2015 World Championships. In 2015 Farah's former coach, Alberto Salazar, was named in a BBC *Panorama* investigation into doping, which led to questions being asked of Farah.[41] In July 2017 the Russian hacking consortium Fancy Bear leaked data from the International Association of Athletics Federations showing that Farah had once been recorded as having suspiciously high readings on his biological passport. He was later cleared of any wrongdoing.[42] Having won gold medals in both the 5,000- and 10,000-metre events at the Rio Olympics in 2016, Farah switched distance; he came third in the 2018 London Marathon, a year after he had been Knighted by the Queen. In July 2022 he revealed in a BBC documentary that his name was in fact Hussein Abdi Kahin and that he had been trafficked to Britain when he was aged nine and forced to work as a domestic servant.

Without competing in any events, Boris Johnson had a good Olympics. He received enormous amounts of free publicity when the zip wire he was riding in Victoria Park to promote London, or himself, or both, lost momentum and left him hanging in mid-air.[43] The *Daily Mirror* later reported that he had arrived late at the opening of the Paralympics after having had an earlier assignation with the American tech-entrepreneur Jennifer Arcuri.[44] Johnson returned to Westminster as MP for Uxbridge and South Ruislip in the 2015 General Election. He finished his second term as London's mayor before being replaced by Sadiq Khan in 2016.

Danny Boyle was offered a Knighthood in late 2012 following the success of the Olympic Opening Ceremony. He turned it down, noting that 'when people say we're all in it together, it's a lovely catchphrase for politicians to use, but I actually do believe it'.[45] He then returned to his day job. In 2013 he directed the psychological thriller *Trance*. In 2015 he directed a film about the life of Steve Jobs, and in 2017 he reunited with the cast of *Trainspotting* to make *T2 Trainspotting*. In 2018 Boyle resigned as the director of the Bond movie *No Time to Die*, citing creative differences, and then in 2019 he released *Yesterday*, a romantic comedy about a struggling musician, Jack Malik, played by Himesh

Patel, who finds fame and fortune after realizing that, somehow, he has entered a parallel universe in which he is the only person in the world who has heard of The Beatles or any of their songs. At one point in the film Ed Sheeran, playing himself, tries to persuade Malik to change the title of his new song to 'Hey Dude' on the grounds that 'Jude is just a bit old-fashioned'.

25
Increasingly Independent

GEORGE SQUARE

George Square sits at the heart of Glasgow's city centre. Planning for the design of the square, which is named after King George III, began in the 1760s. Most of the buildings now lining it were built in the early 1800s. At the middle of the square stands an eighty-foot high statue to Walter Scott, the inventor, in the early 1800s, of a new image of Scotland, one tied to the beauty and romance of the Highlands.[1] One side of the square is occupied by the Millennium Hotel; another by a Wetherspoon's pub, The Counting House, housed in an Italian-style Renaissance building previously used by the Royal Bank of Scotland; and a third by the Glasgow City Chambers, opened in 1888 by Queen Victoria.

George Square has a history. In 1919 engineers campaigning for the introduction of a forty-hour working week held a rally there which ended in a mass brawl when a fight between an off-duty soldier and one of the protestors escalated. Amidst fears the engineers were planning a Bolshevik-style uprising, 10,000 troops were deployed to Glasgow to maintain the peace. A dozen strike leaders were later charged and, following a trial in Edinburgh, some were found guilty of incitement to riot. Although the strike itself was unsuccessful, the Battle of George Square, as it became known, cemented Glasgow's reputation as 'Red Clydeside', the heartland of Scottish political and industrial militancy.[2]

In 2014 George Square was only a few minutes' walk from the headquarters of the official Yes Scotland pro-independence campaign. They set up an open mic in the square so people could talk about why they supported independence.[3] Two days before the referendum, Yes Scotland held its final rally there, with speakers who included Ricky Ross from Deacon Blue and the former professional footballer Martin

Compston, who had made two first-team appearances for Greenock Morton before switching jobs and playing the role of Ewan Brodie in *Monarch of the Glen* and Detective Sergeant Steve Arnott in *Line of Duty*.[4] On the evening of the day of the vote, 18 September 2014, pro-independence supporters congregated in George Square, waiting for the result. They were to be disappointed. Glasgow voted for independence, but Scotland as a whole voted against. The next morning, a number of Scottish papers carried pictures of people, draped in Saltires, crying in George Square.[5] That evening, a Friday night, a group of men marched from the Louden Tavern on Duke Street, a pub known as a gathering point for Unionist Rangers fans, to George Square to celebrate the result.[6] There was lots of singing of 'Rule Britannia' and 'God Save the Queen' and throwing of flares and some fights. According to a report in *The Herald*, a group of young girls with Saltires painted on their faces were chased across George Square.[7] The police arrested six people. It was, all round, a depressing end to the referendum campaign.

'A SENSE OF GRIEVANCE'

The SNP emerged, by the skin of its teeth, as the largest party in the 2007 Scottish Parliament elections. Having shelved any immediate plans for an independence referendum, it set about establishing a reputation for competent, left-of-centre governance. The 2008 financial crisis and the 2009 MPs' expenses scandal strengthened its hand. During the boom years the Scottish economy had grown at a faster rate than any other part of Britain. That made it easier for Labour to argue the case for the value of the Union. But the financial crisis shredded Labour's reputation for economic competence and, at the very least, put a question mark over Britain's future growth prospects. The expenses scandal then reinforced the idea that Westminster MPs were only interested in themselves and could not be trusted. The Scottish Parliament had had more than its own fair share of expenses embarrassments. In November 2001 the Labour leader and first minister Henry McLeish resigned amidst a set of stories about his office expenses.[8] Four years later, the Conservative leader, David McLetchie, resigned after having claimed an ambitious £11,500 on taxi fares. Yet in 2009, the SNP, with only six MPs in Westminster, escaped the majority of the *Daily*

Telegraph's expenses broadsides relatively unscathed. The 2010 General Election, in which the Conservatives won 305 seats in England and Wales and only 1 seat in Scotland, was another godsend to the nationalists. The SNP could now argue that Labour was a busted flush; that they were all that stood between London and a never-ending ideological crusade for economy-busting austerity; and that devolution had failed to offer any protection to Scotland and Scottish interests.

In May 2011 the SNP dominated the Scottish Parliament elections with 45 per cent of the overall vote, winning 69 of the 129 available seats. After the dust had settled, First Minister Alex Salmond demanded that Scotland be granted the independence referendum he had campaigned for. David Cameron, convinced he could win the vote and that blocking Salmond would, in the words of his deputy chief of staff Kate Fall, 'fuel their [the SNP's] sense of grievance', agreed.[9] Cameron's judgement made sense. Opinion polls consistently showed that only around a third of the Scottish electorate would vote for independence.[10] The SNP had done brilliantly in 2011 but as much as a half of its total vote had come from people who did not support independence.[11]

In October 2012 the Westminster and Scottish governments signed the Edinburgh agreement, setting out the basic rules under which the referendum would take place. Most notably, there would only be one question asked – a 'yes' or 'no' to independence. In January 2013 the Electoral Commission recommended that the precise question be, 'Do you agree that Scotland should be an independent country?' This was interpreted as an early win for the Yes campaign in so far as it presented independence as a positive option, which was, for this reason, preferable to asking whether Scotland should remain a part of the United Kingdom.[12] In March 2013 Salmond announced that the referendum, in which sixteen- and seventeen-year-olds would be allowed to vote, would take place in September of the following year.

The decision to restrict the referendum to a straight yes or no question suited both Cameron and Salmond because they thought it would maximize support for each of their own preferred positions.[13] Yet this was something of a carve-up. Opinion polls consistently showed that, if the options had, instead, been independence, the status quo, or a further and substantive devolution of powers to the Scottish Parliament, then the third of these options – 'Devo Max', as it became known – would have received the most support.[14] Devo Max would not have been straightforward. For a start, the Coalition in London and the Scottish Executive in Edinburgh would have strongly disagreed about what it entailed. From London's perspective, the 2012 Scotland Act, which, following a recommendation of the Calman Commission on Scottish devolution (established by Labour with cross-party support in 2007), had given the Scottish Parliament the authority to raise or lower income tax by 10 pence in the pound and to borrow money for capital investment, already constituted something approaching Devo Max.[15] From the SNP's perspective, Calman had been a damp squib and a proper Devo Max would probably have looked a lot like independence. Yet given the way in which the referendum split the Scottish electorate down the middle, it is worth remembering that the two available options on the table were imposed from the top down. Political polarization was as much the effect of the referendum as it was its cause.

During the referendum campaign, Yes Scotland, its campaign coffers boosted by a multimillion-pound donation from Colin and Chris Weir, the winners of a £161-million EuroMillions lottery, conjured an image of a future independent Scotland as a strong, prosperous, inclusive, culturally rich country with its own clear sense of national identity and social justice.[16] Danny Boyle could not have managed to paint a more attractive picture if he had tried. To put some flesh on these bones, Yes Scotland, which was staffed primarily by SNP supporters, offered a rejection of austerity economics; the promise of full-time childcare to boost employment; cuts to corporation tax; and the closure of the Faslane Trident Submarine base in Gare Loch.[17] At a point when austerity was the political order of the day, this was radical stuff. But Yes Scotland was, in its own way, also deeply conservative. It promised continued membership of the European Union and sub-let arrangements on the Royal Family, the BBC and, via a currency union, sterling and the Bank of England. In fact, Yes Scotland, under the banner of full independence, actually offered something which looked a lot like one possible take on what Devo Max might have been.

The No campaign, Better Together, chaired by the former Labour chancellor Alistair Darling, with donations from individual business figures and Edinburgh resident J. K. Rowling, for the most part avoided falling into the trap of arguing that Scotland was not up to the task of governing itself. Instead it chiselled away at Yes Scotland's economic credibility.[18] Creating a new Scottish state would cost billions. The closure of Faslane would result in job losses. A high-tax, high-regulation Scottish economy would struggle to attract foreign investment and would be vulnerable, in the medium term, to falling North Sea oil prices. Above all, Better Together argued that Scotland could not have its cake and eat it. If Scotland chose independence, it would have to apply as a new state to join the European Union and take its chances on Spain – keen to set an example to secessionist Catalonia – vetoing its application. Moreover, it could not expect the rest of Britain to sign-up to a currency union just because it wanted one. As George Osborne put the point, 'the pound isn't an asset to be divided up between two countries after a breakup like a CD collection.'[19] An independent Scotland would have to create its own currency and that would be economically risky. Yes Scotland argued this was a bluff, but if it was a bluff it was one which seemed to have the heavyweight backing of the Treasury's permanent secretary, Nicholas Macpherson, who publicly released his thumbs-down advice to a currency union.[20]

DÉJÀ VU DEVO MAX

Yes Scotland was a slow burn. In February 2013, one poll, which used the exact question approved by the Electoral Commission, was still recording only 34 per cent support for independence.[21] But everyone kept going and the momentum start to change in the spring of 2014 when the negativity of the Better Together campaign, 'Project Fear' as it had been dubbed by its own director of communications, became a story in its own right.[22] By April 2014 a number of opinion polls showed support for independence at around 40 per cent. Then, from 23 July to 3 August, Glasgow hosted the Commonwealth Games: a high-profile platform for Scottish sporting prowess and Scotland's first minister, who comfortably won the 200-metre self-publicity award previously held by Boris Johnson's zip wire. With the wind in its sails, Yes Scotland even started to turn the currency debate to its advantage, arguing that London's rush to rule out a currency union constituted typical English bullying. Then, in early September, a poll put independence ahead for the first time.[23] The Scottish Social Attitudes survey, the fieldwork for which was completed between May and August 2014, offers some clues as to what had happened. Whilst only 9 per cent of people thought they would personally be better off in an independent Scotland, 84 per cent said they did not trust the British government to place the needs of the Scottish nation above that of their own party.[24]

It may be that Yes Scotland peaked too soon. Once independence started to seem a likely outcome, Better Together campaigners redoubled their efforts to place doubts in voters' minds about the possible downsides of independence. They did so by encouraging a number of Scottish-based banks to announce that they might have to move to England and by nudging the Queen to express the hope that voters would 'think very carefully about the future' before voting.* On 8 September Gordon Brown delivered a speech in which he resurrected the option of Devo Max, promising 'nothing less than a modern form of Scottish home rule' if voters rejected independence.[25] Following in his wake, Cameron, Nick Clegg and Ed Miliband were pictured on the front page of the *Daily Record* a week later, just three days before the big referendum day, collectively pledging 'permanent and extensive new powers for the Scottish Parliament'.[26] So, suddenly, the referendum now had as its options Devo Max home rule if voters rejected independence and a form of independence which looked a lot like Devo Max if they voted for it. Yet, in this respect, both sides were now promising to deliver something they could not really guarantee. Yes Scotland's version of independence depended upon the British government playing ball, and it had already said it would not. Better Together's home rule depended upon British party leaders doing what they said they would do to make Devo Max a reality and the Scottish government, the SNP, going along with it.

On 18 September 85 per cent of eligible voters voted. Just over 1.6 million of them (44.7 per cent) voted Yes and just over 2 million (55.3

---

* David Cameron subsequently told the BBC that, having been 'panicked' by the poll suggesting independence might win, he told Palace officials that 'just a raising of the eyebrow' might be enough to suggest the Queen opposed independence and help tip the result. 'I remember conversations I had with my private secretary and he had with the Queen's private secretary and I had with the Queen's private secretary, not asking for anything that would be in any way improper or unconstitutional, but just a raising of the eyebrow, even, you know, a quarter of an inch, we thought it would make a difference.' Cameron did not seem to have considered the possibility that saying that this is what had happened *would* make the Queen's words appear distinctly improper and unconstitutional. Sylvia DeLuca, 'David Cameron asked the Queen if she could "raise an eyebrow" over Scottish independence', LBC News (19 Sept. 2019).

per cent) voted No. A majority of voters in Dundee, Glasgow, North Lanarkshire and West Dunbartonshire voted for independence. A majority in the other twenty-eight council areas in Scotland did not.[27] Support for independence was higher amongst male than female voters; higher amongst younger voters than older ones; higher amongst people self-identifying as working class rather than middle class; and higher amongst Catholics and those with no religion than amongst those self-identifying as Church of Scotland.[28] In March 2015 the *Daily Record* also reported that three-quarters of the 420,000 people living in Scotland who had been born elsewhere in Britain had voted No, and that this may have been enough to swing the result.[29] Yes Scotland did a great job of mobilizing SNP support. Fully 80 per cent of those who had voted for the SNP in the 2011 Scottish Parliament elections, at a point when support for independence was around 30 per cent, ended up voting for independence. On the other hand, the Yes campaign only secured around 30 per cent of those who had voted Labour or Liberal Democrat, and only 12 per cent of Conservative voters.[30]

Alex Salmond, who had described the referendum as a 'once in a generation opportunity' for independence, resigned as leader of the SNP.[31] He was replaced, unopposed, by his deputy Nicola Sturgeon. In August 2018 Salmond, who had stood for and won the Westminster seat of Gordon, in Aberdeenshire, in the 2015 General Election, resigned from the SNP following the publication of allegations of sexual misconduct against him relating to the time whilst he was first minister. Eventually, in March 2020, a few days before the start of the first Covid lockdown, he was acquitted of two counts of attempted rape and nine of sexual assault. Afterwards, Salmond accused the SNP leadership, including Nicola Sturgeon, of a 'malicious and concerted effort' to ruin his reputation and remove him from public life.[32] The Scottish government was eventually forced to concede that its handling of the initial allegations against Salmond had been deeply flawed. A committee of the Scottish Parliament, to which Salmond gave evidence, also found, in March 2021, that Sturgeon had, under oath, given an inaccurate account of when she became aware of the allegations against Salmond and of the contents of a discussion she had had with colleagues about them.[33]

This was a serious allegation, but it was one that had been made by politicians with party political axes to grind. A few weeks later, following an investigation by the independent advisor on the Scottish

Ministerial Code, James Hamilton, a former director of public prosecution in Ireland, Sturgeon was cleared of any wrongdoing.[34] Shortly after, Salmond announced he was forming a new party, Alba, and would contest the forthcoming 2021 Scottish Parliament elections. Alba sank and the SNP won 63 of the 129 available seats. In the end, Sturgeon's reputation was probably damaged by the allegations made by Salmond. But whatever else had happened, it was reasonably clear Sturgeon had not directly intervened at any point to protect Salmond: 'As First Minister I refused to follow the age-old pattern of allowing a powerful man to use his status and connections to get what he wants.'[35]

THE NEW NORMAL

The Scottish referendum result was closer than a lot of people had expected in late 2013. But it was not *that* close, and the British government now had a route forward. Deliver on Devo Max and wait for the SNP to lose their lustre and eventually lose office, and independence would be on the backburner again.

It did not work out like that at first. Instead of fading from view, the referendum became the thing around which everything else realigned; 18 September 2014 became the Groundhog Day to which everyone kept waking up. Those who had voted for independence did not change their minds. Instead, the referendum result led them to switch their lasting support to the SNP. The real loser in the resulting reshuffling was Labour. A lot of Yes voters who had previously voted Labour were angry that the party had campaigned alongside the Conservatives during the referendum campaign. It did not help matters when the party's leader, Johann Lamont, resigned in October 2014, suggesting that Scottish Labour had been treated as a 'branch office' by its English counterparts.[36]

In the 2015 General Election the SNP won 49.9 per cent of the vote, which, whilst only a few percentage points above the Yes vote in 2014, was enough to win fifty-six of the fifty-nine available seats at Westminster. Labour, which had won forty-one Scottish seats in 2010, was now left with exactly as many seats as the Conservatives and Liberal Democrats – which is to say, precisely one. Labour had tried to argue that the SNP was failing to deliver upon its promises and that the independence issue had been settled. It might as well have argued that Nicola Sturgeon had faked her own birth certificate and been born in Surbiton. More than 80 per cent of the large number of people who had voted Labour in the 2010 General Election but then voted Yes in 2014, ended up voting SNP in 2015.[37] In the following Scottish Parliament elections, in May 2016, Labour was squeezed into third place by the Scottish Conservatives.

Brexit made a drama out of a crisis. In May 2016 the Scottish Parliament voted by 106 votes to 8 in favour of staying in the European Union (seven of thirty-one Conservative and one of twenty-four Labour members voted to leave). A few weeks later, 62 per cent of Scottish voters voted to stay in the European Union. Yet Brexit was what then happened. If you were the SNP and you wanted to argue that devolution was a sideshow and that only independence could protect Scotland from being stomped all over by English politicians, Brexit was a bit of a full stop moment. It certainly gave the SNP a plausible opportunity to argue that contrary to Salmond's 'once in a generation' line, a lot had changed and that another independence referendum was now needed. But, for all the heat and light it generated, Brexit did not make any real sustained difference to the overall level of support for independence across an electorate almost all of whom had already made up their minds. In 2016, support for independence rose to 50 per cent. It fell back to around 45 per cent in early 2017. During the Covid pandemic it rose again to 55 per cent before then subsiding to leave a 50/50 split across the balance of opinion polls in 2023.[38] Those who favoured the Union did not seem to be swayed by the possibility that a Union outside a larger European Union might be less attractive. Those who favoured independence did not seem to draw from the Brexit breakdown and the economic costs of leaving the European Union (pp. 482–3) the conclusion that separating Scotland from the rest of UKGBNI might prove equally complicated and costly.

The result was a political stalemate. The SNP kept winning elections and kept arguing that a second referendum was essential. The British government, whilst acknowledging that the Union had to be based on consent, kept arguing that 2014 was not that long ago and that the circumstances were not right for another vote. 'Muscular Unionism' became the new normal within the Conservative Party, with Liz Truss – the international benchmark standard for making friends and influencing people – branding Sturgeon an 'attention seeker' who was best ignored.[39] In December 2019 the Scottish Parliament voted to give the Scottish government the power to call a second referendum. In November 2022 the Supreme Court ruled it did not have the legal authority to do so unilaterally.[40] A few months later, Sturgeon, who had been hinting for some time that she was close to having had enough, resigned in the immediate aftermath of a row over Scottish Parliament legislation relating to transgender rights and the confinement of a convicted rapist, who had begun self-identifying as a woman, in a female prison.

In March 2023, Humza Yousaf, the cabinet secretary for health and social care, won a membership ballot to become the new SNP leader. He had just about put the kettle on in the first minister's office when Peter Murrell, Nicola Sturgeon's husband and the SNP's long-serving chief executive, who had resigned from his role during the leadership campaign after admitting he had misled the press over the size of the party's membership, was arrested. It was in connection with an ongoing investigation by the police into whether some of the £666,000 raised by the SNP to campaign for independence in a second referendum had been improperly spent on other activities. Murrell was released, but the police then arrested the SNP's treasurer, Colin Beattie. In early June, Nicola Sturgeon was herself arrested. To cap it all, the SNP was then trounced in a by-election in Rutherglen and Hamilton West in October 2023. At the time of writing, the final outcome of the police investigation and its political impact on the SNP is unclear. Several commentators have been quick to conclude that the SNP is a spent force and that support for Scottish independence will collapse. That is entirely possible. However, even if the SNP's support proves more resilient, it is hard to see how a British government would countenance a second independence referendum anytime soon.

Yet, in many ways, Scottish independence is already a day-to-day reality. Scotland does not vote or think like the rest of Britain. When it comes to the bread-and-butter issues of health, education, transport and social services it does not have the same policies as the rest of Britain. In October 2022 the Scottish Social Attitudes survey found that 66 per cent of people said they trusted the Scottish government to work in Scotland's best interests 'just about always' or 'most of the time', compared with 22 per cent who trusted the British government to do the same.[41] Amongst younger voters aged between eighteen and thirty-four support for Scottish independence is over 70 per cent.[42] Meanwhile, the most unambiguously pro-unionist political party, the Scottish Conservatives, has learned how to distance itself effectively from large parts of what a Conservative-led Westminster government says and does. Call this (in honour of the bright orange soft drink, manufactured in Cumbernauld, North Lanarkshire, since 1901) Irn-Bru Unionism. Whether or not a second referendum is held, Scotland is quite definitely different from England and, in political terms, has become more different over time.

EVEL

After promising Devo Max if Scotland voted No, David Cameron had to work out what that might mean in practice. He did so by way of a cross-party set of talks chaired by Robert Haldane Smith, a Scottish businessman and banker, which resulted in a government White Paper in January 2015 called – a tad optimistically – *Scotland in the United Kingdom: An Enduring Settlement*.[43] This promised legislation confirming that the Scottish Parliament and government were permanent institutions; the continuation of the Barnett Formula (p. 64); and new powers for the Scottish Parliament to borrow money and set the rates of income tax and the thresholds at which they were paid. The SNP argued that what had been put on the table was a much-watered-down version of what they had been promised. But whether or not this was true, it was still a substantive package that pulled day-to-day Scottish politics further out of the orbit of Westminster.

There was, however, a political sting in the tail. New powers for Scotland were going to be accompanied by 'English Votes for English Laws' (EVEL). If, because of the impact of devolution, a piece of proposed legislation, or a part of a piece of legislation, being debated by the House of Commons related exclusively to England then, in the future, only MPs representing English constituencies would be allowed to vote on it. That sounded straightforward enough. The practice proved more difficult and the resulting procedure was criticized for being overly cumbersome.[44] It was introduced in 2015 but the whole system was suspended in 2020 at the start of the pandemic, in order to streamline procedures, and later was simply and quietly scrapped.[45]

This was, looking back, all very curious. But EVEL was, first and foremost, about party politics, specifically Conservative Party politics. For Cameron, EVEL was a useful thing to be seen to be doing at a point when polls were showing that something like 25 per cent or so of voters in England thought that England was being pushed around and that Scotland ought to be cast aside.[46] During the 2015 General Election campaign, Cameron then pushed a 'coalition of chaos' argument hard, maintaining that a minority Labour government would agree a deal with the SNP who would be left running and ruining the country.[47]

This form of English political chauvinism was a tough act for Cameron to keep playing if all he had to offer in return was a change in parliamentary procedures that made so little practical difference it could be abolished without many people noticing. Which, finally, brings us back to Brexit again. Brexit was not simply an English political movement. A majority of people in Wales as well as a significant minority of people in Northern Ireland and Scotland voted to leave. But Brexit was, it would seem, particularly attractive to people in England with a particularly strong sense of Englishness. Amongst English voters who described themselves as being more British than English, 58 per cent said that they intended to vote to Remain a week prior to the referendum in June 2016. Amongst those who described themselves as being equally British and English, 45 per cent said they intended to vote to Remain and 43 per cent to vote Leave. Amongst voters who described themselves as being English but not British, support for Leave was 73 per cent.[48] It would be pushing things a great deal to say that a narrow No vote in the 2014 Scottish referendum led, just two years later, to a narrow Yes vote to leave the European Union. But there would be at least a grain of truth to doing so.

26

A Hostile Environment

'TENS OF THOUSANDS'

This chapter begins where Chapter 7 on immigration concluded. In February 2006, John Denham, the MP for Southampton Itchen, wrote a memorandum to Tony Blair, Gordon Brown and Charles Clarke, the home secretary, warning them that the number of East European migrants who had travelled to his constituency was far higher than official estimates suggested and that this had resulted in intense pressure upon local public services and in falling wages.[1] He did not receive a reply. But after half a decade in which levels of net migration had risen sharply and opinion polls had consistently found public opposition to higher immigration, New Labour was beginning to rethink its position. In late 2006 the government acknowledged that high levels of immigration had created pressures on local public services and promised new spending to address this. Liam Byrne – he of the 'no money left' note (pp. 285–6) – briefed Parliament on new measures to crack down on employers hiring illegal migrant workers.[2] In March 2007 a new home secretary, John Reid, went further, promising to 'make living and working here illegally even more uncomfortable and constrained'.[3] In September 2007, in his first address to the Labour Party conference as prime minister, Gordon Brown spoke about the need to limit immigration and to create 'British jobs for British workers'.[4] By that point, the government had already imposed transitional border controls to restrict the flow of new immigrants from Romania and Bulgaria when they had joined the European Union. In April 2009 new requirements were introduced in relation to student visas.[5] Shortly after, and on a split decision, the Cabinet agreed to change the tone of the government's statements about immigration to emphasize restraint and control.[6] Quite suddenly, the concept of people and areas being 'left behind', which had been knocking around for a few years, developed a racial dimension. The left behind were the white working class who were failing to get jobs; whose children were failing to do well at school; and whose fears about immigration, Communities Secretary Hazel Blears suggested, had previously been dismissed out of hand.[7]

Labour was, however, rushing to fight a war it had already lost. By August 2008 opinion polls were showing that, when asked which party had the best policies on immigration, 46 per cent said the Conservatives and only 5 per cent Labour.[8] In January 2010, David Cameron, who in his earlier years as leader of the opposition had largely avoided talking about immigration, promised – without, it would seem, much in the way of prior preparation, planning or even cursory analysis – to reduce net immigration to the 'tens of thousands'.[9] Then, during that year's general election campaign a few months later, Brown was inadvertently recorded describing a woman, Gillian Duffy, who had criticized Labour's record on the economy and immigration, as 'bigoted' during a visit to Rochdale.[10] Later that day, Brown, describing himself as a 'penitent sinner', visited Duffy in her house. 'I wanted to come here and say that I made a mistake but also to say I understood the concerns she was bringing to me and I simply misunderstood some of the words she used. I made my apology.' Brown, whose expressions often looked like those of a man who had bought and was wearing new shoes two sizes too small, looked, at this moment, particularly disgruntled with his lot in life.

Immigration was a significant factor in the 2010 General Election. In a paper published in *Political Studies*, Geoffrey Evans and Kat Chzhen found that people who voted Labour in 2005 but disapproved of the government's handling of immigration were particularly likely to have switched their vote in 2010.[11] Labour tended not to lose seats in London and other large cities, where immigration levels had been highest. They lost them instead in places like Morecambe where immigration, although not high in absolute numbers, had increased and where voters believed that Labour's record on this issue was poor (pp. 94–5).

'A REALLY HOSTILE ENVIRONMENT'

David Cameron appointed Theresa May as home secretary and tasked her with meeting the 'tens of thousands' pledge. May was ten years older than Cameron and, in interviews, sometimes showed it, mentioning the 1970s BBC light entertainment comedy show *The Goodies* rather than, as Cameron had done, The Smiths, Snow Patrol and *Desperate Housewives* as a cultural reference point.[12] May had made her name in 2002 when, having been appointed the Conservative Party chairman, she had spoken of how voters still saw the Conservatives as being 'the nasty party'.[13] In 2005 she had considered standing for the Conservative leadership, only to find she had no more than a handful of supporters.[14] When, as home secretary, someone described Cameron and Osborne as the party's modernizers, she was reported to have shouted in reply: 'I'm the original modernizer.'[15] This, however, was not her public image. She was seen as serious but dull; as being ill at ease in the social company of the posh public schoolboys Cameron and Osborne; but as being wholeheartedly determined to deliver upon the promises the Conservatives had made when it came to immigration and, in doing so, to appease 'stealth' voters (p. 259) who just wanted to see politicians deliver on their promises.[16]

May found herself being dealt a very poor hand. Cameron kept talking about how he was going to work day and night to persuade the European Union to either scrap or qualify its Single Market commitment to the freedom of movement of people – or, failing that, to agree to limit welfare payments to recent European arrivals. Yet the European Union was having none of it.[17] When May pushed for tougher rules limiting non-European migration, she ran into a sustained wall of opposition from the Treasury.[18] When she pushed for tighter restrictions on student visas, she ran into opposition from the Liberal Democrat business secretary Vince Cable.[19] Left with a limited set of options, May decided to focus the Home Office's energy on the estimated three-quarters of a million migrants living in Britain who had overstayed or broken the terms and conditions of their visas.[20] May told journalists in 2012 that she wanted to create a 'really hostile environment for illegal migration' in order to deter people from arriving who 'think they can come here and overstay because they're able to access everything they need'.[21]

This 'hostile environment' policy became the trigger for a massive rolling forward of the frontiers of the British state. New legal requirements were imposed upon the NHS to check and confirm the British citizenship of patients. Employers were given new legal responsibilities to check the visa status of potential employees, whilst the maximum fine for employing an illegal worker was doubled to £20,000 per employee. Marriage registrars were required to check the visa status of applicants, as were airlines, the Driving and Vehicle Licencing Agency and landlords. In effect, hundreds of thousands of new immigration officers were recruited to police Britain's boundaries.[22] Meanwhile, actual Home Office employees were set targets to remove illegal migrants and encouraged, when dealing with applications, to be sceptical about what they were being told and to always ask for more evidence.[23] Finally, in a pilot exercise in 2013, the Home Office even paid for vans to travel around London suburbs, on the sides of which was printed the message: 'In the UK illegally? Go home or face arrest'. Speaking on ITV when news of these vans broke, Nigel Farage described their tone as being 'unpleasant and nasty'.[24] (Shortly afterwards pots were reported to have detained and expelled a number of illegal kettles.)

'KICK ME OUT'

Net migration was +294,000 in 2010, down from a peak of +349,000 in 2004.* Over the next few years, and without ever coming within vague shouting distance of the tens of thousands target, net migration fell to +229,000 in 2013. This was explicable primarily in terms of lower economic growth and a falling number of job vacancies. When the economy began to recover from 2012 onwards – and to recover, as we have seen, at a faster rate than many other economies – net migration began to rise again, to +283,000 in 2014 and a new record high of +379,000 in 2015.[25] New Labour had argued that immigration was good for the economy and would make the economic boom boomier (p. 90). This option was not open to the Conservatives, who had framed higher immigration under Labour as a betrayal. Cameron had invited

* See p. 86 for definitions.

voters to 'kick me out' if he failed to deliver upon his tens of thousands promise and, for a while, that began to look like a real possibility.[26] The number of voters seeing immigration as one of the key issues facing the country, which had fallen to around 20 per cent in 2012 and 2013, rose to 47 per cent in 2014.[27]

The Conservative Party's 2015 manifesto restated the tens of thousands objective when it came to net migration, but admitted 'it is clearly going to take more time, more work and more difficult decisions to achieve'.[28] UKIP, predictably, campaigned hard on this issue, mobilizing a tone of what Robbie Shilliam describes as 'racialized melancholia' to argue that the Conservatives had shown themselves to be no different from Labour.[29] Yet, in the end, UKIP, whilst attracting nearly 4 million votes, and over 12 per cent of the total number of votes cast, won just one seat, Clacton, which Douglas Carswell had won for the Conservatives in 2010 before defecting to UKIP in 2014. Having been returned to 10 Downing Street with a narrow overall majority, and minus the Liberal Democrats, Cameron now had to deliver upon his in–out European referendum promise. Immigration was central to that campaign. In the run-up to the referendum Cameron managed to extract from the European Commission an agreement giving UKGBNI the right to apply an 'emergency brake' on the payment of welfare benefits to incoming European migrants in some circumstances – if, and only if, the European Parliament and a majority of other Member States agreed to it doing so. This was not enough to make any real difference.

In August 2015 Nigel Farage predicted immigration would be 'the defining issue' in the Brexit referendum.[30] Shortly after, Vote Leave's director, Dominic Cummings, told Boris Johnson and Michael Gove, the two most prominent Conservatives campaigning to leave, that 'if you want to win this, you have to hit Cameron and Osborne over the head with a baseball bat with immigration written on it'.[31] Which is pretty much what happened. In May 2016 Gove predicted that, with the accession of Albania, North Macedonia, Montenegro, Serbia and Turkey to the European Union, an extra 5 million people would arrive in Britain by 2030. A few weeks later Farage launched a poster showing a large, entirely non-white crowd of queuing refugees under the words 'BREAKING POINT: THE EU HAS FAILED US ALL'. This time round it was Michael Gove's turn to offer a condemnation of the underlying tone.[32]

Figure 4. Word Cloud: What Matters Most to You When Deciding How to Vote in the EU Referendum?

Chris Prosser, Jon Mellon and Jane Green, 'What mattered most to you when deciding how to vote in the EU Referendum?', British Election Study (11 July 2016).

However, more important than any of this was the news from the Office for National Statistics on 26 May 2016, a month before the referendum vote, that net migration in 2015 had been over +330,000.[33] As David Cameron acknowledged in his memoirs, this made the government's 'tens of thousands' target look 'ridiculous'.[34]

The word cloud above shows the results of a question asked by the British Election Study team when, in April and May 2016, they asked voters intending to vote Leave what mattered most to them in deciding how to vote. It does not require much by way of an explanation.[35] Immigration was a house brick of an issue. The 2017 British Social Attitudes survey found 73 per cent of those who were worried about overall levels of immigration voted Leave, compared with 36 per cent of those who did not identify this issue as being of concern.[36]

WINDRUSH

The German cruise ship the *Monte Rosa* was requisitioned by the German government and used to transport troops during the Second

World War. It was captured by the British in 1945 and renamed the *Empire Windrush*. Three years later it was sent to Kingston, Jamaica, in order to ferry British troops home. The captain had spare places on board on the ship's return and sold them to 492 Jamaican migrants who wanted to travel to Britain to work. Under the terms of the 1948 British Nationality Act this group had the legal right to enter Britain as citizens of the United Kingdom and Colonies. In fact, in legal terms, they did not count as migrants at all and were not required to apply for a visa.

The 1971 Immigration Act removed British citizenship rights from Commonwealth citizens, whilst giving Australians, New Zealanders and Canadians preferential terms of access. Foreign nationals who were 'ordinarily' resident in Britain on 1 January 1973, the date on which Britain joined the European Economic Community, were deemed to have 'settled status' and given indefinite leave to remain. Yet no attempt was made to contact and issue *proof* of residency to the estimated 500,000 people who had been born in a Commonwealth country before 1971. Over the next few decades many of those people, and the children and grandchildren of that 'Windrush generation', would have applied for a passport and found they had to prove who they were and why they were British citizens. This was not always an easy task but there are few, if any, reported cases of people being unable to prove their identity.

The Hostile Environment policy changed this dramatically for those people who were entitled to British citizenship but did not have a passport and so had no easy way of proving they were living in Britain legally. Suddenly, and because of the new Hostile Environment rules designed to catch illegal migrants, they were being asked to prove they were British when seeking medical treatment in the NHS or applying for a job or a driving licence or a rental lease. When they could not do that, they found themselves being reported to the Immigration Service, which demanded they provide paperwork proving their residency.

Amelia Gentleman, a journalist at the *Guardian* who was writing stories about the experiences of the Windrush generation long before anyone else, received an email in October 2017 from an immigration charity in Wolverhampton relating the story of Paulette Wilson, a sixty-one-year-old grandmother who had arrived from Jamaica at the age of ten in 1968 and worked for a time in the canteen at the House of Commons. She had been classified as an illegal immigrant; detained at the

Yarl's Wood Detention Centre and was awaiting deportation to Jamaica. She was eventually released but was devastated by her experience. 'I don't feel British. I am British.'[37] Another case Gentleman wrote about concerned a man who had visited Jamaica for his fiftieth birthday but, upon his return, had been told he could not enter Britain on his Jamaican passport. He was forced to live in bedsits and hostels in Jamaica for nearly two years whilst he and his family spent £26,000 in legal fees and accommodation costs working to establish his right to live in Britain. When he eventually managed to do this and returned home, he was told he owed £4,500 in unpaid rent and council tax, taken to court and evicted.[38] In total perhaps as many as 164 people were wrongly held in immigration detention, and 83 of them were deported from Britain.[39] In his book *Empireland*, Sathnam Sanghera suggests that 'Britain has long struggled to accept the imperial explanation for its racial diversity' and that the 'idea that black and brown people are aliens who arrived without permission, and with no link to Britain, to abuse British hospitality is the defining political narrative of my lifetime'.[40] The Hostile Environment made that narrative official government policy.

In February 2018 senior Caribbean diplomats urged the Home Office to suspend deportations and adopt a more compassionate approach towards retired Commonwealth citizens. Seth Ramocan, the Jamaican high commissioner to London, spoke of a 'system [in which] one is guilty before proven innocent rather than the other way round'.[41] In March, Gentleman reported on the experiences of Albert Thompson, a sixty-three-year-old man who had been told to produce a British passport or pay a £54,000 bill for cancer treatment.[42] Jeremy Corbyn then asked Theresa May about this case during Prime Minister's Questions. On 13 April the Church of England's bishops published a joint letter calling on the government to offer an immigration amnesty to Windrush immigrants. Two days later, Downing Street refused a formal diplomatic request to discuss Windrush and the issue of deportations at the Commonwealth Heads of Government meeting.

The dam finally burst on 16 April.[43] On that day more than 140 MPs from all parties signed a letter to the prime minister demanding that she directly intervene to address the crisis. On the same day, Amber Rudd, who had replaced May as home secretary when May had become prime minister in July 2016, acknowledged that there had been Home Office failings and promised nobody else would be deported because of a lack of paperwork. On 17 April a former employee revealed that in 2010 the Home Office had destroyed thousands of landing-card slips recording the arrival dates of Windrush citizens in Britain. On the same day, Theresa May apologized to the Caribbean heads of government at the Commonwealth meeting. On the 23rd Rudd promised that the Windrush generation would all be granted citizenship, resigning on the 30th when it became apparent that, contrary to her earlier assurances to Parliament, the Home Office had in fact set targets for the removal of illegal immigrants. That same day, her replacement as home secretary, Sajid Javid, spoke of how he, as a second-generation migrant, had thought the victims of Windrush could be 'my mum, my brother, my uncle or even me'; he promised to 'do whatever it takes' to correct the injustices that had occurred.[44] A compensation scheme opened in April 2019. By November 2023, 1,532 primary claimants had received compensation payments, out of a total of 7,534 claims.[45]

THREE GREAT SCANDALS

If the 'why did nobody notice' question was a reasonable one to ask about the financial crisis (p. 241), the same was not true of Windrush. Lots of people had seen it coming. In 2014 the charity Legal Action Group published a report highlighting the situation of long-term British residents from the Windrush generation who were unable to prove their citizenship status.[46] Later that year, David Lammy, the MP for Tottenham, raised the Windrush issue in Parliament. In a report, published in 2018, the National Audit Office observed that, by 2014, the Home Office's own analysis had shown that that there were tens of thousands of people who were living legally in Britain but who did not have a biometric passport and so might be affected by the Hostile Environment policy.[47] Over the following few years, a number of other organizations, including Liberty, the Joint Council for the Welfare of Immigrants, the Immigration Law Practitioners Association and the Residential Landlords' Association all raised concerns over the impact of the introduction of Hostile Environment policies on members of the Windrush generation.[48] Caribbean ministers raised Windrush-related cases with the British government from at least early 2016 onwards. These groups weren't saying that some sort of problem might arise in the future. They were saying a very specific problem was already occurring and that the lives of British citizens were being pulled apart by it. Yet nothing was done.

Race is a part of the answer as to why these warnings were ignored. The official 'Windrush Lessons Learned Review', led by Wendy Williams, the inspector of constabulary and fire and rescue services, did not find officials 'deliberately targeted the Windrush generation by reason of their race or otherwise' and had not, as far as she was aware, used 'stereotypical assumptions' about Caribbean or black people. She did, however, find that the Home Office, very few of whose senior staff were black, demonstrated an 'institutional ignorance and thoughtlessness towards the issue of race and the history of the Windrush generation' and that 'some' of the officials she interviewed about what had happened 'when asked about the perception that race might have played a role in the scandal were unimpressively unreflective'.[49]

In a podcast interview recorded in April 2017 Zadie Smith, the author of *White Teeth*, spoke about how, in Britain in the early 2000s, there was a pervasive sense within white Britain that racism was increasingly a thing of the past.[50] Racism still existed. But racist attacks were declining, and everyone thought racists were Neanderthal thugs and that racism was abhorrent. New Labour was on the right side of history. It had commissioned an independent inquiry into the murder of Stephen Lawrence in April 1993. It had acted upon that report to target institutional racism in the Metropolitan Police Service and in 2010, shortly before being removed from power, it had passed an Equality Act placing a statutory duty upon public authorities to consider whether their policies or decisions adversely affected people on the basis of their race, as well as age, disability, sex, religion and sexual orientation.

Looking back, this was, as Smith went on to observe, all a bit naive and somewhat silly. For a start, old-fashioned, in-your-face racism had not gone away. In 2012, the same year that John Terry, Chelsea's captain, was deemed guilty by the Football Association of racially abusing Anton Ferdinand during a Premier League game (p. 143), the English and Welsh police reported that there had been 35,944 racially motivated hate crimes in Britain (a figure which was to rise to 62,685 in 2017 and 109,843 by 2022).[51] But the other increasingly obvious issue in the 2010s was that racism was not simply a matter of agency, of people choosing to be racist, but of structures which created and perpetuated racial inequalities. Immigration officials may not have targeted the Windrush generation because they were black but, as Omar Khan, the former director of the Runnymede Trust, observes, it was an important part of the Windrush story that the Windrush generation were an economically disadvantaged group who, because of the overt racism they had experienced in the labour market when they first arrived in Britain, had been unable to build up any large savings. They had not, for the most part, travelled back to the Caribbean because they could not afford to do so; and so had not previously applied for a passport.[52]

A year before the Windrush scandal had become front-page news, an electrical fault in a refrigerator resulted in a fire which killed seventy-two people in Grenfell Tower, in London, on 14 June 2017. In his address to the Grenfell Tower Public Inquiry, the barrister representing some of the bereaved families, Leslie Thomas, argued that the fire was 'inextricably linked to race'.[53] This was a charged issue. The Fire Brigades Union angrily denied the 'offensive, wrong and unconstructive' charge that firefighters who had attended the Grenfell disaster had demonstrated institutional racism in the assumptions and decisions they had made.[54] Yet race was present in the broader set of economic and social structures within which Grenfell Tower sat. Grenfell provided social housing in an area, Kensington and Chelsea, which was one of the most economically divided in the country.[55] Most of those killed in the fire – 85 per cent – were from ethnic minorities.[56] Zadie Smith, in an interview on the BBC *Today* programme on 5 July 2017, described Grenfell as a 'kind of crime'. She reflected on how private security cars patrolled the 'fancy streets' a few hundred yards away from Grenfell Tower whilst the 'poor were left completely without protection', and of how, in her view, many people in London were only interested in a racially mixed society at a 'very superficial level', which did not extend as far as sending their children to 'mixed schools in really mixed neighbourhoods in mixed communities'.[57]

Yet there is no need to offer one single explanation as to why the Windrush warnings were ignored, or why Grenfell happened. According to Bruce Sounes, an architect working for the firm Studio E that had been awarded the contract to refurbish Grenfell, the proximate cause of the fire was money. He told the Grenfell Inquiry that flammable Reynobond ACM cladding had been used because it was up to £500,000 cheaper than the fire-resistant alternative. Similar cladding on 137 housing blocks across 40 local authorities in England have since failed fire safety tests.[58] And looking back at Wendy Williams' 'Lessons Learned' review, it is also clear that the working culture within the Home Office was one in which questions or concerns about the Hostile Environment policy were discouraged. Williams talks of how ministers 'did not sufficiently question unintended consequences'; of how the Home Office 'tried to put policy intent into practice, which is its function, but did so relentlessly and without proper consideration of the impact of the proposals'; and, finally, of how 'staff across the organisation didn't feel confident enough to raise any doubts of their own'.[59] It appears that, in the Windrush case, a political culture that centralized power within Numbers 10 and 11 Downing Street also operated within government departments to centralize policy-making power in the hands of the secretary of state and their key advisors. A Civil Service staff survey in 2021 – a year after the Home Office's permanent secretary, Philip Rutnam, had resigned citing a 'vicious and orchestrated' campaign by then home secretary, Priti Patel, to undermine him – found just 54 per cent of civil servants agreed that it is 'safe to challenge the way things are done'.[60] Then, during Covid, Anthony Seldon and Raymond Newell, in their account of Boris Johnson's premiership, describe how 'witnesses told us that the fear of blame and for their careers impeded them from being fully frank with their superiors, such was the regime of trepidation and finger-pointing within No. 10'.[61]

There was a third great scandal that unfolded during this period: the unwarranted prosecution, social shaming and financial ruin of more than seven hundred Post Office sub-postmasters who had been incorrectly accused of false accountancy, fraud or theft. In the mid-1990s a contract was awarded to the once British-owned computer firm ICL (which by then had been bought by Fujitsu) to develop and introduce into all the country's post offices the 'Horizon' computer system, in order to track payments and withdrawals and to reduce benefit fraud.[62] Fujitsu's winning bid had come bottom in eight of the eleven scoring criteria used to assess the strengths of each bid. But it had come out cheapest in terms of its overall cost to the government and that was what really counted.[63] By 1999 the system's development and implementation was already behind schedule and beset by reports that the computer systems being used were generating inaccurate data. The Department for Social Security withdrew from a separate contract to use Horizon for these reasons.[64] Ministers, including the prime minister, were warned of these difficulties but decided to press ahead with Horizon's introduction within the Post Office network.[65] From the moment the system went live, local postmasters found that, inexplicably but regularly, their accounts were showing significant imbalances.

As Nick Wallis shows in his detailed account of what happened, Post Office managers encouraged them to submit their data anyway, on the implicit understanding that the problems would be resolved later. In doing so, the postmasters were actually exposing themselves to charges of false accounting. The body representing these workers, the National Federation of Sub-Postmasters, failed to offer them any support. Senior Post Office managers then declined the opportunity to reveal any of their knowledge of the problems which had beset and were still besetting the Horizon system. During the subsequent prosecutions, the Post Office failed to disclose evidence and depended upon amendments to the Police and Criminal Evidence Act (passed when police speed guns had first been introduced) that had established a legal presumption that the technology relevant to a legal case was working unless defendants could prove otherwise. This, of course, the sub-postmasters could not do, because the Post Office did not disclose any of the evidence of any of the problems it had recorded.[66] Senior Post Office managers, it would appear, were reluctant to admit to any potential problems with Horizon for fear their reputation would be tarnished and other postmasters incentivized to commit fraud and to blame account imbalances on their computer systems. Yet, to achieve this, they were willing to accept, or at least close their minds to, the risk that innocent people were being imprisoned – and to keep doing so until 2015. As a Court of Appeal judgment found in April 2021:

> [The Post Office's] failures of investigation and disclosure were so egregious as to make the prosecution of any of the 'Horizon cases' an affront to the conscience of the court. By representing Horizon as reliable, and refusing to countenance any suggestion to the contrary, [the Post Office] effectively sought to reverse the burden of proof: it treated what was no more than a shortfall shown by an unreliable accounting system as an incontrovertible loss, and proceeded as if it were for the accused to prove that no such loss had occurred.[67]

By that point an independent public inquiry into the Post Office scandal had been established at which successive witnesses described the failings of the Horizon system and of Post Office managers and investigators. However, it was only when ITV broadcast a four-part drama about the scandal that the political pressure upon the government became irresistible. In January 2024 the prime minister announced that legislation would be brought forward to exonerate those found guilty on the basis of faulty evidence from the Horizon system, and that victims would be eligible for at least £600,000 compensation payments.

The human costs of the Post Office scandal are immense and have been linked to four suicides.[68] One of those deaths was that of Martin Griffiths, who took his own life in 2013 at the age of fifty-nine. Griffiths had worked at the Ellesmere Port post office since 1995 but had been accused of theft after the accounting system showed a shortfall of £61,000. After he had used his own savings to make up that sum, he was told, in July 2013, that his contract would be terminated. A few months later he deliberately stepped in front of a bus. He was rushed to Aintree hospital but died on 11 October. In his written testimony to the Post Office Inquiry, his brother wrote:

> Every time I read or hear a news item about the Horizon scandal, it brings back all the pain and the anger. My brother tragically lost his life due to a faulty computer system. The Post Office repeatedly denied computer error was the cause of losses amounting to millions. Instead, they arrogantly blamed my brother and thousands of other innocent Sub-postmasters, by wrongly accusing them of theft or false accounting.[69]

There are some differences between the Post Office case and Windrush. There has been no suggestion race was a factor in decisions on whether to prosecute.[70] Instead, the Post Office's failure to recognize and act upon warnings appears to have been driven partly by commercial imperatives. Yet there are other important similarities. In both cases, more junior employees appear to have been reluctant to communicate to more senior managers the extent of their concerns and downplayed the number of cases involved. In both cases, it was only when newspapers and individual constituency MPs became involved and started raising concerns that ministers began asking difficult questions. Finally, and in both cases, undue confidence appears to have been placed in systems because those systems were computerized. Indeed, this was not simply an issue for the Windrush generation but for anyone who was a target of the Hostile Environment policy. One inspection report published in 2016 found that up to 10 per cent of people on Home Office lists had been incorrectly categorized as irregular migrants.[71] In 2008 faulty algorithms were blamed for miscalculating the extent of banks' exposures to balance-sheet risk. In 2010 and 2016 they were blamed for causing 'flash crashes' in stock markets.[72] In 2020 Boris Johnson blamed that year's A-level examination results fiasco on a 'mutant algorithm'.[73] Algorithms and hierarchical decision-making structures do not, it would appear, make for a particularly happy relationship.

Perhaps, more than anything else, the Post Office scandal demonstrated a moral failing on the part of managers of large organizations to care about the consequences of their decisions or to show even the faintest empathy for the lives of the people working in those organizations. There were times, during the 2000s, when identifying and appointing the right kind of managers, and then giving them the authority to get on and do their job and turn things around, came to be seen as the answer to any and all organizational problems. Hospitals, schools, universities and charities were all encouraged to follow the lead set by private firms, most notably the banks, to venerate and empower their managers and, as a part of this, to pay them the going market rate. The Post Office scandal showed what can happen when frameworks are created in which managers are driven by performance targets and subject to not much more than tick-box accountability.

PART SIX

Splintering

In the 1970s and 1980s Margaret Thatcher raged against an earlier era of consensus politics in British national life. 'To me consensus seems to be ... the process of abandoning all beliefs, principles, values and policies in search of something in which no-one believes, but to which no-one objects ... the process of avoiding the very issues that have to be solved, merely because you cannot get agreement on the way ahead.'[1] Consensus politics had empowered the trade unions; weakened the economy; and had encouraged an inevitable sense of decline. For a while, from around 2006 through to perhaps 2015, it nevertheless looked like a certain measure of consensus had re-emerged. Tony Blair had reconciled the Labour Party to large parts of the economic agenda of Thatcherism. David Cameron, 'the heir to Blair' (p. 2), had then reconciled the Conservative Party to large parts of New Labour's policies. The Conservatives had attacked Gordon Brown for having 'splashed the cash like there's no tomorrow', but had not actually opposed the decision to nationalize some of Britain's largest banks when they ran out of cash. For a short while, in the early 2010s, an academic and member of the House of Lords, Maurice Glasman, proselytized on behalf of a 'Blue Labour' focused upon community and solidarity (and, implicitly at least, lower immigration).[2] At the same time, Philip Blond, another former academic who, in 2009, had founded the think tank ResPublica, was arguing the case for a 'Red Toryism', which recognized the significance of ... community and solidarity (and the limits of free markets).[3] Moreover, by 2015, the leaders of all the major parties in Parliament were in favour of Britain staying in the European Union and remained in favour of economic globalization. In Northern Ireland, the draw of consensus politics was weaker but had, nevertheless, been strong enough to sustain co-operation between the Democratic Unionist Party and Sinn Féin since 2007.

That consensus came under tremendous pressure between 2016 and

2019. Some of it survived, some of it did not. All of it was pretty dramatic. The American economist J. K. Galbraith once said that all revolutions are the kicking in of a rotten door.[4] Nobody – his own supporters included – expected Jeremy Corbyn, the subject of this Part's first chapter, to win after he had been persuaded to stand for the Labour Party leadership in 2015. Yet nobody at that point realized just how rotten the Labour Party seemed to many of its members. The most obvious cause of the splintering of British politics was Brexit, which cut across party lines and divided the electorate down the middle. In Chapter 28 I look at the 2016 referendum and how, against the expectations of just about everyone (Nigel Farage included), Leave triumphed. In Chapter 31 I look at what happened after Britain triggered Article 50 in March 2017 and began negotiating its exit from the European Union. It might look a little odd to separate these events in this way. But one of the chapters in between, that on Northern Ireland, provides some of the necessary background to the intricacies of that part-ending finale. Finally, in Chapter 30, I look at the way in which the #MeToo movement, arriving in Britain from the United States in late 2017, shattered a consensus of not doing very much to acknowledge, let alone resolve, cases of sexual misconduct and how this led to both Prince Andrew and the Metropolitan Police being exposed and held accountable for their actions.

27

Oh Jeremy Corbyn

'YOU BETTER MAKE ****ING SURE'

Ed Miliband resigned as Labour leader the day after the 2015 General Election and did so with the air of a man who could not wait for the chance to do something different. With a new leadership contest pending, the left of the Parliamentary Labour Party agreed it ought to nominate a candidate. Jeremy Corbyn put his name forward because, as he told a journalist, nobody else wanted to do so.[1] He reportedly told one confidant, 'you better make f***ing sure I don't get elected.'[2] He just about scraped the thirty-five nominations he needed after several MPs who did not support him agreed to nominate him in order to widen the debate.[3] Within a few weeks, Corbyn was leading the race. He was helped by a prior change to the leadership rules, which allowed anyone who paid £3 to participate in the vote as a registered Labour supporter. He was also helped by the failure of any of the other candidates – Yvette Cooper, Liz Kendall or Andy Burnham – to make a compelling case for how they offered something notably different from Ed Miliband. Corbyn was helped, above all, by a feeling amongst Labour Party members that, after the soft-pedalling of the Miliband years and the painful kicking in the 2015 election by way of thanks, it was time to offer a full-throated, clear-cut, no-half-measures opposition to the Conservatives, austerity and inequality. Corbyn won by a landslide.

The Parliamentary Labour Party and the staff in Labour's Millbank headquarters welcomed Corbyn with the same enthusiasm they would have extended to food poisoning. The bits of New Labour that were still standing were particularly dismissive. Corbyn was a 1970s socialist throwback. He would vacate the electoral centre ground and consign the party to electoral oblivion. He was, in short, everything Tony Blair had not been. But two decades had passed since New Labour had won by moving towards the centre ground. Blair had had the social democratic option available to him of saying New Labour would let the free market do its thing before redistributing the proceeds via higher public spending. That option was not readily available in 2015. The financial crisis had crashed the economy, and growth, wages, productivity and investment had not recovered. Ed Miliband had already argued the case (albeit not hugely successfully) for a very different and un-social democratic approach to the economy (pp. 286–7). It was New Labour, and not the Labour Left, which now looked dated and out of touch.

There was a second problem with the New Labour critique. On lots of issues, Corbyn and the Corbynites could point to the fact that the weight of public opinion, the centre ground of British politics, was now actually quite left-wing. In 2010 the Conservatives had persuaded the majority of voters that there was no alternative to austerity. In 2015 they then persuaded enough of them to stick rather than twist. But the times were changing. The 2017 edition of the British Social Attitudes survey found that for the first time in a long (long) time, a majority of the public said they favoured raising public spending even if that meant higher taxes.[4] Other polls showed widespread support for increasing income tax for the higher paid (65% in favour); renationalizing the railways (52%); banning zero-hour contracts (55%); renationalizing the energy companies (49%); and capping rents (65%).[5]

'I'll believe it when I see it' might have been the response of a New Labour apparatchik. Sure, voters say that they support left-wing policies. But actions speak louder than words and what people tell pollsters they are thinking is not necessarily what they will be thinking about when they come to vote. However, against this Corbyn could argue that voters do not have immutably fixed views and that politics is about persuading people to think and act differently. Here, for example, is Corbyn at the 2017 Labour Party conference: 'It is often said that elections can only be won from the centre ground. And in a way that's not wrong – so long as it's clear that the political centre of gravity isn't fixed or unmovable, nor is it where the establishment pundits like to think it is.'[6]

Labour needed to persuade voters that the economy was failing; that public services were being run into the ground; and that there was a viable alternative to austerity. New Labour had colonized the electoral centre ground in the 1990s. It had done so not only by changing its policies to fit with public opinion. It had done it by successfully arguing that policies such as the minimum wage were not going to lead, as the Conservatives had argued they would, to plague, famine and pestilence.[7] Labour needed to do more of this. It would not be easy, but neither was it impossible. The strength of voters' partisan attachment to parties was waning (p. 260); this made it more, not less, likely voters could be persuaded to switch who they voted for. In the 2015 General Election fully 40 per cent of voters who had voted in two consecutive elections had switched the party they had voted for. The old rules of playing it safe and trying to grab a small number of swing voters by looking as much like your opponents as possible no longer applied.

Corbyn had one more thing going for him from the moment he was elected – authenticity. In a world in which trust in politicians had collapsed and in which it looked like MPs were out to feather their own nests and would say or do anything to get elected, Corbyn was the real deal. He had been opposing public-spending cuts since he was first elected as the member for Islington North in 1983. He had been proved right about the Iraq War. He was not prepared to play party-political tactical games. When, in 2015, the other Labour leadership candidates had abstained on a Conservative-engineered vote to cap total welfare payments, Corbyn had voted against.[8] He was not in it for the money, fame or ministerial chauffeur. He lived modestly and cycled everywhere and spent most of his spare time listening to and helping people in his constituency. Blair had learned how to appear authentic and ordinary. Corbyn did it naturally.

'RISE LIKE LIONS'

Corbynism ticked a lot of boxes, therefore. However, you would not have known that at first. The Conservatives labelled Corbyn and his shadow chancellor, John McDonnell, communists. From early 2016 onwards, the Brexit referendum made a difficult situation for Labour worse. Any leader would have found themselves in an uncomfortable position when it came to Brexit, because, whilst Labour constituency MPs were almost entirely in favour of remaining, Labour voters were evenly split on the issue. But Corbyn played a difficult hand badly. He said he wanted Britain to Remain during the referendum campaign but never really sounded like he meant it. He then argued the day after the result, with close to zero consultation, that the government ought to notify the European Union of its intention to leave immediately.[9]

I am going to turn to the 2016 referendum in the following chapter and to its political aftermath shortly after that. But here, to tell the story of Corbyn's rise and fall I am going to have to break with strict chronology. On 26 June 2016, three days after the European Union referendum, Heidi Alexander, Labour's shadow health secretary, resigned, stating that she had no confidence in Corbyn's leadership. Amidst reports that Hilary Benn, son of Tony and shadow foreign secretary, was plotting to remove him, Corbyn got his retaliation in first by sacking him. This led to a wave of other resignations from the Shadow Cabinet and to a vote of no confidence in his leadership from the Parliamentary Labour Party on 28 June, in which Corbyn won the grand total of forty votes. At that moment, it looked like Corbyn was going to be a proto-Liz Truss. But he did not buckle; he argued that his legitimacy as leader depended not on the support of his MPs but on that of the broader Labour Party. Labour's National Executive Committee endorsed Corbyn's stance and ruled that he could automatically become a leadership candidate (regardless of whether he could attract sufficient nominations). After a legal wrangle the High Court endorsed his position, and in September 2016 Corbyn beat his only rival, Owen Smith, with 62 per cent of the vote.[10]

Labour's civil war came at a cost. In 2015 and early 2016 Labour was rattling along at somewhere between 33 and 35 per cent support in opinion polls. Not great but not too bad. Then, in the final few months of 2016, the Labour vote plummeted and the Conservative vote rose. In February 2017 the Conservatives won a by-election in the Cumbrian seat of Copeland, one which Labour had held since it was created in 1983. At this point, Labour's extenuative was that nobody expected there to be a general election any time soon. After all, Theresa May, when she had replaced David Cameron after the Brexit result, had been crystal-clear in ruling out an early election on the grounds that she did not want to be seen to be playing party-political games with the electorate.[11] But in the end the party-political opportunity looked too great: in April 2017 May announced that she would indeed be seeking an early election to provide clarity and ensure stability (for which read a large-enough majority to pass pending Brexit legislation and wipe out Labour as an opposition party). Under the terms of the Fixed Term Parliament Act passed by the Coalition, the prime minister needed a two-thirds majority to dissolve Parliament (p. 273), which meant Labour could have simply said no. Corbyn decided to go for it. At the start of the resulting election campaign, Labour's internal polling showed it might lose up to half its seats.[12] In local elections on 4 May, a few weeks later, Labour lost 382 council seats and got just 27 per cent of the vote. The Conservatives gained 563 seats and overall control of 11 councils. Everything seemed to be going the way Corbyn's critics had argued it would go, and lots of Labour parliamentary candidates started to expunge references to Corbyn in their own local campaign literature.

What happened next was almost completely unexpected.* From around mid-May onwards, Labour started to pick up support at a faster (and then faster) rate. On election day, 8 June 2017, Labour achieved 40 per cent of the vote (up 9.6 percentage points from 2015) and 262 seats (up 30). The Conservatives got 758,000 more votes than Labour and won 55 more seats, but fell short of an overall majority thanks to having 13 fewer seats than they had managed in 2015. What saved them was an unexpectedly strong showing by the Scottish Conservative Party, which won twelve additional seats; the collapse of UKIP, which, under its new leader Paul Nuttall, went from over 12 per cent of the vote to less than 2 per cent; and, behind that, a 'grey wall' of retired voters (whereas only 23% of voters in their twenties voted Conservative, 58% of those aged sixty to sixty-nine, and 69% of those aged seventy or over did so).[13] But if the Conservatives had just about held on, nobody was in any doubt that the election had been a disaster for them. The results were so shocking one senior Conservative Party official collapsed and had to be taken to hospital by ambulance.[14] May (just about) survived and eventually negotiated a loose 'supply and confidence' alliance with the Democratic Unionist Party. The former promised an extra £1 billion in funding for Northern Ireland whilst, in return, the latter promised to

* We now know that the Conservative Party's own polling showed that calling an early election would be deeply unpopular with voters; that the Conservatives' lead was largely down to a dislike of the other parties rather than deep-seated support for them; and that, therefore, up to a quarter of its current support might switch during the course of the campaign. Tim Bale, *The Conservative Party After Brexit* (Cambridge, 2023), p. 33.

support May's minority government when it came to the Queen's Speech, the Budget and finance bills, and legislation relating to national security and Britain's withdrawal from the European Union.[15]

In the months that followed, Corbyn's critics within the Labour Party regrouped. Labour had done unexpectedly well in the 2017 election but had still fallen a long way short of winning. It had stolen seats in places like Canterbury, Kensington and Reading where it had not won before. It had, however, also lost seats in heartland areas like Mansfield and Middlesbrough. Labour had done well because the Conservatives and Theresa May had campaigned so badly. May had never convincingly managed to explain why she had called an early general election when she had previously said she would not. She had appeared painfully uncomfortable during interviews. She had endlessly repeated a line that the country needed a 'strong and stable' government, to a point where it was beyond parody. She had launched a new set of proposals to reform the social care system, had then struggled to explain what those proposals were and then, having almost immediately abandoned those proposals when they were labelled a 'dementia tax', denied she had changed anything.[16] As her joint chief of staff Nick Timothy subsequently wrote, if 'they say you campaign in poetry and govern in prose, we were campaigning in sullen, monosyllabic grunts'.[17]

Yet whilst some of these caveats around the 2017 General Election now look reasonable enough, at the time they seemed simply churlish. Labour had secured more votes and a larger share of the vote than it had in any general election since 1997. Corbyn had persuaded millions of people to switch their vote and support him. In doing so he had redefined where the centre ground was in British politics and had proved himself to be an effective campaigner. The day after the general election, Jon Snow, on Channel 4 news, put it as follows. 'I know nothing. We, the media, the pundits, the experts, know nothing. We simply didn't spot it.'[18] Opposition to Corbyn within the Parliamentary Labour Party receded further, and the number of people joining the Labour Party continued to rise.[19] On 24 June Corbyn introduced Run The Jewels at the Glastonbury Festival, where he was serenaded by an audience singing 'Oh Jeremy Corbyn' to the tune of the White Stripes' 'Seven Nation Army'. Corbyn spoke about his childhood visits to Glastonbury Tor and about the election: 'What was fascinating about the last seven weeks of election campaigning around Britain is that the commentariat got it wrong, the elites got it wrong.' Labour had narrowly lost but 'politics has got out of the box' and people would continue to demand 'something very different in our society'. Corbyn concluded by quoting lines from Percy Bysshe Shelley's 'Masque of Anarchy', a poem written in 1819 in the aftermath of the Peterloo Massacre: 'Rise like Lions after slumber / In unvanquishable number, / . . . Ye are many – they are few.'[20]

THE FALL FROM GRACE

Labour did as badly in the 2019 General Election as it had done unexpectedly well in the 2017 one. It lost 2 million votes and over sixty seats, many of them so-called 'Red Wall' seats in the North of England. Partisan de-alignment and electoral volatility had leveraged Labour's result in 2017. They compounded its downturn in 2019. May had malfunctioned in 2017. Boris Johnson, her replacement, had a few rough moments in 2019 (most notably when he appeared to steal a journalist's phone during a visit to a hospital), but for the most part he played it safe and stayed on-script.[21] In 2017 Corbyn had been new and different and had benefited from being the underdog. In 2019, Corbyn simply looked hangdog.

The two issues that, more than any other, killed the Corbyn project – and had killed it long before Johnson called a general election – were Brexit and antisemitism. In 2017 Theresa May had called the election to strengthen her hand in Brexit negotiations but had refused to say anything about what form Brexit might take. This suited Labour, which wanted to make the election about economic issues and, as a result, were able to appeal to voters in Remain- *and* Leave-voting constituencies.[22] But, once the election was over and the Brexit negotiations had started, and a 'hard Brexit' had come to look increasingly likely (p. 405), Corbyn struggled to hold his party together. In June 2017 Chuka Umunna, a Labour MP who had sat in Ed Miliband's Shadow Cabinet as shadow secretary of state for business, innovation and skills and had returned to the backbenches after the 2015 election, tabled an amendment to the Queen's Speech. In it he called for Britain to remain a member of the European Single Market, which guaranteed the free movement of goods, people and capital. Corbyn ordered Labour MPs to abstain from voting on it and sacked several frontbench shadow ministers who defied him and voted for it.[23] Then, in February 2018, Corbyn announced that Labour wanted to negotiate a bespoke customs union with the European Union. In terms of the menu of Brexit options, ranging (as we will later see) from withdrawing Britain's application to leave right through to a no-deal Brexit, this option was somewhere a little to the hard-Brexit side of the middle. As such, it enraged Remainers within the party, and at that year's Labour Party conference a motion was approved to hold a second referendum.

After the vote of no confidence in 2016, 'members of the Labour Party disagree with Jeremy Corbyn' was not exactly a shocking news story. But the problem Corbyn faced this time round was that lots of the people supporting either a second referendum or a super-soft Brexit were his own natural supporters. It was the grassroots group Momentum, which had been established to support Corbyn, that had sponsored the 2018 Labour Party motion on holding a second referendum. Moreover, it was becoming clear that Corbyn was on a different political page not only from his Brexit minister, Keir Starmer, who wanted to remain within the European Union's Customs Union (and quite possibly its Single Market), but from his shadow chancellor and long-time political ally John McDonnell.[24] In the end, and come the 2019 General Election, Labour's position was that it would renegotiate Theresa May's deal and put the results to a second referendum. This was a position of sorts, but it was not a particularly clear one as Corbyn seemed reluctant to say how he would vote in such a second referendum. At one level this was defensible. He could argue that it would all depend upon the deal he had secured. But, to a lot of people, it looked like Labour's policy on the single most contentious issue in British politics for a long time was to not really have a policy. Labour lost an average of 8.7 percentage points of its 2017 vote in constituencies that had voted Leave in the 2016 referendum, and 6.2 percentage points of its vote in those which had voted Remain.[25]

In August 2015 the *Jewish Chronicle* published a critical story about the links between Jeremy Corbyn and a Palestinian solidarity organization, Deir Yassin Remembered, some of whose members were intensely antisemitic.[26] Following a number of other stories about antisemitic comments and bullying by Labour Party members, Corbyn, in April 2016, asked Shami Chakrabarti, the former director of Liberty, to investigate antisemitism within the party. Chakrabarti, who was a short while later appointed by Corbyn to the House of Lords, concluded that Labour was 'not overrun by antisemitism, Islamophobia, or other forms of racism'.[27] Then, in March 2018, the Jewish Labour MP Luciana Berger reposted another *Jewish Chronicle* story about a Facebook comment Corbyn had made in support of a graffiti artist, Mear One, who had pictured hook-nosed bankers playing Monopoly on the backs of the poor. The picture was about as obviously antisemitic as it could have been. Corbyn responded that he was simply defending free speech and had not looked at the pictures closely enough and was sorry for his mistake.[28] (Berger was the recipient of numerous threats to her life and had to be given a police escort to protect her at that year's Labour Party conference.[29])

In an article he wrote for the *Evening Standard* not long after, Corbyn accepted that there was an issue with antisemitism within the Labour Party.[30] This looked like progress, but Corbyn next ran headlong into a row about whether to fully endorse the International Holocaust Remembrance Alliance definition of antisemitism – or, rather, the full range of illustrative examples that definition included.[31] This was a strange hill to choose to fight and risk dying on, and in July 2018 the *Jewish Chronicle*, *Jewish News* and *Jewish Telegraph* all ran the same front-page editorial suggesting that a Corbyn government would pose an 'existential threat to Jewish life'.[32] In May 2019 the Equalities and Human Rights Commission launched an inquiry into antisemitism within the Labour Party. A lot of Corbyn's political enemies had a strong incentive to run as hard as they could with the accusations of antisemitism and bullying. But, in a careful and balanced retrospective on events, two academics, Matthew Bolton and Harry Pitts, also observe that Corbyn's populist critiques of Britain's rigged economic system and the baleful effects of financial capitalism, when run together with his principled anti-Zionism and anti-imperialism, created a productive environment within which antisemitism could flourish within the Labour Party.[33]

From the moment he was first elected in 2015, the Conservatives and the Conservative-supporting press presented Corbyn as a dangerous extremist. One of the ways in which they did this was to find statements Corbyn had made years before which could be interpreted as offering support for the IRA or other terrorist movements.[34] By and large, those stories fell flat. Following the 2017 election, however, the accusation of antisemitism, together with Corbyn's initial and seemingly sceptical response to what we now know, beyond any reasonable doubt, to have been the Russian state-sponsored poisoning of Sergei and Yulia Skripal in March 2018, did his political enemies' work for them.[35] After Labour looked as if it were carving out a new political centre in 2017, one fixed around a state-led socialist approach to the economy, by the time of the 2019 election, 46 per cent of voters had come to regard Labour as an extreme party; fewer than 5 per cent saw it as being at the political centre.[36]

'IT'S TIME TO REMEMBER THE GOOD GOVERNMENT CAN DO'

It is tempting, looking back, to see Corbyn as a left-wing aberration; someone who, having eventually been replaced by a conviction centrist, Keir Starmer, left no discernible trace. That would be a mistake. The most interesting quality of the 2017 General Election is that it resulted in one increasingly left-wing party, Labour, facing-off against another increasingly left-wing one, the Conservatives.

After David Cameron resigned following the result of the Brexit referendum, Theresa May won the 2016 Conservative Party leadership contest because her key rivals – Boris Johnson, Michael Gove and Andrea Leadsom – imploded, and because she was seen as a safe pair of hands. She had plenty of ministerial experience and, despite having voted Remain, would honour the referendum result. May, at the time, was known largely for her hard-line views on immigration and was seen, on that basis, as being on the right of the Conservative Party. Which made what happened next all the more interesting. Addressing reporters outside 10 Downing Street on 13 July 2016, May spoke about

> [the] burning injustice that if you are born poor, you will die on average nine years earlier than others. If you're black, you're treated more harshly by the criminal justice system than if you are white. If you're a white, working-class boy, you're less likely than anyone else in Britain to go to university. If you're at a state school, you're less likely to reach the top professions than if you were educated privately. If you are a woman, you will earn less than a man. If you suffer from mental health problems, there's not enough help to hand.[37]

A few months later, at the Conservative Party conference, May told delegates 'it's time to remember the good government can do', arguing that 'where markets are dysfunctional, we should be prepared to intervene' and that 'people with assets have got richer' and that 'people without them have suffered'.[38] The party's 2017 manifesto opened with a promise that a Conservative government led by her would not 'drift to the right'. It added that Conservatives 'reject the cult of selfish individualism' and 'abhor social division, injustice, unfairness and inequality' whilst promising a raft of new workers' rights; changes to corporate governance laws; an industrial strategy; more research and development spending; a new regional development fund; more investment in technical education; and caps on energy bills.[39] This all looked very different to anything Margaret Thatcher, Iain Duncan Smith, Michael Howard or, even at his most modernizing, David Cameron might have thought or said. Theresa May's brand of Conservatism had a certain hard-edged, 'One Nation' flavour to it. But what seemed to hold it together more than anything else was a deep-seated suspicion of free market *and* social liberalism.

In many ways, it is hard to think of two politicians more different than Theresa May and Jeremy Corbyn. There was certainly very little warmth between them. In their book *Left Out*, the journalists Gabriel Pogrund and Patrick McGuire quote a source as saying that the face-to-face talks between May and Corbyn over Brexit in May 2019 were like 'tinder dates from hell' with 'neither having the hinterland to sustain a conversation beyond the dry matter at hand'.[40] Certainly, when it came to immigration and foreign policy issues they were poles apart. But when it came to Brexit, May and Corbyn both thought the referendum result had been driven by a rejection of the economic status quo and that voters were crying out for radical change. May, for example, described Brexit as being driven by 'a sense – deep, profound, and let's face it, often justified – that many people have today, that the world looks well for a privileged few, but not for them'.[41]

In the end, Theresa May's Conservative revolution did not amount to much. Her attention and political capital were consumed by Brexit negotiations and internal party management. She was consistently stymied by her chancellor, Philip Hammond, who was an ardent supporter of fiscal austerity and free markets.[42] May also struggled to delegate decisions to other ministers. In a book that is part memoir and part philosophical treatise, Nick Timothy writes that 'the role of the prime minister is not to play every instrument in the orchestra, but to write the score and conduct the musicians. Too often, Theresa was trying to play the strings, woodwind, brass and percussion all at the same time.'[43] Finally, and perhaps most obviously, the 2017 General Election debacle, which cost Timothy his job, robbed May of not only her majority but her political credibility. To the relief of many of her Conservative MPs, the post-election Queen's Speech simply shelved all the earlier manifesto talk of ending the 'triple lock' on pensions, means-testing the Winter Fuel allowance, reforming social care and overhauling corporate governance. There are, however, two parallel universes out there. In the first, the 2017 General Election campaign lasted a few weeks longer and Labour overtook the Conservatives, won a narrow majority and oversaw a set of economic policy reforms which would have left Tony Blair's head spinning.[44] In the second, the 2017 General Election campaign was a month shorter and the Conservatives maintained their polling lead, won a huge majority and oversaw a set of economic policy reforms that would have been startlingly different from those pursued by David Cameron and the Coalition.

28

Brexit: Should I Stay or Should I Go Now?

RIDING THE TIGER

David Cameron's strategy, when he became Conservative Party leader and was earning 'the right to be heard', was to stop the rest of his party from 'banging on about Europe'.[1] Voters, he argued, cared about the NHS and their taxes. Europe was a sideshow. But, at the same time, Cameron was happy to offer a notably Eurosceptic manifesto in the 2010 General Election: one which ruled out future membership of the Single Currency and promised a referendum on any future European treaty that entailed a substantial transfer of powers.[2] That probably felt like a safe-enough promise to make. After French and Dutch voters had rejected a proposed European Constitution treaty in 2005 and Irish voters had, at the first time of asking, rejected its successor, the Lisbon Treaty, in a referendum held in June 2008, the general view was that nobody was going to be proposing any new treaties any time soon.[*]

Events then got in the way. The Eurozone crisis began in earnest in late 2009 and, with Greece in a mess and Spain, Portugal and Italy wobbling, the European Union decided it needed new powers to deal with the crisis, and that this would require a new treaty. Cameron needed this like a hole in the head and in December 2011, to the joy of his Eurosceptic Conservative backbenchers, he vetoed the proposed

---

[*] The Lisbon Treaty, the replacement for the failed European Union Constitution, was eventually approved, at the second time of asking, by Irish voters in October 2009. It was a bit of a hodgepodge of different measures but included an extension in the use of qualified majority voting within the Council of Ministers and new powers for the European Parliament. Although little noticed at the time, it also confirmed that member states could withdraw from the European Union in accordance with their own constitutional requirements and specified a procedural route for them to do so via its 50th article.

treaty. Sir Ivan Rogers, who was the UK's permanent representative to the European Union before he resigned over Brexit, argues that this led to a significant shift in Cameron's thinking.[3] Europe, he suggests Cameron concluded, would always look for more opportunities for more integration. Britain would not. So, something needed to be done and Europe needed to change. At the following year's Conservative Party conference, Cameron launched into a red-meat attack on 'fat, sclerotic, over-regulated' countries continuing to 'spend money on unaffordable welfare systems, huge pension bills and unreformed public services'. He did not mention the European Union by name. He didn't need to.[4]

Having decided to ride the tiger, Cameron then found he was unable to dismount. The more critical of Europe he was, the more some of his Conservative colleagues argued that the only answer was to leave. Conservative Party Euroscepticism was nothing new. Margaret Thatcher had taken aim at the European Commission in her 1988 Bruges speech: 'We have not successfully rolled back the frontiers of the state in Britain, only to see them re-imposed at a European level with a European superstate exercising a new dominance from Brussels.'[5] In the early 1990s getting on for thirty Conservative MPs had voted against the Maastricht Treaty.[6] Yet right through the 1990s and well into the 2000s Eurosceptics had been fighting for a renegotiation of Britain's membership terms. Relatively few Eurosceptics advocated simply leaving.[7] However, when UKIP started to threaten the Conservative Party's right flank after Cameron's election as Conservative leader, this began to change. Within the 2010 intake of Conservative MPs, undiluted, leave-if-we-can, come-what-may Euroscepticism became a real force.[8] In 2011 a public petition calling for a referendum on Britain's future membership garnered more than 100,000 signatures and was, as a result, timetabled for a debate in the House of Commons. Conservative MPs were instructed to vote against the motion. Eighty-one of them refused to do so.[9] Add to that the growing support of a large part of the Conservative-supporting press for an in–out referendum, and growing levels of support for UKIP in opinion polls, and Cameron was in a tight spot. It got tighter when he ran into trouble over same sex marriage in the House of Commons (pp. 298–9) and reports surfaced that up to twenty Conservative MPs might be planning to defect to UKIP.[10]

In January 2013 Cameron, with, it would seem, very little consultation and no Cabinet discussion, decided that the quickest way to end a war might be to lose it.[11] In a speech at the London headquarters of the Bloomberg media company he defended the basic principle of European governments co-operating with each other through the European Union to address issues like trade, terrorism and climate change. At the same time, he attacked a federalist mindset which, he argued, lacked democratic legitimacy and resulted in 'spurious regulation which damages Europe's competitiveness'.[12] This was, by now, the standard Cameron text. But this time he went further; he promised, if re-elected, to renegotiate the terms of Britain's EU membership and, having done so, to put the successful results to an in–out referendum in which he would campaign to remain.

The promise of a future referendum on Europe was largely – but not entirely – about managing the Conservative Party's divisions. Cameron had reached the view that the question of Britain's membership would, sooner or later, need resolving and that a referendum offered the best and most democratic way of doing this. But the timing of the announcement was all about shoring up his own political position. And it worked. Cameron, whose continued leadership had been in doubt, survived. In May 2013 well over a hundred backbench Conservative MPs voted to demand immediate legislation to hold a referendum. In late 2013 Cameron ended up in a running battle over the creation of a Banking Union to support the Single Currency.[13] In May 2014 the Conservatives were beaten into third place in the European Parliament elections, trailing both UKIP and Labour. Not long after, Cameron lost a vote in the European Council over whether to appoint the federalist-inclined Jean-Claude Juncker as president of the European Commission. That was embarrassing and, to make matters worse, two Conservative MPs, Douglas Carswell and Mark Reckless, left to join UKIP shortly after. Nevertheless, Cameron not only avoided a leadership challenge but in the 2015 General Election did enough to win a narrow overall majority, seeing off not only Ed Miliband but also the challenge of UKIP – who won over 12 per cent of the vote but only one parliamentary seat.

REFERENDUM COUNTDOWN

Although he had spent so much of his first term trying (and failing) to not talk about Europe, Cameron now wanted to get the promised referendum out of the way sooner rather than later.[14] So a Referendum Bill was tabled and in June 2015 secured the overwhelming support of 544 MPs, with Labour voting in favour. In early September, the Electoral Commission recommended that the referendum question ought to be: 'Should the United Kingdom remain a member of the European Union or leave the European Union?'*[15]

From late October 2015 onwards, Cameron focused on his promised renegotiation of Britain's membership terms: a renegotiation which would allow him to argue that Britain had reset the federalist dial and that remaining made sure-fire sense. Prior to the 1975 referendum on Britain's membership of what was then the European Economic Community (EEC), Harold Wilson had pulled off this trick, securing a package of concessions that provided a platform for a strong vote to remain.[16] In late 2015 polls suggested that support for remaining might rise dramatically – from around 31 per cent to 49 per cent – if Cameron also struck a good deal (at this point in time, around 25 per cent said they would not vote or did not know how they would vote).[17] But he didn't. Cameron never seemed entirely clear about what he wanted to achieve in the renegotiations he had demanded and, insofar as he had promised to do something to curtail the right to freedom of movement within the European Single Market, he did not come close to getting what he wanted.[18] Cameron eventually extracted a vague statement that Britain need not worry too much about Europe's future plans for political integration and a heavily qualified temporary brake on the payment of in-work benefits to European citizens living in Britain.[19] One of the Eurosceptic Conservative backbenchers, Steve Baker, got a long and heartfelt laugh when, during the subsequent Commons debate in early February 2016, he asked the minister for Europe, David Lidington, whether he had been reduced to 'polishing poo'.[20]

On 20 February Cameron confirmed that the date of the referendum would be 23 June 2016. Later that day, six members of his Cabinet, including his previously close political ally Michael Gove, announced they would be campaigning to leave. The following day, Boris Johnson, the mayor of London who had, in the past, defended Britain's membership of the EU as a vital cog in London's economic fortunes, said he

* In the initial Referendum Bill, the mooted draft question was the one-way 'Should the United Kingdom remain a member of the European Union?'. That question was expected to favour Remain because it made remaining the positive option.

would also be campaigning to leave. George Osborne was later to describe his decision as 'one thousand percent cynical'.[21] Johnson, he and others concluded, had looked at the way the wind was blowing and had decided the Conservative Party was becoming more clearly Eurosceptic, and that anyone campaigning to lead it in the future had better be onboard first. Either way, Johnson's declaration made a difference. He provided a high-profile and moderate-looking face to the official Vote Leave campaign. According to the Conservative Remainer Anna Soubry, at that point the minister of state for small business, later the leader of the Independent Group for Change, 'Boris was critical. That was a killer blow for remain.'[22] Nevertheless, opinion polls seemed to be showing Remain was ahead. Of the sixteen polls conducted between 20 February and 20 March 2016, ten put Remain ahead, two put Leave ahead and two reported a tie.[23]

In April the Treasury published a forecast that households would be £4,300 a year worse off if Britain left.[24] Piling in on the Remain side of the argument, the Bank of England warned Brexit could trigger a recession.[25] The Confederation of British Industry predicted it could lead to a million lost jobs and £100 billion in annual losses.[26] The largest banks then joined the chorus, arguing that leaving would be an act of economic self-harm. HSBC and JP Morgan suggested they might have to relocate abroad.[27] On 22 April, during a state visit, President Obama said that Britain would be at 'the back of the queue' for a trade deal with the United States if it left.[28] Johnson countered this with a claim that leaving would save Britain £350 million a week, money which could then be spent on the NHS. The statistical basis for the argument was that Britain made a £19 billion gross contribution to the European Union budget each year, which translated to something like £350 million a week. Critics, including the chair of the UK National Statistics Authority, argued that this number was glaringly misleading because it ignored the £4 billion rebate negotiated by Margaret Thatcher in the early 1980s (or, as others added, the estimated £11 billion spent directly in Britain by the European Union each year).[29] The Leave campaign argued in response that its gross figure was correct and that, when it came to issues like salaries, it was the gross figure people usually spoke about. In his *Secret Brexit Diary* (so secret, he published it) the European Union's chief negotiator, Michel Barnier, says he spoke to Nigel Farage about the £350 million figure and that Farage had said, 'Yes, that was a mistake. I told Boris not to do it.'[30] Whether or not that is true, it misses the point. The £350 million claim got the media talking about the costs of European Union membership and even if the correct figure was £250 million, that still seemed like a large sum.[31]

From early May onwards, the two groups campaigning to leave, the official Vote Leave campaign, associated with Johnson, Gove and Dominic Cummings, and Leave.EU, backed by the businessman and UKIP donor Arron Banks and associated with Farage, increasingly focused on immigration. This paid off when, on 26 May, the Office for National Statistics published data showing that net migration had risen to +333,000 in 2015.[32] This was the point at which Remain's (increasingly) narrow polling lead evaporated. Twelve of twenty-one opinion polls conducted in May put Remain ahead. In June, Remain was ahead in just fifteen of forty-five.[33] On 16 June the Labour MP for Batley and Spen, Jo Cox, was murdered by a white supremacist who had shouted 'This is for Britain', 'Keep Britain independent' and 'Put Britain first'.[34] Campaigning was suspended for three days before the vote then took place.

Although a majority of opinion polls taken over the final month of the campaign showed Leave either neck-and-neck or slightly ahead, almost everyone, Nigel Farage included, expected Remain to win, even if only narrowly.[35] By around 4 a.m. on 24 June it had become clear that the result would be different. Britain voted to leave the European Union by a margin of 17.4 million votes (51.9 per cent) to 16.1 million (48.1 per cent) on a turnout of just over 72 per cent.[36] Scotland and Northern Ireland voted to Remain (by margins of 24 percentage points and 12 percentage points respectively). England and Wales voted to Leave (by margins of 7 and 5 per cent). The largest cities, with the exceptions of Birmingham and Sheffield, voted to Remain. In London, Remain led by 20 percentage points. Leave did best in smaller towns and rural areas, securing its largest majorities in Boston (75% of the vote) and South Holland (73%), both in Lincolnshire, and Castle Point in Essex (72%).* Age mattered: 64 per cent of those aged over sixty-five voted to Leave

---

* As we saw in Chapter 7, immigration in the 2000s was generally highest in the largest cities. In many rural areas the percentage of the population born outside the UKGBNI remained below 2%. Boston, which had become a regional hub for seasonal agricultural work, was an exception. By 2010 13% of Boston's population had been born outside the UKGBNI.

compared with only 25 per cent of those aged between eighteen and twenty-four. Education also mattered: 70 per cent of people whose highest qualification was GCSEs voted to Leave compared to only 32 per cent of those with degrees.[37] Ethnicity also made a difference: 69 per cent of black, Asian and minority ethnic voters voted to Remain.[38]

Social class also mattered, albeit by not nearly as much. Using the standard classification system, the Remain vote within social classes A and B (upper-middle and middle class) was 59 per cent. Amongst C1 (lower-middle class) voters it was 52 per cent. Amongst C2 (skilled working class) voters it was 38 per cent. Amongst social classes D and E (working class and not working) it was 36 per cent.[39] But social class was not decisive. There were significantly more middle-class households than working-class ones in Britain by 2016. This, combined with differences in turnout, meant that there were more middle-class Leave voters than there were working-class ones.[40] Finally, left and right, the old standby of British politics in the early 2000s (pp. 51–2), also registered. The 2016 British Social Attitudes survey found that if you divided people into three groups according to their underlying left–right position, then 55 per cent of the most left-wing third of voters opted to vote to Leave compared with 48 per cent of the most right-wing third.[41]

WHY? PART I

If you wanted to focus on the campaign to explain the eventual result, then the damp squib of Cameron's renegotiation in late 2015, Boris Johnson's decision to campaign to Leave in February 2016 and the release of the ONS data on migration in late May all stand out as important moments. But there is also a more general point to make here. The Leave campaign successfully mixed an instrumental argument that Britain (and ordinary British people) would be better-off leaving with a positive emotional argument about taking back control and regaining sovereignty. The sovereignty argument was a bit of a show-stopper. Britain had been a sovereign country and the mark of that sovereignty had been the absolute and indivisible right of Parliament 'to make or unmake any law whatever'.[42] That sovereignty had been not simply compromised but lost when Britain had joined the European Economic Community and Britain's inability to control its own borders was the proof of that. The counter-argument – that sovereignty is a slightly outdated concept and that countries can achieve far more by working together – looked, by comparison, rather anodyne.

On the other side of the Brexit divide, a number of those involved in the Remain campaign have since acknowledged that they were over-reliant on instrumental arguments about the potential costs of leaving. Will Straw, the executive director of Britain Stronger in Europe, has spoken of how 'we never managed to get across ... the need for a more emotional case on both the benefits of being in along with the risks of leaving'. For Dominic Grieve, the former Conservative Party attorney general,

> the campaign [to Remain] was dreadful ... we had to make a positive case for the benefits of EU membership, and there was an emotional case that could be made even in the United Kingdom, which was really all about the First and Second World War, about bringing people together, preventing conflict, and building a future with a group of partners with whom we were going to be inevitably entangled, whether we remained or whether we left.[43]

If you wanted to look beyond the immediate confines of the campaign to offer a longer history of Brexit, there are also plenty of options. You could go back around 450,000 years to the moment when, following a catastrophic megaflood, the land bridge connecting the British Isles to the Continent collapsed (Brexit 1.0 as the team from Imperial College London documenting this process have described it).[44] Or you could go back just a few hundred years to the Tudors and the gradual emergence, with the help of a succession of wars against the French, of a modern-looking, centralized state in which, over time, sovereignty came to be defined in an absolute and distinctly un-pluralist way. Or you could go back to the Second World War and the idea that Britain had 'stood alone' and won and in winning had shown its political system to be superior to all others.* As Jean Monnet, one of the key drivers of European integration, put it, Britain was different because Britain 'felt no need to exorcise history'.[45] Or, in the aftermath of that

---

* In reality, Britain had never stood alone. In 1940/41, prior to the USA's entry to the war, it had benefited from lend-lease arrangements and from several million troops from the Empire and Dominions.

war, you could point to the economic draw of the Commonwealth or the hope of the 'special relationship' with the United States.

This book has, however, been focused on the political history of Britain since the year 2000 and over this more recent period three factors stand out as being of significance in explaining the decision to leave. First, immigration. Rightly or wrongly, New Labour was seen to have chosen to ignore the weight of public opinion when it came to immigration in the 2000s. Cameron recognized this and made a great play of promising to reduce net migration to the 'tens of thousands'. But he had no real plan to deliver upon this promise. The issue, however, was not simply about the overall numbers. It was about control. Randall Hansen, an academic at the University of Toronto, observes that, across the democratic world, public attitudes towards immigration do not appear to have any connection to actual levels of immigration in those countries. Quite the opposite seems to be true. Immigration is, if anything, more popular in countries with high levels of immigration. What seems to drive hostility towards immigration, he argues, is, above all, a sense that governments have lost control of their borders and cannot choose who to let in.[46] That was true of Australia in the early 2000s when the country was split over the arrival of migrants on boats. It became true of the United States a few years later when illegal crossings from Mexico became a headline political concern. It was also true of Britain where the Leave campaign linked high net migration to the free movement of people within the European Single Market and a loss of British sovereignty via the slogan 'take back control'. I have already noted Dominic Cummings' advice to Johnson and Gove: 'If you want to win this, you have to hit Cameron and Osborne over the head with a baseball bat with immigration written on it.'[47]

It is one of the oddities of post-Brexit British politics that overall levels of net migration, having fallen between 2017 and 2019, then rose to a new high of +606,000 in 2022 and did so, in part, as a result of decisions taken by Johnson, whilst prime minister, to significantly relax the salary threshold required to move to Britain and to further increase the number of designated 'shortage' occupations where migration rules are relaxed further.[48] Moreover, this happened at a point when the proportion of people telling pollsters that immigration was one of the key issues facing the country had fallen to around 10 per cent (compared to around 40 per cent-plus in early 2016).[49] The lesson to be drawn from this might be that public concern about migration was a passing fad or that, post-Brexit, attitudes towards immigration have become more positive. Yet whilst there is some evidence public opinion shifted and became slightly *more* favourable towards immigration in the year *prior* to the 2016 referendum, attitudes since then have largely stabilized.[50] It could of course be that other issues – Covid-19 and the cost-of-living crisis – simply squeezed immigration down the list of people's priorities. But it might also be that, post-Brexit, the sense Britain *had* regained control also mattered.

The second issue is the economy. The economy grew at a steady but unspectacular rate between 2010 and 2015, whilst median household income *after* housing costs rose by just over 4 per cent.[51] This is, however, only a part of the story. Average weekly *earnings* fell. Between January 2000 and December 2007 average real seasonally adjusted pay, adjusted for inflation and at 2015 prices, rose by 21 per cent, from £425 to £513. Over the next eight years, until December 2015, it then fell by 5 per cent to £487. A large part of this was due to the impact of the financial crisis. But, even after the economy had started to grow again, pay stagnated. Between April 2013 and December 2015 average real total pay rose by just £1.[52] In 2015 the Conservatives nevertheless won a general election fought largely over the issue of austerity. Yet, as we have also seen, attitudes towards austerity and public spending subsequently turned (p. 352). It would be a mistake to try to reduce Brexit solely to economics. There were plenty of well-off, economically secure people in London and the Home Counties who voted for Brexit. And there were, no doubt, plenty of people who voted for Brexit regardless of whether they thought they might end up worse-off. In their study of the Brexit vote, Maria Sobolewska and Robert Ford find that, whilst perceptions of the current state of the economy were closely linked to the probability of someone voting Labour in the 2015 General Election, they were not statistically linked to voting Remain.[53] Yet, against this, the extent to which particular areas were exposed to austerity-linked spending cuts does go some way towards predicting whether an area voted to stay or go during the referendum.[54] As we have seen, both Jeremy Corbyn and Theresa May regarded the vote to Leave as being propelled by low economic growth and stagnating wages (p. 361). In the 2000s we saw how the rise of a populist opposition to Blair and New Labour, which first bubbled to the surface during the September

2000 fuel crisis, was ultimately contained by the economic boom and rising household incomes. By the time of the 2016 referendum, those economic good times were long gone.

The final issue is trust. During the 1975 referendum on whether to remain within the EEC, the main party leaders, backed by business, had campaigned to remain and voters had eventually followed their lead. The patrician's patrician, Roy Jenkins, Labour home secretary and soon-to-be president of the European Commission, mused that in 1975 'the British electorate took the advice of the people they were used to following'.[55] In 2016 the leaders of all the major political parties campaigned to remain (albeit with a somewhat limited degree of enthusiasm in Jeremy Corbyn's case, p. 354). The Remain campaign group, Britain Stronger in Europe, backed this with endorsements from the Bank of England, the Treasury and the CBI, all three living former prime ministers, President Obama, the former heads of MI5 and MI6, trade union leaders and an assortment of former NATO secretary generals and US secretaries of state *and* James Bond (or, rather, Daniel Craig). But by 2016 far fewer people were willing to accept being told how to vote. The financial crisis had happened. The MPs' expenses scandal had happened. Only a few months before the referendum David Cameron had been forced to admit that he had benefited from a tax-friendly, Panama-based, offshore trust his father had established.[56] The strength of people's identification with political parties was down (p. 260) and only 15 per cent of people trusted politicians to tell the truth.[57]

Mistrust was the sentiment Michael Gove ran hard with when he was interviewed by Faisal Islam on Channel 4 three weeks before the referendum vote. The famous line from this interview is Gove's claim that 'the people of this country are tired of experts'.[58] For many Remainers this was proof-positive of the populist, post-truth, know-nothing message of the Leave campaign. This was to risk missing the point of what Gove was saying, however. Rewind a few seconds and Islam had begun by quoting a long list of people and organizations backing Remain. He then asked Gove why the public should trust him over them. Gove responded by arguing that it was not about him and that he wanted people to make their own minds up. He then went on to say that he wanted the British people to 'take back control of our destiny from those organisations which are distant, unaccountable, elitist and don't have their interests at heart'. This was not just about the European

Union. It was about the political establishment more generally. Having been accused by Islam of sounding like a conspiracy theorist, Gove suggested that 'the people who are backing the Remain campaign are people who have done very well, thank you, out of the European Union.' To this he then added the 'enough of experts' payoff. Gove was not, in other words, simply having a pop at expertise. He was responding to and exploiting a sense of inequality and lack of trust in much the same way that the fuel protestors had done in 2000, the Occupy movement had done in 2011 and Jeremy Corbyn was to do in the 2017 General Election. It worked. In a country full of people who mistrusted politicians and the government, 65 per cent of people who said that they distrusted the government voted Leave.[59]

WHY? PART II

In 1996 John Howard, the new Australian prime minister, inherited from his predecessor, Labor's Paul Keating, growing calls for Australia to become a Republic. Howard, a committed monarchist, convened a constitutional convention and invited those favouring the Republic to agree upon a model for selecting the head of state who would replace the Queen prior to a referendum. The delegates to the convention considered three alternative models: direct election, parliamentary election by special majority, and appointment by a special council following a prime ministerial nomination. It all became quite messy, with pro-Republic delegates falling out with each other over the best model. Eventually, a complex hybrid model was agreed upon and put to the vote in a referendum in November 1999. But the wind had been taken out of the sails of the Republican movement by the arguments during the convention and the Republican option lost with 45 per cent of the vote.[60]

In 2013 Cameron promised a referendum if the Conservatives were re-elected but did not require that those in favour of leaving agree upon a model of what Brexit would entail. As a result, divisions within the Leave camp between those who favoured a relatively 'soft' Brexit with Britain remaining in the European Union's Customs Union and those favouring a 'hard' Brexit remained largely hidden. As did divisions between those who wanted to leave because they favoured cutting taxes and regulation and turning Britain into a 'Singapore-on-Thames' and those who wanted to leave because they saw the opportunity to break free from European Union restrictions on state aid and use Brexit as a means to promote the goal of 'levelling-up'. As Alan Finlayson observes, many of those who voted to Leave were voting against the acceleration of economic and cultural globalization, whilst many of those who led the campaign to Leave were arguing that Brexit would provide Britain with the opportunity to globalize further.[61] It has routinely been argued that Brexit was driven by a nostalgia for and some sort of attempt to recreate a British Empire 2.0. Yet as the historian Robert Saunders demonstrates, advocates for Brexit, with all their talk of buccaneering and of Drake, were in fact harking back to a pre-Empire age, in which Britain was a small island nation with a large trading presence. On this account of British history, as Saunders goes on to argue, Britain was not great because it eventually gained an Empire. It gained an Empire because it was great and could become great again, Empire or not.[62] Either way, the absence of an agreed alternative also made it much easier for Leavers to suggest that striking a post-Brexit deal with the European Union would be 'the easiest deal in human history', and that Britain could keep all the trade advantages of being in the European Union whilst striking its own trade deals, controlling immigration and providing free ice cream for everyone on hot days.[63]

The 2015 British Election Study invited respondents to select their preferred position along an 11-point scale, running from uniting fully with the European Union on the one side to doing everything possible to protect Britain's independence from the European Union on the other. The results are shown in Figure 5. On the one hand, it shows not only that more voters tended towards a more Eurosceptic position (positions 7–11) than a Euro-enthusiast one (positions 1–5) but that a significant number of people (just under 18 per cent) took the extreme position of wanting to do everything possible to leave. This is not the kind of 'bell curve' distribution we saw in Chapter 4 on the fuel crisis in relation to people's sense of their left and right political positioning where the centre-ground positions were dominant. On the other hand, and that said, the three centrist positions (5, 6 and 7) attracted the combined support of nearly a third of people, whilst steadfast Europeanism (positions 1, 2 and 3) attracted the support of a further 13 per cent. A year later, in 2016, Leave nevertheless won because the very fact of the

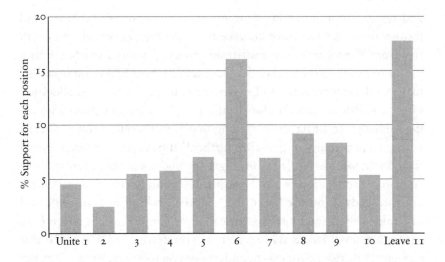

Figure 5. Attitudes towards Britain's Membership of the European Union, 2015

Note: 10% of respondents answered 'don't' know'.

UK Data Service, 'British General Election Study of 2015: Face-to-face post-election survey', variable p03_1 (http://nesstar.ukdataservice.ac.uk/webview/).

referendum forced most people's pretty-nuanced views on Europe through a binary mangle, requiring them to choose between stay or go. There was no split-the-difference, centre-ground option in 2016 that could appeal to the median voter.

Many of those in favour of Brexit, most notably Theresa May's one-time joint chief of staff Nick Timothy, were convinced that, when it came to Europe, there was no centre ground.[64] Britain either had to be in the European Union or out of the European Union. This was the logic which drove a large part of the Brexit argument and a large part of Theresa May's post-referendum negotiations. There is no middle ground. 'Brexit means Brexit.'[65] Or, more precisely, Brexit, if it meant anything, had to mean leaving the European Single Market guaranteeing the freedom of movement of people, goods, services and capital, the European Union's Customs Union and the jurisdiction of the European Court of Justice, because that was what the European Union *was*. This was, however, debatable. Prior to 2016 Britain had, for better or worse, carved out over several decades a centre-ground position when it came to Europe, which broadly reflected public opinion. Britain was in the

European Union and in the Single Market and had (belatedly, in 1997) signed the Social Chapter Protocol of the Maastricht Treaty. Yet Britain had opted-out of European Monetary Union, the Schengen Agreement (abolishing internal borders and most forms of passport control) and the 2011 Treaty on Stability, Co-ordination and Governance (which, after the British veto, most other European countries pressed ahead with anyway) and the subsequent Banking Union. Michel Barnier quotes Luxembourg's prime minister, Xavier Bettel, as saying of the British that, prior to 2016, 'they were in and they had many opt-outs; now they want to be out with many opt-ins.'[66]

That in-out, hokey-cokey membership was becoming harder to sustain in the early 2010s. Out-and-out leave-now-and-don't-look-back-in-anger Euroscepticism was becoming more popular with voters and Conservative MPs. At the same time, integrate-everything-and-integrate-it-now federalism was also gaining ground within Europe. In June 2015, no doubt to David Cameron's deep irritation, the presidents of the European Council, European Parliament, European Commission and European Central Bank published a joint report arguing the case for a deeper economic, financial, fiscal and political union.[67] As was the case with the Scottish referendum in 2014, the Brexit referendum was, however, more the cause of political polarization than its effect. It forced people to make a choice where no choice had been necessary before.

29

Northern Ireland: From Ashes to Dust

On 12 January 2017 the *Irish Times* reported that Northern Ireland's deputy first minister, Martin McGuinness, was suffering from amyloidosis, a rare and incurable disease.[1] Three days before, McGuinness, who had been the deputy first minister since May 2007, had resigned over the failure of Arlene Foster, the first minister and leader of the Democratic Unionist Party, to step aside while a preliminary investigation was carried out in the so-called 'cash for ash' scandal (pp. 382–3). McGuinness's resignation effectively killed the existing Stormont Executive and triggered another set of elections to the Northern Ireland Assembly. In his resignation letter McGuinness argued that the 'equality, mutual respect and all-Ireland approaches enshrined in the Good Friday Agreement have never been fully embraced by the DUP' and that 'successive British Governments have undermined the process of change by refusing to honour agreements, refusing to resolve the issues of the past while imposing austerity and Brexit against the wishes and best interests of people here'.[2]

McGuinness was hospitalized and passed away on 21 March. His funeral was held in his hometown of Derry where, as a young man, McGuinness had been second-in-command of the local IRA Brigade. The service was held at St Columba's Church, only a few hundred yards away from 'Free Derry Corner', commemorating the once self-declared nationalist part of Derry. McGuinness's coffin, covered in the Irish Tricolour, was paraded past this symbol of Republican nationalism before it entered the church. Amongst the fifteen hundred people who attended the service were the Irish president and taoiseach, the secretary of state for Northern Ireland, James Brokenshire, Arlene Foster, and the former US president Bill Clinton.

Clinton released a statement immediately following McGuinness's death in which he revealed McGuinness had personally overseen the decommissioning of the IRA's weapons a decade before.[3] At the funeral itself, he delivered the final eulogy. He praised McGuinness's role in the peace process and the risks he had taken in chancing 'the rejection of his comrades and the wrath of his adversaries'. He argued McGuinness 'had made honourable compromises and was strong enough to keep them'. He was 'a good husband, a good father, a follower of the faith of his father and mother and a passionate believer in a free, secure, self-governing Ireland'. Clinton concluded by telling the assembled mourners: 'if you really came here to celebrate his life and honour the contribution of the last chapter of it, you have to finish his work.'[4]

Clinton's words were impeccably and typically well-delivered. They constituted a defiant plea for the future of a peace process which he, McGuinness and others had worked to realize. Yet by the point he delivered his eulogy, that process, whose painful development was described in an earlier chapter, was already in a lot of trouble.

THE FRESH START

Ian Paisley of the DUP and McGuinness were sworn in as first and deputy first minister in May 2007. They worked together until June 2008 when Paisley, upon his retirement, was replaced by Peter Robinson.[5] From that moment until January 2016, when Robinson himself retired shortly after suffering a major heart attack, McGuinness and Robinson, Sinn Féin and the DUP, continued to disagree about just about everything but just about held everything together. As Ian Paisley Jnr describes it in the journalist Brian Rowan's account of this period, 'maybe we'll get to the point where trust comes into the equation, but at the moment we have politics without trust, but we've got politics.'[6] In March 2009, when dissident Republicans killed two soldiers collecting pizzas outside Massereene Barracks in County Antrim and, shortly after, a policeman, Stephen Carroll, in Craigavon, County Armagh, McGuinness stood alongside Peter Robinson and the chief constable of the Police Service of Northern Ireland to condemn the attacks and describe those involved as 'traitors to Ireland'.[7]

In February 2010, after lengthy talks at Hillsborough Castle, the official residence of the secretary of state for Northern Ireland, Sinn Féin and the DUP reached a final agreement on the devolution of policing and justice matters to the Northern Ireland Executive. In June 2010, following the publication of the Saville Report into Bloody Sunday, the shooting dead of twenty-six unarmed protestors in Derry in 1972 by soldiers of the Parachute Regiment, David Cameron offered a full and evidently sincere apology in the House of Commons. 'What happened on Bloody Sunday was unjustified and unjustifiable.'[8] In elections to the Northern Ireland Assembly, in May 2011, voters then offered a broad endorsement of the political status quo – the DUP and Sinn Féin winning three additional seats between them. Not long after, the Queen made a state visit to the Republic of Ireland, the first by a British monarch since her grandfather, King George V, in 1911. She visited the Gaelic Football Museum at Croke Park, where British soldiers had shot dead fourteen people during the Irish War of Independence. In a speech delivered during a state banquet in Dublin Castle, the opening line of which she delivered in Irish, she spoke of the 'sad and regrettable reality that through history our islands have experienced more than their fair share of heartache, turbulence and loss' but also of the way in which, as a result of the Good Friday Agreement, 'what were once only hopes for the future have now come to pass'.[9] In June 2012, as a part of the Diamond Jubilee Celebrations, the Queen visited Northern Ireland and met and shook hands with McGuinness.

In December 2012 Belfast City Council announced it was going to restrict the number of days during which the Union Jack would be flown from City Hall. The result was a series of riots and street protests. Tensions between the DUP and Sinn Féin were also rising over a number of other 'legacy' issues, including parades; the search for the remains of the people who had disappeared, presumed murdered, during the Troubles; the recording of the oral history of the Troubles; an increasingly sharp argument about the official status of the Irish language, Gaelic, in Northern Ireland; and, finally, the impact of austerity-led public spending cuts. In 2015 the murders of Gerard 'Jock' Davison and Kevin McGuigan, during a feud the *Belfast Telegraph* linked to the proceeds of the 2004 Northern Bank robbery, was blamed on figures linked to the IRA.[10]

Times were tough but the DUP and Sinn Féin had each decided, back in May 2007, that they had more to gain from being in government than they had from remaining outside, and neither Robinson nor

McGuinness changed their minds on that basic issue. So, in December
2014, after another marathon set of talks, the Stormont House agreement was reached relating to the establishment of a Commission on
Flags, Identity, Culture and Tradition; the creation of an Oral History
Archive; and the formation of an independent Historical Investigations
Unit to probe outstanding criminal killings and alleged police misconduct. All of this was washed down with a commitment, on the part of
the Northern Ireland Executive, to pass a balanced budget in return
for an additional £2 billion in support from the Treasury.[11] A year
later, and after another set of talks, the agreement which had been
reached at Stormont House was finally translated into the 'Fresh Start'
agreement.[12]

'IF YOU FEED A CROCODILE'

In January 2016 Arlene Foster was elected, unopposed, as Peter Robinson's replacement as DUP leader and first minister. The hot take on
Foster was that she represented a generational shift and something different. She was twenty years younger than Robinson and had not been
elected to the Northern Ireland Assembly until 2003. Moreover, Foster
was a woman and an Anglican in a male-dominated political party with
umbilical ties to the Free Presbyterian Church of Ulster.

Arlene Kelly had been raised in rural County Fermanagh, close to the
border with the Irish Republic. When she was eight years old, her father,
John, a part-time police reservist, had been shot and seriously wounded
by the IRA outside the family house. Years later, Foster recalled how
she had watched him crawl back into the kitchen with blood pouring
from his head.[13] Nearly a decade later, Foster was travelling to school
on a bus that was attacked by the IRA: they were aiming to kill its
driver, Ernie Wilson.[14] After studying law at Queen's University Belfast
and qualifying as a solicitor, Kelly, who married Brian Foster, a police
officer, in 1995, stood for election to the Northern Ireland Assembly in
2003, not as a Democratic Unionist but as a member of the Ulster
Unionist Party. Not long after, she resigned and joined the DUP in protest at what she considered to be David Trimble's appeasement of the
IRA. By the time Ian Paisley finally agreed to become first minister in
2007, alongside Martin McGuinness, Foster had already developed

something of a reputation for being a hardliner in a party not exactly known for being full of softies.

In January 2016, shortly before she assumed office as first minister, Foster went out of her way to let it be known she would not be travelling to Dublin for the official centenary celebrations of the 1916 Easter Rising against British rule a few months later because she viewed it as having been 'an attack on democracy'.[15] Then, in her inaugural address as first minister, she promised never to forget the past; to honour the memory of those who had served in the security forces during the Troubles; and suggested that their reward and legacy could be seen in a stable and secure Northern Ireland within UKGBNI.[16] As textbook examples of political emollience go, this was not going to win any awards.

Events then took an unexpected turn. Before she had become first minister Foster had been the finance minister in the Assembly, and before that she had been the minister for enterprise, trade and investment, during which time she oversaw the establishment of the Renewable Heat Incentive (RHI) scheme. The idea here was to provide local businesses with a taxpayer-funded incentive to switch from using fossil fuels to renewable fuel systems, such as wood-pellet burners. There was, however, a massive flaw in the initiative. Because there was no overall cap on the amount which could be claimed under the terms of the scheme, businesses had every reason to burn more and more fuel in order to claim more money. Hence the name of the scandal, 'cash for ash'. On three occasions between 2013 and 2015, a local businesswoman, Janette O'Hagan, contacted Foster to warn her that the scheme was being abused.[17] She was ignored and, she said, made to feel like a liar.[18] Only in 2015, after Foster had become finance minister, did her replacement, Jonathan Bell (another DUP politician), close the scheme to new applicants. Suddenly, it became apparent that 'cash for ash' could end up costing the taxpayer hundreds of millions of pounds. At the same time, rumours began to swirl that the scheme had been left in place because DUP-supporting local businessmen had done really well out of it.[19]

In December 2016 Jonathan Bell alleged Foster and two of her top advisors had intervened to prevent him from closing the scheme earlier.[20] Sinn Féin joined the UUP and the Social Democratic and Labour Party (SDLP) in demanding Foster step aside whilst a public inquiry began. Foster, who was also coming under intense pressure to step aside

from colleagues within the DUP, refused, saying she did not take instructions from Sinn Féin.[21] A few weeks later, McGuinness, to return to the
point where this chapter started, resigned as deputy first minister. In his
resignation letter he argued that the RHI scandal had led to a 'crisis of
confidence' in Northern Ireland's political institutions. But, as we have
seen, he also went out of his way to suggest that the Good Friday Agreement had 'never been fully embraced by the DUP'. Indeed if there was
one single issue which fractured the coalition between Sinn Féin and the
DUP it was not 'cash for ash', but, rather, the DUP's refusal to move
forward with an Irish Language Act – something which had been agreed
to in principle as long ago as 2006.[22] Cash for ash was the proverbial
straw that had broken the back of power-sharing.

In January 2017 Martin McGuinness's resignation triggered a fresh
set of elections to the Northern Ireland Assembly. Foster did not flinch.
During the campaign, she ruled out any future deal on an Irish Language Act, warning that 'if you feed a crocodile it will keep coming back
and looking for more'.[23] The DUP just about held on, winning one seat
more than Sinn Féin and seeing off, once again, the challenge from the
ultra-hardline Traditional Unionist Voice party, which had been formed
in 2007 when Jim Allister, its leader, had resigned from the DUP. Foster's position nevertheless looked precarious. She was saved because the
public inquiry into the RHI scheme took three years to do its work and
because the June 2017 General Election left the Conservatives short of
an overall majority in Westminster and needing to do a deal with the
DUP to stay in office.[24] Foster, who had looked like damaged goods,
was suddenly indispensable and, as we have seen, extracted a £1-billion
promise of extra public spending in return for a commitment to vote
with the government in the Westminster Parliament on key issues.

Following the Northern Ireland Assembly and Westminster general
elections, talks about relaunching the Northern Ireland Executive,
chaired by the Northern Ireland secretary James Brokenshire, began but
broke down over a number of issues, including Foster's continued
opposition to an Irish Language Bill. Sinn Féin, the nationalist SDLP
and Irish government ministers all argued, with varying levels of intensity, that the British government was now effectively a prisoner of the
DUP. Eventually, and after a long period in which it was left to Northern Irish civil servants to just about keep things ticking along, a deal of
sorts was struck in 2020 and Arlene Foster returned as first minister

alongside Michelle O'Neill, Sinn Féin's vice president following Gerry Adams' retirement in 2018.[25] It did not work. The DUP and Sinn Féin struggled to agree on anything and after one row after another the DUP walked out once again in February 2022.

By that time, Brexit had already added another layer of disagreement. In 2016 Sinn Féin, the SDLP, UUP and the Alliance Party supported Remain. The DUP supported Leave. An estimated 85 per cent of Catholics voted to Remain whilst 60 per cent of Protestants voted to Leave.[26] But that was not the real problem. The real problem, as John Major and Tony Blair (amongst others) had warned would be the case during the referendum campaign, was that Brexit put firmly back on the table the issue of Northern Ireland's border with the Republic to its south.[27] The nationalist side feared Brexit would mean UKGBNI leaving the European Single Market; that leaving the Single Market would mean customs checks and a 'hard border' between Northern Ireland and the Republic of Ireland; that a hard border would amount to a betrayal of the Good Friday Agreement; and that this would lead to a breakdown in the peace process.[28] Meanwhile, the Unionist side feared that any attempt by the British government to appease the Republic of Ireland and avoid a hard border would threaten Northern Ireland's place within UKGBNI.

This was the problem Theresa May inherited in July 2016. From the time of the October 2016 Conservative Party conference onward, it gradually became clear that she favoured a hard-ish Brexit which would entail leaving the Single Market (p. 408). This, together with May's later 'confidence and supply' alliance with the DUP, heightened fears Britain could no longer play the role of an 'honest broker' and that a hard border was in the offing.[29] But May seemed to be fully committed to the Good Friday Agreement and to the peace process and, besides this, knew that the European Union would never accept the return of a hard border either. So, in December 2017, at the conclusion of the first stage of the Brexit talks, May signed an agreement with the European Union settling the terms of Britain's divorce, whilst seeming to promise that there would be no future hard border between Northern Ireland and the Republic of Ireland.[30]

The problem came in reconciling May's determination to leave the Single Market with the pledge to avoid a hard border. In February 2018 the European Union proposed an arrangement whereby Northern Ireland would remain *within* the European Single Market for goods, obviating the need for customs checks and a hard border between the Republic of Ireland and Northern Ireland, but in which the rest of UKGBNI would leave the Single Market and the European Union's Customs Union. There was however a catch. If Northern Ireland was in and the rest of UKGBNI was out, there would have to be some form of de facto border and customs checks between Northern Ireland and mainland Britain. Theresa May rejected this option out of hand. In July 2018 she instead proposed a 'Facilitated Customs Arrangement', under which UKGBNI and the European Union would collect customs duties on each other's behalf but in which UKGBNI would be free to set its own differing tariffs if it wanted, whilst also, and alongside this, maintaining shared regulatory standards. If it had been accepted, Facilitated Customs would have removed the need for a hard border between Northern Ireland and the Republic. But the problem was that the European Union had already indicated that it was not interested in such a deal, which, it suggested, was impracticable. May persisted but the European Union eventually did what it had said it would do and rejected this option in September 2018.

An alternative was needed and May eventually suggested a 'backstop' arrangement, the Northern Ireland Protocol, whereby UKGBNI would form a single customs union; in which UKGBNI would align itself with the European Union's 'level playing field' provisions on state aid, labour and the environment; and in which, in addition, Northern Ireland would also align itself with other European Single Market rules in relation to agriculture, taxation and energy.[31] This was basically a very complicated way of squaring a circle and avoiding the need for a border between Northern Ireland and the Republic or between Northern Ireland and the rest of UKGBNI. Which looked like a good idea – unless you wanted to leave the European Union. If you had campaigned to Leave, the backstop looked a lot like Remaining, with Northern Ireland still in the Single Market and the rest of UKGBNI agreeing to follow large parts of the European rule book, with no real say over what those rules would be. May argued that the backstop would be a temporary arrangement, to be left in place until a long-term deal could be agreed with the European Union. But, as the attorney general, Sir Geoffrey Cox, was eventually forced to confirm to Parliament, unless Britain *and* the European Union could *both* agree to a longer-term trade deal which avoided the need for a hard border between

Northern Ireland and the Republic, Britain would have to remain in the backstop indefinitely.[32]

To cut short the story I will tell in Chapter 31, 'Getting Brexit Done', May tried but failed to get her backstop deal over the line. She resigned and was replaced by Boris Johnson who, according to May's chief of staff, Gavin Barwell, regarded the Northern Irish border as being 'the tail wagging the Brexit dog' (i.e., as being rather less important than May had considered it to be).[33] Johnson promised his party a brand new deal with no downsides and no backstop. In reality, after talks with the Irish taoiseach Leo Varadkar, what he did in October 2019 was to go back to a version of the deal which the European Union had put on the table in February 2018 and May had rejected. Northern Ireland would remain within the European Single Market, so removing the need for a border between the Republic of Ireland and Northern Ireland. Meanwhile, the rest of UKGBNI would leave the European Union and the European Union's Customs Union and would be free to strike its own trade deals, including a trade deal with the European Union. Northern Ireland would formally remain a part of Britain's customs territory. But there would be customs checks and a de facto border between Northern Ireland the rest of Britain.

A crucial difference between this version of the Northern Ireland Protocol and the one May had negotiated was that it was not a 'backstop'. This was simply how it would be going forward. The other main difference was that Northern Ireland's Assembly would be given the opportunity, every four years, through a simple majority vote, to review these arrangements.[34] If it wanted to, it could, therefore, ditch Single Market alignment and so remove the need for the customs checks between Northern Ireland and the rest of Britain. Looking ahead, the medium-term problem the Protocol created was that if this ever happened, it would be likely to result in the return to a hard border between Northern Ireland and the Republic – something Sinn Féin and the other nationalist parties could be relied upon to reject as a betrayal of the Good Friday Agreement. The short-term problem these arrangements created was that the DUP also hated the Protocol. Economically, it meant it was going to become a lot more time-consuming and expensive to move goods across the Irish Sea from Liverpool or Cairnryan to Belfast. Politically, it meant Northern Ireland was going to be treated differently from the rest of

UKGBNI. But Conservative MPs, who were now desperate to 'Get Brexit Done', were happy enough and Johnson, having won a large majority in the 2019 General Election, no longer needed the DUP's support and was happy enough to wave them goodbye.

In April 2021 Foster resigned from the DUP's leadership, having lost the confidence of just about all of her party. She was replaced, on 28 May, by Edwin Poots – who also proceeded to lose the confidence of his party and was replaced by Jeffrey Donaldson, a long-time opponent of the Good Friday Agreement, a month later.[35] This looked like a real mess and in the 2022 Northern Ireland Assembly elections the DUP's vote fell by just short of 7 percentage points. It lost three seats and found itself in a position where Sinn Féin now had the most seats in the Assembly. Would the DUP be prepared to go back into a coalition with Sinn Féin and accept the position of deputy first minister? On the one hand, this may not have looked like a hugely important question. Under the Good Friday rules, the first and deputy first ministers had identical powers. But in other respects this could not have mattered more. Accepting the deputy role meant accepting minority status. The DUP's eventual answer to this question was that it would not play ball until the British government had renegotiated the Protocol.[36] After a lot of huffing and puffing, that renegotiation was settled in 2023 via the 'Windsor Framework'. This allowed for a new system of 'green lanes' to allow pre-approved traders to export goods from mainland Britain to Northern Ireland (but not to the Republic) with minimal border checks.* The Windsor Framework looked like a triumph for the British government because in many ways it was.[37] The difference by 2022 was that the European Union did not have to worry about striking a tough deal in order to deter other countries from following Britain out of the Union. It wanted to normalize relations with Britain, and playing good cop and revising the terms of the Protocol by softening (but not eliminating) the de facto customs border between Northern Ireland and 'mainland' Britain was a small price to pay for doing so. The

* The Windsor Agreement left the European Court of Justice as, on paper, the ultimate arbiter of European Single Market rules in Northern Ireland. But it also created a 'Stormont brake' under which thirty members of the Northern Ireland Assembly, from at least two parties, could ask the British government to veto changes in European Union Single Market rules; *The Economist*, 'Explaining what is in the Windsor Framework' (2 Mar. 2023). This was, in other words, a messy compromise. But most compromises are.

DUP remained unimpressed and continued to block the re-establishment of the Northern Ireland Assembly and Executive until early 2024.

'AN ENJOYABLE PASTIME'

Brexit was a jolt – a big jolt – to the Northern Irish political system and the Good Friday Agreement. There is, however, also another factor at play here. In the 1971 census, right at the start of 'the Troubles', around 35 per cent of Northern Ireland's population stated, when asked, that they were Catholic. By 1991 that proportion had grown, to just over 38 per cent, but Catholics remained a minority.[38] That was why the peace process, once it got going again in the early 1990s, was always going to have to be built upon power-sharing. A majoritarian system, as successive elections to the Northern Ireland Parliament from 1921 to 1969 had shown, simply made it too easy for the Protestant and Unionist majority to sideline the Catholic and nationalist minority.[39] However, as these numbers also show, the Catholic population was growing at a faster rate than the Protestant one and this created the demographic possibility of the Catholic minority one day becoming Northern Ireland's new majority. During an interview in 2001, Gerry Adams quipped that 'outbreeding unionists may be an enjoyable pastime ... but it hardly amounts to a political strategy'.[40] Yet when the results of the 2021 Census were published in September 2022, they showed that there were more people who said they were Catholic or had been raised as a Catholic in Northern Ireland than there were people who were Protestant or had been raised as a Protestant.[41]

This matters because it has left many in the Protestant and Unionist community feeling entirely embattled – a minority within the Island of Ireland; a minority within Northern Ireland; and cast asunder from mainland Britain via Johnson's Brexit deal. It also matters because it potentially offers to Sinn Féin and the nationalist Catholic community an alternative to power-sharing, or, more accurately given what has happened since 2017, intermittent power-sharing. The Good Friday Agreement had required the SDLP and Sinn Féin to accept that any future reunification of Ireland would require majority support in Northern Ireland. In 1998 that looked a long way off. By 2022 less so. Indeed, such was the economic strain being posed by Brexit, it was suddenly not even that hard to imagine, at a pinch, some Unionists voting for reunification, alongside those not identifying as belonging to either community. In June 2021, on the occasion of Northern Ireland's Centenary celebrations, the journalist Susan McKay predicted 'there isn't going to be a second centenary for Northern Ireland. It might not even last another decade.'[42]

Irish reunification, if it happens, is not going to happen by Tuesday next week. For a start, the authority to call a 'border poll' referendum is held by the British secretary of state for Northern Ireland. The Good Friday Agreement says he or she must call a referendum if 'it appears likely' that a majority would be in favour of reunification.[43] But there is no clear text around how to define 'appears likely', which means that, as with a second Scottish referendum, the status quo has a built-in advantage. The next problem is that any reunification would require majority support not only amongst Northern Irish voters but, in practice, a majority of voters in the Republic of Ireland as well.[44] Finally, whilst the proportion of people in the Northern Ireland Life and Times survey who say they favour reunification as a long-term political solution has been rising, it remains very much a minority taste. In 2021 37 per cent of people favoured Northern Ireland remaining a part of UKGBNI but with devolved government (the Good Friday Agreement solution); 12 per cent favoured Northern Ireland remaining a part of UKGBNI but with direct rule from London and no devolution; 7 per cent favoured Northern Ireland becoming an independent state; 14 per cent did not know or had another idea; and only 30 per cent favoured reunification.[45]

There is, however, another demographic and political story to tell about Northern Ireland. On the one hand, Northern Irish party politics retains a sectarian base. In 2003 the Northern Ireland Life and Times survey found that fewer than 1 per cent of Catholics supported either the DUP or UUP and that only 2 per cent of Protestants supported the nationalist SDLP, with 0 per cent supporting Sinn Féin.[46] Move forward to 2018 and it remains the case that very few self-identifying Catholics support a Unionist party or Protestants a nationalist party.* On the

* In 2018 1% of self-identifying Catholics said that they felt closest to the UUP (and 0% the DUP) whilst 1% of Protestants said they felt closest to Sinn Féin and 1% the SDLP. By 2022 a recorded 0% of Catholics said they felt closest to either the UUP or the DUP whilst 1% of Protestants said they felt closest to Sinn Féin and 4% to the SDLP. Note the change in question here, from 'Which Northern Ireland political party do you support?' to 'Which of these

other hand, whilst in 2003 (a perhaps surprisingly high) 35 per cent identified as *neither* nationalist nor Unionist, that number had risen to fully 50 per cent by 2018 (before falling back to 38 per cent in 2022).[47] But, even more strikingly, whilst the avowedly non-sectarian Alliance Party had received just 3.7 per cent of the vote in the 2003 Northern Ireland Assembly elections, in the 2022 elections it secured 13.5 per cent.

The Alliance Party is not about to sweep the board. In 2022 13.5 per cent of the vote translated to third place: a long way behind either the DUP or Sinn Féin. Yet this is not simply about votes. The Alliance has developed a critique of the political status quo which may well attract the support of the two smaller nationalist and unionist parties it is currently ahead of. The problem with the Good Friday Agreement, this critique runs, is that it has paralysed decision-making and embedded divisions by effectively guaranteeing a power-sharing role for the largest political party from each community whilst, at the same time, making it far too easy for that party to walk away from the responsibility of government when it suits its political interests to do so.[48] What is needed, the Alliance argues, is a different system: one which is still based on power-sharing, but which recognizes how Northern Ireland has changed and does not require parties to designate themselves as being nationalist or Unionist and in which the participation of the largest nationalist and largest Unionist party is not required within the Executive. This would obviously benefit the Alliance because if it ever overtook Sinn Féin or the DUP in the future, it would be able to enter the power-sharing Executive with its leader becoming either first or deputy first minister in a way that, at the moment, would not be constitutionally possible. So far, that is straightforward enough. The Alliance has also suggested that if the two largest parties resign from or refuse to join the Executive, as Sinn Féin and the DUP have done in the past, all the other parties ought to be allowed to negotiate with each other to see whether any of them can form a coalition which commands majority support in the Assembly.

political parties do you feel closest to?' Northern Ireland Life and Times Survey, 'Interest in politics/party affiliation' (https://www.ark.ac.uk/nilt/results/polatt.html#identity).

30
Me Too

HARVEY WEINSTEIN

On 5 October 2017 two journalists working for the *New York Times*, Jodi Kantor and Megan Twohey, published a story with the self-explanatory headline 'HARVEY WEINSTEIN PAID OFF SEXUAL HARASSMENT ACCUSERS FOR DECADES'.[1] Weinstein, who had founded the independent film distribution company Miramax (named after his parents Miriam and Max) and had later founded a film studio, The Weinstein Company, issued a statement via his lawyers that appeared alongside the article.[2] Weinstein apologized for his behaviour and explained, unconvincingly, that 'I came of age in the '60s and '70s, when all the rules about behaviour and workplaces were different'. He added that he planned to take a leave of absence from work. A few days later, the *New York Times* published fresh allegations from thirteen other women, which included an allegation of rape. Journalists also noted other reporters had previously investigated Weinstein but had been stymied by the reluctance of actresses to talk about him for fear of damaging their career, and by nondisclosure agreements attached to legal settlements.[3] Reacting to these stories, the Academy of Motion Picture Arts and Sciences stripped Weinstein of his previous awards and expelled him from the organization in order to 'send a message that the era of wilful ignorance and shameful complicity in sexually predatory behaviour and workplace harassment in our industry is over'.[4]

On 15 October the American actor Alyssa Milano tweeted: 'if all the women who have been sexually harassed or assaulted wrote "me too" . . . we might give people a sense of the magnitude of the problem.'[5] Within a day #MeToo was the top-trending hashtag in the United States. Over the next six months, the number of accusations publicly levelled against men in the American media and entertainment industry spiralled. On 17 October Roy Price, the head of Amazon Studios, resigned after the film producer Isa Hackett accused him of lewd behaviour. On 18 October the Olympic gymnast McKayla Maroney revealed she had been sexually assaulted by former team doctor Larry Nassar. On 29 October the actor Anthony Rapp accused Kevin Spacey of making sexual advances towards him when he was just fourteen.* On 9 November the *New York Times* published a story about the predatory behaviour of the comedian Louis C.K.[6] On 29 November the co-anchor of the *Today* programme on NBC News, Matt Lauer, was fired for sexual misconduct. In December the Democrat Senator Al Franken resigned following a series of allegations of sexual misconduct. In April 2018 the comedian and actor Bill Cosby was convicted of drugging and molesting a woman. In May 2018 Weinstein was charged with rape and in March 2020 was sentenced to twenty-three years in prison.

#MeToo was a monumental moment, the significance of which was underlined by the American feminist, legal scholar and activist Catharine MacKinnon:

> The #MeToo movement is accomplishing what sexual harassment law to date has not. This mass mobilization against sexual abuse, through an unprecedented wave of speaking out in conventional and social media, is eroding the two biggest barriers to ending sexual harassment in law and in life: the disbelief and trivializing dehumanization of its victims.[7]

ME TOO – UK

#MeToo was always likely to cross the Atlantic. In February 2018 a group of British-based female actors, producers and writers announced the formation of the 'Time's Up' movement.[8] Not long after, a fund established by a number of prominent female actors, including Emma Watson, Keira Knightley and Jodie Whittaker, donated £1 million to a number of groups advocating for women who had been the victims of sexual

* Spacey was charged by the Crown Prosecution Service with four counts of sexual assault in May 2022. Following a trial at Southwark Crown Court, he was found not guilty on all charges in July 2023.

harassment and abuse.[9] Over the following years, a series of media reports highlighted systematic patterns of harassment and abuse in schools, the armed forces, universities and the police.[10] Yet until the duke of York agreed to be interviewed by Emily Maitlis for the BBC, the initial focus of the #MeToo movement in Britain was on Westminster politics.

On 29 October 2017 Mark Garnier, the Conservative MP for Wyre Forest and a parliamentary under-secretary, admitted calling his assistant 'sugar tits' and asking her to purchase sex toys for his wife but argued this did not constitute harassment.[11] The next day the political website Guido Fawkes published a list of thirty-plus Conservative MPs alongside allegations about their behaviour compiled by aides working with them. The names of the MPs themselves had been redacted. Shortly after, the journalist Julia Hartley-Brewer alleged that Michael Fallon, the secretary of state for defence, had repeatedly and inappropriately touched her knee during a dinner in 2002. The next day, on 1 November, Fallon resigned, telling journalists, in a presumably unintentional pastiche of Weinstein's statement to the *New York Times*, that 'the culture has changed over the years. What might have been acceptable 10, 15 years ago is clearly not acceptable now.'[12] The Labour MP Tom Blenkinsop and the former Olympic rower and Conservative Party candidate Alex Story both accused Chris Pincher, a Conservative Party whip, of making unwanted sexual advances towards them. Story described Pincher as a 'pound shop Weinstein'.[13] In December, Damian Green, the first secretary of state and minister for the Cabinet Office, was accused of sexual harassment by a Conservative Party activist and, separately, of viewing pornography on a work computer. After a Cabinet Office inquiry he resigned.

The Labour Party was also the subject of serious allegations. Bex Bailey, a Labour Party activist and member of the party's National Executive Committee, revealed she had been raped by someone who was more senior than her within the party when she was nineteen years old, and that when she 'summoned up the courage' to report the incident she had been told she might damage her career if she made a formal complaint.[14] Shortly after, Kelvin Hopkins, the Labour MP for Luton North, was suspended from the party because of sexual harassment allegations. Ivan Lewis, the MP for Bury South, was accused of sexually harassing a young party member at a Labour Party event. He apologized for any behaviour that was 'unwelcome or inappropriate in the circumstances and caused anyone to feel awkward' but was suspended.[15] It was during this period that the Scottish government was also notified of a number of sexual harassment complaints against Alex Salmond relating to the period when he was first minister (p. 327).

When the allegations against MPs first appeared, Theresa May stated that unwanted sexual behaviour was 'completely unacceptable' and wrote to the speaker of the House of Commons, John Bercow, calling for the establishment of a new grievance procedure to deal with complaints at Westminster. May later promised cross-party talks on the issue, but amidst a dispute with the Labour leadership about whether and to what extent trade union representation was the answer to the problem, these talks went nowhere and the political caravan moved on. The specific problem faced by MPs' researchers and assistants, that they were directly employed by an MP, quite possibly the MP they were being harassed by, and that they were working on short-term contracts which could easily be terminated, was left unaddressed. In July 2022 Channel 4 News reported that more than one in ten staff working for MPs said they had been sexually harassed, and that over 70 per cent thought that speaking out about sexual harassment or bullying would harm their careers.[16]

If there was a change of culture and practices amongst MPs after 2017 it was hard to spot. Chris Pincher resigned but was reappointed as deputy chief whip in February 2022, before resigning once again having been accused of sexually assaulting two men during an event at the Carlton Club a few months later (p. 445). In January 2022 the parliamentary commissioner for standards found the former speaker John Bercow guilty of a series of allegations of bullying behaviour.[17] In April 2022 the Conservative MP Neil Parish resigned having gone one better than Damian Green and watched pornography on his phone (inadvertently, he maintained) whilst sitting in the Chamber of the House of Commons. Not long after, another Conservative MP, Imran Ahmad Khan, resigned after being convicted of sexually assaulting a fifteen-year-old boy. Finally, in June 2023, David Warburton resigned as an MP a year after having been suspended by the Conservative Party in relation to allegations of taking drugs and making inappropriate sexual advances towards two women.[18] All of this made the issue of political trust seem kind of quaint. The bar was, it seemed, now set at the level of non-criminal behaviour.

A TENDENCY TO BE TOO HONOURABLE

Duke of York has not been the happiest of titled lineages. The first recipient, Edmund of Langley, did all right for himself and died of natural causes at the ripe old age of sixty-one in 1402. His son, Edward, the second duke of York, was killed at the Battle of Agincourt in 1415. Half a century later, Prince Richard of Shrewsbury, duke of York and second son of King Edward IV, disappeared from in the Tower of London along with his brother, Edward V, both presumed murdered on the orders, it has generally been assumed, of Richard III. In 1625 Charles Stuart, second son of James I and duke of York, was crowned Charles I. He was executed in 1649. The title was then bestowed on James Stuart, the second son of Charles I. He converted to Catholicism; resigned as lord high admiral rather than take an oath denying transubstantiation; and went into exile in Brussels before becoming king after his brother, Charles II, died in 1685. James II then ruled with Trussian levels of incompetence before eventually being deposed by William of Orange in the 'Glorious Revolution' of 1688. Frederick Augustus, the second son of George III, whose setbacks during the War of the Second Coalition were immortalized in the song 'The Grand Old Duke of York', resigned as commander-in-chief of the British army in 1809 after his mistress, Mary Anne Clarke, had apparently received bribes from officers in return for promises of rapid promotion (Frederick was judged not to have directly received bribes but did not come out of the affair particularly well).[19]

The dukedom was created for the eighth time for Andrew Windsor, the Queen's second son, in 1986 on the day he married Sarah Ferguson. In 1999 Andrew was introduced to Jeffrey Epstein, the investment banker and financier, by a mutual friend, Ghislaine Maxwell, the daughter of the former publisher and newspaper owner Robert Maxwell. In 2021, during Ghislaine Maxwell's trial for sex trafficking, a photograph was published of the three of them at the Queen's Balmoral residence shortly after they had met. In 2008 Epstein was convicted in a Florida court of soliciting a minor for prostitution and of soliciting a prostitute. He was eventually sentenced to thirteen months in jail, much of which time he spent on work-release programmes. In 2010, shortly after Epstein's release from prison, Andrew visited him at his New York apartment. In February 2011 the *Daily Mail* published a photograph, taken in March 2001, of Andrew with his arm around a young woman, Virginia Giuffre.[20] Giuffre had met Maxwell in 2000 when she had been working as a spa attendant at Donald Trump's Mar-a-Lago club. Maxwell had offered her a job working for Epstein before she was, in Giuffre's own words, 'passed round like a platter of fruit' to Epstein's associates.[21] When Andrew met her, she was seventeen years old. In April 2015 court documents became public which alleged Andrew had pressured Giuffre into having sex with him when they had met in 2001. Buckingham Palace steadfastly denied the allegations.

In 2016 Sam McAlister, a producer for BBC *Newsnight*, contacted Andrew to ask whether he would be prepared to be interviewed on television. The answer was no, but six months later the duke's aides got back in touch to say he might be interested but that the issue of Andrew's relationship with Epstein would be off-limits. McAlister walked away. In July 2019 Epstein was arrested again and a month later killed himself. At this point McAlister persuaded Amanda Thirsk, Andrew's private secretary, that his 'position of silence in the face of global scrutiny was untenable'.[22] A deal was struck for an interview, this time with no questions off-limits. The interview would be conducted by Emily Maitlis who had first presented *Newsnight* in 2006 and had become its lead anchor in 2018. It took place in Buckingham Palace on 14 November 2019. In an interview for the Full Disclosure podcast, James O'Brien subsequently asked Maitlis how she had felt at the end of the interview. She replied that she had spent a lot of the interview and the period after worrying about whether she had asked all the right questions. But when pushed by O'Brien on whether she knew 'what you'd got', she accepted that 'I knew what we had was pretty extraordinary'.[23]

The interview was broadcast on 16 November.[24] Andrew denied meeting Giuffre on 10 March 2001 because he had been at a Pizza Express in Woking. He added that her recollection of how much he had sweated when they were at Tramps nightclub was also false because, ever since serving in the Falklands War, where he had 'an overdose of adrenalin', it had been 'almost impossible for me to sweat'. Maitlis asked whether he regretted his relationship with Epstein. He said he did not because of 'the people that I met and the opportunities that I was given to learn either by him or because of him'. Asked why he had stayed with Epstein after his release from prison, Andrew said his apartment was a convenient place to stay and 'I felt it was the honourable and right thing to do and I admit fully that my judgement was probably coloured by my tendency to be too honourable.' Towards the end of the interview Maitlis asked him whether he had any sense of 'guilt, regret or shame' as a result of his friendship with Epstein. Andrew replied that he regretted how Epstein 'has quite obviously conducted himself in a manner unbecoming'. Maitlis replied: 'Unbecoming? He was a sex offender.' Andrew responded 'Yeah, I'm sorry, I'm being polite.'

The instant reaction to the interview was 'nuclear level bad'.[25] Within a few days, Andrew had announced that he planned to 'step back from public duties for the foreseeable future'.[26] In July 2020 Maxwell, who had gone into hiding, was arrested on multiple criminal charges related to the trafficking and sexual abuse of young women and girls. In December 2021 she was found guilty and sentenced to a maximum of sixty-five years. A few months before, Virginia Giuffre had sued Andrew in a Federal District Court in New York, accusing him of 'sexual assault and intentional infliction of emotional distress'. Andrew promised to co-operate fully. His lawyers then sought, unsuccessfully, to have the case dismissed. In January 2022, Buckingham Palace issued a statement saying that Andrew would face the lawsuit as a private citizen and that his military affiliations and Royal patronages had been returned to the Queen.[27] In February he agreed to settle the case and to pay £10 million to support victims of trafficking. This begged an obvious question – one asked by Emily Maitlis during an interview published in *Tatler* in 2022 – about why he had chosen to settle.[28]

Is it too simple to draw a straight line between Weinstein's downfall in October 2017 and the launch of the #MeToo movement and Andrew's disgrace two years later? There was, after all, nothing particularly new in the allegation that Giuffre had been trafficked by Epstein and Maxwell; that Andrew had met with Giuffre in London; or even that she had been pressured into having sex with him – any more than there was anything new in the *New York Times* allegation that Weinstein had harassed and abused women. As had been the case with the Windrush, Post Office and Weinstein scandals, the allegations against Andrew had been hiding in plain sight. Yet, in other ways, the line between #MeToo and Andrew is in fact reasonably clear. Andrew had only agreed to be interviewed at a point when the world had changed and saying nothing about his relationship with Epstein was no longer tenable. The world had changed because Epstein had been arrested again and had killed himself. But it had also changed because of #MeToo and a sense that behaviour which was intolerable should actually be publicly described as intolerable. Writing in the *Guardian* in August 2019, prior to the Maitlis interview but after Epstein's suicide, the columnist Marina Hyde chewed over the details of Andrew's friendship with Epstein and spoke of 'the kind of man – and we've all met them – who has a two-tier view of the female sex. There is a world for their daughters, hopefully insulated from men like their friend Jeffrey, and then there is another world for the girls who service their friend Jeffrey.'[29] #MeToo had pushed those worlds closer together.

CRIME

On several occasions earlier, I've cited the results of polls asking people what they consider to be the most important issues facing the country – immigration, the environment, Europe, and so on. Yet there is one issue that has, traditionally, come consistently close to topping these lists which I've barely mentioned so far: crime. The numbers here waxed and waned but between 2000 and 2007 around 30 per cent of people consistently mentioned crime when asked about the most important issues facing the country. That number fell to around 20 per cent at the time of the 2010 General Election and to 10 per cent by the 2015 General Election, before climbing again to 20 per cent in 2018.[30] In terms of party politics, 'tough on crime and tough on the causes of crime' was one of the issues and one of the soundbites which helped define New Labour's Third Way in the late 1990s. In 2006 David Cameron's 'hug a hoodie' speech signalled Conservative modernization (p. 74). Having earned the 'right to be heard', his 'broken Britain' campaign then hit Labour over the head with a half-brick of arguments about social disorder and spiralling crime. In the run-up to the EU referendum, Nigel Farage and the Leave.EU campaign linked European Union membership and the freedom of movement within it to crime and, specifically, a Romanian crime wave.[31] Finally, and in the 2019 General Election campaign, whenever he talked about anything other than getting Brexit done, Boris Johnson was usually talking about recruiting 20,000 new police officers to tackle crime.[32]

Most people are convinced not only that crime is an important issue, but that levels of crime are rising. In 2009 more than 80 per cent of people believed that crime had gone up 'in the past few years in the country as a whole'.[33] That number fell to around 60 per cent but there has never been a time when a majority of people thought crime was falling. Yet the evidence here is that people's perceptions are mistaken.* The National Crime Survey for England and Wales, the Scottish Crime and Justice Survey and the Northern Ireland Safe Community Survey provide the key sources of data here (the figures below relate to England and Wales, and those in the endnote to Scotland and Northern Ireland).[34] The number of domestic burglaries rose from 0.97 million a year in 1981 to a peak of around 2.4 million in 1993. Since then, that number has fallen steadily to 1.8 million in 1999, 0.9 million in 2010 and 0.7 million in 2019. The number of incidents of violent crime has also fallen from a peak of 4.4 million in 1995 to 1.8 million in 2010 and to 1.1 million in 2022. The number of homicides and the number of firearms offences have also nearly halved since the early 2000s. Given just how many other things have gone wrong in other areas of public policy these are noteworthy figures – even if, as is the case, crime rates in Britain are still higher than those across most of the rest of Western Europe.[35]

The standout exceptions to this generally positive story are sexual harassment and sexual crime. In 2014, three years prior to the launch of the #MeToo movement in America, Laura Bates published a book, *Everyday Sexism*, and launched an associated website, The Everyday Sexism Project, detailing women's everyday experiences of verbal abuse, intimidation, indecent exposure, sexual harassment, assault and rape.[36] When her book was published, there was almost no available data on the prevalence of sexual harassment. That has now changed. In 2020, in a first of its kind, a Government Equalities Office survey found that over 70 per cent of the British population, men and women, had experienced at least one form of sexual harassment in their lifetime and that over 40 per cent had been sexually harassed during the previous year: the most common experiences being unwelcome sexual jokes, staring or looks, and sexual comments.[37]

Bates's argument is that harassment is one part of a broader culture, a patriarchy, of crime up to and including sexual offences and murder.

* They are mistaken in relation to overall crime levels. This does not mean that people are necessarily wrong to think that crime is increasing in the area in which they live.

The available evidence suggests she is right. The total number of rapes recorded by police forces in England and Wales rose from 15,074 in 2010 to 59,921 in 2019. The total number of sexual offences rose from 53,006 to 164,308 over the same period.[38] To put these figures into context, only an estimated one in six women who are raped report that rape to the police for fear of embarrassment, fear that nothing will be done or fear of humiliation.[39] Meanwhile, the number of successful prosecutions for rape in England and Wales fell from 2,581 in 2014/15 to 1,439 in 2019/20.[40] In November 2020 a coalition of charities working with the victims of rape and sexual assault published a report concluding that 'rape and sexual abuse have been effectively decriminalised'. The Home Office's own figures, the report noted, suggest that there was only a 1 in 70 chance that an initial complaint of rape made to the police would even result in a charge, let alone a conviction.[41]

The crime which galvanized public attention to sexual violence against women in Britain came during the third national Covid lockdown in 2021. On the evening of 3 March Sarah Everard, a marketing executive for a digital media agency, was walking home from a friend's house in Brixton Hill, near Clapham Common, when she disappeared. The next morning her boyfriend, Josh Lowth, reported her missing and the case was escalated to the Specialist Crime Unit. On 9 March police arrested Wayne Couzens, a serving member of the Metropolitan Police's Parliamentary and Diplomatic Protection Command. The next day Sarah Everard's body was found in woodland near Ashford, Kent, close to a piece of land Couzens owned. He was charged with kidnapping and murder. In June 2021 he pleaded guilty to Everard's kidnapping and rape and in July to her murder. He was sentenced to life imprisonment with a whole life order in September 2021. It had now become apparent that Couzens, whose nickname when he had worked at the Civil Nuclear Constabulary had been 'the Rapist', had previously exposed himself on three occasions. Witnesses had recorded either partial or full details of vehicles he was driving each time but the police had failed to properly investigate the crimes.[42]

Everard's murder, and the fact her murderer was a serving police officer, was truly shocking. But as Bates has gone on to observe in *Fix the System, Not the Women*, it formed part of a more general pattern of femicide: one which has not always attracted as much media interest.[43] The day before Sarah Everard's disappearance, Samantha Heap was found dead at her house in Congleton in Cheshire. She had been murdered by her neighbour, David Mottram, who had tricked his way into her house after saying he had lost his keys and needed to use her phone to call a family member to get a spare key. The day after Sarah went missing, Geetika Goyal was found dying of stab wounds on a Leicester pavement. Her husband was later convicted of her murder. On the same day, Imogen Bohajczuk was found dead at a property in Oldham, her body so badly mutilated she had to be identified by dental records. In March 2023 the Labour MP Jess Phillips read in Parliament the names of women killed by men or where a man was the prime suspect during the previous twelve months.[44] It stretched to well over a hundred names.

MET TOO

On the evening of 13 March, only a few days after the police had arrested Couzens, a vigil was held for Sarah Everard on Clapham Common. The duchess of Cambridge attended and later revealed she had sent a personal letter to Sarah's family.[45] Most of those present left after a few hours. Some stayed and then refused to leave when asked to do so by Metropolitan Police officers. Shortly after, the police intervened to break up the crowd and disperse those present. Four people were arrested for public order offences and breaching Covid lockdown restrictions. The mayor of London, Sadiq Khan, directed Her Majesty's Inspectorate of Constabulary and Fire and Rescue Services to conduct a review of policing at the event. It found that the Metropolitan Police had acted justifiably given the risk of Covid transmission.[46] What was not clear, however, is why the police had decided to intervene in this case when one of their own officers had just been arrested for rape and murder and when, only a few weeks later, little apparent effort was made to intervene and break up rather larger public events when football fans, most of them male, gathered to celebrate Liverpool's and Rangers' football titles.

In October 2022 an interim report into the Metropolitan Police's internal misconduct system by the former victims' commissioner Louise Casey found that 'cases are taking too long to resolve' and that 'allegations are more likely to be dismissed than acted upon'.[47] In his reply, the new commissioner of the Met, Mark Rowley, who had replaced Cressida Dick after she had lost the confidence of the London mayor and resigned in February 2022, accepted 'our organisation is being undermined by corrupting behaviours that have gone unchallenged and been allowed to multiply'.[48] In January 2023 David Carrick, who was also serving as an armed police officer in the Parliamentary and Diplomatic Protection Service, pleaded guilty to multiple counts of rape and was sentenced to life imprisonment. It transpired that he had previously been investigated in relation to nine allegations of rape, domestic violence and harassment. In July 2021, four months after Sarah Everard's murder, Carrick had been placed on restricted duties after being arrested on suspicion of rape, but he had not been suspended.[49] Vera Baird, another former victims' commissioner, commented that 'the Metropolitan police seem incapable of not employing – and furthermore retaining – some quite evil people'.[50] Mark Rowley apologized and, in doing so, revealed that a new Domestic Abuse and Sexual Offences Unit he had established to consider allegations against serving officers was investigating more than eight hundred officers and that one in fifty of all serving officers had been taken off frontline duties as a result.[51] Casey's final report, published in March 2023, concluded that 'racism, misogyny and homophobia are present within the [Met's] organisational processes and systems' and that 'public consent is broken'.[52]

In 1997 a record number of 120 female MPs were elected, 101 of them representing the Labour Party. New Labour was committed to promoting greater gender equality and, to its credit, invested political time and effort into issues like childcare, flexible working, violence against women and pensions.[53] The gender pay gap, the difference between average hourly earnings (excluding overtime) of men and women as a proportion of men's average hourly earnings (again, excluding overtime) fell from nearly 27 per cent in 2000 to 20 per cent by 2010.[54] Yet it would be hard, looking back, to argue that New Labour showed itself ready to take real political risks on this issue. When it came to childcare, career breaks and promotion to the most senior positions in large public- and private-sector firms, New Labour opted, for the most part, for nudges and incremental progress rather than legislative sticks. By the early 2020s, the world looked very different. The gender pay gap had continued to fall, to around 15 per cent in 2020. Yet levels of sexual violence against women had risen and a key organization tasked with responding to and reversing that rise, the Metropolitan Police, had come to be seen as part of the problem.

31
Getting Brexit Done

THE ENDURANCE

Between 1982 and 1988 the Australian critic, writer and poet Clive James presented *Clive James on Television* on Sunday nights on London Weekend Television. The programme consisted of clips of odd or funny TV programmes from other countries, with James, who passed away in 2019, offering a sardonic commentary. Today, that kind of format feels tired. But in the 1980s it seemed original and became wildly popular, regularly attracting more than 10 million viewers. Insofar as *Clive James on Television* is remembered at all though, it is probably for its regular slot featuring the Japanese game show *Za Gaman, The Endurance*. Week after painful week, teams of contestants put themselves through trials of endurance with the weakest being gradually eliminated. In one episode, contestants were fed sheep's brains and tabasco sauce. In another, they were tied to a post and charged at by a (fake) bull. In Egypt, contestants were taken to the desert and made to do a headstand against a metal pyramid structure, wearing only their underwear, whilst heated sand was poured on them and they were burned with magnifying glasses. Later, on a freezing cold day in Holland, they were made to sit in a bath of ice cubes whilst, for some reason, eating frozen spaghetti.

Clive James's commentary on all of this does not stand up well. There is a basic undertone that foreigners are crazy and that the Japanese shout a lot. James recognized this. In the fifth volume of his memoirs, *The Blaze of Obscurity: The TV Years*, he talks about *Endurance* whilst adopting a tone of bemused detachment from it all. When a stringer in Tokyo first posted clips of the programme to Britain, James writes that it was 'like tasting an electric light socket'.[1] He accepts that, in broadcasting the clips, his team were constantly on the 'lip of an ethical precipice'. He nevertheless maintains that the programme was not racist. 'It was a question of culture, and what we were seeing was a cultural nightmare being turned into a playground before our eyes.' In the 1990s Paul Ross, the elder brother of Jonathan, hosted a British version of *Endurance* on Challenge, a TV channel owned and broadcast by Sky. Some of the character of *Endurance* was then picked up by and embedded within *I'm a Celebrity . . . Get Me Out of Here!* from 2002 onwards.

Between 2016 and 2020 the spirit of *Endurance* was on constant display in the negotiations with the European Union, which began once Theresa May's letter triggering Article 50 had arrived in Brussels via Eurostar. In the aftermath of the referendum results, but before the negotiations had begun, there was a widespread assumption that reaching a deal would be easy. Europe wanted to export things to Britain. Britain wanted to buy those things and export to Europe. A deal was in everyone's interest. The reality was a great deal more painful. Over the next couple of years, Theresa May had to endure a series of trials which, whilst not quite as innovative as those on *Endurance*, must nevertheless have felt endless.

£985.50

The immediate aftermath of the June 2016 referendum result was chaos. Civil servants had not done any planning for what would happen in the event of a Leave vote because David Cameron had forbidden them from doing so.[2] Cameron, who had repeatedly said he would not resign if Leave won, promptly resigned, quoting Enoch Powell's adage that 'all political lives end in failure'.[3] Nigel Farage resigned as leader of UKIP in early July, remarking that 'my political ambition has been achieved' (his replacement, Diane James, resigned shortly after).[4] Jeremy Corbyn argued that the government should immediately trigger Article 50 and in doing so provoked a reaction that soon led to mass resignations and a leadership challenge (p. 354).

Eventually, though, it began to settle down. Whilst the value of the pound slid by more than 10 per cent on foreign exchange markets, there was no immediate economic meltdown of the sort predicted by George

Osborne and the Treasury prior to the referendum. In mid-July, Theresa May was appointed prime minister having made it clear, during her leadership campaign, that 'there must be no attempts to remain inside the European Union, no attempts to rejoin it through the back door, and no second referendum'.[5] At the Conservative Party conference in October she announced that the government she led would, by the end of March 2017, trigger Article 50, kick-starting formal negotiations about the terms and conditions of Britain's exit from and future relationship with the European Union. She also seemed to signal, to the joy of the largest part of the Conservative Party activists present, that Brexit would mean an end to free movement of people and the legal authority of the European Court of Justice. Her self-imposed timetable hit a pothole in November 2016 when the High Court ruled that the government could not leave the European Union without Parliament having first voted for it, an outcome which led the *Daily Mail* to denounce the judges involved as 'enemies of the people'.[6] The government appealed to the Supreme Court but lost. This looked, initially, like a major setback for Theresa May, one which many Remainers hoped would pave the way for Parliament to vote against leaving or for a second referendum. Yet the enemies of the people ended up doing the government a favour. Having just about reconciled itself to what the court had done, May put before Parliament a wafer-thin Bill running to a dozen lines requiring 'Her Majesty's Government to notify the European Council by 31 March 2017 of the United Kingdom's intention to withdraw from the European Union'. This meant that the vote about Article 50 was not going to be about the terms of Britain's departure but the fact of the departure itself.

On 1 February 2017 498 MPs, including the majority of Labour MPs, voted in favour of Article 50. The SNP, the Liberal Democrats, the Social Democratic and Labour Party, Plaid Cymru, forty-seven dissident Labour MPs, the Green MP Caroline Lucas and one lone Conservative, Ken Clarke, voted against.[7] The government had an overwhelming majority of 384. On 29 March, with two days to spare, two civil servants, travelling via a Eurostar train to Brussels, delivered a letter to Donald Tusk, the president of the European Council, triggering Article 50. The two business premier tickets, it was later reported, cost £982.50 plus £3 in booking fees.[8]

THE DIVORCE TERMS

Plenty of senior Conservatives wanted to launch straight into negotiations about Britain's future economic and political relationship with the European Union once Article 50 had been triggered. The European Union disagreed. Before there could be any talks about the future, Britain first had to settle the terms and conditions of its exit. Britain snarled and growled and then gave way and on 19 June 2017 David Davis, the secretary of state for exiting the European Union, and Michel Barnier, the European Union's chief negotiator, met for the first time in Brussels. This was the moment when a populist, emotional, say-what-you-think-when-you-think-it Brexit disappeared behind closed doors and suddenly became quite complex and difficult (not least because, as it soon became clear, Davis had close to zero authority from 10 Downing Street to do any actual negotiating).*

There were three main issues to be decided on at this first stage: the rights of European Union citizens living in Britain and British citizens living in the European Union; financial liabilities; and Northern Ireland.[9] The first of these was settled relatively quickly. Europeans living in Britain would be allowed to stay and vice versa. The next issue, money, proved trickier. The European negotiating team had been encouraged to seek a tough deal with a view to discouraging any other country from leaving the European Union any time soon. 'There must be a threat, there must be a risk, and there must be a price for leaving the European Union', as the French president somewhat bluntly put it.[10] So Europe argued Britain had entered into all sorts of budgetary and pension commitments and needed to find £70 billion down the back of the sofa. Various Brexiteers, Boris Johnson included, suggested in response that Britain ought to offer the square root of nothing and walk away if need be.[11] Donald

* If you choose to believe Dominic Cummings – who, it is probably fair to say, has plenty of bad things to say about plenty of people – it probably did not help matters that Davis was 'as thick as mince'. Owen Bennett, 'David Davis is "thick as mince" says Vote Leave campaign chief Dominic Cummings', Huffington Post (17 July 2017). The more striking problem was that the British government did not enter the negotiations with any clear sense of what it wanted. Raoul Ruparel, an advisor to Davis, later recalled that at the beginning of the talks the government 'still didn't have a particularly clear policy on anything'. Meg Russell with Lisa James, *The Parliamentary Battle over Brexit* (Oxford, 2023), p. 127.

Trump, who was elected US president in November 2016, said Britain ought to sue the European Union for billions of dollars.[12] May told Davis to compromise and a figure of £35 billion was eventually agreed.

The third and toughest issue, and the one I have already discussed separately, was Northern Ireland (Chapter 29). The Irish government, backed by the other EU members, was adamant that a hard border between Northern Ireland and the Republic had to be avoided at all costs. Theresa May did not disagree but could not say what ought to happen instead. So the can got kicked down the road and in December 2017 negotiators published a joint report that repeated the promise to avoid a hard border and added to it a British 'commitment to preserving the integrity of its internal market and Northern Ireland's place within it'.[13] There were plenty of Conservative Party Brexiteers who looked at the terms of this deal and hated it, and they found eager allies in the Democratic Unionist Party, who thought May had conceded too much to the Irish government. Yet May called her critics' bluff and secured the support of her Cabinet, and on 15 December Donald Tusk announced sufficient progress had been made on the divorce terms and that second-stage discussions about Britain's future trade and political relationship could begin, whilst detailed negotiations over the precise text of the Withdrawal Agreement would continue.

DEAL OR NO DEAL

Given just how messy everything got over the next eighteen months, it is worth emphasizing that, at the start of this second stage, relatively little seemed to separate the British and European Union positions. The Europeans wanted to keep the European Single Market, that is, the legal commitment to the free and effectively borderless movement of goods, services, capital and people, whole. If Britain wanted a post-Brexit deal in which there was no freedom of movement of people, there could be no completely free movement of goods, services or capital either. But this did not mean that the European Union was against a zero-tariff free trade deal. What the European Union wanted instead was a set of assurances that there would be a 'level playing field' when it came to trade: that Britain would not walk out the door and then, for example, ramp up state aid to British companies who could then export to Europe more cheaply. It also wanted to avoid a 'no-deal' Brexit, where Britain exited and trade reverted to operating under World Trade Organization rules, meaning tariffs on imports and exports.

In a centralized winner-takes-all political system (even one in which, in this case, the winner was in a hugely precarious position following the 2017 General Election) Britain's position was set by the prime minister following consultation with her personal Brexit advisor, the civil servant Olly Robbins. Boris Johnson, now foreign secretary, was kept at arm's length. When he tried to arrange to meet with May, he was routinely told she was too busy.[14] The chancellor, Philip Hammond, was also sidelined. He later described May's habit of outlining Britain's Brexit stance in set-piece speeches without any consultation with the Cabinet as amounting to, effectively, a 'coup'.[15] So Britain's negotiating position was really just one person's position. Theresa May was clear, right from the start, that she wanted an end to the free movement of people, one leg of the European Single Market. Over time, it became clear that she also wanted Britain to exit the other legs, the free movement of goods, services and capital, for fear of otherwise remaining subject to the legal authority of the European Court of Justice, which enforced the Single Market rules. Britain did not, in other words – and contrary to the fear of many European leaders – want to 'have its cake and eat it'.[16]

In a speech in January 2017 delivered at Lancaster House, the neoclassical mansion near Buckingham Palace commissioned by Frederick Augustus, the 'Grand Old Duke of York', in 1825 and now managed by the Foreign Office, May said she wanted 'the freest possible trade in goods and services'. In order to achieve this, she added, she would be willing to 'take in elements of current Single Market arrangements'.[17] So Britain would leave the Single Market but agree to follow a tranche of Single Market rules. That was not a million miles away from the European position. To try and extract as good a deal as possible, May also warned in that Lancaster House speech that, as far as she was concerned, 'no deal is better than a bad deal'.[18] This threat scared the bejeezus out of Hammond and some other Cabinet ministers. But there is very little evidence that May was really prepared to drop the British economy off a cliff and go for a no-deal Brexit, and very little evidence the European Union thought she would do it either.

So, a deal was there to be done on a future trade relationship. The main problem was that, following the 2017 General Election, May lacked a parliamentary majority and was being pulled in different directions by different parts of her own party who, in return for their support, were demanding concessions which could be relied upon to inflame their opponents. The Conservative-supporting press focused their attention on 'Remoaners' within the Conservative Party, and there can be no doubt that a number of Conservative MPs favoured the 'softest' of Brexits and that some of them came to support a second referendum. But most of the Conservative Party opposition to the prime minister came from committed Eurosceptics within the European Research Group who were wary of a super-soft 'Brexit in Name Only'. In theory, May could have cut herself free from the hard core of her Conservative Party opponents by holding cross-party talks to see if a deal could have been struck around a soft Brexit (a point I return to later in this chapter). Prior to May's arrival in 10 Downing Street, Oliver Letwin, Cameron's chancellor of the Duchy of Lancaster and Euro-fixer, had been preparing for cross-party talks.[19] But May, an exceptionally tribal politician, was not much interested in talking to members of her own Cabinet, let alone to politicians in other political parties.[20]

In July 2018, following a punishingly long meeting at the prime minister's country retreat, Chequers, May just about got her Cabinet to agree to a deal to put to the European Union (albeit at the expense of the resignations of her Brexit secretary, David Davis, and foreign secretary Boris Johnson).[21] This was the Facilitated Customs Arrangement discussed in the chapter on Northern Ireland (p. 385). If this was a breakthrough though, it was a short-lived one. The European Union rejected May's Chequers deal out of hand at the European Union summit meeting in Salzburg in September. May fizzled and fumed and walked out of the room. She had hoped to have in place a final Withdrawal Agreement (the divorce terms) *and* a future trade and political deal signed, sealed and delivered by the time the Article 50 countdown had wound down to zero in March 2019. After the Salzburg snub, that looked increasingly unlikely to happen. With time running short and under intense pressure, May was forced back to the negotiating table.

The result was the Northern Ireland Protocol and the 'backstop' in which 'mainland' Britain would agree to follow a large part of the Single Market rule book and Northern Ireland would abide by even more of it, to avoid a hard Irish border. May argued that this would be a temporary arrangement until an agreement could be reached on a longer-term trade deal (presumably some version of the Plan A Facilitated Customs Agreement). But, as it eventually became clear, if no deal could be reached, Britain would remain within the backstop indefinitely. For hardline Brexiteers, this was a Grade I betrayal. However, on 14 November May just about got the Cabinet to endorse what she had agreed with the European Union, albeit at the political cost of the resignation of four ministers, including Dominic Raab, the new Brexit secretary who had replaced David Davis. The question now was whether Parliament would also toe the line.

PARLIAMENT SAYS NO

In Chapter 28 on the 2016 referendum, I noted that voters had all sorts of views on what Britain's relationship with the European Union should be (pp. 375–6). The same was true of MPs. There were some who nominally wanted to leave but who also wanted to remain within the Single Market for goods, people, capital and services, either by negotiating a special deal with the European Union or by joining the European Economic Area. There were some who were prepared to leave the Single Market but who wanted to remain within the European Union's Customs Union, which would have meant tariff-free and customs checks-free movement of goods in and out of the European Union but also accepting the Common External Tariff on goods imported from outside the European Union. There were some who wanted a 'Canada-style' free-trade deal for goods with the European Union, which would have left Britain free to strike its own trade deals and set its own tariffs with other countries. There were some who were prepared to accept extensive 'level playing field' standards to make such a trade deal possible. There were others who were not. There were some who were so annoyed by the European Union and so opposed to any restrictions upon trade that they genuinely wanted a no-deal Brexit and a completely fresh start. Whilst, right at the other end of the spectrum, there was a block of MPs who wanted, in some shape or form, a second referendum in the hope of blocking Brexit altogether.

For better or worse, the 2016 referendum took a whole range of possible opinions in terms of Britain's relationship with the European Union and required people to choose between staying or leaving. May's political instincts would have been to try and avoid asking Parliament what it thought altogether. Failing that, she would probably have tried to fix things so that MPs had a choice between her deal or Britain joining a political federation and everlasting union with the Democratic People's Republic of Korea. But she couldn't do this. MPs, led into battle by the former Conservative attorney general Dominic Grieve, had voted to be given a 'meaningful vote' on the Draft Withdrawal Agreement and the 'Backstop' within it.

There was still a centre ground here. If you had lined up every MP in a row from the most committed, 'leaving is utter madness', on the one side, to the most Eurosceptic 'leave at any cost', on the other, then the median position would probably have been a new free trade customs union with the European Union.[22] So if Brexit had worked like the British electoral system had worked in the 2000s, favouring the party, New Labour, which moved to and said it had moved to the centre ground, Parliament should, sooner or later, have coalesced around a not too hard, not too soft, just right Goldilocks Brexit which commanded majority support. However, this was not what happened. The divisions over Brexit were now running so deep that deals between the different camps proved elusive. Those who favoured a second referendum and Remaining believed in this cause so passionately that they were not prepared to vote for a softer Brexit in order to avoid a harder one. Those who favoured a harder Brexit than May had put on the table and thought that Britain risked getting trapped in the Backstop indefinitely, believed in the virtues of a hard Brexit so passionately they were not prepared to vote for a softer version in order to forestall the risk of Brexit simply not happening at all. Moreover, by the time they started voting, MPs were not just voting about Brexit. Labour MPs knew they were also voting to topple the prime minister and to boost Labour's electoral chances. Add to this the complete breakdown of party-political discipline within the Conservative Party and the result was chaos.

MPs rejected, once, twice, three times, the Draft Withdrawal Agreement: by the historic record-breaking margin of 432 to 202 votes on 15 January 2019; by 391 to 242 votes on 12 March; and, finally, by 344 to 286 votes on 29 March. If Parliament did not want the Draft Withdrawal Agreement, what did it want? In two sets of so-called 'indicative votes' on 27 March and on 1 April MPs were given the opportunity to vote for or against a whole set of Brexit-related options. On 1 April a majority of MPs came close to supporting the creation of a new customs union (273 votes in favour and 276 against, with 100 abstentions).[23] But no option commanded majority support and there was a lot of tactical voting. Tellingly, a vote on whether to hold a third round of indicative votes on 3 April was tied.[24] What MPs could agree on at this stage was the need to avoid a no-deal Brexit, taking that option off the table in a vote on 8 January 2019 and, once again, on 13 March.

Theresa May, meanwhile, kept herself busy. In December 2018 she survived a vote of no-confidence by Conservative MPs at the price of saying that she would stand down before the next election. In January 2019 she survived a vote of no-confidence in the House of Commons. On 20 March she broadcast to the nation. 'You are tired of the infighting. You are tired of the political games and arcane procedural rows. Tired of MPs talking about nothing else but Brexit.'[25] Replace 'you' with 'I am' and you can get a sense of her mood. But the idea that 'the people' were a unified block and that Parliament was standing in the way of their will was a nonsense. On 22 March the European Union granted Britain a temporary extension of Article 50 until something, anything, could be settled. In early April, May opened talks with Labour to explore whether some form of cross-party deal could be carved out (p. 361). On 17 May those talks collapsed having accomplished almost nothing. On 5 April she asked for, and eventually received, a second extension from the European Union on the *Za Gaman*-like condition that Britain contested the forthcoming European Parliament elections on 23 May. This was a car-crash moment for the government. Nigel Farage's new Brexit Party won 30 per cent of the vote. The unambiguously Pro-Remain parties – the Liberal Democrats (20%), the Greens (12%) and the SNP (38% of the vote in Scotland) – also did well. Labour, which was trying and failing to find a middle-ground position, got run over from both sides (14%). The Conservatives came fifth (9%). The following day Theresa May resigned.[26]

'GETTING BREXIT DONE'

Boris Johnson saw off nearly a dozen rivals to become Conservative Party leader on 23 July 2019. The following day he promised to 'come

out of the EU on October 31 . . . no ifs or buts'.[27] Publicly, Johnson then
went all Tony Montana from *Scarface*. He purged the Cabinet of anyone
who looked remotely soft on Brexit. All the members of his new Cabinet were required to agree in advance that there would be no further
Article 50 extension. He put no-deal back on the table as the only alternative to passing the Withdrawal Agreement. He withdrew the
Conservative whip from twenty-one Conservative MPs, including Ken
Clarke and the now former chancellor Philip Hammond, who voted
against a no-deal Brexit. In late August, he took a leaf out of King James
I's seventeenth-century playbook and prorogued Parliament in order to
stop MPs from causing any more mischief.* In doing so, Johnson was
not only goading his opposition and seemingly undermining the concept of parliamentary sovereignty, around whose defence the Brexit
campaign had mobilized, but was risking drawing the Queen, who had
approved the prorogation, into the front line of politics.[28]

Johnson's hardline approach initially looked like it had failed. The
day before Parliament was suspended, MPs voted to make a no-deal
Brexit illegal. On 24 September the Supreme Court ruled that the prorogation had been illegal on the grounds that it had 'the effect, of
frustrating or preventing, without reasonable justification, the power of
Parliament to carry out its constitutional functions as a legislature and
as the body responsible for the supervision of the executive'.[29] Behind
the scenes, however, Johnson met with the Irish taoiseach, Leo Varadkar, to get a deal. That new deal was a version of the old deal Theresa
May had rejected in early 2018. Northern Ireland would remain within
the European Single Market. Britain as a whole would leave the European Union's Customs Union and would be free to strike its own trade
deals with other countries. There would be no tariffs or quotas on trade
with the European Union but there would be customs checks and,
to ensure a 'level playing field', Britain would have to broadly adhere to

---

* James I of England (James VI of Scotland) had prorogued Parliament for eighteen months
in 1604/5 after being riled by its debates over Church reform and the statutory union of
England and Scotland. As far as James was concerned, 'nothing is heard [in Parliament] but
cries, shouts and confusion. I am surprised that my ancestors should ever have allowed such
an institution to come into existence.' Johnson may well have been thinking along the same
lines. But whereas the 1604 proroguing ended when the Gunpowder Plot was discovered,
Johnson's was undone by the courts. BBC News, 'From Civil War to the Glorious Revolution' (19 May 1998).

existing European Union rules on a range of issues, including state aid, competition policy and climate change.[30] There would be no Backstop. There would, however, be a customs border for goods going from mainland Britain to Northern Ireland. Finally, there would be a Northern Irish consent mechanism through the Assembly.

On 22 October 2019 Parliament approved the Withdrawal Agreement and Johnson's new deal by 329 votes to 299. But, if this was a triumph, it was a short-lived one because Parliament also voted to reject the government's timetable for the passage of the rest of the Withdrawal Agreement, arguing that it left insufficient time to effectively scrutinize the deal. With the clock running down on May's earlier Article 50 extension, and Parliament having also voted, hours before it had been prorogued back in August to rule out a no-deal Brexit, Johnson was now forced to do what he said he would never do and to seek yet another extension. This was a huge embarrassment. But it was a Pyrrhic victory for his critics because it allowed Johnson, with a deal now done, to argue that Parliament was blocking the will of the people and had 'outlived its usefulness' (very King James) and that the only way forward was a general election.[31] The Fixed Term Parliament Act passed by the Coalition meant Johnson needed the support of two-thirds of MPs to dissolve Parliament. Labour had initially refused to play ball. But with a no-deal Brexit off the table and Johnson embarrassed, the Liberal Democrats and the SNP decided that they fancied their chances in an early election and let it be known they would now support the government. On 29 October Parliament voted by 438 to 20 for an election on 12 December. The Liberal Democrats and the SNP abstained after their preferred day for the election to be held, 9 December, was rejected. Around half of the Parliamentary Labour Party either voted against an early election or abstained.

The 2019 General Election was decisive. Johnson, borrowing freely from May's 2017 General Election campaign agenda, and freed from the need to run any expenditure commitments past the Office for Budget Responsibility (as would have been the case with a budget statement prior to the dissolution of Parliament), waxed lyrical about 'levelling up', the recruitment of 20,000 more police officers, 40 new NHS hospitals, £14 billion extra for schools and more money for green energy and transport infrastructure. When it came to Brexit he spoke about his 'oven-ready' deal; how voters had been 'betrayed' by politicians (the lack of progress so far being 'orchestrated from Islington by politicians who sneer at your values and ignore your votes'); and, above all, by the need to just get Brexit done.[32] Asked whether his new deal would require there to be customs checks between Northern Ireland and the rest of Britain, Johnson said it absolutely would not and advised anyone given a customs form to simply 'throw it in the bin'.[33]

In total, anti-Brexit parties got 52 per cent of the vote on 12 December. However, vote was split between Labour, the Liberal Democrats, the Scottish National Party, Plaid Cymru and the Greens.[34] The Conservatives secured 43.6 per cent of the vote (their highest share since 1979), and 73 per cent of the votes of those who had voted to leave in 2016, for an overall majority of eighty seats.[35] In New Labour's 1997 landslide, social class had still mattered in electoral terms. Unskilled working-class voters (social classes D and E) were almost twice as likely to vote Labour as higher and intermediate managerial, administrative and professional (AB) voters.[36] In Johnson's 2019 landslide, those differences had practically disappeared. The Conservatives won 45 per cent support amongst AB voters and 41 per cent amongst DE voters.[37] Economic position did matter even if class did not. The Conservatives did particularly well amongst voters who regarded themselves as being economically secure.[38] Beyond that, the divisions which drove the 2019 General Election results were the same as those which had been exposed by the 2016 referendum: age (the Conservatives won 19% of the votes of those aged eighteen to twenty-four and 64% of those aged sixty-five or over); qualifications (the Conservatives won 59% of the vote of those with no qualifications and 34% of those with degrees); and geography (the Conservatives won just about everywhere other than in London, the larger Northern cities, Scotland and parts of Wales).[39]

On 20 December 2019 the new Parliament voted to approve the Withdrawal Agreement (the divorce proceedings) *and* a guillotine motion to curtail debate on it. The British and European Union negotiating teams then resumed their meetings about Britain's future trade relationship. Barnier and the Europeans thought this would involve little more than dotting i's and crossing t's on the pre-election deal. They were mistaken. At their first meeting, Britain's lead negotiator, David Frost, told Barnier that Johnson did not feel bound by that deal. 'We can accept some elements [of it] but not all.'[40] In particular, whilst Johnson was still happy enough with the basic idea of a zero-tariff trade deal he was not at all happy with some of the 'level playing field' reciprocal conditions being put around it. Johnson accused the European Union of acting in bad faith and said he would not hesitate to revert to a no-deal Brexit unless something changed. To add to the pressure, he also toyed with an Internal Market Bill, which would have made it legally impermissible to have customs checks between different parts of UKGBNI and so would render the Northern Ireland leg of his deal null and void as well.[41]

After their first meeting with Frost, some of the European Union negotiators must have been sorely tempted to simply book six months off work. But they stuck at it and started the negotiations again. Eventually, and after some last-minute wrangles about fishing quotas, a new deal was struck and on 30 December 2020 Parliament was recalled to approve the European Union (Future Relationship) Bill. In 2016 Johnson had promised leaving the European Union would result in 'frictionless' trade with the European Union.[42] That was not going to be the case. There were going to be no tariffs and no quotas for goods, but there would be customs checks and other non-tariff barriers between Northern Ireland and mainland Britain, and between mainland Britain and continental Europe. The new deal was an improvement on a no-deal Brexit – which would have meant tariffs between Britain and the European Union. But it had clear limits. It contained no provisions for mutual recognition of product testing; no process for recognizing equivalence of food safety measures; and no framework for the mutual recognition of professional qualifications.[43] These all constituted significant non-tariff barriers to trade. In a report published by the Resolution Foundation in 2022, several economists estimated that, cumulatively, these new barriers to trade were the equivalent of a 9 per cent increase in tariffs for manufacturing, and a 14 per cent increase for services.[44]

The difference in these two numbers is important. One specific problem with the terms of the new deal was that it was mostly about trade in goods. But it is services which, for the most part, constitute Britain's comparative economic advantage and account for nearly 50 per cent of all exports (twice the OECD average).[45] In particular, there was very little in the new deal to please the City of London. There were no 'passporting' arrangements whereby Financial Conduct Authority-approved British firms would be able to operate in the European Union (or vice versa). Instead, UK-based financial firms would need to offer services through EU-based entities.[46] Finance and banking, a mainstay of the British economy for decades, suddenly looked like it was facing a much tougher ride when it came to fending off Frankfurt, Paris and other wannabe global financial centres.[47]

Nevertheless, Brexit had been done. Nigel Farage declared that 'the war is over'.[48] What's more it had been done with a deal rather than a no-deal, and without Theresa May's Backstop. But it was a (very) hard kind of Brexit: much harder than the kind most Leavers had envisaged in 2016; much harder than the Brexit May had negotiated; and harder than Johnson's pre-election deal had envisaged. In an interview in July 2021 David Davis, the Brexit secretary who resigned over the Chequers deal, described it as 'marginally better than no deal'.[49] But, whatever the economic costs in terms of amorphous sounding (but real enough) non-tariff barriers to trade, Brexit was a political triumph. Johnson had broken the logjam. He had got Brexit done. He had won a thumping majority in a general election. He had united the Conservative Party (not a single Conservative MP voted against the Withdrawal Agreement on 20 December). If Johnson had decided to retire in December 2020, Conservative Party MPs would probably have stumped up the cash to build a statue of him and place it on the fourth plinth at Trafalgar Square.

PART SEVEN

Quartered

In the opening chapter I cited Zhou Enlai's 'too early to tell' comments about the 1789/1968 revolutions. This is the part of the book where the events I'm writing about, Covid-19, 'Partygate', deteriorating relations with Russia and China, and the cost-of-living crisis, are, by any measure, still very much unfolding. That made it very tempting to conclude the book in the relatively well-charted waters of 2019. Nevertheless, I think that doing so would have been a mistake because events since then, unfolding or not, have been so obviously tumultuous. There are other reasons to plough ahead. The first of these is simple entertainment. Some of the details of what happened during Partygate and Liz Truss's rapid rise and even more rapid fall are simply too tempting to resist. The second reason is more substantive. Many of the decisions taken since 2019 reveal significant flaws in the way in which decisions are taken in the British system: flaws that speak to some of the issues raised in previous chapters and which I will pursue in more detail in the Conclusion.

It is worth acknowledging that there are (at least) three important issues that, right now, it feels too soon to say a great deal about, and which get no more than a passing mention here. The release of Chat-GPT and, in March 2023, a petition signed by the tech entrepreneurs Elon Musk and Steve Wozniak requesting a pause to the further development of Artificial Intelligence (AI), pushed what had been a background policy issue onto the front pages.[1] Plenty of books and reports on AI have already been published.[2] What is not yet remotely clear is quite how much difference AI will make over the next decade; how, if at all, its development will be regulated; and whether, as the results of a survey published by the American Research Group suggest, there really is a 5 per cent chance of AI causing an 'extremely bad outcome' such as human extinction.[3] A second and very different issue is the future of the Monarchy following the death of Queen Elizabeth and the accession of Charles III. Charles has at various moments indicated that he will not 'meddle' in politics but will continue to publicly talk about issues he feels most passionately about.[4] Quite what will happen if Charles does interpret his role very differently to his mother is an interesting but difficult question to answer. Third, at the time of writing (the summer of 2023) there are some possible signs that climate change is reaching a 'tipping point': that average global temperatures are increasing at an accelerating rate; that the ice caps are melting at a faster rate; and that the Gulf Stream may be collapsing.[5] I discuss the politics and economics of climate change in Chapter 36, but if these early warning signs prove to be correct, what I say there may soon feel obviously inadequate.

I've selected the title *Quartered* for this part of the book for a number of reasons. First, it is meant to underline just how quickly we are now approaching the end of the first quarter of the twenty-first century and, as such, how recent history has a habit of becoming just history. By 2025 Tony Blair's arrival in Downing Street in 1997 as the youngest prime minister since the 2nd earl of Liverpool in 1812 will be further in the past than either Abba's triumph in the 1974 Eurovision Song Contest, the 1973 OPEC oil crisis or the Bloody Sunday shootings in Derry had been in May 1997. *Quartered* is also an allusion to hanging, drawing and quartering, the formal and distinctly grizzly British punishment for High Treason until 1870. The last few years have not been as painful as being hanged by the neck until nearly dead and then disemboweled. They have not been great either. The comedian Stewart Lee had a nice line he would deliver during the opening moments of a gig in his 2022 *Snowflake/Tornado* tour: 'It's nice to be here in the brief interlude between the pandemic and the start of nuclear war.' That has sometimes felt about right.

32
Covid

'YOU MUST STAY AT HOME'

June Almeida, a Scottish virologist who worked at St Thomas' Hospital Medical School, and David Tyrrell, who studied medicine at Sheffield before becoming director of the Common Cold Unit at Harnham Down in Wiltshire, discovered and named the first human coronavirus in the late 1960s.[1] Coronaviruses can cause cases of the common cold. They have also been responsible for outbreaks of Severe Acute Respiratory Syndrome (SARS) and Middle East Respiratory Syndrome (MERS). In December 2019 doctors in Wuhan, a city in the central belt of China with a population of over 10 million, began to report cases of patients suffering from acute breathing difficulties. The first death from this coronavirus, one which we now know was a variant of the SARS-CoV-1 virus which had caused a SARS outbreak in China in the early 2000s, was reported on 11 January 2020.[2] As the number of new cases continued to rise, the Chinese authorities finally confirmed, on 20 January 2020, that human transmission of SARS-CoV-2 was likely. Shortly after, Wuhan was locked down. By the end of that month there had been around 10,000 confirmed cases and over 200 deaths in and around Wuhan.

There are dozens of direct flights each day from Wuhan to other Asian countries and to the United States and Europe. By mid-December, traces of the virus had already been detected in sewage water in Northern Italy.[3] The first case in France was recorded on 27 December. In Britain the first meeting of the Scientific Advisory Group for Emergencies (SAGE) was held on 22 January. Yet the initial policy response to Covid was, to say the least, measured. On 30 January the chief medical officers for England, Wales, Scotland and Northern Ireland recommended raising the threat level from low to moderate. On 3 March, at a moment when Italian hospitals were being overwhelmed, the British government announced a Coronavirus Action Plan, focused on tracing the contacts of people with Covid-19, as it had been named, and slowing the spread of the disease.[4]

For a while, ministers and officials flirted with the idea of some sort of herd-immunity strategy. On 5 March Johnson told viewers of ITV's *This Morning* that one option was to 'take it [the virus] on the chin, take it all in one go and allow the disease ... to move through the population, without taking as many draconian measures'.[5] As late as 11 March, the government's chief scientific advisor, Patrick Vallance, told listeners to the BBC's *Today* programme that, since the majority of people catching Covid would get a mild illness, the government's aim was to 'build up some degree of herd immunity ... so that more people are immune to the disease and we reduce the transmission'.[6] At this stage, stronger social-distancing measures were also being considered, but at its meeting on 5 March SAGE agreed 'there is no evidence to suggest that banning very large gatherings would reduce transmission'.[7] A full lockdown was not even on the agenda.

The direction of travel then changed and changed quite suddenly. In terms of making policy decisions, the key figure in 10 Downing Street at this time was Johnson's chief advisor, the former director of Vote Leave Dominic Cummings. Cummings, rather like Gordon Brown before him, believed that, as a condition of accepting the job, he had made a deal with the prime minister and would be given personal control over domestic policy. Johnson would front the Downing Street operation but Cummings would call the shots.[8] Ben Warner, a data scientist working for Cummings, had a brother who worked at a senior level in the NHS who told Warner his managers were increasingly worried that the expected numbers of Covid-19 patients would overwhelm and might even break the NHS. Ben Warner told Cummings what his brother had said, and on the evening of 11 March Cummings texted the prime minister to suggest more needed to be done to slow the spread of the virus, and that it needed to be done quickly.[9] On 12 March Johnson held a press conference in which he said that whilst 'some people compare it [Covid] to seasonal flu ... alas, that is not right'.[10] If herd immunity had been close to emerging as the default strategy, everything, from this moment on, was about 'flattening the curve' and protecting the NHS.

The question was about how best to do this. One problem was that Johnson was initially reluctant to agree to much in the way of additional social-distancing measures, let alone a lockdown. He did say that people with Covid symptoms would be required to self-isolate. But that was about it.

Over the next couple of days, the sense grew that Covid was going to be bad – really bad – and that not enough was being done to slow its spread. On 16 March researchers at Imperial College London, led by Neil Ferguson, published a paper predicting over 500,000 Covid deaths in Britain in the event of an 'unmitigated epidemic'.[11] An unmitigated epidemic – one in which nobody did anything to stop the spread of the virus – was never likely. But 500,000 was obviously an eye-catching number. On 18 March schools were closed. By then, most universities had already switched to online learning. On the 19th the government unveiled new emergency powers allowing the police and public health and immigration officers to detain people suspected of having Covid-19 and to fine them £1,000 if they refused to be tested.[12] Finally, at 8.30 p.m. on Monday 23 March, to an estimated live television audience of over 27 million people, Johnson finally announced the first national lockdown:

> Without a huge national effort to halt the growth of this virus, there will come a moment when no health service in the world could possibly cope; because there won't be enough ventilators, enough intensive care beds, enough doctors and nurses ... so it's vital to slow the spread of the disease ... and that's why we have been asking people to stay at home during this pandemic. And though huge numbers are complying – and I thank you all – the time has now come for us all to do more. From this evening I must give the British people a very simple instruction – you must stay at home.[13]

FIFTEEN MONTHS

Lockdown was not about eliminating Covid. It was about slowing its spread, and, in that respect, it broadly worked. Recorded hospital admissions across Britain peaked at just under 3,000 a day in early April.[14] The seven-day rolling average of people across the United

Kingdom dying within twenty-eight days of being identified as having Covid-19 rose from 103 to 296 to a peak of 938 on 14 April.[15] It helped that people had *already* adjusted their behaviour and reduced their social contacts *before* the lockdown began. It also helped that the virus itself was less deadly than had initially been feared. In the early stages of the pandemic some reports published by the World Health Organization suggested a mortality rate amongst Covid-19 patients of 3.4 per cent.[16] That would have had catastrophic implications. In fact, the actual number in Britain turned out to be less than 1 per cent (although amongst those aged over seventy it was closer to 10 per cent and amongst those over eighty, 15 per cent).

Yet, if lockdown worked, it was, as Wellington once said of Waterloo, 'the nearest run thing you ever saw'. The seven 'Nightingale' hospitals, built in a hurry to provide extra NHS capacity, remained mostly empty. But more than 10 per cent of NHS staff were unable to work because of Covid for much of April. Ventilators were in desperately short supply and, at the peak of the first wave, they were being rationed on the basis of age and prior health.[17] In order to empty NHS beds, large numbers of elderly patients were discharged to care homes, where they subsequently caught Covid or unwittingly transmitted Covid to those care homes from the hospitals. Most routine consultations and operations were cancelled. Thousands of people caught Covid but decided against going to hospital, many of whom then died at home.

Once new case numbers started to fall in April, the 'what next' question became more acute. From the start it was obvious that easing restrictions would, sooner or later, result in an increase in the numbers of new cases. If the good news was that the mortality rate from Covid was lower than expected, the bad news was that it was highly transmissible, especially within *indoor* spaces. By late March it was also clear that people who had caught Covid could infect others before they themselves displayed any symptoms. By May 2020 it had also become apparent that a worryingly large number of people could infect others without *ever* showing any symptoms. So, what could be done to avoid an endless cycle of rising infections, lockdown, falling infections, looser lockdown and then rising infections? The long-term hope was for a vaccine. There was, however, a broad consensus in the spring of 2020 that it would be at least two years before an effective vaccine could be developed and made available. After all, no vaccine had yet been developed for either SARS or MERS. For a while, that left a policy of contact tracing and self-isolation as the best-case alternative. This was not, by any means, a crazy plan. Singapore, South Korea, Taiwan and, to a lesser but still significant extent, Germany and the Netherlands put in place effective national testing systems. It nevertheless took Britain a long time to even get close to falling short of those benchmarks. On 31 March, the health secretary, Matt Hancock, set a target of completing 100,000 tests a day by the end of April.[18] That target was just about met, but the NHS-branded contact-tracing phone app, in which great hopes had been invested, was abandoned in mid-June not long after its launch.[19]

When the summer arrived and case numbers were still (just about) falling, lockdown restrictions were gradually eased, more out of hope than any great expectation. Schools were reopened, followed by non-essential shops and, finally, in early July, pubs, restaurants and hairdressers. In August, to push the economic recovery along, the taxpayer-funded 'eat out to help out' scheme was launched. By that point, we now know, the number of new cases was once again rising. On 21 September SAGE recommended a 'package of interventions' to reverse an 'exponential rise in cases' and, in doing so, referred to the need for a 'circuit-breaker' lockdown.[20] Johnson was reluctant to do this. Eventually, he announced a 10 p.m. curfew on pubs and a complicated three-tier geographic system of social-distancing restrictions. None of this made any great difference to the underlying infection rate, which continued a steady upward trajectory. By the end of October, over 1,000 new patients were being admitted to hospital a day with Covid.[21] When the chief executive of NHS England, Simon Stevens, warned that the NHS risked being overwhelmed by new cases, déjà vu hit with a second national lockdown being declared on 5 November. To add to the strain, it became clear that a new and more lethal 'Kent' variant had now emerged and was spreading rapidly across the country. After a short amnesty for Christmas, during which it might have been appropriate for government ministers and members of SAGE to play a football match in the no man's land of their policy disagreements, the second lockdown morphed into a third national lockdown, which began on 5 January 2021. Hospital admissions subsequently peaked at just over 4,000 a day in mid-January and deaths at a little over 1,200 a week later.

The third national lockdown was bleak. The weather was foul and for those who were lucky enough to be safe and well, any novelty to be had from staying at home had worn off. There was, however, a sliver of hope. In November 2020, Pfizer and AstraZeneca had announced positive results from their vaccine trials. On 2 December the Medicine and Healthcare Products Regulatory Agency (MHRA) had approved the use of the Pfizer-BioNtech vaccine in patients. Six days later, at Coventry University Hospital, Margaret Keenan became the first person in the world outside a clinical trial to be vaccinated. On 30 December, the Oxford AstraZeneca vaccine was approved. In January, the Moderna vaccine was added to the approved list and by the end of February 2021 over 20 million people had been vaccinated. The sudden sense of progress was rocked, briefly, in late March by evidence that a small but statistically significant number of younger people receiving the Oxford AstraZeneca vaccine were dying from blood clots they had developed shortly after being vaccinated. On 7 April the MHRA announced that anyone under the age of thirty would be given a different vaccine.[22] Reports that up to a third of people would decline the opportunity to be vaccinated nevertheless proved to be wide of the mark. Amongst over seventies, the key at-risk group, take-up of the vaccine was over 90 per cent.[23]

With the numbers of people being vaccinated continuing to rise, lockdown was gradually lifted. Limited outdoor gatherings were allowed from late March. Pubs and restaurants were allowed to reopen outdoor areas for customer service from mid-April. International travel was permitted from mid-May. Fears about the spread of the 'Delta' variant, and an anxious wait to see whether it would prove vaccine-resistant, delayed the final lifting of lockdown restrictions in July. Yet whilst there was huge relief when that moment finally came, there was no sense of triumph. Johnson had accepted that 'we cannot simply eliminate Covid – we must learn to live with it'.[24] In late 2021 the emergence of the 'Omicron' variant resulted in the closure of borders and the introduction of a requirement to wear face coverings in shops and on public transport, together with an accelerated vaccine 'booster' programme. A lockdown was avoided, however, and Omicron did not, in the end, prove to be resistant to existing vaccines. By the end of March 2022, two years after the start of the first lockdown, over 187,000 people had died in Britain as a result.[25] By January 2023 around 2 million people were experiencing self-reported 'long Covid'.[26]

DIFFERENT CLASS

There was a moment, during the first wave of Covid-19 in the spring of 2020, when it felt nothing would ever be the same again. In his book *A Duty of Care*, published in March 2022, the historian Peter Hennessy talks about a world *before* and a world *after* Covid.[27] Yet the pandemic was, in other respects, simply a reminder of things we had forgotten or chosen to avoid publicly talking about – such as the failure of successive governments to do anything remotely meaningful to fix a social care system that, by 2020, was not just close to breaking but had already broken.

Covid was, in particular, an enduring reminder of the importance of social class not just as an indicator of voting behaviour, but as a determinant of life chances. In October 2021 two books were published which, in very different ways, spoke to the enduring issue of class in Britain. The first, *There is Nothing For You Here*, was written by Fiona Hill, a Harvard professor who had served on Donald Trump's National Security Council. The daughter of a miner and a midwife, she had grown up in Bishop Auckland, County Durham, before leaving Britain.[28] The second, *A Class Act*, was by the comedian Rob Beckett who went to Coopers School in Bromley before studying tourism management at Canterbury Christ Church University in Kent. Of the two books, Beckett's is the more moving because it is written by someone who still feels acutely working class even though he knows he is living in a middle-class world.

> As much as we laugh it off, there is a huge class divide in this country, between the varying types of privilege and lack of it. Confidence and opportunity are not a luck-of-the-draw commodity. They are normally inherited or maybe bought from previously successful generations through education and assets.[29]

Beckett talks about how his lack of confidence and an insecurity about money drove him to accept any comedy work going early in his career, and how the lockdown forced him to stop, giving him time to reflect. Yet Beckett also knows enough to know that his experience was a fortunate one. As the art critic J. J. Charlesworth put it on Twitter, there was no national lockdown. What there was instead was a world in which middle-class people stayed at home whilst working-class people brought them parcels.[30] If that sounds flippant, the Social Mobility Commission found that professionals had home-working rates more than 40 percentage points higher than that of any working-class occupation.[31]

In 2019, prior to the start of the pandemic, males living in the least deprived 10 per cent of areas in England could expect to live for almost a decade longer than those in the most deprived 10 per cent. For females, the difference was about eight years.[32] Covid then had a further and direct impact upon mortality rates in ways which were largely explicable in terms of social class. The most detailed analysis here was conducted by a team composed of researchers from the London School of Hygiene and Tropical Medicine, the Office for National Statistics and the University of Manchester and published in *BMJ Occupational and Environmental Medicine* in 2022.[33] Using public health data the authors calculate age-standardized mortality rates for Covid per 100,000 people, stratified by sex and occupations, for England between January and December 2020, using a sample comprising over 14 million people aged between forty and sixty-four who were employed in 2011 and completed the 2011 Census. It finds that the highest rates of death were amongst taxicab drivers and chauffeurs (120 per 100,000 for men), care workers and home carers (99 for men and 39 for women), elementary security occupations (94 and 40), bus and coach drivers (91 for men) and cleaners (84 and 40). It was lowest amongst teaching and educational professionals (26 and 11), corporate managers and directors (26 and 13) and science, research, engineering and technology professionals (21 and 10).*

DOING IT DIFFERENTLY

The two radical alternatives to lockdown would have been zero Covid and herd immunity. During the first national lockdown, in the spring of 2020, the idea of keeping restrictions in place until there were zero, or

---

* The obvious exception to the class-based rule was healthcare. Amongst health and social care associate professionals the age-standardized mortality rate was 59 for men and 20 for women. Amongst health professionals it was 54 and 19.

close to zero, new infections became, for a brief while, quite fashionable. China, it seemed, had shown that if you locked-down for long enough and hard enough then you could subsequently lift lockdown indefinitely.[34] Operating a zero-Covid policy in Britain would have been a tough ask. By early July 2020, three months after the start of the lockdown, there were still around six hundred new cases per day. That tough task was effectively made impossible by the failure to develop an efficient and capable test-and-trace system. Zero Covid was still a possible long-term policy goal, but eventually, as Covid numbers began to spike in China and the length and ferocity of its lockdowns escalated, its sheen gradually wore off.

At the other extreme, a strategy of letting Covid rip and achieving herd immunity also had its adherents, not least amongst those who regarded the lockdowns as constituting an intolerable breach of civil liberties and as being, in addition, economically suicidal.[35] In October 2020, forty-two Conservative MPs voted against the introduction of a 10 p.m. curfew for that reason. One of them, Sir Graham Brady, the chair of the Conservative Party's backbench 1922 Committee, suggested a month later that new lockdown measures then being introduced would, 'if they had been taken in any totalitarian country around the world', have been denounced 'as a form of evil'.[36] There were, however, clear objections to the herd-immunity strategy. For a start, lifting lockdown restrictions in the expectation of achieving herd immunity might well have come close to precipitating the collapse of the NHS, as patient numbers increased and the number of medical staff with the virus rose. It is also quite likely that many people would have simply chosen to self-isolate once the number of hospital admissions started to rise, making it harder to achieve herd immunity. This would also have meant the economy, far from being turbo-charged by the lifting of formal social-distancing restrictions, would – at least in a dramatic short term – have contracted further, unless the government had been prepared to order people to go to work and legally enforce this edict.

Moreover, it was also clear, from about the summer of 2020 onwards, that people could catch Covid multiple times. Whilst most people tended to get a much milder version of the virus the second or third time round, reinfection would also have made it much harder to achieve a level of herd immunity. Finally, a herd-immunity strategy would almost certainly have resulted in the additional deaths of tens or even hundreds of thousands of elderly and medically vulnerable people. Faced with this final objection, advocates tended to fall back on the employment of a 'shielding' strategy. The problem here was that shielding was, in practice, extremely difficult to achieve, as the number of deaths in care homes demonstrated. As for the libertarian argument, it was premised on the idea that people could and should be trusted to make their own informed decisions, having weighed the risks and benefits of social contact. At one level that made perfect sense. But one of the problems with Covid was that it was only possible to know what was happening – the number of new cases and, as a result, the risks of catching Covid – *after* the event, once data had been collected and collated. The risk argument also had a potentially long tail. I might weigh the risks and decide to go out. But the people I meet the next day, in the shops or at work, can't know what I have done and so can't easily make their own informed decisions.[37]

The libertarian argument was an intellectually coherent one. But it also leaked into conspiracy theories that Covid was being caused by the new 5G mobile phone network; that Covid had been developed by China as a bio-weapon; that it had been stolen from a Canadian virus research lab; that it had been engineered by the CIA; that it had been manufactured by Jewish capitalists in order to trigger a stock market collapse; that it was part of a population control scheme created by the Pirbright Institute in England and Bill Gates; that case numbers were being deliberately faked; that chloroquine was an effective treatment; that vaccines would, variously, cause infertility or modify your DNA and had killed millions of people.[38] For the most part, conspiracy theories were relatively peripheral to mainstream political debate. In 2023 Andrew Bridgen MP was suspended and eventually expelled from the Conservative Party for suggesting that the British Heart Foundation was engaged in a cover-up in relation to evidence that specific types of Covid vaccines increased inflammation of the arteries; that this was responsible for a huge number of deaths; and that one consultant he had spoken to had suggested 'this is the biggest crime against humanity since the Holocaust'.[39] But Britain (mostly), in this respect, still looked very different to the United States. There, and in the context of an existing culture war, attitudes towards Covid polarized across party-political lines, with Anthony Fauci, the director of the National Institute of Allergy and Infectious Diseases, becoming a particularly divisive figure.[40]

For that reason, Covid was seen by some people as offering an overdue antidote to populism and Brexit with, for example, the vice-chancellor of Oxford University, Louise Richardson, commenting in September 2021 that 'with the [Covid] vaccine, it seems like the public can't get enough of experts' and adding, for good measure, that she was embarrassed the 'enough of experts' Cabinet minister Michael Gove had graduated from Oxford.[41] There is, no doubt, an element of truth to this: in Britain, the pandemic did result in an increase in public trust in science.[42] Yet Richardson's comment also ignores not only the specific context in which Gove had made his 'enough of experts' comments (pp. 373–4), but the extent to which, when it came to, for example, the issue of climate change, the sceptic's objection was not necessarily to science per se but to the sense that expert scientists were out of touch and pursuing their own interests and agendas – and, as such, were not living up to the standards set by science (pp. 127–9). Finally, whilst, for the most part, conspiracy theories about Covid were relatively peripheral to public debate, subsequent polling has shown that around 10 per cent of people in the UK believed it was 'definitely true', and around 20 per cent 'probably true', that the Covid-19 pandemic was part of a global effort to force everyone to be vaccinated, and that the 'Great Reset' announced by the World Economic Forum during the pandemic was a conspiracy to impose a totalitarian world government.[43]

I'll come back to a third and more plausible policy alternative presently. For now, it is worth asking how effective the policy route taken, one of tightening and loosening lockdowns, proved to be. In certain respects, there is a good argument for concluding that the answer is reasonably so. The NHS did not collapse. The number of hospital admissions and deaths was curtailed far below the levels they would otherwise have been. The 'what next' question was ultimately answered by the arrival, ahead of schedule, of the vaccines. Yet it is also obvious that significant mistakes were made in the implementation of that policy. One of the most egregious was the discharge of untested NHS patients into care homes. Another was the failure to develop an effective contact-tracing system. The attempt to use new technology, rather than the systems that could have been provided by Apple and Google, wasted huge amounts of time and money. More fundamentally, the failure to develop and rigidly enforce a system of self-isolation of the sort employed in, for example, Singapore, or, alternatively, to put in place a financial support system that gave people sufficient financial incentive to self-isolate, made a significant difference; some existing evidence suggests that only around 20 per cent of people who had Covid symptoms fully complied with self-isolation requirements.[44]

Finally, and standing above everything else, was the timing of the lockdowns themselves. The logic of lockdown is that if you are going to do it, you are better doing it sooner rather than later. The longer you leave it, the more cases and hospital admissions there will be and the longer it will take to get back to the baseline you started at. The British government consistently acted as if the opposite were true. In June 2020 Neil Ferguson told MPs that locking down one week earlier in March would have halved a death toll which, at that point, stood at around 40,000 people.[45] The government had a partial excuse for its tardiness in March 2020. There was a huge amount of uncertainty about the virus and SAGE, for whatever reason, was not arguing – at least not in a robustly clear-cut fashion – the case for an immediate lockdown. The same was not true of the second Covid wave in the autumn of 2020. SAGE couldn't have been clearer about the need for a 'circuit-breaker'. According to Dominic Cummings, Johnson's response was 'I'm not doing it. It's politically impossible and lockdowns don't work.'[46]

In March 2011, whilst he was mayor of London, Johnson told journalists that one of his political heroes was Larry Vaughn, the fictional mayor of Amity Island in the film *Jaws*. 'He kept the beaches open . . . I don't know what happened to his political career thereafter, but he did the right thing.'[47] In the summer of 2020, with case numbers rising again, Johnson repeated this line, telling Cummings he wished he'd 'kept the beaches open' six months earlier and adding, on some accounts, 'I don't believe in any of this, it's all bullshit. I wish I'd been the mayor in Jaws and kept the beaches open.'[48] Yet this is a strange reading of the movie in question. The viewer has the great advantage of knowing from the very start of *Jaws* that there is a Great White Shark off Amity. It is, nevertheless, just about possible to sympathize with Vaughn's view that the shark's first victim, Chrissie Watkins, had been killed as the result of a boating accident. When, shortly after, a young boy is killed in full view of a crowded beach it is blindingly clear Vaughn had made the wrong call. Refusing to call a second lockdown in September 2020 was like saying the boy had swallowed too much sea water.

There are various sources of comparative data on the number of deaths caused by Covid. One measure has been compiled by the Johns

Hopkins Coronavirus Research Center and tracks the number of deaths from Covid per 100,000 of the population through until October 2023.[49] It reports a mortality rate in Britain of 325 per 100,000. The equivalent figures for other G7 economies are 58 for Japan; 135 for Canada; 203 for Germany; 255 for France; 311 for Italy; and 341 for the United States (and 66 for Korea and 29 for Singapore, two countries which, along with Japan, introduced effective test-and-trace systems at the start of the pandemic). So, on this measure, Britain's Covid performance was a notably poor one. The same applies to Britain's economic performance. Using World Bank figures, the world economy shrank by 3.1 percentage points in 2020.[50] In the United States it fell by 2.8 points; in Germany by 3.8 points; in Japan by 4.3 points; in Canada by 5.1 points; in France 7.5 points; in Italy by 9 points; and in Britain by 10.4 points. Moreover, as we will see later, the British economy was also the slowest to recover to its pre-pandemic baseline (p. 478). Returning to the mortality-rate figures, there is no single factor which can explain why Britain's numbers were so high. Prior relatively low levels of health mattered, as did associated high levels of obesity.[51] Yet slow lockdowns were also, without doubt, an important factor.

There was, however, a viable alternative strategy to tackling the pandemic. In *The Year the World Went Mad*, a book whose title does close to 0 per cent justice to the subtlety of the author's argument, Mark Woolhouse, a professor of infectious disease epidemiology at the University of Edinburgh and a member of one of the SAGE subcommittees and of the C19 Advisory Group for the Scottish government, argues that Britain became way too dependent upon lockdowns as a policy tool.[52] Woolhouse argues not only that the economic and social costs of lockdowns were immense, but that there was a consistent failure to undertake a thorough cost–benefit analysis of the merits of lockdown versus a balanced programme of other interventions, including social-distancing measures and ongoing restrictions on known high-risk venues and activities such as nightclubs, indoor concerts and crowded pubs. Sweden, he suggests, offers the clear example of how a more limited but carefully targeted policy might have worked. It maintained clear social-distancing requirements and backed this with a test-and-trace system, but kept schools open and avoided any lockdowns. Using the same Johns Hopkins and World Bank figures, its excess mortality was 235 per 100,000 (well below Britain's), whilst its economy shrank by just 2.2 per cent in 2020.

Woolhouse is not arguing that the beaches should have been kept open. His contention is, rather, that by thinking almost exclusively in terms of lockdown or not lockdown in the first place, Britain ended up choosing between two unpalatable and extreme policy alternatives and did so without consistently considering and weighing-up the possible long-term social costs of lockdown. As time has passed, these costs have become more apparent. Despite the operation of the furlough scheme to protect jobs between 1 March 2020 and 30 September 2021, around 400,000 people were made redundant during the first three months of the pandemic. Disproportionately, those people were the youngest and oldest workers, low-paid workers, disabled people and people from minority ethnic groups.[53] Some of those who were furloughed enjoyed having more time for themselves and eventually decided against returning to work. But for many furlough was a profoundly lonely and alienating experience: one associated with higher levels of self-reported poor mental health.[54] We can now also see that lockdown not only directly impacted pupils' learning at the time, but that this loss of learning has not been reversed and has had the largest impact on children from disadvantaged backgrounds.[55] Finally, it is now clear that lockdown has had a significant impact on school attendance levels. In 2017/18, just over 11 per cent of pupils at state schools were absent for ten or more half-days over the course of the school year. By 2021/2 that had already risen to over 23 per cent.[56] Woolhouse's argument, when put alongside some of the data we now have on the social costs of lockdown, is compelling. Yet the kind of policies Woolhouse describes would have required some deft decision-making: loosening and tightening policies at the margins in response to the latest data and, as he accepts, escalating to a lockdown if needed. It is hard to conclude that, in the place it mattered most, 10 Downing Street, Britain had that kind of leadership on offer.

£271 BILLION AND COUNTING

Covid-19 was, as Johnson said in March 2020, 'the worst public health crisis for a generation'.[57] But it was also an economic calamity. Between 14 February 2020 and 23 March 2020, as the pandemic unfolded, the market value of the US Dow Jones stock market index fell by 43 per cent. That was bad. What made it worse was the evidence that investors were losing confidence in and were selling US Treasury Bonds at a loss, in order to buy gold or hoard US dollars.[58] This was something new. In September 2008, when many of America's largest banks were imploding, Treasury Bonds were still considered to be as safe as houses (or, at least, non-subprime-financed houses). In 2020 this was no longer the case. Investors seemed to be losing confidence in the long-term solvency of the US government. At which point, the Federal Reserve stepped in and reran its 2008 playbook: cutting interest rates to zero and announcing a plan to buy $500 billion in US Treasuries and $200 billion in mortgage-backed securities and to keep doing this for as long as it took to start to restore market confidence. Something similar happened in Britain. The stock exchange crashed, and markets showed signs of losing confidence in Treasury Gilts. The Bank of England responded by cutting interest rates to 0.1 per cent whilst announcing that it would be buying an initial £200 billion in government debt on the secondary market from other financial institutions.[59]

Monetary and financial policy was supported by changes in fiscal policy. On 27 March President Trump approved and signed into law the Coronavirus Aid, Relief and Economic Security Act: a $2.2 trillion stimulus package worth around 10 per cent of the country's GDP. In Britain, the Keynesian lifejacket was donned by the chancellor, Rishi Sunak. Sunak was a fiscal hawk who later argued with Johnson over the prime minister's ambitions to raise public spending and cut taxes. But in March 2020 Sunak nevertheless found himself assuring MPs that 'now is not a time for ideology and orthodoxy'.[60] He was not joking. Over the next eighteen months £70bn was invested in the Coronavirus Job Retention (furlough) Scheme; £28bn on the Self-Employment Income Support Scheme; nearly £9bn on an 'uplift' to Universal Credit and Working Tax Credits; £12bn on the Small Business Grant Fund; £900m on the 'Eat Out to Help Out' scheme; and £285m on the Test and Trace Payment Support Scheme.[61] VAT was also cut at a cost of around £8 billion.[62] Largely as a result of additional NHS procurement and the development of the national test-and-trace scheme, overall public health expenditure, adjusted for inflation, rose from £173 billion to £218 billion in the space of a year.[63] Finally, and on top of all of this, around £100 billion was also made available in various kinds of business loans.

Britain did not become a socialist state in 2020. Public money was being used to keep private-sector jobs and save capitalist businesses rather than to replace them. Yet the frontiers of the state were, once again, being rolled forward. In 2019 total managed public expenditure was the equivalent of around 39 per cent of GDP. In 2020/21 it rose to over 51 per cent.[64] In 2009 and 2010 the government borrowed a total of something like £280 billion to stave off a full-blown depression. That was meant to be a short-term measure. But by 2019 it was still borrowing £44 billion a year. In 2020, to pay for all that it was doing, it borrowed a cool £313 billion.[65] They key to all of this was more quantitative easing. The Bank of England went into the market to buy Treasury Gilts and then, to help balance demand and supply, bought some more. The Bank of England's balance sheet showed its total loans to the Asset Purchase Facility (which did its actual buying and selling on the secondary market) grew from £444 billion in March 2020 to £840 billion in June 2021.[66] The Bank of England and its governor, Andrew Bailey, argued that it was doing all of this in order to preserve financial stability rather than directly to finance government debt.[67] This was a moot point. True, the Bank of England was not buying Gilts directly from the Treasury. But, to protect financial stability, the Bank found itself in a position where it was buying government debt, which meant that the government, knowing that the Bank of England was doing this, could keep borrowing money. The question of whether (and when) there would be a price to pay for this is one of the subjects of the final chapter of this Part.

33

From Trust to Truss

A HUMAN SHIELD

Boris Johnson did not cover himself in Churchillian glory during the opening salvos of the Covid pandemic. When COBRA, the Civil Contingencies Committee, began meeting to discuss what should be done, Johnson skipped its first five meetings.[1] According to Dominic Cummings, his one-time chief advisor later turned nemesis, Johnson spent most of February 2020 'dealing with a combination of divorce, his current girlfriend wanting to make announcements about their relationship, an ex-girlfriend running around the media, financial problems exacerbated by the flat renovation, his book on Shakespeare, and other nonsense, because obviously he never took the whole thing seriously'.[2] On 3 March, with the infection rate rising, he told reporters he had met Covid-19 patients in hospital. 'I shook hands with everybody, you'll be pleased to know.' SAGE had advised against shaking hands that morning.[3] On 20 March, eight days after he had told a press conference Covid posed 'the worst public health crisis for a generation', he bunked-off another COBRA meeting.[4]

On Thursday 26 March, three days after announcing the first national lockdown and a few hours after meeting with the Queen, Johnson stood outside 10 Downing Street to participate in the first 'clap for our carers'. A few hours later he tested positive for Covid (as did the health secretary Matt Hancock and the chief medical officer Chris Witty at around the same time). He went into self-isolation. A week later, his condition deteriorated. On the late afternoon of Sunday 5 April, he was driven to St Thomas' hospital and admitted to a private room and given oxygen. The next day Johnson was transferred to critical care. But although he was seriously ill, he did not deteriorate further and was not put on a ventilator. On the Thursday he was transferred back to a general ward. He recovered and was discharged on Easter Sunday, 12 April. That evening, he recorded a video message expressing gratitude to the nursing team who had cared for him, whilst thanking the rest of the country for the sacrifices 'you have made and are making'.[5]

It was reported afterwards that, whilst recuperating, Johnson, in conversation, had taken to quoting the Roman statesman and philosopher Cicero's line *salus populi suprema lex esto*, 'the health of the people is the supreme law'.[6] The implication was that Johnson, a natural libertarian who, according to one of his biographers, Sonia Purnell, thought 'illness is for weak people', had been converted to the lockdown cause.[7] That, as we have already seen, was not actually the case. *Salus populi suprema lex esto* has a bit of a history. In the early 1600s James I took to citing it in support of the principle of Royal Absolutism and, in particular, of the right of the king to raise new taxes without the consent of Parliament if he believed that the security of the nation was threatened. In this context, the idea that the health of the people is the supreme law was contrasted with *Salus Populi*, the idea sovereignty resided in and with the people as represented by and through Parliament.[8] Johnson, fresh from his 2019 General Election triumph, was, it may be thought, signalling an intention to do things his way.

THE BAT SIGNAL

In an earlier chapter on the MPs' expenses scandal, I suggested that political mistrust can be associated with higher levels of electoral volatility and a lower level of willingness to comply with policies requiring some measure of personal sacrifice (pp. 258–9). Trust was, obviously, an acute issue in March 2020. People had plenty of entirely selfish reasons to change their behaviour and comply with lockdown restrictions. Doing so would reduce their own chances of infection. Yet, in a situation in which it was already clear the risks of serious illness were going to be highest for the elderly and those with prior medical conditions, the government wanted to emphasize that people owed it to their local communities and to the NHS and its staff to stay at home, regardless of whether, left to their own devices, they would have done so.

The problem was that overall levels of trust in politicians, prior to the start of the pandemic, were vanishingly low. After the debacle of the MPs' expenses, overall levels of trust in politicians to tell the truth and to be guided by the national interest recovered somewhat with the formation of the Coalition in 2010. Yet the revelation contained within the 'Panama Papers' (p. 373) that David Cameron had profited from an offshore investment fund established by his father, followed by the long post-Referendum Brexit breakdown, reduced that still-fragile trust. By 2019 only 14 per cent of people trusted politicians to tell the truth, and only 15 per cent trusted the government to place the needs of the nation above the interests of their own party 'just about always' or 'most of the time'.[9]

There is some suggestive evidence that countries with higher levels of trust achieved higher levels of compliance with Covid restrictions. Drawing on European Social Survey data, Olivier Bargain and Ulugbek Aminjonov found that the sharpest reductions in mobility following the imposition of a national lockdown occurred in countries with the highest levels of political trust.[10] Yet the bigger and unexpected story here is not about the relationship between *prior* levels of trust and compliance but, rather, about the extent to which, at the start of the crisis, overall levels of public trust surged, as if being summoned by a Bat Signal placed on the top of a building in Whitehall, and how that surge sustained lockdown compliance.

In December 2019, shortly after his election victory, polls showed that only around 28 per cent of people said they trusted Johnson. By the end of March 2020, after a month in which he had skipped meetings and delayed the start of lockdown, the number trusting him had risen to 50 per cent.[11] Shortly after he had been released from hospital, Johnson's *approval* ratings climbed towards 70 per cent.[12] Britain was not the only country in which overall levels of trust rose as a result of a 'rally around the flag' effect.[13] During the spring of 2020 the approval ratings of Chancellor Merkel, presidents Trump and Macron and prime ministers Trudeau in Canada and Morrison in Australia also climbed. Yet in Britain levels of trust rose more than in any other country. This might in part have been because levels of trust started from a lower base. But there is another side to this story. According to a former advisor who had worked with Johnson when he was mayor of London, Guto Harri, Johnson's hospitalization served not, as many might have expected, to underline the mistakes he had previously made, but, rather, to turn him, in his own moment of sickness and then recovery, into a symbol of the nation.[14]

Resurgent levels of trust sustained high levels of compliance during the early stages of the pandemic. YouGov found that the number of people who said they were avoiding crowded places was still over 70 per cent by early May 2020.[15] We know people don't always answer survey questions wholly accurately. However, in an online paper published at the end of May 2020, a team of researchers at Imperial College used anonymized and aggregated mobile phone data to calculate that, by the end of March 2020, the number of journeys people were making had fallen to around 40 per cent of the pre-pandemic level on workdays and just 15 per cent of the pre-pandemic baseline levels at weekends, and there was no significant tailing-off in these numbers in April or early May.[16]

Compliance was not perfect. During the first two months of the national lockdown the England footballers Jack Grealish and Kyle Walker (twice), the epidemiologist Neil Ferguson and the Scottish chief medical officer, Catherine Calderwood, were publicly busted for apparently flouting lockdown restrictions. Newspapers carried stories of people driving hundreds of miles to buy groceries, and the National Police Chiefs' Council revealed in mid-April that over a thousand fines had been issued by local police forces in England and Wales in relation to breaches of lockdown restrictions.[17] Yet, to an extent which might have seemed unlikely when the pandemic began, overall levels of compliance with lockdown were remarkably high.[18]

SHOULD HAVE GONE TO SPECSAVERS

On Friday, 22 May 2020, the *Guardian* and the *Daily Mirror* reported that a neighbour had seen Dominic Cummings in the driveway of his parents' farmhouse in County Durham towards the end of March. The neighbour, it transpired, had been alerted to his presence by the sound of Abba's 'Dancing Queen' being played.[19] This immediately raised the question of what Cummings was doing in Durham when he worked in London and there was a national lockdown. Cummings, who had acquired a measure not just of political fame but of actual fame when Benedict Cumberbatch was cast to play him in a TV dramatization of the Brexit referendum, was, to put it mildly, a Marmite figure. There were plenty of people, plenty of whom were in the Conservative Party, who were more than happy not to give him the benefit of the doubt.

The following day, Robin Lees, a retired Chemistry teacher, rang a newspaper to say he had seen Cummings at Barnard Castle on Easter Sunday, 12 April, the day Johnson had been discharged from hospital. It was for this reason that, two days later, Cummings found himself addressing a socially distanced press conference in the garden at 10 Downing Street.[20] Looking more like Phil Collins' older brother than Benedict Cumberbatch, Cummings confirmed he and his wife had driven to Durham on 27 March at a point when she had fallen ill, and that they had self-isolated in a cottage on his parents' farm. He added he had also developed Covid symptoms during this time. Cummings argued he had acted entirely in accordance with the lockdown regulations in driving to Durham, because he and his wife needed to ensure that his parents could look after their child if they both became ill.[21] He then described how, on Easter Sunday, they had contemplated returning to London:

> My wife was very worried, particularly given my eyesight seemed to have been affected by the disease. She didn't want to risk a nearly 300-mile drive with our child, given how ill I had been. We agreed that we should go for a short drive to see if I could drive safely. We drove for roughly half an hour and ended up on the outskirts of Barnard Castle town ... We parked by a river ... I felt a bit sick. We walked about 10 to 15 metres from the car to the river bank nearby. We sat there for about 15 minutes. We had no interactions with anybody. I felt better. We returned to the car.

Cummings offered a robustly aggressive defence of his actions and did not wilt under questioning. Yet he never really explained why he had decided to go for a test drive with the rest of his family in the car or why they had chosen to drive to a local beauty spot. Neither did he mention that 12 April happened to be his wife's birthday. On 28 May the Durham Constabulary released a statement saying that whilst Cummings might have committed a minor breach of lockdown regulations in driving to Barnard Castle, it did not plan to do anything about it because it had a general rule of not taking retrospective action.[22]

Cummings survived but his relationship with Johnson was already deteriorating. Johnson was tiring of Cummings' obvious contempt for him and, egged on by his new wife, Carrie, kept intervening on policy matters which Cummings believed he ought to be in sole charge of. Carrie, to complete the *Dynasty* saga, then sought to undermine Cummings by placing her own allies into key roles. Eventually, in mid-November 2020, following the ousting of his ally Lee Cain as Downing Street's director of communications, Cummings decided he had had enough and, displaying both pride and prejudice, walked away.[23] Long before that happened, graffiti on a sign on the A66 directing visitors to Barnard Castle read FREE EYE TESTS HERE.

Two studies, one published in the *Lancet* in August 2020 and another in Nature's *Humanities and Social Science Communications* in July 2021, used survey data to show there was a significant rise in levels of mistrust in the government and its handling of the Covid crisis in the immediate aftermath of Cummings' misadventures.[24] The Nature study found that the proportion of people expressing mistrust in the government nearly doubled, from 37 per cent in mid-May to 66 per cent in the days immediately following Cummings' press conference. The *Lancet* study showed that this effect was quite localized. It was levels of mistrust in the British government which spiked at this time. There was no equivalent increase in the mistrust in either the Scottish or Welsh devolved governments or the health service more generally. There is some evidence that levels of compliance with lockdown restrictions had already started to fray from around the middle of May onwards. YouGov, for example, found that the number of people reporting that they were avoiding crowded places had fallen from 80 per cent in the middle of April to 70 per cent by the middle of May. That tail-off in compliance accelerated in June.[25] To what extent was this due to a 'Cummings effect'? One academic study, drawing on data running through until early June 2020, found that there was already a level of cynicism about the degree to which 'people can bend the rules when they need to' and that this increased following Cummings' press conference. It also found that this kind of cynicism was linked to lower levels of social-distancing compliance. On the other hand, the same study found that people who were most angry about Cummings' actions said they were *more* likely to comply with lockdown restrictions as a result.[26] On balance, it feels reasonable to suggest that Cummings undermined the lockdown he had pressed for.

BJORN AGAIN

On 1 December 2021, when Cummings was long gone but new Omicron-related lockdown restrictions were being debated in Parliament, the *Daily Mirror* reported that a series of 'gatherings' had been held in Downing Street before Christmas 2020. Over the next few months, the *Guardian*, the *Independent*, ITV and the *Daily Telegraph* published a deluge of increasingly lavish stories about who had drunk what with whom and when in Downing Street over the course of the pandemic. Highlights included a drinks party in the garden of 10 Downing Street on 20 May 2020 for which Martin Reynolds, Johnson's principal private secretary, had issued a 'bring your own booze!' invitation; a surprise birthday party held for Johnson on 19 June at which a cake covered in a Union Jack had been served; a video recording of a mock press conference in December 2020 in which the newly installed Downing Street press secretary, Allegra Stratton, joked about how she would respond to questions about whether there had been parties in Downing Street; a party, at which a child's swing had been broken, on 16 April 2021, the day before Prince Philip's funeral and for which the Queen sat alone; assorted 'Wine Time Friday' and leaving events, at one of which, the one for Lee Cain, Johnson had joked about this being 'the most unsocially distanced party in the UK right now'; and an Abba party held in Johnson's flat on the evening of Cummings' resignation, at which Carrie Johnson, who seemed to dislike Cummings as much as he seemed to dislike her, reportedly played Abba's 'The Winner Takes It All' at full volume.[27] Benny Andersson who, along with Björn Ulvaeus, Anni-Frid Lyngstad and Agnetha Fält-skog, was reforming Abba in a virtual reality format at the time, released a statement to the press: 'You can't call it an Abba Party. It's a Johnson Party where they play Abba.'[28] Andersson and Ulvaeus had written 'The Winner Takes It All', a lament to love lost, shortly after Ulvaeus and Fältskog had separated. As such, Andersson might have added that Carrie Johnson was not playing the song in the spirit in which it had been originally intended.

When the first 'Partygate' reports surfaced, Johnson's initial public reaction was to categorically assure the House of Commons there had been no parties and that all Covid regulations had been followed at all times. As the *Financial Times* journalist Sebastian Payne makes clear in his account of Johnson's downfall, this was a huge mistake.[29] Johnson had no clear idea at that moment what events had or had not happened and had a sometimes-sketchy knowledge of the detail of the Covid regulations themselves. As more details emerged, Johnson appointed the Cabinet secretary, Simon Case, to investigate. Embarrassingly, Case had to step aside when it transpired that he had hosted a party in December 2020. He was replaced by Sue Gray, the former head of the Propriety and Ethics Team within the Cabinet Office, who began collecting photos of events and tallying them against the logbooks kept at Downing Street detailing the times people had entered and left the building. On 25 January 2022, the Metropolitan Police, who had initially adopted the live-and-let-live stance of their Durham colleagues, announced that they were launching a formal investigation into breaches of lockdown restrictions.

Gray published her interim report on 31 January. In it she listed sixteen gatherings that had taken place in Downing Street, twelve of which, she added, had become the subject of police inquiries.[30] On 12 April 2022 it was reported that Boris and Carrie Johnson and Rishi Sunak would be fined in relation to Johnson's surprise birthday party. On 19 May the Metropolitan Police announced they had completed their investigations and had issued a total of 126 fixed penalty notices. A week later, Gray published her final report, which, in addition to providing more details about some of the parties, described a 'lack of respect and poor treatment of security and cleaning staff' at Number 10 who had raised concerns about what they had seen and heard.[31]

On 6 June 2022, the final day of the Queen's Jubilee Celebrations, Graham Brady, the chairman of the Conservative backbench 1922 Committee, revealed that the required number of Conservative MPs had written to him requesting a Conservative Party leadership contest. The next day, when the vote took place, 211 Conservative MPs expressed their continuing confidence in Johnson, whilst 148 expressed their desire to see him gone. Not long after, the Conservatives were mauled in two parliamentary by-elections triggered by the resignations of Neil Parish and Imran Ahmad Khan (p. 394). However, for a while it looked like Johnson might nevertheless survive. He argued hard that, following Russia's invasion of Ukraine (pp. 468–9), what Britain needed, above all else, was political stability. What's more, under the Conservative Party's rules, there was, in theory at least, no scope to hold another leadership contest until June 2023.

Johnson then self-immolated. In February 2022 he had appointed Chris Pincher deputy chief whip. On 1 July the press reported that Pincher had assaulted two men during an event at the Carlton Club. Pincher resigned and was eventually suspended from the Parliamentary Conservative Party, but only after Johnson had denied knowing anything about his past behaviour (p. 393).[32] On 5 July the retired Foreign Office permanent secretary Simon McDonald, who had previously been in touch with Downing Street to ask them to correct the record, published correspondence showing Johnson had, contrary to his own public assurances, been told about those concerns.[33] Johnson was left with no alternative but to say he had forgotten. A few hours later, Sunak resigned as chancellor and Sajid Javid, who had replaced Matt Hancock as health secretary when Hancock had himself been caught breaking lockdown regulations, followed. Johnson's immediate reaction was to stay and fight.* Yet, with dozens more ministers resigning and more set to follow, Johnson bowed to the inevitable and announced his exit on 7 July. 'The herd is powerful and when the herd moves, it moves ... no one is remotely indispensable.'[34] Meanwhile, Partygate had had an unsurprising but significant impact on political trust. A report published by the Institute for Public Policy Research in 2023 found that Covid flattened levels of public trust. Asked whether 'British politicians are out merely for themselves, for their party, or to do what is best for their country', the number answering 'for themselves', which had approached 50 per cent in the aftermath of the 2009 expenses scandal, stood at nearly 70 per cent.[35]

Eleven Conservative MPs announced their intention to stand for the

---

* Sebastian Payne reports that when Michael Gove told him he thought he needed to resign Johnson responded with a story of an uncle of his who, during a dispute with his employers, had 'failed to take his meds one day' and barricaded himself into his office at East Ham Town Hall with a shotgun before being removed by the police. 'That', he added, 'is going to be me. I'm going to fight; they're going to have to prise me out of here.' Sebastian Payne, *The Fall of Boris Johnson* (London, 2022), p. 193. Johnson's plan may have been to ask the Queen for an early general election. After he had resigned there were reports arrangements had been put in place to ensure that, if Johnson had called the Palace to seek a dissolution of Parliament, he would have been told the Queen was unavailable. Dominic Penna, 'Queen to have been unavailable if Boris Johnson had tried to call snap election, sources claim', *Daily Telegraph* (20 Nov. 2022).

Conservative Party's leadership, with eight making it to the first ballot of MPs on 13 July. Seven days and four votes later Rishi Sunak (with 137 votes) and Liz Truss (113 votes) went forward to contest the run-off amongst Conservative Party members. In policy terms, Truss ran on an argument that the economy needed growth and that the way to get growth was to cut taxes. Sunak, who had clashed with Johnson over the issue of tax cuts prior to his resignation, was more circumspect. He agreed tax cuts were needed to drive growth but argued that they would have to wait until the economy had started to recover.[36] Neither candidate raised any doubts about the economic merits of Brexit, and neither spent a great deal of time (in fact any time) talking about Johnson's pet project of 'levelling-up'.[37] The turn away from the free market the Conservative Party had taken following Theresa May's arrival in 2016 had now seemingly reversed itself.

Truss and her campaign managers did a good job of implying Sunak had consistently undermined Johnson before eventually stabbing him in the back. Sunak did a good job of consistently denigrating Truss's 'fantasy economics'.[38] Finally, Truss, who had grown up in Roundhay, a green and pleasant suburb in Leeds, with a father who was a professor of mathematics and a mother who was a nurse and a teacher, did a good job of presenting herself as someone who had clawed her way out of a childhood of grinding poverty and so understood the challenges faced by ordinary people in a way that Sunak, educated at Winchester College and married to the daughter of a billionaire, did not. On 5 September it was announced that Truss had beaten Sunak by a grand total of 81,000 votes to 60,000. The next day, Johnson departed, promising, like the Roman dictator Cincinnatus, to return to his plough, albeit, in his case, to do so after a long holiday in Barbados.[39]

A 'HIGH PRIORITY'

Boris Johnson's political downfall made for a compelling political drama. Yet if you were looking for the strongest evidence of declining standards in governance, 'Partygate' might well be a bit of a side-show. During the 1980s and 1990s a key argument in British politics centred upon the composition and respective sizes of the public and private sectors. The de facto nationalizations of some of Britain's largest banks in 2009 and Jeremy Corbyn's 2017 General Election campaign revived that argument. Yet, in some respects, the key political question of the last decade has not been about where to draw the boundary between public and private but of how best to manage the relationship between them.

Public-sector organizations are increasingly required to act like private-sector firms and, in doing so, to outsource slices of their work to private companies. As a result, those private firms have become increasingly dependent upon contracts from the public sector to survive. That creates a powerful incentive for firms to lobby ministers in relation to outsourcing arrangements and other regulatory rules. The results can sometimes be spectacularly awful. In 2010 the Labour MP Stephen Byers was recorded describing himself as 'a bit like a sort of cab for hire' (p. 257). In 2023 the Conservative MP Scott Benton reportedly offered to lobby ministers on behalf of the gambling industry and to leak a confidential policy document, in return for payments of up to £4,000 a month.[40]

Lobbying is not inherently improper. Governments potentially benefit from knowing what businesses are thinking and how policies are being implemented. Yet, increasingly, business operates within a privileged position within those lobbying relationships. During the Coalition years, around 45 per cent of the six-thousand-plus recorded meetings government ministers held with outside organizations included business. In over 80 per cent of those meetings business was the only kind of organization represented at that meeting.[41] Lobbying blurs the lines between public interest and private gain, and between the legitimate exchange of views and trading in contacts and favours. The Covid pandemic exposed two such cases.

Greensill Capital was founded by the Australian businessman Alexander 'Lex' Greensill in 2011 and specialized in supply chain financing.* During the Coalition years, Greensill was encouraged to work with government departments by Jeremy Heywood, the then Cabinet secretary who, like Greensill, had previously worked at the investment bank Morgan Stanley.[42] As a result, Greensill was introduced to David

---

* Supply chain financing involves a third party with a high credit rating, such as a company like Greensill Capital, entering an arrangement whereby it pays a supplier as soon as an invoice has been issued and the buyer subsequently pays the third party.

Cameron and, shortly after, had business cards printed on which he described himself as a senior advisor to the prime minister.[43] After leaving office, Cameron then began working for Greensill Capital, earning upwards of £7 million for his troubles.[44] In 2019 Cameron and Greensill met the health secretary Matt Hancock for a 'private drink' to discuss a new payment scheme for NHS staff.[45] In January 2020 Cameron and Greensill flew to Saudi Arabia to meet Crown Prince Mohammed bin Salman, who at that point was still being treated as something of an international pariah following the American Central Intelligence Agency's conclusion that he had ordered the murder of the journalist Jamal Khashoggi in 2018. In March 2021 the *Financial Times* reported that Cameron had directly lobbied ministers to allow Greensill Capital to join the Corporate Covid Financing Facility, which would have allowed the company to issue loans, insured by the government, during the pandemic.[46] Cameron and his staff had sent nine WhatsApp messages to the chancellor Rishi Sunak and twelve text messages to the Treasury permanent secretary Tom Scholar. In one of those messages Cameron asks Scholar whether he can 'give you lunch once the budget is done' and whether he has a number for the Bank of England's deputy governor for financial stability, Sir Jon Cunliffe, before signing off 'love DC'.[47]

Cameron's efforts to secure Covid-related support for Greensill were unsuccessful and the company itself went bust in March 2021. To this extent, it might be argued, the system worked. The Treasury, for its part, argued that Cameron was treated no differently to anyone else and that his lobbying efforts made absolutely zero difference. This was by any standards a heroic line of argument to adopt. The Treasury Select Committee reacted to it with evident irony: 'We are very surprised about this, given that Mr Cameron was an ex-Prime Minister, who had worked with those he was lobbying, had access to their mobile phone numbers, and appears to have been able to negotiate who should attend meetings.'[48]

David Cameron, whilst defending his involvement with Greensill Capital and the lobbying he had undertaken on its behalf, eventually seemed to reach a similar conclusion. In a statement released in April 2021 he accepted that, as a former prime minister, 'communications with the government need to be done through only the most formal of channels, so there can be no room for misinterpretation'.[49]

The second scandal is, at the time of writing, still unfolding. At the start of the pandemic there was a huge shortage of personal protective equipment (PPE) for healthcare workers in the NHS and care homes. Large parts of the existing stockpiles of equipment had rotted and the key manufacturer of PPE, China, was reluctant to export material for obvious reasons.[50] The result, during the first few weeks and months of the pandemic, was an adrenaline-fuelled rush to find new sources of supply in an incredibly tight market. With ministers and officials constantly being approached by potential new suppliers, the government established a 'high-priority lane' to assess and process potential leads from officials, ministerial offices, MPs and members of the House of Lords, senior NHS staff and other health professionals. These leads were treated as being prima facie more credible than others and treated with more urgency.[51] A National Audit Office report found that about one in ten suppliers processed through the high-priority lane (47 out of 493) subsequently obtained contracts, compared to less than one in a hundred suppliers that came through the ordinary channels (104 of 14,892).[52]

In December 2020 the *New York Times* reported that, of the initial contracts it had analysed (many of which went through the high-priority lane), around half, measured in terms of the value of the contracts, went to companies run by friends and associates of politicians in the Conservative Party or by companies that had controversial histories and either poor credit records or histories of fraud and tax evasion.[53] The government initially published a 'nothing to see here' response that amounted to a claim that the journalists who had written the story did not understand how the British government worked.[54] The National Audit Office, which continued to investigate what had happened, later reported that a significant number of the contracts that had been awarded to high-priority firms prior to May 2020 had, in fact, not been subjected to the same financial, commercial and legal checks as other applications.[55]

In February 2021 the High Court ruled that Hancock, whilst he was health secretary, had 'acted unlawfully' by failing to comply with the government's Transparency Policy and publish the details of contracts.[56] In a separate case the High Court ruled in June 2021 that a decision by the Cabinet Office to award a £500,000 contract to a research firm, Public First, whose owners had links to Dominic Cummings, 'gave rise to apparent bias' and was unlawful (that judgment was subsequently overturned on appeal in January 2022).[57] In November 2021 it was then reported that Michelle Mone, a business leader who had been appointed a Conservative peer in 2015, had personally recommended PPE Medpro under the high-priority scheme. The company had been formed at the start of the pandemic and was led by Anthony Page, a business associate of Mone's, and Mone's husband, Doug Barrowman.[58] PPE Medpro was awarded a £122-million contract. In November 2022 the *Guardian* reported that an Isle of Man trust, of which Mone and her adult children were beneficiaries, had received £29 million from the company.[59] In December it emerged that the government was suing PPE Medpro for the value of its contract, plus costs, on the grounds that the medical gowns it had supplied were defective. On 6 December Mone announced that she was taking a 'leave of absence' from the House of Lords in order to clear her name. A year later, and with a National Crime Agency investigation still on-going, Mone admitted that she had repeatedly lied about her connections to PPE Medpro. If the Covid pandemic did not constitute the finest hours of Boris Johnson, Dominic Cummings or Matt Hancock, Greensill and PPE Medpro constituted, at best, rather grubby codas to them. They seemed to show that the British administrative system, the state, could be bent out of shape by the people who were or had been involved in running it.

34
Culture Wars

'THE PRIG AND THE PRUDE'

In one of the opening chapters I described New Labour's successful electoral strategy as being one of positioning itself at the centre-ground between left and right and, in doing so, quoted Tony Blair as saying: 'We have to stay bang in the centre ground. I am where the country is. Hague is more right-wing than the country and GB [Gordon Brown] is more left wing than the country.'[1] In an endnote to this discussion – one you would have been excused for missing – I linked New Labour's strategy to the median voter argument as it was initially outlined by the American political scientist Anthony Downs in his 1957 book *An Economic Theory of Democracy*.[2] In the kind of political world Downs imagined, voters are defined in terms of where they sit on a left–right political spectrum. In such a situation, there will, by definition, be a median voter: a person with exactly as many people to the left of them as to the right. Downs' simple argument was that a party which positions itself at the location of the median voter will triumph.

Over the years, Downs' argument has been critiqued and developed in several different ways.[3] One common line of argument is that voters don't simply choose between parties based on their spatial position. Voters also care about the character and qualities of party leaders; about the underlying performance of the economy; and about the integrity of a party's politicians. Left and right positions can tell you something, but it certainly does not tell you all you need to know in order to predict how someone will vote. An alternative argument here is that, whilst a party's spatial position matters, politics is not simply about left and right. I have already touched upon this. The fuel protestors did not position themselves as being simply left or right. They framed their position as being one of defending the interests of ordinary voters against an out-of-touch, metropolitan elite who did not understand them (pp. 52–3). We might also think of there being a second dimension of politics relating to attitudes towards individual freedom. Here we have, on the one side, liberal progressives who believe personal freedom should be maximized. And, on the other, socially conservative authoritarians who, when it comes to issues like freedom of speech, respect for authority and traditional values and attitudes towards censorship, emphasize social order and responsibility and duties over rights.[4]

The roots of this cultural division over social freedom run deep. In England in the 1630s, it pitted Puritanism against Arminianism and, eventually, once the Civil War had begun, Roundheads against Cavaliers.[5] In the early 1790s, after The Three Estates had made their mark but before King Louis had lost his head, Edmund Burke, via his *Reflections on the Revolution in France* and, a year later, Thomas Paine in his response, *Rights of Man*, were the leading British players in a nascent culture war argument about the likely consequences of levelling the established French order in the name of freedom and equality.[6] In his 1956 book *The Future of Socialism*, Anthony Crosland set not only an economic agenda for future Labour governments (p. 39) but a social and cultural one as well. He railed against 'socially-imposed restrictions on the individual's private life and liberty'; argued that in the 'blood' of socialists 'there should always run a trace of the anarchist and the libertarian, and not too much of the prig and the prude'; and set an agenda for the reform of laws relating to divorce, censorship, abortion, capital punishment, the rights of women and the rights of gay men which provided a template for Harold Wilson's Labour governments.[7] In the late 1960s would-be revolutionaries mounted sit-ins and staged street protests to express their disdain for capitalism, liberal democracy and American imperialism in Vietnam. This was Zhou Enlai's 'too early to tell' moment. In Britain, on 17 March 1968 hundreds of people, including a young Mick Jagger, protested outside the American Embassy in Grosvenor Square.[8] Some of them had been inspired by Maoism and by Chairman Mao's own Cultural Revolution, which had got underway in 1966.

The 1980s begat a set of related culture war battles in Britain over 'loony left' councils; gay rights and Section 28 (p. 296); unilateral nuclear disarmament and the Greenham Common Women's Peace Camp; and the anti-Apartheid movement and whether Nelson Mandela was a terrorist. Moving on, Daniel Hooper, aka 'Swampy', became a culture war icon in 1996 when he was the last person to be removed from a tunnel that protestors had dug underneath the route of a proposed new extension to the A30 in Devon. Adding to his already considerable lustre, the Conservative transport minister John Watts said he'd like to see him 'buried in concrete'.[9] In 1999 a Norfolk farmer, Tony Martin, shot dead sixteen-year-old Fred Barras after he had broken into his home. Martin was convicted of murder: a judgment which provoked a campaign to secure his release or, as eventually happened, to reduce his conviction to one of manslaughter.[10] The Conservative Party's new leader, William Hague, pledged to change the law under which Martin had been convicted and announced he was 'on the side of the people who protect their homes'.[11] In the early 2000s the culture war mantle was passed on to protestors campaigning against foxhunting and for transgender rights (a subject to which we will return).[12]

BREXITLAND

The existence of a second, social-cultural political dimension, alongside a left–right one, complicates the dynamics of party competition. Put simply, parties must choose where to position themselves across a range of different *kinds* of policy issues, which means that the location of the centre-ground is not always as obvious. As another American political scientist, William H. Riker, argued, in a notable development of Downs' work, it also creates opportunities.[13] Parties don't have to take the existence of these dimensions of politics as fixed and given. They can instead try to raise the relative salience of dimensions in voters' minds or even try to establish new ones to split their opponents' vote.

Riker's most famous example is drawn from the study of American politics. In the first part of the nineteenth century the salient dimension of conflict within American politics was socio-economic and recognizably left–right. The Democrats stood for agrarian expansionism, for easy credit and low tariffs. The opposition, whose name went from Federalist to National Republican to Whig to Republicans, stood for commercial expansionism, for tight credit and high tariffs. With politics cast in this mould the Democrats built a winning coalition out of the support of the agricultural southern and northwestern states. Therefore, the opposition, who relied on the votes of the northeastern states, managed to elect only one president with a majority of the popular vote between 1800 and 1864. Riker argues that in the late 1850s, the Republicans, led by Abraham Lincoln, were able to overcome their political exclusion by igniting a second, previously dormant party-political dimension of conflict: slavery. They used this, he argues, to break the coalition between the northwestern states, which were against the admission of new slave states to the union, and the south, who argued this was exclusively a matter for the states concerned. Riker is not arguing, it should be emphasized, that Lincoln was simply using the issue of slavery as an electoral ruse. But politicians can be both principled and sincere and calculating and ambitious. It was Lincoln's political art, an art Riker labels 'heresthetics', to combine these two.

In the early 2000s, William Hague, Iain Duncan Smith and Michael Howard sought not simply to position the Conservative Party as a socially conservative and right-of-centre alternative to Labour but, at a point when the economy was doing well, to raise the salience of the social-cultural dimension by highlighting issues such as crime, poor behaviour in schools, the development of a 'something-for-nothing culture' and an over-emphasis on people's rights at the expense of their responsibilities. As strategies go, it was not a notable success. The Conservatives badly lost the 2001 and 2005 elections having acquired a reputation for being, in Theresa May's words, the 'nasty party'. In opposition and then in government, David Cameron took a different tack. He downplayed the social-cultural dimension and focused on positioning the Conservatives at the centre of the left–right spectrum. In relation to issues like same sex marriage, this led, as we have seen, to some turbulence within the Conservative Party. But Cameron was a sincere social liberal who also had an electoral game plan for holding power and who was also helped by the 2008 financial crisis and the return of left–right economic issues around tax, spending and debt to the political stage.

Looking back at the early 2010s, we can see there were some issues which looked like they offered likely grounds for some culture war fighting. The most obvious of these was same sex marriage, complete with its slippery-slope fears of whether people might one day be allowed to marry their pets (p. 265). A second candidate was the 2011 London riots, where people polarized between thinking that everything that happened had happened because of austerity or, alternatively, thinking that it was all down to bad parenting and the pernicious influence of *Grand Theft Auto*.[14] The 2013 conviction of Sergeant Alexander Blackman for fatally shooting an injured Taliban fighter in Afghanistan also divided opinion around the question of whether or not it was reasonable to try British soldiers for their actions in situations in which they had been in constant danger and had had to make split-second decisions about whether to open fire or not.[15] Although it looked like a classic economic, left–right issue, austerity also had a cultural dimension, framed around arguments about the morality of debt, the identities of the deserving and undeserving poor, and pitting hardworking but struggling families against welfare scroungers 'sleeping off a life on benefits' as George Osborne described it (p. 288).[16]

Then came Brexit. As far as Remainers were concerned, Britain's continued membership of the European Union was, first and foremost, an economic issue. This is how Britain Stronger in Europe sought to frame the referendum campaign, by way of support from the CBI, the Bank of England and assorted banks. Insofar as immigration was an issue, and Stronger in Europe knew it was, the focus of the campaign was on the economic benefits of the free market in people. For those campaigning to leave, the economic opportunities offered by Brexit were not insignificant. But leaving was also framed in cultural and emotive terms, relating to notions of sovereignty and of Britishness and the cultural impact of immigration. The Leave campaign won the her-esthetic war. In 2016 people's self-identified position along the left–right political spectrum did not provide much of a clue as to whether they voted leave or remain. But as Maria Sobolewska and Robert Ford have shown in *Brexitland*, people's social and cultural attitudes and identities did:

> Brexit is the expression of conflicts which have been building in the elect-
> orate for decades, not their cause. Brexitland is the name we give to our
> divided nation, but while Brexit gives a name and a voice to these divides,
> they are not new. They have their roots in trends which have been run-
> ning for generations – educational expansion, mass immigration and
> ethnic change.[17]

What's more, the three-year-long *Za Gaman* slow motion car crash of Britain's exit entrenched those differences, giving the two sides a clear sense of themselves as social groups with shared views and a common sense of contempt for their opponents.[18] As a result, and six years after the referendum, the British Social Attitudes survey found that people's attitudes towards Brexit continued to be predictive of other social-cultural attitudes. For example, whilst two-thirds of Leave supporters felt 'very strongly' British compared with less than a third of their Remain counterparts, they also had a different view on what Britishness meant: 65 per cent of Leavers thought that to be 'truly British' it was important to have been born in Britain, compared to only 34 per cent of Remainers. To take another issue, whereas 60 per cent of Remainers thought equal opportunities for black and Asian people had 'not gone far enough', the same was true of only 23 per cent of Leavers.[19]

'GUARDIAN-READING, TOFU-EATING, WOKERATI'

By 2020, with Brexit close to being concluded, a key question for Conservative strategists would have been how to maintain the coalition which had triumphed in the 2016 referendum and the 2019 General Election. The answer, when it arrived, came via the United States.

In the late 1960s, President Nixon and Vice President Spiro T. Agnew stoked a culture war in the name of the 'silent majority' and against what Agnew memorably described as the 'nattering nabobs of negativism' in the press.[20] In the 1980s and 1990s, the Christian right, led by figures like Pat Robertson, constructed a new religious base to the Republican Party (p. 303). In August 1992 the political commentator and former White House director of communications Pat Buchanan addressed delegates to the Republican National Convention. 'There is a religious war going on. It is a cultural war, as critical to the kind of nation we shall be as was the Cold War itself, for this war is for the soul of America.'[21] This was the political line Nixon and Agnew had previously played. Now it was back. Over the next two decades, America's culture war, fought over abortion, gun control and prayer in schools, gathered momentum. When Donald J. Trump declared his candidacy to be the Republican candidate for president in June 2015 he added to that line a nativist, populist ideology and a sure-fire sense of how best to use social media to mobilize support and antagonize his opponents.

It was the murder of an African American, George Floyd, in Minneapolis on 25 May 2020 by Derek Chauvin, a white police officer, and Trump's reaction to it, which was probably most impactful. On the evening of 25 May Trump described Floyd's death as being 'very sad and tragic', adding that he had asked the FBI and Justice Department to investigate what had happened.[22] Following protests and riots in Minneapolis the following evening, Trump called upon the police to restore order, declaring – in a divisive phrase dating back to the 1960s Civil Rights protests – 'when the looting starts, the shooting starts'.[23] Over the following months Black Lives Matter protests and campaigns to 'defund the police' rubbed up against All Lives and Blue Lives Matter demonstrations. Trump embraced what became a highly polarizing debate. In one incident, on 1 June 2020, police used tear gas to clear protestors from Lafayette Square in Washington to allow Trump to pose with a Bible outside the square's St John's Episcopal Church. Trump did not create, as if out of thin air, an anti-racism protest movement in Britain. Black Lives Matter UK had been formed in 2014 and had organized protests in relation to both the Windrush scandal and Grenfell. Yet the murder of George Floyd triggered a reaction not only in Washington but in Britain.

In June 2020 a series of antiracism marches took place in British cities. During one of these, in Bristol on 7 June, protestors toppled and threw into Bristol harbour a statue of Edward Colston, a local seventeenth-century merchant and slave trader, which had been erected in 1895. The following day, at a Black Lives Matter protest in London, 'was a racist' was daubed on a statue of Churchill in Parliament Square. These events triggered a series of counterprotests intended to protect statues. During one of these, on 13 June, one such protestor, Andrew Banks (who later told magistrats he had drunk sixteen pints the night before), was pictured relieving himself next to a plaque erected in memory of PC Keith Palmer, who had been stabbed to death in a terrorist attack on Parliament in March 2017.

Race and the legacy of the Empire became central components of other culture war issues. During June 2020, English Premier League football players began 'taking the knee' prior to the start of matches: a practice which had originated in the US in 2016 when the National

Football League player Colin Kaepernick had knelt on one knee during the playing of the American anthem to protest against racial inequality and police brutality. When England players took the knee prior to the start of the European Championship Finals, they were booed by significant sections of the crowd at Wembley. In August 2020 the former Yorkshire cricketer Azeem Rafiq described, initially in an interview with the cricket magazine *Wisden*, his long-standing experiences of racism within a team that had not selected a Yorkshire-born player of Asian descent until 2004.[24] After his remarks were reported by the national press, Rafiq's experiences led, variously, to an Employment Tribunal, parliamentary hearings, Yorkshire's suspension from hosting test match cricket, the temporary resignation of Yorkshire's chairman and other board members, and a disciplinary hearing against six former Yorkshire players or coaches.[25]

Race and accusations of racism also fuelled a multi-series culture war over the lives, experiences and responsibilities of the duke and duchess of Sussex. It began in 2016 when the *MailOnline* published a story with the headline '(ALMOST) STRAIGHT OUTTA COMPTON' and the *Mail on Sunday* published a column citing Meghan Markle's 'exotic DNA'. Both were later cited by Markle as examples of the casual racism of the British press.[26] The following year, Princess Michael of Kent, who, in 2004, had told a group of black diners at a New York restaurant to 'go back to the colonies', apologized for wearing a Blackamoor Brooch depicting an African man wearing a crown and jewels at a lunch event hosted by the Queen, where she had met Markle for the first time.[27] The stakes were raised in January 2020 when Harry and Meghan announced their decision to 'step back' as senior members of the Royal Family and move to America.[28] In March 2021, during an interview with Oprah Winfrey, Meghan described how she had been told by Harry of 'several conversations' he had had with 'senior' members of the Royal Family about how dark a colour of skin the couple's expected child might have.[29] By this point, Meghan had become a front-line figure in Britain's polarizing culture wars, offering enough mileage for Jeremy Clarkson to later write of how 'I hate her [Meghan Markle]. Not like I hate Nicola Sturgeon [the Scottish first minister] or Rose West [serial killer]. I hate her on a cellular level.'[30]

Race was perhaps the central and defining issue of Britain's culture war in the 2020s. But that war, which came attached with its own vocabulary of 'woke', 'cancel culture', 'virtue signalling' and 'intersectionality', ranged across a broad array of other social–cultural issues, including protests against the Metropolitan Police following the murder of Sarah Everard and a series of linked controversies over climate change. These included the rights and wrongs of direct action to block roads or, in October 2022, of throwing tomato soup over Van Gogh's 'Sunflowers' at the National Gallery, as well as the location of wind farms, the merits of fracking and the need for a referendum on Britain's net zero legislation.[31]

The other major issue that polarized public debate related to transgender rights. In 2004, following a ruling by the European Court of Human Rights, the Labour government passed the Gender Recognition Act. This made it possible for transgender adults, having received a diagnosis of gender dysphoria from a medical practitioner working in that area, to apply for a Gender Recognition Certificate.[32] In the 2010s transgender rights groups began to rally around an argument that the processes involved in the 2004 Act were too bureaucratic, invasive and expensive, and rested on the assumption that a transgender identity was a medical condition.[33] They argued people should be allowed to self-identify as being transgender and that this ought to be a basis on which an application for a Gender Recognition Certificate could be made. Theresa May's government publicly supported this principle.[34] This led several other groups, including Fair Play for Women and Mayday-4women, to argue that self-identification risked allowing predatory men to self-identity as women in order to gain access to women-only spaces. Beyond this, some of these campaigners, labelled TERFs (Trans-Exclusionary Radical Feminists) by their opponents as a term of abuse, argued that self-identification risked erasing the biological reality of womanhood and that, as the author J. K. Rowling pointed out, 'woman is not a costume'.[35]

Eventually, in 2020, the government, now led by Boris Johnson, announced that self-identification would not be adopted. By this point however, the argument about transgender rights had inflated to include several other issues, including the use of puberty blockers for children, the participation of trans men and women in sport, a ban on trans-conversion therapy and, following the resignation of a philosopher from Sussex University, Kathleen Stock, who had been accused of transphobia, freedom of speech within universities. In December 2022 the Scottish Parliament voted to remove the need for a psychiatric diagnosis of gender dysphoria, accepting the case for self-identification. Shortly after, the case of Isla Bryson, a transgender woman who had been convicted of the rape of two women before her gender transition, became a headline story when she was remanded to a women's prison, HMP Cornton Vale, prior to sentencing.

The Conservative Party did not create Britain's culture wars. But it is fair to say they seized upon them for reasons both principled and calculative because they offered the prospect of holding together the Brexit coalition and of deterring socially conservative voters from ever returning to the Labour fold. Britain has, overall, as we saw earlier in Chapter 23, become a notably more liberal country over time when it comes to issues like same sex relationships, cohabiting before marriage and working women. But on these culture war issues public opinion seemed more febrile and polarized. That is why, as well as being the subject of endless Tweets by Conservative MPs, such issues became the subject of speeches by Boris Johnson, Jacob-Rees Mogg, Michelle Donelan, Oliver Dowden and Suella Braverman (who blamed '*Guardian*-reading, tofu-eating, wokerati' for disruption caused by direct-action climate protesters) and prompted legislation relating to the right to protest and free speech within universities and a series of government announcements in relation to restarting coal mining, the ending of the 'war on motorists' and the housing of asylum-seekers.[36] If, as Carl von Clausewitz once said, 'war is the continuation of politics by other means', then Britain's culture wars in the early 2020s were the continuation of Brexit by other means.

WAXING AND WANING

One of the recurring features of culture wars over the ages is that they are conducted in an all-or-nothing, polarizing manner in which participants all view each other as either friends or enemies.[37] For all the issues discussed here, it is entirely possible to conceive of middle-ground positions. Edward Colston's statue should have been removed and placed in a museum. Megan Markle may have been treated badly by members of the Royal Family and may well have been the victim of racial prejudice, but she may also fall someway short of being a candidate for deification. There is a strong case for reforming and streamlining the process of applying for a Gender Recognition Certificate, but this does not mean that someone who identifies as a woman need, in all possible contexts, be treated entirely the same as someone who was born a woman.

That said, social media perhaps made the 2020 culture wars particularly divisive. Twitter (rebranded as X in 2023) was established in 2006 but it was in the early 2010s that the platform began to attract millions of users, and it was in 2014, during the Scottish independence referendum, that it was first credited with having had a decisive political impact.[38] There was a hope, in the early 2010s, that Twitter and other social-media platforms would offer politicians a way of updating their constituents and humanizing politics by showing, in real time, the dilemmas involved in making political decisions.[39] Some went further, imagining a world in which Twitter would encourage constant debate and a form of deliberative democracy in which people's views shifted in response to arguments and evidence. In fact, as it turned out, social media in general, and Twitter in particular, were a Petri dish for group polarization which gave users the easy option of choosing which conversations to be part of; filtering out alternative views; and, if they wanted, demonizing and abusing their opponents.[40] In 2018 Jack Dorsey, the former chief executive of Twitter, announced changes to the platform's algorithms which were intended to have the effect of discouraging 'troll-like behaviors' and promoting 'healthy conversations'.[41] It is telling that, having done this, Twitter's share price fell and continued falling. When Elon Musk accidentally-on-purpose bought Twitter in October 2022, he reversed the changes Dorsey had made whilst defending an absolute right to freedom of speech.

A second, recurring featuring of culture wars is that they tend to wax before then waning. In early 2022, the start of a real war in Ukraine and the beginning of the cost-of-living crisis which followed it, took some of the intensity out of the debate. The slow fading of the culture wars was probably helped by the refusal of the Labour Party, or, more precisely, of its new leader, Keir Starmer (who had been elected in April 2020), to consistently engage with many of the culture war issues of the day. The Labour Party has, at times, found itself discomforted over debates about statues and, in particular, trans rights.[42] Yet this did not preclude Labour from surging ahead in opinion polls from around 2021 onwards as a result, largely, of the lead it established over the Conservatives on the very traditional and non-cultural-looking issues of the economy and the

NHS. In this respect, it may well be that, in terms of electoral strategy, Starmer called it correctly. Whilst it was a characteristic of the culture wars that seemingly everyone had an opinion about a lot of the issues involved, the number of people actively engaging in marches, counter-marches or Twitter spats about these issues was always quite limited. A poll for Times Radio in February 2021 asked people what they thought politicians meant when they spoke about a culture war. Only 7 per cent of people offered a relevant answer, 15 per cent got it wrong, and 76 per cent said they didn't know.[43] It may be that voters were not alone in this regard. In March 2021, Boris Johnson's official spokesman told journalists, during a routine briefing, that he did not know what 'woke' meant before seemingly linking the issue to levelling-up and transport infrastructure. Shortly before, in a news interview, Johnson had stumbled over a question about whether the new US president, Joe Biden, was woke. Johnson had every reason to avoid directly criticizing Biden but, even so, his response – that 'there's nothing wrong with being woke' – was a strange one for him.[44]

35
Great Powers

ABERYSTWYTH MON AMOUR

Aberystwyth is one of the more beautiful (and improbably remote) British seaside towns. The promenade, tucked within Cardigan Bay, stretches from the ruins of Aberystwyth Castle on the one side to the funicular railway running to the top of Constitution Hill on the other. Aberystwyth hosts the National Library of Wales in a building faced, like those on Regent Street in London, with Portland stone. It is also the setting for Malcolm Pryce's six-part Welsh Noir comic detective series, starring private eye Louie Knight, opening with *Aberystwyth Mon Amour* in 2001 and concluding with *The Day Aberystwyth Stood Still* in 2011.[1] Besides being the birthplace of the biologist and television presenter Steve Jones and the eventual home of the painter and sculptor Mabel Pakenham-Walsh, Aberystwyth's other claim to (a sort of) fame is that, in 1919, its university was the world's first to establish a Department of International Politics through the establishment of the Woodrow Wilson Professor and Chair of International Politics.[2]

For a long time, the academic study of international politics was dominated by 'realism', a theory that traces its intellectual origins back to Thucydides and Machiavelli but which became closely associated, in Britain at least, with the work of the former diplomat E. H. Carr, the author of *The Twenty Years' Crisis* (in 1939) and *What is History?* (in 1961), who held the Woodrow Wilson Chair between 1936 and 1950.[3] Realism argues that the international environment is a nasty and brutish place characterized by the absence of any sovereign authority; that states and their leaders are driven by their own interests to exploit opportunities and to take advantage of each other where they can; that security is underpinned by military power and a lack of sentimentality;

and that peace is fragile and best maintained through the careful construction of a balance of power.[4] Realists like Carr argued that peace-seeking politicians like President Woodrow Wilson, who, in the immediate aftermath of the First World War, pushed for the establishment of the League of Nations in the hope of securing a new and peaceful age, were utopian fools.[*] The world is what it is and what it has always been, and any attempt to pretend otherwise will end in disaster.

The main theoretical alternative to realism is liberalism. Liberals recognize that the world is a potentially dangerous place and that war is always possible but are more optimistic about people's capacity to make it a safer place. Trade can create interdependencies between countries and raise the costs of going to war.[5] States can learn to manage their differences through the development of international organizations within which norms of restraint and compromise can develop.[6] Realists claim to be the no-nonsense tell-it-like-it-is bouncers standing outside the nightclub. But liberals argue that realism is itself unrealistic. War is not inevitable. The League of Nations may have flopped, with a Second World War following the First. But by the time Carr passed away, aged ninety in 1982, France and Germany were bound peacefully together within the European Economic Community. Here at least, the utopian had become normal.

A LIBERAL AGE

Realism was the go-to practitioner's theory of the Cold War. The Soviet Union was bent on world domination and on exploiting Western weakness. A collective security system in the form of NATO, backed by a US-led nuclear deterrence, was essential. Diplomacy, as practised by arch-realists like Henry Kissinger, the US secretary of state from 1973

---

[*] The funding for the establishment of the Department of International Politics in Aberystwyth in 1919 was provided by the Davies family, who gave £20,000 to honour the memory of students of the University who had died in the First World War. The Davieses were committed liberals and proponents of the League of Nations. It is for this reason that the new Professorship was named after Woodrow Wilson. They were not overjoyed when Carr was appointed to the position they had paid for and proceeded to bite the hand which was feeding him.

to 1977, was about creating alliances and maintaining a balance of power, something in which he and President Richard Nixon excelled, brokering China's rapprochement with the West (p. 12). By the time Tony Blair arrived in 10 Downing Street the world looked very different. The economy was booming. The Cold War was over. The Soviet Union had collapsed. American hyper-power was unchallenged. History, Francis Fukuyama was arguing, had ended. There was no plausible alternative to liberal capitalism.[7] As a result, the British government's 1998 Strategic Defence Review could talk of a 'transformed' international situation, the absence of a 'direct military threat to the United Kingdom' and 'a cooperative partnership with Russia'.[8]

Blair welcomed American-led plans to expand NATO eastwards.* He was, however, keen to avoid isolating Russia. He backed the NATO–Russia Permanent Joint Council; pushed for Russia's inclusion within the G7; and spoke, warmly, about co-operation to fight terrorism.[9] Blair, as a good liberal, was also keen to strengthen Britain's economic relationship with Russia. Between 2000 and 2008 the total value of British exports to Russia increased from £1,392 million to £5,674 million a year, with BP and one of Russia's largest oil companies, TNK, signing a huge deal in 2003 to produce oil and gas in Russia.[10] Britain, as we have seen, was also more than happy to welcome the transfer of Russian wealth to the City of London, the London property market and its surrounding public schools (p. 99).

One of Tony Blair's first overseas trips as prime minister, in June 1997, was to watch the Union Jack being lowered for the last time whilst colonial Hong Kong was returned to China amidst the pomp and ceremony of a grand naval review and the last voyage of the Royal Yacht *Britannia*. After exiting stage left, Britain then tried, not always entirely successfully, to build a new relationship with China around trade and economics. China was liberalizing. In December 2001 it joined the World Trade Organization and became a fully-fledged, A-list member of the global capitalist economy, with an average growth rate of over 10 per cent a year (to put this into context, this growth rate meant adding something the size of the Greek economy to the Chinese

---

* The Czech Republic, Hungary and Poland joined NATO in 1999. They were followed, within a few years, by Bulgaria, Estonia, Latvia, Lithuania, Romania, Slovakia and Slovenia.

one every four months).[11] Chinese trade liberalization and growth boosted the British economy. It opened up new export and investment opportunities for British companies, with the value of British exports rising from £2,549 million to £11,002 million a year between 2000 and 2008.[12] More importantly, Chinese imports and China's increasingly central position within global value chains (pp. 114–15) kept British consumer prices, inflation and interest rates much lower than they would otherwise have been, sustaining the economic boom.[13]

In August 2008 Beijing hosted the Summer Olympics. A month later, Lehman Brothers declared bankruptcy and the financial crisis began. China, which had accumulated a stock of over $900 billion in US Treasury Securities as part of its efforts to peg the value of its currency against the dollar, decided not to kick America when it was down by selling these assets.[14] Instead, the president of the China Investment Corporation, Gao Xiqing, affirmed his confidence in what he described – in a real zinger of a reference to the bank bail-outs – as 'American socialism with Chinese characteristics'.[15] Shortly after, when the world economy stumbled and China's exports fell, the Chinese government unveiled a 4-trillion-yuan stimulus package, focused on infrastructure spending and healthcare, which kick-started Chinese and world economic growth. As George Osborne acknowledged in a speech delivered to the Shanghai Stock Exchange in September 2015, the global economy in 2008/9 was 'like a damaged aeroplane, flying with one engine, China's engine'.[16]

Even after HMY *Britannia* had set off into the sunset, Britain's relationship with China was not all plain sailing. In 1999, during NATO's bombing campaign against Serbia in support of Kosovo, the Chinese Embassy in Belgrade was accidentally (possibly accidentally on purpose) bombed by NATO jets and three Chinese citizens killed.[17] Tibet, which had been occupied and effectively annexed by China in the 1950s, posed another complication: the Chinese government froze diplomatic relations whenever a British politician dared meet with the exiled Dalai Lama. Yet, overall, Britain's relationship with China, which had previously been dominated by Hong Kong, improved during the 2000s, offering, so it would seem, a good case-study in the political virtues of economic interdependence.

THE OLYMPIC SPIRIT

In November 2006 Russian Federal Security Service agents, using highly radioactive polonium-210, poisoned and killed Alexander Litvinenko, a former Russian agent who had defected to Britain in 2000. After Russia refused to extradite the prime suspects – two Russian agents, Andrei Lugovoy and Dmitry Kovtun – Britain, no doubt with one eye on its burgeoning trade relationship, responded with a damp squib of a diplomatic retaliation, expelling four Russian diplomats and suspending negotiations for a bilateral visa-facilitation agreement.[18] It is hard to think President Putin would have been left terrified. Then, in August 2008, Putin read but apparently misunderstood a memo about how the Olympics, taking place in Beijing, were meant to foster international co-operation and invaded Georgia. That was a turning point. Britain, America and several other Western countries now concluded that Putin was a nationalist dictator who was fundamentally anti-liberal and who posed a threat to international security. Realism was suddenly back in fashion and, when Putin decided to use the Winter Olympics being held in Sochi in February 2014 as the launchpad for an invasion of the Crimea, Britain was towards the front of the queue in arguing the case for Russia's suspension from the G8, economic sanctions and a strengthened NATO military presence on the alliance's eastern border.

Putin, for what it is worth, had decided long before that Britain and the West could not be trusted and were out to weaken, if not destroy, Russia. In 1999 Russia (and China) had objected vigorously to the NATO bombing campaign against Serbia, which had taken place in the absence of any UN mandate. The then Russian president, Boris Yeltsin, maintained that the West was guilty of an act of 'open aggression'.[19] Putin, who replaced Yeltsin as president in May 2000, quickly approved a new Russian Security Strategy that sought to counter 'attempts to create an international relations structure based on domination by developed Western countries'.[20] In 2014, in a speech defending Russia's actions in Crimea, he was still referencing what had happened in Kosovo. 'Our Western partners, led by the United States of America, prefer not to be guided by international law ... but by the rule of the gun ... they have come to believe [that] they can decide the destinies of the world. This happened in Yugoslavia; we remember 1999 very well.'[21]

After the Russian invasion of Crimea, attention started to focus on the military security of the rest of Ukraine. In 1994 the 'Budapest Memorandum' had been signed by the Russian Federation, the United States and the United Kingdom. It prohibited these three signatories from threatening or using military or economic force against three others: Belarus, Kazakhstan and Ukraine. In return, the governments of these three now-independent countries agreed to give up the nuclear weapons that had been left on their territory when the USSR fell apart. NATO had subsequently expanded eastwards and, in 2008, had formally welcomed Ukraine's aspirations to join the alliance (p. 137). In 2014 the Ukrainian Parliament renounced Ukraine's non-aligned status and reiterated the country's desire to join NATO. In 2016 Britain and Ukraine signed a defence co-operation agreement and in February 2021 the NATO general secretary confirmed that Ukraine was a candidate for membership. Shortly after, Putin published a magnificently long and rambling essay about Western aggression and double standards. In it, he ominously described Russians and Ukrainians as 'one people – a single whole'.[22]

On 4 February 2022 Putin travelled to Beijing to attend the opening ceremony of the Winter Olympic Games. Given his Olympic record, that in itself should probably have been taken as a warning sign that Russia was planning military action. Putin and President Xi met and released a statement opposing 'further enlargement of NATO'.[23] Ukraine was not mentioned by name. It did not need to be. That evening, at the opening ceremony, when the Ukrainian athletes entered the arena Putin was filmed closing his eyes. At the time, journalists speculated that he had fallen asleep.[24] Perhaps not. On 21 February, a day after the Olympics had ended, Putin declared that Ukraine was an integral part of Russia; that the Ukrainian president Volodymyr Zelenskyy was the public face of a puppet regime managed by foreign powers; and that he had authorized the deployment of Russian peacekeeping forces to eastern Ukraine. A full-scale invasion, centred upon an attempt to occupy Kyiv, followed.

The Russian invasion was unsuccessful. The armoured column dispatched to Kyiv was repulsed. In September, Ukraine, which had been given tens of billions of dollars of economic and military aid, counterattacked. It retook territory within the Kharkiv Oblast and the city of Kherson. (At the time of writing, a further counteroffensive, which began in June 2023, has made limited progress.) Russian firms and exports were sanctioned by Western countries, which outlined plans (with varying degrees of conviction) to phase out the import of Russian oil and gas. Russia found itself isolated on the diplomatic stage with the UN passing a resolution in October 2022 condemning its 'attempted illegal annexation' of Ukrainian provinces.[25] China, along with thirty-four other countries, abstained. Putin must have been disappointed that China had not voted against the resolution, yet the proto-alliance between the two countries held. China remained reluctant to export weapons to Russia in 2022 but agreed a $150 billion central bank liquidity swap to help Russia reduce the impact of Western financial sanctions.[26] Meanwhile, the Russian state's revenue from the sale of oil and gas increased by around $26 billion that year.[27]

At a first glance, the Russian invasion of Ukraine looked like it marked not only the return to a new Cold War, but a vindication of realist thinking. Countries are driven by narrow calculations of national interest. Peace is fragile. Economic interdependence is illusory. War is always possible and hard military power is the unavoidable bedrock of the international system. Politicians who thought Russia (or China) might be liberalized by trade and would become peace-loving liberal democracies were utopian fools. This does not, however, mean realists were necessarily happy with what had happened. In the early 2000s the American academic John J. Mearsheimer opposed the Iraq War on the brutally realist ground that the threat of a massive American nuclear retaliation would be enough to deter Saddam Hussein from deploying weapons of mass destruction in a context in which there was no other 'compelling strategic rationale' for the invasion.[28] Twenty years later, when it came to Ukraine, he argued that the West, by consistently pushing the boundaries of NATO further east, and, in particular, by welcoming Ukrainian aspirations to join NATO back in 2008 but then not actually letting it join, had backed Russia into a corner. Meanwhile, another realist, Kissinger, who had in his 1994 book, *Diplomacy*, highlighted Russia's enduring conviction that Georgia and Ukraine were within its sphere of influence, suggested that Ukraine trade territory for peace.[29] Mearsheimer is no apologist for Putin or for Russia. But, he argues, the West badly misplayed its hand. It provoked Russia by hinting at the prospect of its immediate neighbour joining NATO, but without then providing Ukraine with any firm security guarantees.[30]

Mearsheimer's realist analysis of the Ukrainian conflict had a precedent. During the original Cold War, the realist Hans Morgenthau argued that a third world war was most likely to be triggered not by an unexpected shift in the balance of power, but by the excessive ideological idealism of leaders 'imbued with the crusading spirit of the new moral force of nationalistic universalism'.[31] Wars, in other words, are caused not by realist warmongering but by misplaced liberal idealism. Liberals might reply that liberal values are worth fighting for and that, if NATO had not expanded eastwards in the 1990s and 2000s, Latvia, Estonia, Lithuania and Poland would not have had the opportunity to transform, for the better, their political systems. Liberalism has, in other words, a principled reason for being 'muscular' (pp. 153–4) even if realists have good reason to worry about the consequences those principles have had, whether in Iraq or, Mearsheimer would argue, in Ukraine.

A GOLDEN AGE

China helped bail out America in 2008. Yet over the next half-dozen years a broad consensus formed within America that Xi Jinping, who had become general secretary of the Chinese Communist Party in November 2012, was a stridently authoritarian and nationalist leader with zero interest in economic or political liberalization, and that China posed a growing political, economic and military threat to American global power. Realism was back, big time. America needed to 'pivot' to Asia and to stand up – and be seen to stand up – to Chinese expansionism, whether that took the form of threats to Taiwan, the construction of artificial islands in the South China Sea, or the violation of international trading rules.[32]

This shift in American foreign-policy thinking was crystallized by another realist theorist, Graham Allison, in an article first published in *The Atlantic* in September 2015. Allison, referencing the proto-realist Athenian historian and military general Thucydides' account of the origins of the war between Athens and Sparta, argued that, throughout history, when a rising power has confronted a ruling power the result has usually been war.[33] Rising and risen powers are bound to view each other's ambitions with suspicion and to assume the worst of each other's actions. Established powers will always be tempted to confront their rival before it is too late. A rising power will always be looking for opportunities to flex its muscles. This does not make war inevitable; the transition between British and American world power was, at times, a bumpy one, but it did not result in a war. But war is more common than not. Allison suggests that, since 1500, twelve out of sixteen cases of 'hegemonic transition' have led to war.[34] The defining question of our age is, he suggests, whether China and the United States can learn from history and escape Thucydides' 'trap'.

Historians have challenged the accuracy of Allison's history and his twelve out of sixteen numbers.[35] Joseph Nye, the liberal international-relations theorist who developed the idea of 'soft power' (p. 5), has argued that the huge economic interdependencies between America and China mean that their respective situations are fundamentally different from those of Sparta and Athens.[36] Other academics have argued that China, far from seeking to eclipse America, is, in its words and deeds, simply seeking a share of international political leadership to match its growing economic power, along with territorial reunification and a limited regional hegemony in Southeast Asia.[37] Yet it was Allison's hyper-pessimistic realist analysis which stuck, in part because it had already taken root within the American foreign-policy establishment.

America has not disengaged from China economically. To do so would, as the US treasury secretary Janet Yellen has argued, be disastrous.[38] In 2022 American exports to China totalled around $160 billion and Chinese exports to America $500 billion. By January 2023 China still held $850 billion in US Treasury Securities.[39] Yet the political tone of that trade has changed to one which can perhaps be best described as one of 'weaponized interdependence' in which trade has gone hand-in-hand with stand-offs, sanctions and threats.[40] In October 2022 the Biden administration announced a ban on microchip exports to China, targeting both American companies trading with China and overseas companies using American-made semiconductors. Biden has also signalled an intention to reverse a decade-long process by which the most advanced microchips are increasingly manufactured by the strategically vulnerable Taiwan Semiconductor Manufacturing Company and to repatriate that work to America.[41] Apple, which continues to manufacture its microprocessors in Taiwan before assembling its final products in China, has been lambasted for its close ties with Beijing by both Democrats and Republicans.[42]

Britain, it almost goes without saying, usually sticks close to the coat-tails of American foreign policy.[43] Yet when it came to China, Britain, for a long time, went its own way. David Cameron and George Osborne arrived in office in 2010 determined to forge a deeper economic relationship with China. There was nothing particularly exceptional about this at the time. Yet Britain stuck to this position long after American thinking had changed. In October 2013 Osborne visited Shanghai and, in a keynote speech, reminisced about his time backpacking around the country as a student whilst looking forward to a 'golden decade for both our countries'. In March 2015, Britain, despite loud objections from America, became one of the founding members of the Chinese-led Asian Infrastructure Investment Bank. The Obama administration accused Britain of a 'constant accommodation' of China and, for a while, briefed that Britain's intelligence relationship with America might be jeopardized.[44] Britain did not seem to mind and seven months later Xi Jinping arrived in Britain on a state visit, which featured a state banquet at Buckingham Palace; talks with Cameron at the prime minister's country house, Chequers (during which Cameron bought Xi a pint of Greene King IPA and a mini-basket of fish and chips at the nearest pub, The Plough, at Cadsden); and an overnight trip to Manchester to visit the National Graphene Institute at the University of Manchester, followed by a visit to the National Football Museum to witness the former Manchester City defender Sun Jihai being inducted into the English Football Hall of Fame.*

When Theresa May replaced Cameron as prime minister in 2016, she said some nice things about his legacy as a 'great, modern prime minister' and then proceeded, for the most part, to shred his policy legacy.[45] But when it came to China, May decided that, with Brexit looming, Britain needed new economic and political friends more than ever. In September 2017 she spoke to President Xi to discuss trade, security co-operation and North Korea and agreed, as the official summary of the conversation put it, that 'the UK and China should continue to consolidate the "Golden Era" of bilateral relations and deepen our strategic

---

* The Plough is the pub where, three years earlier, the Camerons had accidentally managed to leave their daughter behind when they had visited for lunch but left separately. After Xi's visit The Plough became a tourist attraction for Chinese visitors and, in 2016, it was bought by a Chinese firm, SinoFortone.

partnership'.[46] In January 2018 May arrived in China to talk, once again, about trade and, specifically, the timetable for a future, post-Brexit, free-trade agreement. At the end of that meeting, the Chinese media praised her for her 'pragmatic collaboration' and willingness to ignore the 'noise and nagging' of 'radical public opinion'.[47] This was probably about as much media praise as May received in 2018 and she was rewarded when, in August, the Chinese Commerce Ministry announced the start of formal talks to reach a 'top notch' trade deal.[48] In 2019 May then resisted American demands that Britain terminate a 5G contract it had signed with the Chinese company Huawei in 2012.[49]

Having held the line when it came to prioritizing trade over just about anything else, Britain's relationship with China began to deteriorate in 2019. On 14 July, a few days before Boris Johnson won the race to replace her as prime minister, May announced Huawei's contract would, after all, be ended and that any material the company had already installed would be removed.[50] In June 2020, following earlier protests over a proposed extradition treaty, China mounted a direct takeover of Hong Kong, arresting activists, politicians and newspaper editors. Britain declared this to be a breach of the terms of the Joint Declaration under which Hong Kong had been returned to China and offered – to China's evident fury – resettlement and potential British citizenship to up to 3 million Hong Kong residents. In October of that year, the new director general of the security service (MI5), Ken McCallum, warned that whilst the Russian intelligence services could provide 'bursts of bad weather', China 'is changing the climate' and posed a threat to Britain's core national interests.[51]

In March 2021 the Ministry of Defence published a new Integrated Defence Review, which described China as a 'systematic competitor' to Britain. This was, in some ways, relatively dovish: Russia got labelled as an 'acute and direct threat'.[52] But in his evidence to a parliamentary committee a month later, the foreign secretary Dominic Raab went further, warning that China 'wants to ransack the international system'.[53] In April, the House of Commons endorsed a motion describing China's mass detention of upwards of a million Uyghur people in Xinjiang province to constitute an act of genocide.[54] In July, a new National Security and Investment Act gave the government new powers to block the foreign takeover of British firms across a range of security-related industries[55] and, in September, Britain, Australia and America announced the formation of a new AUKUS Security Partnership designed to counter Chinese military and political influence in the Pacific. (The alliance had, for the British, the added advantage of profoundly annoying the French, too.[56])

In November 2021 the chief of the Secret Intelligence Service, Richard Moore, warned of the dangers of Chinese interference in domestic British politics and of China's growing determination to resolve the Taiwan issue by force if necessary.[57] In January 2022 MI5 went public with a warning that an alleged Chinese agent, Christine Lee, had made a series of donations to MPs – the largest, totalling over £400,000, to Labour's Barry Gardiner – designed to win political favour.[58] Britain now saw itself as being back in a big, bad, post-liberal world composed of not simply threatening but conspiring great powers who wished to do Britain harm. Rather like a teenager who rows with their parents, sleeps on a friend's sofa and talks about renting a small flat before doing the sums and moving back home, Britain had, for a short while, experimented with the idea of pursing foreign-policy independence, at least when it came to China, but had come to think better of it.

FLYING THE FLAG

How well equipped is Britain to thrive and survive in a realist world in which China and Russia both constitute security threats? Britain remains one of five permanent members of the UN Security Council. Its political and security relationships with France and Germany were strained by Brexit (and, with France, additionally by the AUKUS Treaty). Yet the Ukraine crisis has brought Britain back into the fold: Rishi Sunak and Emmanuel Macron held a highly performative best-friends-forever summit in March 2023. Britain also patched up its differences with America and Joe Biden over Northern Ireland through the Windsor Framework (p. 387). Yet, during her brief period in office, Liz Truss could not hide her visible disappointment in having to admit, following a flying visit to New York in September 2022, that America had as much enthusiasm for a post-Brexit free-trade agreement with Britain as most people do in renewing their car insurance.[59]

Realists place a great deal of emphasis on 'hard' military power as the ultimate guarantor of security.[60] In real, inflation-adjusted terms (and at 2021/2 prices) defence expenditure grew from £40bn in 2000 to £47bn in 2009/10 before falling to £42bn in 2015/16 and rising again to £49bn in 2021/2 (a sum which is equivalent to 2 per cent of GDP).[61] By comparison, China's estimated annual defence budget is around £234bn and America's £645bn. The size of the regular British Army fell from 207,000 in 2000 to 147,000 in 2022.[62] With coastal patrol vessels excluded, the number of ships in the Royal Navy has declined by around 74 per cent since the Falklands War in the early 1980s.[63] And the number of front-line fighter jets has fallen by 40 per cent since 2007, to just 119.[64] In 2016 a former chief of the defence staff, General Sir Richard Barrons, warned there was no military plan to defend Britain in a conventional conflict and that a Russian air campaign would quickly overwhelm existing defences.[65] That sounded controversial at the time. But by 2023 Defence Secretary Ben Wallace accepted that Britain's armed forces had been 'hollowed out and underfunded'.[66]

Britain still maintains a nuclear deterrent; Parliament voted in 2016 to replace the existing Vanguard Class submarines with four new Dreadnought ones at an estimated cost of over £31 billion.[67] Britain has also commissioned two new aircraft carriers, HMS *Queen Elizabeth* and HMS *Prince of Wales*. In September 2021, and following an earlier promise by Boris Johnson to return 'east of Suez', the *Queen Elizabeth*, which had been joined by a detachment of American fighter planes, sailed through the South China Sea for a freedom of navigation exercise, whilst one of its escorts, HMS *Richmond*, sailed through the Strait of Taiwan itself.[68] China warned it would not continue to tolerate incursions into what it claims as sovereign waters and denounced Britain's colonial mindset.[69] The head of the Royal Navy, Admiral Tony Radakin, was quoted as saying the *Queen Elizabeth* was 'flying the flag for Britain and carrying forward the prime minister's vision of a Global Britain'.[70] But, in the event of any sustained military conflict with China over Taiwan, Britain's new carriers would have no alternative but to retreat hundreds (and hundreds) of miles because they are exceptionally vulnerable to missile attack.[71] That also applies to the larger US carriers (and to China's as well). But the *Queen Elizabeth* and the *Prince of Wales* would be more vulnerable than most because, as two other former chiefs of the defence staff, General Sir David Richards and General Sir Nicholas Houghton, have suggested, the new carriers were so expensive that the Ministry of Defence had to cannibalize other parts of the Armed Forces' budget to pay for them. One casualty has been the construction of a series of frigates and destroyers whose job it would have been to protect the aircraft carriers from attack.[72]

In 1987 the British historian Paul Kennedy published *The Rise and Fall of the Great Powers*.[73] Looking ahead to the 2000s, Kennedy took the continued relative decline of Britain and France for granted; anticipated the rise of China (and Japan); and predicted the relative decline of America. Kennedy was right about Britain but, despite the huge failures of Afghanistan and Iraq and the challenge now posed by China, it is not yet obvious that the sun is setting on American power. Britain needed American economic and military power to fight the Second World War. In the aftermath of the Suez crisis in 1956 it then accepted that it could not afford to operate independently of America. The Conservative Party's dalliance with China in the 2010s constituted, in this respect, an interesting and important moment. But in answer to the question posed at the start of this section, Britain's fortunes in a realist world remain dependent on America.

36
In the Red

A BAD YEAR

From around September 2007 onwards, there was never a point when it felt that the British economy was doing brilliantly, even when it was growing steadily. From about late 2021 onwards, it became increasingly obvious that the economy was, in fact, doing spectacularly badly in all sorts of different ways. Covid-19 had knocked around 11 per cent off GDP and added more than £300 billion in additional public debt. It had also had the effect of reducing the available workforce by over a million. Some of this was due to people in their fifties and upwards deciding to retire early rather than return to work after being furloughed. The largest part of that fall was, however, a knock-on effect of the near doubling of the number of people on hospital waiting lists waiting for consultant-led elective care.[1] On some estimates around 300,000 people who had been working prior to 2020 said that they were no longer working by 2022 because of long-term illness.[2]

A second problem was inflation. Covid disrupted global supply chains, whilst ongoing lockdowns in China in the pursuit of zero Covid further flattened productivity capacity. With too much pent-up demand chasing too little supply, inflation was running at over 5 per cent by December 2021. As a result – and starting that month – the Bank of England began increasing interest rates. The Russian invasion of Ukraine in February 2022, as well as causing the deaths of over 200,000 people over the following year, also led to a huge spike in energy and grain prices.[3] By August of that year, it was estimated that the average household heating bill in Britain would rise from around £1,200 a year in 2021 to over £6,000 by April 2023.[4] Higher energy prices had pushed inflation to an annual rate of over 9 per cent, and interest rates to 3.5 per cent, by December 2022.

High inflation added something like £3,000 to average mortgage costs for anyone renewing their policy in 2022.[5] It also triggered outbursts of industrial action in the public sector where average pay rises in the summer of 2022 were 2.7 per cent (compared to 7 per cent in the private sector).[6] By the end of that year, nurses, doctors, ambulance workers, railway workers, teachers, postal workers, barristers, civil servants, university lecturers and, in Scotland, refuse workers, had gone on strike. Less noticed, rising interest rates also impacted hugely on the cost of servicing Britain's public debt. Recall here that whilst public-sector borrowing remained high in the 2010s, the interest rate cost of serving that debt was stable at around £40 billion (p. 282). As inflation rose, that changed – and changed dramatically. By March 2022, the Office for Budget Responsibility was forecasting that government debt interest payments would rise to a cool £114 billion in 2022/3.[7] At that point, it is estimated, Britain's debt repayments, equivalent to over 10 per cent of GDP, would be the highest of any high-income country.[8] Put all of this together and low growth and high inflation combined to squeeze household incomes. The Resolution Foundation estimated that average household disposable income fell by 3.3 per cent in 2022, the biggest annual fall in a century.[9] As 2022 slid into 2023, 'non-core' inflation, exclusive of energy and food prices which had been badly impacted by Covid and by Ukraine, was running at over 6 per cent by April 2023: its highest rate for over thirty years.[10]

Covid, inflation and the Russian invasion of Ukraine damaged economies across the world. The British one was harder hit than most, however. In 2020 the British economy contracted by more than that of almost any other country (p. 433). In 2021 it then grew by 8.7 per cent, well above the European trend. Between the first quarter of 2022 and the end of the second quarter of 2023 the British economy then grew by an average of 0.2 per cent a quarter, compared to an average of 0.3% in France, 0.5% in Canada and Germany, 0.6% in Italy and America and 0.9% in Japan.[11]

NOT JUST A BLIP

Britain's *annus horribilis* in 2022 had been a long time in the making. In the boom years of the 2000s the economy had grown by an average of 2.7 per cent a year. That was reasonably impressive but, as we have seen, also a little misleading as the boom was followed by a crash which wiped out some of the earlier gains. Taken as a whole, between 2000 and 2010, the economy grew by an average of just 1.7 per cent a year. Between 2010 and 2019, prior to the pandemic shock, it then grew by an average of 2.2 per cent a year. Between 2010 and 2022, taking account of the pandemic, economic growth averaged, again, 1.7 per cent.[12] To see what kind of a difference low long-term growth makes, take note of the 'Rule of 72'. Divide 72 by the rate of growth in a country. The resulting number is how long it will take for the economy to double in size. For China, ticking along at 10 per cent growth in the 2000s, the economy will double in size every seven years. For Britain, during the boom years at 2.7 per cent growth, it would take just over twenty-six years. At 1.7 per cent it will take forty-two years.

If the numbers when it comes to growth are distinctly ordinary, those for household income are worse. Between 2000/1 and 2007/8 average median household income *after* housing costs grew by 16 per cent to a total of £456 a week. By the end of 2019/20, more than a decade later, it had grown by just over another 9 per cent to £499. By 2021/2 it was just 27 pence higher.[13] These figures on household income include the effect of tax credits. If you look at average total pay, then the picture starts to look bleak. Between January 2000 and December 2007 average weekly real seasonally adjusted pay, adjusted for inflation and at 2015 prices, grew by just under 20 per cent, from £425 to £513. The financial crash took some of the sheen off that figure. By the end of December 2010 average pay had fallen to £492. Since then, and through to the end of 2022, average pay has risen by a grand total of 0.6 per cent to £495 – in other words, to below the level it had been in 2007.[14]

If there is a positive story here, it is that levels of income and wealth inequality have not increased over the last decade or so. The Gini Coefficient for household income *after* housing costs rose slightly, from 0.389 in 2000/1 to 0.402 in 2007/8. It fell during the austerity years to 0.396 in 2015/16, before falling again to 0.383 in 2021/2.[15] For overall levels of wealth, the Gini Coefficient rose fractionally, from 0.61 between 2006 and 2008 to 0.62 between 2018 and 2020.[16] Yet, if you are looking for a cloud to go with this silver lining, overall levels of income inequality remain high by international standards. Of the G7 economies only the United States had a (slightly) higher level of income inequality than Britain's.[17] Stagnant wages, low growth in household income, low overall rates of growth and relatively high levels of income inequality have combined to generate high levels of relative and absolute poverty. The Institute for Fiscal Studies estimates that by 2021/2 10 per cent of the population had a household income which was less than 50 per cent of the median household income *before* housing costs, and that 14 per cent did so *after* housing costs.[18] To take just two absolute measures of poverty, in 2023 the Trussell Trust estimated that 11.3 million people, 14 per cent of all adults or their households, experienced food insecurity in the twelve months to June 2022.[19] And the estimated number of people sleeping rough in England has increased from 1,768 in 2010 to 3,069.[20]

Regarding public expenditure, New Labour made a social democratic virtue of increasing spending; the Coalition made it a priority to cut public expenditure; and the pandemic resulted in a huge jump in the other direction. At the end of it all, total managed public expenditure, measured as a share of GDP, rose from 35 per cent of GDP in 2000/1 to a peak of 46 per cent in 2009/10, before falling to a low of 39 per cent in 2018 and, after spiking during the pandemic, falling again to 44.6 per cent in 2021/2.[21] But although public expenditure has waxed and waned whilst increasing overall, the aggregate tax burden has pretty much flatlined at between 36 and 38 per cent of GDP between 2000 and 2020, before rising to 39.3 per cent in 2021/2.[22] You don't need a Nobel Prize in economics to spot the discrepancy here. Public expenditure as a share of GDP has been consistently higher than the tax take. Andrew Turnbull, the former treasury permanent secretary and, later, Cabinet secretary, observed in 2019 that 'what we're trying to do is run public services on a kind of north European level on tax rates that are much lower, probably 10% of GDP lower'.[23] That is an inescapable truth of the British political economy. It is one that has been avoided by borrowing on a gargantuan scale. In 2000 public sector net debt was £334 billion. By March 2008, as the boom was about to end abruptly, it was £543 billion. By 2022 total public debt exceeded £2,200 billion and by 2023 it had risen again and was the equivalent of more than 100 per cent of GDP.[24] If interest payments on that debt do rise to anything like £114 billion a year, the headroom for any government of any political stripe will be exceptionally limited. To put this sum into context, £114 billion is around £10 billion more than the British government anticipated spending on education in 2022/3.[25]

The scale of the economic challenges Britain faces in the future will be compounded by an ageing population. Low growth, stagnating wages and increased NHS backlogs have slowed (and possibly already reversed) previous increases in average life expectancy. During the 2000s there was an average annual fall of around 26 deaths per 100,000 people. Between 2010 and 2018 that improvement tailed off, with the annual fall averaging just under 2 deaths per 100,000. Over this period, overall life expectancy for men living in the most deprived areas of the country stalled, and it actually decreased for women.[26] In April 2023 the Office for National Statistics reported that the age-standardized mortality rate had risen by a statistically significant amount when compared to both 2021 and 2022.[27] Increasing life expectancy in Britain has been replaced by falling life expectancy. Yet, even so, an ageing population is nevertheless going to pose an economic challenge in the coming decades. Almost one in five people are currently aged sixty-five or over. By 2050 that is projected to rise to one in four.[28] If the retirement age keeps being raised, an ageing population need not necessarily lead to an equivalent rise in the dependency ratio, i.e., the proportion of the population of non-working age. Yet, however this works out in practice, none of the options – dying younger, working longer, or being poorer – is, it must be said, hugely attractive.

With regards to climate change, British *territorial* greenhouse gas emissions (see p. 122 on the importance of the word territorial in this context) have continued to fall, from around 800 million tonnes in 1990 to 600 million tonnes by 2010 and to 425 million tonnes in 2021.[29] Reaching the statutory Net Zero target by 2050 is, however, likely to require significant further levels of public and private investment over the next decade. In particular, it is estimated that a capital spend of around £39 billion on energy efficiency measures (primarily insulating walls and roofs) and £37 billion on cleaner and more energy-efficient heating systems is likely to be required between 2022 and 2032.[30] In the longer term, these investments, if they are made, will not only reduce emissions but save money on energy costs. Yet if there was a list of things that Britain has been particularly bad at getting right, housing and long-term investment would be quite near the top. In March 2023, the government seemed to accept that its newly published 'Net Zero' strategy would not do enough to hit its own legally enforceable target.[31] Three months later, the Climate Change Committee suggested that 'the UK has lost its clear global leadership role on climate action' and that its 'confidence in the UK meeting its medium-term targets has decreased'.[32] Shortly after, business leaders and a group of climate scientists, including Sir Nicholas Stern, wrote to the prime minister to warn that Britain was in danger of losing any credible claim to international leadership on the issue of climate change.[33] Rishi Sunak responded, shortly after, by saying that, whilst he remained committed to the net zero 'agenda', it had to be pursued in a 'proportionate and pragmatic way'.[34] Meanwhile, total global emissions of carbon dioxide, which were 22 billion tonnes in 1990 and 25 billion tonnes in 2000, had risen to 37 billion tonnes by 2022.[35]

It is also increasingly clear that Brexit has come at an economic cost and that it is going to take a spectacular reversal of fortunes for that to change. In 2020 Britain left the European Union's Single Market and Customs Union and accepted significant non-tariff barriers to trade with its largest trading partners. One detailed estimate by John Springford, at the Centre for European Reform, is that Brexit, by the spring of 2022, had reduced Britain's trade in goods by 7 per cent and its GDP by 5.5 per cent.[36] In 2016 Britain was the thirteenth largest carmaker in the world, producing around 1.7 million vehicles a year. By 2022 it had fallen to eighteenth having produced 775,000 cars.[37] Brexit also seems to be contributing to the ongoing relative decline of the City of London. In the early 2000s the firms listed on the London Stock Exchange accounted for around 13 per cent of global equity value. By 2022 that number had fallen to just 4 per cent. In that same year only around 1 per cent of the money raised through Initial Public Offerings (that is, of shares sold in privately owned firms for the first time) was raised in London.[38] Brexit has not been a 'here today but zombie apocalypse tomorrow' kind of an economic disaster. It has, instead, taken the form of a slow puncture, one which the former governor of the Bank of England Mark Carney argues also goes some way to explaining why inflation has been higher in Britain than in most other European countries.[39]

Over time, it is possible new trade deals will offset some of the losses incurred in trade with the European Union. This was certainly the payoff from Brexit envisaged by most of the key figures in the officially designated Vote.Leave campaign. The problem with the European Union, as they saw it, was not its internal free-trade arrangements but its protectionist instincts towards the rest of the world. A new global, buccaneering Britain would be free to strike new trade deals and, in doing so, become a 'Singapore-on-Thames'.[40] Since then, the results have been largely underwhelming. New free-trade deals with Australia and Japan have been concluded. In March 2023 it was announced that Britain would become the first European country to join the Comprehensive and Progressive Agreement for Trans-Pacific Partnership. Yet nearly all the seventy or more trade deals which Britain has signed since leaving the European Union, including the one with Japan, have basically rolled-over the terms and conditions of existing European deals. That was not true of the deal with Australia, but that deal was not a particularly great deal: the access it offered Australian farmers to the British market was notably greater than that offered to British farmers to the Australian one. In November 2022 the Conservative MP and former secretary of state for the environment, food and rural affairs George Eustice said of the Australian deal that it 'gave away far too much for far too little in return'.[41] Meanwhile, proposed free trade deals with America and India have stalled, whilst the one with China has disappeared without trace.

If this economic assessment sounds like miserabilism of the highest order, it is probably worth emphasizing just how widespread that miserabilism has become. In September 2022, Penny Mordaunt, the minister of state for trade policy, was one of the candidates to replace Boris Johnson. In the fifth and final ballot of Conservative MPs she came third, eight votes behind Liz Truss. In January 2023, after she had become leader of the House of Commons, she delivered a wide-ranging speech to the Institute of Government. Echoing Theresa May's analysis when she entered Downing Street in 2016 (p. 360), Mordaunt argued that for many people 'the whole system can seem rigged against them'. To this she added the singularly downbeat assessment that 'the very continuation and success of capitalism and democracy hangs in the balance'.[42] By that point, the person who had narrowly beaten her in the race to become prime minister had come and gone.

THE LIZ TRUSS EXPERIENCE

On 6 September 2022, addressing the country from behind a new Jenga-style lectern of blocks of wood, costing (reportedly) £4,175, the new prime minister, Liz Truss, fresh from her defeat of Rishi Sunak in the Conservative Party leadership contest, promised to 'get Britain working again' with a 'bold plan to grow the economy through tax cuts and reform'.[43] Over the next thirty-six hours she sacked the permanent secretary at the Treasury, Tom Scholar; appointed a new Cabinet, minus Sunak and anyone who had ever been alone in the same room as Sunak; and announced a new plan to freeze household energy bills at £2,500 a year for two years, at a cost of around £150 billion.[44]

On the afternoon of 8 September Queen Elizabeth died after a short illness. Just over two thousand people, including nearly ninety world leaders, attended her funeral on Monday 19 September. Public reactions varied, but after seventy years during which she had been a stable fixture in national life there was a palpable sense of an era closing. After fourteen days of national mourning, politics returned with the bang of a mini-budget on 23 September, in which the new chancellor, Kwasi Kwarteng, scrapped the 45 pence rate of higher tax for those earning £150,000; brought forward Sunak's planned 1 pence cut in the basic rate of taxation to April 2023; cancelled Johnson's proposed 1.25 per cent national insurance rise to pay for NHS and social care; and cut stamp duty for property buyers.

In a world of low political trust, Truss had done exactly what she said she would do: cut taxes. What she had not done was to let the Bank of England know what she was doing; let the Office for Budget Responsibility cost the proposals; or say anything about how the tax cuts and the £150 billion to be spent on household energy bills would be paid for.[45] It is probably fair to assume that, in the medium term, Kwarteng's budget would have required some combination of higher borrowing and spending cuts. We never quite found out for sure because the markets tanked. Sterling fell. The interest rate the Treasury needed to offer on its 10-year Gilts, which had already risen from practically zero in 2020 to 3.2 per cent in August 2022, jumped to nearly 5 per cent. On 27 September the IMF called on Truss to reverse her economic policies.[46] The next day, amidst reports several pension funds were close to collapse, the Bank of England did what it had been doing for the best part of a decade: it rode to the rescue by promising to start buying Treasury Gilts in whatever quantity was needed to restore market stability.[47]

On 14 October, with her support within the parliamentary Conservative Party draining away, Truss sacked Kwarteng. He was replaced by Jeremy Hunt, who proceeded to junk those bits of the September mini-budget which had not already been abandoned. On 11 October *The Economist* had published a leader which observed that it had only taken Truss a week to 'blow up her own government': a period which, it noted, is 'roughly the shelf-life of a lettuce'.[48] A few days later, Denis Mann, deputy editor at the *Daily Star*, had the idea of buying a lettuce and livestreaming a picture of it alongside a framed photograph of Truss and the caption 'Will Liz Truss outlast this lettuce?' Within a few days it had attracted 350,000 viewers. On the day of Truss's eventual resignation, 20 October, 'God Save the King' was played and the portrait of Truss was turned face-downwards. Shortly after, the musical accompaniment switched to the 1980 hit 'Celebration' by Kool & the Gang.[49]

After Truss resigned, Boris Johnson flew back into the country to contest the new leadership contest. But despite receiving the required number of nominations, he withdrew, leaving Rishi Sunak to become prime minister on 25 October 2022.[50] Sunak came under immediate pressure to reduce inflation, reduce interest rates and to intervene to reduce mortgage payments, whilst also cutting taxes in the run-up to the next general election. With hardly any room for economic manoeuvring, in January 2023 Sunak prioritized halving inflation, growing the economy, reducing the overall national debt, reducing NHS waiting lists, and passing new laws to stop boats carrying asylum-seekers from crossing the English Channel.[51] There was very little in this list Conservative backbenchers could easily have disagreed with. But in the immediate aftermath of Johnson's resignation from Parliament, a few days in advance of publication of a report detailing the ways in which he had previously misled the House over 'Partygate', reports were already surfacing of a potential leadership challenge against Sunak.[52]

GROWING BACK

Liz Truss was right about one thing. Economic growth in Britain has been low for a long time. There are a set of related reasons as to why that is so that can probably command a fair degree of consensus amongst economists and across large (but not all) parts of the political spectrum. First, low growth is umbilically connected to low productivity. I have already noted that productivity growth, understood as increases in the amount produced for every hour worked, stagnated between 2010 and 2015. The OECD estimates that, by 2022, and using 2015 as a baseline (=100), GDP per hour worked had risen to an average of 107 across the 38 member countries of OECD as a whole; to 107 in the United States; 105 in countries using the European Single Currency; 106 in Germany; 111 in Portugal; and to 104 in Britain.[53] So it is fair to say that productivity is still an issue.

Second, low productivity is connected to low levels of investment. Between 2010 and 2015 Gross Capital Formation (the fixed assets of the economy, measured as a percentage of GDP) was 16.6 per cent, which, as we have seen, put Britain in 150th place out of 174 countries for which the World Bank keeps records (p. 290). Since then, and between 2015 and 2021, investment has risen to an average of 18 per cent, putting Britain in a not much higher position of 145th.[54] The story here is not, as it was during the Coalition years, primarily about declining public-sector investment. That has risen in real, inflation-adjusted terms from £36 billion in 2015 to £64 billion in 2021/2 and is, at the time of writing, projected to rise to £67 billion in 2023/4.[55] Britain's poor investment levels are now more closely connected to low levels of business investment as a share of GDP. As previously noted, the Office for National Statistics dataset here uses 1997 as a baseline measurement (=100). In Q1 of 2016, immediately prior to the European Union referendum, investment stood, using this measure, at 163. It had declined to 162 by Q1 of 2019 and then fell to just 128 at the start of the pandemic, before recovering to 162 in Q4 of 2022.[56]

One issue when it comes to business investment is the short-term view of the City of London. In the mid-1990s, as a part of his ill-fated 'stakeholding' speech, Tony Blair railed against the short-termism of the City: 'It is surely time to assess how we shift the emphasis in corporate ethos from the company being a mere vehicle for the capital market – to be traded, bought and sold as a commodity.'[57] That argument made a comeback after the boom had ended. In a review of corporate governance commissioned by Gordon Brown and published in 2009, Sir David Walker, a former chairman of Barclays and Morgan Stanley, bemoaned a 'myopic' focus on short-term company profits and share price.[58] In 2012 a government-sponsored review of equity markets by Sir John Kay also identified short-termism as a key economic problem, pointing to the need to 'reduce the pressures for short-term decision making that arise from excessively frequent reporting of financial and investment performance'.[59] The short-termism of the City as a factor explaining Britain's relatively poor economic performance was subsequently highlighted by Ed Miliband, Jeremy Corbyn and Theresa May.[60] Yet there is no evidence here of any great change having occurred. The London Stock Exchange may have a declining share of the global equity market, but the firms listed on it have nevertheless done extraordinarily well over the last decade. The FTSE 250 index surged from just over 6,000 in January 2009 to 19,928 by March 2023.[61] It is hard to explain this sustained rise in terms of underlying corporate profit levels. The average net rate of return for non-financial corporations – a standard measure of profitability which averaged 10.9 per cent between 2000 and 2007 – rose slightly to an average of 11.1 per cent between 2010 and 2015, before falling to an average of 10.4 per cent between 2015 and 2019 and then to 9.6 per cent in 2020 and 2021.[62] Instead, it is higher short-term dividend payments, which have increased from £43 billion in 2010 to £84 billion in 2022 across FTSE 100 firms, that seem to be most closely linked to and best explain rising overall capital market values.[63]

A second part of the story of Britain's poor productivity and investment performance is regional inequality. This is not exactly a new insight. As chancellor, Gordon Brown prioritized regional economic development in the 2000s.[64] George Osborne committed himself to 'rebalancing' the economy. Boris Johnson preferred 'levelling-up'.[65] Yet if anything has changed here, it has changed for the worse. Figure 6 shows levels of output per worker across different regions in Britain in 2020, as measured against a baseline of 100 for the country. What is immediately striking here is that output only exceeded the UKGBNI

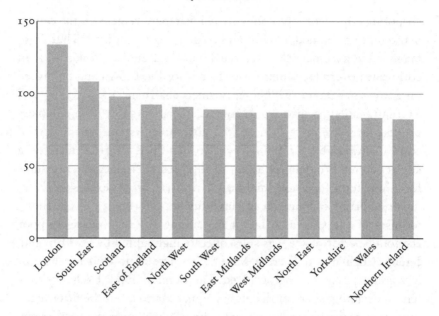

Figure 6: Output per Worker by Region, 2020

UK = 100

Office for National Statistics, 'Regional labour productivity, UK: 2020', Figure 3 (16 June 2022).

average in London and the Southeast. When compared with the year 2000, only two areas, London and Scotland, *improved* their relative productivity performance when measured in this way.*[66] Everywhere else has, in effect, been levelled down. The announcement in October 2023 that plans to extend the HS2 rail line from Birmingham to Manchester were being abandoned felt, in this respect, emblematic.

Finally, and perhaps a little bit more left field, whilst under-investment will render British firms increasingly uncompetitive in global markets over the longer term, those same firms can nevertheless afford to under-invest right now because they operate within increasingly uncompetitive

---

* Relative to a baseline of 100 for each year, London's output per hour was estimated to be 129 in 2000, 137 in 2010 and 133 in 2020. The equivalent figures for Yorkshire and Humberside were 88, 87 and 85; for Wales 87, 82 and 84; for the Northeast 88, 87 and 86; for the Northwest 91.5, 92 and 91; for Northern Ireland 84, 80 and 83; for the East Midlands 88, 86 and 87; for the West Midlands 90, 86 and 87; and those for Scotland 91, 97 and 98.

markets domestically. The four largest firms operating in their respective industries now account for 80 per cent of all personal current accounts, 90 per cent of the broadband market, 70 per cent of the grocery market and 60 per cent of the domestic electricity and gas markets.[67] In a working paper for the Centre for Competition Policy, Stephen Davies reviews the data and finds that, across the economy as a whole, market concentration levels rose by about 30 per cent between 1998 and 2011; that, by 2018, around 30 per cent of industries could be classified as concentrated or highly concentrated, using traditional Competition Authority guidelines, and that firms with the largest market shares in an industry in any one year have become *more* likely to retain those – or higher – market shares in later years.[68]

SHIFTING GROUND

The ideas of free market economists such as the Austrian-born Friedrich Hayek retained a cult status in the post-war years but were, by the early 1970s, of only marginal significance within the mainstream of economics thought. In 1969 Hayek moved to the University of Salzburg where he lived in a run-down suburb and worked in a department where he had few colleagues and, he complained, a substandard library in which to work.[69] His fortunes only began to improve a few years later when he published the first volume of his magnum opus, *Law, Legislation and Liberty*, and his free market ideas came increasingly to be seen as the solution to the West's economic malaise.[70] By the early 2000s, where we started this book, free market ideas were, if not dominant, then firmly ascendant. Tony Blair was not, I have argued, a neoliberal Thatcherite (p. 23). But he was a social democrat who was prepared, for the most part, to let the market do its thing with a view to redistributing the proceeds. More than that, he was someone who believed that the discipline of the market and the rigour of private-sector businesses could be applied more broadly. Need a Dome to host a party? Get some business sponsorship. Need to put some delivery oomph into public services? Inject a bit of competition and shadow market pricing. Need a fast-growing global financial centre? Head this way and walk through the door marked 'light-touch'. What's more, it seemed to be working. The British economy was growing, and wages and household income were rising. Having won a viable parliamentary majority in just two of the previous eleven general elections between 1950 and 1997, Labour won by a landslide in 1997 and 2001 and came away with a healthy majority in 2005.

Britain was not the only country that seemed to be swimming with the free market current. In the United States, the Republican Party, which, between 2002 and 2006, controlled the presidency and the House of Representatives, passed two major pieces of legislation to cut income and capital gains tax and eliminate estate tax. The European Union, which Margaret Thatcher and, later, David Cameron regarded as a backwater of statist planning and over-generous welfare systems, approved, in 2000, the pro-market 'Lisbon Strategy', intended to 'open up hitherto sheltered and protected sectors . . . and secure more flexibility and adaptability in the labour market'.[71] In Germany, the Social Democratic Chancellor Gerhard Schröder bet the bank on 'Agenda 2010': a set of reforms that included tax cuts, cuts in pension and unemployment benefits, and labour market deregulation.[72] Finally, in China, accession to the World Trade Organization in 2001 was matched with deregulation of banking, the privatization of state-owned enterprises and the dismantling of much of the existing social welfare system.[73]

Looking back, the 2008 financial crisis was the turning point. In an interview in 2008 the American economist Joseph Stiglitz, who had won a Nobel Prize in 2001 for his work showing how, in conditions of asymmetric information, competitive markets – contra Hayek – predictably generated inefficiencies, said:

> The fall of Wall Street is for market fundamentalism what the fall of the Berlin Wall was for communism. It tells the world that this way of economic organization turns out not to be sustainable. In the end, everyone says that model doesn't work. This moment is a marker that the claims of financial market liberalization were bogus.[74]

It did not, safe to say, feel like that at the time. In Britain, following the financial crisis public spending came to be seen as the cause of the economic downturn, rather than, as Keynesians would have wanted, the answer to it. Yet by the time of the 2017 General Election Jeremy Corbyn and Theresa May were both talking about the need to roll forward the frontiers of the state. That, in the end, came to very little, but skip forward to the end of the first quarter of the twenty-first century and it seems clear that the ideological tide, which was flowing in one direction in the 1970s, is now reversing.

Efforts to reduce carbon emissions are one part of the story here. Great power rivalry is another. The American sociologist and historian Charles Tilly has shown how, over the last thousand years, mobilizations for warfare have provided the chief occasions for the expansion, consolidation and creation of state authority.[75] In Britain, the wars Britain fought over the course of the eighteenth and early nineteenth centuries against the French led to the emergence of a centralized state army, a centralized system of taxation to pay for it and, Linda Colley argues, a growing sense of a shared British national identity (p. 15).[76] A century later, the frontiers of the state were rolled forward again by the two world wars, after which a post-war consensus centred on nationalization, economic planning, the welfare state and Keynesianism fell like a branch of ripe plums into the lap of the newly elected Labour government, as the historian Paul Addison describes it.[77] We might now be seeing early signs of the same process. China has not abandoned the market but has, in recent years, prioritized growth within state-owned enterprises and, under the banner of 'Made in China 2025', an increasingly mercantilist set of policies designed to reduce its dependence upon overseas technology and, in particular, on imported advanced semiconductors.[78] In America, President Biden has secured congressional support for a $1.2 trillion Infrastructure Investment and Jobs Act; a $280 billion CHIPS (semiconductor) and Science Act; a $390 billion Inflation Reduction Act centred on investments in alternative energy and climate change mitigation; a ban on the export of any semiconductor technology to be used in China (p. 471); and new antitrust measures to boost competitiveness.[79] Meanwhile, Labour's shadow chancellor, Rachel Reeves, has picked up and run with some of these ideas under the headline banner of 'securonomics'.[80] In the European Union, a Green Deal Industrial Plan is being put in place, focused on climate change, skills training and the partial reversal of previous rules precluding state aid for domestic industries.[81] Even Liz Truss, a simulacrum of an imagined version of Thatcherism minus the statecraft, was happy to stake £150 billion of public money on price-fixing energy bills. Increasingly, it would seem, market forces and market prices are no longer the final word.

It is not hard to understand how, in the 1970s, free market Hayekian-inspired economics came to be seen as providing plausible answers to the problems posed by low growth and rising inflation and unemployment. Given the strength of the global economic boom, which was already under way when he became leader, nor is it hard to see how Tony Blair came to put his ideas about stakeholding on a shelf in a cupboard at the back of the garage. It is, however, increasingly hard to see how free market ideas could still provide the solutions to the structural problems Britain now confronts. In terms of political economy this book opened during one era. It is ending at what feels to be the start of another.

Conclusion

THE EIGHTEENTH BRUMAIRE

In the summer of 1852 Karl Marx published a short essay, *The Eighteenth Brumaire of Louis Napoleon*, discussing the historical and political significance of the constitutional *coup d'état* staged by Napoleon Bonaparte's nephew the year before.[1] Not entirely surprisingly, the analysis can probably be best described as Marxist. Louis Napoleon's moves are interpreted within the context of the class struggle within France and the legacy of the 1848 revolutions. Whatever your political taste, the opening paragraphs are, however, something classic. Marx starts with the line about history appearing first time as tragedy and then repeating itself as farce. Shortly after, he says this:

> Men make their own history, but they do not make it just as they please; they do not make it under circumstances chosen by themselves, but under circumstances directly encountered, given and transmitted from the past. The tradition of all the dead generations weighs like a nightmare on the brain of the living.

Whoever comes to occupy 10 Downing Street over the next few years might want to consider framing that excerpt and putting it on their desk (but probably not telling the *Daily Mail* where it comes from). That is because the current circumstances really are weighing heavily. Economic growth and standards of living have flatlined. Public debt and interest payments on that debt are extraordinarily high. Political trust is low. The SNP may, for the first time since 2003, be retreating rapidly, but the state of the Union nevertheless remains precarious. The choices political leaders can make in these circumstances will be constrained. The bond markets flexed their muscles to put an end to Liz Truss and there is nothing to prevent them, if they want, from biting again. The prospects of returning to high and sustained 2000s-style economic growth any time soon do not seem great and could become a whole lot worse if the great power rivalry between China and America deteriorates, or if the Ukrainian war inflates further. The evidence of the economically deleterious effects of Brexit continue to accumulate. Reclaimed sovereignty or not, the number of asylum-seekers arriving in Britain and the cost of exporting and importing goods will continue to remain reliant upon the goodwill of other European countries. Capitalist economic systems, Britain's included, continue to depend upon favourable economic assessments being made about them by business executives deciding whether and where to invest, as Marx would have appreciated more than most.

Yet politicians still have choices to make. That is one of the obvious lessons of the last quarter of a century. Politics makes a difference. It was a choice to increase NHS spending in 2000. It was a choice, a few years later, to commit British troops to the Iraq War. David Trimble had a choice about whether to sign the Good Friday Agreement in 1998. Seven years later, Gerry Adams and Martin McGuinness had a choice about whether to end the IRA's armed struggle. The following year ministers chose to deploy thousands of British troops to Helmand. A choice was made to promote light-touch regulation. Tony Blair made a choice to regard economic globalization as an unavoidable fact of life and to present it as such. It was a choice to bail out the banks in 2008 and, having done so, it was a further choice to commit to a general principle of non-interference in their economic management. It was David Cameron's and Nick Clegg's choice to form a Coalition and the Coalition's choice to go all-out on austerity. Cameron had a choice about whether to risk the ire of parts of his own party by committing himself to legalizing same sex marriage and, not long after, about whether to dangle before his backbench critics the offer of a future referendum on Britain's membership of the European Union. After that referendum had taken place, a whole lot of choices were made about how to define Brexit. When it came to Covid, the virus itself held most of the important cards. But there were choices to be made about the timing of lockdowns and the levels of and targets for financial support. Politicians don't get to make history in circumstances of their own choosing. But through the choices they make they do get to make history. Quite a lot of it in recent times.

PARTY TIME

The sledgehammer theme of this book is that Britain has endured, and is enduring, a succession of deep, connected and, in terms of the scale of their effects, often avoidable political and economic crises. I recognize, in saying this, that the term 'crisis' is routinely over-used, with any passing mini-drama being repackaged and described as a crisis by one or other breathless journalist or media outlet competing to attract attention. I also recognize that, whether something gets to be called a crisis, and what that crisis is thought to consist of, is an irreducibly political process. Crises are not brute facts. They are politically constructed and contested. Finally, I recognize that a sense of never-ending decline and crisis seems to be hardwired into the British psyche and that plenty of other countries have been left bruised and battered by the events of the last few decades. The financial crisis, Covid and the spike in energy prices that followed the Russian invasion of Ukraine were global events. Yet, I come back to where I began. A measure of despondency about the course of Britain's history over the last quarter of a century is warranted. Haywire crises, which could have been avoided, have happened. Crises which could not have been avoided have been handled badly. There are not many people sitting in France, Germany, Australia, America, Canada, South Korea or Japan thinking 'if only we could be more like Britain'.

In earlier chapters I've kept scratching away at and highlighting enduring flaws in the way in which political choices are made in Britain. Rather than simply revisit those arguments, I'm going to jump right in at the deep end here and suggest that one underlying – and increasingly acute – problem is the dominant role accorded to adversarial political parties in Britain's political system. That may, initially at least, seem like quite an abrupt departure. But given the amount of time I've spent referencing Britain's 'partyocracy' it will, I hope, soon make sense.

The emergence of a strong party system in Britain is usually traced to the aftermath of the 1832 Reform Act and the gradual evolution of existing Tory and Whig factions within Parliament into the Conservative and Liberal parties. By the start of the 1920s at the very latest, a party-political system which would be instantly recognizable to anyone today was already part of the furniture. A small number of nationally based parties founded on distinct political ideologies. The use of pre-election manifestos to make policy commitments. A first-past-the-post plurality voting system to deliver one of those parties a clear working majority in the House of Commons. The House of Commons outranking the House of Lords. Strong internal party discipline, with backbench MPs whipped into supporting their party leadership. A 'loyal' opposition party whose job it is to oppose anything and everything the government of the day does whilst remaining wholly and solely committed to the electoral process. And, finally, a high level of executive autonomy with the governing party setting Parliament's agenda.

To its critics, including, perhaps most famously, Quintin Hogg, Baron Hailsham, the Conservative lord chancellor from 1970 to 1974, and again from 1979 to 1987, this amounted to an 'elective dictatorship'.* To its supporters it was and remains the virtuous expression of democratic values. In a system in which millions of people get to vote, and most of them have different opinions, political parties offer a way of structuring political competition and linking public opinion to policy outcomes. Parties offer voters a set of alternatives between reasonably coherent ideological and policy alternatives. Equipped with a working majority in Parliament, a winning party has a strong incentive to try to deliver upon its policy promises and, in doing so, to claim a legitimate democratic mandate for its actions. The losing parties, for their part, have an equally strong incentive to hold the government to account and expose its shortcomings, and to try, next time round, to offer a package of policies which appeal to more people. Meanwhile, political parties offer forums for the selection, training and competitive promotion of new generations of political leaders.[2] That pure system of partyocracy has taken some knocks in recent years. Scottish and Welsh devolution has resulted in policy-making powers being shared across different governments composed of rival political parties. Hailsham's elective dictatorship has been diluted by the transfer of significant powers to an

---

* Quintin Hogg, 'The Richard Dimbleby Lecture' (14 Oct. 1976). Hogg later developed the basic thesis of his argument in a book, *The Dilemma of Democracy: Diagnosis and Prescription* (London, 1978). Parliamentary sovereignty, he argued, had allowed the House of Commons to make or undo any law and this, in turn, meant that any party which commanded a parliamentary majority could exercise absolute political power. 'Only a revolution, bloody or peacefully contrived, can put an end to the situation,' he concluded in a notably pessimistic assessment.

independent Bank of England and by the establishment of the Supreme Court. The capacity of the first-past-the-post system to generate significant majorities for the largest political party may, to judge by the results of the 2010 and 2017 general elections, be waning. The Coalition which assumed power in 2010 was based on co-operation between parties and *post*-election negotiation over manifesto commitments. Between 2016 and 2019 Brexit shattered the parliamentary coherence of the Conservative Party and badly damaged that of Labour.[3]

Yet political parties remain utterly central to the way in which Britain is governed. Government is and remains government by political party. The number of non-partisan outsiders appointed to ministerial positions, and the number of independent MPs elected to the House of Commons, remain vanishingly small. After a brief period in the mid-2010s when it looked like Britain was set to become a genuinely multiparty system, Labour and the Conservatives struck back, accumulating 80 per cent of votes cast in the 2017 General Election and nearly the same amount in the 2019 follow-up. Post-Brexit, *most* MPs still vote as a bloc on party lines during *most* parliamentary divisions. MPs do sometimes defect to another party, but that happens once in a blue moon. Manifestos remain a bedrock of election campaigning, post-election legitimacy and opposition taunts about broken promises. The business of His Majesty's Loyal Opposition remains one of opposition. Beyond this, and whether on Twitter (X), in speeches, in interviews or in Prime Minister's Questions, parties spend vast amounts of their time attacking other parties and trying to raise the salience of issues which they think will discomfort their opponents and potentially split their vote.

It is true that the Bank of England and other bodies, including the Office for Budget Responsibility and the Climate Change Committee, have been largely pulled out of the orbit of party politics. Yet, looked at in another way, the fact that this has happened – and that its happening has attracted sustained political support – is testimony to the strength of the conviction that elected politicians would, if given the opportunity, allow narrow considerations of party-political advantage to influence their decision-making. Moreover, the reach of political parties has, in other ways, been extended. The number of cross-bench (independent) peers sitting within and being appointed to the House of Lords has dwindled.[4] Ministers, prime ministers included, are more ready than they once were to remove departmental permanent secretaries they do not feel a great political or personal affinity with (p. 202).[5] Finally, whilst it is a requirement for ministers to make appointments to quasi-independent quangos without regard to applicants' party-political affiliations, New Labour ministers in the 2000s and Conservative ministers in the 2010s and early 2020s have, surprisingly often, reached the considered conclusion that the person who has the best qualities to perform a role also just happens to be a keen supporter of their party.[6]

DOWNSIDES

For a long, long time demands for constitutional reform in Britain have centred upon the case for adopting some form of proportional representation to ensure that the share of the national vote a party receives in a general election broadly tallies with its share of MPs in the House of Commons. That argument, which was tried, tested and rejected in the 2011 referendum on the Alternative Vote, still attracts considerable support – particularly from activists on the centre-left frustrated at the capacity of the Conservative Party to keep winning general elections with only a minority of the vote.[7] Yet electing a slightly different set of MPs from a slightly different mixture of parties would still leave the basic role of political parties unchallenged. The bigger question, which is, to my mind, now increasingly worth asking, is whether the growing political problem Britain faces is not one to do with the way in which votes for political parties are translated into seats, but with the dominant role of political parties as currently constituted.

In the opening chapter I cited the results of a focus group my colleague Kate Dommett conducted about how people view political parties. The punchline, you may recall, was that party activists have as low an opinion of political parties as most ordinary voters (pp. 8–9). To mention some of her other findings, this time from survey questionnaires rather than focus groups, when asked how well parties run the country, 1% said very well; 26% said fairly well; 39% not very well; and 26% not well at all (8% did not know). When asked how well parties represent the people who vote for them, 2% said very well; 27% fairly well; 41% said not very well; and 10% said not well at all. When asked whether parties deliver upon their promises and deliver good outcomes, the results were not hugely different – which is to say they were pretty bad.[8]

Activists and ordinary voters are not alone when it comes to their distaste for party politics. Most recently, the former Cabinet minister and former MP Rory Stewart has decried the 'rigidity and shallowness' of political parties:

> Our life as politicians has rewired our synapses, just as profoundly as the study of London streets has enlarged the hippocampuses of London cabbies. In our case, the profession has developed not an expanded memory centre, but a capacity for shortcuts and sinuous evasions. Our brains have become like the phones in our pockets: flashing, titillating, obsequious, insinuating machines, allergic to depth and seriousness.[9]

Before launching into an assault on the political status quo, it is first worth saying that politics, as well as being an important human activity, is also a profoundly challenging and invariably disappointing one. Politics is, as the German sociologist Max Weber once said, a strong and slow boring of hard boards.[10] It entails endless trade-offs, compromises, betrayals and setbacks. It is exhausting to do and easy, after the event, to second-guess and pick apart. Yet, even so, and acknowledging all of this to be true, I do think it is reasonable to believe that political parties have now become more of the problem than they are the solution to a problem.

Here, we might start by returning, briefly, to the issue of proportional representation. Proponents of electoral reform argue that the current system leads to the election of an unrepresentative legislature because it does not come close to balancing the share of the vote a party receives with the number of seats in Westminster that it wins. That is certainly true. But the larger problem here surely is that political parties are profoundly unrepresentative in a whole series of other ways, relating not only to the gender, race and age of candidates but in terms of the basic attachment of those candidates *to* a political party.[11] The basic problem with a partyocracy – whatever voting system it is underpinned by – is that the number of people who strongly identify with, let alone contribute to or join, a political party is quite low (and falling) and that the number of people who dislike and distrust political parties is high and growing.[12] Political parties offer a thin reed on which to hang the legitimacy of a political system.

Party-based representative democracy is unrepresentative. It also leads to predictably poor standards of governance. High levels of partisanship and the never-ending search for party-political advantage consistently impedes effective decision-making. Governing parties routinely find themselves trapped into defending the indefensible for fear of being seen to be weak or of having to admit failure. At the same time, they have little alternative but to dismiss opposition ideas or suggestions out of hand as being wildly impracticable. Conversely, opposition parties are expected to express their steadfast, principled opposition to policies which, once they are elected, they then routinely resign themselves to. The demands of constant electioneering discourage parties from addressing deep-seated policy issues where the political costs of action are likely to be short term and the benefits long term. The constant shadow of the next general election (or local election, or even opinion poll) creates a constant temptation to take decisions and allocate funding with one eye on gaining a party-political advantage and, increasingly, when the political going gets tough, to dump an incumbent leader.

Think back here to the list of issues where, I have suggested, calculations of political interest, whether in terms of an advantage within a party or relative to another party, have loomed large: social care; housing; Labour's kill-nationalism-'stone-dead' assessments of the likely effects of devolution; the Conservatives' opposition to increases in fuel duty in the early 2000s; Blair's out-of-hand dismissal of concerns expressed within the Labour Party about Iraq; the death of Dr David Kelly; the policy paralysis caused by the TB-GBs; David Cameron's 'tens of thousands' pledge on immigration; Cameron's promise to hold a referendum on Britain's European Union membership; the choice of the question for the 2014 Scottish independence referendum; the initial refusal to take seriously or respond to the Windrush scandal; the creation and then, not long after, the abandonment of 'English Votes for English Laws'; Labour's reframing of the Conservative Party's proposals in relation to social care as a 'dementia tax' in 2017 (following a similar trick by the Conservatives in 2010); the reaction of both Jeremy Corbyn's critics and supporters to allegations of antisemitism within the Labour Party; the motives of MPs during the 'indicative votes' over Brexit; and the stoking of culture wars.

In 1776 the Scottish economist Adam Smith published *The Wealth of*

Nations. In it he argued that competitive markets harness the self-interest of producers in ways which, as if by 'an invisible hand', promote an end 'which was no part of their intention' in benefiting consumers through lower prices and better products.[13] The argument for relying upon political parties as the engines of democracy takes a similar form. Parties have a self-interest in identifying and selecting popular policies and credible leaders who will help get them elected. Once elected, parties have a strong incentive to keep their election promises to develop a reputation for being honest and trustworthy. That invisible hand no doubt sometimes works. You may not have liked the policy or the way in which it was announced or packaged, but New Labour (eventually) got it right when it identified higher NHS spending as a vote-winner in the early 2000s. Similarly, and putting aside the intricacies of the debate about an expansionary fiscal contraction (p. 281), David Cameron, in reversing his earlier pledge to abide by Labour's spending plans if elected, spotted and responded to a strong groundswell of opinion in the aftermath of the financial crisis that Labour had wasted money and that public borrowing was too high. But you would need a particularly robust cognitive constitution to spot the *consistent* operation of an invisible hand in British politics that has, year after year, successfully reconciled calculations of party-political advantage with standards of good governance.

To pursue this reasoning further, partyocracy works to preclude principled policy compromises on tough issues where a consensus, if one could be forged, might increase the legitimacy of a policy and make it more likely to endure beyond the shelf-life of any one administration. I don't want to sound too naive about this. Politics is about disagreement. Political parties with very different ideologies and very different views on policy issues may, even with the best will in the world, fail to identify or see any merits in compromise positions. Moreover, voters may come to regard any compromise which is made as unprincipled horse-trading motivated by political ambition. That is how most voters came to regard the formation of the Coalition in 2010. Yet the search to achieve a principled compromise based on a recognition of the validity of alternative views can, nevertheless, be reasonably seen as embodying democratic principles of equality and mutual respect.[14] That is certainly how, for example, many people viewed the compromises entailed within the Good Friday Agreement. By comparison, the failure of the established political parties to engage in any meaningful discussions over Brexit in the hope of finding a compromise position now appears deeply unprincipled. Not all sincere searches for a compromise will be successful. But this does not mean that none will be.

Partyocracy also seems to exacerbate and at least partly account for two other problems that have been recurring themes in earlier chapters: the perils of centralization and of short-termism. National political parties exist to contest elections, beat their opponents and implement their policies. This does not sit comfortably with an ethos of power-sharing or of decentralization. Devolution is now a fact of political life which politicians based in London have, by and large, learned to live with. Yet, at the same time, over the last few decades local government has gone from weak to weaker, becoming, in the process, little more than a delivery unit for central government policy initiatives and (to judge by the political make-up of the constituencies that have disproportionately benefited from government largesse) further vectors of party-political advantage.[15] Meanwhile, and within the central government, decision-making authority has continued to be centralized within Number 10 Downing Street, checked only by the authority of the Treasury next door and the Bank of England a couple of miles down the road. In the cases of Iraq, Brexit and Covid, policy discussions within the Cabinet were led from the front by prime ministers whose views were known in advance to those around the table.

Political careers, as well as policy horizons, are increasingly short. The average tenure of a secretary of state occupying a Cabinet-level position is around two years. One rung down the political ladder and the average tenure for a junior minister in a department is closer to a year.[16] Given that most former ministers say it takes at least two years to properly understand a role and to reach a considered view on what needs to be done and how it might be best achieved, that feels far from ideal.[17] Chief executives of British firms, a group not exactly renowned for their long-term decision-making (pp. 290–91), serve, by comparison, for an average of five years.[18] Rory Stewart, who was shuffled between the positions of environment minister, minister of international development, minister of the foreign office and international development in Africa and prisons and probation minister over the course of just three years, has suggested that party leaders sign up to a pledge to keep ministers in their appointed positions for at least two years. It is a nice idea but one which ignores the party political reasons leaders have to shuffle ministers around every few months to reward, punish or just fill in gaps left by resignations or scandals.[19] Constant reshuffles in which ministers are plucked up and put down somewhere else within Whitehall are one reason why average tenures are so short. Turmoil within political parties as leaders are toppled and replaced and purge their rivals is another. At one end of this pipeline, MPs are appointed to ministerial office whilst they are still relatively inexperienced. In April 2023 seven of the twenty-two elected members of the Cabinet had first been elected as MPs in 2015, and three in 2019.* At its other end, Cabinet ministers then tend to disappear quickly and without much of a trace. Only seven members of the Cabinet in April 2023 had been Cabinet ministers in the second Johnson administration formed after the 2019 General Election (all of them serving, at that time, in different roles). Only three were there at the start of the second May administration in June 2017. Moreover, the short shelf lives of ministerial careers has been matched by increasing levels of turnover within senior Civil Service positions, where career development has become linked to rapid moves between jobs. Several departments, including the Treasury and the Cabinet Office, lose a quarter of their staff each year.[20]

PLAN B

What can be done? Keeping Winston Churchill's famous dictum about democracy being 'the worst form of government except all those other forms that have been tried from time to time' firmly in mind, the answer is not to abandon the principle of democratic election.[21] Nor is the answer, tempting as it may sometimes seem, to dispense with political parties altogether. They are too embedded within the political system and, for all their faults, provide a valuable point of linkage between voters and policy decisions. This is not, however, an all-or-nothing choice. Even if political parties are here to stay, much more can be done to redesign democratic institutions in such a way as to give representatives

* By comparison, in the Coalition government formed in 2010, three of its initial Cabinet members were first elected in 2005, five in 2001, eight in 1997, four in 1992 and one, Ken Clarke, in 1970.

elected under a party-political label more of an incentive to put their narrow party interests aside and, at the same time, to increase the representation of independents. I'll start here with some relatively modest proposals and work my way up.

Private Members Bills (PMBs) already give backbench MPs, usually working on a cross-party basis, the opportunity to develop legislation independent of the government.* Most of the nearly four hundred PMBs that have become parliamentary acts since 1983 relate to relatively narrow and politically uncontroversial issues.[22] That is not surprising. In order to attract cross-party support and avoid being filibustered, they must be designed that way. That does not mean that the resulting legislation is unimportant, however, or that select committees have already reached the limits of their utility.[23] More time could be allocated to the discussion of PMBs (currently limited to thirteen Fridays in a parliamentary year) and, at the same time, it could be made much harder to block them except by way of a majority vote.

The development of the select committee system within the House of Commons has been a notable success story of parliamentary reform over the last half-century.[24] Although constituted in such a way that the balance of MPs on a committee broadly matches the balance of parties in Parliament, they operate on a surprisingly consistent, non-partisan basis to scrutinize government departments, make policy recommendations and, increasingly, to campaign for political change.[25] Yet it remains relatively easy for the government, if it wants, to brush aside select committee recommendations.[26] The future role of select committees could be enhanced by giving them a leading role in pre-legislative scrutiny and in setting aside more parliamentary time for debates on and votes in relation to committee recommendations. Select committees could also be given the opportunity to sponsor PMBs. Finally, and in terms of incremental changes, if the democratic mandate of the second chamber, the House of Lords, could be enhanced (an admittedly big *if* right now), the powers accorded to it to revise rather than simply delay government legislation could then be extended. The House of Lords, in its current format, routinely inflicts dozens of defeats each year on government

---

* At the start of each parliamentary session, twenty backbench MPs are selected by ballot to introduce a PMB. Additional bills may be introduced via the 'Ten Minute rule' but are exceptionally unlikely to be successful. UK Parliament, 'Private Members' Bills'.

legislation, most often inserting new clauses to alter the reach or content of a proposed law.[27] Sometimes, these are accepted by the government. Yet the government can, if it wants, simply reverse any defeats it has suffered and eventually impose its will.[28] If a reformed second chamber were granted additional powers, the government would then have a stronger incentive to reach principled compromises with it.

The secret ballot system is, nowadays, considered an absolutely essential feature of free and fair elections: one that is protected as a universal right by Section 3 of Article 21 of the Universal Declaration of Human Rights.[29] In Britain, its use dates back to a by-election in Pontefract in 1872 (the seals on the ballot boxes were apparently stamped not with the Great Seal of the Royal Borough of Pontefract, granted by Richard III, but by the one used at the time to distinguish genuine Pontefract cakes).[30] The rationale for secret ballots is clear. It makes corruption and intimidation less likely and, as such, gives voters the opportunity to express their views sincerely.[31] Yet, in Parliament, the party-imposed whipping system has the opposite effect.[32] MPs know that, if they vote against their party, they risk, at the very least, their future career advancement and, potentially at least, reselection in their constituency. In other words, whipping gives MPs every reason, if they remain unpersuaded by the arguments advanced by their party leader, to express their views insincerely. In the workshops she conducted, Kate Dommett notes that objections to the whipping system were 'particularly prominent' and seen as 'emblematic' of the flaws of parties.[33]

In January 2022, whilst the 'Partygate' scandal was unfolding and dissident MPs were seeking to collect enough signatures to trigger a confidence vote in Boris Johnson's leadership, the Conservative MP Will Wragg, who was also the chair of the Public Administration and Constitutional Affairs Committee, accused government whips, ministers and Number 10 advisors of blackmail.[34] He said that he and other MPs had been told that, if they continued to destabilize Johnson, embarrassing stories about their private lives would be leaked to the press and funding withdrawn from their constituencies. Christian Wakeford, a Conservative MP who defected to the Labour Party at this time, alleged that he had been told by the whips that he would lose funding for a new secondary school in his constituency if he voted against the government.[35] Wragg subsequently met with Metropolitan

Police officers. A few weeks later the Metropolitan Police issued a short statement saying it would be taking no further action because 'there is no evidence of any criminal offence'.[36] At that point, the world moved on. Yet threats of the sort described by Wragg – threats which it is difficult to believe had not been made plenty of times before by whips of all party-political stripes – would seem to breach the spirit of the Seven Principles of Public Life adopted in the wake of the 'sleaze' allegations of the early 1990s and to potentially constitute not only blackmail as defined under Section 21 (1) of the Theft Act, but the further criminal offence of Misconduct in Public Office.[37] If there was a lack of evidence of a criminal offence being committed, it is unclear why the Metropolitan Police did not launch an inquiry in order to collect evidence. Putting the immediate legal issue to one side, there is clearly a lack of transparency around the whipping process. That is, however, one which can be addressed. The existing MPs' Code of Conduct could be amended to specify precisely what threats and offers it is permissible for a whip or someone acting on their behalf to make. That could be combined with the establishment of a specific duty upon MPs to report possible breaches of those rules, together with a duty upon parliamentary authorities and the Committee of Standards in Public Life to investigate alleged breaches.

Finally, an alternative solution to encourage party politicians to act in a less party-political way is to find ways of electing fewer party politicians. This would be easiest to achieve in a reformed second chamber, where a requirement could be imposed that, for example, at least 40 per cent of new peers be cross-bench independents rather than party appointees. In the House of Commons, the barriers to the election of independents are higher, which is why, despite the contempt in which parties are generally held, so few independents are elected to Parliament. There are exceptions. In 1997 the former BBC journalist Martin Bell stood against Neil Hamilton, the Conservative MP at the centre of the mid-1990s 'cash-for-questions' scandal and won. In 2001 Richard Taylor, a former consultant at Kidderminster General Hospital and president of the Independent Kidderminster Hospital and Health Concern group, was elected as the MP for Wyre Forest. In 2005 Peter Law, who had resigned from the Labour Party over the issue of all-women candidate shortlists, was re-elected as the independent MP for Blaenau Gwent. But such examples are few and far between.[38] It is not impossible that, one day, this might eventually change of its own accord. In Australia – another political system traditionally dominated by a handful of political parties, albeit whilst using a more proportional voting system – independents, the so-called teals, won six seats in the House of Representatives in 2022.[39] But the chances of something similar happening in Britain could also be increased by asking voters, in the context of a general election, whether they would like to see a minimum number of independent MPs sitting in the House of Commons and, if so, what number – with options ranging from, perhaps, 5 to 15 per cent. That number could then be selected from the pool of independent candidates who attracted the most constituency votes at a local level or from a national pool or, more radically, by sortition.[40] The democratic mandate of representatives elected in this way would differ from those elected through a first-past-the-post (or, for that matter, proportional) voting system. But their mandate would derive from a democratically expressed meta-preference to have different kinds of representatives.

RAHM'S LAW

At the end of the opening chapter, I listed a set of people and events – Kevin Keegan, *Gladiator* and DVDs – the memory of which was meant to underline just how long ago the year 2000 is. Since then, I've spent a lot of time describing how much Britain has changed and how those changes have been propelled by assorted political crises. Describing what changes have occurred and why is the historian's stock-in-trade. Very few histories start with a preface from the author emphasizing that the most important aspect of the period they are writing about is that very little happened during it. Yet having devoted so many pages to documenting crises, dramas and change, it is worth concluding things here by underlining just how instantly recognizable Britain's political system remains, not only to anyone who was around in the year 2000 but to the system that had been put in place by the 1920s.

True, Welsh, Scottish and Northern Irish devolution are now here to stay (even if, in Northern Ireland, the principle of devolution has been more often honoured in the breach than the observance). An independent Bank of England and Supreme Court have also been established. But it is hard to think of many more political innovations. The Fixed Term Parliament Act and English Votes for English Laws (p. 331) have come and gone. Political and economic power remains concentrated within a couple of square miles of central London (and, thanks to devolution, in an additional few blocks of land in Edinburgh and Cardiff). The Crown Prerogative, the constitutional mechanism by which the principle of parliamentary sovereignty is fused to the day-to-day reality of minister-ial power, remains largely unchallenged. Local government remains marginalized. Republicanism remains, at this point, a largely minority interest. Voters rejected a change to the voting system in 2011, rejected Scottish independence in 2014 and rejected the relative constitutional novelty of a Coalition when given the opportunity to do so in the 2015 General Election. Brexit was a huge moment of political rupture, but it was, in many respects, a counter-revolution: seeking to undo to Britain what Edward Heath had done to it in the early 1970s.

Party politicians have come and gone in large numbers. Yet the par-ties themselves remain largely recognizable. The Conservative Party (formed in 1834) and the Labour Party (formed in 1900) continue to dominate general elections. UKIP was a massively influential force in British politics for a short while but is now moribund. Its natural suc-cessor, the Reform Party, is, at the time of writing, consistently recording around 7 per cent support in opinion polls but has not yet had a polit-ical breakthrough moment. Change UK disappeared without a trace. The Green Party has failed to make a significant breakthrough at national level. After squeezing past Labour by the narrowest of margins in 2007, the SNP went on a decade-long run of electoral shock and awe. Yet, even at its peakiest peak, the SNP has struggled to translate this into consistent majority support for independence. The issue here is not simply that the political parties on offer remain broadly the same. It is also that they are still articulating many of the same arguments. If you were teleported from the year 2000 to today you might struggle for a few seconds to work out how to listen to the news on a digital radio, or slightly longer to access it via the Internet, but, when you got there, the content of party-political argument would all seem familiar: tax and spend, cutting red tape, postcode lotteries, nanny states, trickle-down, picking winners and Britain punching above its weight. Meanwhile, policy problems such as housing, social care, social mobility, public debt, regional inequality, the asylum system and the railways, which waves of ministers from different political parties have, at various points, promised to fix, still need fixing. In 2008, Barack Obama's chief of staff, Rahm Emanuel, first coined what has since become known as Rahm's Rule: 'You never want to let a serious crisis go to waste.'[41] Britain was in the middle of its financial crisis at that time and has had plenty of crises since. Yet Rahm's Rule does not seem to have travelled particularly well across the Atlantic. The haywire crises Britain has experienced have been immensely costly but, judged in terms of the changes they have resulted in, what seems equally notable is that they have, so far, been wasted.

The historian Peter Hennessy has been writing about the state of Whitehall and the vagaries of British politics since the mid-1970s when he worked at *The Times*. In recent years he has drawn our attention to the baseline assumption of the British political system – that decision-makers will be 'good chaps' and act in the national interest – and the extent to which this assumption is no longer tenable.[42] Hennessy is far from being sanguine about Britain's current position. 'We haven't got time to muck about in this country any more. There are so many deep-set problems. They need the best attention and effort of the best of the political and administrative classes all the time, and we're not getting it.' Yet a 'Pollyana by temperament', he is not without hope: 'I'm not a Whig historian – that everything gets better – but there are moments when we take ourselves by surprise as a country.'[43] The fragile state of the Union, low economic growth, political mistrust, the security challenges posed by authoritarian Russia and China and the acceleration of climate change are, at this point, the known unknowns. But there is still time to take ourselves by surprise and to change who makes political decisions and how.

Timeline of Key Events

2000

16 January	Whilst being interviewed on the BBC Tony Blair announces plans to raise NHS expenditure.
11 February	The Royal Bank of Scotland succeeds in its hostile takeover bid for the NatWest bank.
11 February	The Northern Ireland Executive is suspended resumes following an impasse over arms decommissioning.
19 April	Norfolk farmer Tony Martin is sentenced to life imprisonment for the murder of sixteen-year-old burglar Fred Barras.
4 May	Ken Livingstone, standing as an independent, becomes the first elected mayor of London.
7 September	Fuel protestors blockade Stanlow Refinery, marking the start of the 'fuel crisis'.
11 October	Scottish First Minister Donald Dewar dies following a fall outside his house.
31 December	Millennium Dome exhibition closes after one year.

2001

19 February	Start of the foot-and-mouth crisis.
16 May	Deputy Prime Minister John Prescott punches a protestor during a visit to Rhyl.
26 May	Disturbances in Oldham, the first of a series in towns across the North of England that summer.

TIMELINE OF KEY EVENTS

7 June	General Election. The Labour Party is re-elected with a narrowly reduced overall majority.
11 September	Al-Qaeda terror attacks on New York and Washington.
13 September	Iain Duncan Smith becomes leader of the Conservative Party following the resignation of William Hague.
7 October	Military attacks on Afghanistan begin.
23 October	The IRA issues a statement confirming that it has begun decommissioning arms.
9 November	The first Harry Potter movie, *Harry Potter and the Philosopher's Stone*, opens in London.

2002

14 January	Britain is declared to be free of foot-and-mouth disease.
30 March	The Queen Mother dies aged 101.
5–7 April	Tony Blair meets with President Bush at Crawford, Texas, to discuss Iraq.
3 June	The 'Party in the Palace' takes place in Buckingham Palace as a part of the Golden Jubilee.
25 July	The Commonwealth Games open in Manchester.
24 September	The government publishes a dossier alleging that Iraq possesses weapons of mass destruction which can be deployed within 45 minutes of an order to do so.
14 October	The Northern Ireland Assembly is suspended following allegations of spying.

2003

15 February	Protest marches across Britain against military intervention in Iraq.
18 March	Parliament authorizes British military action in Iraq. Two days later military action against Iraq begins.
1 May	President Bush declares 'mission accomplished' in relation to Iraq War.

3 May	Elections to the Scottish Parliament and the Welsh National Assembly. Labour remains the largest party in both.
29 May	Journalist Andrew Gilligan alleges that the 2002 government dossier in relation to weapons of mass destruction had been edited to make it 'sexier'.
18 July	Weapons scientist Dr David Kelly is found dead near his Oxfordshire home.
24 October	The final British Airways flight of Concorde.
29 October	Iain Duncan Smith resigns as leader of the Conservative Party.
22 November	England beat Australia in the final of the Rugby Union World Cup in Sydney.

2004

28 January	The Hutton Inquiry report into the death of Dr David Kelly is published and largely exonerates Tony Blair and the government from any wrongdoing.
6 February	Chinese cockle pickers working in Morecambe Bay are killed by the incoming tide.
28 April	A new building, 'the Gherkin', opens in London.
1 October	Tony Blair confirms that he will seek a third and final term as prime minister.
2 October	The first Park Run takes place at Bushy Park in London.
4 November	Voters reject the proposal to create an elected Regional Assembly in the Northeast of England.
18 November	Legislation relating to the establishment of Civil Partnerships for same sex couples and a ban on foxhunting are given parliamentary approval.

2005

| 4 April | The Gender Recognition Act allowing transgender people to have their reassigned gender legally recognized comes into effect. |

5 May	General Election. Labour wins but with a significantly reduced majority.
6 July	London is selected as the host city for the 2012 Summer Olympics.
7 July	Terrorist attacks in London.
28 July	The IRA announces an end to its armed struggle.
9 November	Proposals to extend detention of suspected terrorists to 90 days rejected by House of Commons.
6 December	David Cameron is elected as the new leader of the Conservative Party.

2006

6 September	Tom Watson resigns as a Labour minister, precipitating a Labour Party leadership crisis.
9 October	YouTube, which had been launched in February 2005, is bought by Google for $1.6bn.
30 October	The Stern Review into the economics of climate change is published.
16 November	The new James Bond film *Casino Royale*, starring Daniel Craig, is released.
23 November	Russian defector and naturalized British citizen Alexander Litvinenko dies having been poisoned with polonium-210 in London.
30 December	Former Iraqi President Saddam Hussein is executed.

2007

26 January	Former *News of the World* Royal Editor Clive Goodman jailed having pleaded guilty to phone hacking charges.
1 February	Tony Blair is interviewed by Metropolitan Police officers for a second time in relation to the cash-for-honours affair.

8 May	Ian Paisley and Martin McGuinness sworn in as first minister and deputy first minister of Northern Ireland.
17 May	Scottish National Party leader Alex Salmond sworn in as first minister of Scotland.
27 June	Tony Blair officially resigns as prime minister and is replaced by Gordon Brown.
13 September	BBC Business Editor Robert Peston reports that the Northern Rock bank has sought emergency support from the Bank of England.
18 December	Nick Clegg is elected leader of the Liberal Democrats.

2008

22 February	Having been unable to find a buyer, the government confirms that Northern Rock bank is to be nationalized.
1 May	The Conservative Party candidate Boris Johnson beats Ken Livingstone to become mayor of London.
7 April	A jury finds that Diana, Princess of Wales, was unlawfully killed by her driver, Henri Paul.
9 June	At the conclusion of its Second Reading in the House of Commons, the Climate Change Act receives overwhelming support.
15 September	Lehman Brothers investment bank collapses.
8 October	The British government unveils a multibillion-pound rescue package for British banks.
18 December	Woolworths announces that it will soon cease trading.

2009

| 23 January | The Office for National Statistics confirms that Britain has entered a recession after successive quarters of negative growth. |
| 22 February | The Danny Boyle film *Slumdog Millionaire* wins eight Oscars. |

26 February	The Royal Bank of Scotland announces losses of over £24bn, the largest in British corporate history.
2 April	The G20 meet in London, where discussion is dominated by the financial crisis.
22 April	Chancellor Alistair Darling announces the introduction of a new 50 per cent rate of taxation for those earning in excess of £150,000.
30 April	British military operations in Iraq are formally declared to be over.
8 May	The *Daily Telegraph* publishes the first of an avalanche of stories in relation to MPs' expenses.

2010

29 January	Tony Blair gives evidence to the Chilcot Inquiry into the war in Iraq.
22 March	The Labour Party suspends a number of senior MPs following the 'cash for influence' scandal.
15 April	The eruption of the Eyjafjallajökull volcano in Iceland leads to the closure of European air space.
6 May	General Election. The Conservatives win the most votes and seats but fall short of an overall majority.
12 May	The Conservative and Liberal Democrat parties agree to form a Coalition.
15 June	David Cameron apologizes for the 1972 'Bloody Sunday' shootings in Derry.
22 June	The new Conservative chancellor addresses the House of Commons and reveals plans to raise taxes and cut public spending to reduce the borrowing deficit.
25 September	Ed Miliband elected as the new leader of the Labour Party.
5 November	Nigel Farage elected as the new leader of UKIP.

2011

25 January	Sky Sports presenter Andy Gray is sacked following comments he made about a female referee.
19 March	British troops join a coalition of forces to intervene in Libya following the approval of a United Nations resolution.
5 May	The Alternative Vote is rejected in a referendum on the electoral system.
5 May	Elections to the Scottish Parliament give the Scottish National Party an overall majority.
17 May	Queen Elizabeth starts a state visit to the Republic of Ireland.
7 July	The *News of the World* ceases publication after allegations of phone hacking.
4 August	Mark Duggan is shot dead by police in London leading, a few days later, to riots in London and other cities.
21 October	St Paul's Cathedral is closed to the public as a result of the 'Occupy' protests.
9 December	David Cameron blocks a proposed new European Union treaty to manage the Eurozone crisis.

2012

3 January	Gary Dobson and David Norris are found guilty of the racist murder of Stephen Lawrence in London in 1993.
10 January	The Scottish government confirms plans to hold a referendum on independence in September 2014.
31 January	The former chairman of the Royal Bank of Scotland, Fred Goodwin, is stripped of his knighthood.
3 February	The England football player John Terry is suspended as England captain following allegations that he racially abused Anton Ferdinand during a game.

27 July	The opening ceremony of the London Olympics is held.
30 September	ITV broadcasts a documentary revealing the long history of allegations of sexual abuse which had been made against Jimmy Saville.
14 October	The Ministry of Defence confirms that five Royal Marines have been charged with murder in relation to the shooting of an insurgent in Afghanistan.

2013

23 January	David Cameron promises a referendum on Britain's European Union membership if the Conservatives are re-elected.
4 February	Former Cabinet minister and Liberal Democrat MP Chris Huhne pleads guilty to perverting the course of justice.
8 April	Former Conservative prime minister Margaret Thatcher dies.
22 May	British soldier Lee Rigby is stabbed to death by two men in Woolwich.
7 July	Andy Murray becomes the first British man to win Wimbledon since 1936.
21 July	MPs vote in favour of same sex marriage.
29 August	Parliament, which had been recalled, debates and then rejects the option of military intervention in Syria.
20 November	The General Synod of the Church of England votes to allow the ordination of women as bishops.

2014

22 May	UKIP wins the largest share of the vote and the most seats in elections to the European Parliament.
24 June	Former *News of the World* editor and Downing Street director of communications, Andy Coulson, is found guilty of conspiring to hack phones.

5 July	The opening stage of the Tour de France begins in Leeds.
23 July	The Commonwealth Games open in Glasgow.
28 August	Conservative MP Douglas Carswell defects to UKIP and is followed (in September) by Mark Reckless.
18 September	Scottish independence referendum.
15 October	Nicola Sturgeon becomes leader of the SNP when it is announced that no other candidate has stood against her.

2015

10 March	Presenter Jeremy Clarkson is suspended from *Top Gear* following a fracas with a producer.
7 May	General Election. The Conservatives win a narrow overall majority.
12 September	Jeremy Corbyn is elected leader of the Labour Party.
19 October	Start of a state visit to Britain by the Chinese leader Xi Jinping.
30 October	The last British detainee being held at Guantanamo Bay is released.
2 December	MPs vote to authorize air strikes against Islamic State forces in Syria.
15 December	British astronaut Tim Peake arrives at the International Space Station.

2016

11 January	Arlene Foster, who had become the leader of the Democratic Unionist Party in December, is sworn in as first minister of Northern Ireland.
20 February	David Cameron announces the date of the European Union referendum. The following day, Boris Johnson announces he will campaign to leave.
5 May	Labour's Sadiq Khan elected mayor of London.
23 June	Britain votes to leave the European Union. David Cameron resigns as prime minister the following day.

28 June	Jeremy Corbyn loses a vote of no confidence by the Parliamentary Labour Party.
13 July	Theresa May becomes prime minister.
1 September	The Francis Crick biomedical research centre opens in London.
24 September	Jeremy Corbyn is re-elected leader of the Labour Party following a membership ballot.

2017

9 January	Martin McGuinness resigns as Northern Ireland's deputy first minister.
1 February	MPs vote to trigger Article 50 and start Britain's withdrawal from the European Union.
22 May	Manchester Arena terrorist attack, the deadliest since the 2005 London bombings.
8 June	General Election. The Conservative majority is reduced.
14 June	Grenfell Tower fire.
26 June	Parliamentary agreement between the Conservative and Democratic Unionist Party finalized.
8 December	The British government and the European Union reach an agreement on the first stage of the negotiations over Britain's withdrawal.

2018

4 March	Former Russian double agent Sergei Skripal and his daughter, Yulia, are poisoned with a nerve agent in Salisbury.
29 April	Amber Rudd resigns as home secretary during the Windrush scandal.
6 July	Following discussions at Chequers, the Cabinet agrees Britain's negotiating position for a future political and trade relationship with the European Union.
29 August	Former SNP leader Alex Salmond resigns from the party following allegations made against him of sexual misconduct.

21 September	European Union leaders reject the Chequers deal at a summit meeting in Salzburg.
25 November	Britain and the European Union reach a revised agreement on a Brexit withdrawal agreement.
12 December	Theresa May wins a vote of no confidence in her leadership by Conservative MPs.

2019

15 January	MPs vote to reject Theresa May's November 2018 deal to leave the European Union.
18 February	Seven Labour MPs announce that they have resigned from the Labour Party and are forming the Independent Group. They are followed, a few days later, by several Conservative MPs.
20 March	Theresa May requests a three-month extension to Britain's withdrawal from the European Union.
12 April	Nigel Farage launches the new Brexit Party.
18 May	Britain's entry to the Eurovision Song Contest, 'Bigger than Us', finishes in last place.
24 May	Theresa May announces her intention to resign as prime minister.
24 July	Boris Johnson becomes prime minister.
28 August	Boris Johnson requests that the Queen suspend Parliament.
24 September	The Supreme Court rules that the suspension of Parliament was illegal.
16 November	In an interview with Emily Maitlis, Prince Andrew denies having had sex with Virginia Giuffre when she was a teenager.
12 December	General Election. The Conservative Party win a landslide majority.

2020

8 January	Prince Harry and Meghan Markle announce plans to 'step back' as senior members of the Royal Family.
11 January	The Northern Ireland Assembly reconvenes for the first time in three years.
23 January	The European Union Withdrawal Agreement Bill receives Royal Assent.
23 March	Boris Johnson announces the first Covid lockdown.
27 March	Boris Johnson tests positive for Covid-19.
4 April	Keir Starmer elected leader of the Labour Party.
23 May	News breaks that Dominic Cummings travelled to his parents' house near Durham at the start of lockdown.
7 June	Protestors topple a statue of Edward Colston and throw it into Bristol Harbour.
4 July	Lockdown restrictions in England are eased as pubs, restaurants and hairdressers reopen.
12 October	New three-tier Covid alert and lockdown system is introduced.
8 December	Margaret Keenan is the first person vaccinated against Covid-19.

2021

4 January	Third Covid-19 lockdown for England begins.
3 March	Sarah Everard is kidnapped and murdered.
26 June	Matt Hancock resigns as health secretary having admitted breaking lockdown restrictions.
19 July	Most remaining Covid-19 restrictions are lifted in England.
10 August	A lawsuit against Prince Andrew, accusing him of sexually abusing Virginia Giuffre, is filed in New York.
15 August	Taliban forces seize control of the Afghan capital, Kabul.
19 December	Pictures are published of Boris Johnson and other staff members at 10 Downing Street drinking wine together during the first lockdown.

2022

10 February	Cressida Dick resigns as Metropolitan Police commissioner, having lost the confidence of the London mayor.
15 February	It is announced that Prince Andrew has agreed to settle the legal case brought against him by Virginia Giuffre.
24 February	Russia invades Ukraine.
13 April	It is confirmed that Boris Johnson and Chancellor Rishi Sunak have been fined in relation to a breach of Covid lockdown regulations.
5 May	Northern Ireland Assembly elections held, the results of which show that Sinn Féin has become the largest party.
7 July	Boris Johnson announces his intention to resign as prime minister.
31 July	The England Women's football team beats Germany in the final of the European Championships.
6 September	Liz Truss becomes prime minister, having won the Conservative Party leadership contest.
8 September	Queen Elizabeth dies.
20 October	Liz Truss resigns as prime minister.

2023

29 January	Conservative Party chairman Nadhim Zahawi is sacked by the new prime minister, Rishi Sunak, following an investigation into his tax affairs.
15 February	Scottish First Minister Nicola Sturgeon announces her intention to resign.
27 February	A new set of rules regulating the movement of goods to and from Northern Ireland, the Windsor Framework, is agreed with the European Union.
29 March	Humza Yousaf is sworn in as Scottish first minister.
6 May	Coronation of King Charles III.
15 June	The House of Commons Privileges Committee concludes that Boris Johnson knowingly misled the House over his knowledge of lockdown gatherings.

List of Abbreviations

AI	Artificial Intelligence
ASBO	Antisocial Behaviour Order
ATP	Association of Tennis Professionals
BES	British Election Study
CBI	Confederation of British Industry
DUP	(Northern Irish) Democratic Unionist Party
EEC	European Economic Community (forerunner of the European Union)
EVEL	English Votes for English Laws
FIFA	Fédération Internationale de Football Association
FSA	Financial Services Authority
G7	Group of Seven. An established intergovernmental forum consisting of Canada, France, Germany, Italy, Japan, the United Kingdom and the United States.
G8	Group of Eight. An intergovernmental forum between 1997 and 2014 that, in addition to the members of the G7, included Russia.
GDP	Gross Domestic Product. The total estimated value of goods and services produced in a country in a year.
IBGYBG	'I'll be gone. You'll be gone.'
IED	Improvised Explosive Device
IMF	International Monetary Fund
IPCC	Intergovernmental Panel on Climate Change
IRA	Irish Republican Army. Technically, the 'Provisional' IRA (hence 'the Provos').
MERS	Middle East Respiratory Syndrome
MHRA	Medicine and Healthcare Products Regulatory Agency
MSP	Member of the Scottish Parliament

NATO	North Atlantic Treaty Organization
OBR	Office for Budget Responsibility
OECD	Organisation for Economic Co-operation and Development
ONS	Office for National Statistics
OPEC	Organization of the Petroleum Exporting Countries
PPE	Personal Protective Equipment
PMB	Private Member's Bill
QE	Quantitative Easing. A form of monetary policy where the central bank purchases assets (usually government bonds) in order to reduce effective interest rates and stimulate economic activity.
RBS	Royal Bank of Scotland
SAGE	Scientific Advisory Group for Emergencies
SARS	Severe Acute Respiratory Syndrome
SDLP	(Northern Irish) Social Democratic and Labour Party
Snafu	'Situation normal, all fouled up'. Originally a Second World War military term (with 'fouled' sometimes being replaced with a stronger alternative).
SNP	Scottish National Party
TUC	Trades Union Congress
UKGBNI	The United Kingdom of Great Britain and Northern Ireland
UKIP	United Kingdom Independence Party
UUP	(Northern Irish) Ulster Unionist Party
UN	The United Nations
WMD	Weapons of Mass Destruction

Acknowledgements

I have accumulated a number of debts in writing this book which I would like to take the time to acknowledge here.

The Leverhulme Trust offered me a research fellowship, giving me the time I needed to start this project. Bill Hamilton at AM Heath and my editor at Penguin, Stuart Proffitt, and Charlotte Ridings have consistently offered the perfect balance of encouragement, constructive advice and detailed feedback. Richard Duguid, Sandra Fuller and Francisca Monteiro have each managed elements of the production process with impressive professionalism.

A number of academic colleagues have read and commented on drafts of earlier chapters or have taken the time to discuss their take on my ideas and arguments. They include Kate Dommett, Scott Lavery, Karl Pike and Peter Allen. Conversations with Kate about her book *The Reimagined Party* pushed me towards the conclusions I have reached here about the increasingly baleful effects of political parties. Jamie Johnson guided me through the twists, turns and subtleties of the realist theory of international relations, whilst Feargal Cochrane lent me a small share of his very large and detailed knowledge of Northern Ireland and its peace process. My former PhD student at the University of Exeter, Kathleen Lund, who has had a long and distinguished public service career, read and commented upon an early draft of the entire manuscript and, in doing so, pointed to the many and various ways in which academics (this academic) need to learn to write more clearly. Jim Colvin pointed me to the (dis)parallel between the Brexit Referendum vote and the 1999 Australian Republican vote. Last, but by no means least on this list, Michael Jacobs has offered, over several years, consistently invaluable advice and ideas.

Over the summer of 2023 The Sheffield Undergraduate Research

Experience scheme supported Tom Owen, a student in the Politics Department, to work with me in preparing the final manuscript, constructing the timeline and fact-checking data and references. Tom is blessed with an eye for detail and added huge amounts to the book by identifying things which needed to be taken out. For much of the time I was writing this book I was editing the academic journal *Political Studies*. I did this alongside my colleagues Charles Pattie, Matt Sleat and Hayley Stevenson, who made this work much more enjoyable than it would otherwise have been.

My daughter, Asha, shotgunned the dedication at the start, but Jane was there throughout and Jordan was there to share an office with for the best part of the year whilst he was studying for his master's degree and was always great company. I owe a great deal to my friend and long-time co-author Steve Bell, who had to adjust to my leaving Australia in order to return to Sheffield; then had to tolerate my disappearing for several years when I was serving as head of department; and then, at the end of all of this, graciously stood back whilst I devoted large parts of my time to writing this book at the expense, at the time, of writing with him. My colleague at Sheffield Liam Stanley had a great sense of when and how to keep pushing me on through the iterations of revisions to the manuscript and, above all, was the person who first told me that I should spend three or four years writing a book on modern British history. It is now at least three or four years later.

Notes

1 BRITAIN ON THE EDGE

1 *The Economist*, 'The strange case of Britain's demise' (12 December 2022). 2. Nick Clegg, *Politics Between the Extremes* (London, 2016), p. 224. 3. BBC News, 'On This Day, 1979: No chaos here' (10 January 1979). 4. US News, 'Quality of life' (undated) and World Population Review, 'Country rankings: standard of living: quality of life by country 2023' (undated). 5. The Soft Power 30 (https://softpower30.com/). 6. Chris Patten, 'Is Britain becoming a failed state', Project Syndicate (20 August 2019). 7. Nick Clarke, Jonathan Moss, Will Jennings and Gerry Stoker, *The Rise of Anti-Politics in Britain* (Southampton, 2014), p. 1. 8. James Robinson, 'Nadhim Zahawi sacked: the seven major findings from ethics investigation', Sky News (30 January 2023). Andrew McDonald, 'UK Deputy PM Dominic Raab resigns after bullying probe', Politico (21 April 2023). 9. Ipsos, 'Ipsos veracity index 2022' (23 November 2022). 10. Elizabeth Clery, John Curtice, Morgan Frankenburg, Hannah Morgan and Susan Reid, 'Brexit, the pandemic and trust and confidence in government', *British Social Attitudes: The 38th Report* (London, 2021), p. 1. 11. The Hansard Society, *Audit of Political Engagement, 16* (London, 2019), pp. 9–10. 12. Kate Dommett, *The Reimagined Party: Democracy, Change and the Public* (Manchester, 2020), pp. 144–5. 13. This is not to suggest that the history of England's engagement with Ireland began with Cromwell. Henry VIII had been declared the king of Ireland in 1541. 14. Norman Davies, *The Isles: A History* (Basingstoke, 1999), pp. 557–84. Christopher Whatley, 'Economic causes and consequences of the Union of 1707: a survey', *The Scottish Historical Review*, 68, 186 (pt 2) (1989): 150–81. 15. David Graham, 'The strange friendship of Martin McGuinness and Ian Paisley', *The Atlantic* (21 March 2017). 16. See, for example, Heather Stanfiel, 'New research yields unexpected results in Northern Irish border poll', Keough School of Global Affairs (7 December 2022). 17. Will Hayward, 'Support for Welsh independence at its lowest in three years, St David's Day poll for Wales Online', Wales Online (1 March 2023). 18. Chris Smith, 'Quantitative Easing', House of Lords Library (11 November 2021). 19. The World Bank, Data, 'Gross Capital Formation (% of GDP)' (undated). 20. OECD, Data, 'GDP per hour worked' (undated). 21. Office for National Statistics, 'Public sector finances, Tables 1 to 10: Appendix A (21 July 2023). To access this data, open the excel file for the relevant date. Table 'PSA 1', Column E, 'Public sector net debt excluding public sector banks and Bank of England'. 22. Median household weekly income after housing costs was £393 in 2000/1; £456 in 2007/8; and £499 in 2021/2. Institute for Fiscal Studies, 'Living standards, poverty and inequality in the UK' (undated). The data used in this spreadsheet is regularly updated. The data cited here was correct as of July 2023. 23. Office for National Statistics, 'Average weekly earnings in Great Britain: March 2023' (14 March 2023) (X09: Real average weekly earnings using Consumer Price Inflation). 24. Resolution Foundation, *Stagnation Nation: Navigating a Route to a Fairer and More Prosperous Britain* (London, 2022), p. 10.

25. Interview, 'Keir Starmer on the trial, the judge and Dave and Helen's legal career' (1997) (https://www.mcspotlight.org/people/interviews/starmer.html). 26. W. Joseph Campbell, '"Too early to say": Zhou was speaking about 1968, not 1789', Media Myth Alert (14 June 2011). Also see 'A very diplomatic guy', Week in China (17 June 2011). 27. Mayumi Itoh, *The Origins of Contemporary Sino-Japanese Relations: Zhou Enlai and Japan* (Basingstoke, 2016). 28. Andrew Marr, 'Teaching History', BBC *Start the Week* (30 December 2013). 29. Vladimir Lenin, *What is to Be Done?* [1902] (Oxford, 1963). 30. Nicholas Canny, *Making Ireland British, 1580–1650* (Oxford, 2001). 31. Linda Colley, *Britons: Forging the Nation 1707–1837* (New Haven, CT, 1992). 32. Stuart Ward, *Untied Kingdom: A Global History of the End of Britain* (Cambridge, 2023), p. 123.

PART ONE

1 Fran Abrams, 'Blair: I think I'm a pretty straight sort of guy', *Independent* (17 November 1997). 2. Richard Stevenson, 'Man in the News: Tony Blair, a Laborite with elan', *New York Times* (22 July 1994).

2 A DOME WITH NO POINT

1 Rowan Moore, 'The Millennium Dome twenty years on ... revisiting a very British fiasco', *Guardian* (1 December 2019). 2. Mark Henderson, 'Taste walks a high wire', *The Times* (30 December 1999). 3. Tony Blair, *A Journey* (London, 2010), p. 261. 4. Andy Beckett, 'The bug that didn't bite', *Guardian* (24 April 2000). 5. Stephanie Barczewski, *Heroic Failure and the British* (New Haven, CT, 2016). 6. Clive Gray, 'The Millennium Dome: falling from grace', *Parliamentary Affairs*, 56, 3 (2003): 441–55. 7. Joanna Moorhead, 'Our year at the Dome', *Guardian* (28 December 2000). 8. The National Archives, 'Cabinet Conclusions: Minutes of Meetings', CAB 128/126 (25 May 2000). 9. Nigel Hemmington, David Bowen, Evgenia Wickens and Alexadros Paraskevas, 'Satisfying the basics: reflections from a consumer perspective of attractions management at the Millennium Dome', *International Journal of Tourism Research*, 7, 1 (2005): 1–10. 10. Colin Brown, 'Blair: we're centre party now', *Independent* (11 April 1996). 11. Tony Blair, 'The Young Country', Speech, Brighton (3 October 1995). Reprinted in Tony Blair, *New Britain: My Vision of a Young Country* (London, 1996), pp. 62–72. 12. *The Economist*, 'What Tony taught Boris' (28 August 2021). 13. William Hague, Speech, 'Remember the Dome' (16 May 2001). 14. Shiv Malik, 'Peter Mandelson gets nervous about people getting "filthy rich"', *Guardian* (26 January 2012). 15. Designing Buildings, The Construction Wiki, 'Millennium Dome' (3 January 2023). 16. Treasury figures show Total Managed Expenditure constituted 35.4% of GDP in 1996/7 and 35.2% in 2000/1. HM Treasury 'Public expenditure statistical analyses', Chapter 4 (Table 4.1) (20 July 2022). 17. Tony Blair, Labour Party Conference Speech (1 October 2002). 18. Fiachra Gibbons, 'Mandelson made Dome third rate', *Guardian* (13 January 2000). 19. BBC News, 'Dome should close, say public' (26 May 2000). 20. Tony Blair, 'The Stakeholder Economy', Speech to the Singapore Business Community (8 January 1996). Reprinted in Blair, *New Britain*, pp. 291–6. 21. Philip McCann, *The UK Regional–National Economic Problem* (London, 2016), p. 125. 22. James Robertson, 'The News Where You Are' (2014) (https://www.youtube.com/watch?v=ZhL57cjN8xY). 23. Office for National Statistics, 'Personal wellbeing in the UK, 2012/13' Section 5, 'Areas of persistently high and low well-being, Figure 6' (30 July 2013). 24. McCann, *The UK Regional–National Economic Problem*, p. 125. 25. Paul Swinney and Marie Williams, *The Great British Brain Drain: Where Graduates Move and Why* (London, 2016), p. 1. 26. Evans and Evans, 'A hipster's guide to

London' (undated) (https://evanevanstours.com/blog/a-hipsters-guide-to-london). Andrew Anthony, 'Shoreditch: is hipster heaven now falling prey to cultural cleansing?', *Guardian* (22 July 2018). **27.** Gov.UK, 'Regional Ethnic Diversity' (22 December 2022). **28.** Mathilde Bourge, 'London is voted best food city in the world', Fine Dining Lovers (29 March 2019). **29.** Moore, 'The Millennium Dome twenty years on'. **30.** John Curtice and Holli Semetko, 'Does it matter what the papers say?', in Anthony Heath et al. (eds.), *Labour's Last Chance? The 1992 Election and Beyond* (Aldershot, 1994), p. 55. **31.** Stephen Cushion, Allania Kilby, Richard Thomas, Marina Moore and Richard Sambrook, 'Newspapers, impartiality and television news: intermedia agenda-setting during the 2015 UK General Election campaign', *Journalism Studies*, 19, 2 (2018): 162–81. **32.** George Brock, 'Tony Blair's Millennium Bug (and media studies)' (undated) (http://georgebrock. net/tony-blairs-millennium-bug-and-media-studies/). **33.** Queen Elizabeth II, 'A Speech by the Queen on her Golden Wedding Anniversary' (20 November 1997). **34.** Peter Oborne, 'How Blair betrays the Crown', *Spectator* (9 April 2005). **35.** Jonathan Brown, 'Duchess of York "devastated" after newspaper sting', *Independent* (23 October 2011). **36.** Andy McSmith, 'Scandal-hit Prince Andrew to step down as UK trade envoy emissary', *Independent* (23 October 2011). **37.** *Observer*, 'What we think of the Royals: The Observer poll in full' (30 December 2001). **38.** *The Economist*, 'The monarchy is at its strongest in years, unlike the government' (19 May 2018). **39.** Jonathan Healey, *The Blazing World: A New History of Revolutionary England* (London, 2023), pp. 353–4.

3 THE NHS

1 Quoted in Owen Jones, 'Frank Dobson: Labour needs to be "knocking lumps" off this government', *Guardian* (30 July 2014). **2.** British Social Attitudes Survey, 'Key time series', 37 (2021), p. 2. **3.** BBC News, 'Woman dies after surgery cancelled' (1 June 2000). **4.** Mary Riddell, 'The New Statesman Interview – Robert Winston', *New Statesman* (17 January 2000). **5.** BBC *Breakfast With Frost*, 'Transcript of interview with Tony Blair'. **6.** Michael Gove, 'Frost turns to slush, *The Times* (17 January 2000). **7.** More precisely, Brown's reported response to Blair's interview was: 'you've stolen my f**ing budget'. Matthew Tempest, 'Brown and Blair: the top five TB-GB moments', *Guardian* (19 June 2007). **8.** Trevor Kavanagh, 'Blair's U-turn on NHS', *Sun* (19 January 2000). **9.** Robert Peston, *Brown's Britain* (London, 2005), p. 268. **10.** William Hague, House of Commons Debate, 19 January 2000 (Hansard, col. 838). **11.** Nicholas Timmins, *The Most Expensive Breakfast in History: Revising the Wanless Review 20 Years On* (London, 2021). **12.** Derek Wanless, 'Securing our future health: taking a long-term view. Final report', HM Treasury (April 2002), p. 118. **13.** HM Treasury, 'Public expenditure statistical analyses', Chapter 4 (Tables 4.3 and 4.4) (20 July 2022). **14.** Lucina Rolewitz, Billy Palmer and Cyril Lobont, 'The NHS workforce in numbers' (chart, number of people per GP, nurse and medical and dental staff since 1949), Nuffield Trust (12 October 2022). **15.** The King's Fund, 'An independent audit of the NHS under Labour, 1997–2005' (March 2005), p. 4. **16.** Ruth Thorlby and Jo Maybin, 'A high performing NHS? A review of progress, 1997–2010', The King's Fund (April 2010), p. 15. **17.** OECD Statistics, 'Avoidable mortality' (undated). **18.** OECD Statistics, 'Maternal and infant mortality' (undated). **19.** Cancer Research UK, 'Trends over time survival for all cancers combined' (undated). **20.** Rajeev Syal, 'Abandoned NHS IT system has cost £10bn so far', *Guardian* (18 September 2013). **21.** BBC News, 'Blair defends higher GP salaries' (18 April 2006). **22.** OECD Statistics, 'Health expenditure and financing' (undated). **23.** The King's Fund, 'Social care: what has been achieved?' (2010). **24.** The King's Fund, 'British Social Attitudes Survey 2011: Public satisfaction with the NHS and its services' (17 July 2012). The figures here relate to the proportion either satisfied or very satisfied with the NHS. **25.** Nigel Lawson,

The View from Number 11 (London, 1992), p. 613. **26.** BBC, *Breakfast with Frost*, 'Transcript'. **27.** Tony Blair, 'Speech by the Prime Minister at St Thomas' Hospital, London (29 February 2000). **28.** Wanless, 'Securing our future health', p. 152. **29.** James Heilbrun, 'Baumol's cost disease', in Ruth Towse (ed.), *Handbook of Cultural Economics* (Cheltenham, 2020), pp. 91–101. *The Economist*, 'Governments are not going to stop getting bigger' (20 November 2021). **30.** Peter Mandelson, *The Third Man* (London, 2011), p. 227. **31.** Ruth Alexander, 'Which is the world's largest employer?' *BBC News* (20 March 2012). **32.** Kelly Shuttleworth and Elspeth Nicholson, 'Devolution and the NHS', Institute for Government (18 August 2020). **33.** Nichola Mays and Anna Dixon, 'Assessing and explaining the impact of New Labour's reforms', in *Understanding New Labour's Market Reforms of the NHS* (London, 2011). **34.** BBC News, 'Q and A: Foundation Hospital row' (20 November 2003). Peston, *Brown's Britain*, pp. 301–2. **35.** Anthony Crosland, *The Future of Socialism* (London, 1956). **36.** Patrick Diamond, *The Crosland Legacy* (Bristol, 2016). **37.** Tony Blair, *The Third Way: New Politics for the New Century* (London, 1998). **38.** Andrew Hindmoor and Karl Pike, 'Past, present and future: Tony Blair and the political legacy of New Labour', in Nathan Yeowell (ed.), *Rethinking Labour's Past* (London, 2021). **39.** Tara McCormack, 'From "ethical foreign policy" to national security strategy: exporting domestic incoherence', in Oliver Daddow and Jamie Gaskarth (eds.), *British Foreign Policy* (London, 2011). David Leigh and Rob Evans, 'How Blair put pressure on Goldsmith to end BAE investigation', *Guardian* (21 December 2007). Ben Russell and Nigel Morris, 'Court condemns Blair for halting Saudi arms inquiry', *Independent* (11 April 2008). **40.** For discussions see Michael Foley, *The Rise of the British Presidency* (Manchester, 1993). **41.** John Rentoul, *Heroes or Villains: The Blair Government Reconsidered* (Oxford, 2019), p. 56. **42.** *Evening Standard*, 'Dictator Blair: Premier could not see why Cabinet should have a voice on key economic decisions' (13 April 2012). **43.** Lucy Ward, '"President Blair killed Cabinet", says Mowlam', *Guardian* (17 November 2001). **44.** BBC News, 'Mowlam sidelined by Blair' (10 September 2000). **45.** Peter Hennessy, 'The Blair style of government: an historical perspective and an interim audit', *Government and Opposition*, 33, 1 (1998): 3–20. **46.** Jackie Ashley, 'The rise and rise of President Blair', *New Statesman* (5 November 2001) and Michael Foley, *The British Presidency: Tony Blair and the Politics of Public Leadership* (Manchester, 2000). **47.** Centre for Public Impact, 'The Prime Minister's Delivery Unit (PMDU) in the UK'. **48.** *Independent*, 'Inside Blair Force One' (20 November 2005). **49.** Keith Dowding, 'The prime ministerialization of the British prime minister', *Parliamentary Affairs*, 66, 3 (2013): 617–35. **50.** Robert Anderson and Geoff Evans, 'Who Blairs wins? Leadership and voting in the 2001 election', *British Elections and Parties Review*, 13, 1 (2003): 229–47. **51.** Greg Hurst, 'Just call me Gordon. Yes, Prime Minister', *The Times* (28 June 2007). **52.** Decca Aitkenhead, 'Tony Blair on ambition, housework and still living like a prime minister', *The Times* (28 June 2020).

4 FUEL ON A FIRE

1 Essar, 'Stanlow' (undated) (https://www.essaroil.co.uk/our-locations/stanlow/). **2.** *The Economist*, 'Standstill Britain' (14 September 2000). **3.** Associated Press International, 'Fishermen block ports, farmers block ports and roads to protest rising fuel prices' (25 August 2000). **4.** Brian Doherty, Matthew Paterson, Alexandra Plows and Derek Wall, 'Explaining the fuel protests', *British Journal of Politics and International Relations*, 5, 3 (2003): 1–23. **5.** John Prescott, *Prezza: My Story, Pulling no Punches* (London, 2008), p. 244. **6.** Chris Mason, 'What exactly is a COBRA meeting', BBC News (23 July 2012). **7.** *The Economist*, 'Paying fealty to farmers' (12 March 2015). **8.** Tim Bale, *The Conservative Party from Thatcher to Cameron* (Cambridge, 2010), p. 107. **9.** Jonathan Powell, *The*

New Machiavelli: How to Wield Power in the Modern World (London, 2010), p. 43. 10. Andrew Rawnsley, *The End of the Party: The Rise and Fall of New Labour* (London, 2010), p. 4. 11. Alastair Campbell, *The Blair Years* (London, 2007), p. 471. 12. Press Association, 'Emergency powers on way as fuel crisis grows' (11 September 2000). 13. Press Association, 'British unions close ranks behind government in fuel crisis' (13 September 2000). 14. Jill Sherman and James Doran, 'Milburn puts NHS on alert', *The Times* (14 September 2000). 15. Nick Robinson, 'Fuel protests: governing the ungovernable?', *Parliamentary Affairs*, 56, 3 (2003): 423–40. 16. Thomson Financial News, 'UK fuel protesters end blockade at Stanlow' (14 September 2000). 17. BBC News, 'The men behind the fuel protests' (3 November 2000). 18. Paul Eastham, 'Fuel fiasco will cost Blair votes', *Daily Mail* (16 September 2000). 19. Chris Riches, 'EggMan hard boiled', *Sun* (18 May 2001). 20. David Millward, 'Labour to scrap national road pricing plans', *Daily Telegraph* (15 October 2007). 21. Victoria Johnson, Graham Currie and Janet Stanley, 'Measures of disadvantage: is car ownership a good indicator?', *Social Indicators Research*, 97, 3 (2010): 439–50. 22. Kiron Chatterjee et al., 'Young people's travel – what's changed and why?', Report to the Department of Transport (January 2018). 23. Department for Transport, 'Region and Rural-Urban Classification, NTS9902: Household car ownership by region and rural-urban classification' (30 July 2013) (click on the tab for the time series data, NTS 9902). 24. Mircea Panait, '*Top Gear Germany* to start airing in 2016', *Autoevolution* (11 July 2015). 25. Jess Denham, '*Top Gear* investigated for racism and offensive language after Jeremy Clarkson's final warning', *Independent* (6 August 2014). 26. BBC News, 'Jeremy Clarkson dropped from *Top Gear*, BBC confirms' (25 March 2015). 27. *The Economist*, 'The petrol party: Boris Johnson's strained love affair with the motorist' (14 August 2021). 28. Alastair Campbell, *Diaries, Volume 3: Power and Responsibility* (London, 2011), p. 319. 29. Anthony Heath, Roger Jowell and John Curtice, *The Rise of New Labour: Party Policies and Voter Choices* (Oxford, 2001) pp. 118–20. 30. See Andrew Hindmoor and Brad Taylor, *Rational Choice*, 2nd edn (Basingstoke, 2015), pp. 48–78. 31. Matthew Smith, 'Left-wing vs. right-wing: it's complicated', YouGov (14 August 2019). 32. Margaret Canovan, *Populism* (New York, 1981), p. 294. 33. Bryn Morgan, 'General Election Results, 1st May 1997', House of Commons Library, Research Paper 01/38 (29 March 2001). 34. Lady Margaret Jay, the leader of the House of Lords and lord keeper of the privy seal between 1998 and 2001, was the daughter of James Callaghan. 35. Tony Blair, *A Journey* (London, 2010), p. 293. 36. Oliver Heath, 'Policy representation, social representation and class voting in Britain', *British Journal of Political Science*, 45, 1 (2015): 173–93 (p. 182). 37. Catherine Johnson and Gemma Rosenblatt, 'Do MPs have the "right stuff"?', *Parliamentary Affairs*, 60, 1 (2007): 164–9, and Kai Arzheimer and Jocelyn Evans, 'Geolocation and voting: candidate voter distance effects on party choice in the 2010 UK General Election in England', *Political Geography*, 31, 5 (2012): 301–310. 38. Sarah Childs and Philip Cowley, 'The politics of local presence: is there a case for descriptive representation?', *Political Studies*, 59, 1 (2011): 1–19. 39. Institute for Fiscal Studies, 'Living standards, poverty and inequality in the UK' (undated). These figures are routinely updated. The ones used here were taken in June 2023. 40. Between 2000/1 and 2006/7 the average income of the median household grew by 13.6%. Below that threshold, that is, in the poorest half of households, it grew by between 14 and 15% with the (notable) exception of the poorest 5% of households, where it grew by only 7%.

5 DEVOLUTION

1 Linda Colley, *Britons: Forging the Nation 1707–1837* (New Haven, CT, 1992). 2. Daniel Defoe, *Union and No Union* [1713]. Quoted in Norman Davies, *The Isles:*

A History (Basingstoke, 1999), p. 583.   3. David Edgerton, *The Rise and Fall of the British Nation: A Twentieth Century History* (London, 2018), p. 26.   4. Tom Nairn, *The Break-Up of Britain* (London, 1977).   5. James Mitchell, *Devolution in the UK* (Manchester, 2009), pp. 29–30.   6. In 1979 Just over 51% of voters in Scotland voted for devolution. As a result of a successful amendment proposed by the Labour MP George Cunningham, a successful result had, however, been made contingent upon 40% of the electorate supporting devolution. As a result, and with turnout just 64%, the proposal failed.   7. Ben Jackson, *The Case for Scottish Independence: A History of Nationalist Thought in Modern Scotland* (Cambridge, 2020), p. 141.   8. BBC News, 'UK Politics: Talking politics. The history of Scottish devolution' (1 June 1998).   9. Brian Taylor, 'How is the killing the SNP stone dead project going?' BBC News (4 February 2015).   10. Tony Blair, *A Journey* (London, 2010), p. 251.   11. A clear but lower majority of 62% gave a positive answer to a second question asking whether the new Scottish Parliament should have tax-raising powers.   12. Rachel Borrill, 'Labour attempts to defuse Blair's "parish council" power for Scots', *Irish Times* (5 April 1997).   13. Ross Burnside, *The (Budgetary) Times They are A'Changin: 20 Years of Devolved Budgets* (Edinburgh, 2019).   14. Donald Dewar, 'Speech at the Opening of the Scottish Parliament' (1 July 1999).   15. James Kellas, *The Scottish Political System* (Cambridge, 1973) and James Mitchell, *Governing Scotland: The Invention of Administrative Devolution* (Basingstoke, 2003).   16. Tony Blair, John Smith Memorial Lecture (7 February 1996), reprinted in Tony Blair, *New Britain: My Vision of a Young Country* (London, 1996), pp. 310–21.   17. Blair, *A Journey*, p. 516.   18. Paul Cairney, *The Scottish Political System Since Devolution* (Exeter, 2011), p. 185.   19. Paul Cairney, 'Public policies', in Scottish Devolution Monitoring Report (UCL Devolution Monitoring Programme, January 2006), pp. 119–21.   20. Scottish Centre for Social Research, 'Public perceptions of Scotland after devolution: findings from the 2004 Scottish Social Attitudes Survey', Chapter Three, Trust in Government, Figure 3.1 (11 September 2005).   21. John Osmond and Jessica Mugaseth, 'Assembly Government' (UCL, Quarterly Monitoring Programme, February 2003), pp. 2–4.   22. Ron Davies, *Devolution: A Process Not an Event* (Cardiff, 1999). From the moment of its establishment in 1999 through to May 2020 the Senedd was formally known as the National Assembly for Wales, although the nomenclature of Senedd had informally been used.   23. Democratic Audit, 'The Scottish Parliament's record on women's representation is in the balance' (13 September 2013).   24. James Mitchell, 'The narcissism of small differences: Scotland and Westminster', *Parliamentary Affairs*, 63, 1 (2010): 98–116.   25. Jones changed his mind a few months later and was subsequently re-elected as leader.   26. Michael Kenny, *The Politics of English Nationhood* (Oxford, 2014), p. 43.   27. Alisa Henderson and Richard Wyn Jones, *Englishness: The Political Force Transforming Britain* (Oxford, 2022), pp. 39–42.   28. Institute for Government, 'Barnett Formula' (25 November 2020). When asked whether Scotland got more than its fair share of resources, something like 20–30% of English people said this was indeed the case. Henderson and Wyn Jones, *Englishness*, p. 64.   29. The National Archives, 'Cabinet Conclusions: Minutes of Meetings', CAB 128/126 (10 February 2000).   30. John Hibbing and Elizabeth Theiss-Morse, *Stealth Democracy: Americans' Beliefs about How Government Should Work* (New York, 2002).   31. Office for National Statistics, 'Regional Gross Domestic Product: All ITL Regions', 1998 to 2019 edition (26 May 2021) (Table 7).   32. BBC News, 'McLetchie resigns as Tory leader' (31 October 2005).   33. John Mullin, 'Alex Salmond: the new king of Scotland' *Independent* (10 August 2008).   34. Rob Johns and John Mitchell, *Takeover: Explaining the Extraordinary Rise of the SNP* (London, 2016), pp. 105–12.   35. Severin Carrell, 'Alex Salmond: a canny political operator, but not infallible', *Guardian* (11 January 2012).   36. For the evidence on this see Johns and Mitchell, *Takeover*, pp. 104–6.   37. The sticking point in discussions with the Liberal Democrats was the SNP's pledge to hold a referendum on independence. Mullin, 'Alex Salmond'.   38. BBC News, 'Labour Plaid coalition sealed' (7 July 2007).   39. Scottish Government, 'Your

Scotland, your voice: a national conversation' (14 August 2007). **40.** *The Economist*, 'Reforming the selection of leaders is only the start of Sir Keir's troubles' (23 September 2021). **41.** Johns and Mitchell, *Takeover*, p. 76. **42.** Scotland's Census, 'National Identity' (3 August 2021). **43.** Johns and Mitchell, *Takeover*, p.121.

6 CENTRISM

1 Ipsos, 'Labour Leader Image' (25 September 2016) and Ipsos, 'Labour Party Image' (25 September 2015). **2.** Sam Lister, 'In the doghouse', *The Times* (6 June 2001). **3.** David Cracknell and Eben Black, 'The incredible shrinking Tories', *Sunday Times* (10 November 2002). **4.** Peter Snowdon, *Back From the Brink: The Inside Story of the Tory Resurrection* (London, 2010), p. 191. **5.** Oliver Letwin, *Hearts and Minds: The Battle for the Conservative Party from Thatcher to the Present* (London, 2017), p. 131. **6.** David Cameron, 'Change to Win', Speech at Conservative Party Conference (4 October 2005). **7.** Michael Ashcroft and Isabel Oakeshott, *Call me Dave: The Unauthorised Biography of David Cameron* (London, 2015), p. 250. **8.** Peter Oborne, 'Ken and the Kid', *Daily Mail* (6 October 2005). **9.** Matthew D'Ancona, 'The race to take on David Davis is no longer an open and shut case', *Daily Telegraph* (6 October 2005). **10.** Benedict Brogan, James Chapman and Tim Shipman, 'D-Day: a dismal day for Davis', *Daily Mail* (6 October 2005). **11.** David Cameron, *For the Record* (London, 2019), p. 87. **12.** Tania Branigan and Julian Glover, 'The drugs question that won't go away: Davis says any recent use must disqualify candidate', *Guardian* (15 October 2005). **13.** Andrew Denham and Pete Dorey, 'A tale of two speeches? The Conservative leadership election of 2005', *Political Quarterly*, 77, 1 (2006): 35–42. **14.** Steve Richards, *The Prime Ministers: Reflections on Leadership from Wilson to Johnson* (London, 2020), p. 311. **15.** Andrew Rawnsley, '"I'm not a deeply ideological person. I'm a practical one"', *Observer* (18 December 2005). **16.** Tim Shipman, 'Blair is a lame duck who must go now, says Murdoch', *Daily Mail* (8 October 2006). **17.** George Jones, 'You were the future once', *Daily Telegraph* (8 December 2005). **18.** David Cameron, 'Modern Conservatism', Speech at Demos (30 January 2006). **19.** British Election Study, 2005: face-to-face survey, questions Bq39a and Bq39c (via http://nesstar.ukdataservice.ac.uk/webview/. **20.** *The Economist*, 'A brief history of One Nation Conservatism' (9 May 2017) and David Seawright, *The British Conservative Party and One Nation Politics* (London, 2009). **21.** Tim Bale, *The Conservative Party from Thatcher to Cameron* (Cambridge, 2010), pp. 190–91, 244–5, 248–9. **22.** Francis Maude, 'Britain Today Needs a Successful and Appealing Conservative Party', Speech to Conservative Party Conference (3 October 2005). George Jones, 'Rifkind states claim as party's one nation man', *Daily Telegraph* (4 October 2005). **23.** Snowdon, *Back From the Brink*, p. 188. **24.** Jesse Norman and Janah Ganesh, *Compassionate Conservatism: What it is and Why We Need it* (London, 2006), p. 1. **25.** Aisah Gani, 'Clause IV: a brief history', *Guardian* (9 August 2015). **26.** David Cameron, 'Speech to the Centre for Social Justice' (18 January 2006). **27.** Lee Glendinning, 'Cameron's secret shoe chauffeur', *Guardian* (28 April 2006). **28.** David Cameron, 'The Best is Yet to Come', Conservative Party Conference Speech (4 October 2006). **29.** Will Woodward, 'Cameron to party: choose more women candidates', *Guardian* (22 August 2006). **30.** Alex Barker, 'Osborne makes key spending pledge', *Financial Times* (3 September 2007). **31.** Patrick Wintour, 'Cameron aide warns of Tory backbench misgivings', *Guardian* (12 July 2006). **32.** Conservative Home, 'Tebbit attacks Cameron for "trying to purge the memory of Thatcherism"' (30 January 2006). **33.** Brendan Carlin, 'Off-the-cuff Cameron accuses UKIP of being "fruitcakes and closet racists"', *Daily Telegraph* (5 April 2006). **34.** Bale, *The Conservative Party*, p. 340. **35.** Ben Macintyre, 'Who cares about the E word?', *The Times* (9 December 2005). **36.** Ian Kirby, 'Posh? I voted in Pop Idol', *News of the World* (20 May 2005). **37.** Mark Bentham, 'Tories' young pretender insists on a fair chance for all', *Guardian* (15 May 2005). 38. Ned Temko and David Smith, 'Cameron admits: I used dope at Eton', *Guardian* (11 February 2007). 39. BBC News, 'Brown Eton class comment spiteful, says Cameron' (6 December 2009). 40. Guy Adams, 'Cameron's cronies: the Bullingdon class of '87', *Independent* (13 February 2007). 41. Tony Blair, 'Leader's Speech', Labour Party Conference, Bournemouth (28 September 1999). 42. David Turner, 'From Walpole to Boris: a brief history of Eton College and the 20 prime ministers it has produced', *History Extra* (1 August 2019). 43. Rosemary Bennett, 'Eton pledges to decolonise its teaching after parents' appeal', *The Times* (26 June 2020). 44. Christopher de Bellaigue, 'Eton and the making of a modern elite', *1843 Magazine* (16 August 2016). 45. David Renton, 'The Tories, Eton and private schools', *International Socialism* (15 April 2011). 46. de Bellaigue, 'Eton and the making of a modern elite'. 47. Cameron, *For the Record*, p. 25. 48. Michael White and Anne Perkins, 'Nasty party warning to Tories', *Guardian* (8 October 2002). 49. David Cameron, 'Leader's Speech', Conservative Party Conference (4 October 2006). 50. Cameron, *For the Record*, p. 64. See also Bale, *The Conservative Party*, ch. 7. 51. David Cameron, 'Living within our Means', Speech (19 May 2008).

PART TWO

1 The World Bank, 'GDP growth (Annual %)'. 2. The respective figures for median monthly income were £459 in 2000/1 and £526 in 2007/8. Institute for Fiscal Studies, 'Living standards, poverty and inequality in the UK', (undated). These figures are routinely updated. The ones here were taken in June 2023. 3. Robert Joyce, Alastair Muriel, David Phillips and Luke Sibieta, *Poverty and Inequality in the UK, 2010* (London, 2010), p. 61. 4. Joseph Stiglitz, Amartya Sen and Jean-Paul Fitoussi, 'Report by the Commission on the Measurement of Economic Performance and Social Progress' (14 Dec. 2009). 5. Oliver James, *Affluenza* (London, 2007). For an earlier account by the Australian writer Clive Hamilton see *Affluenza: When Too Much is Never Enough* (London, 2005).

7 IMMIGRATION

1 David Ward, 'Why is Morecambe Bay so dangerous?', *Guardian* (12 Feb. 2004). 2. Kari Fey, 'Morecambe Bay cockle picking disaster', *Great Disasters* (15 Feb. 2019). Helen Pidd, 'Man who guided people across Morecambe Bay for 56 years dies aged 88', *Guardian* (20 Nov. 2021). 3. Mark Oliver, 'Tides kill 19 cockle pickers', *Guardian* (6 Feb. 2004). 4. BBC News, 'Morecambe Bay's cockling disaster's lasting impact' (3 Feb. 2014). 5. To this day, nobody can be completely sure how many people died in the Morecambe Bay tragedy. Jason Cowley, *Who Are We Now? Stories of Modern England* (London, 2022), p. 49. *Westmorland Gazette*, 'Walkers find human skull buried in Morecambe Bay sands' (14 July 2010). 6. BBC News, 'Morecambe Bay cockling disaster's lasting impact' (3 Feb. 2014). 7. BBC News, 'Man guilty of 21 cockling deaths' (24 Mar. 2006). 8. BBC News, '58 dead in lorry port' (19 June 2000). 9. Hsiao-Hung Pai, 'The lessons of Morecambe Bay have not been learned', *Guardian* (3 February 2014). Paul Broadbent, 'Don't claim we didn't act on gangmasters after Morecambe Bay', *Guardian* (16 Feb. 2014). 10. Simon Heffer, 'We are all victims of this lunacy', *Daily Mail* (7 Feb. 2004); Alison Little, 'No wonder you look so worried Mr Blair, the immigrant backlash is turning into a vote winner for the Tories', *Daily Express* (16 Feb. 2004); *Daily Express*, Editorial, 'Migrant proposals will still leave us picking up the bill' (24 Feb. 2004); and *Daily Mail*, Editorial, 'Effective policy or just an illusion?' (25 Feb. 2004). 11. Matthew Tempest,

'Howard visits scene of cockle-pickers tragedy', *Guardian* (18 Feb. 2004).   12. House of Commons Select Committee on Home Affairs, 'Asylum Applications', Vol. 1, HC 218-I (26 Jan. 2004), p. 41.   13. Erica Consterdine, *Labour's Immigration Policy: The Making of the Migration State* (London, 2018), pp. 138–40, 177–9.   14. UK in a Changing Europe, 'Brexit Witness Archive'. Also see Will Somerville and Sara Wallace Goodman, 'The role of networks in the development of UK migration policy', *Political Studies*, 58, 5 (2010): 951–70.   15. BBC News, 'Call for immigration rethink' (12 Sept. 2000).   16. Tony Blair, 'The Global Economy', Speech to the Keidanren, Tokyo (5 Jan. 1996), reprinted in Tony Blair, *New Britain: My Vision of a Young Country* (London, 1996), pp. 118–29.   17. Tony Blair, 'Forward', 'New Labour Because Britain Deserves Better' (Labour Party Manifesto, 1997).   18. Tony Blair, 'Speech, Labour Party Conference (1 Oct. 2001).   19. Tony Blair, 'Speech, Labour Party Conference (27 Sept. 2005).   20. Tony Blair, quoted in Ryan Bourne, 'Tony Blair is right – globalisation is a fact not a choice', Cato Institute, Commentary (1 Mar. 2019).   21. Ed Lowther, 'Prof says his "13,000 EU migrants" report misinterpreted', BBC News (7 Mar. 2013).   22. Harry Lambert, 'Labour's lost future: the inside story of a 20-year collapse', *New Statesman* (2 Sept. 2021). Louise Radnofsky, '750,000 East Europeans have come to UK since 2004, figures show', *Guardian* (26 Feb. 2008).   23. Office for National Statistics, 'Local area migration indicators UK' (27 Aug. 2020).   24. Rob Ford, Gareth Morrell and Anthony Heath, 'Fewer but better? Public views about immigration', *British Social Attitudes: The 29th Report* (London, 2012), p. 30.   25. Robert Ford and Anthony Heath, 'Immigration: a nation divided?', in Alison Park et al. (eds.), *British Social Attitudes: The 31st Report* (London, 2014), p. 81.   26. British Social Attitudes Survey, 2009, Immigration, questions A935 and A937 (http://nesstar.ukdataservice.ac.uk/webview/).   27. Ipsos, 'Most important issues facing Britain' (1 Dec. 2022).   28. Richard Littlejohn, 'No ceasefire in Labour's war against the English', *Daily Mail* (1 Aug. 2006).   29. Ben Page, *British Attitudes to Immigration in the 21st Century*, Transatlantic Council on Migration (Washington, DC, 2009), p. 11.   30. Nancy Kelley, Omar Khan and Sarah Sharrock, 'Racial prejudice in Britain today', National Centre for Social Research (Sept. 2017), p. 6.   31. Lauren McLaren, Hajo Boomgaarden and Rens Vilegenthart, 'News coverage and public concern about immigration in Britain', *International Journal of Public Opinion Research*, 30, 2 (2018): 173–93.   32. Ford, Morrell and Heath, 'Fewer but better?', p. 34.   33. Stephen Nickell and Jumana Saleheen, 'The impact of immigration on occupational wages: evidence from Britain', Staff Working Paper 574, Bank of England (Dec. 2015). Also see Christian Dustmann, Francesca Fabbri and Ian Preston, 'The effect of immigration along the distribution of wages', *Review of Economic Studies*, 80, 1 (2012): 145–73.   34. Lauren McLaren, 'Immigration and trust in politics in Britain', *British Journal of Political Science*, 42, 1 (2012): 163–85.   35. This data is collated and published by the Office for National Statistics. For an explanation of how it is calculated see 'Measuring the Data', Office for National Statistics, 'Regional economic activity by Gross Domestic Product, UK: 1998 to 2011', Section 7 (25 Apr. 2023).   36. Office for National Statistics, 'Regional Gross Domestic Product: All ITL Regions', 1998 to 2019 edition (26 May 2021) (Table 7).   37. Michelle Blade, '29 pictures of Morecambe's long gone Central and West End piers bring back fond memories', *Lancaster Guardian* (5 May 2023).   38. Neil Turner, 'Morecambe: the decline, fall and rejuvenation of a seaside resort (part Two)' (29 Aug. 2017).   39. Sam Jordison and Dan Kieran, *Crap Towns: The 50 Worst Places to Live in The UK* (London, 2003).   40. Christina Beatty, Steve Fothergill and Ian Wilson, 'England's seaside towns: a benchmarking study', Department for Communities and Local Government (Nov. 2009).   41. Richard Cracknell, Oliver Hawkins, Nicholas Duckworth and Matthew Keep, 'Census 2011 constituency results: United Kingdom', House of Commons Library, Research Briefing 14/10 (26 Feb. 2014). It is then possible to download individual constituency profiles via 'Data for Census 2011 Constituency Results: United Kingdom'.

8 ALL THE MONEY IN THE WORLD

1 Martin Waller, 'Lehman's profile on a high', *The Times* (6 Apr. 2004). 2. Ben Shimshon (ed.), *Civilised Capitalism* (London, 2004). 3. Hannah Furness, 'Regulating the banks: what politicians used to say about the City', *Daily Telegraph* (4 July 2012). 4. James Blitz, 'Brown bid to woo City ahead of election', *Financial Times* (6 Apr. 2004). Larry Elliott, 'Brown hints at City tax breaks', *Guardian* (6 Apr. 2004). 5. Gary Burn, 'The State, the City and the Euromarkets', *Review of International Political Economy*, 6, 2 (1999): 225–61. 6. Catherine Schenk, 'Summer in the City: banking failures of 1974 and the development of international banking supervision', *English Historical Review*, 129 (2014): 1129–56. 7. Quoted, Bethany McLean and Joseph Nocera, *All the Devils Are Here: The Hidden History of the Financial Crisis* (New York, 2010), p. 53. 8. Royal Bank of Scotland Group, Annual Reports and Accounts 2007, p. 66. 9. Stephen Bell and Andrew Hindmoor, *Masters of the Universe but Slaves of the Market* (Cambridge, MA, 2013), p. 103. 10. Banks Daily, 'The World's Largest Ten Banks by Total Assets' (undated) (https://banksdaily.com/topbanks/World/2007.html). 11. *The Economist*, 'Why is London so attractive to tainted foreign money?' (7 May 2022). 12. Oliver Bullough, *Butler to the World: How Britain Became the Servant of Tycoons, Tax Dodgers, Kleptocrats and Criminals* (London, 2022), p. 4. 13. *The Economist*, 'How to solve Britain's dirty money problem' (7 May 2022). 14. Michael Bloomberg and Charles Schumer, *Sustaining New York's and the US' Global Financial Services Leadership* (New York, 2007), p. 14. 15. Sam Miller, 'Regulating financial services in the United Kingdom – an American perspective', *The Business Lawyer*, 44, 2 (1989): 323–64. 16. Robert Wright, 'Gordon Brown held "gun to head" of Eddie George over BoE independence', *Financial Times* (20 July 2021). 17. James Kwak and Simon Johnson, *13 Bankers: The Wall Street Takeover and the Next Financial Meltdown*. (New York, 2010), p. 5. On the efficient market hypothesis see Burton G. Malkiel, 'The efficient market hypothesis and its critics', *Journal of Economic Perspectives*, 17, 1 (2003): 59–82. 18. Philip Augar, *Chasing Alpha: How Reckless Growth and Unchecked Ambition Ruined the City's Golden Decade* (London, 2009) p. 47. 19. Jean Eaglesham, 'Brown ally backs record bank profits', *Financial Times* (11 Oct. 2006). 20. Peter Gowan, 'Crisis in the heartland', *New Left Review*, 55 (2009): 5–30. 21. Warren Buffett, 'Chairman's Letter', Berkshire Hathaway Annual Report 2002, p. 15. 22. Shawn Tully, 'How JP Morgan steered clear of the credit crunch, *Fortune* (2 Sept. 2008). 23. Michael Lewis, *The Big Short: Inside the Doomsday Machine* (London, 2010). 24. Andrew Hindmoor and Allan McConnell, 'Why didn't they see it coming? Warning signs, acceptable risks and the global financial crisis', *Political Studies*, 61, 3 (2013): 543–60. 25. Andrew Hindmoor and Allan McConnell, 'Who saw it coming? The UK's great financial crisis', *Journal of Public Policy*, 35, 1 (2015): 63–96. 26. Alistair Darling, *Back from the Brink* (London, 2011), p. 3. 27. Georgina Hutton and Ali Shalchi, 'Financial Services: Contribution to the UK Economy', House of Commons Library, Briefing Paper 6193 (1 Sept. 2022), p. 13. City of London, *Total Tax Contribution of UK Financial Services*, 9th edn (London, 2016). The business of calculating tax yield is a contentious one. There can be a reasonable suspicion that the banks have a clear vested interest in inflating estimates of their economic impact. The House of Commons briefing paper cited above offers, in this respect, a more modest assessment of the tax revenue of finance. Finally, note the figures here are for the whole financial sector, not just for the City of London. 28. HM Treasury 'Public Expenditure Statistical Analyses', Chapter 4 (Table 4.3) (20 July 2022). 29. Gordon Brown, 'Mansion House Speech' (20 June 2007). 30. Charles Lindblom, *Politics and Markets: The World's Political Economic Systems* (New York, 1977). 31. Stephen Bell and Andrew Hindmoor, 'Taming the City? Structural power and the evolution of British banking policy amidst the great financial meltdown', *New Political Economy*, 20, 3 (2014): 454–74. Stephen Bell and Andrew Hindmoor, 'Structural power and the politics

of bank capital regulation in the United Kingdom', *Political Studies*, 65, 1 (2017): 103–21. **32.** Office for National Statistics, 'Household Income Inequality, UK: Financial Year Ending 2020', Figure 4 (28 Mar. 2021). **33.** Andrew Haldane, 'The doom loop', *London Review of Books* (23 Feb. 2012). **34.** Brian Bell and John Van Reenen, 'Bankers and their bonuses', *The Economic Journal*, 124, 574 (2014): F1–21. **35.** John Lanchester, *Capital* (London, 2012). **36.** Thomas Piketty, *Capital in the Twenty-First Century* (Cambridge, MA, 2014). **37.** Ibid., p. 344. **38.** Adair Turner, *Between Debt and the Devil: Money, Credit, and Fixing Global Finance* (Princeton, NJ, 2015). **39.** Christophe André, *Improving the Functioning of the Housing Market in the United Kingdom* (Paris, 2011), p. 13. **40.** Turner, *Between Debt and the Devil*, p. 71. **41.** Natural Resource Governance Institute, 'The resource curse: the political and economic challenges of natural resource wealth' (Mar. 2015). **42.** Nicholas Shaxon, *The Finance Curse: How Global Finance is Making Us Poorer* (London, 2018). Andrew Baker, Gerald Epstein and Juan Montecino, *The UK's Finance Curse: Costs and Processes* (Sheffield, 2018).

9 OPENING THE APPLE

1 I-Regent, 'The history of Regent Street' (undated). Culture Trip, 'The history of Regent Street, London' (undated). Jonathan Prynn, 'Apple changes Regent Street to its core', *Evening Standard* (13 Apr. 2012). **2.** Paula Dear, 'Apple's flock worships new store', BBC News (20 Nov. 2004). **3.** Zoe Wood, 'Apple opens biggest store to date in Covent Garden', *Guardian* (8 Aug. 2010). **4.** *Guardian*, 'Tony Blair's full speech' (7 Mar. 2000). **5.** Timothy Leary, *Chaos & Cyberculture* (Berkeley, CA, Ronin Press, 1994). Quoted in Luke Dormehl, *The Apple Revolution: Steve Jobs, the Counterculture and How the Crazy Ones Took over the World* (London, 2012), p. 234. **6.** Nick Rawlinson, 'History of Apple: The story of Steve Jobs and the company he founded', *Macworld* (25 Apr. 2017). **7.** Minda Zetlin, 'These old Apple computers are worth up to $905,000 – and you might have one sitting in your basement', CNBC (23 Jan. 2020). **8.** Aaron Smith, 'Apple's iconic "1984" spot: behind the scenes', CNN Business (22 Jan. 2014). **9.** Danielle Ryan, 'Ridley Scott's infamous Apple commercial', Fandom (30 Nov. 2016). **10.** John Markoff, 'Apple expects it will lose $700m', *New York Times* (28 Mar. 1996). **11.** Michael Simon, 'Apple gets its ultimate revenge on Michael Dell with the world's first trillion-dollar market cap', *Macworld* (2 Aug. 2018). **12.** Jack Schofield, 'Steve Jobs: obituary', *Guardian* (6 Oct. 2011). **13.** *The Economist*, 'Steve Jobs: obituary' (6 Oct. 2011). **14.** Jason Snell, '2010 in review: Apple as a business', *Macworld* (30 Dec. 2010). **15.** Nick Bilton, 'The 30-year-old Macintosh and a lost conversation with Steve Jobs', *New York Times* (24 Jan. 2014). **16.** Office for National Statistics, 'Family Spending Workbook 4: Expenditure by household characteristic', FYE 2001 to FYE 2019 edition of the dataset (excel file), which is Table A45. **17.** Aditya Raghunath, 'Apple app store will be available in 175 countries from April 2020', The Motley Fool (24 Mar. 2020). Andrew Orr, 'Apple brand recognition beats other tech companies, shows study', The Mac Observer (7 Sept. 2018). **18.** Simon Lavington, 'A brief history of British computers: the first twenty-five years', BCS (1 Sept. 2010). **19.** Georgina Ferry, *A Computer Called Leo: Lyons Tea Shops and the World's First Office Computer* (London, 2003). **20.** David Edgerton, *The Rise and Fall of the British Nation: A Twentieth Century History* (London, 2018), p. 412. **21.** Giles Turner and Kitty Donaldson, 'UK sold off $42bn of semiconductor firms before review', Bloomberg (11 July 2021). Mark Swenry, 'Chinese-owned firm acquires UK's largest semiconductor manufacturer', *Guardian* (5 July 2021). **22.** James Thompson, 'Kraft is "truly sorry" for U-turn over closure of Cadbury's Somerdale plant', *Independent* (17 Mar. 2010). **23.** Will Hutton, *The State We're In* (London, 1995). Will Hutton, 'UK for sale, one careless owner', *Observer* (12 Feb. 2006). Will Hutton, 'A real loss of sovereignty', *Guardian* (25 June 2007). Will Hutton,

'Foreign ownership may be fun, but beware the penalties', *Guardian* (7 Sept. 2008). For evidence of Blair's brief conversion see Tony Blair, 'The Stakeholder Economy', Speech to the Singapore Business Community (8 Jan. 1996), reprinted in Tony Blair, *New Britain: My Vision of a Young Country* (London, 1996), pp. 291–6. **24.** United Nations Conference on Trade and Development, *World Investment Report 2013, Global Value Chains* (New York, 2013), p. x. **25.** John West, *Asian Century . . . on a Knife Edge: A 360 Degree Analysis of Asia's Recent Economic Development* (London, 2019), p. 91. **26.** Apple, Supplier List (2020) (https://www.apple.com/supplier-responsibility/pdf/Apple-Supplier-List.pdf). **27.** Patrick McGee, 'How Apple tied its fortunes to China', *Financial Times* (17 Jan. 2023). **28.** Kenneth L. Kraemer, Greg Linden and Jason Dedrick, 'Capturing value in global networks: Apple's *iPad* and *iPhone*' (July 2011). **29.** Scott Berg, 'The human cost of an iPhone', *Washington Post* (2 Mar. 2018). **30.** Brian Merchant, 'Life and death in Apple's forbidden city', *Observer* (18 June 2017). **31.** Apple was allowed, by the Irish Revenue Commissioners, to use a single Irish company, split into two branches, for the purpose of tax accounting. **32.** Naomi Fowler, 'Is Apple paying less than 1% tax in the EU?', Tax Justice Network (25 June 2018). **33.** Liam Kelly, 'Apple pays just £3.8m tax on £1.2bn sales', *The Times* (30 June 2019). **34.** Prices through Pcworld.co.uk via the Wayback Machine Internet Archive. **35.** Dan Farber, 'What Steve Jobs really meant when he said: "Good artists copy; great artists steal"', C/Net (28 Jan. 2014). **36.** EveryMac.com, 'UK Mac Prices' (undated). **37.** Salary figures from Payscale.com and glassdoor.co.uk. **38.** OpenUK, 'Open source software contributed an estimated £46.5bn to UK business in 2020, according to OpenUK', Press Release (13 Oct. 2021). **39.** *The Economist*, 'Wikipedia is 20 and its reputation has never been higher' (7 Jan. 2021). **40.** Amber Berson, 'How to be Included on Wikipedia' (8 Mar. 2018). **41.** Jim Giles, 'Internet encyclopaedias go head to head', *Nature*, 438 (2005): 900–901.

10 A CHANGING CLIMATE

1 Howard Davies, *The Chancellors: Steering the British Economy in Crisis Times* (Cambridge, 2022), p. 73. **2.** *Sydney Morning Herald*, 'A man for all seasons' (24 Mar. 2007). **3.** Sir Nicholas Stern, *The Stern Review: The Economics of Climate Change* (London, 2006). **4.** Ibid., p. ii. **5.** *The Economist*, 'How about that Stern Report?' (2 Nov. 2006). **6.** Ros Taylor, 'The wrap: you can take an eco-hike', *Guardian* (30 Oct. 2006). **7.** William Nordhaus, 'A review of the Stern Review on the Economics of Climate Change', *Journal of Economic Literature*, 45, 3 (2007): 686–702. *The Economist*, 'How to value a grandchild: first choose your discount rate' (4 Dec. 2006). Geoff Mann, 'Check your spillover', *London Review of Books* (Feb. 2022). **8.** *The Economist*, 'We're all green now up to a point' (4 Nov. 2016). **9.** Margaret Thatcher, 'Speech to the Royal Society' (27 Sept. 1988). **10.** Margaret Thatcher, 'Speech at Second World Climate Conference' (6 Nov. 1990). **11.** Conservative Party, 'You can Only Be Sure With the Conservatives' (1997 Conservative Party Manifesto). **12.** Liberal Democrat Party, 'Make the Difference' (1997 Liberal Democrat Manifesto). **13.** Labour Party, 'New Labour Because Britain Deserves Better' (1997 Labour Party Manifesto). **14.** Nigel Lawson, *An Appeal to Reason: A Cool Look at Climate Change* (London, 2008). **15.** On New Labour's early record see Neil Carter, 'Combating climate change in the UK: challenges and obstacles', *Political Quarterly*, 79, 2 (2008): 194–205. **16.** Department for Environment, Food and Rural Affairs, 'The UK's initial report under the Kyoto Protocol' (20 Nov. 2006). **17.** Department for Environment, Food and Rural Affairs, 'Carbon footprint for the UK and England to 2019' (28 June 2022). **18.** Grant Jordan and Irene Lorenzoni, 'Is there now a political climate for policy change? Policy and politics after the Stern Review', *Political Quarterly*, 78, 2 (2007): 310–19. **19.** The Institute for Government, 'The Climate Change Act' (2008), p. 112. In

2008 a review published by the Policy Exchange think tank found that, of 138 high-level government targets in relation to the environment, 60% were either going to be missed or were so vague that missing them was not possible. Thomas Sweetman, 'Green dreams: a decade of missed targets', Policy Exchange (1 May 2008).   **20.** Martha Kirby, 'Modelling the fall and rise in the importance of the environment to the British public: 2006–2019', *British Journal of Politics and International Relations*, 25, 2 (2022): 199–218.   **21.** BBC News, 'Cameron visits Norwegian glacier' (20 April 2006).   **22.** Institute of Government, 'The Climate Change Act', p. 118.   **23.** On the Treasury's position see the Institute of Government, 'The Climate Change Act', p. 119.   **24.** Public Whip, 'Climate Change Bill – Third Reading' (28 Oct. 2008).   **25.** Peter Burnham, 'New Labour and the politics of depoliticisation', *British Journal of Politics and International Relations*, 3, 2 (2001): 127–49.   **26.** Michael Jacobs, 'Copenhagen was not a (complete) failure', *Inside Story* (9 Nov. 2010).   **27.** Ibid.   **28.** Ipsos, 'Most Important Issues Facing Britain' (11 Apr. 2014).   **29.** Eleanor Taylor, 'Concern about climate change: a paler shade of green?', in Alison Park et al., *British Social Attitudes: The 28th Report* (London, 2012), p. 94.   **30.** Ibid., p. 95.   **31.** Ibid., p. 103.   **32.** Otto Kirchheimer, 'The transformation of the Western European party systems', in Joseph La Palombara and Myron Weiner (eds.), *Political Parties and Political Development* (Princeton, NJ, 1966).   **33.** Niels Mede and Mike Schafer, 'Science-related populism: conceptualising populist demands towards science', *Public Understanding of Science*, 29, 5 (2020): 473–91. Matthew Lockwood, 'Right-wing populism and the climate change agenda: exploring the linkages', *Environmental Politics*, 27, 4 (2018): 712–32.   **34.** Sheila Jasanoff, 'Breaking the waves in science studies: comment on H. M. Collins and Robert Evans, 'The Third Wave of Science Studies', *Social Studies of Science*, 33, 3 (2003): 389–400.   **35.** John Durant and Nicola Lindsey 'The great GM food debate', Parliamentary Office of Science and Technology, Report 138 (May 2000).   **36.** Andea Stöckl and Anna Smajdor, 'The MMR debate in the United Kingdom: vaccine scares, statesmanship and the media', in Christine Holmberg, Stuart Blume and Paul Greenough (eds.), *The Politics of Vaccination: A Global History* (Manchester, 2017). On the failings of media coverage see Roger Dobson, 'Media misled the public over the MMR vaccine, study says', *British Medical Journal*, 326 (2003): 1107.   **37.** Richard Black, 'Climate email hack "will impact on Copenhagen Summit"', BBC News (3 Dec. 2009).   **38.** Harry Collins, *Are We All Scientific Experts Now?* (Cambridge, 2014).   **39.** Harry Collins and Robert Evans, *Rethinking Expertise* (Chicago, 2007).   **40.** Mark Brown, 'Climate science, populism and the democracy of rejection', in Deserai Crow and Maxwell Boykoff, *Culture, Politics and Climate Change: How Information Shapes our Future* (London, 2014). For a more general discussion from which the argument in this section draws see John Meyer, 'Power and truth in science-related populism: rethinking the role of knowledge and expertise in climate politics', *Political Studies*, Published Online Mar. 2023.   **41.** Medhi Hasan, 'Why is climate change denier Owen Patterson still in his job?', The Huffington Post (23 Apr. 2014).   **42.** Rowena Mason, 'David Cameron at centre of "get rid of all the green crap" storm', *Guardian* (21 Nov. 2013).   **43.** Philip Oldfield, 'UK scraps zero carbon homes plan', *Guardian* (10 July 2015). Gary King, 'The way the wind blows', *Worldwind Technology* (21 Dec. 2022).   **44.** Institute for Government, 'UK Net Zero Target' (20 Apr. 2020).   **45.** Tristan Rayner, 'UK power generation in 2020: renewables up to 43%', *PV Magazine* (29 July 2021).   **46.** Going back to the earlier ground of how to count emissions, Britain's overall, consumption-led, carbon footprint, fell by around 12% between 2000 and 2018.   **47.** *The Economist*, 'How Britain decarbonised faster than any other rich country' (15 Feb. 2021). Michael Jacobs, 'Glasgow kiss', *Inside Story* (15 Nov. 2021).   **48.** Bill McLoughlin, 'Just Stop Oil: two charged after throwing soup at Van Gogh painting', *Evening Standard* (15 Oct. 2022). Sean Ingle, 'World Snooker Championships disrupted by Just Stop Oil protests in Sheffield', *Guardian* (17 Apr. 2023).   **49.** Glen Owen, 'Nigel Farage's new drive for vote to kill off Boris's "ruinous" green agenda: he got us out of the EU . . . now the former UKIP chief demands a referendum on net zero', *Daily Mail* (5 Mar. 2022). 50. Ipsos, 'Important issues facing Britain' (1 Dec. 2022). 51. Daniel Phillips, John Curtice, Miranda Phillips and Jane Perry, *British Social Attitudes, The 35th Report* (London, 2018), pp. 151, 152, 155. 52. Intergovernmental Panel on Climate Change, 'Climate Change 2023: Synthesis Report, Summary for policymakers', (2023), p. 5.

11 A GLOBAL GAME

1 Ian Herbert, 'Ronaldo: I am a slave', *Independent* (11 July 2008). 2. Barnaby Feder, 'Theodore Levitt, 81, who coined the term globalization, is dead', *New York Times* (6 July 2006). 3. David Scott, *Leviathan: The Rise of Britain as a World Power* (London, 2013). 4. Richard Price, 'One big thing: Britain, its empire, and imperial culture', *Journal of British Studies*, 45, 3 (2006): 602–27. 5. John Maynard Keynes, *The Economic Consequences of the Peace* (London, 1919), p. 6. 6. Martin Wahl, 'Athletic Bilbao', Football History (undated). 7. David Storey, 'Football, place and migration: foreign footballers in the FA Premier League', *Geography*, 96, 2 (2011): 86–94. Jeff Lawrence, 'Jack Reynolds: The father of Ajax Amsterdam', Football Times (9 Nov. 2014). 8. Aidan Scott, 'Lisbon Lions Week: Jock Stein's heroes were all born within 30 miles of Celtic Park – how do Real Madrid's 2016 Champions League Winners compare?', *Scottish Sun* (24 May 2017). 9. 'Foreign players in the Premiership, 1992/3', *Guardian* (28 Feb. 2002). Overseas here is, rightly or wrongly, defined as non-British *and* non-Irish players. 10. Soccerex, 'Market Insight, The Rights Track: a history of the Premier League's UK TV deals' (13 Feb. 2018). 11. Sports Business Group, 'Lost in translation: football money league', Deloitte (Feb. 2009). 12. John Binder and Murray Findlay, 'The effects of the Bosman ruling on national and club teams in Europe', *Journal of Sports Economics*, 13, 2 (2011): 107–29. In Germany the figure was 51%, in Spain 41% and in Italy 36%. 13. David Conn, 'Cost of Glazers' takeover at Manchester United reaches £500m', *Guardian* (22 Feb. 2012). Strother Scott, 'A bad deal: the flawed logic of the Hicks and Gillett takeover', *Live4Liverpool* (25 Aug. 2010). 14. Tony Blair, 'Speech, Labour Party Conference (27 Sept. 2005). 15. NATO News, 'NATO decisions on open-door policy' (3 Apr. 2008). 16. Thomas Friedman, *The Lexus and the Olive Tree: Understanding Globalization* (New York, 1999). 17. Charles Goodhart, 'How should we regulate bank capital and financial products? What role for living wills?', in Adair Turner (ed.), *The Future of Finance: The LSE Report* (London, 2010). 18. Undiscovered Scotland, 'William McGregor' (undated). 19. Welsh Gull, 'A league of their own' (undated). 20. Graeme Lloyd, 'Hammam dreams of Wales United', *Guardian* (8 Aug. 2000). 21. David Goldblatt, *The Game of Our Lives: The Meaning and Making of English Football* (London, 2014), pp. 212–15. 22. Alan Bairner and Peter Shirlow, 'Territory, politics and soccer fandom in Northern Ireland and Sweden', Online Research Bank (2000). 23. Goldblatt, *The Game of Our Lives*, p. 207. 24. Dominic Cummingham, 'LVF threat forces out football star', *Independent Ireland* (22 Aug. 2002). 25. BBC News, 'Nine jailed over Kevin McDaid death in Coleraine' (1 July 2014). 26. Goldblatt, *The Game of our Lives*, p. 224. 27. Paul McDonald, 'SPL TV: a television soap opera', *NutMeg* (1 Sept. 2016). 28. CNBC, 'Super League near collapse as the six English clubs withdraw' (20 Apr. 2021). 29. *Guardian*, 'Full Text of Blair's Speech' (18 Sept. 2002). 30. Report from the Independent Commission on Social Mobility: Summary Document (Jan. 2009), p. 1. 31. OECD, *Going for Growth* (Paris, 2010), p. 186. 32. Maya Bello-Taylor, 'Arthur Wharton – probably the first Black professional footballer in the world', Black History Month (12 Dec. 2022). 33. Jack Leslie was called up to the England squad in 1925 but denied an appearance because of the colour of his skin. A BBC investigation in 2013 identified Benjamin Odeje, who was born in Nigeria, as the first black Three Lions player when he was selected for England schoolboys, as a

15-year-old in March 1971. Sami Mokbel, 'The FA to finally recognise Benjamin Odeje as first Black man to play for England after a 51-year wait', *Mail Online* (19 Sept. 2022). **34.** Goldblatt, *The Game of Our Lives*, p. 167. **35.** Lucy Tobin, 'Why aren't there more Black football managers?' *Guardian* (28 Mar. 2011). **36.** Culture, Media and Sport Committee, Racism in Football, Vol. 1, HC 89 (19 Sept. 2012), p. 3. **37.** BBC Sport, 'John Terry banned and fined by FA over Anton Ferdinand incident' (27 Sept. 2012). **38.** Donald McRae, 'Anton Ferdinand: I have kicked myself for years for not speaking out', *Guardian* (20 Nov. 2020). **39.** BBC News, 'The Boxing Day game that changed women's football' (26 Dec. 2020). **40.** Victoria Gosling, 'Girls allowed? The marginalization of female sports fans', in Jonathan Gray, Cornel Sandvoss and C. Lee Harrington (eds.) *Fandom: Identities and Communities in a Mediated World* (New York, 2007), p. 253. **41.** The FA Premier League, 'National fan survey report 2005/6 season'. **42.** Goldblatt, *The Game of Our Lives*, p. 280. **43.** *Independent*, 'Newell avoids sack over "sexist" comments' (16 Nov. 2006). **44.** Owen Gibson, 'Andy Grey sacked by Sky for "unacceptable and offensive" behaviour', *Guardian* (25 Jan. 2011).

PART THREE

1 Tony Blair, Speech, Labour Party Conference (1 Oct. 2001). **2.** Tony Blair, 'Farewell Speech' (10 May 2007).

12 GIVING WAR A CHANCE

1 BBC News, 'Blair's statement in full' (11 Sept. 2001). **2.** Jason Burke, *The 9/11 Wars* (London, 2011), p. 25. **3.** BBC News, 'Blair pledges solidarity with US' (21 Sept. 2001). **4.** CNN, 'Transcript of President Bush's address' (21 Sept. 2001). **5.** Ben Smith and Arabella Thorp, 'The legal basis for the invasion of Iraq', House of Commons Library, SN/IA/5340 (26 Feb. 2010). **6.** Jessica Hodgson, 'BBC liberated Kabul says Simpson', *Guardian* (13 Nov. 2001). **7.** 'Text of President Bush's 2002 State of the Union Address', *Washington Post* (29 Jan. 2002). **8.** Tony Blair, 'Press Conference with President George Bush' (6 Apr. 2002). **9.** United Nations Security Council, 'Resolution 1441' (8 Nov. 2002). **10.** CNN International, 'Woodward: Tenet told Bush WMD case a "slam dunk"' (19 Apr. 2004). **11.** Gordon Corera, '10 new things we've learned about the Iraq War and its legacy', *Shock and War*, BBC Radio 4. Jeremy Greenstock, *Iraq: The Cost of War* (London, 2016), p. 181. **12.** Roger Mortimore, 'Iraq, the last pre-war polls', Ipsos (21 Mar. 2003). **13.** John Chilcot, *The Report of the Iraq Inquiry, Executive Summary* (London, 2016), p. 46. **14.** The vote authorizing the use of force was carried by 412 votes to 149. **15.** Paddy Ashdown, *The Ashdown Diaries, Volume II, 1997–99* (London, 2001), p. 127. **16.** Tony Blair, House of Commons Liaison Committee, Minutes of Evidence, Examination of Witness (21 January 2003). **17.** Tony Blair, 'Speech at the George Bush Senior Presidential Library' (7 Apr. 2002). **18.** *Guardian*, 'Full text of Blair's TUC address', (10 Sept. 2002). **19.** Kenneth Clarke, *Kind of Blue: A Political Memoir* (London, 2016), p. 421. **20.** John Chilcot, *The Report of the Iraq Inquiry, Volume IV* (London, 2016), p. 372. **21.** Paul Bignell, 'Secret memos expose link between oil firms and invasion of Iraq', *Independent* (19 Apr. 2011). **22.** Tim McMahon, 'Historical oil prices chart' (14 Mar. 2023). **23.** Tony Blair, *A Journey* (London, 2010), p. 424. **24.** Corera, '10 new things we've learned about the Iraq War'. Also see BBC News, 'US ready to fight without UK' (12 Mar. 2003). **25.** Tony Blair, 'Doctrine of the International Community', Speech, Chicago (22 Apr. 1999). **26.** Blair goes so far as to cite Gladstone's campaign whilst defending the Iraq invasion. Blair, *A Journey*, p. 225. **27.** Chilcot, *Executive Summary*, p. 45. **28.** John

Chilcot, *The Report of the Iraq Inquiry, Volume V* (London, 2016), p. 363. **29.** Catherine Shoard, '"It was such obvious bullshit": The Rock writer shocked film may have inspired false WMD intelligence', *Guardian* (8 July 2016). **30.** Robin Butler, *Review of Intelligence on Weapons of Mass Destruction*, Command paper 6492 (London, 2004), paras. 270 and 331. **31.** 'The secret Downing Street memo', *Sunday Times* (1 May 2005). **32.** Chilcot, *Executive Summary*, pp. 83–4. **33.** John Rentoul, 'Chilcot Report: politicians', *Political Quarterly*, 87, 4 (2016): 498–9. **34.** Andrew Rawnsley, *The End of the Party: The Rise and Fall of New Labour* (London, 2010), p. 185. **35.** Anthony Seldon, *Blair* (London, 2004), p. 574. **36.** Bob Woodward, *Plan of Attack* (New York, 2004), pp. 296–7. **37.** BBC News, 'Clare Short interview' (10 Mar. 2003). **38.** Peter Mandelson, *The Third Man* (London, 2011), pp. 353–4. Butler, *Review of Intelligence*, para. 61-11. **39.** Chilcot notes that Iraq was raised at twenty separate meetings of the Cabinet. Chilcot, *Executive Summary*, pp. 55–62. **40.** Seldon, *Blair*, p. 580. **41.** Chilcot, *Executive Summary*, p. 56. **42.** Butler, *Review of Intelligence*, para. 61-11. **43.** John Kampfner, 'War and the law: the inside story', *New Statesman* (8 Mar. 2004). **44.** John Reynolds, 'Ministers "told to burn" Iraq War legal advice', *The Times* (1 Nov. 2015). **45.** Chilcot, *Executive Summary*, pp. 83–4.

13 IRAQ AND AFGHANISTAN

1 The banner had been placed there as a direct result of a request from the White House. Dana Bush, 'White House pressed on Mission Accomplished sign', CNN (29 Oct. 2003). **2.** Tom Happold, 'Middle East more secure, PM tells troops', *Guardian* (29 May 2003). **3.** John Chilcot, *The Report of the Iraq Inquiry, Executive Summary* (London, 2016), p. 120. **4.** YouGov, 'Iraq Trends' (undated) (http://cdn.yougov.com/cumulus_uploads/document/raghpsamvo/YG-Archives-Pol-Trackers-Iraq-130313.pdf). **5.** CNN, 'Blair flies into Iraq weapons row' (29 May 2003). **6.** HM Government, 'Iraq's weapons of mass destruction: the assessment of the British government' (24 Sept. 2002). **7.** *Guardian*, 'Full transcript of Gilligan's "sexed up" broadcast' (9 July 2003). **8.** Lord Hutton, *Report of the Inquiry into the Circumstances Surrounding the Death of Dr David Kelly CMG* (London, 2004), p. 20. **9.** Ben Russell and Andy McSmith, 'The case for war is blown apart', *Independent* (29 May 2003). **10.** Paul Waugh, 'Revealed: the pressure on Dr Kelly in the weeks, days and hours before his death', *Independent* (15 Aug. 2003). **11.** Hutton, *Report of the Inquiry*, p. 29. He was told this by Richard Hatfield, the personnel director of the Ministry of Defence. **12.** Tony Blair, *A Journey* (London, 2010), p. 456. **13.** Hutton, *Report of the Inquiry*, p. 49. **14.** Ibid., p. 15. **15.** Norman Baker, *The Strange Death of David Kelly* (London, 2007). Hutton, *Report of the Inquiry*, p. 101. Miles Goslett, 'Mystery of the helicopter that landed at the scene of Dr Kelly's death after his body was found', *Daily Mail* (14 May 2011). **16.** Robert Lewis, *Dark Actors: The Life and Death of David Kelly* (New York, 2013). Robert Lewis, 'David Kelly: an end to the conspiracy theories', *Guardian* (4 July 2013). **17.** David Singleton: 'Jonathan Oliver exclusive: the man who embarrassed Tony Blair over David Kelly', *PR Week* (27 Sept. 2011). **18.** Matthew Tempest, 'Blair: I accept responsibility', *Guardian* (28 Aug. 2003). **19.** *The Economist*, 'Fatal words' (21 Aug. 2003). **20.** Hutton, *Report of the Inquiry*, p. 153. **21.** Chilcot, *Executive Summary*, p. 46. **22.** *Independent*, 'US forces "used chemical weapons" during assault on city of Fallujah' (8 Nov. 2005). **23.** Paul Bremer, *My Year in Iraq: The Struggle to Build a Future of Hope* (New York, 2006), p. 112. **24.** Binns told the Chilcot inquiry that he had concluded that 'the best way to stop looting was just to get to a point where there was nothing left to loot'. Chilcot, *Executive Summary*, p. 87. **25.** BBC News, 'Iraq abuse case soldiers jailed' (25 Feb. 2005). **26.** Matthew Taylor, 'Beginner's luck', *Guardian* (13 Sept. 2008). **27.** John Chilcot, *The Report of the Iraq Inquiry, Volume IX* (London, 2016),

p. 76.   28. Ben Barry, *Blood, Metal and Dust: How Victory Turned into Defeat in Afghanistan and Iraq* (London, 2020), p. 312.   29. Chilcot, *Executive Summary*, p. 103.   30. John Chilcot, *The Report of the Iraq Inquiry, Volume VIII* (London, 2016), p. 224.   31. Simon Akam, *The Changing of the Guard: The British Army since 9/11* (London, 2021), p. 258. Chilcot, *Executive Summary*, p. 108.   32. BBC News, 'UK troops deployed to Afghanistan "to avoid cuts"' (13 Jan. 2011). Dannatt vigorously denied the claim, calling it 'somewhere between misjudged and mischievous'.   33. Akam, *The Changing of the Guard*, p. 204.   34. Mike Martin, *An Intimate War: An Oral History of the Helmand Conflict* (London, 2017), p. 54.   35. Barry, *Blood, Metal and Dust*, p. 395.   36. Steve Chapman, 'Obama's memoir highlights his Afghanistan failure', *Chicago Tribune* (25 Nov. 2020).   37. Theo Farrell, *Unwinnable: Britain's War in Afghanistan* (London, 2017), p. 357.   38. Hannah O'Grady and Joel Gunter, 'SAS unit repeatedly killed Afghan detainees, BBC finds', BBC News (12 July 2022).   39. Around this time, the Afghan Central Bank was looted of $1 billion, through business loans to politically connected local leaders. Jon Boone, 'The financial scandal that broke Afghanistan's Kabul Bank', *Guardian* (16 June 2011).   40. Evan Solomon, 'Fighting in Afghanistan: "You have the watches. We have the time"', *Maclean's* (2 Sept. 2017).   41. Jonathan Powell, 'The lesson we failed to learn from 9/11: peace is impossible if we don't talk to our enemies', *Guardian* (10 Sept. 2021).   42. Elisha Fieldstadt, 'The last soldier to leave Afghanistan – nicknamed "Flatliner" – was uniquely prepared for that moment', NBC News (1 Sept. 2021).   43. David Wilcock, 'Boris is caught in another lie: damning emails prove he did help Carrie's friend Pen Farthing airlift dogs out of Kabul while people died – despite his adamant denials', *Mail Online* (26 Jan. 2022). Peter Davidson, 'Foreign secretary "regrets" going on holiday to 5-star beach resort as Taliban swept across Afghanistan', *Daily Record* (17 Aug. 2021).   44. James Hider and Michael Evans, '655,000 Iraqis have died in war, says Lancet', *The Times*, (12 Oct. 2006). BBC News, 'Iraq study estimates war-related deaths at 461,000' (16 Oct. 2013).   45. Ellen Knickmeyer, 'Costs of the Afghan War', AP (17 Aug. 2021).   46. Carol Giacomo, 'Suicide had been deadlier than combat for the military', *New York Times* (1 Nov. 2019).   47. Victoria Basham, 'Gender, race, militarism and remembrance: the everyday geopolitics of the poppy', *Gender, Place and Culture*, 23, 6 (2016): 883–96.   48. Ipsos, 'Labour leader image' (25 Sept. 2016).   49. In a CNN interview in 2015 Blair apologized for aspects of the Iraq War for the first time and said that there were 'elements of truth' in the theory that the invasion helped feed the rise of Isis. Richard Osley, 'Tony Blair apologises for "mistakes" over Iraq War and admits "elements of truth" to view that invasion helped rise of Isis', *Independent* (24 Oct. 2015).   50. Peter Ricketts, 'After Iraq: the great unravelling', *New Statesman* (15 Mar. 2023).

14 THE HOME FRONT

1 BBC News, '7th July bombings. What happened that day?' (3 July 2015).   2. BBC News, 'Obituary: Carrie Taylor' (15 Nov. 2010).   3. BBC News, 'Obituary: Atique Sharif' (20 Jan. 2011).   4. BBC News, 'Obituary: Samantha Badham' (17 Dec. 2010). BBC News, 'Obituary: Lee Harris' (10 Jan. 2011).   5. BBC News, 'Obituary: Giles Hart' (20 Jan. 2011).   6. BBC News, '7 July shutdown criticised' (1 Mar. 2006).   7. Sandra Laville and Haroon Sidique, 'Jean Charles de Menezes inquest records open verdict', *Guardian* (12 Dec. 2008).   8. 'Report of the Official Account of the Bombings in London on 7th July 2005', HC 1087 (11 May 2006), p. 8.   9. Ibid., p. 14.   10. Aidan Kirby, 'The London bombers as "self-starters": a case study in indigenous radicalization and the emergence of autonomous cliques', *Studies in Conflict and Terrorism*, 30, 5 (2007): 415–28.   11. BBC News, 'London bomber: text in full' (1 Sept. 2005).   12. BBC News, 'Video of 7th July bomber released' (6 July 2006).   13. 'Report of the Official Account of the Bombings in London', p. 26.

14. Richard Norton-Taylor, 'Iraq Inquiry: Eliza Manningham-Buller's devastating testimony', *Guardian* (20 July 2010). 15. Norton-Taylor, 'Iraq Inquiry'. Also see John Chilcot, *The Report of the Iraq Inquiry, Executive Summary* (London, 2016), p. 50. 16. Clare Feikert-Ahalt, 'The UK's legal response to the London bombings of 7/7', Library of Congress Blogs (13 May 2013). 17. Jenny Percival and Elizabeth Stewart, 'Timeline: 42-day detention', *Guardian* (13 Oct. 2008). 18. Peter Clarke, 'Learning from experience: counter-terrorism in the UK since 9/11', Policy Exchange (1 June 2007). 19. Joint Committee on Human Rights – Third Report, 'The Terrorism Bill' (28 Nov. 2005). 20. David Anderson QC, 'The Terrorism Acts in 2015' (Dec. 2016), pp. 90–91. 21. Andrew Gamble, *The Free Economy and the Strong State: The Politics of Thatcherism* (London, 1988). 22. Tony Blair, 'Tough on Crime and Tough on the Causes of Crime', Speech, Labour Party Conference (30 Sept. 1993). 23. Britain was far from being unique in reaching such a conclusion. In Spain, France, Germany and America the state also assumed new powers during this period to fight terrorism. 24. 'Oldham Riots – 10 years on: kids' fight that sparked worst riots for a generation', *Manchester Evening News* (23 May 2011). 25. Mike Makin-Waite, *On Burnley Road* (London, 2021), p. 90. 26. BBC News, 'Businessman jailed over Bradford riots' (3 July 2003). 27. Ted Cantle, 'Community Cohesion: A report of the Independent Review Team', Home Office (2001), p. 16. 28. Ibid. 29. Nick Adams et al., 'Households below average income: an analysis of the income distribution – 1994/5 to 2008/9', Department for Work and Pensions (2013), p. 38 30. Office of the Deputy Prime Minister, 'Communities and neighbourhoods: indices of deprivation: district indices' (2000). 31. Cantle, 'Community Cohesion', p. 9. 32. Khizar Humayun Ansari, *The Infidel Within: Muslims in Britain since 1800* (Oxford, 2018). 33. Samuel Huntington, *The Clash of Civilizations and the Remaking of World Order* (New York, 1996). 34. Munira Mirza, Abi Senthilkumaran and Zein Ja'far, *Living Apart Together: British Muslims and the Paradox of Multiculturalism* (London, 2007), p. 14. 35. For a careful analysis of the limitations of opinion polling on this issue and the way individual polls are reported see Adrian Cousins, 'Muslim opinion and the myth of "tacit support" for terrorism', Counterfire (20 Mar. 2015). 36. Martyn Frampton, David Goodhart and Khalid Mahmood MP, *Unsettled Belonging: A Survey of Britain's Muslim Communities* (London, 2016), p. 67. For other survey data see Ridhi Kashyap and Valerie Lewis, 'British Muslim youth and religious fundamentalism: a quantitative investigation', *Ethnic and Racial Studies*, 36, 12 (2013): 2117–40 and Ipsos, 'A review of survey research on Muslims in Britain' (21 Mar. 2018). 37. Ben Pitcher, *The Politics of Multiculturalism: Race and Racism in Contemporary Britain* (London, 2009), p. 2. 38. Robin Cook, 'Robin Cook's Tikka Masala speech', *Guardian* (19 Apr. 2001). 39. BBC News, 'Straw's veil comments spark anger' (5 Oct. 2006). 40. BBC News, 'Conform to society says PM' (8 Dec. 2006). 41. David Cameron, 'Foreign Policy in the National Interest', Speech to the Lord Mayor's Banquet (14 Nov. 2011). Oliver Daddow and Pauline Schnapper, 'Liberal intervention in the foreign policy thinking of Tony Blair and David Cameron', *Cambridge Review of International Affairs*, 26, 2 (2013): 330–49. 42. For a detailed account based on access to and interviews with those delivering the 'Prevent' programme see Helen Warrell, 'Inside Prevent: the UK's controversial anti-terrorism programme', *Financial Times* (24 Jan. 2019). 43. David Cameron, Speech at Munich Security Conference (5 Feb. 2011). 44. Ian Kershaw, 'Investigation Report: Trojan Horse Letter' (21 July 2014). 45. Michael Gove, *Celsius 7/7* (London, 2006), Kindle Loc. 81. 46. Peter Clarke, 'Report into allegations concerning Birmingham schools arising from the "Trojan Horse" letter', HC 576 (July 2014), p. 12. 47. Kershaw, 'Investigation Report', p. 4. Khalid Mahmood, 'What the New York Times gets wrong about the Trojan Horse Affair', *Spectator* (24 Feb. 2022). Sonia Sodha, 'The Trojan Horse Affair: how serial podcast got it so wrong', *Guardian* (20 Feb. 2022). 48. *New York Times*, 'The Trojan Horse Affair' (undated) (https://www.nytimes.com/interactive/2022/podcasts/trojan-horse-affair.html). John Holmwood and Therese O'Toole, *Countering Extremism in British*

Schools? The Truth About the Birmingham Trojan Horse Affair (Bristol, 2018). Gove, for his part, has described the *New York Times* as 'useful idiots'. Richard Adams, 'Michael Gove calls *New York Times* "useful idiots" for Trojan Horse podcast', *Guardian* (11 Dec. 2022). 49. Tony Blair, 'PBS frontline, "Interview: Prime Minister Tony Blair', (8 May 2002). 50. The National Archives, 'Cabinet Conclusions: Minutes of Meetings', CAB 128/127 (13 Sept. 2001). 51. George Bush, 'Remarks by the President Upon Arrival', The White House South Lawn (16 Sept. 2001). 52. These particular lines are taken from a speech by Blair to an 'Islam and Muslims in the World Today' Conference. BBC News, 'Full Text: Blair speech on Islam' (4 June 2007). 53. Tony Blair, *A Journey* (London, 2010), p. 348.

15 NORTHERN IRELAND

1 Sinn Féin, 'IRA Statement' (28 July 2005). 2. 'Reaction from Tony Blair and Bertie Ahern', *Guardian* (28 July 2005). 3. 'Statement by Tony Blair on the Ending of the IRA Armed Campaign' (28 July 2005). 4. William Butler Yates, 'The Lake Isle of Innisfree' (1888), quoted in Feargal Cochrane, *Belfast: The Story of a City and its People* (New Haven, CT, 2023), p. 17. 5. Harold Jackson and Anne McHardy, *The Two Irelands: The Problem of the Double Minority* (London, 1984). 6. In 1981, Danny Morrison, an IRA volunteer and one of Adams' key advisors, asked two questions at a meeting: 'Who here really believes we can win the war through the ballot box?' and 'Will anyone here object if, with a ballot paper in this hand and an Armalite [rifle] in the other, we take power in Ireland?' Quoted in *The Economist*, 'The quest for respectability – and votes – has transformed Sinn Fein' (4 Dec. 2021). Claire Simpson, 'Gerry Adams has always denied being an IRA member', *Irish News* (9 May 2019). 7. The Anglo-Irish Agreement, enshrined within an international treaty, gave the Republic of Ireland a limited consultative role in Northern Irish politics. The unionist side, which had not believed Thatcher capable of reaching the deal, despised and opposed the Agreement, arguing that it effectively gave the Republic executive rights in the governance of Northern Ireland (which it did not). 8. Ralph Riegel, 'Secret state papers reveal the genesis of Northern peace process', Independent.ie (27 Dec. 2020). 9. Niall Ó Dochartaigh, 'Good Friday Agreement: the early 1990s back-channel between the IRA and British government that made peace possible', The Conversation (6 Apr. 2023). 10. Feargal Cochrane, *Northern Ireland: The Fragile Peace*, 2nd edn (New Haven, CT, 2021), p. 122. 11. Ibid., pp. 126–7. Owen Bennett-Jones, 'What Fred did', *London Review of Books* (Jan. 2015). 12. Brian Rowan, *How the Peace was Won* (Dublin, 2008), pp. 53–7. 13. Cited in Jonathan Powell, *Great Hatred, Little Room: Making Peace in Northern Ireland* (London, 1999), p. 94. 14. Mo Mowlam, *Momentum: The Struggle for Peace, Politics and the People* (London, 2000), p. 145. 15. Northern Ireland Office, 'The Belfast Agreement' (10 Apr. 1998). 16. Ibid., p. 2. 17. Gavin Esler, *How Britain Ends: English Nationalism and the Rebirth of Four Nations* (London, 2021), p. 162. 18. Northern Ireland Life and Times Survey, 1998, 'Which Northern Ireland political party would you support?' (https://www.ark.ac.uk/nilt/1998/Political_Attitudes/NIPARTY.html). 19. Cochrane, *Northern Ireland: The Fragile Peace*, p. 213. 20. Irish Republican Army, 'Statement on Decommissioning' (30 April 1998). 21. Ella Alexander, 'Ian Paisley's most caustic quotes: Catholics "breed like rabbits and multiply like vermin"', *Independent* (12 Sept. 2014). 22. Tony Blair, *A Journey* (London, 2010), p. 178. 23. Brian Hanley and Scott Millar, *The Lost Revolution: The Story of the Official IRA and the Workers' Party* (London, 2010). 24. Northern Ireland Office, 'The Belfast Agreement'. 25. David Trimble, *To Raise Up a new Northern Ireland, Articles and Speeches 1998–2000* (Belfast, 2001), p. 36. Blair, *A Journey*, p. 175. 26. Jonathan Powell, *Great Hatred, Little Room*, p. 147. 27. Mitchell had initially become involved in 1995 when he led an international

commission to review options for paramilitary arms decommissioning. **28.** The National Archives, 'Cabinet Conclusions: Minutes of Meetings', CAB 128/126 (10 Feb. and 17 Feb. 2000). **29.** Jason Burke, Henry McDonald and John O'Farrell, 'IRA agrees to open up its weapons dumps', *Guardian* (7 May 2000). **30.** BBC News, 'IRA weapons dump inspected' (26 June 2000). Katri Merikallio and Tapani Ruokanen, 'How a Finn and a South African brought peace to Northern Ireland', Politico (23 Feb. 2016). **31.** BBC News, 'Trimble resigns over arms row' (1 July 2001). **32.** Powell, *Great Hatred, Little Room*, p. 202. Brendan O'Leary, *A Treatise on Northern Ireland: Volume III, Consociation and Confederation* (Oxford, 2019) p. 238. **33.** *Guardian*, 'Full text of Adams' Speech' (22 Oct. 2001). **34.** Statement by the Independent International Commission on Decommissioning (23 Oct. 2001). **35.** Rosie Cowan et al., 'Castlereagh break-in an "inside job"', *Guardian* (22 June 2002). **36.** Henry McDonald, 'Unionists threaten to topple Executive', *Guardian* (21 Apr. 2002). **37.** In December 2005 the charges against Donaldson were dropped. Shortly after, Gerry Adams held a press conference in which he announced Donaldson had been a British spy. **38.** Cochrane, *Northern Ireland: The Fragile Peace*, p. 221. **39.** Powell, *Great Hatred, Little Room*, p. 17. The National Archives, 'Cabinet Conclusions: Minutes of Meetings', CAB 128/127 (12 July 2001). **40.** Northern Ireland Life and Times Survey, 'Constitutional preference' (27 July 2022). **41.** The DUP had eventually agreed to take up positions within the power-sharing Executive but had adopted a policy of 'critical engagement'. This had meant constantly rotating positions to stymie decision-making. **42.** Ian Paisley, 'Extracts from Speech by Ian Paisley at the North Antrim DUP Association Annual Dinner, Ballymena' (27 Nov. 2004). **43.** Powell, *Great Hatred, Little Room*, p. 244. Richard Sackford, 'Ian Paisley: why "Dr No" finally said yes to peace', *Irish Examiner* (13 Sept. 2014). **44.** David Mitchell, 'Sticking to their guns? The politics of arms decommissioning in Northern Ireland, 1998–2007', *Contemporary British History*, 24, 3 (2010): 341–61. **45.** *Irish Times*, 'Adams says he sees future without IRA' (26 Oct. 2002). **46.** David McGinn, 'My war is over, says Martin McGuinness', *Belfast Telegraph* (29 Oct. 2002). **47.** Jenny Booth, 'IRA offered to shoot McCartney killers', *The Times* (8 Mar. 2005). **48.** Philip Sherwell, 'I'll never deal with Adams again, says Bush', *Daily Telegraph* (13 Mar. 2005). **49.** Tony Blair, 'Speech on the Resumption of Devolved Government in Northern Ireland, Stormont' (8 May 2007). **50.** BBC News, 'Ian Paisley's speech in full' (8 May 2007). **51.** Table NI-SEC-04 'Deaths (Number) Due to the Security Situation in Northern Ireland (only), 1969–2015', CAIN, Background Information on Northern Ireland Society – Security and Defence (https://cain.ulster.ac.uk/ni/security.htm#05).

16 THE TB-GBS

1 Peter Mandelson, *The Third Man* (London, 2011), p. 160. **2.** Paul Routledge, *Gordon Brown* (London, 1998), p. 62. **3.** Tony Blair, *A Journey* (London, 2010), p. 72. **4.** Gordon Brown, *My Life, Our Times* (London, 2018), p. 100. See also Blair, *A Journey*, p. 69; Ed Balls, *Speaking Out: Lessons in Life and Politics* (London, 2016), p. 63; and Mandelson, *The Third Man*, p. 172. **5.** See Robert Peston, *Brown's Britain* (London, 2006), p. 74 and Phillip Whitehead, 'The second consul', *Guardian* (22 Jan. 2005). **6.** John Rentoul and Jon Davis, *Heroes or Villains: The Blair Government Reconsidered* (Oxford, 2019), p. 87. **7.** 'New Labour Because Britain Deserves Better', The Labour Party Manifesto (May 1997). **8.** Andrew Rawnsley, *Servants of the People: The Inside Story of New Labour* (London, 2000), pp. 76–82. **9.** *The Economist*, 'Tomorrow, perhaps' (1 Nov. 1997). **10.** Andrew Rawnsley, 'What Blair really thinks of Brown', *Observer* (18 Jan. 1998). **11.** Michael White, 'Blair balances the power', *Guardian* (28 July 1998). **12.** In his memoirs Blair describes how, at this point, he 'was a bit like a Zombie' and feeling acutely strained. Blair, *A Journey*, p. 424. **13.** Andrew Rawnsley, 'It's never been worse', *Observer* (24 Nov.

2002). TB-GBs was a political play of words on the 'heebie jeebies', a nonsense rhyming pair coined in America in the 1920s. 14. John Prescott, *Prezza: My Story, Pulling no Punches* (London, 2008), pp. 314–15. Helen Rumbelow, 'Prescott served up pie of peace for feuding party rivals', *The Times* (10 Jan. 2005). Mandelson, *The Third Man*, p. 372. 15. Jean Eagleshom, 'Blair pledges to stand for full third term', *Financial Times* (1 Oct. 2004). 16. John Rentoul, 'The Top 10: political operations', *Independent* (13 Feb. 2016). Mandelson, *The Third Man*, p. 369. 17. Chris Giles and George Parker, 'Liz Truss accused of "ideological purge" in sacking of top UK civil servant', *Financial Times* (10 Sept. 2022). 18. Paul Brighton, 'Book Review: *Inside the Department of Economic Affairs: Samuel Brittan, The Diary of an Irregular, 1964–6*', LSE Blog (17 Aug. 2012). For a longer history and assessment of this argument, published a few months before Liz Truss's dramatic rise and fall, see Howard Davies, *The Chancellors: Steering the British Economy in Crisis Times* (Cambridge, 2022), especially ch. 9, 'The Treasury's changing shape'. 19. Mandelson, *The Third Man*, p. 250. 20. Prescott, *Prezza: My Story*, p. 308. 21. Peston, *Brown's Britain*, p. 99. Whitehead, 'The second consul'. 22. For the full YouTube version, see https://www.youtube.com/watch?v=7-gfVy4gHLU. 23. Prescott, *Prezza: My Story*, p. 311. 24. Mark Brown, 'Revealed: why Sir Cliff gave Blair a summer holiday', *Guardian* (24 Aug. 2006). 25. Blair, *A Journey*, pp. 613–15. Philip Webster and Peter Riddel, 'Blair defies his party over departure date', *The Times* (1 Sept. 2006). 26. James Blitz and Jean Eaglesham, 'Blair refuses to set departure timetable', *Financial Times* (1 Sept. 2006). 27. *The Economist*, 'Moving towards the exit' (9 Sept. 2006). 28. *Guardian*, 'Full text of Tom Watson's letter' (6 Sept. 2006). 29. Steve Richards, *Whatever it Takes: The Real Story of Gordon Brown and New Labour* (London, 2010), p. 231. 30. Will Woodward and Patrick Wintour, 'Resignation and threats: the plot to oust the prime minister', *Guardian* (7 Sept. 2006). 31. CNN News, 'Blair – I will resign within a year' (7 Sept. 2006). 32. Peter Riddell, 'Blair: Gordon will be an excellent prime minister', *The Times* (28 Apr. 2005). 33. Andrew Adonis, *Education, Education, Education: Reforming England's Schools* (London, 2012), p. 116. 34. Blair, *A Journey*, p. 617. 35. Ibid., p. 605. 36. Peston, *Brown's Britain*, p. 186. 37. Tony Blair, Speech, Labour Party Conference (1 Oct. 2001). 38. John Kampfner, *Blair's Wars* (London, 2003), p. 252. 39. Peston, *Brown's Britain*, p. 238. 40. Ed Potton, 'The Euro: background to the five economic tests', House of Commons Library, Research Paper 03/53 (4 June 2003). 41. Davies, *The Chancellors*, pp. 95–6. 42. Gordon Brown, Speech, Labour Party Conference (27 Sept. 2004). 43. Gordon Brown, 'Foreword', *The Future of Socialism* (London, 2006). 44. Department for Work and Pensions, 'Benefit and tax credit expenditure in Great Britain' (tables) (Table 1) (January 2013). 45. James Browne and David Phillips, 'Tax and benefit reforms under Labour', Institute for Fiscal Studies, 2010 Election Briefing Note No. 1, p. 16. 46. Institute for Fiscal Studies, 'Living standards, poverty and inequality in the UK' (undated). On the significance and limitations of the Gini Coefficient see Thomas Piketty, *Capital in the Twenty First Century* (Cambridge, MA, 2014), pp. 266–7. I provide figures for after housing-cost income inequality in a later chapter. 47. Robert Shrimsley, 'Boris Johnson has backed Dominic Cummings over Sajid Javid – and there will be a cost', *Financial Times* (13 Feb. 2020). 48. Rentoul and Davis, *Heroes or Villains*, p. 50. 49. Prescott, *Prezza: My Story*, p. 306. 50. Andrew Rawnsley, 'Moody, angry, naive: yes, he was flawed but Gordon Brown did save the world, *Observer* (7 Dec. 2014).

17 BROKEN HOMES

1 Hugh Graham, 'Phil and Kirstie's biggest lessons after 20 years of *Location, Location, Location*', *The Times* (20 Sept. 2020). 2. Sam Adams, 'The golden age of TV is over', Slate (31 Oct. 2019). 3. Department of Housing, Communities and Local Government, 'House

prices from 1930, annual house price inflation, United Kingdom, from 1970' (Table 502) (10 Nov. 2012). **4.** Department of Housing, Communities and Local Government, 'Simple average house prices' (Table 503) (10 Nov. 2012). **5.** These figures are taken from the Land Registry, 'UK house price index: average price by type of property' (undated). **6.** Office for Science, *Land Use Futures: Making the Most of Land in the 21st Century* (London, 2010), p. 181. **7.** Office for National Statistics, 'Overview of the UK population: August 2019' (Figure 1) (23 Aug. 2019). **8.** Office for National Statistics, 'Families and households' (2 Mar. 2021). Excel file. Table 5, 'Households by size, United Kingdom'. **9.** David Miles and Vladimir Pillonca, 'Financial innovation and European housing and mortgage markets', *Oxford Review of Economic Policy*, 24, 1 (2008): 145–75. **10.** Filipa Sa, 'The effect of foreign investors on local housing markets: evidence from the UK', CFM Discussion Paper, DP2016-39 (2016). **11.** Transparency International, 'Stats reveal extent of suspect wealth in UK property and Britain's role as global money laundering hub' (18 Feb. 2022). **12.** Office for National Statistics, 'House building, UK: permanent dwellings started and completed by country' (Table 2a) (24 Feb. 2023). **13.** Alex Morton, *Making Housing Affordable* (London, 2009) p. 14. **14.** OECD, 'Housing stock and construction', Figure HM1.1, 'Dwellings per thousand inhabitants', (18 Oct. 2022), p. 2. **15.** See Matt Griffith, *We Must Fix It: Delivering Reform of the Building Sector to Meet the UK's Housing and Economic Challenges* (London, 2011); Brian Green, 'Is it time for housing policy to pay more heed to the costs and benefits of location?', *Building* (23 July 2013); Kate Barker, *Review of Housing Supply: Delivering Stability: Securing our Future Housing Needs* (London, 2004); and Martin Wolf, 'The big problem with UK housing', *Financial Times* (6 Oct. 2005). **16.** *The Economist*, 'Why Britain cannot build enough of anything' (1 Sept. 2022). **17.** OECD, 'Fiscal Decentralisation database', 'Tax autonomy of state and local government' (Table 1, 2000–2018) (undated). **18.** Rowland Atkinson and Keith Jacobs, *Housing* (London, 2020), p. 19. **19.** BBC News, 'Right to buy homes made £2.8m in profit "in weeks"' (14 Mar. 2019). **20.** Office for National Statistics, 'House building, UK: permanent dwellings' (Table 2a). Full Fact, 'Social housing stock has fallen over the last 30 years' (9 Mar. 2018). **21.** Office for National Statistics, 'House building, UK: permanent dwellings' (Table 2b). Wendy Wilson and Cassie Barton, 'Social rented housing (England): past trends and prospects', House of Commons Library, Briefing Paper, 8963 (12 Aug. 2022). **22.** Office for Science, *Land Use Futures*, pp. 74–5. **23.** Ibid., p. 60. **24.** Edward Clarke, Nada Nohrová and Elli Thomas, *Delivering Change: Building Homes Where We Need Them* (London, 2014). Alan Evans and Oliver Hartwich, *The Best Laid Plans: How Planning Prevents Economic Growth* (London, 2007). Philip McCann, *The UK Regional–National Economic Problem* (London, 2016), pp. 324–5. **25.** Office for Science, *Land Use Futures*, pp. 154–5, 178. Asa Bennett, 'Golf courses in England use twice as much land as housing', The Huffington Post (12 Nov. 2013). **26.** John Hind, 'Did I say that? – John Prescott', *Guardian* (27 Apr. 2008). **27.** Office of Fair Trading, *Homebuilding in the UK: A Market Study* (London, 2008), p. 132. **28.** Brett Christophers, *Rentier Capitalism: Who Owns the Economy, and Who Pays for It?* (London, 2020), pp. 328–30. **29.** Ibid., p. 344. A 2015 survey published by *Inside Housing* suggests that up to 40% of former council houses may now be rented out. Nate Kitch, 'Right to buy to let', *Inside Housing* (14 Aug. 2015), cited in Christophers, *Rentier Capitalism*, p. 344. **30.** Abdulkader Mostafa and Colin Jones, 'Rent or buy: does the British obsession with home ownership pay off?', The Conversation (4 Apr. 2019). **31.** Department for Work and Pensions, 'Pensioners' income series: financial year 2010/11' (12 July 2012), p. 40. **32.** Resolution Foundation, 'As time goes by: shifting incomes and inequality between and within generations', Figure 11. 'Typical pensioner incomes are now above working-age ones' (13 Feb. 2017), p. 25. **33.** Department of Housing, Communities and Local Government, 'Private registered provider: average weekly rents by district, from 1997' (Table 704) (10 Nov. 2012). **34.** Department of Housing, Communities and Local Government, 'Private landlords survey' (18 Oct.

2011). More generally see Matthew Watson, 'House price Keynesianism and the contradictions of the modern investor subject', *Housing Studies*, 25, 3 (2010): 413–26. In total, the number of private landlords jumped from around 900,000 in 2000 to 1.7 million by 2010. Richard Ronald and Justin Kadi, 'The revival of private landlords in Britain's post-homeownership society', *New Political Economy*, 23, 6 (2018): 786–803. **35.** Liam Reynolds et al., *Breaking Point – How Unaffordable Housing is Pushing Us to the Limit* (London, 2008). **36.** The Health Foundation, 'Proportion of households living in non-decent homes by tenure' (27 Apr. 2023). **37.** Department of Housing, Communities and Local Government, 'Gross weekly income of household by tenure' (Table FA1341) (14 Nov. 2012). Peter Malpass and Ceri Victory, 'The modernisation of social housing in England', *International Journal of Housing Policy*, 10, 1 (2010): 3–18. **38.** David Willetts, *The Pinch: How the Baby Boomers Stole their Children's Future* (London, 2010). **39.** Chloe Timperley, *Generation Rent: Why You Can't Buy a Home or Even Rent a Good One* (London, 2019). **40.** Bobby Duffy, *Generations: Does When You're Born Shape Who You Are?* (London, 2021), p. 42. **41.** Harriet Sherwood, 'Pasta one-liner wins best joke award at Edinburgh Festival Fringe', *Guardian* (22 Aug. 2022). **42.** Also see Andrew Hindmoor, *What's Left Now? The History and Future of Social Democracy* (Oxford, 2018), pp. 149–54. **43.** The data used in this online Institute for Fiscal Studies spreadsheet is regularly updated. The data here was downloaded in July 2023. **44.** Institute for Fiscal Studies, 'Living standards, poverty and inequality in the UK' (undated). **45.** Thomas Piketty, *Capital in the Twenty-First Century* (Cambridge, MA, 2014), p. 344. **46.** Office for National Statistics, 'Wealth in Great Britain: Dataset, Gini Coefficients for aggregate total wealth by components' (Table 2.4) (5 Dec. 2019). **47.** Department of Housing, Communities and Local Government, 'Repayments as a percent of income and deposit as a percent of purchase price' (Table 539) (10 Nov. 2012). **48.** BBC News, 'Architects say new houses are "shameful shoebox homes"' (14 Sept. 2011). **49.** Bank of England, 'Further details about total lending to individuals data'. Click on the link 'Lending secured on dwellings'. **50.** Colin Crouch, 'Privatised Keynesianism: an unacknowledged policy regime', *British Journal of Politics and International Relations*, 11, 3 (2009): 382–99. **51.** Department for Work and Pensions, 'Benefit expenditure and caseload tables, 2023', Outrun and Forecast Tables: Spring Budget 2023 (Table 1a) (25 Apr. 2023).

18 THE RUN ON THE ROCK

1 BBC News, 'Northern Rock gets bank bail-out' (13 Sept. 2007). Material in this chapter draws significantly upon two of my earlier books, *12 Days that Made Modern Britain* (Oxford, 2020) and *Masters of the Universe but Slaves of the Market* (Cambridge, MA, 2014, the latter written with my colleague Stephen Bell. **2.** Richard Smith, 'Boss held hostage by £1m couple', *Daily Mirror* (15 Sept. 2007). **3.** Specifically, since the collapse of Overend, Gurney and Company in 1866. Treasury Select Committee, 'The Run on the Rock, Volume 1', HC 56-I (24 Jan. 2008), p. 8. **4.** Vince Cable, *The Storm: The World Economic Crisis and What It Means* (London, 2009), p. 12. **5.** Treasury Select Committee, 'Run on the Rock, Volume 1', pp. 38–9. **6.** Mervyn King, 'Letter to Treasury Select Committee', in Treasury Select Committee, 'The Run on the Rock, Volume II', HC 56-II (24 Jan. 2008), Ev. 214. Also see Mervyn King, *The End of Alchemy: Money, Banking and the Future of the Global Economy* (London, 2016), p. 268. **7.** Patrick Kinsley, 'Financial crisis: timeline', *Guardian* (7 Aug. 2012). **8.** Martin Arnold, 'Northern Rock in facts and figures', *Financial Times* (31 Aug. 2017). **9.** Gordon Brown, *Beyond the Crash: Overcoming the First Crisis of Globalization* (London, 2010), p. 23. **10.** Arnold, 'Northern Rock in facts and figures'. Philip Augar, *Chasing Alpha – How Reckless Growth and Unchecked Ambition Ruined the City's Golden Decade* (London, 2009) p. 149. **11.** Alex Brummer,

The Crunch, The Scandal of Northern Rock and the Escalating Credit Crisis (London, 2008), p. 9.   12. See 'Third arrears fine in Northern Rock case', *Yorkshire Post* (30 July 2020) and Northern Rock, 'Annual Report and Accounts, 2006', p. 6.   13. *The Times*, Editorial, 'Northern crock' (20 Nov. 2007).   14. Alistair Darling, Speech to the Worshipful Company of International Bankers (4 Feb. 2008).   15. Augar, *Chasing Alpha*, p. 154. National Audit Office, 'The nationalisation of Northern Rock', HC 298 (18 Mar. 2009), Appendix 4, 'Northern Rock's use of securitisation and its relationship with granite'.   16. Northern Rock, 'Annual report and accounts' (2007), p. 31. Hyun Shin, 'Reflections on Northern Rock: the bank run that heralded the global financial crisis', *Journal of Economic Perspectives*, 23, 1 (2009): 101-19.   17. Bell and Hindmoor, *Masters of the Universe but Slaves of the Market*, pp. 56-7.   18. Hans Blummenstein, Ahmet Keskinler and Carrick Lucas, 'Outlook for the securitisation market', *OECD Journal: Financial Market Trends*, 1 (2011): 4.   19. Bell and Hindmoor, *Masters of the Universe but Slaves of the Market*, p. 56.   20. Northern Rock, 'Summary annual report' (2006), p. 1.   21. Andrew Haldane and Piergiorgio Alessandri, 'Banking on the State', Conference Paper, Federal Reserve Bank of Chicago, Twelfth Annual International Banking Conference (25 Sept. 2009), p. 14.   22. See Daniel Sanches, 'Shadow banking and the crisis of 2007-8', *Business Review*, Federal Reserve Bank of Philadelphia, Q2 (2014), pp. 7-14 and Gaston Gelos and Nico Valckx, 'The growth of shadow banking', IMF Blog (3 Oct. 2014).   23. Treasury Select Committee, 'Run on the Rock, Volume 1,' p. 16.   24. Gretchen Morgensen, 'Small unit in London pushed AIG into the skid that nearly destroyed it', *New York Times* (28 Sept. 2008).   25. Financial Services Authority, 'Internal audit – FSA's supervision of Northern Rock' (26 Mar. 2008).   26. Alistair Darling, *Back from the Brink* (London, 2011), p. 318.   27. Andrew Farlow, *Crash and Beyond: Causes and Consequences of the Global Financial Crisis* (Oxford, 2013), p. 315.   28. Financial Services Authority, 'The failure of the Royal Bank of Scotland: Financial Services Authority board report' (Dec. 2011), p. 29.   29. James Kirkup, 'Mervyn King: regulators unable to stop City banks taking risks due to government', *Daily Telegraph* (26 Feb. 2009).   30. Mark Williams, *Uncontrolled Risk: The Lessons of Lehman Brothers and how Systemic Risk Can Still Bring Down the World Financial System* (New York, 2010), p. 168.   31. For compelling accounts of this moment, see Philip Augar, *The Bank That Lived a Little: Barclays in the Age of the Very Free Market* (London, 2018) and Andrew Sorkin, *Too Big To Fail: Inside the Battle to Save Wall Street* (London, 2009).   32. Tim Geithner, *Stress Test: Reflections on Financial Crises* (London, 2014), p. 186.   33. BBC News, 'The day Lehman Brothers went under' (14 Sept. 2008).

19 FALLING DOWN

1 Quoted in Adam Tooze, *Crashed: How a Decade of Financial Crises Changed the World* (New York, 2019), p. 162.   2. See Joseph Stiglitz, *Freefall: America, Free Markets and the Sinking of the Global Economy* (New York, 2010).   3. Quoted in Anthony Seldon and Peter Snowdon, *Cameron at 10: The Inside Story* (London, 2015), p. 9.   4. Karl Marx, *The Communist Manifesto*, in Karl Marx and Friedrich Engels, *Selected Works, Volume 1* (Moscow, 1969), p. 16.   5. Andrew Pierce, 'The Queen asks why no one saw the credit crunch coming', *Daily Telegraph* (5 Nov. 2008).   6. Alistair Darling, *Back from the Brink* (London, 2011), p. 3.   7. Quoted in Stephen Bell and Andrew Hindmoor, *Masters of the Universe but Slaves of the Market* (Cambridge, MA, 2013), p. 201.   8. Adair Turner, *The Turner Review: A Regulatory Response to the Global Banking Crisis* (London, 2009), p. 88.   9. Adair Turner, 'Reforming Finance: Are We Being Radical Enough?' The 2011 Clare Distinguished Lecture in Economics and Public Policy, Clare College, Cambridge, 18 Feb. 2011.   10. Ben Shimshon, 'Poster-truth politics: the Gordon Brown posters for the election that never was', *Prospect* (10 Dec. 2017).   11. Kirsty Walker, 'Brown wasted my New

Labour legacy: Blair savages successor for losing centre ground', *Daily Mail* (9 July 2011).   12. Allegra Stratton and Patrick Wintour, 'James Purnell quits Cabinet and calls on Gordon Brown to stand aside now', *Guardian* (5 June 2009).   13. John Rentoul, 'Ed saved Gordon to get his job', *Independent* (21 Nov. 2010). Allegra Stratton, 'Geoff Hoon's unsent letter and a secret plot to oust Gordon Brown', *Guardian* (6 Jan. 2010).   14. Patrick Wintour, 'Gordon Brown hit by fresh bullying allegations', *Guardian* (21 Feb. 2010).   15. BBC News, 'Gordon Brown staff "contacted bullying helpline"' (21 Feb. 2010).   16. Paul Krugman, 'Gordon does good', *New York Times* (12 Oct. 2008). Also see William Keegan, *Saving the World? Gordon Brown Reconsidered* (London, 2012).   17. Gordon Brown, *Beyond the Crash: Overcoming the First Crisis of Globalization* (London, 2010), p. xvii.   18. See Barack Obama, *A Promised Land* (London, 2020), p. 334.   19. See Frederico Mor, 'Bank rescues of 2007–9: outcomes and cost', House of Commons Library, Briefing Paper 5748 (8 Oct. 2018), p. 5 and National Audit Office, 'Taxpayer support for UK banks, FAQs' (20 Nov. 2020).   20. Geoff Mann, *In the Long Run We Are All Dead: Keynesianism, Political Economy and Revolution* (London, 2019).   21. Bank of England, 'Official bank rate history' (undated) (https://www.bankofengland.co.uk/boeapps/database/BankRate.asp).   22. Tooze, *Crashed*, pp. 210–15.   23. Stephen Bell and Andrew Hindmoor, 'Taming the City? Structural power and the evolution of British banking policy amidst the great financial meltdown', *New Political Economy*, 20, 3 (2014): 454–74; Stephen Bell and Andrew Hindmoor, 'The ideational shaping of state power and capacity: winning battles but losing the war over bank reform in the US and UK', *Government and Opposition*, 49, 3 (2014): 342–68; Stephen Bell and Andrew Hindmoor, 'Structural power and the politics of bank capital regulation in the UK' *Political Studies*, 65, 1 (2017): 103–21; and Stephen Bell and Andrew Hindmoor, 'Are the major global banks now safer? Structural continuities and change in banking and finance since the 2008 crisis', *Review of International Political Economy*, 25, 1 (2018): 1–27.   24. Quoted in Patrick Jenkins, 'Banks: too dull to fail?', *Financial Times* (6 Sept. 2016).   25. Eric Helleiner, *The Status Quo Crisis: Global Financial Governance after the 2008 Meltdown* (Oxford, 2014).   26. Timothy Edwards, 'The Independent Commission on Banking: The Vickers Report', House of Commons Library, Research Briefing 6171 (30 Dec. 2013).   27. Bell and Hindmoor, 'Are the major global banks now safer?'   28. Bell and Hindmoor, *Masters of the Universe but Slaves of the Market*, pp. 98–9.   29. BBC News, 'JP Morgan to move into Lehman London headquarters' (20 Dec. 2010).   30. Bruno Iksil, 'London Whale complains of unfair blame for $6.2bn JP Morgan losses', *Financial Times* (23 Feb. 2016).   31. Neil Irwin, *The Alchemists: Three Central Bankers and a World on Fire* (New York, 2013), p. 233. *Financial Times*, 'Text of Mervyn King's speech to the Lord Mayor's banquet' (17 June 2009).   32. Quoted in Irwin, *The Alchemists*, p. 235.   33. *The Economist*, 'Emerging markets' experiments with QE have not turned out too badly' (29 Oct. 2020).   34. Filippo Busetto et al., 'QE at the Bank of England: a perspective on its functioning and effectiveness', *Bank of England Quarterly Bulletin* (18 May 2022), Chart 1.   35. Technically, purchases were routed through an Asset Purchase Facility, which was lent money by the Bank of England. Hence by December 2014 the Bank of England's own balance sheet recorded as an asset a £315bn loan to the APF. Bank of England, 'Consolidated balance sheet' (31 Dec. 2014).   36. As a secondary effect, it was expected QE would also stimulate the economy by weakening the pound on international markets, boosting exports. *The Economist*, 'QE or not QE' (14 July 2012).   37. Delphine Strauss, 'BoE is financing UK's coronavirus measures, Bailey acknowledges', *Financial Times* (14 May 2020).   38. Chris Smith, 'Quantitative Easing', House of Lords Library (11 Nov. 2021).   39. Bank of England, 'The distributional effects of asset purchases', *Bank of England Quarterly Bulletin* (13 Sept. 2013) and Philip Bunn, Alice Pugh and Chris Yeates, 'The distributional impact of monetary policy easing in the UK between 2008 and 2014', Bank of England Staff Working Paper, 720 (Mar. 2018).   40. Bank of England, 'The distributional effects of asset purchases'.   41. Fraser Nelson,

'QE – the ultimate subsidy for the rich', *Spectator* (23 Aug. 2012). 42. Richard Murphy, 'The political economy of people's quantitative easing', Tax Research UK (17 Aug. 2015). 43. Irwin, *The Alchemists*, p. 256. 44. Larry Elliott, 'Bank of England rebuts May and Hague's attacks on quantitative easing', *Guardian* (19 Oct. 2016). 45. Andrew Baker, Andrew Hindmoor and Sean McDaniel, 'Performing central bank independence: the Bank of England's communicative financial stability strategy', *Regulation and Governance* (https://onlinelibrary.wiley.com/doi/10.1111/rego.12564). 46. Barry Eichengreen and Kevin O'Rourke, 'A tale of two depressions', VoxEU (8 Mar. 2012). 47. Daniel Drezner, *The System Worked: How the World Stopped Another Great Depression* (Oxford, 2014), pp. 31–8. 48. By 2013, the World Trade Organization estimated that new protectionist measures had reduced global trade by only around 0.2%. Drezner, *The System Worked*, p. 41. 49. International Energy Agency, 'Global annual change in real gross domestic product (GDP), 1900–2020' (4 May 2020). 50. Institute for Fiscal Studies, 'Living standards, poverty and inequality in the UK' (undated). 51. Office for National Statistics, 'Gross domestic product: year on year growth' (22 Dec. 2021). 52. UK Data Service, 'British General Election study of 2010' (questions bq31a and bq31b) (http://nesstar.ukdataservice.ac.uk/webview/). 53. Leeds University, 'Academics rate Brown one of the worst post-1945 PMs' (2 Aug. 2010) (https://web.archive.org/web/20101104123616/http://www.leeds.ac.uk/news/article/867/academics_rate_brown_one_of_the_worst_post_1945_pms). 54. Royal Holloway Group, 'The prime ministerial ratings game: a parliamentary perspective' (5 May 2015).

20 AN EXPENSES BUSINESS

1 The material in this chapter draws upon some of my earlier published work on the expenses scandal, in Andrew Hindmoor, *12 Days that Made Modern Britain* (Oxford, 2020). Two *Telegraph* journalists, Robert Winnett and Gordon Rayner, have offered a detailed account of the unfolding of the story from the inside. Robert Winnett and Gordon Rayner, *No Expenses Spared* (London, 2009). 2. Rosa Prince and Holly Watt, 'MPs' expenses: Gordon Brown's house swap that let him claim thousands', *Daily Telegraph* (8 May 2009). 3. *Guardian*, 'Humiliated Tory MP Peter Viggers quits over duck island expense claim' (23 May 2009). 4. Ben Leapman, 'MPs expenses: the Saints', *Daily Telegraph* (18 May 2009). 5. Suzy Jagger and Philip Webster, 'MP Nadine Dorries censured by Tories over expenses suicide remark', *The Times* (23 May 2009). 6. BBC News, 'Stop MP humiliation – archbishop' (23 May 2009). 7. Nigel Allington and Gillian Peele, 'Moats, duck houses and bath plugs: Members of Parliament, the expenses scandal and the use of web sites', *Parliamentary Affairs*, 63, 3 (2010): 385–406. 8. Kathy Marks, 'Peter Foster: from "Cheriegate" to fresh claims of fraud', BBC News (6 Apr. 2017). 9. Vikram Dodd and Patrick Wintour, 'No one to face charges in cash for honours inquiry', *Guardian* (20 July 2007). 10. Paul Valley, 'Michael Levy: Lord Cashpoint', *Independent* (18 Mar. 2006). Michael Levy, *A Question of Honour* (London, 2008), p. 252. 11. *Sunday Times*, 'Lords for hire' (1 Feb. 2009). 12. Deborah Summers, 'MPs must disclose expenses, High Court rules', *Guardian* (16 May 2008). 13. Winnett and Raynor, *No Expenses Spared*, pp. 80–84. 14. *Daily Telegraph*, 'IPSO upholds Gordon Brown expenses complaint' (15 May 2017). 15. Andrew Thomas, 'Brown says sorry over expenses', Channel 4 News (11 May 2009). 16. This was compared to just 20% of MPs who were not directly targeted for criticism during the expenses scandal. Charles Pattie and Ron Johnson, 'The electoral impact of the UK 2009 MP's expenses scandal', *Political Studies*, 60, 4 (2012): 730–50. 17. BBC News, 'MPs told to repay £1.1m expenses' (4 Feb. 2010). 18. Phillip Clothier, 'MPs cash-for-influence: the inside story', *Prospect* (25 Mar. 2010). 19. *Sunday Times*, 'Stephen Byers: "I'm like a cab for hire"' (21 Mar. 2010). 20. Tom Whitehead,

'European Elections 2009: UKIP claims breakthrough', *Daily Telegraph* (8 June 2009).   **21.**
Andrew Rawnsley, *The End of the Party: The Rise and Fall of New Labour* (London, 2010),
p. 649.   **22.** Royal College of Physicians, 'Annual survey of public trust in professions'
(Sept. 2009).   **23.** World Values Survey, Wave 5 (2005–9), 'Confidence in political parties',
online analysis (https://www.worldvaluessurvey.org/WVSOnline.jsp).   **24.** Ipsos, 'Trust in
professions: long-term trends' (30 Nov. 2017).   **25.** Tom Tyler, *Why People Obey the Law*
(New Haven, CT, 1992). Harry Quilter-Pinner, Rachel Statham, Will Jennings and Viktor
Valgarosson, *Trust Issues: Dealing with Distrust in Politics* (London, 2021), pp. 2–12.
Susan Dodsworth and Nic Cheeseman, 'Political trust: the glue that keeps democracies
together', International Development Department, University of Birmingham, May 2020,
pp. 5–6.   **26.** Colin Hay and Gerry Stoker, 'Understanding and challenging populist negativity towards politics: the perspectives of British citizens', *Political Studies*, 65, 1 (2017):
4–23. John Hibbing and Elizabeth Theiss-Morse, *Stealth Democracy: America's Beliefs
about How Government Should Work* (Cambridge, 2002).   **27.** Will Jennings, Nick Clarke
and Jonathan Moss, 'The decline in diffuse support for national politics: the long view on
political discontent in Britain', *Public Opinion Quarterly*, 81, 3 (2017): 748–58.   **28.**
Maria Sobolewska and Robert Ford, *Brexitland* (Cambridge, 2020), p. 136.   **29.** Edward
Fieldhouse et al., *Electoral Shocks: The Volatile Voter in a Turbulent World* (Oxford, 2019),
p. 13. An online summary can be found at British Election Study, 'Electoral shocks: the volatile voter in a turbulent world' (13 Dec. 2019).   **30.** Press Gazette, 'British Press Awards
2010: full list of winners' (24 Mar. 2010).   **31.** See Nick Davies, *Flat Earth News* (London,
2008).   **32.** John Lloyd, *What the Media Do to Our Politics* (London, 2004), p. 20.   **33.**
Tony Blair, Speech, 'The Media', Reuters (12 June 2007).   **34.** Simon Kelner, 'When the
"feral beast" of the *Independent* bit back at Tony Blair', *Independent* (26 Mar. 2016).   **35.**
House of Commons, Home Affairs Committee, 'Unauthorised tapping into or hacking of
mobile communications', HC 907 (19 July 2011), pp. 3–4.   **36.** Jennifer Saba, 'Could
Murdoch deputy Hinton take the fall?', Reuters (9 July 2011).   **37.** Nick Davies, 'Phone
hacking approved by top *News of the World* executive – new files', *Guardian* (15 Dec.
2010).   **38.** Nick Davies and Amelia Hill, 'Missing Milly Dowler's voicemail was hacked
by *News of the World*', *Guardian* (4 July 2011). There was some dispute after this about
whether the messages would have been deleted automatically.   **39.** BBC News, 'Rupert
Murdoch: the most humble day of my life' (19 July 2011).   **40.** Tom Watson and Martin
Hickman, *Dial M for Murdoch* (London, 2012).   **41.** Martin Hickman, 'News Inter-
national "tried to blackmail Select Committee"', *Independent* (28 May 2012).   **42.** Mark
White, 'Major: Murdoch asked me to change policy', Sky News (12 June 2012).   **43.** Andre
Tartar, 'David Cameron met 26 times with Murdoch, his editors', *New York Magazine* (26
July 2011). Harriet Sherwood, 'Quiet, pretty ... and notorious: Chipping Norton in the
spotlight again', *Guardian* (28 June 2014).   **44.** James Robinson, 'David Cameron, Ed
Miliband and Co flock to pay homage at Rupert Murdoch's summer party', *Guardian* (20
June 2011).   **45.** Wikiwand, 'List of newspapers in the UK by circulation' (undated).   **46.**
Charlotte Tobitt, 'UK local newspaper closures: at least 265 titles gone since 2005, but pace
slowed', Press Gazette (Aug. 2020).   **47.** Melanie Weaver, 'Ofcom: BBC One, ITV and
Facebook are the most used news sources in the UK. In that order', Journalism.co.uk (3
Aug. 2021).   **48.** Charlotte Tobitt, 'Ofcom survey: news consumption via social media and
Google is down', Press Gazette (13 Aug. 2020).

PART FIVE

1 Benedict Anderson, *Imagined Communities: Reflections on the Origin and Spread of
Nationalism* (London.1983).   **2.** Andrew Hough, 'Gay marriage? We may as well allow it
with animals, says Christian Tory', *Daily Telegraph* (13 Oct. 2011).   **3.** Conservative Party,

Invitation to Join the Government of Great Britain (London, 2010), p. 21. **4.** Judy Griffith, 'Perspectives on the Windrush Generation scandal: an interview with Judy Griffith', *The British Library* (4 Oct. 2018). **5.** BBC News, 'London Olympics: how volunteers made the games' (10 Aug. 2012).

21 THE COALITION

1 Martin Kettle, 'Nick Clegg was the winner in this historic leaders' debate', *Guardian* (15 Apr. 2010). Katy Parry and Kay Richardson, 'Political imagery in the British general election of 2010: the curious case of Nick Clegg', *British Journal of Politics and International Relations*, 13, 4 (2011): 474–89. **2.** Richard Watson, 'Cameron's big, open, comprehensive offer to Clegg', *The Times* (8 May 2010). On Cameron's earlier discussions with Osborne see Janan Ganesh, *George Osborne: The Austerity Chancellor* (London, 2012), p. 253. **3.** Matt Chorley, 'Hugh Grant lookalike who used to get Cameron's coffee now runs the world', *The Times* (18 Feb. 2022). **4.** Philip Webster, Tom Baldwin and Roland Watson, 'His parting shot', *The Times* (11 May 2010). **5.** David Cameron, *For the Record* (London, 2019), p. 141. **6.** Ray Dunne, 'SDP: breaking the mould', BBC News (25 Jan. 2001). **7.** Paddy Ashdown, *The Ashdown Diaries, Volume 1, 1988–1997* (London, 2000), p. 273. **8.** Sarah Schaefer, 'Prescott: I would have resigned over Lib-Lab deal', *Independent* (23 Oct. 2000). **9.** Tony Blair, *A Journey* (London, 2010), p. 120. **10.** Andrew Russell and Edward Fieldhouse, *Neither Left nor Right? The Liberal Democrats and the Electorate* (Manchester, 2005). **11.** Paul Marshall and David Laws (eds.), *The Orange Book: Reclaiming Liberalism* (London, 2004). A second book, published in 2007, restated the Plan B case for a left-of-centre liberalism. Duncan Brack et al. (eds.), *Reinventing the State: Social Liberalism for the 21st Century* (London, 2007). **12.** Philip Patrick, 'Ming Campbell on the first Tokyo Olympics: I was bored out of my head', *The Scotsman* (11 July 2021). **13.** George Parker and Alex Barker, 'Man in the news: Nick Clegg', *Financial Times* (9 Apr. 2010). **14.** See, for example, James Blitz, 'Can UK Coalition go the distance?', *Financial Times* (14 May 2010). **15.** Liberal Democratic Party, 'Liberal Democrat Manifesto 2010', p. 33. **16.** Holly Watt and Laura Roberts, 'I have the nuclear option: it's like fighting a war', *Daily Telegraph* (20 Dec. 2010). **17.** Toby Helm, 'Nick Clegg targeted as anti-AV campaign links him to broken promises', *Guardian* (5 Feb. 2011). **18.** Cameron, *For the Record*, p. 293. **19.** Hélène Mulholland and Patrick Wintour, 'Ed Miliband faces AV battle as MPs and peers back No vote', *Guardian* (16 Mar. 2011). **20.** Cameron, *For the Record*, p. 294. **21.** Nick Clegg, *Politics: Between the Extremes* (London, 2016), p. 134. **22.** Sky News, 'Lords Reform: Lib Dems threaten Tories' (6 July 2012). **23.** Cameron, *For the Record*, p. 264. **24.** Nicholas Watt, 'Nick Clegg boasts of blocking 16 Tory policies in "tooth and nail" fight', *Guardian* (18 Sept. 2013). **25.** Cameron, *For the Record*, p. 510. **26.** Blitz, 'Can UK Coalition go the distance?'. **27.** David Laws, *Coalition: The Inside Story of the Conservative–Liberal Democrat Coalition Government* (London, 2016), p. 67. **28.** Isaiah Berlin, *The Hedgehog and the Fox* (London, 1953). **29.** Clegg, *Politics: Between the Extremes*, pp. 28–9. **30.** Ganesh, *George Osborne*, p. 277. **31.** John Harris, 'The strange death of the Liberal Democrats', *Guardian* (12 June 2015). For polling data during this period see Ipsos, 'Voting intentions in Great Britain, 2002–present' (18 Feb. 2023). **32.** Sky News, 'Clegg crowned "most disliked leader" in poll' (1 June 2014). **33.** David Cutts and Andrew Russell, 'From coalition to catastrophe: the electoral meltdown of the Liberal Democrats', *Parliamentary Affairs*, 68, Sup, 1 (2015): 70–87. **34.** Adrian Slade, 'Coalition and the deluge', *Journal of Liberal History*, 88 (Autumn, 2015). **35.** Thomas Quinn, Judith Bara and John Bartle, 'The UK Coalition agreement of 2010: who won?', *Journal of Elections, Public Opinion and Parties*, 21, 2 (2011): 295–312. **36.** Kate Dommett, 'A miserable little compromise: exploring Liberal

Democrat fortunes in the UK Coalition', *Political Quarterly*, 84, 2 (2013): 218–27.   37. British Election Study, 2015, 'Face-to-face post-election survey' (question: q01:3).   38. Clegg, *Politics: Between the Extremes*, p. 26.   39. Libby McEnhill, 'Unity and distinctiveness in UK Coalition government: lessons for junior partners', *Political Quarterly*, 86, 2 (2015): 101–9.   40. Edward Fieldhouse et al., *Electoral Shocks: The Volatile Voter in a Turbulent World* (Oxford, 2019), pp. 118–19.   41. Iain McLean, '"England does not love coalitions": the most misused political quotation in the book', *Government and Opposition*, 47, 1 (2012): 3–20.   42. Laws, *Coalition*, pp. 85–6.   43. In 2009 Rennard resigned as chief executive of the Liberal Democrats amidst allegations of sexual misconduct. Haroon Siddique and Patrick Wintour, 'Lord Rennard did not resign purely on health grounds, Nick Clegg admits', *Guardian* (27 Feb. 2013).   44. Clegg's successor, Jared O'Mara, was subsequently suspended from the Labour Party and, later, charged with fraud and sentenced to four years in prison.   45. Henry Mance, 'My trip into the Metaverse with Facebook defender in chief, Nick Clegg', *Financial Times* (16 Dec. 2021).   46. Caroline Graham, 'How Uber-Liberal Nick Clegg is living the Californian dream in "America's most expensive zip code" – with his millions from Facebook, the world's "most illiberal firm"', *Daily Mail* (20 Feb. 2021). In August 2022 Clegg became one of a number of senior executives at Meta (as Facebook had become) to move to London. Gareth Corfield and James Warrington, 'Sir Nick Clegg returns to London in latest Meta move', *Daily Telegraph* (3 Aug. 2022).   47. Mance, 'My trip into the Metaverse'.

22 CALLING AN AUSTERITY EMERGENCY

1 George Osborne, 'Queen's Speech Economy Debate' (8 June 2010).   2. See Alberto Alesina and Silvia Ardagna, 'Large changes in fiscal policy: taxes versus spending', National Bureau of Economic Research, Working Paper 15438 (Oct. 2009) and Francesco Giavazzi and Marco Pagano, 'Can severe fiscal contractions be expansionary? Tales of two small European countries', National Bureau of Economic Research, Working Paper 3378 (May 1990).   3. Nicholas Wapshott, *Keynes Hayek: The Clash that Defined Modern Economics* (London, 2011).   4. Robert Skidelsky, *John Maynard Keynes: Economist, Philosopher, Statesman* (London, 2013), p. 533.   5. For a highly critical review, from a broadly Keynesian perspective, of the theory of the Expansionary Fiscal Contraction and of austerity see Mark Blyth, *Austerity: The History of a Dangerous Idea* (Oxford, 2013), pp. 212–20.   6. Adam Tooze, *Crashed: How a Decade of Financial Crises Changed the World* (London, 2018), pp. 101–2.   7. Office for Budget Responsibility, '% debt interest (central government, net of APF)' (6 May 2022). The APF in this title is Asset Purchase Facility, the conduit through which the Bank of England conducts quantitative easing.   8. Jonathan Portes, 'The Coalition's confidence trick', *New Statesman* (8 Aug. 2011).   9. HM Treasury, 'Budget 2010' (22 June 2010), p. 15.   10. Fawcett Society, 'The impact of austerity on women' (19 Mar. 2012).   11. Ben Quinn, 'Anti-cuts groups descend on banks in NHS protest', *Guardian* (28 May 2011).   12. The main effect of these proposed changes was, at least in their first version, to require NHS Trusts and other bodies to tender for health services and to choose private providers if they offered potential cost savings.   13. BBC News, 'Budget 2012: Labour attack package for millionaires' (21 Mar. 2012).   14. James Orr, 'Nadine Dorries: David Cameron and George Osborne are just arrogant posh boys', *Daily Telegraph* (23 Apr. 2012).   15. Ipsos, 'Voting intentions in Great Britain, 2002–present' (18 Feb. 2013).   16. YouGov, 'Government cuts', Archive (undated) (https://d25d2506sfb94s.cloudfront.net/cumulus_uploads/document/xjt2iq1a7v/YG%20trackers%20-%20Government%20Cuts.pdf).   17. Michael White, 'Series of political knocks took toll on loyal Brownite, Tom Watson', *Guardian* (2 June 2009).   18. Alan Travis, 'Officials launch drive to seek out illegal migrants at work', *Guardian* (16 May 2007).   19. David Laws,

Coalition: The Inside Story of the Conservative–Liberal Democrat Coalition Government (London, 2016), pp. 29–31. 20. See Rafael Behr, 'The making of Ed Miliband', *Guardian* (15 Apr. 2015). On the underlying academic theory see Peter Hall and David Soskice (eds.), *Varieties of Capitalism: The Institutional Foundations of Comparative Advantage* (Oxford, 2001). 21. Ivor Gaber, 'The "othering" of "Red Ed", or how the *Daily Mail* framed the British Labour leader', LSE Blogs (10 Mar. 2015). On the deleterious effects of inequality see Ed Miliband, 'The Hugo Young Lecture', reproduced in *Prospect* (10 Feb. 2014). 22. Geoffrey Levy, 'The man who hated Britain: Red Ed's pledge to bring back socialism is a homage to his Marxist father. So what did Miliband Snr really believe in? The answer should disturb everyone who loves this country', *Daily Mail* (27 Sept. 2013). 23. James McCandless, 'How a bacon sandwich derailed Ed Miliband's UK political career', The Huffington Post (12 Oct. 2018). 24. Bryne himself was tasked by Ed Miliband with leading Labour's post-election inquest and then became the shadow secretary of state for work and pensions. 25. Liam Byrne, 'I'm afraid there is no money: the note I will regret forever', *Guardian* (9 May 2015). 26. Independent Inquiry into Why Labour Lost, 'Labour's future: why Labour lost in 2015 and why it can win again' (2016), p. 7. Jon Cruddas, 'Labour lost because voters believed it was anti-austerity', LabourList (5 Aug. 2016). 27. HM Treasury 'Public expenditure statistical analyses', Chapter 4 (Tables 4.1 and 4.3) (20 July 2022). 28. Channel 4 News, 'Osborne unveils £10bn benefits cut package' (8 Oct. 2012). 29. Department for Work and Pensions, 'Benefit expenditure and caseload tables 2016', Outrun and Forecast: Autumn Statement 2016 (table 1a) (7 April 2016). The figure on overall social protection expenditure is taken from the same source as above, HM Treasury, 'Public expenditure statistical analyses' (Table 4.4). 30. Institute for Fiscal Studies, 'Living standards, poverty and inequality in the UK' (undated). 31. Andy Haldane, 'Whose Recovery?', Speech in Port Talbot (30 June 2016). 32. Jonathan Watkins et al., 'Effects of health and social care spending constraints on mortality in England: a time trend analysis', *BMJ Open*, 7 (2017). Also see Georgina Lee, 'Did austerity kill 120,000 people?', Factcheck, Channel 4 News (20 Sept. 2019). 33. Office for National Statistics, 'Gross domestic product: year on year growth: CVM SA %' (12 May 2023). 34. OECD Statistics, 'Gross domestic product – annual growth rates' (undated). 35. Office for National Statistics, 'Public sector finances tables 1 to 10: appendix A' (21 July 2023). To access this data, open the excel file for the relevant data. Table 'PSA 1', Column E, 'Public sector net debt excluding public sector banks and Bank of England'. For budget deficit figures see the Office for National Statistics, 'Public sector finances, UK', Figure 3 (25 May 2023). 36. Robert Chote, 'Letter to the Prime Minister' (8 Mar. 2013) and George Eaton, 'The OBR rebukes Cameron for claiming that austerity has not hit growth', *New Statesman* (8 Mar. 2013). 37. OECD, 'Elusive global growth outlook requires urgent policy response', *Economic Outlook* (18 Feb. 2016). 38. The World Bank, Data, 'Gross capital formation (% of GDP)' (undated). 39. Office for National Statistics, 'Profitability of UK companies, October to December 2019' (Figures 1 and 4) (28 April 2020). 40. AJ Bell, 'Dividend dashboard' (Q2 2022). 41. Office for National Statistics, 'Business investment in the UK: October to December 2022: revised results' (31 Mar. 2023) (Figure 1). 42. HM Treasury, 'Public expenditure', Chapter 4, Table (4.1). 43. Paul Krugman, *The Age of Diminished Expectations* (Cambridge, MA, 1994), p. 11. 44. *The Economist*, 'Britain's productivity problem is long-standing and getting worse' (9 June 2022). 45. OECD Data, 'GDP per hour worked' (undated). 46. The Resolution Foundation, *Stagnation Nation: Navigating a Route to a Fairer and More Prosperous Britain* (London, 2022), p. 8. 47. Conservative Party, 'Strong Leadership, A Clear Economic Plan, A Brighter, More Secure Future', Conservative Party Manifesto (2015), p. 8. 48. BBC News, 'Iain Duncan Smith, resignation letter' (18 Mar. 2016). 49. YouGov, 'Government cuts'. 50. Elizabeth Clery, John Curtice and Roger Harding, *British Social Attitudes: The 34th Report* (London, 2017), p. 67. 51. Anthony Seldon, *May at 10* (London, 2019), p. 77. 52. James Watts,

'Conservative Conference: Theresa May declares "end of austerity" with boost to new homes', *Independent* (3 Oct. 2018). **53.** Rowena Mason, 'George Osborne criticised for gruesome remarks against Theresa May', *Guardian* (13 Sept. 2017). **54.** James Warrington, 'George Osborne takes up full-time banking role at Robey Warshaw', *City A.M.* (1 Feb. 2021).

23 SAME SEX MARRIAGE

1 Ipsos, 'Voting intentions in Great Britain, 2002–present' (18 Feb. 2003). **2.** *Guardian*, 'UN Security Council Resolution 1973 (2011) on Libya – full text' (17 Mar. 2011). **3.** BBC News, 'President Obama: Libya aftermath "worst mistake" of presidency' (11 Apr. 2016). **4.** *Guardian*, 'David Cameron's Conservative Party conference speech in full' (5 Oct. 2011). **5.** Nicola Oakley, 'Man who had UK's first civil partnership recalls tragic moment his partner passed away just hours later', *Daily Mirror* (4 Dec. 2015). **6.** Elizabeth Clery, John Curtice and Roger Harding, *British Social Attitudes: The 34th Report* (London, 2017), p. 89. **7.** David Cameron, *For the Record* (London, 2019), p. 438. **8.** BBC News, 'Cameron Speech in full' (4 Oct. 2006). **9.** Michael Ashcroft and Isabel Oakeshott, *Call Me Dave: The Unauthorised Biography of David Cameron* (London, 2016), p. 405. **10.** Gerri Peev, 'Revealed: David Cameron privately attacked Tory opponents of gay marriage as "Neanderthals"', *Daily Mail* (6 Sept. 2015). **11.** BBC News, 'George Osborne says Tories will "consider gay marriage"' (11 Apr. 2010). **12.** Anthony Seldon and Peter Snowdon, *Cameron at 10: The Inside Story* (London, 2015), p. 274. **13.** Government Equalities Office, 'Equal marriage consultation' (15 Mar. 2012). **14.** Maria Miller, 'Parliamentary statement on equal civil marriage' (18 Dec. 2012). **15.** Catherine Fairburn, Oliver Hawkins, Nerys Roberts, Doug Pyper and Djuna Thurley, 'Marriage (Same Sex) Couples Bill', House of Commons Library, Briefing Paper 13/08 (14 Jan. 2013). **16.** Ben Clements, 'Public attitudes on the gay marriage debate are divided along party lines', LSE Blog (12 Dec. 2012). **17.** Robert Booth, Rajeev Syal and Nicholas Watt, 'Tories prepare for gay marriage vote amid defections and resignations', *Guardian* (1 Feb. 2013). **18.** 'The government has no mandate to redefine the meaning of marriage', Letter, *Daily Telegraph* (17 Dec. 2012). **19.** Seldon and Snowdon, *Cameron at 10*, p. 277. Also see Andrew Pierce, 'I'm a gay man who opposes gay marriage. Does that make me a bigot, Mr Cameron?', *Mail on Sunday* (12 June 2012). **20.** Ashcroft and Oakeshott, *Call Me Dave*, p. 408. **21.** BBC News, 'EU referendum: 100 Tory MPs back call for vote' (28 June 2012). **22.** Sadie Gray and Soraya Kishtwari, 'Labour to back Tory rebellion over EU budget' *The Times* (31 Oct. 2012). **23.** David Cameron, 'Speech on Europe', Bloomberg (23 Jan. 2013). **24.** BBC News, 'Gay marriage: MPs back bill despite Conservative backbench opposition' (5 Feb. 2013). **25.** Caroline Davies, 'Couple plan to tie knot at midnight on day UK gay marriage becomes legal', *Guardian* (11 Dec. 2013). **26.** Ashley Cowburn, 'Andrea Leadsom: I didn't like gay marriage law because it hurts Christians, admits Tory contender to be PM', *Independent* (7 July 2016). **27.** BBC News, 'Heterosexual couple win civil partnership case' (27 June 2018). **28.** Christian Voice, 'The trivialisation of matrimony', Government Equalities Office, Equal Marriage Consultation (15 Mar. 2013). **29.** Government Equalities Office, Equal Marriage Consultation. **30.** Steven Kettell, 'I do, thou shalt not: religious opposition to same-sex marriage in Britain', *Political Quarterly*, 84, 2 (2013): 247–55. **31.** Office for National Statistics, 'Religion in England and Wales, 2011' (11 Dec. 2012); Scottish Local Government and Communities Directorate, 'Census 2011 equality results, Part Two. Chapter 3. Religion' (26 Mar. 2014); and Northern Ireland Assembly, Research and Information Service, 'Census 2011: key statistics', NIAR 005-13 (20 Feb. 2013). **32.** Peter Brierley, 'Estimates of Church attendance in Britain, 1980–2015', British Religion in Numbers (undated). **33.** Peter Brierley, *Capital Growth: What the 2012 London Church*

Census Reveals (Tonbridge, 2013). **34.** Linda Woodhead, 'The rise of "no religion" in Britain: the emergence of a new cultural majority', The British Academy Lecture, *Journal of the British Academy*, 4 (2016): 245–61. **35.** Charles Taylor, 'Western secularity', in Craig Calhoun (ed.), *Rethinking Secularism* (Oxford, 2011). **36.** *The Times*, 'Man and God' (24 Dec. 2007). **37.** Ben Leach, '*Slumdog Millionaire* director Danny Boyle almost became a priest', *Daily Telegraph* (14 Jan. 2009). **38.** Evangelical Alliance, 'Tributes to the nation's most openly Christian prime minister' (8 Apr. 2013). **39.** Alan Wilkinson, *Christian Socialism: Scott Holland to Tony Blair* (London, 2012). **40.** Colin Brown, 'Campbell interrupted Blair as he spoke of his faith: "We don't do God"', *Daily Telegraph* (4 May 2003). **41.** John Rentoul, 'Blair converts to Catholicism', *Independent* (23 Dec. 2007). **42.** Premier Christianity, 'Here's what our next prime minister has said about Christianity' (19 June 2019). **43.** John Green and James Guth, 'The Christian right in the Republican Party: the case of Pat Robertson', *Journal of Politics*, 50, 1 (1988): 150–65. **44.** Jeffrey Jones, 'Belief in God in US dips to 81%, a new low', Gallup (17 June 2022). David Roach, 'Church attendance dropped among young people, singles, liberals', *Christianity Today* (9 Jan. 2023). **45.** Stella Rouse and Shibley Telhami, 'Most Republicans support declaring the United States a Christian nation', Politico (21 Sept. 2022). **46.** William Martin, *With God on our Side: The Rise of the Religious Right in America* (New York, 1996). **47.** Grace Davie, *Religion in Britain: A Persistent Paradox*, 2nd edn (London, 2015). **48.** John Curtice, Elizabeth Clery, Jane Perry, Miranda Phillips and Nilufer Rahim, *British Social Attitudes: The 36th Report* (London, 2019), p. 28. **49.** Simon Jenkins, *England's Cathedrals* (London, 2016), pp. xx–xxiv. Simon Jenkins, 'Our cathedrals lift the spirit, standing proud amidst the chaos below', *Evening Standard* (20 Dec. 2016). **50.** Paul Heelas, *The New Age Movement: Religion, Culture and Society in the Age of Postmodernity* (Oxford, 1996). Charles Taylor, *A Secular Age* (Cambridge, MA, 2007), p. 489. **51.** Muhammad Al-Hussaini, 'Occupy: the fault line between St Paul's and the Corporation of London', *Guardian* (28 Nov. 2011). **52.** Fraser McDonald, 'In time of schism', *London Review of Books* (16 Mar. 2023). **53.** The Church of England was first described as the 'Tory party at prayer' in 1917 by Agnes Maude Royden, an English preacher, suffragist and campaigner for women's rights within the Church. **54.** *The Economist*, 'Why Boris bashes the archbishop' (22 Apr. 2022). **55.** Madeleine Davies, 'Bishops gather in House of Lords to vote against gay marriage bill', *Church Times* (7 June 2013). **56.** Harriet Sherwood, 'Church of England bishops want immigration amnesty for Windrush Generation', *Guardian* (13 Apr. 2018). **57.** Church of England, 'Church schools and academies' (undated). **58.** Department for Education, 'Collective worship in schools' (31 Jan. 1994). **59.** Philip Williamson, 'How King Charles's coronation will reflect his desire to be defender of all faiths', The Conversation (5 May 2023). **60.** Ben Clements, 'Attitudes towards gay rights', British Religion in Numbers (Jan. 2017), Figure 9. **61.** Rob Johns and James Mitchell, *Takeover: Explaining the Extraordinary Rise of the SNP* (London, 2016), p. 226. **62.** James Tilley, '"We don't do God"? Religion and party choice in Britain', *British Journal of Political Science*, 45, 5 (2015): 907–27. **63.** Office for National Statistics, 'Religion, England and Wales: Census, 2021' (29 Nov.2022). **64.** William Wallis, 'How England and Wales lost their religion', *Financial Times* (22 Dec. 2022). **65.** Ridhi Kashyap and Valerie Lewis, 'British Muslim youth and religious fundamentalism: a quantitative investigation', *Ethnic and Racial Studies*, 36, 12 (2013): 2117–40. **66.** Ben Clements, 'Religious affiliation and party choice at the 2017 General Election', British Religion in Numbers (11 Aug. 2017). **67.** Curtice et al., *British Social Attitudes: The 36th Report*, p. 135. **68.** John Curtice, Nathan Hudson and Ian Montagu, 'Family life', in *British Social Attitudes: The 37th Report* (London, 2020), p. 20. **69.** Elizabeth Clery, John Curtice, Sarah Frankenburg, Hannah Morgan and Susan Reid, 'New values, new divides?', in *British Social Attitudes: The 38th Report* (London, 2021), p. 20. **70.** Press release, 'Support for the death penalty falls below 50% for first time' (26 Mar. 2015). **71.** Alison Park, Caroline Bryson,

Elizabeth Clery, John Curtice and Miranda Phillips, *British Social Attitudes: The 30th Report* (London, 2013), p. 119. 72. Curtice et al., *British Social Attitudes: The 36th Report*, p 139. 73. *The Economist*, 'Many Britons have changed their minds on gay marriage' (13 July 2023).

24 ISLES OF WONDER

1 Amy Raphael, *Danny Boyle: Creating Wonder* (London, 2013), Kindle edn, loc. 783. 2. This description of the film was offered by Lias Saoudi, the lead singer of Fat White Family. Barry Nicholson, '*Trainspotting*: An oral history of the cult film and its sequel', *NME* (27 Jan. 2017). 3. Jonathan Freedland, 'Danny Boyle: champion of the people', *Guardian* (9 Mar. 2013). 4. *The Economist*, 'The greatest sideshow on earth' (22 July 2010). 5. Inside the Games, 'Blair Sees the Olympics as an example of Britain's multiculturalism' (18 Aug. 2009). 6. Robert Tombs discusses the history of declinism and acutely challenges many of the assumptions about it in *The English and their History* (London, 2014), pp. 759–61. 7. Jim Tomlinson, 'Thrice denied: "declinism" as a recurrent theme in British history in the long twentieth century', *Twentieth Century British History*, 20, 2 (2009): 227–51. 8. Michael Shanks, *The Stagnant Society: A Warning* (Harmondsworth, 1961). Arthur Koestler (ed.), *Suicide of a Nation?* (London, 1963). 9. Andrew Gamble, *Britain in Decline* (London, 1981). 10. Conservative Party, 'Conservative General Election Manifesto, 1979' (11 Apr. 1979). 11. Tony Blair, 'The Young Country', Speech, Brighton (3 Oct. 1995). Reprinted in Tony Blair, *New Britain: My Vision of a Young Country* (London, 1996), pp. 62–74. 12. Conservative Party, *Invitation to Join the Government of Great Britain* (London, 2010). 13. Office for National Statistics, 'Personal well-being in the UK, 2012/13' (30 July 2013), Figure 2., p. 9. 14. 'Frankie Boyle's best jokes on Mock the Week: too hot for TV 2' (https://www.youtube.com/watch?v=ghZ5pcYbCDM). 15. BBC News, 'London 2012: Olympic missiles put in position' (12 July 2012). 16. *The Economist*, 'The rings cycle' (30 June 2012). 17. Bloomberg UK, 'The PR disaster of London's Olympic traffic lanes' (14 March 2012). 18. Robert Booth and Nick Hopkins, 'London 2012 Olympics: G4S failures prompt further military deployment', *Guardian* (24 July 2012). 19. Nicholas Watt, Hélène Mulholland and Owen Gibson, 'Mitt Romney's Olympics blunder stuns No 10 and hands gift to Obama', *Guardian* (27 July 2012). 20. BBC News, 'London 2012: North Koreans walk out after flag row' (26 July 2012). 21. Raphael, *Danny Boyle*, loc. 7482. 22. Samuel Osborne, 'Danny Boyle claims Tories tried to axe NHS celebration in London 2012 Olympics Opening Ceremony', *Independent* (10 July 2016). 23. David Cameron, *For the Record* (London, 2019), p. 377. 24. Raphael, *Danny Boyle*, loc. 7078. 25. Nick Clegg, *Politics: Between the Extremes* (London, 2016), p. 224. 26. Avril Ormsby, 'London 2012 Opening Ceremony draws 900 million viewers', Reuters (7 Aug. 2012). 27. Gabriel Power, 'Most watched UK TV broadcasts ever: from Boris's lockdown address to Princess Diana's wedding', *The Week* (25 Mar. 2020). 28. The Huffington Post, 'Curse of Cameron: is the prime minister jinxing our Olympic medal hopefuls?' (31 July 2012). 29. BBC News, 'Olympics "dominated by privately educated"' (3 Aug. 2012). 30. Greg Rutherford, *Unexpected: The Autobiography* (London, 2017). 31. BBC News, 'UK GDP: economy shrank at end of 2012' (25 Jan. 2013). 32. Tom Clark, 'Britain's end-of-year Olympic verdict: it was worth every penny', *Guardian* (25 Dec. 2012). 33. HM Government and Mayor of London, 'Inspired by 2012: the legacy from the Olympic and Paralympic Games, Fourth Annual Report' (Aug. 2016). 34. Rowan Moore, '"The kind of place planners have dreamed of": the London Olympics site 10 years on', *Guardian* (24 July 2022). 35. House of Lords, Select Committee on Olympic and Paralympic Legacy, 'Keeping the flame alive', Report of Session 2013–14, HL Paper 78 (18 Nov. 2013). 36. Andy Bull, 'The dirty games: how London 2012 became tainted',

Guardian (17 July 2021). **37.** Martha Kelner, 'Para-swimmers are "exaggerating their disabilities" MPs are told', *Guardian* (1 Nov. 2017). **38.** *Cycling News*, 'British Cycling accused of burying 2012 report detailing bullying' (21 Feb. 2017). BBC News, 'Gymnastics abuse: Whyte Review finds physical and emotional abuse issues were "systemic"' (16 June 2022). **39.** Ella Alexander, 'Jessica Ennis-Hill receives Twitter rape threats, after taking a stand against potential Ched Evans Sheffield United re-signing', *Independent* (14 Nov. 2014). **40.** Alex Spink, 'Greg Rutherford targets Winter Olympic glory – and he's not taking the piste', *Daily Mirror* (27 Oct. 2021). In the end, Rutherford did not make the cut for the Olympic team. Mark Stainforth, 'Greg Rutherford misses out on Great Britain bobsleigh team for Winter Olympics', *Independent* (20 Jan. 2022). **41.** BBC News, 'Mo Farah: Olympic champion says new questions over Alberto Salazar are "not fair"' (29 Feb. 2020). **42.** Martha Kelner, 'Mo Farah was suspected, then cleared, of doping by IAAF expert', *Guardian* (6 July 2017). **43.** Hannah Furness, 'Boris Johnson gets stuck on zip wire carrying two Union flags', *Daily Telegraph* (1 Aug. 2012). **44.** Rosaleen Fenton, 'Boris Johnson dashed to 2012 Paralympics Ceremony with Royals after sleeping with Arcuri for first time', *Daily Mirror* (28 Mar. 2021). **45.** Freedland, 'Danny Boyle: champion of the people'.

25 INCREASINGLY INDEPENDENT

1 Charlotte Higgins, 'Scotland's image-maker Sir Walter Scott, invented "English" legends', *Guardian* (16 Aug. 2010). **2.** Ann Fotheringham, 'Remembering Glasgow's Battle of George Square 101 years on', *Glasgow Evening Times* (18 Jan. 2020). **3.** Iain MacWhirter, *Disunited Kingdom: How Westminster Won a Referendum but Lost Scotland* (Glasgow, 2015), p. 14. **4.** BBC News, 'Scottish Independence: Yes campaigners stage Glasgow rally' (16 Sept. 2014). **5.** Chris Green and Nigel Morris, 'Scottish Referendum result: Yes voters grieve the Scotland that could have been', *Independent* (19 Sept. 2014). **6.** Libby Brooks, 'Violence in Glasgow as Loyalists attack pro-Independence supporters', *Guardian* (20 Sept. 2014). **7.** *The Herald*, 'Stand-off between pro-UK and Independence supporters in Glasgow's George Square' (19 Sept. 2014). **8.** BBC News, 'McLeish steps down' (8 Nov. 2001). **9.** Kate Fall, *The Gatekeeper: Life at the Heart of No 10* (London, 2020), p. 196. **10.** Rob Johns and James Mitchell, *Takeover: Explaining the Extraordinary Rise of the SNP* (London, 2016), p. 189. John Curtice, 'The 2011 Scottish Election: records tumble, barriers breached', *Scottish Affairs*, 76, 1 (2011): 51–73. **11.** John Curtice, 'One year on: the legacy of the independence referendum', University of Strathclyde and David Hume Institute, 2015. **12.** As Alex Salmond observed at the time, the agreed question gave the Yes campaign a 'firm platform' because 'it is simply not possible to enthuse people on a negative'. Alex Salmond, *The Dream Shall Never Die: 100 Days that Changed Scotland Forever* (London, 2015), p. 33. **13.** Michael Keating and Nicola McEwan, 'The Scottish Independence debate', in Michael Keating (ed.), *Debating Scotland: Issues of Independence and Union in the 2014 Referendum* (Oxford, 2017), p. 8. **14.** Hannah Thompson and Laurence Janta-Lipinski, 'The Scottish Referendum', YouGov (18 Jan. 2012). Arno van der Zwet and Craig McAngus, 'National identity and party affiliation are set to play a key role in the Scottish Referendum, whose result is more uncertain than opinion polls suggest', LSE Blog (11 Dec. 2013). **15.** Scotland Office, *Scotland's Future in the United Kingdom: Building on Ten Years of Scottish Devolution*, Cm 7738 (London, Nov. 2009). **16.** Libby Brooks, 'Lottery winners Colin and Chris Weir donate 79% of Yes Scotland funds', *Guardian* (11 May 2014). **17.** Scottish Government, 'Scotland's economy: the case for independence' (26 Nov. 2013). **18.** BBC News, 'Scottish Independence: JK Rowling donates £1m to pro-UK group' (11 June 2014). **19.** Andrew Black and Aiden James, 'Scottish Independence: "Yes" vote means leaving pound, says Osborne', BBC News (13 Feb.

2014). 20. Severin Carrell, 'Civil servants accused of bias during Scotland's independence referendum', *Guardian* (23 Mar. 2015). Peter Spence, 'Currency union is incompatible with Scottish independence', *Daily Telegraph* (9 Sept. 2014). 21. *The Economist*, 'Scottish Independence: battle of the profs' (16 Feb. 2013). 22. Tom Gordon, 'I admit it: the man who coined Project Fear label', *The Herald* (21 Dec. 2014). 23. Curtice, 'One year on', p. 4. 24. Scottish Social Attitudes Survey, 2014. 25. Simon Johnson, 'Gordon Brown unveils cross-party deal on Scottish powers', *Daily Telegraph* (8 Sept. 2014). 26. David Clegg, 'David Cameron, Ed Miliband and Nick Clegg sign joint historic promise which guarantees more devolved powers for Scotland and protection of NHS if we vote No', *Daily Record* (15 Sept. 2014). 27. *Guardian*, 'Scottish independence referendum: final results in full (18 Sept. 2014). 28. Johns and Mitchell, *Takeover*, p. 226. 29. David Clegg, 'Independence referendum figures revealed: majority of Scots born here voted YES while voters from elsewhere in UK said No', *Daily Record* (26 Mar. 2015). 30. Ailsa Henderson and James Mitchell, 'Referendums as critical junctures? Scottish voting in British elections', *Parliamentary Affairs*, 71, supp. 1 (2018): 109–24 p. 112. 31. BBC News, 'Salmond: referendum is once in a generation opportunity' (14 Sept. 2014). 32. Mure Dickie, 'Salmond claims malicious and concerted effort to remove him from public life', *Financial Times* (22 Feb. 2021). 33. Mure Dickie, 'Scottish committee members find Nicola Sturgeon misled Parliament', *Financial Times* (23 Mar. 2021). 34. Scottish Government, 'Independent Report by James Hamilton on the First Minister's self-referral under the Scottish Ministerial Code' (22 Mar. 2021). 35. Nicola Sturgeon, 'Opening Statement to the Holyrood Inquiry', SNP (3 Mar. 2021). 36. BBC News, 'Johann Lamont resignation: Scottish Labour leader stands down immediately' (25 Oct. 2014). 37. Henderson and Mitchell, 'Referendums as critical junctures?', p. 114. 38. Ben Walker, 'Scottish Independence poll tracker', *New Statesman* (14 Jan. 2021). 39. BBC News, 'Truss says best to ignore attention-seeking Sturgeon' (2 Aug. 2022). On the concept of 'Muscular Unionism' see Ciaran Martin, 'Can the UK survive Muscular Unionism?', *Political Insight*, 12, 4 (2021): 36–9. 40. David Allen Green, 'Ruling against Scottish Independence vote throws ball back into political arena', *Financial Times* (23 Nov. 2022). 41. Scottish Social Attitudes Survey 2021/22, 'Attitudes data' (31 Oct. 2022). 42. Chris McCall, 'Scottish Independence support soars among young Scots with almost three in four backing Yes', *Daily Record* (17 Sept. 2020). 43. HM Government, *Scotland in the United Kingdom: An Enduring Settlement*, Cm 8990 (London, Jan. 2015). 44. Daniel Gover and Michael Kenny, 'What's going wrong with English Votes for English Laws and how can it be improved?', Democratic Audit (8 Dec. 2016). 45. BBC News, 'Commons scraps English Votes for English Laws' (13 July 2021). 46. Alisa Henderson and Richard Wyn Jones, *Englishness: The Political Force Transforming Britain* (Oxford, 2022), p. 69. 47. Nigel Morris, 'General Election 2015: Labour–SNP "coalition of chaos" would threaten UK, says David Cameron', *Independent* (16 Apr. 2015). 48. Henderson and Wyn Jones, *Englishness*, p. 83.

26 A HOSTILE ENVIRONMENT

1 Nicholas Watt and Patrick Wintour, 'How immigration came to haunt Labour: the inside story', *Guardian* (24 Mar. 2015). 2. 'Liam Byrne, Minister for Immigration, Citizenship and Nationality', House of Commons (4 Dec. 2006). 3. James Slack, 'Labour texts immigrants "pls can u go home"', *Daily Mail* (6 Mar. 2007). 4. BBC News, 'What does British jobs pledge mean?' (16 Nov. 2007). 5. Jessica Shepherd, 'International students may spurn UK because of new visa rules', *Guardian* (1 Sept. 2009). 6. Watt and Wintour, 'How immigration came to haunt Labour'. 7. Jon Swaine, 'White working class "feels ignored on immigration"', *Daily Telegraph* (2 Jan. 2009). Robbie Shilliam, *Race and the*

Undeserving Poor (Newcastle, 2018), pp. 2–3.   8. Ipsos, 'Best party on key issues: asylum and immigration' (20 Apr. 2015).   9. *Guardian*, 'Tories would limit immigration to "tens of thousands" a year, says Cameron' (11 Jan. 2010). The 2010 Conservative Manifesto repeated this promise. 'We will take steps to take net migration back to the levels of the 1990s – tens of thousands a year, not hundreds of thousands'. Conservative Party, *Invitation to Join the Government of Great Britain* (London, 2010), p. 21.   10. Matthew Weaver, 'The Gordon Brown and Gillian Duffy transcript', *Guardian* (28 Apr. 2010).   11. Geoffrey Evans and Kat Chzhen, 'Explaining voters' defection from Labour over the 2005–10 electoral cycle: leadership, economics and the rising importance of immigration', *Political Studies*, 61, 1 suppl. (2013): 138–57.   12. Elizabeth Day, 'Theresa May – what lies beyond the public image?', *Guardian* (27 July 2014).   13. Michael White and Anne Perkins, 'Nasty party warning to Tories', *Guardian* (8 Oct. 2002).   14. Rosa Prince, *Theresa May: The Enigmatic Prime Minister* (London, 2017), ch. 10.   15. Anthony Seldon, *May at 10* (London, 2019), p. 12.   16. David Runciman, 'Do your homework', *London Review of Books* (16 Mar. 2017).   17. ITV News, 'Cameron was forced to retreat over EU migrant plan' (29 Nov. 2014). Steven Swinford, 'Angela Merkel: freedom of movement cannot be questioned "in any way"', *Daily Telegraph* (7 Jan. 2015). Anthony Seldon and Peter Snowdon, *Cameron at 10: The Inside Story* (London, 2015), pp. 451–62.   18. Alan Travis, 'UK Cabinet in fresh spat over immigration', *Guardian* (2 Dec. 2015).   19. David Matthews, 'Cable fires latest salvo on student visas', *Times Higher Education* (13 July 2012).   20. The Migration Observatory, 'Irregular migration in the United Kingdom' (11 Sept. 2020).   21. James Kirkup and Robert Winnett, 'Theresa May interview: "We're going to give illegal migrants a really hostile reception"', *Daily Telegraph* (25 May 2012).   22. Melanie Griffiths and Colin Yeo, 'The UK's Hostile Environment: deputising immigration control', *Critical Social Policy*, 41, 4 (2021): 521–44.   23. On the existence of Home Office targets see Alan McGuiness, 'Home Office did set targets for voluntary removal of illegal immigrants', Sky News (26 Apr. 2018). On the application process see the evidence of Lucy Morton, the general secretary of the Immigration Services Union in Home Affairs Select Committee, 'The Windrush Generation', HC 990 (27 June 2018), p. 12.   24. BBC News, 'Farage attacks "nasty" immigration posters' (25 July 2013).   25. Madeleine Sumption and Peter Walsh, 'Net Migration to the UK', The Migration Observatory (20 Dec. 2022), p. 6.   26. Matt Chorley, '"I'll cut immigration or kick me out": what Cameron told voters at the last election before numbers arriving soared to 300,000', *Daily Mail* (4 Mar. 2015).   27. Ipsos, 'Issues index, 2007–2017' (4 Oct. 2022).   28. Conservative Party, 'Strong Leadership, A Clear Economic Plan, A Brighter, More Secure Future' (14 Apr. 2015), p. 29.   29. Shilliam, *Race and the Undeserving Poor*, p. 154.   30. 'Nigel Farage: immigration will be the defining issue of this EU referendum campaign', *Daily Telegraph* (21 Aug. 2015).   31. Geoffrey Evans and Anand Menon, *Brexit and British Politics* (Cambridge, 2017), p. 53.   32. BBC News, 'Michael Gove "shuddered" at UKIP migrants poster' (19 June 2016).   33. BBC News, 'Net migration rises to 330,000 – second highest on record' (26 May 2016).   34. David Cameron, *For the Record* (London, 2019), p. 670.   35. See Tessa Buchanan, 'Brexit behaviourally: lessons learned from the 2016 referendum', *Mind and Society*, 18 (2019): 13–31. Also see Matthew Goodwin and Caitlin Milazzo, 'Taking back control? Investigating the role of immigration in the 2016 vote for Brexit', *British Journal of Politics and International Relations*, 19, 3 (2017): 450–64; John Curtice, 'Why Leave won the EU referendum', *Journal of Common Market Studies*, 55, S1 (2017): 19–37; and Harold Clarke, Matthew Goodwin and Paul Whiteley, *Brexit: Why Britain Voted to Leave the European Union* (Cambridge, 2017), pp. 146–74.   36. Elizabeth Clery, John Curtice, and Roger Harding, *British Social Attitudes: The 34th Report* (London, 2017), p. 158.   37. Amelia Gentleman, 'Perspectives on the Windrush Generation scandal: an account by Amelia Gentleman', *The British Library* (4 Oct. 2018).   38. Sarah Marsh, Haroon Siddique and Caroline Bannock, 'Windrush Generation tell of holidays that led to exile and heartbreak', *Guardian* (19 Apr. 2018). **39.** Amelia Gentleman, 'Windrush row: Javid's apology overshadowed by new removal figures', *Guardian* (21 August 2018). Kevin Rawlinson, 'Windrush: 11 people wrongly deported from UK have died – Javid', *Guardian* (12 Nov. 2018). **40.** Sathnam Sanghera, *Empireland: How Imperialism Has Shaped Modern Britain* (London, 2021), p. 73. **41.** Amelia Gentleman, 'Caribbean diplomats ask UK for more compassion for citizens', *Guardian* (22 Feb. 2018). **42.** Amelia Gentleman, 'Londoner denied NHS cancer treatment: "It's like I'm being left to die"', *Guardian* (10 Mar. 2018). **43.** Kevin Rawlinson, 'Windrush-era citizens row: timeline of key events', *Guardian* (16 Apr. 2018). **44.** Pippa Crear, 'Sajid Javid pledges to "urgently do right" by Windrush Generation', *Guardian* (30 Apr. 2018). **45.** Home Office, 'Windrush compensation scheme data, November 2023' (4 Jan. 2024). **46.** Fiona Bawdon, 'Chasing status: if not British then what am I?', Legal Action Group (Oct. 2014). **47.** National Audit Office, 'Handling of the Windrush Situation', HC 1622 (5 Dec. 2018), p. 8. **48.** Home Affairs Select Committee, 'The Windrush Generation', p. 30. **49.** Wendy Williams, 'Windrush, lessons learned review', HC 93 (Mar. 2020), pp. 13, 49. **50.** The Adam Buxton Podcast, 'Zadie Smith', Episode 40. Zadie Smith, *White Teeth* (London, 2020). **51.** Grahame Allen and Yago Zayed, 'Hate crime statistics', House of Commons Library, 8357 (2 Nov. 2022), p. 10. **52.** Omar Khan, 'Windrush, racism, and freedom', in Tony Buckle (ed.), *What is Freedom?* (Oxford, 2021). **53.** BBC News, 'Grenfell Tower Inquiry: fire "inextricably linked with race"' (7 July 2020). **54.** Fire Brigades Union, 'Grenfell Tower Inquiry: suggestion of institutional racism' (19 June 2018). **55.** Amelia Gentleman, 'Grenfell Tower MP highlights huge social divisions in London', *Guardian* (13 Nov. 2017). **56.** Mark Townsend, 'Grenfell families want Inquiry to look at role of "race and class" in tragedy', *Guardian* (26 July 2020). **57.** BBC *Today* Programme, 'Zadie Smith speaks out on Grenfell Tower' (5 July 2017). Also see Zadie Smith, 'Fences: A Brexit Diary', *The New York Review* (18 Aug. 2016), reprinted in Zadie Smith, *Feel Free* (London, 2018), pp. 20–34. **58.** Nathaniel Barker, 'ACM was "cheaper option", Grenfell Inquiry hears', *Inside Housing* (15 July 2020). Also see Richard Waite, 'Specified cladding on Grenfell switched to "cheaper version"', *Architects' Journal* (30 June 2017); BBC News, 'Grenfell Tower: cladding "changed to cheaper version"' (30 June 2017); and Andrew Griffin, 'Grenfell Tower cladding that may have led to fire was chosen to improve appearance of Kensington block of flats', *Independent* (14 June 2017). **59.** Williams, 'Windrush, lessons learned', pp. 7, 119. **60.** Sebastian Payne, 'Home Office chief Philip Rutnam quits', *Financial Times* (29 Feb. 2020). *The Economist*, 'The machine that runs Britain's state needs an overhaul' (23 Mar. 2023). **61.** Anthony Seldon and Raymond Newell, *Johnson at 10: The Inside Story* (London, 2023), p. 250. **62.** Nick Wallis, *The Great Post Office Scandal* (Bath, 2021), p. 7. **63.** Ibid., p. 8. **64.** Gareth Corfield, 'Tony Blair was warned about Post Office IT deal', *Daily Telegraph* (21 Aug. 2022). **65.** Alan Johnson, 'Witness Statement', Post Office Horizon IT Inquiry' (13 Sept. 2022). Geoff Mulgan, 'Witness Statement', Post Office Horizon IT Inquiry (21 Sept. 2022). **66.** Wallis, *The Great Post Office Scandal*, pp. 125–6. **67.** Lord Justice Holroyde, Mr Justice Picken and Mrs Justice Farbey DBE, 'Josephine Hamilton and Others v Post Office Limited', Judiciary of England and Wales (23 Apr. 2021), p. 3. **68.** Mark Sweney, 'Post Office: Horizon scandal victims to receive £600,000 compensation each', *Guardian* (18 Sept. 2023). **69.** The Post Office IT Inquiry: Written Statement Regarding Human Impact/Cost. **70.** But see Harry Taylor, 'Post Office used racist term for black people, documents show', *Guardian* (27 May 2023). **71.** Colin Yeo, 'Inspection report on "Hostile Environment" finds hundreds wrongly denied services', Free Movement (14 Oct. 2016). **72.** Alexis Madrigal, 'Regulators finger dumb algorithm in "flash crash"', *The Atlantic* (1 Oct. 2010). Jamie Condliffe, 'Algorithm probably caused a flash crash of the British pound', *MIT Technology Review* (7 Oct. 2016). **73.** BBC News, 'A-levels and GCSEs: Boris Johnson blames "mutant algorithm" for exam fiasco' (26 Aug. 2020).

PART SIX

1 Margaret Thatcher, 'Sir Robert Menzies Lecture', Monash University (6 October 1981). 2. Maurice Glasman, 'Labour as a Radical tradition', in Maurice Glasman, Jonathan Rutherford, Marc Stears and Stuart White (eds.), *Labour and the Politics of Paradox, The Oxford–London Seminars* (eBook, 2011). 3. Philip Blond, *Red Tory: How the Left and Right Have Broken Britain and How We Can Fix It* (London, 2010). 4. John Kenneth Galbraith, *The Age of Uncertainty* (London, 1977), p. 96.

27 OH JEREMY CORBYN

1 Steve Richards, *The Prime Ministers We Never Had: Success and Failure from Butler to Corbyn* (London, 2021), p. 342. 2. James Butler, 'Failed vocation: the Corbyn project', *London Review of Books* (3 Dec. 2020). 3. BBC News, 'Margaret Beckett: I was a moron to nominate Jeremy Corbyn' (22 July 2015). 4. Elizabeth Clery, John Curtice and Roger Harding, *British Social Attitudes: The 34th Report* (London, 2017), p. 77. 5. Philip Cowley and Dennis Kavanagh, *The British General Election of 2017* (London, 2018), p. 393. 6. Jeremy Corbyn, 'Labour Party Speech' (27 Sept. 2017). 7. Andrew Hindmoor, *New Labour at the Centre: Constructing Political Space* (Oxford, 2004). 8. Patrick Wintour, 'Welfare Bill: Labour in disarray as 48 MPs defy whips to vote no', *Guardian* (21 July 2015). Labour's other leadership candidates toed the line. Corbyn did not. 9. In an interview on 11 June 2016, Corbyn tellingly rated his commitment to remaining in the European Union as 'seven, or seven and a half, out of ten'. BBC News, 'Corbyn, "I'm seven out of ten" on EU' (11 June 2016). 10. Paul Dallison, 'Jeremy Corbyn can stay on Labour leadership ballot, court rules', Politico (28 July 2016). 11. Tim Shipman, 'The owl unseats the No 10 pussycat', *The Times* (2 Oct. 2016). 12. Tim Shipman, *Fallout: A Year of Political Mayhem* (London, 2017), p. 213. 13. Chris Curtis, 'How Britain voted at the 2017 General Election', YouGov (13 June 2017). 14. Nick Timothy, *Remaking One Nation: The Future of Conservatism* (Cambridge, 2020), p. 2. 15. Aubery Allegretti, 'What is in the DUP confidence and supply deal keeping Tories in power', Sky News (21 Nov. 2018). 16. George Parker, 'Theresa May backs down on "dementia tax" social care plans', *Financial Times* (22 May 2017). 17. Timothy, *Remaking One Nation*, p. 16. The poetry/prose line is most closely associated with Bill Clinton but appears to have been coined by the former New York governor Mario Cuomo. 18. Jack Summers, 'Jon Snow says he, journalists and pundits "know nothing" after mis-calling General Election', Huffington Post (9 June 2017). 19. Paul Whiteley, Monica Poletti, Paul Webb and Tim Bale, 'Oh, Jeremy Corbyn! Why did Labour membership soar after the 2015 General Election', *British Journal of Politics and International Relations*, 21, 1 (2019): 80–98. 20. Pascale Hughes, 'Jeremy Corbyn tells Glastonbury crowds to "Rise, like lions after slumber"', *inews* (24 June 2017). 21. ITV News, 'Boris Johnson takes ITV reporter's phone after refusing to look at photo of boy on hospital floor' (9 Dec. 2019). 22. Geoffrey Evans and Anand Menon, *Brexit and British Politics* (Cambridge, 2017), p. 103. 23. Jon Stone, 'Jeremy Corbyn sacks Labour shadow ministers for defying him over Brexit vote', *Independent* (29 June 2017). 24. Gabriel Pogrund and Patrick Maguire, *Left Out: The Inside Story of Corbyn Under Labour* (London, 2020), pp. 135–43. 25. Robert Ford, Paul Surridge, Will Jennings and Tim Bale, *The British General Election of 2019* (Basingstoke, 2021), p. 464. 26. *Jewish Chronicle*, 'The key questions Jeremy Corbyn must answer' (12 Aug. 2015). 27. The Labour Party, 'The Shami Chakrabarti Inquiry' (30 June 2016). 28. Heather Stewart, 'Corbyn in antisemitism row after backing artist behind "offensive" mural', *Guardian* (23 Mar. 2018) 29. Oliver Milne, 'Jewish MP Luciana Berger flanked by police protection at Labour Conference after months of antisemitic threats', *Daily Mirror* (24 Sept. 2018). Berger left the

Labour Party in 2019 but rejoined in 2023. **30.** Jeremy Corbyn, 'What I'm doing to banish antisemitism from the Labour Party', *Evening Standard* (24 Apr. 2018). **31.** International Holocaust Remembrance Alliance, 'What is antisemitism? Non-legally binding working definition of antisemitism' (undated). BBC News, 'A guide to Labour Party antisemitism claims' (18 Nov. 2020). **32.** *Jewish Chronicle*, 'Jewish papers take unprecedented step of publishing the same page on Labour' (25 July 2018). **33.** Matthew Bolton and Harry Pitts, *Corbynism: A Critical Approach* (Bingley, Yorkshire, 2018), pp. 104–7. Also see Jessica Elgot and Peter Walker, 'Antisemitism issue used as a "factional weapon" in Labour, report finds', *Guardian* (19 July 2022). **34.** Andrew Gilligan, 'Revealed: Jeremy Corbyn and John McDonnell's close IRA links', *Daily Telegraph* (10 Oct. 2015). **35.** Tom Rayner, 'Salisbury attack: "sheer fury" at Corbyn's response to spy poisoning', Sky News (14 Mar. 2018). **36.** YouGov, 'Is the Labour Party moderate or extreme?' (undated). **37.** Theresa May, 'Statement from the New Prime Minister' (13 July 2016). **38.** Theresa May, 'The New Centre Ground', Leader's Speech, Conservative Party Conference (5 Oct. 2016). **39.** The Conservative Party Manifesto, 'Our Plan for a Stronger Britain and a Prosperous Future' (2017), p. 9. **40.** Pogrund and Maguire, *Left Out*, p. 197. **41.** May, 'The New Centre Ground'. **42.** Timothy, *Remaking One Nation*, pp. 7, 18. **43.** Ibid., p. 8. **44.** Sebastian Whale, 'John McDonnell: Jeremy Corbyn would be in No 10 if election campaign was two weeks longer', PoliticsHome (16 Sept. 2017).

28 BREXIT

1 David Cameron, 'Leader's Speech', Conservative Party Conference (1 Oct. 2006). This was the first of two speeches Cameron delivered at that year's conference. **2.** The Conservative Party, *Invitation to Join the Government of Great Britain* (London, 2010), p. 113. **3.** Ivan Rogers, 'The inside story of how David Cameron drove Britain to Brexit', *Prospect* (25 Nov. 2017). **4.** Matthew D'Ancona, *In It Together: The Inside Story of the Coalition Government* (London, 2013), p. 240. **5.** Margaret Thatcher, 'Speech to the College of Europe, Bruges' (20 Sept. 1988). **6.** Stephen Castle, 'Major says three in Cabinet are bastards', *Independent* (25 July 1993). **7.** Oliver Letwin, *Hearts and Minds: The Battle for the Conservative Party from Thatcher to the Present* (London, 2019), pp. 14–16. **8.** Luke Moore, 'What explains Euroscepticism in the Conservative Party?', OxPol Blog (20 Nov. 2015). **9.** James Kirkup, 'EU referendum: David Cameron "loses control of backbench" in biggest Conservative rebellion', *Daily Telegraph* (25 Oct. 2011). **10.** BBC News, 'Nigel Farage calls on Conservative MPs to join UKIP' (6 May 2012). James Rodger, 'David Cameron "feared being ousted if he didn't agree to EU referendum"', *Birmingham Live* (8 Jan. 2018). **11.** The quickest way to end a war line was offered by George Orwell in his 1946 essay 'Second Thoughts on James Burnham'. **12.** David Cameron, 'Speech on Europe', Bloomberg (23 Jan. 2013). **13.** Alex Barker, 'The Brits and Banking Union: bad omens for Cameron's referendum', *Financial Times* (18 Dec. 2013). **14.** Kate Fall, *The Gatekeeper: Life at the Heart of No 10* (London, 2020), p. 269. **15.** Nicholas Watt and Rajeev Syal, 'EU Referendum: Cameron accepts advice to change wording on question', *Guardian* (1 Sept. 2015). **16.** David Cowling, 'A tale of two referendums', UK in a Changing Europe (12 May 2016). David Butler and Uwe Kitzinger, *The 1975 Referendum* (London, 1976), p. 62. **17.** Harold Clarke, Matthew Goodwin and Paul Whiteley, *Brexit: Why Britain Voted to Leave the European Union* (Cambridge, 2017), p. 21. **18.** In his memoirs Ken Clarke argues that Cameron never really 'had a clear idea of what he wanted to get out of his EU reform negotiations' because 'they had mainly been a tactical device to kill the time between calling the referendum in 2013 and holding it years later'. Kenneth Clarke, *Kind of Blue: A Political Memoir* (London, 2016), p. 485. **19.** Sir Ivan Rogers, UK in a Changing Europe, 'Brexit Witness Archive' (https://ukandeu.ac.uk/brexit-witness-archive/). **20.** Owen

Bennett, '"You are polishing poo", Watch Tory MP's insult to government minister over EU deal', The Huffington Post (2 Feb. 2016). **21.** Anthony Seldon and Raymond Newell, *Johnson at 10: The Inside Story* (London, 2023), p. 38. **22.** Quoted in Tim Shipman, *All Out War* (London, 2016), p. 179. **23.** *Financial Times*, 'Brexit Poll Tracker' (undated). **24.** HM Treasury, 'HM Treasury Analysis: The long-term economic impact of EU membership and the alternatives' (18 Apr. 2016). **25.** Chris Giles, Gemma Tetlow and George Parker, 'Brexit carries risk of recession, warns Bank of England', *Financial Times* (12 May 2016). **26.** Julia Kollewe, 'Brexit could cost £100bn and nearly 1m jobs, CBI warns', *Guardian* (21 Mar. 2016). **27.** Jill Treanor, 'HSBC could switch 1,000 banking jobs to France after a Brexit vote', *Guardian* (15 Feb. 2016). Sean Farrell, 'JP Morgan boss: up to 4,000 jobs could be cut after Brexit', *Guardian* (3 June 2016). **28.** BBC News, 'Barack Obama says Brexit would leave UK at the "back of the queue" on trade' (22 Apr. 2016). Greg Heffer, 'Cameron "personally requested" Obama's back of the queue Brexit warning', Sky News (2 July 2018). **29.** Sir Andrew Dilnot, 'Statement on the use of Official Statistics on contributions to the European Union', UK Statistics Authority (27 May 2016). **30.** Michel Barnier, *My Secret Brexit Diary* (Cambridge, 2021), p. 103. **31.** Seldon and Newell, *Johnson at 10*, p. 39. **32.** BBC News, 'Net migration to UK rises to 330,000 – second highest on record' (26 May 2016). **33.** *Financial Times*, 'Brexit Poll Tracker'. **34.** Ed Caesar, 'Jo Cox, the Brexit vote, and the politics of murder', *The New Yorker* (24 June 2016). **35.** Charlie Cooper and Katie Forster, 'EU Referendum: Nigel Farage says it "looks like Remain will edge it" as polls close', *Independent* (23 June 2016). **36.** See Clarke, Goodwin and Whiteley, *Brexit*, pp. 208–12. **37.** Peter Moore, 'How Britain voted at the EU Referendum', YouGov (27 June 2016). **38.** Ipsos, 'How Britain voted in the 2016 EU Referendum' (5 Sept. 2016). **39.** Ibid. **40.** Danny Dorling, 'Brexit: the decision of a divided country', *British Medical Journal*, 354 i3697 (6 July 2016). George Arnett, 'UK became more middle class than working class in 2000, data shows', *Guardian* (26 Feb. 2016). **41.** Sarah Butt, Elizabeth Clery, John Curtice and Roger Harding, 'Culture wars', in *British Social Attitudes: The 39th Report* (London, 2022), p. 6. **42.** Albert Venn Dicey, *Introduction to the Study of the Law of the Constitution* (London, 1889), p. 38. **43.** UK in a Changing Europe, 'Brexit Witness Archive'. **44.** Imperial College London, Department of Earth Science and Engineering, 'How Britain Became an Island (Brexit 1.0)' (undated). **45.** Tony Judt, *Postwar: A History of Europe Since 1945* (London, 2005), p. 160. **46.** Randall Hansen, 'Making immigration work: how Britain and Europe can cope with their immigration crises', The *Government and Opposition* Leonard Schapiro Lecture, University of Sheffield, March 2015. *Government and Opposition*, 51, 2 (2016): 183–208. **47.** Geoffrey Evans and Anand Menon, *Brexit and British Politics* (Cambridge, 2017), p. 53. **48.** Rob Picheta, Luke McGee and Christian Edwards, 'Britain sees record net migration levels, increasing pressure on government', CNN (25 May 2023). Mattha Busby, 'Government reduces minimum salary for migrants to settle in UK', *Guardian* (24 Oct. 2020). **49.** Ipsos, 'Issues index: 2018 onwards' (4 Oct. 2022). John Burn-Murdoch, 'Britain is now a high-immigration country and most are fine with that', *Financial Times* (12 May 2022). **50.** Ipsos, 'Attitudes towards immigration' (2022). **51.** Institute for Fiscal Studies, 'Living standards, poverty and inequality in the UK' (undated). *After* housing costs median household income grew by nearly 6% over the same period. The data in this spreadsheet is routinely updated. This data was taken in July 2023. **52.** Office for National Statistics, 'Average weekly earnings time series' (14 Mar. 2023). X09. Real average weekly earnings using Consumer Price Inflation. **53.** Maria Sobolewska and Robert Ford, *Brexitland* (Cambridge, 2020), pp. 231–2. **54.** Dorling, 'Brexit: the decision of a divided country'; Danny Dorling and Sally Tomlinson, *Rule Britannia: Brexit and the End of Empire* (London, 2019); and Thiemo Fetzer, 'Did austerity cause Brexit?', *American Economic Review*, 109, 11 (2019): 3849–86. **55.** Quoted in Evans and Menon, *Brexit and British Politics*, p. 71. **56.** Robert Booth, Holly Watt and David Pegg, 'David Cameron admits he profited from father's Panama offshore trust', *Guardian* (7 Apr. 2016). Daniel Boffey, 'Cameron faces questions over £200,000 gift from mother', *Guardian* (10 Apr. 2016). 57. Ipsos, 'Trust in professions: long-term trends' (30 Nov. 2017). 58. Henry Mance, 'Britain has had enough of experts, says Gove', *Financial Times* (3 June 2016). 59. Elizabeth Clery, John Curtice and Roger Harding, *British Social Attitudes: The 34th Report* (London, 2017), p. 158. 60. John Higley and Ian McAllister, 'Elite division and voter confusion: Australia's Republic Referendum in 1999', *European Journal of Political Research*, 41, 6 (2002): 845–61. 61. Alan Finlayson, 'Who won the referendum?', Open Democracy (26 June 2016). 62. Robert Saunders, 'Brexit and Empire: "Global Britain" and the myth of imperial nostalgia', *Journal of Commonwealth and Imperial History*, 48, 6 (2020): 1140–74. 63. Matthew Weaver, 'Liam Fox: EU trade deal after Brexit should be "easiest in history" to get', *Guardian* (20 July 2017). 64. 'Britain is either a member of the European Union or it is not.' Nick Timothy, *Remaking One Nation: The Future of Conservatism* (Cambridge, 2020), p. 191. 65. Mark Mardell, 'What does "Brexit means Brexit" mean?', BBC News (14 July 2016). 66. Barnier, *My Secret Brexit Diary*, p. 128. 67. Jean-Claude Juncker with Donald Tusk, Jeroen Dijsselbloem, Mario Draghi and Martin Schulz, *Completing Europe's Economic and Monetary Union* (Brussels, 2015).

29 NORTHERN IRELAND

1 Paul Cullen, 'Martin McGuinness receiving treatment for amyloidosis', *Irish Times* (12 Jan. 2017). 2. Martin McGuinness, 'Resignation Letter' (9 Jan. 2017). 3. Bill Clinton, 'Statement from President Bill Clinton on the Passing of Martin McGuinness' (21 Mar. 2017) 4. Gregg Ryan, 'Bill Clinton speaks at McGuinness funeral', *Church Times* (31 Mar. 2017). 5. David Graham, 'The strange friendship of Martin McGuinness and Ian Paisley', *The Atlantic* (21 Mar. 2017). 6. Brian Rowan, *How the Peace was Won* (Dublin, 2008), p. 141. 7. Owen Bowcott, 'Hardliners vent their fury at Martin McGuinness', *Guardian* (14 Mar. 2009). 8. BBC News, 'Bloody Sunday killings unjustified and unjustifiable' (15 June 2010). 9. Queen Elizabeth, 'A Speech by the Queen at the Irish State Banquet' (18 May 2011). 10. Jim Cusack, 'Provos murdered Kevin McGuigan in a row over proceeds from the Northern Bank robbery', *Belfast Telegraph* (20 Sept. 2015). 11. The Northern Ireland Office, 'The Stormont House Agreement' (23 Dec. 2014). 12. The Northern Ireland Office, 'A fresh start for Northern Ireland' (17 Nov. 2015). 13. Liam Clarke, 'Arlene Foster relives horror of father's shooting by IRA and tells how bus blast could have killed her', *Belfast Times* (18 Dec. 2015). 14. Suzanne McGonagle, 'Driver of school bus blown up by IRA tells of personal heartache 30 years on', *Irish Times* (26 June 2018). 15. Gerry Moriarty, 'Incoming first minister urged to reconsider her decision not to attend Easter Rising events in Dublin', *Irish Times* (11 Jan. 2016). 16. *Belfast Telegraph*, 'First Minister Arlene Foster's inaugural speech' (8 Jan. 2016). 17. Will Leitch, 'RHI inquiry: whistleblower would take same actions again', BBC News (9 Feb. 2018). 18. Robin Sheeran and Iain McDowell, 'Cash for Ash whistleblower made out to be liar', BBC News (9 Feb. 2018). 19. Eventually, and because of reforms to payment systems, the final cost of the RHI scheme was around £240m. Jonathan Bell, 'Stormont officials confirm RHI to cost £240m as concerns raised over unspent millions', *Belfast Telegraph* (12 Nov. 2019). 20. ITV News, 'Foster ordered me to keep renewable scheme open – Bell' (16 Dec. 2016). 21. BBC News, 'RHI scandal: McGuinness calls on NI first minister to step aside' (16 Dec. 2016). 22. The DUP had accepted the outcome of the so-called St Andrews Talks but had not, at that time, formally said it would back an Irish Language Act. On this basis, the DUP argued it had not reneged upon any promises it had made. 23. Niall Carson, 'Arlene Foster on Sinn Féin: "If you feed a crocodile it will keep coming back for more"', TheJournal.ie (6 Feb. 2017). 24. When the Cash

for Ash report was eventually published, it was something of an anticlimax. Suzanne Breen, 'Explainer: Why Arlene Foster's job is safe after RHI Report targets civil servants', *Belfast Telegraph* (13 Mar. 2020). **25.** UK Government, 'New decade, new approach' (Jan. 2020), p. 15. BBC News, 'Stormont Deal: one year on, what's changed?' (11 Jan. 2021). **26.** John Garry, 'The EU Referendum vote in Northern Ireland: Implications for our understanding of citizens' political views and behaviour', Knowledge Exchange Seminar Series, 2016/17 (12 Oct. 2016), p. 2. **27.** Lesley-Anne McKeown, 'Tony Blair and John Major warn a Brexit could threaten peace process during visit to Derry', *Irish Times* (9 June 2016). Laura Hughes, 'EU Referendum: John Major and Tony Blair warn Brexit would "jeopardise the unity" of the United Kingdom', *Daily Telegraph* (9 June 2016). **28.** Feargal Cochrane, *Northern Ireland: The Fragile Peace*, 2nd edn (New Haven, CT, 2021), p. 285. **29.** Connor Murphy, 'Gerry Adams says Tory–DUP deal in breach of Good Friday Agreement', Politico (15 June 2017). BBC News, 'Leo Varadkar "reassured" about DUP–Tory deal' (19 June 2017). Jonathan Powell, 'Mrs May's deal with the DUP threatens twenty years hard work in Ireland', *Guardian* (11 June 2017). **30.** Prime Minister's Office and Department for Exiting the European Union, 'Joint report on progress during phase 1 of negotiations under Article 50 on the UK's orderly withdrawal from the EU' (8 Dec. 2017), p. 7. **31.** Department for Exiting the European Union, 'Agreement on the withdrawal of Great Britain and Northern Ireland from the European Union and the European Atomic Energy Community, as endorsed by leaders at a special meeting of the European Council on 25 November 2018' (25 Nov. 2018), p. 309. **32.** Sir Geoffrey Cox, 'Legal Effect of the Protocol on Ireland/Northern Ireland' (13 Nov. 2018). **33.** Gavin Barwell, *Chief of Staff: Notes from Downing Street* (London, 2021), p. 271. **34.** 'Did Unionism always oppose the Northern Ireland Protocol?', FactcheckNI (23 Mar. 2022). **35.** Jonathan Tonge, '"And I hereby declare the runner-up to be the winner": the extraordinary 2021 DUP leadership election', *Political Quarterly*, 92, 3 (2021): 506–11. **36.** *Irish Times*, 'Jeffrey Donaldson: "I won't be going back into Executive until Protocol dealt with"' (12 Mar. 2022). **37.** Indeed, in many ways, it resembled the 'maximum facilitation' arrangements favoured by the Eurosceptic members of Theresa May's Cabinet as an alternative to the Facilitated Customs Agreement. Under the terms of this alternative, technology would have been used to minimize the need for border checks between Northern Ireland and the Republic. **38.** CAIN (Conflict Archive on The Internet), 'Background information on Northern Ireland society – population and vital statistics' (undated). **39.** One important way in which it did so was by giving the Parliament of Northern Ireland and the government of Northern Ireland the opportunity to set the terms of the electoral franchise. A crucial way in which it did this was by denying the vote to those renting a property and so not paying rates. *Irish Legal News*, 'Irish legal heritage: one man, one vote' (12 Oct. 2018). **40.** Simon Hattenstone, 'The Monday Interview: The survivor', *Guardian*, 30 Apr. 2001). **41.** Northern Ireland Statistics and Research Agency, MS-B23, 'Religion or religion brought up in' (22 Sept. 2022). Using this census question there were, at the time of the 2021 Census, 869,000 Catholics in Northern Ireland, 827,000 Protestants and other Christians; 28,515 people of other religions; and 177,360 people who refused to answer the question. **42.** Susan McKay, 'Northern Ireland is coming to an end', *New York Times* (30 June 2021). **43.** Northern Ireland Office, 'The Belfast Agreement' (10 Apr. 1998), p. 3. **44.** John Coakley, 'A farewell to Northern Ireland? Constitutional options for Irish Unity', *Political Quarterly*, 93, 2 (2022): 307–15, p. 312. **45.** Northern Ireland Life and Times Survey, 2021. **46.** Northern Ireland Life and Times Survey, 'Interest in politics/party affiliation'. **47.** Northern Ireland Life and Times Survey, 'Identity'. **48.** See John Cushnahan, 'The Effectiveness of the Belfast/Good Friday Agreement' (Dec. 2022). Alliance Party, 'Together We Can', 2022 Manifesto for the Northern Ireland Assembly Elections (Apr. 2022), pp. 89–92.

30 ME TOO

1 Jodi Kantor and Megan Twohey, 'Harvey Weinstein paid off sexual harassment accusers for decades', *New York Times* (5 Oct. 2017). 2. *New York Times*, 'Statement from Harvey Weinstein' (5 Oct. 2017). 3. See Liam Stanley, Ellie Gore, Genevieve LeBaron, Sylvie Craig, Remi Edwards, Sophie Wall and Tom Watts, 'The political economy of the Weinstein scandal', *Global Society*, 37, 1 (2023): 93–113. 4. Rachel McGrath, 'Harvey Weinstein expelled from the Academy after Oscars board vote', The Huffington Post (18 Oct. 2017). 5. The black activist Tarana Burke had founded the 'Me Too' programme in 2006 to support girls and young women of colour in deprived areas of America who were survivors of sexual violence. Penny Griffin, '#MeToo, white feminism and taking everyday politics seriously in the global political economy', *Australian Journal of Political Science*, 54, 4 (2019): 86–104. 6. Melena Ryzik, Cara Buckley and Jodi Kantor, 'Louis C.K. is accused by five women of sexual misconduct, *New York Times* (9 Nov. 2017). 7. Catharine MacKinnon, '#MeToo had done what the law could not do', *New York Times* (4 Feb. 2018). 8. 'Sisters, this is our moment to say time's up', Letter, *Observer* (18 Feb. 2018). 9. BBC News, '#MeToo: UK stars give £1m to sexual harassment victims' (18 Oct. 2018). 10. Women and Equalities Committee, 'Sexual harassment and sexual violence in schools', House of Commons, HC 826 (29 Nov. 2016); Christina Dodds, 'Sexual harassment is a real problem in the Armed Forces', The Conversation (23 July 2019); David Batty and Elena Cherubini, 'UK universities accused of failing to tackle sexual misconduct', *Guardian* (28 Mar. 2018); and Joe Lewis, 'Sexual harassment and violence in further and higher education', House of Commons Library, Research Briefing 9438 (9 Feb. 2022). 11. BBC News, 'MP Mark Garnier cleared of breaking Ministerial Code' (21 Dec. 2017). 12. Steven Swinford, Kate McCann and Christopher Hope, 'Sir Michael Fallon quits as Westminster sex scandal claims its first scalp', *Daily Telegraph* (2 Nov. 2017). 13. Ned Simmons, 'Tory MP Chris Pincher refers himself to police after "pound shop Harvey Weinstein" claim', The Huffington Post (5 Nov. 2017). 14. BBC News, 'Bex Bailey: I was raped at a Labour Party event in 2011' (31 Oct. 2017). 15. Rowena Mason, 'Labour suspends ex-minister Ivan Lewis over sexual harassment claim', *Guardian* (23 Nov. 2017). 16. Cathy Newman, 'Exclusive: scale of misconduct in Westminster revealed', Channel 4 News (12 July 2022). 17. Sophie Morris, 'John Bercow: former speaker banned from Parliament for life after bullying inquiry finds him guilty', Sky News (8 Mar. 2022). 18. Chay Quinn, 'Tory MP David Warburton resigns after sex and drugs investigation – triggering new by-election headache for Sunak', LBC News (18 June 2023). 19. Linda Colley, *Britons: Forging the Nation 1707–1837* (New Haven, CT, 1992), p. 222. 20. Sharon Churcher, 'The full incredible story of the picture of Andrew with Virginia Giuffre and Ghislaine Maxwell', *Daily Mail* (19 Feb. 2022). 21. BBC News, 'Virginia Giuffre: what we know about Prince Andrew's accuser' (12 Jan. 2022). 22. Juliet Rieden, 'Inside Prince Andrew's infamous BBC Newsnight interview that damaged the Royal Family', ABC News (12 July 2022). 23. James O'Brien, 'Full Disclosure with Emily Maitlis' (15 Sept. 2022). 24. BBC News, 'Prince Andrew Newsnight interview: transcript in full' (17 Nov. 2019). 25. Zoe Drewett, 'Prince Andrew interview described as "nuclear explosion level bad"', *Metro* (17 Nov. 2019). 26. David Mercer, 'Prince Andrew steps back from public duties over Jeffrey Epstein scandal', Sky News (6 Dec. 2019). 27. Mikhaila Friel, 'The Queen strips Prince Andrew of royal patronages and military titles', The Insider (13 Jan. 2022). 28. Hope Coke, 'Former *Tatler* cover star Emily Maitlis on why Prince Andrew's Newsnight interview is even more significant right now', *Tatler* (17 Feb. 2022). 29. Marina Hyde, 'Poor Prince Andrew is "appalled" by Epstein. Let that be an end to it', *Guardian* (23 Aug. 2019). 30. Ipsos, 'Important issues facing Britain' (22 Dec. 2022). 31. Michael Savage, 'Nigel Farage warns of Romanian crime wave once EU restrictions are lifted', *The Times* (20 Sept. 2013). 32. Gordon Rayner, 'Boris Johnson unveils £1bn plan to put bobbies back on the

beat', *Daily Telegraph* (4 July 2019). **33.** Office for National Statistics, 'Public perceptions of crime in England and Wales: year ending March 2016', Figure 1 (7 Sept. 2017). **34.** Office for National Statistics, 'Crime in England and Wales, year ending June 2022' (27 Oct. 2022). Broadly speaking, the patterns of crime rates in Scotland map those in England and Wales. The 2019/20 Scottish Crime and Justice Survey found that 'Scotland has become a safer place over the last decade or so, following large falls in both the overall level of crime and the likelihood of being a victim of crime since 2008/09'. *Scottish Crime and Justice Survey 2019/20*, 'Main findings, executive summary' (16 Mar. 2021). Crime has also fallen – and fallen from a lower initial base – in Northern Ireland, with the proportion of people experiencing any personal (rather than household) crime falling from 5.6% to 1.9% in 2018. Department of Justice, '*Experience of crime: findings from the 2019/20 Northern Ireland Safe Community Survey*', Experience of crime findings, 2019–20 data tables (Table 2) (26 Feb. 2021). **35.** Our World in Data, 'Homicide rate per 100,000 population' (undated). **36.** Laura Bates, *Everyday Sexism* (London, 2014). The website can be found at: https://everydaysexism.com/. **37.** Lorna Adams, Laura Hilger, Emma Moselen, Tanya Basi, Oliver Gooding and Jenny Hull, '2020 sexual harassment survey', Government Equalities Office (2020). **38.** Office for National Statistics, 'Sexual offences prevalence and trends, England and Wales: year ending March 2022' (Figure 4). Also, Office for National Statistics, 'Sexual offences in England and Wales overview: year ending March 2020' (Figure 2) (18 Mar. 2021). **39.** Rape Crisis, 'Statistics about sexual violence and abuse' (undated). **40.** Home Affairs Select Committee, 'Investigation and prosecution of rape' (12 Apr. 2022) (Figure 7). **41.** Centre for Women's Justice, End Violence Against Women Coalition, Imkaan and Rape Crisis England and Wales, 'The decriminalisation of rape' (Nov. 2020), p. 1. **42.** Tristan Kirk, 'Met Police "sorry" Wayne Couzens wasn't arrested for indecent exposure', *Evening Standard* (6 Mar. 2023). **43.** Laura Bates, *Fix the System: Not the Women* (London, 2022). **44.** Alexandra Topping, 'Jess Phillips reads to MPs list of women killed over past year', *Guardian* (9 Mar. 2023). **45.** Kate Ng, 'Kate Middleton has reportedly written an emotional letter to the family of Sarah Everard', *Independent* (26 Mar. 2021). **46.** Her Majesty's Inspectorate of Constabulary and Fire and Rescue Services, 'An Inspection of the Metropolitan Police Service's policing of a vigil held in commemoration of Sarah Everard' (30 Mar. 2021). **47.** Baroness Casey of Blackstock, 'Letter sent via email to Commissioner of the Metropolitan Police Service Sir Mark Rowley' (17 Oct. 2022). **48.** Mark Rowley, 'Letter sent to Baroness Casey of Blackstock' (17 Oct. 2022). **49.** Samuel Osborne, 'David Carrick: timeline of Met Police's missed opportunities to stop serial rapist', Sky News (17 Jan. 2023). **50.** Jamie Grierson, 'Ex-victims' commissioner hits out at "evil" in Met amid David Carrick fallout', *Guardian* (17 Jan. 2023). **51.** *The Economist*, 'The toxic culture of the Metropolitan Police Service' (18 Jan. 2023). **52.** Baroness Casey Review, 'Final Report: an independent review into the standards of behaviour and internal culture of the Metropolitan Police Service' (Mar. 2023), pp. 17, 22. **53.** Katherine Rake, 'Women', in *Closer to Equality? Assessing New Labour's Record on Equality After 10 Years in Government* (London, 2007). **54.** Office for National Statistics, 'Gender pay gap in the UK: 2021' (26 Oct. 2021).

31 GETTING BREXIT DONE

1 Clive James, *The Blaze of Obscurity: The TV Years* (London, 2009), p. 17. **2.** Geoffrey Evans and Anand Menon, *Brexit and British Politics* (Cambridge, 2017), p. 93. **3.** David Rankin, 'Brexit's a bad move, but Cameron will not quit if Britain disagrees', *The Times* (10 Jan. 2016). Adam Withnall, 'David Cameron says he will not stand down – even if he loses the EU referendum', *Independent* (12 June 2016). Katie Forster, 'David Cameron's first words when he realised he had lost EU referendum', *Independent* (2 July 2016). **4.** David

Hughes and Andrew Woodcock, 'Nigel Farage resigns as UKIP leader after achieving his political ambition', The Huffington Post (5 July 2016). **5.** Reuters, 'UK's May, launching leadership bid, vows to honour Brexit vote' (30 June 2016). **6.** James Blitz, 'Brexit Briefing: Enemies of the people?' *Financial Times* (4 Nov. 2016). **7.** Votes in Parliament, 'European Union (Notification of Withdrawal) Bill: Second Reading' (1 Feb. 2017). **8.** Andrew Woodcock, 'Hand-delivering Article 50 letter cost almost £1,000', The Huffington Post (10 Feb. 2018). **9.** The other issue which ended up being resolved at this stage was that of a transition period after Britain formally left the European Union. Chris Grey, *Brexit Unfolded: How No One Got What They Wanted (and Why They Were Never Going To)* (London, 2021), p. 102. **10.** Anne-Sylvaine Chassany, 'Hollande demands tough Brexit negotiations', *Financial Times* (7 Oct. 2016). **11.** Tim Shipman, *Fallout: A Year of Political Mayhem* (London, 2017), p. 93. **12.** Gavin Barwell, *Chief of Staff: Notes from Downing Street* (London, 2021), p. 213. **13.** Prime Minister's Office and Department for Exiting the European Union, 'Joint report on progress during phase 1 of negotiations under Article 50 on the UK's orderly withdrawal from the EU' (8 Dec. 2017), p. 7. **14.** Anthony Seldon and Raymond Newell, *Johnson at 10: The Inside Story* (London, 2023), p. 50. **15.** Tim Bale, *The Conservative Party After Brexit* (Cambridge, 2023), p. 21. **16.** BBC News, '"Have cake and eat it" Brexit notes played down by government' (29 Nov. 2016). **17.** Theresa May, 'The Government's Objectives for Exiting the European Union', Lancaster House Speech (17 Jan. 2017). **18.** Ibid. **19.** Meg Russell with Lisa James, *The Parliamentary Battle Over Brexit* (Oxford, 2023), p. 70. **20.** Dominic Grieve, UK in a Changing Europe, 'Brexit Witness Archive'. **21.** Christopher Hope, 'No 10 warns taxis on standby for ministers who resign today over Brexit as May exerts authority', *Daily Telegraph* (6 July 2018). BBC News, 'Boris Johnson's resignation letter and May's reply in full' (9 July 2018). **22.** According to Theresa May's post-2017 chief of staff, Gavin Barwell, a customs union was, give or take, the deal she had negotiated with the European Union. Barwell, *Chief of Staff*, p. 280. **23.** Elise Uberoi, 'Indicative Votes 2.0: where did support lie?', House of Commons Library, Insight (23 Apr. 2019). **24.** LBC News, 'MPs reject plan for more indicative Brexit votes after John Bercow breaks tie' (3 Apr. 2019). **25.** Theresa May, 'PM Statement on Brexit' (20 Mar. 2019). **26.** She did so having been warned that Conservative MPs were about to change the rules to allow for a second vote of no confidence in her leadership and that she would lose. **27.** Boris Johnson, 'First Speech as Prime Minister' (24 July 2019). **28.** Laura Beers, 'Why the Queen said yes to Boris Johnson's request to suspend Parliament', The Conversation (29 Aug. 2019). **29.** Rachel Hogarth, 'Supreme Court decision on prorogation', Institute of Government (11 Sept. 2019). **30.** Michel Barnier, *My Secret Brexit Diary* (Cambridge, 2021), pp. 280–82. **31.** Jonathan Read, 'Boris Johnson claims Parliament has outlived its usefulness', *New European* (24 Oct. 2019). **32.** Tom Newton Dunn, 'Brexit betrayal: Boris Johnson slams "sneering" Jeremy Corbyn's "betrayal" of Brexit voters as he launches 72-hour Labour heartland blitz', *Sun* (9 Dec. 2019). **33.** BBC News, 'General Election 2019: Boris Johnson "does not understand" deal treaty checks' (8 Nov. 2019). Rebecca Taylor, 'General Election: Leaked Treasury document "wrong" on Brexit checks, Boris Johnson claims', Sky News (9 Dec. 2019). **34.** Nigel Farage initially threatened to run Brexit Party candidates in every constituency. In the end, he opted to give pro-Brexit Conservative MPs a free run whilst standing against pro-Remain Labour MPs. **35.** The Conservatives secured the votes of only 20% of those who had voted to Remain in 2016. Labour secured the votes of 48% of those who had voted to Remain but only 15% of those who had voted to Leave. Gideon Skinner, Roger Mortimore and Dylan Spielman, 'How Britain voted in 2019', Ipsos (20 Dec. 2019). **36.** Ipsos, 'How Britain voted in 1997' (31 May 1997). **37.** Skinner, Mortimore and Spielman, 'How Britain voted in 2019'. **38.** Jane Green and Roosmarijn de Geus, 'Red Wall or Red Herring? Economic insecurity and voter intention in Britain' (24 May 2022). **39.** Skinner, Mortimore and Spielman, 'How Britain voted in 2019'. **40.** Barnier, *My Secret Brexit Diary*,

p. 316. **41.** BBC News, 'Northern Ireland secretary admits new bill will break international law' (8 Sept. 2020). **42.** Thomas Colson, 'Boris Johnson promised frictionless trade after Brexit but now his government admits new border checks are "inevitable"', *Business Insider* (11 Feb. 2020). **43.** Anton Spisak, 'Unpacking the Brexit deal: what it means and where it takes future UK–EU relations', Tony Blair Institute for Global Change (31 Dec. 2020). **44.** Swati Dhingra, Emily Fry, Sophie Hale and Ningyuan Jia, 'The Big Brexit: an assessment of the scale of changes to come from Brexit', Resolution Foundation (June 2022), p. 39. Also see Jan Bakker, Nikhil Datta, Richard Davies and Josh de Lyon, 'Non-tariff barriers and consumer prices: evidence from Brexit', Centre for Economic Performance, 1888 (December 2022). **45.** Resolution Foundation, 'Stagnation nation: navigating a route to a fairer and more prosperous Britain' (2022), p. 107. **46.** European Banking Authority, 'EBA informs customers of UK financial institutions about the end of the Brexit transition period' (8 Dec. 2020). **47.** Sam Fleming, Philip Stafford and Laura Noonan, 'The EU vs the City of London: a slow puncture', *Financial Times* (10 Jan. 2022). **48.** Jim Pickard and Sebastian Payne, 'The war is over, we have won declares jubilant Farage', *Financial Times* (31 Jan. 2020). **49.** UK in a Changing Europe, 'Brexit Witness Archive'.

PART SEVEN

1 Future of Life Institute, 'Pause giant AI experiments: an open letter' (22 Mar. 2023). **2.** Michael L. Littman et al., 'Gathering strength, gathering storms: the one hundred year study on Artificial Intelligence (AI100)' 2021 Study Panel Report, Stanford University (September 2021); Cade Metz, *Genius Makers* (London, 2021); Melanie Mitchell, *Artificial Intelligence: A Guide for Thinking Humans* (London, 2019); and Stuart Russell, *Human Compatible: Artificial Intelligence and the Problem of Control* (New York, 2019). **3.** *The Economist*, 'How generative models could go wrong' (19 Apr. 2023). **4.** Gordon Raynor, 'Why King Charles will not reign in the same way as Queen Elizabeth II', *Daily Telegraph* (10 Sept. 2022). William Booth and Karla Adam, 'What kind of monarch will King Charles be? Different from his mum', *Washington Post* (9 Sept. 2022). That said, Charles, when still Prince of Wales, also told a BBC interviewer that 'I do realise it's a separate exercise being sovereign'. Sean Coughlan, 'What kind of king will Charles be?', BBC News (9 Sept. 2022). **5.** F. D. Flam, 'The earth is dancing close to a temperature tipping point', *Washington Post* (19 July 2023); Andrea Thompson, 'July 2023 is hottest month ever recorded on earth', *Scientific American* (27 July 2023); World Metrological Organization, 'Past eight years confirmed to be the eight warmest on record', Press Release (12 Jan. 2023); Damian Carrington, 'Climate crisis: scientists spot warning signs of Gulf Stream collapse', *Guardian* (5 Aug. 2023).

32 COVID

1 Sydney Combs, 'She discovered coronaviruses decades ago – but got little recognition', *National Geographic* (17 Apr. 2020). Elisabeth Mahase, 'Covid-19: first coronavirus was described in the BMJ in 1965', *British Medical Journal*, 369 (16 Apr. 2020). **2.** It seems quite likely, given the ongoing reluctance of the Chinese government to publicly investigate the issue, that we may never be able to pinpoint the origins of Covid-19. See, variously, Amy Maxman, 'Wuhan market was epicentre of pandemic's start, studies suggest', *Nature*, 603 (Mar. 2022); Jeremy Farrar with Anjana Ahuja, *Spike: The Virus vs The People* (London, 2021), p. 52; the BBC Radio series *Fever: The Hunt for Covid's Origins*; and Jonathan Calvert and George Arbuthnott, *Failures of State: The Inside Story of Britain's Battle with*

Coronavirus (London, 2021), pp. 40–50. **3.** BBC News, 'Coronavirus was already in Italy by December, wastewater study finds' (19 June 2020). **4.** Department of Health and Social Care, 'Coronavirus (Covid 19) action plan' (3 Mar. 2020). **5.** Rachael Krishna, 'Here is the transcript of what Boris Johnson said on *This Morning* about the novel coronavirus', Full Fact (10 Mar. 2020). It is important to underline that Johnson was describing this as one possible option. He was not announcing it as government policy. **6.** Heather Stewart and Mattha Busby, 'Coronavirus: science chief defends UK plan from criticism', *Guardian* (13 Mar. 2020). **7.** Addendum to Thirteenth SAGE Meeting on Covid-19 (5 Mar. 2020). **8.** Anthony Seldon and Raymond Newell, *Johnson at 10: The Inside Story* (London, 2023), p. 255. **9.** Dominic Cummings, Health and Social Care Committee and Science and Technology Committee, 'Oral Evidence Transcripts' (26 May 2021). **10.** Prime Minister's Office, 10 Downing Street, 'Prime Minister's Statement on Coronavirus' (12 Mar. 2020). **11.** Neil Ferguson et al., 'Impact of non-pharmaceutical interventions to reduce COVID-19 mortality and healthcare', Imperial College Covid-19 Response Team (16 Mar. 2020). **12.** Kate Proctor, Peter Walker and Rajeev Syal, 'Police and health officials to get powers to detain under UK Coronavirus Bill', *Guardian* (19 Mar. 2020). That legislation was then debated in Parliament and approved. It was given Royal Assent and became law on 25 March. **13.** Prime Minister's Office, 10 Downing Street, 'Prime Minister's Statement on Coronavirus' (23 Mar. 2020). **14.** Our World in Data, 'UK daily new hospital admissions for Covid-19'. I say recorded because the complete veracity of statistics in February and early March 2020, when Covid was still a largely unknown quantity and tests may not always have been run, is uncertain. **15.** Our World in Data, 'UK daily new confirmed Covid-19 deaths'. **16.** Berkeley Lovelace and Noah Higgins-Dunn, 'WHO says coronavirus death rate is 3.4% globally, higher than previously thought', CNBC (3 Mar. 2020). **17.** Calvert and Arbuthnott, *Failures of State*, pp. 250–55. **18.** Health and Social Care Committee and Science and Technology Committee, 'Coronavirus: lessons learnt to date', HC 92 (21 Sept. 2021). David Norgrove, 'Letter to Matt Hancock regarding Covid-19 testing' (11 May 2020). **19.** Jacqui Wise, 'Covid-19: UK drops its own contact tracing app to switch to Apple and Google model', *British Medical Journal*, 369 (19 June 2020). **20.** Scientific Advisory Group for Emergencies, 'Sage 58 Minutes: Coronavirus (Covid-19) response, 21 September 2020' (12 Oct. 2020). **21.** Our World in Data, 'UK daily new hospital admissions for Covid-19'. **22.** Medicine and Healthcare Products Regulatory Agency, 'MHRA issues new advice, concluding a possible link between COVID-19 Vaccine AstraZeneca and extremely rare, unlikely to occur blood clots' (7 Apr. 2021). **23.** Office for National Statistics, 'Coronavirus and vaccination rates in people aged 70 years or over by socio-demographic, England: 8 December 2020 to 11 March 2021' (29 Mar. 2021). **24.** Prime Minister's Office, 10 Downing Street, 'PM Statement at Coronavirus Press Conference' (14 June 2021). **25.** Healthcare in the United Kingdom, 'Deaths in the United Kingdom', Weekly deaths with Covid-19 on the death certificate by date registered, total registered deaths. **26.** Office for National Statistics, 'Prevalence of ongoing symptoms following Coronavirus (Covid-19) infection in the UK' (2 Feb. 2023). **27.** Peter Hennessy, *A Duty of Care: Britain Before and After Covid* (London, 2022). **28.** Fiona Hill, *There is Nothing for You Here: Finding Opportunity in the Twenty First Century* (London, 2021). **29.** Rob Beckett, *A Class Act: Life as a Working-Class Man in a Middle-Class World* (London, 2021), p. 6. **30.** J. J. Charlesworth, Tweet, 14 October 2020. **31.** The Social Mobility Commission found that 55% of workers in households with an annual income greater than £20,000 worked from home compared with 19% for those below £20,000. Social Mobility Commission, 'State of the Nation 2021: social mobility and the pandemic' (July 2021), p. 15. **32.** In Wales the respective gaps were 9.5 years (male) and 7 years (female). In Scotland they were 13.7 years (male) and 10.5 years (female). The Health Foundation, 'Life expectancy and healthy life expectancy at birth by deprivation' (6 Jan. 2022). **33.** Vache Nafilyan et al., 'Occupation and Covid-19 mortality in England:

a national linked data study of 14.3 million adults', *BMJ Occupational and Environmental Medicine*, 79, 7 (2022): 433–41. **34.** A Zero Covid policy for the UK became, for a while, the key policy demand of the 'Independent' SAGE group. Laurie Clarke, 'Covid-19's rebel scientists: has iSAGE been a success?', *British Medical Journal* (20 Oct. 2021). **35.** 'The Great Barrington Declaration', written by Jay Bhattacharya (Stanford), Sunetra Gupta (Oxford) and Martin Kulldorff (Harvard) and published in October 2022 offered the clearest (and one of the most controversial) statements of this strategy. Jonathan Sumption, 'Set us free from lockdown, ministers, and stop covering your backs' *Sunday Times* (17 May 2020). Jonathan Sumption, 'Boris Johnson's "strongman" government is destroying democracy', *Daily Telegraph* (2 Oct. 2020). **36.** Chris Slater, 'Greater Manchester MP joins Tory revolt over new lockdown', *Manchester Evening News* (2 Nov. 2020). **37.** Jonathan Compton, 'Lord Sumption is wrong on lockdown liberty', *Law Gazette* (19 May 2020). **38.** Ed Pertwee, Clarissa Simas and Heidi Larson, 'An epidemic of uncertainty: rumours, conspiracy theories and vaccine hesitancy', *Nature Medicine*, 28 (2022): 456–9 and Saiful Islam et al., 'Covid-19 rumors and conspiracy theories: the need for cognitive inoculation against misinformation to improve vaccine adherence', *PLoS One*, 16 (12 May 2021). **39.** Tim Baker, 'Andrew Bridgen: MP kicked out of Tory Party after comparing Covid vaccines to Holocaust', Sky News (26 Apr. 2023). **40.** Rob Stein, 'Fauci reveals he has received death threats and his daughters have been harassed', NPR (5 Aug. 2020). On the polarizing party political effects of Covid in America see Austen Hegland, Annie Zhang and Josh Pasek, 'A partisan pandemic: how Covid-19 was primed for polarization', *The American Academy of Political and Social Science*, 700 (Mar. 2022). **41.** Nadeem Badshah and Richard Adams, 'Oxford vice chancellor "embarrassed" to have Michael Gove as alumnus', *Guardian* (1 Sept. 2021). **42.** Oxford University, 'Covid-19 increased public trust in science, new survey shows' (25 Jan. 2023) and Gideon Skinner, Cameron Garrett and Jayesh Navin Shah, 'How has Covid-19 affected trust in scientists?', Ipsos (Sept. 2020). **43.** The Policy Institute, King's College London, 'Conspiracy belief among the UK public and the role of alternative media' (June 2023), p. 3 (https://www.kcl.ac.uk/policy-institute/assets/conspiracy-belief-among-the-uk-public.pdf). **44.** Adam Forrest, 'Only 18 per cent of people self-isolate after developing coronavirus symptoms, UK study finds', *Independent* (25 Sept. 2020). **45.** Health and Social Care Committee and Science and Technology Committee, 'Oral Evidence Transcripts' (26 May 2021). **46.** Farrah with Ahuja, *Spike*, pp. 173–4. In April 2021 several newspapers reported that Johnson, in the midst of a heated policy discussion, also said 'no more fu**ing lockdowns – let the bodies pile high in their thousands'. Reuters, 'UK denies that Johnson said let the bodies pile high' (25 Apr. 2021). **47.** Ian Dunt, 'Boris reveals his political hero: the mayor from *Jaws*', Politics. Co.UK (18 Oct. 2011). Also see Tim Wyatt, 'Boris Johnson has history of comparing himself to *Jaws*' reckless mayor who kept beaches open', *Independent* (27 Apr. 2021). **48.** Health and Social Care Committee and Science and Technology Committee, 'Oral Evidence Transcripts' (26 May 2021). Jeremy Farrar and Ajana Ahuja, 'Out of control: the moment Boris Johnson let Covid run rampant', *Sunday Times* (17 July 2021). **49.** Johns Hopkins University, Coronavirus Research Center, 'Mortality analyses' (undated), deaths per 100,000. **50.** World Bank, 'GDP growth (Annual %)', (undated). **51.** Jacqui Wise, 'Covid-19: highest death rates seen in countries with most overweight population', *British Medical Journal*, 372 (2021). **52.** Mark Woolhouse, *The Year the World Went Mad: A Scientific Memoir* (Muir of Ord, 2022), p. 94. **53.** Andrew Powell, Brigid Francis-Devine and Harriet Clarke, 'Coronavirus: impact on the labour market', House of Commons Library, CBP8898 (9 Aug. 2022). **54.** Heather Wilson and David Finch, 'Unemployment and mental health: why both require action for our Covid-19 recovery', The Health Foundation (Apr. 2021), p. 3. **55.** Education Endowment Foundation, 'The impact of Covid-19 on learning: a review of the evidence' (May 2022). **56.** Andrew Eyles, Esme Lillywhite and Lee Elliot Major, 'The rising tide of school absences in the post-pandemic era', LSE Blog

(28 June 2023). 57. Prime Minister's Office, 10 Downing Street, 'Prime Minister's State-ment on Coronavirus' (12 Mar. 2020). 58. Adam Tooze, *Shutdown: How Covid Shook the World's Economy* (London, 2021), pp. 111–14. 59. Bank of England, 'Bank rate reduced to 0.1 per cent and asset purchases increased by £200bn – March 2020' (19 Mar. 2020). 60. HM Treasury, 'Chancellor of the Exchequer, Rishi Sunak on Covid-19 Response' (17 Mar. 2020). 61. Robin McKie and Toby Helm, 'Sunak under fire as "stupid" eat out to help out scheme to be focus of Covid Inquiry', *Guardian* (3 June 2023). 62. Thomas Pope, 'Coronavirus: what support did government provide for individuals and businesses?', Institute for Government (31 Mar. 2022). Also see Office for Budget Respon-sibility, 'Economic and fiscal outlook' (Nov. 2020), pp. 79–81. 63. HM Treasury, 'Public expenditure statistical analyses', Chapter 4 (Table 4.3) (20 July 2022). These are inflation-adjusted figures at 2021/2 prices. 64. HM Treasury, 'Public expenditure statistical analyses', Chapter 4 (Table 4.1) (20 July 2022). 65. Office for National Statistics, 'Public sector finances, UK: April 2023', Figure 3 (23 May 2023). The figures here are exclusive of the public sector banks. 66. Bank of England Database, Bank of England Weekly Report (undated) (https://www.bankofengland.co.uk/weekly-report/balance-sheet-and-weekly-report). Data can then be downloaded via an Excel file in which weekly amounts outstanding of central bank sterling loan-to-asset purchase facility total (in sterling millions) (not sea-sonally adjusted) are shown in Column J. 67. Andrew Bailey, 'Bank of England is not doing monetary financing', *Financial Times* (5 Apr. 2020).

33 FROM TRUST TO TRUSS

1 Peter Walker, 'Boris Johnson missed five coronavirus Cobra meetings, Michael Gove says', *Guardian* (19 Apr. 2020). 2. Jeremy Farrah with Anjana Ahuja, *Spike: The Virus vs The People* (London, 2021), p. 125. 3. Andrew Woodcock, 'Coronavirus: scientists advised against handshakes on day Boris Johnson boasted of "shaking hands continuously"', *Inde-pendent* (5 May 2020). 4. Farrah with Ahuja, *Spike*, p. 139. 5. Boris Johnson, 'Coronavirus Speech Transcript: Announcement After Release from Hospital' (12 Apr. 2020). 6. Peter Jones, 'Cicero would have been quick to end the lockdown', *Spectator* (9 May 2020). 7. Sonia Purnell, who had worked alongside Johnson whilst he was a journalist at the *Daily Telegraph*'s office in Brussels, spoke of his 'very weird attitude to illness . . . he was intoler-ant of anybody who was ill. Until now, he has had a very robust constitution. He has never been ill until now, and this will be a huge shock to him. His outlook on the world is that illness is for weak people.' Quoted in Robert Mendick, 'The inside story of Boris Johnson's coronavirus battle', *Daily Telegraph* (6 Apr. 2020). 8. Jonathan Healey, *The Blazing World: A New History of Revolutionary England* (London, 2023), p. 169. 9. Ipsos, 'Veracity index: trust in professions survey' (26 Nov. 2019). Elizabeth Clery, John Curtice, Morgan Frankenburg, Hannah Morgan and Susan Reid, 'Brexit, the pandemic and trust and confi-dence in government', in *British Social Attitudes: The 38th Report* (London, 2021), p. 7. 10. Olivier Bargain and Ulugbek Aminjonov, 'Trust and compliance to public health poli-cies in times of Covid-19', IZA Institute of Labour Economics (May 2020). Also see James Weinberg, 'Can political trust help to explain elite policy support and public behaviour in times of crisis? Evidence from the United Kingdom at the height of the 2020 coronavirus pandemic', *Political Studies*, 70, 3 (2022): 655–79. 11. For this and other data on levels of trust see Fanny Lalot, Ben Davies and Dominic Abrams, 'Trust and cohesion in Britain during the 2020 COVID-19 pandemic across place, scale and time', Report for the British Academy (Nov. 2020), pp. 12–14. 12. YouGov, 'How well is Boris Johnson doing as prime minis-ter?' (undated). 13. Lalot, Davies and Abrams, 'Trust and cohesion in Britain', p. 9. 14. Max Colchester and Anna Isaac, 'Inside Boris Johnson's tangle with Covid-19', *Wall Street Journal* (15 May 2020). 15. YouGov, 'Personal measures taken to avoid Covid-19'

(undated).   16. Benjamin Jeffrey et al., 'Anonymised and aggregated crowd level mobility data from mobile phones suggests that initial compliance with Covid-19 social distancing interventions was high and geographically consistent across the UK', Imperial College Covid-19 Response Team (17 July 2020).   17. National Police Chiefs' Council, 'Fixed penalty notices issued under Covid' (29 May 2020).   18. Jonathan Calvert and George Arbuthnott, *Failures of State: The Inside Story of Britain's Battle with Coronavirus* (London, 2021), p. 188.   19. *Northern Echo*, 'Dominic Cummings defends Durham trip as "right" following calls for PM's aide to quit' (23 May 2020).   20. A full transcript of the press conference was published by the *Independent*: 'Dominic Cummings: full transcript of Boris Johnson's aide's statement from Downing Street', *Independent* (25 May 2020). Cummings pointed out that the lockdown rules contained a proviso that it would sometimes be difficult for parents with children to follow all the guidelines and that they should 'keep following this guidance to the best of your ability': something which, he argued, he and his wife had done.   21. Full Fact, 'What did the lockdown rules say when Dominic Cummings travelled to Durham?' (27 May 2020).   22. Kirsteen Paterson, 'Full Durham Police statement on Dominic Cummings' lockdown breach', The National (28 May 2020).   23. For more details of the relationship between Carrie Johnson, Boris Johnson and Dominic Cummings see Anthony Seldon and Raymond Newell, *Johnson at 10: The Inside Story* (London, 2023), ch. 6. Toby Helm, 'More questions for Civil Service boss who said Carrie Johnson was PM', *Guardian* (15 Oct. 2023).   24. Daisy Fancourt, Andrew Steptoe and Liam Wright, 'The Cummings effect: politics, trust and behaviours during the Covid-19 pandemic', *The Lancet*, 396, 10249 (15 Aug. 2020). Ben Davies et al., 'Changes in political trust in Britain during the Covid-19 pandemic in 2020: integrated public opinion evidence and implications', *Humanities and Social Science Communications*, 8, art. 166 (9 July 2021), pp. 1–9.   25. YouGov, 'Personal measures taken to avoid Covid-19' (undated).   26. Jonathan Jackson et al., 'Public compliance and Covid-19: did Cummings damage the fight against the virus, or become a useful anti-role model?', LSE Blog (15 June 2020).   27. ITV News, 'ITV News podcast reveals Boris Johnson joked about "the most unsocially distanced party in the UK"' (12 Jan. 2023). Aubrey Allegretta, 'Music from "Abba Party" could be heard all over Number 10, says Cummings', *Guardian* (31 May 2022).   28. Nick Duffy, 'Abba's Benny Andersson on Downing Street party row: "You can't call it an Abba Party, it is a Johnson Party"', *The i* (7 Feb. 2022).   29. Sebastian Payne, *The Fall of Boris Johnson* (London, 2022), pp. 27–30.   30. Cabinet Office, 'Investigation into alleged gatherings on government premises during Covid restrictions – update' (31 Jan. 2022), p. 8.   31. Cabinet Office, 'Findings of Second Permanent Secretary's investigation into alleged gatherings on government premises during Covid restrictions' (25 May 2022), p. 36. Alain Tolhurst, 'MPs left puzzled at "Abba Party" being abandoned by Sue Gray investigation', PoliticsHome (25 May 2022).   32. Ben Quinn, 'Byelection likely as Chris Pincher faces suspension over groping claims', *Guardian* (6 July 2023).   33. Henry Dyer, 'Downing Street "still not telling the truth" over Chris Pincher, former head of Foreign Office claims', *Business Insider* (5 July 2022). Glen Owen and Dan Hodges, 'He grabbed me', *Mail on Sunday* (2 July 2022).   34. Boris Johnson, 'Statement in 10 Downing Street' (7 July 2022).   35. Parth Patel, Ryan Swift and Harry Quilter-Pinner, 'Talking politics: building support for democratic reform', Institute for Public Policy Research (June 2023), p. 10.   36. George Parker, Jim Pickard and Jasmine Cameron-Chileshe, 'Rishi Sunak refuses to match Liz Truss on tax cuts', *Financial Times* (21 July 2022).   37. Insofar as there was a dispute about Brexit, it was a dispute about who had supported it first and supported it most passionately since. Few hustings went by without Sunak emphasizing that Truss had voted to Remain in 2016.   38. During their early leadership debates, Sunak's habit of interrupting Truss to attack the plausibility of her economic plans led to accusations of 'mansplaining'. Caroline Davies, 'Sunak's interruptions ignite debate over "mansplaining" in politics', *Guardian* (26 July 2022).   39. Boris Johnson, 'Final Speech as Prime Minister' (6 Sept. 2022).   40. Aubery Allegretti and Donna

Ferguson, 'Tory MP Scott Benton has whip suspended after newspaper sting', *Guardian* (5 Apr. 2023). **41.** Katharine Dommett, Andrew Hindmoor and Matthew Wood, 'Who meets whom: access and lobbying during the Coalition years', *British Journal of Politics and International Relations*, 19, 2 (2017): 389–407. For a discussion see Martin Kettle, 'It's time to give unions a seat at the table in talks about how Britain is run', *Guardian* (15 Dec. 2022). **42.** Nigel Boardman, 'Review into the development and use of supply chain finance (and associated schemes) in government, Part 1: report of the facts' (21 July 2021), p. 8. Jeremy Heywood's widow, Suzanne, has defended his actions. Toby Helm, 'My Jeremy was made scapegoat for Greensill affair, says Lady Heywood', *Guardian* (23 Jan. 2022). **43.** Heather Stewart and Kalyeena Makortoff, 'Business card puts Greensill founder at the heart of Downing Street', *Guardian* (30 Mar. 2021). **44.** BBC News, 'Greensill: David Cameron "made $10m" before company's collapse' (9 Aug. 2021). **45.** Gabriel Pogrund and Caroline Wheeler, 'David Cameron lobbied Number 10 and Hancock for Greensill', *The Times* (10 Apr. 2021). **46.** Jim Pickard, Cynthia O'Murchu and Robert Smith, 'David Cameron lobbied for Greensill access to Covid loan schemes', *Financial Times* (18 Mar. 2021). **47.** Alan McGuiness, 'Greensill lobbying scandal: the texts ex-PM Cameron sent to Sunak, Gove and top officials to lobby for Greensill', Sky News (12 May 2021). **48.** Treasury Select Committee, 'Lessons from Greensill Capital', HC 151 (20 July 2021), para 204. **49.** BBC News, 'In full: David Cameron's statement on Greensill row' (12 Apr. 2021). **50.** Channel 4 News, 'Revealed: PPE stockpile was out-of-date when coronavirus hit UK' (7 May 2020). **51.** Nigel Boardman, 'Boardman Review of government procurement in the Covid-19 pandemic' (8 Dec. 2020), pp. 23–4. **52.** National Audit Office, 'Investigation into government procurement during the Covid-19 pandemic', HC 959 (26 Nov. 2020), p. 9. **53.** Jane Bradley, Selam Gebrekidan and Allison McCann, 'Waste, negligence and cronyism: inside Britain's pandemic spending', *New York Times* (17 Dec. 2020). **54.** Cabinet Office, 'Response to article published by the *New York Times* on UK government procurement' (23 Dec. 2020). **55.** National Audit Office, 'Investigation into the management of PPE contracts', HC 1144 (30 Mar. 2022), p. 8. **56.** Andrew Woodcock, 'Matt Hancock acted unlawfully over Covid contract details, High Court judge rules', *Independent* (19 Feb. 2021). **57.** David Conn, 'Covid contract for firm run by Cummings' friends unlawful, finds judge', *Guardian* (9 June 2021). **58.** Martin Williams, 'Why government awarded "urgent" PPE contract to firm run by ex-associate of Tory peer Michelle Mone', *The Herald* (8 Oct. 2020). **59.** David Conn, 'Revealed: Tory peer Michelle Mone secretly received £29m from "VIP lane" PPE firm', *Guardian* (23 Nov. 2022).

34 CULTURE WARS

1 Alastair Campbell, *Diaries, Volume 3: Power and Responsibility* (London, 2011), p. 319. **2.** Anthony Downs, *An Economic Theory of Democracy* (New York, 1957). **3.** For a general review see Andrew Hindmoor and Taylor Brad, *Rational Choice*, 2nd edn (Basingstoke, 2015), pp. 48–78 for a more detailed account. **4.** On the nature of this second political dimension see the 'Political Compass' (https://www.politicalcompass.org) and Sarah Butt, Elizabeth Clery and John Curtice, *British Social Attitudes, 39th Report* (London, 2022), 'technical details'. **5.** See Robert Tombs, *The English and their History* (London, 2014), pp. 212–15 and Kevin Sharpe, 'Culture, politics, and the English Civil War', *Huntington Library Quarterly*, 51, 2 (1988): 95–135. **6.** Edmund Burke, *Reflections on the Revolution in France* (Stanford, CA, 2001 [1790]). Thomas Paine, *Rights of Man* (Cambridge, 2012 [1791]). **7.** Anthony Crosland, *The Future of Socialism* (London, 1956), p. 403. **8.** BBC News, 'On This Day: 1968, I remember being terrified'. **9.** Colin Brown, 'Bury Swampy remarks fuel gaffe machine', *Independent* (15 Mar. 1997). **10.** 'Tony Martin: Man who shot burglars knows he still divides opinion', BBC News (17 Aug.

2019). **11.** *Guardian*, 'Hague: I am on the side of people who protect their homes against criminals' (26 Apr. 2000). **12.** On foxhunting see Tony Blair, *A Journey* (London, 2010), p. 305. **13.** William Riker, *Liberalism Against Populism: A Confrontation Between the Theory of Democracy and the Theory of Social Choice* (San Francisco, 1982); William Riker, *The Art of Political Manipulation* (New Haven, CT, 1986); William Riker, 'The heresthetics of constitution-making: the presidency in 1787', *American Political Science Review*, 78, 1 (1984): 96–111; William Riker, *The Strategy of Rhetoric: Campaigning for the American Constitution* (New Haven, CT, 1996). Riker's focus is on American politics. Iain McLean has developed a series of clever applications relating to British politics in *Rational Choice and British Politics: An Analysis of Rhetoric and Manipulation from Peel to Blair* (Oxford, 2001). **14.** Liam Martin, '*Grand Theft Auto* blamed for London Riots', The Huffington Post (8 Aug. 2011). **15.** Sergeant Blackman's conviction was subsequently reduced to manslaughter in the light of new medical evidence presented by his defence team. He was released from prison in April 2017. **16.** See Liam Stanley, '"We're reaping what we sowed": Everyday crisis narratives and acquiescence to the age of austerity', *New Political Economy*, 19, 6 (2014): 895–917 and Liam Stanley, *Britain Alone: How a Decade of Conflict Remade the Economy* (Manchester, 2022). **17.** Maria Sobolewska and Robert Ford, *Brexitland* (Cambridge, 2020), p. 2. **18.** By the summer of 2019 only 6% of voters did not self-identify as either Leavers or Remainers. Robert Ford, Paula Surridge, Will Jennings and Tim Bale, *The British General Election of 2019* (Basingstoke, 2021), p. 29. **19.** Sarah Butt, Elizabeth Clery and John Curtice, 'Culture wars', in *British Social Attitudes, 39th Report* (London, 2022). **20.** John Dombrink, 'The withering of the culture war', The Conversation (5 Aug. 2015). Norman Lewis, 'The myth of Spiro Agnew's nattering nabobs of negativism', *American Journalism*, 27, 1 (2010): 89–115. **21.** Pat Buchanan, 'Culture War Speech', Voices of Democracy (17 Aug. 1992). **22.** Maggie Astor, 'What Trump, Biden and Obama said about the death of George Floyd', *New York Times* (29 May 2020). **23.** Michael Wines, 'Looting comment from Trump dates back to racial unrest of the 1960s', *New York Times* (29 May 2020). **24.** Taha Hashim, 'The extraordinary life of Azeem Rafiq', *Wisden* (17 Aug. 2020). **25.** Josh Noble, 'Racism and sexism "widespread" in English Cricket, report finds', *Financial Times* (27 June 2023). **26.** Emily Burack, 'Meghan Markle addresses that "straight outta Compton" story', *Town and Country* (24 Aug. 2022). **27.** Phil McCausland, 'Princess apologizes after wearing brooch deemed "racist" to lunch with Megan Markle', ABC News (22 Dec. 2017). On the 2004 incident see Marcus Warren, 'Princess Michael "told black diners to go back to colonies"', *Daily Telegraph* (27 May 2004). **28.** BBC News, 'Prince Harry and Meghan to step back as senior royals' (8 Jan. 2020). **29.** BBC News, 'Meghan and Harry interview: Racism claims, duke "let down" by dad, and duchess on Kate' (9 Mar. 2021). **30.** Georgia Aspinall, 'Here's the story behind Jeremy Clarkson's strange obsession with Meghan Markle', *Grazia* (19 June 2022). **31.** Pressure for a net zero referendum was initially mobilized by Nigel Farage. Glen Owen, 'Nigel Farage's new drive for vote to kill off Boris's ruinous green agenda', *Mail on Sunday* (5 Mar. 2022). **32.** Catherine Fairbairn, Doug Pyper and Bukky Balogun, 'Gender Recognition Act Reform: consultation and outcome', House of Commons Library, Briefing 09079 (17 Feb. 2022). **33.** Ruth Pearce, Sonja Erikainen and Ben Vincent, 'TERF wars: an introduction', *The Sociological Review*, 68, 4 (2020): 677–98. **34.** Rowena Mason, 'Theresa May plans to let people change gender without medical checks', *Guardian*, (18 Oct. 2017). **35.** J. K. Rowling, 'J. K. Rowling writes about her reasons for speaking out on sex and gender issues', Blogpost (10 June 2020). **36.** Boris Johnson, 'Conservative Party Speech' (6 Oct. 2020); Adrian Zozsut, 'Jacob Rees-Mogg in bizarre speech thanks "woke brigade" for tearing down historical statues', *The European* (21 Jan. 2021); Michelle Donelan, 'Minister Addresses Policy Exchange' (26 Apr. 2022); Oliver Dowden; 'Standing Up for our Values', Speech at the Heritage Foundation, Washington DC (15 Feb. 2022); and Faye Brown, 'Home Secretary Suella Braverman blames protest disruption on tofu-eating wokerati', Sky News (18 Oct. 2022). Also see *The Economist*, 'Tories bet on culture wars to unite disparate voters' (18 Feb. 2021); Robert Shrimsley, 'Conservative culture war is fight for new establishment', *Financial Times* (14 July 2021); and Sky News, 'Rishi Sunak attacks "hare brained" traffic schemes and vows to "slam the brakes on the war on motorists"' (30 Sept. 2023). The Conservatives also established a Commission on Race and Ethnic Disparities, the broad conclusions of which were that Britain had become a less racist society over time and that racism was not a systemic feature of British life. Commission on Race and Ethnic Disparities, 'The Report of the Commission on Race and Ethnic Disparities' (28 Apr. 2021). 37. Carl Schmidt, *The Concept of the Political* (Chicago, 1996). 38. See Stuart Ward, 'Independence referendum: how Yes won the social media war', The National (5 Sept. 2019) and Ana Langer, Michael Comerford and Des McNulty, 'Online allies and tricky freelancers: understanding the differences in the role of social media in the campaigns for the Scottish independence referendum', *Political Studies*, 67, 4 (2019): 834–54. 39. Stephen Coleman, 'New mediation and direct representation: reconceptualising representation in the digital age', *New Media and Society*, 7 (2005): 177–98. 40. Stephen Ward and Liam McLoughlin, 'Turds, traitors and tossers: the abuse of UK MPs via Twitter', *The Journal of Legislative Studies*, 26, 1 (2020): 47–73. 41. Georgia Wells, 'Twitter makes tweaks to punish "troll-like" behavior', *Wall Street Journal* (15 May 2018). 42. Ailbhe Rea, 'Inside Labour's "clusterfuck" week on trans rights', *New Statesman* (3 Apr. 2022). Joe Pike, 'Keir Starmer will lose election campaign on day one unless he shifts his trans rights position, Labour strategists warn', Sky News (24 Mar. 2023). 43. Andrew Anthony, 'Everything you wanted to know about the culture wars – but were afraid to ask', *Guardian* (13 June 2021). Sam Coates, 'Is Joe Biden woke? Boris Johnson says there's "nothing wrong" if he is', Sky News (21 Jan. 2021). 44. Coates, 'Is Joe Biden woke?'

35 GREAT POWERS

1 'The Kingdom of Welsh Noir' (https://www.malcolmpryce.com/). 2. Aberystwyth University, Department of International Politics, 'Timeline of events' (undated). 3. Aberystwyth's connection to realism was then maintained through the later appointments of Laurence Martin, Trevor Evans and, in the early 1980s, John Garnett. E. H. Carr, *The Twenty Years' Crisis* (London, 2001). E. H. Carr, *What is History?* (London, 1964). 4. The thumbnail description of realism offered here brushes over important differences between 'classical' and 'structural' realism. See Kenneth Waltz, *Theory of International Politics* (New York, 1979). 5. See Henry Farrell and Abraham Newman, 'The new interdependence approach: theoretical development and empirical demonstration', *Review of International Political Economy*, 23, 5 (2016): 713–36. 6. Stephen Krasner (ed.), *International Regimes* (Ithaca, NY, 1983). 7. Francis Fukuyama, *The End of History and the Last Man* (New York, 1992). 8. Ministry of Defence, *Strategic Defence Review: Modern Forces for the Modern World* (London, 1998), p. 2. 9. Claire Bigg, 'Russia: Putin, Blair meet to mend fences', Radio Free Europe (5 Oct. 2005). 10. Office for National Statistics, 'UK total trade: all countries, non-seasonally adjusted' (11 Aug. 2023). This dataset is regularly updated (although it is possible to access previous versions through an available link). The figures can be downloaded via an Excel file and these numbers are taken from tab 1. 11. Graham Allison, *Destined for War: Can China and America Escape Thucydides' Trap* (Cambridge, MA, 2017), p. 7. 12. Office for National Statistics, 'UK total trade: all countries'. 13. See Michael Francis, 'The effect of China on global prices', *Bank of Canada Review* (Autumn 2007), pp. 13–25. 14. See Larry Summers, 'The United States and the Global Adjustment Process', The Stavros Nicarchos Lecture, Institute for International Economics (23 Mar. 2004). 15. James Fallows, 'Be nice to the countries that lend to you',

The Atlantic (Dec. 2008). **16.** George Osborne, 'Speech to the Shanghai Stock Exchange' (22 Sept. 2015). **17.** See John Sweeney, Ed Vulliamy and Jens Holsoe, 'NATO bombed Chinese deliberately', *Observer* (17 Oct. 1999). **18.** Duncan Allan, 'Managed confrontation: UK policy towards Russia after the Salisbury attack', Chatham House Research Paper (30 Oct. 2018), p. 3. **19.** BBC News, 'Russia condemns NATO at UN' (25 Mar. 1999). **20.** Arms Control Association, 'Russia's national security concept' (2000). **21.** Christian Snyder, 'How a 1999 NATO operation turned Russia against the West', *The Pitt News* (6 Sept. 2017). **22.** The President of Russia, Vladimir Putin, 'On the Historical Unity of Russians and Ukrainians' (12 July 2021). **23.** The President of Russia, 'Joint Statement of the Russian Federation and the People's Republic of China on International Relations Entering a New Era and Global Sustainable Development' (4 Feb. 2022). **24.** Meredith Cash, 'Putin appeared to get caught sleeping during the opening ceremony at the Beijing Olympics', Insider (4 Feb. 2022). **25.** UN News, 'Ukraine: UN General Assembly demands Russia reverse course on 'attempted illegal annexation' (12 Oct. 2022). **26.** Bloomberg News, 'Sanctions on Russia puts focus on China's Central Bank' (28 Feb. 2022). **27.** Enerdata, 'Russia's oil and gas revenues grew by 28% in 2022' (17 Jan. 2023). **28.** John J. Mearsheimer and Stephen M. Walt, 'An unnecessary war', Foreign Policy (Jan. 2003). **29.** Henry Kissinger, *Diplomacy* (New York, 1994). Timothy Bella, 'Kissinger says Ukraine should cede territory to Russia to end war', *Washington Post* (24 May 2022). **30.** See John J. Mearsheimer, 'Why the Ukraine crisis is the West's fault: the liberal delusions that provoked Putin', *Foreign Affairs*, 93, 5 (2014): 77–127; John Mearschemier, 'Why the West is principally responsible for the Ukrainian crisis', *The Economist* (19 Mar. 2022); and Isaac Chotiner, 'Why John Mearsheimer blames the U.S. for the crisis in Ukraine', *The New Yorker* (1 Mar. 2022). **31.** Hans Morgenthau, *Politics Amongst Nations: The Struggle for Power and Peace* (New York, 1948), p. 430. **32.** Kenneth Liebertha, 'The American pivot to Asia', The Brookings Institute (21 Dec. 2011). **33.** Graham Allison, 'The Thucydides Trap: are the U.S. and China headed for war?', *The Atlantic* (24 Sept. 2015). Allison developed the argument further in his *Destined for War*. **34.** Allison, *Destined for War*, p. 244. **35.** Michael Beckley, 'The power of nations: measuring what matters', *International Security*, 43, 2 (2018): 7–44. **36.** Joseph Nye, 'How not to deal with a rising China: a US perspective', *International Affairs*, 98, 5 (2022): 1635–51. **37.** See Rosemary Foot and Amy King, 'China's world view in the Xi Jinping era: where do Japan, Russia and the USA fit?', *British Journal of Politics and International Relations*, 23, 2 (2021): 210–27 and Shaun Breslin, 'Divided but not poles apart: Europe, the United States, and the rise of China', *Asian Perspective*, 45, 1 (2021): 177–90. **38.** Alan Rappeport, 'Yellen says bid to decouple from China would be disastrous', *New York Times* (13 January 2023). **39.** Jamie McGeever, 'China slips away from Treasuries but sticks with dollar bonds, Reuters (23 Feb. 2023). **40.** Daniel Drezner, Henry Farrell and Abraham Newman (eds.), *The Uses and Abuses of Weaponized Interdependence* (Washington, DC, 2021). **41.** See Chris Miller, *Chip War: The Fight for the World's Most Critical Technology* (New York, 2022). **42.** See Patrick McGee, 'How Apple tied its fortunes to China', *Financial Times* (17 Jan. 2023). **43.** See John Kampfner, *Blair's Wars* (London, 2003), p. 117 and Annabelle Dickson, 'Boris Johnson's parting shot: "Stay close to the Americans"', Politico (20 July 2022). **44.** Geoff Dyer and George Parker, 'US attacks UK's "constant accommodation" with China', *Financial Times* (12 Mar. 2015). **45.** Theresa May, 'Statement from the New Prime Minister' (13 July 2016). **46.** Prime Minister's Office, 10 Downing Street, 'PM call with President Xi' (25 Sept. 2017). **47.** Ross Gibson, 'Chinese repression of Muslims in Xinjiang: economic benefit can no longer be valued over human rights', The Organization for World Peace (9 June 2019). **48.** Reuters, 'China says agrees with Britain to discuss "top notch" free trade deal' (25 Aug. 2018). **49.** See Guy Faulconbridge and Kylie MacLellan, 'British PM on Huawei: We will do 5G without hurting security', Reuters (27 Jan. 2020). **50.** Leo Kelion, 'Huawei 5G kit must be removed from UK by 2027', BBC News (14 July

2020). 51. Dominic Nicholls, 'MI5 chief: Russia's intelligence services provide "bursts of bad weather", China is "changing the climate"', *Daily Telegraph* (14 Oct. 2020). 52. Natasha Kuhrt, 'Why the Integrated Defence Review treats Russia and China differently', King's College London, News Centre (19 Mar. 2021). 53. International Relations and Defence Committee, 'The UK and China's security and trade relationship: a strategic void', House of Lords, HL62 (10 Sept. 2021), p. 53. 54. Patrick Wintour, 'UK MPs declare China is committing genocide against Uyghurs in Xinjiang', *Guardian* (22 Apr. 2021). 55. *The Economist*, 'Britain's government is trying to protect national security' (8 Jan. 2022). 56. BBC News, 'AUKUS: France pulls out of UK defence talks amid row' (20 Sept. 2021). 57. Richard Moore, Speech, International Institute for Strategic Studies (30 Nov. 2021). 58. Fiona Hamilton, 'Minister promises inquiry into Chinese "agent" with links to Labour', *The Times* (14 Jan. 2022). 59. George Parker and Felicia Schwartz, 'Liz Truss admits UK trade deal with US is not on the agenda', *Financial Times* (20 Sept. 2022). 60. Waltz, *Theory of International Politics*, p. 153. 61. HM Treasury, 'Public Expenditure Statistical Analyses', Chapter 4, Table 4.3 (20 July 2022). 62. Ministry of Defence, 'Quarterly Service Personnel Statistics' (10 Mar. 2022). *Guardian*, Data Blog, 'Army cuts: how have UK Armed Forces personnel numbers changed over time?'. The figures here relate to regular personnel and are exclusive of part-time territorial forces. 63. Historic UK, 'The Royal Navy's size throughout history' (undated). 64. Joel Adams, 'Exclusive: RAF has smallest combat force in history with fewest fighter jets after shrinking by nearly half in just 12 years', *Daily Mail* (26 June 2019). 65. Sam Jones, 'Britain's "withered" forces not fit to repel all-out attack', *Financial Times* (16 Sept. 2016). 66. Kit Heren, 'Government has "hollowed out and underfunded" the British Army, Defence Secretary Ben Wallace admits', LBC News (30 Jan. 2023). 67. Claire Mills and Esme Kirk-Wade, 'The cost of the UK's strategic nuclear deterrent', House of Commons Library Briefing 8166 (3 May 2023), p. 4. 68. Boris Johnson, Speech, 'Britain is Back East of Suez' (9 Dec. 2016). 69. Global Times, 'UK should not tempt its own fate in South China Sea' (29 July 2021). 70. Jonathan Beale, 'HMS *Queen Elizabeth*: Why is a UK aircraft carrier going on a world tour?', BBC News (21 May 2021). 71. *The Economist*, 'Carriers are big, expensive, vulnerable and popular' (14 Nov. 2019). 72. Sir David Richards, *Taking Command* (London, 2014), p. 5 and Ben Glaze, 'Lack of investment is damaging Britain's "Jedi Knight" Army', *Daily Mirror* (13 May 2019). 73. Paul Kennedy, *The Rise and Fall of the Great Powers* (New York, 1987).

36 IN THE RED

1 British Medical Association, 'NHS backlog data analysis' (undated). 2. John Burn-Murdoch, 'Chronic illness makes UK workforce the sickest in developed world', *Financial Times* (21 July 2022). *The Economist*, 'Illness is stopping Britons coming back to work' (26 Jan. 2023). 3. James Billot, 'What's the truth about casualty numbers in Ukraine?', UnHerd (25 Jan. 2023). 4. David Sheppard, 'Why are UK home energy bills going through the roof?', *Financial Times* (26 Aug. 2022). 5. *The Economist*, 'Britain well-placed to cope with a downturn in the housing market, but it will still hurt' (19 Jan. 2023). 6. Office for National Statistics, 'Average weekly earnings in Great Britain, December 2022' (13 Dec. 2022). 7. Office for Budget Responsibility, '% debt interest (central government, net of APF)' (March 2022). Also see Paul Tucker, 'Quantitative easing, monetary policy implementation and the public finances', Institute for Fiscal Studies (14 Oct. 2022), p. 2. 8. Mary McDougall, 'UK to run up highest debt interest bill in developed world', *Financial Times* (25 July 2023). 9. Torsten Bell, 'New Year's Outlook, 2023: They think it's all over ... it isn't now', The Resolution Foundation (30 Dec. 2022). 10. Office for National Statistics, 'Consumer Price Inflation, UK: May 2023' (21 June 2023). 11. Office for

National Statistics, 'Gross Domestic Product: year on year growth' (11 Aug. 2023). Office for National Statistics, 'GDP quarterly national accounts, UK: April to June 2023', (8) international comparisons' (29 Sept. 2023). The ONS revised its figures for post-Covid GDP in September 2023. See Roula Khalaf, 'UK economy bounced back from Covid, ONS revisions reveal', *Financial Times* (1 Sept. 2023). **12.** Office for National Statistics, 'Gross Domestic Product: year on year growth' (11 August 2023). **13.** Institute for Fiscal Studies, 'Living standards, poverty and inequality in the UK' (undated). These figures are routinely updated. The ones used here were downloaded in June 2023. **14.** Office for National Statistics, 'Average weekly earnings in Great Britain: March 2023' (14 March 2023) (X09: Real average weekly earnings using Consumer Price Inflation). **15.** Institute for Fiscal Studies, 'Living standards, poverty and inequality'. *Before* housing cost inequality fell from 0.358 in 2007/8 to 0.347 in 2015/16, before then falling to 0.342 in 2021/2. **16.** Office for National Statistics, 'Household total wealth in Great Britain: April 2018 to March 2020' (7 Jan. 2022). **17.** OECD Data, 'Income inequality' (on the basis of the most recent available figures). In 2020 the US Coefficient was 0.377 and the British one 0.355. **18.** Institute for Fiscal Studies, 'Living standards, poverty and inequality'. **19.** The Trussell Trust, 'Hunger in the UK' (June 2023), p. 12. **20.** Department for Levelling-Up, Housing and Communities, 'Rough sleeping snapshot in England: Autumn 2022' (28 Feb. 2023). **21.** HM Treasury, 'Public expenditure statistical analyses 2022', Chapter Four, Tables, Table 4.1 (20 July 2022). **22.** Institute for Fiscal Studies, Tax Lab, 'How have government revenues changed over time?' (undated). **23.** Andrew Turnbull, 'Overcoming barriers to tax reform', Institute for Government (12 Sept. 2019), p. 8. **24.** Office for National Statistics, 'Public sector finances', Tables 1 to 10: Appendix A (21 July 2023). Mehreen Khan, 'UK net debt above 100% of GDP for the first time since 1961', *The Times* (22 June 2023). **25.** HM Treasury, 'Public expenditure statistical analyses 2022', Chapter Four, Table 4.1 (20 July 2022). **26.** Louise Marshall, David Finch, Liz Cairncross and Jo Bibby, 'Mortality and life expectancy trends in the UK', The Health Foundation (Nov. 2019), p. 2. **27.** Office for National Statistics, 'Monthly mortality analysis: England and Wales: March 2023' (25 Apr. 2023). Also see *The Economist*, 'Britain has endured a decade of early deaths. Why?' (9 Mar. 2023). **28.** Office for National Statistics, 'Living longer and old-age dependency – what does the future hold?' (24 June 2019). **29.** Department for Business, Energy and Industrial Strategy, '2021 UK greenhouse gas emissions, provisional figures' (31 Mar. 2022). **30.** Resolution Foundation, *Stagnation Nation: Navigating a Route to a Fairer and More Prosperous Britain* (London, 2022), pp. 75–6. **31.** Attracta Mooney, Camila Hodgson and Jim Pickard, 'UK admits revised net zero strategy will fail to hit emission targets', *Financial Times* (30 Mar. 2023). **32.** Climate Change Committee, 'Progress in reducing emissions' (June 2023), p. 13. **33.** Adam Vaughan, 'Net Zero: UK is being left behind, big business warns Rishi Sunak', *The Times* (19 July 2023). Jim Pickard and Attracta Mooney, 'UK's green halo fades under Sunak leadership', *Financial Times* (20 July 2023). **34.** BBC News, 'Rishi Sunak: Banning things not right approach to net zero' (29 July 2023). Also see Rishi Sunak, 'PM Speech on Net Zero' (20 Sept. 2023). **35.** Our World in Data, 'CO2 emissions from fossil fuels' (undated). International Energy Agency, 'CO2 emissions in 2022' (Mar. 2023). **36.** John Springford, 'The cost of Brexit until June 2022', Centre for European Reform (21 Dec. 2022). **37.** *The Economist*, 'Britain's car making industry is increasingly under threat' (24 Jan 2023). **38.** *The Economist*, 'Britain's stockmarket has languished. Its gilt market may be next' (2 Mar. 2023). **39.** Szu Ping Chan and Tim Wallace, 'Brexit is to blame for inflation, claims Mark Carney', *Daily Telegraph* (16 June 2023). **40.** Tom McTague and Francesco Guerrera, 'Britain's Singapore threat', Politico (25 Nov. 2020). **41.** Henry Zeffman, 'UK trade deal with Australia gave too much away', *The Times* (15 Nov. 2022). **42.** Penny Mordaunt, 'Speech to the Institute for Government Annual Conference' (18 Jan. 2023). **43.** Prime Minister's Office, 10 Downing Street, 'Liz Truss's Statement' (6 Sept. 2022). Aletha Adu, 'Liz Truss Jenga-style podium cost taxpayers £4,175', *Guardian* (18 Jan. 2023). **44.** George Parker, Jim Pickard and Chris Giles, 'Liz Truss unveils £150bn UK energy plan but limits business support', *Financial Times* (8 Sept. 2022). **45.** Henry Zeffman, 'Liz Truss accused of trying to avoid scrutiny over Budget', *The Times* (22 Aug. 2022). BBC News, 'Bank of England wasn't briefed on mini-budget' (19 Oct. 2022). **46.** Tom Rees, Ben Riley-Smith, Tim Wallace and Hannah Boland, 'IMF urges Truss to reverse top rate tax cut in rare intervention', *Daily Telegraph* (27 Sept. 2022). **47.** Bank of England, 'Bank of England announces gilt market operation' (28 Sept. 2022). **48.** *The Economist*, 'Liz Truss has made Britain a riskier bet for bond investors' (11 Oct. 2022). **49.** Truss later described the joke as 'puerile' and argued that the media had not engaged with or properly understood her economic programme. Sky News, 'Liz Truss says lettuce live stream was "puerile" and claims of dressing similar to Thatcher are lazy thinking' (19 June 2023). **50.** Jamie Grierson, 'Boris Johnson had enough backers to challenge Rishi Sunak, says 1922 chair', *Guardian* (4 Nov. 2022). **51.** Prime Minister's Office, 10 Downing Street, 'Prime Minister Outlines his Five Key Priorities for 2023' (4 Jan. 2023). **52.** Katy Balls, 'The plot against the PM', *Spectator* (17 June 2023). Faye Brown, 'Boris Johnson stands down as MP with immediate effect', Sky News (10 June 2023). **53.** OECD, 'Productivity per hour worked' (undated). **54.** The World Bank, Data, 'Gross Capital Formation (% of GDP)' (undated). **55.** HM Treasury, 'Public expenditure statistical analyses 2022', Chapter Four, Table 4.1 (20 July 2022). **56.** Office for National Statistics, 'Business investment in the UK: October to December 2022: revised results', Section (3), whole economy investment (31 Mar. 2023). **57.** Tony Blair, 'The Stakeholder Economy', Speech to the Singapore Business Community, 8 Jan. 1996, in Tony Blair, *New Britain: My Vision of a Young Country* (London, 1996), p. 295. **58.** David Walker, 'A review of corporate governance in UK Banks and other financial industry entities: final recommendations' (26 Nov. 2009). **59.** John Kay, 'The Kay Review of UK equity markets and long-term decision making, final report' (July 2012), p. 10. **60.** Theresa May made reform of corporate governance a priority when she became prime minister. See Department for Business, Energy and Industrial Strategy, 'Corporate governance reform, Green Paper' (Nov. 2016), p. 32. **61.** London Stock Exchange, 'FTSE 250' (undated). **62.** On overall levels of profit see OECD, *Economic Outlook*, Issue 1 (2023), Box 1.2, 'The Contribution of Unit Profits to Domestic Inflationary Pressures'. **63** AJ Bell, 'Dividend dashboard' (2021). During the pandemic dividend payments fell but still exceeded £60bn. **64.** See, for example, HM Treasury, 'Productivity in the UK: the regional dimension' (Nov. 2001); HM Treasury, 'A Modern regional policy for the United Kingdom' (Mar. 2003); and Ed Balls, 'Britain's new regional policy: sustainable growth and full employment for Britain's regions', in Ed Balls and John Healey (eds.), *Towards a New Regional Policy: Delivering Growth and Full Employment* (London, 2000). **65.** Department for Levelling-Up, Housing and Communities, 'Levelling-Up the United Kingdom' (2 Feb. 2022). **66.** Office for National Statistics, 'Regional labour productivity, UK: 2020' (16 June 2022). **67.** Scott Corfe, Aveek Bhattachyra and Richard Hyde, 'Banking and competition in the UK economy', Social Market Foundation (May 2021), p. 17. **68.** Stephen Davies, 'Competition and concentration: charting the fault lines', Centre for Competition Policy, Working Paper 21-11 (2 Dec. 2021). Also see Competition and Markets Authority, 'The state of UK competition' (30 Nov. 2020) and The Resolution Foundation, 'Is everybody concentrating? Recent trends in product and labour market concentration in the UK' (26 July 2018). **69.** Bruce Caldwell, 'Hayek's Nobel', in Peter Boettke and Virgil Storr (eds.), *Revisiting Hayek's Political Economy* (Bingley, 2017), pp. 1–20. **70.** *Rules and Order* was first published in 1973. The following year Hayek was awarded the Nobel Prize for Economics. *The Mirage of Social Justice* was published in 1976 and *The Political Order of a Free People* in 1979. *Law, Legislation and Liberty* was first published as a single volume in 1982. Friedrich Hayek, *Law, Legislation and Liberty* (London, 1982). **71.** European Commission, Secretariat-General, *Facing the Challenge:*

The Lisbon Strategy for Growth and Employment: Report from the High Level Group Chaired by Wim Kok (Brussels, 2004), p. 8.   72. Eurofound, 'Chancellor Proposes Agenda 2010 to Revive Economy' (30 Mar. 2003).   73. International Monetary Fund, 'People's Republic of China: Staff Report for the 2004 Article IV Consultation' (5 Nov. 2004). Loren Brandt and Thomas Rawski, *China's Great Economic Transformation* (Cambridge, 2010).   74. Nathan Gardels, 'Stiglitz: The fall of Wall Street is to market fundamentalism what the fall of the Berlin Wall was to Communism', The Huffington Post (17 Oct. 2008).   75. Charles Tilly, *Coercion, Capital and European States, AD 990–1990* (Cambridge, MA, 1990), p. 70. Also see Charles Tilly, 'Reflections on the history of European state making', in Charles Tilly (ed.), *The Formation of National States in Western Europe* (Princeton, NJ, 1975).   76. Linda Colley, *Britons: Forging the Nation 1707–1837* (New Haven, CT, 1992), p. 1.   77. Paul Addison, *The Road to 1945* (London, 1975), p. 14.   78. Chris Miller, *Chip War: The Fight for the World's Most Critical Technology* (New York, 2022), Part VII. Qianer Liu, 'China gives chipmakers new powers to guide industry recovery', *Financial Times* (21 Mar. 2023).   79. Laura Tyson and Lenny Mendonca, 'America's new era of industrial policy', Project Syndicate (2 Jan. 2023). *The Economist*, 'Joe Biden attempts the biggest overhaul of America's economy in decades' (27 Oct. 2022). On new antitrust measures see Joe Biden, 'Remarks by President Biden at Signing of Executive Order Promoting Competition in the American Economy', The White House (9 July 2021).   80. Rachel Reeves, 'Securonomics', Speech, Peterson Institute, Washington DC (24 May 2023).   81. European Commission, 'The green deal industrial plan: Putting Europe's net zero industry in the lead' (1 Feb. 2023).

CONCLUSION

1 Karl Marx, *The Eighteenth Brumaire of Louis Napoleon* (London, 2013 [1852]).   2. A strong defence of the role of parties within a democracy is offered by Robert Goodin, *Innovating Democracy: Democratic Theory and Practice* (Oxford, 2008), pp. 204–34. Also see Jonathan White and Lea Ypi, *The Meaning of Partisanship* (Oxford, 2016).   3. See Meg Russell and Philip Cowley, 'The policy power of the Westminster Parliament: the "parliamentary state" and the empirical evidence', *Governance*, 29, 1 (2016): 121–37.   4. See Richard Kelly, 'Peerage creations since 1997', House of Commons Library, Briefing Paper 5876 (Feb. 2020).   5. Catherine Haddon, 'Permanent secretaries', Institute of Government (12 Mar. 2020) and Patrick Diamond and Dave Richards, 'What does Dominic Raab's resignation tell us about the current state of minister–civil servant relations?', Mile End Institute (22 Apr. 2023).   6. See BBC News, 'In Graphics: The politics of quangos' (3 Feb. 2014); Commissioner for Public Appointments, 'Annual report, 2021–22' (Jan. 2023), pp. 52–5; and George Grylls and Oliver Wright, 'Tories make donors and friends directors of Civil Service boards', *The Times* (5 Aug. 2020).   7. Michael Savage and Toby Helm, 'Keir Starmer defies call for changes to first past the post voting system', *Guardian* (24 Sept. 2022). David Ward and Abbie Jones, 'Electoral reform has gone from niche to consensus view – Labour must back PR', Labour List (16 June 2023).   8. Kate Dommett, *The Reimagined Party: Democracy, Change and the Public* (Manchester, 2020), pp. 118, 122.   9. Rory Stewart, *Politics on the Edge: A Memoir from Within* (London, 2023), p. 4.   10. Max Weber, 'Politics as a vocation', in H. H. Gerth and C. Wright Mills (eds.), *From Max Weber: Essays in Sociology* (London, 1970 [1919]), p. 128.   11. See Richard Cracknell and Richard Tunnicliffe, 'Social background of MPs, 1979–2019', House of Commons Library, Briefing Paper 7483 (15 Feb. 2022); Timothy Peace, 'Scottish Parliament Election 2021: What happened? Where do we go from here?', Race.Ed (17 May 2021); and Senedd Research, 'Election 2021: How diverse is the sixth Senedd?' (11 May 2021).   12. See Matthew Burton and Richard Tunnicliffe, 'Membership of political parties in Great Britain',

House of Commons Library, Research Briefing SN05125 (30 Aug. 2022). **13.** Adam Smith, *An Inquiry into the Nature and Causes of the Wealth of Nations* (Oxford, 1992 [1776]), p. 349. **14.** On the democratic virtues of compromise see Richard Bellamy, *Liberalism and Pluralism: Towards a Politics of Compromise* (London, 1999); Richard Bellamy, 'Democracy, compromise, and the representation paradox: coalition government and political integrity', *Government and Opposition*, 47, 3 (2012): 441–65; Christian Rostboll, 'Democratic respect and compromise', *Critical Review of International Social and Political Philosophy*, 20, 5 (2017): 619–35; and Simon May, 'Principled compromise and the abortion controversy', *Philosophy & Public Affairs*, 33, 4 (2005): 317–48. **15.** See Andy Bounds and Alan Smith, 'Levelling up bias in favour of Tory seats "pretty blatant"', *Financial Times* (5 Mar. 2021) and Samir Jeraj and Ben Walker, 'The return of pork barrel politics', *New Statesman* (13 Sept. 2021). **16.** Tom Sasse, Tim Durrant, Emma Norris and Ketaki Zodgekar, 'Government reshuffles: the case for keeping ministers longer', Institute for Government (Jan. 2022). **17.** See ibid., pp. 7–8. **18.** Spencer Stuart, 'Board Composition, 22 UK Spencer Stuart Board Index'. **19.** Ryan Bembridge, 'Rory Stewart: Time for ministers to serve two years minimum', Property Wire (13 Nov. 2023). **20.** Rhys Clyne and Maddy Bishop, 'Staff turnover in the Civil Service', Institute of Government (12 Apr. 2022) and Emma Norris and Tom Sasse, 'Moving on: the cost of high staff turnover in the Civil Service', Institute of Government (15 Jan. 2019). **21.** Winston Churchill, Parliament Bill, House of Commons Debates (11 Nov. 1947). **22.** Sarah Piddy and Daniel Rogers, 'Successful Private Members' Bills since 1984', House of Commons Library (9 May 2022). **23.** In recent years successful PMBs have, for example, resulted in British Sign Language being recognised as an official language and imposed a legal requirement upon the Secretary of State to give guidance to relevant authorities on steps they must take to meet the needs of people with Down's syndrome. **24.** UK Parliament, 'Select committees'. **25.** See Philip Lynch and Richard Whitaker, 'Unity and divisions on departmental select committees: a Brexit effect?', *The British Journal of Politics and International Relations*, 23, 3 (2021): 471–87 and Adam Mellows-Facer, Chloe Challender and Paul Evans, 'Select committees: agents of change', *Parliamentary Affairs*, 72, 4 (2019): 903–22. **26.** See Andrew Hindmoor, Philip Larkin and Andrew Kennon, 'Assessing the influence of select committees in the UK: the Education and Skills Committee, 1997–2005', *The Journal of Legislative Studies*, 15, 1 (2009): 71–89. **27.** The Constitution Unit, 'Government defeats in the House of Lords'. **28.** UK Parliament, 'The Parliament Acts'. **29.** The Universal Declaration states that: 'The will of the people shall be the basis of the authority of government; this will shall be expressed in periodic and genuine elections which shall be by universal and equal suffrage and shall be held by secret vote or by equivalent free voting procedures.' **30.** Thomas Smith, 'Democracy and Pontefract cakes: the story of the secret ballot', *Pomfretian* (May 2019). **31.** For a rare argument advancing the case for open (non-secret) ballots as a way of enhancing legitimacy see Geoffrey Brennan and Philip Pettit, 'Unveiling the vote', *British Journal of Political Science*, 20, 3 (1990): 311–33. **32.** See Jennifer Walpole and Richard Kelly, 'The Whip's Office', House of Commons Library, Research Briefing SN/PC/02829 (10 Oct. 2008), p. 2. **33.** Dommett, *The Reimagined Party*, p. 149. **34.** ITV News, 'Tory MP Will Wragg accuses No 10 of "blackmailing" MPs over opposition to Boris Johnson' (20 Jan. 2022). **35.** Peter Walker and Jessica Elgot, 'Tory defector says whips told him to back PM or lose school funds', *Guardian* (20 Jan. 2022). **36.** Kevin Schofield, 'Met Police will not take any action over allegation of bullying by Tory MPs', The Huffington Post (9 Feb. 2022). **37.** The Seven Principles of Public Life (also known as the Nolan Principles after Lord Michael Nolan, the first chair of the Committee on Standards in Public Life established in 1994) apply to anyone who works as a public officeholder. Committee on Standards in Public Life, 'The Seven Principles of Public Life' (31 May 1995). **38.** A larger number of MPs have sat as independents either when they have resigned from or been suspended by their party. **39.** So-called because the candidates mixed 'blue' conservative economic policies with a 'green' priority on climate change. Calla Wahlquist, 'Teal independents: who are they and how did they upend Australia's election?', *Guardian* (23 May 2022).   40. Sortition, that is lottery, was a staple of Athenian notions of democracy and was seen as embodying the democratic principle of equality. See Bernard Manin, *The Principles of Representative Government* (Cambridge, 2010).   41. Rahm Emanuel, 'CEO Council', *Wall Street Journal* (19 Nov. 2008). Winston Churchill is often said to have said the same thing when working to establish the United Nations, although no formal record of his doing so exists.   42. Andrew Blick and Peter Hennessy, 'Good chaps no more? Safeguarding the constitution in stressful times', The Constitution Society (18 Nov. 2019). Tom Clark, 'Johnson has killed off the "good chaps" theory of government', *Prospect* (21 Jan. 2022). *The Economist*, 'Britain's good chap model of government is coming apart' (18 Dec. 2018).   43. Henry Mance, 'Peter Hennessy on Boris Johnson's government', *Financial Times* (23 May 2022).

Index

armed forces – *cont'd.*
145, 159–60, 164–6, 170, 171;
occupation of Helmand Province,
145, 167–8, 171, 494; 'Operation
Enduring Freedom' in Afghanistan,
148; provides security at 2012
Olympics, 311; shrinking size of
Army and Navy, 475
Armitage, Richard, 155
Arsenal FC, 141
Ashdown, Paddy, 151, 268–9, 277
Ashley, Mike, 137
Asian Infrastructure
Investment Bank, 472
Aston Villa FC, 135, 139
AstraZeneca, 426
asylum-seekers, 84, 85, 285, 297–8,
494, 508–9; boats carrying in
English Channel, 10, 485; housing
of as culture war issue, 460;
Rwanda plan, 304–5
Athletic Bilbao, 134
Atkinson, Rowan, 313
Attlee, Clement, 251
austerity, Coalition, 3, 80, 297, 299,
494; arguments against, 282–3,
288–9; arguments in favour of,
280–82, 287–8, 289, 291; and
Brexit vote, 372; broad measure of
public support for, 259, 284–5, 352;
Clegg and Alexander as unwavering
on, 273–4; Corbyn's opposition to,
293, 351, 352–3; and culture wars,
455; economic consequences of,
287–92, 317, 479; and fairness,
281, 283; financial crisis provides
context for, 2, 10, 212; and
inequality, 283, 288–9, 479;
investment during, 105, 290–91;
Labour viewed as to blame for, 285,
286, 287, 501; NHS as exempt
from, 280, 281, 288; political mood
over changes (from 2016), 292–3,
351, 352, 372; possible excess

deaths due to, 289; presented as
solution to emergency, 279–80, 281,
282, 290; productivity during, 290,
292, 486; protest marches against
spending cuts, 284, 294; public
sector debt increases during,
289–90; rising welfare expenditure
during, 288; SNP opposition to, 68,
323, 324; spending cuts in northern
Ireland, 378, 380; 'we're all in it
together' framing of, 265,
283, 284, 319
Australia, 371, 374, 439, 473–4, 483,
507
autism, 128

Badham, Samantha, 173
BAE Systems, 40
Bailey, Andrew, 436
Bailey, Bex, 393
Baird, Vera, 402
Baker, Norman, 162
Baker, Steve, 366
Baldwin, Stanley, 73
Balls, Ed, 100–101, 263, 286
Bank for International Settlements,
101
Bank of America, 240
Bank of Credit and Commerce
International, 100, 233
Bank of England: and bank credit
creation, 98; and Brexit campaign,
367, 373, 455; Court of, 227*, 227;
and financial crisis (2008), 211, 236,
241–2, 245–6; independence of, 17,
41, 61, 88–9, 100, 125, 200, 214,
496–7, 507–8; inflation targeting,
214, 245; inflation/cost-of-living
crisis (from 2022), 477–8; King's
Mansion House speech (2009), 247,
248, 285–6; and Kwarteng's mini
budget, 484, 485; and light-touch
regulation, 100, 236; and Northern
Rock, 227–8; and party politics,

history, British – *cont'd.*
emergence of mutual/building
societies, 228; Gladstone's liberal
interventionism, 154; gradual
formation of United Kingdom, 9;
James I's treatment of Parliament,
413*, 438; mobilizations for
warfare, 491; no golden age of
politics in Britain, 6; prequels to
recent crises, 4; previous eras of
globalization, 133–4, 135–6; roots
of cultural division over social
freedom, 452–3; Suez crisis (1956),
145*, 251, 476
Hitchens, Christopher, 302
Hodge, Margaret, 243
Hogg, Quintin, Baron Hailsham,
496*, 496
homosexuality: and age of consent,
296; attitudes of religious
organizations, 298, 300–301, 305;
and civil partnership, 296, 297; gay
marriage, 74, 265, 295, 297–300,
305, 307, 364, 454, 460, 494;
homophobia, 50; legalization in
1960s, 452; New Labour's record
on, 296, 298; Section 28
controversy, 296, 297, 452
Hong Kong, 465, 473
Hoon, Geoff, 151, 158, 243, 256
Hopkins, Kelvin, 393
'Horizon' computer system, 344–5
Houghton, General Sir Nicholas,
475–6
House of Lords, 25, 61, 259, 273,
305, 496, 497, 504–5, 506
housing market: and 'Baby Boomers',
219–20, 221; 'buy-to-let' mortgages,
220; development firms' large
profits, 218–19; 'Generation Rent',
221; and green belts, 217–18;
history of mutual/building societies,
228; and house building, 215–17;
housing associations, 217;

housing-benefit expenditure, 224–5;
housing/design/DIY TV
programmes, 213–14; impact of
boom on inequality, 221–3, 222;
impact of financial crisis, 216;
impact of partyocracy, 500; land
banking by developers, 218–19;
landlords, 220, 221; low interest
rates in 2000s, 215, 217, 219, 223,
224; and New Labour, 10, 212,
217–18, 223–5; owner-occupiers,
219–20, 221; and planning system,
216–17; proliferation of 'shameful
shoebox homes' in 2000s, 224;
rising prices in 2000s, 105, 213–16,
218–19, 223–4; Russian ownership
of property, 215, 465; taxpayers
money thrown at, 224–5; tenants/
renters as losers in, 220–21;
Thatcher's 'right to buy'
programme, 212, 217, 219
Howard, John, 374
Howard, Michael, 69, 73, 74, 79, 84,
454
HSBC, 103, 367
Huawei, 473
Huhne, Chris, 270, 271
Hume, John, 187, 189, 190
Huntingdon, Samuel, 180–81
Hurd, Douglas, 76
Hutton, Brian, 6, 163, 202, 261
Hutton, Will, 114, 115, 137
Hyde, Marina, 398

I'm a Celebrity (TV show), 253, 404
IBM, 113
'Ice Bucket' challenge (2014), 292
Icera (semiconductor firm), 113
ICL, 113, 344–5
Iksil, Bruno, 247
Ilyas, Mohammed, 179
Imagination Technologies, 113
immigration: and 2010 general
election, 334; and 2015 general

politicians: absence of public trust in,
6–7, 29–30, 34, 65, 69, 92, 128,
211–12, 258–60, 353, 373–4,
438–9, 445; careers as increasingly
short, 502–3; choices of, 494; and
Christianity, 302–3; expenses
scandal (2009), 2, 3, 7, 211–12,
243, 252–3, 255–60, 322–3, 439;
greater trust in Scottish government,
330–31; and #MeToo movement,
393–4; no golden age of trust in,
6–7; number of female MPs, 63, 75,
402; overuse of terms 'crisis' and
'emergency', 279, 495; politics as
profoundly challenging activity,
499; and Richard Scarry Rule, 46;
soaring of trust levels during
pandemic, 439–40; and strong prior
local connections, 54; 'Veracity
Index' (Ipsos), 7
Poots, Edwin, 387
populist politics: attacks on experts,
129, 373–4; and climate change,
127, 129; and Covid-19 pandemic,
430–31; and the EU, 54–5; and the
fuel crisis (2000), 52–4, 92; and
immigration, 54, 89–90; Johnson's
2019 election campaign, 414–15;
narrative of out-of-touch elite, 53,
127, 373–4, 451–2; New Labour's
vulnerability to, 53–6, 92, 127,
128–9, 372–3; politics as dull/
duplicitous narrative, 65; strong
comeback in 2010s, 54, 56; and
Trump, 456–7 see also culture wars
Portillo, Michael, 73
Post Office scandal, 344–7
Powell, Colin, 154
Powell, Jonathan, 40–41, 47, 151, 193
PPE Medpro, 450
Prescott, John, 41*, 46, 53, 202, 203,
209–10, 218, 252, 269; thumps
Craig Evans (2001), 48–9
Price, Roy, 392

HMS *Prince of Wales*, 475–6
printing technology, 111*
Private Eye, 262
Provisional IRA, 3, 9, 146, 186, 188,
190, 191–4, 195–7, 380, 381, 494
Pryce, Malcolm, 463
Public First (research firm), 449–50
Purnell, James, 243
Purnell, Sonia, 438
Putin, Vladimir, 171, 467, 468

Al-Qaeda, 147–8, 166, 169, 175, 176
Quakers, 301
Quantitative Easing (QE), 248–50,
282, 289, 435, 436
HMS *Queen Elizabeth*, 475–6

Raab, Dominic, 7, 169, 410, 473
race/ethnicity: and 2001 riots,
178–80; antisemitism row under
Corbyn, 307, 358–9, 500; Black
Lives Matter movement, 457–8;
and Brexit referendum result, 369;
and Cameron's Conservatives, 75,
76; and Cantle Report, 179, 180,
182; 'clash of civilizations'
language, 180–83; and *Clive James
on Television*, 403–4; as culture war
issue, 181–3, 457–8; diversity in
London, 26; economic disparities,
179–80; and football, 142–3, 342;
and Grenfell Tower disaster, 343–4,
457; and Immigration Act (1971),
339; imperial explanation for racial
diversity, 340; and public opinion,
89, 91; religious framing for
post-11 September world, 180–84;
'Windrush Generation', 265–6, 305,
338–44, 457, 500
racism: anti-Apartheid movement,
453; and attitudes to immigration,
90, 91; in football, 142–3, 342; and
the Royal Family, 458, 460; 'taking
the knee' by EPL players, 457–8;

(October 2022), 485; fined in relation to 'Partygate', 444; loses leadership election to Truss, 446, 484

Sunday Times, 70, 254

Supreme Court, 41, 330, 497, 507

Sutton, Willie, 102

'Swampy' (Daniel Hooper), 453

Swansea City FC, 139

Sweden, 85, 433

Syed, Hamza, 183

Taiwan, 114, 425, 470, 471, 474, 475

Taliban, Afghanistan, 148, 156, 166, 167, 168–9

Tarbel, Fethi, 294

Tax Justice Network, 116

taxation: Apple's globalized arrangements, 115–16; Blair sees higher taxes as death trap, 32, 42, 208–9; Brown's U-turn on 10p starting rate, 243; and Cameron's Conservatives, 74, 76, 78, 79, 80, 124; centralized system of emerges, 15, 491; and climate change, 121, 122, 123, 124, 130; and Crosland's *The Future of Socialism*, 39; 'Double Irish' corporate tax tool, 116; fuel escalator, 44–5, 49, 50, 121; and the housing boom, 224–5; inheritance tax, 243, 273; local taxes, 61, 62, 216, 217; and the NHS, 32, 34, 37, 42; overall burden (2000–2022), 480; populist 'stealth tax' arguments, 44, 55, 123; revenues from financial sector, 102–3, 104, 106, 242, 244; Scotland Act (2012), 324; tax breaks for City of London, 97, 103; tax credits, 11, 23, 208; windfall tax on privatized utility companies, 17, 23, 208

Taylor, Carrie, 172–3

Taylor, Richard, 506

Tebbit, Norman, 75

Tenet, George, 150

terrorism: 7/7 terrorist attacks in London, 3, 146, 172–8, 181–2, 184; attack on Glasgow Airport (2007), 242; Brown defeated over pre-trial detention extension (2008), 243; centralizing of counter-terrorism work, 177; Coalition's policies, 182; by dissident Republicans, 379; failed suicide attacks (21 July 2005), 174; IRA's London Docklands bomb (1996), 188; loyalist groups in Northern Ireland, 191*; Omagh bombing (August 1998), 192; post-7/7 anti-terrorism measures, 176–8; 'Prevent' programme, 182; Provisional IRA, 3, 9, 146, 186, 188, 190, 191–4, 195–7, 380, 381, 494; 'Real IRA', 192; September 11 attacks, 3, 145, 147–8, 184, 193, 262–3

Terry, John, 133, 143, 342

Thatcher, Margaret: abolishes exchange controls (1979), 135; Anglo-Irish Agreement (1985), 187; Bruges speech (1988), 364; and Cabinet system of collective government, 41; Christianity of, 302; and City's 'Big Bang' deregulation, 100; on dangers of climate change/global warming, 121; and Falklands War (1982), 145*, 310; neoliberal Thatcherism, 2, 17, 178, 349; place in ranking of post-war prime ministers, 251; presidential style of, 40; promises to reverse national decline, 310; rejects consensus politics, 310, 349; 'right to buy' programme, 212, 217, 219; social conservatism/prurient individualism of, 298

Thijssen, Frans, 136

Thirsk, Amanda, 396